AND BEAUTY ANSWERS

ELSPETH CAMERON
AND BEAUTY ANSWERS
THE LIFE OF FRANCES LORING AND FLORENCE WYLE

Cormorant Books

Canada Council Conseil des Arts
for the Arts du Canada

The publisher gratefully acknowledges the support of the
Canada Council for the Arts and the Ontario Arts Council
for its publishing program. We acknowledge the financial support
of the Government of Canada through the Book Publishing
Industry Development Program (BPIDP) for our publishing activities.

Printed and bound in Canada

Library and Archives Canada Cataloguing in Publication

Cameron, Elspeth, 1943–
And beauty answers: the life of Frances Loring & Florence Wyle / Elspeth Cameron.

Includes bibliographical references and index.
ISBN 978-1-897151-13-6

1. Loring, Frances, 1887–1968. 2. Wyle, Florence, 1881–1968.
3. Women sculptors — Canada — Biography.
4. Sculptors Society of Canada. I. Title.

NB249.L6C35 2007   730.92'271   C2007-902753-9

Editor: Marc Côté
Cover design: Angel Guerra/Archetype
Front cover image: Frances Loring and Florence Wyle by
Robert Flaherty, 1919; courtesy of the Art Gallery of Ontario
Spine image: *Sun Worshipper*, Florence Wyle, 1916; courtesy of the
National Gallery of Canada
Text design: Tannice Goddard/Soul Oasis Networking
Printer: Friesens

CORMORANT BOOKS INC.
215 SPADINA AVENUE, STUDIO 230, TORONTO, ONTARIO, CANADA M5T 2C7
www.cormorantbooks.com

For Frances Gage and Rebecca Sisler

Contents ⋙

SONG

Out of agony is music born —
With love broken and hopeless
Man turns to beauty's self for peace
And beauty answers, looking in his eyes,
There is no peace,
Save that which time or death may bring, but one word holds;
I bid you "sing."

(Florence Wyle, Poems, 1959)

Introduction ⁓

Conventional wisdom has it that Frances Loring and Florence Wyle are difficult to tell apart. Even their first names, which begin with the letter "F" and denote two European centres of art, are confusing. And both names contain the syllable "lor." Their work is not easily told apart either. Frances Gage, a younger sculptor who knew them and their work well, recalls having difficulty identifying a work before finding Wyle's signature on it. As one writer observed in 1977, a decade after their deaths, "Loring and Wyle, who were 'among the last of the salon-and-academy romantics to retain some relevance in Canadian art, should really be viewed as a single talent, not two ... [E]ach drew upon the other's strength to create a joint body of work that transcended the individual.'"[1]

After studying The Girls — as they were known — and their work for a few years, I disagree. Although they shared neoclassical training, they were different individuals. There was more life force in Frances, more agitation. Her work is more ruffled and powerful than Florence's. Frances more often depicted motion; Florence created serenity. Florence was more spiritual than Frances and, paradoxically, more earthy. For her, the life force was in all nature, and in nature's creatures. It was her privilege to record it. Frances was a flamboyant extrovert; Florence was a tough-minded introvert. Even their methods differed. Frances dashed off her creations in energetic spurts; whereas Florence worked regularly and hard. Frances sculpted with empathy, projecting herself into her portrait busts and statues. Florence worked with sympathy, honouring otherness. There were class differences too. Frances had been raised amid wealth and culture in a family that prized women. Florence grew up among farming people who were not well educated and who regarded girls as second-class citizens. There is something quintessential in the roles they played late in their lives. Florence patiently answered the door like a servant and said, "Come in, and meet Miss Loring,"[II] whom she fittingly nicknamed "Queenie." And Frances would receive their guests lounging like royalty on a bank of pillows.

Whenever they were asked about whether they influenced each other, they said no. Typically, Frances once said, "neither of [us] ever interferes with the work of the other and while [we] criticize each other's output, it is usually only in a very slight and friendly fashion."[III]

There have been several proposals for a book about Frances Loring and Florence Wyle. Immediately after they died, an informal group who called themselves the Friends of Loring and Wyle tried to find an author for such a book and raised a subsidy for it.[IV] The original idea was for a book that would be composed of about two-thirds sculpture illustrations and one-third biographical and critical text. The Friends knew the two women wanted such a book. Loring and Wyle actually initiated the project five or six years before they died. They gathered several photographs of their work and approached Clare Bice — then president of the Royal Canadian Academy of Arts in Toronto — for advice about publishers. All three thought the Canada Council might fund it.

Frances made it clear that she did not want a thorough investigation into her private life. "Miss Loring was upset that everyone got into her life," Lawrence Hayward, a neighbour who befriended the two sculptors in their old age, reported. "She wanted closure when she died. She wanted [the comments of] her friends to die with her. She wished to have [only] her works and efforts as an artist written about."ᵛ

Clare Bice approached Montreal art critic Robert Ayre to write the text in February 1968. Frances Gage, as one of The Girls' executors, went to see him armed with a sheaf of photographs, but Ayre declined.ᵛᴵ Hayward himself proposed writing such a book, but his background as a dancer and his later career as a massage therapist made him inadequate to the task. "I do not think that Mr. Hayward would be a suitable collaborator," publisher Jack McClelland, of McClelland & Stewart, informed the trustees in 1969.ᵛᴵᴵ Hayward failed to get a Canada Council grant to undertake the project. That same year, biographer Lois Milani approached Frances Gage to discuss writing a book about The Girls. That, too, did not materialize.ᵛᴵᴵᴵ

In 1972, an affectionate, anecdotal biography of Loring and Wyle by their friend, sculptor Rebecca Sisler, appeared. Sisler complained that the $2,000 Canada Council grant she received was not enough to do justice to her subjects. But her short book, *The Girls*, is lively and informative throughout. In 1987, as part of a large retrospective of The Girls' work, art historian Christine Boyanoski prepared a handsome and thorough catalogue that includes several photographs of The Girls and their works, a chronology of their lives, a bibliography, and a brief biographical summary.

It is not surprising that a full biography of Loring and Wyle seemed desirable. Their work was essential to the development of Canadian sculpture. As early as 1925 one journalist predicted, "Anyone with even a little knowledge of sculpture can safely prophesy that both they and their church will, some time, be very well and widely known indeed."ᴵˣ Both of them — but especially Wyle — were well trained at the Art Institute of Chicago in the neoclassical tradition, a style of sculpture based on Greek and Roman classics that valued the accurate representation of anatomy and espoused beauty as an elevating principle. Without the high standards they brought to their art as a result of their training, Canadian sculpture in the first half of the twentieth century could not have developed as it did. Loring, who tended to the grandiose Roman side of neoclassicism, created large monuments that defined "Canadian." Wyle favoured the simple purity of the Greek aspect of neoclassicism, which, in an age that called upon Canadian sculptors to express and establish national sentiments, positioned her further from the centre than Frances. The neoclassical tradition was eminently suited to the war memorials that made them both famous after the Great War. Its dignity and sense of occasion suited the sombre Canadian temperament and the era's nationalist purpose.

Loring and Wyle were part of the small group of English and French Canadian sculptors who formed the Sculptors' Society of Canada in 1928. Their place within that group is made clear in a lecture that sculptor Emanuel Hahn gave on 12 March 1928 at the Art Gallery of Toronto. "Up to the 1880s," he said, "there had been scarcely any effort in the plastic art in Canada. During the past 30 years, however, the progress has been considerable." He especially singled out for praise "the bronze work of Walter S. Allward of Toronto and the late Louis-Philippe Hébert of Montreal; while others whose work is becoming well-known are Alfred Howell, Frances Loring and Florence Wyle of Toronto, and Alfred Laliberté, George W. Hill and Henri Hébert of Montreal."[x] Both Héberts, father and son, were monumentalists who celebrated French-Canadian history. So was George W. Hill, whose main contributions — like those of Louis-Philippe Hébert — stood on Parliament Hill in Ottawa. Laliberté depicted the bucolic *habitant* life. No one yet thought of Canada's aboriginals as serious sculptors.

French-Canadian sculpture either glorified French-Canadian historical figures and an agricultural *habitant* past, or it continued in the liturgical tradition established by early woodcarvers. But as Frances Loring soon realized, it was possible in the late 1920s — before French-Canadian nationalism was not yet antagonistic to its federal context — to forge bonds between the only sculptors practising in Canada in Ontario and Quebec. Her initiation of the Sculptors' Society of Canada in 1928 had a ripple effect that lasted for at least the next decade.

The fact that The Girls were both from the American midwest and had been taught at Chicago was a crucial aspect of their success in Canada. In the Art Institute they had been told that the future of American sculpture would depend on midwestern independence to buck tradition, and in this way would be free from the slavish imitation of European art. It required only a slight lateral shift to adapt the enthusiastic rhetoric about the vitality of the midwestern United States to the rhetoric in Canada at the time that extolled the pioneer spirit in the arts.[xi] This attitude positioned them much closer to the Canadian nationalism that was defining a new nation than either the French-trained Howell or the German-trained Hahn.

Had Loring and Wyle stayed in the United States, as they fully intended to do, their lives would have been entirely different. Because of her upbringing in mining camps, Loring would probably have worked — for a time at least — in New York's Ashcan school, which championed society's underdogs. Florence might have continued in the profitable fountain sculpture popular at the time. It is even possible that both of them might have been inspired by New York's 1913 Armory Show (which they certainly would have seen had they stayed in Greenwich Village) and developed along modernist lines, as many of their male and female American contemporaries did. An important contact who might have prodded Loring and Wyle into more experimental work was their fellow student in Chicago: Georgia O'Keefe. Although they did not know O'Keefe well at the Institute, the three would probably have met at the Gallery 291 nearby, after O'Keefe became the partner of the Gallery owner, Alfred Stieglitz, in 1918.

If Loring and Wyle had stayed in the United States, Canadian sculpture would have lacked the high level of professionalism that resulted from their training. By coming to Canada, The Girls helped advance Canadian sculpture out of its fledgling phase of historical hagiography into the next important stage of monumentalization. They were instrumental in establishing a sound neoclassical base. And, later on, they were instrumental in nudging Canadian sculpture from its initial "celebration of the nation's heroes, institutions and middle-class values," — which were meant "to educate, elevate and delight"[xii] in that order — towards an aesthetic of fine art for all Canadians. They never abandoned the concept that art should elevate, but they thought it should delight more than it should educate. Above all, it should be beautiful. As Loring said late in life, "The evolution toward the fuller consciousness of beauty is slow, but once it has captured your soul, nothing else will do."[xiii]

It is unfortunate that the social and cultural revolution of the 1960s threw Loring and Wyle into the shadows of Canadian sculptural history. As with all revolutions, the new ousted the old. The onset of modernism, with its new, more subjective concepts for three-dimensional works and the new materials they could be made of, provoked an over-reaction against the work that had gone before. Beaux-arts neoclassicism — including the later style of Rodin, the art-deco stylizations of the 1920s and 1930s, and New York's socially conscious Ashcan school approach, which Loring and Wyle had begun to apply to their work — were viewed as hopelessly outdated. Works by sculptors like Loring and Wyle suddenly became almost invisible. As time passed and modernism took hold in the arts in the 1960s, they were often dismissed or ridiculed.

In their heyday from about 1920 to 1950, their contribution to Canadian sculpture was enormous. Beyond that, these two women led remarkable lives. While they were alive, Loring and Wyle spawned a widespread mythology. It was essentially romantic. Even though they met as classmates, their early contact had a mentor-student aspect. Florence did not teach Frances directly, but she was six years older than Frances and was already established as an assistant teacher at the Art Institute of Chicago. At the beginning of their friendship she played Pygmalion to Frances's Galatea. Perhaps because of this, Frances always claimed that Florence was the better sculptor. And Frances brought with her the romance of having spent seven years in Europe with her mother and brother. She had *experienced* many of the world's most famous sculptures and had dipped in and out of a number of art institutions abroad.

Their own accounts of meeting are in the tradition of "love-at-first-sight." They "clicked" immediately, they later said. Sharing a studio in Greenwich Village in 1910 was also romantic — and adventurous, especially for two women. It suggested elopement. When Frances's father arbitrarily closed down their studio in New York after a year, while they were away, it smacked of the heavy-handed father attempting to thwart young lovers. Certainly, concern for the morals of his daughter was paramount, though he encouraged her friendship with Wyle, whom he hoped might settle head-strong Frances down.

The continuation of Florence and Frances's Bohemian life in Toronto in 1911–12 suggested a deep commitment. Frances used the word "romantic" to describe their discovery of the old red church building that became their studio-home in 1920. Their other, outrageously squalid country property corroborated the romantic myth of an artistic retreat close to nature. The informal gatherings held at both locations were the closest Toronto came to having a Bohemian salon like those of various North American expatriates in Paris or the Bloomsbury Group in England in the 1920s. Even their poverty — on and off through the years — fit the stereotype of the struggling artist. The dusty, bare church was their "garret." The fact that they died within three weeks of each other suggested to many a spiritual bond and a reunion of their "inseparable spirits" in some other world.[xiv]

Had either Florence or Frances been a man, the implication of this romantic myth would have been that they were deeply in love, a couple who lived and worked together in the sixty years between when they met and when they died.

But were they a couple? Were they lesbian?

Many have thought so. In 1911, their instructor at the Art Institute of Chicago, Lorado Taft, sabotaged the jobs they wanted as assistants to the New York sculptor Daniel Chester French with a letter of reference that claimed they were lesbian. The sobriquet "The Girls," by which they were commonly known once they set up their studio in the church building in Toronto in 1920, had overtones of homosexuality. So did the term "The Boys," already widely used for their friends, Charles Ashley and James Crippen, the well-known Toronto photographers of famous Canadians[xv] who lived a block from their studio.

As time passed and homosexuality gradually became more visible in Toronto society, the couple — also known as the "Loring-Wyles" or the "Loringwyles"[xvi] — were assumed to be lovers. Writing in the *Toronto Star* in 1979, Donald Jones describes Loring as "an unusual and talented woman who shocked and fascinated this city for more than half a century."[xvii] Alluding to the TV show *The Odd Couple*, which slyly made fun of homosexuality by depicting two men living together, Jones refers to Loring and Wyle as the "odd-couple sculptors" in his 1983 column "Historical Toronto."[xviii] Robertson Davies based his characters "The Ladies" in his 1994 novel *The Cunning Man* on The Girls. Like The Girls, Davies's two women artists — one an etcher (as was The Girls' friend Dorothy Stevens), the other a sculptor — live in a church building. Davies hints at their lesbianism by naming them Miss Pansy Freake and Miss Emily Raven-Hart. Though Davies denied any reference to Loring and Wyle, the coincidental similarities[xix] are too many to ignore. Davies disingenuously claimed he was inspired by "two women artists he had known in England ... who were people of a type which has always interested me."[xx] Both Loring and Wyle also have entries in the 2004 edition of *The Queer Encyclopedia of the Visual Arts*.[xxi] But defenders of lesbianism who later addressed The Girls did them a disservice. Since they did not investigate the situation deeply, their tributes are either superficial or inaccurate. One article misspells both their names (as Francis Loring and Florence Wylie).[xxii] The use of their studio as one of the settings in a 1989 gay film called *Urinal* is utterly misleading.[xxiii]

There is no way of knowing whether Loring and Wyle had a sexual relationship. Just as we cannot know the sexual details of relationships between men and women (unless they choose to tell us), in the absence of letters or any other evidence from The Girls, there is only silence. This absence or scarcity of materials is typical of female biographical subjects. Certainly the men I have written about arrived complete with extensive archival materials. Hugh MacLennan's mother kept his first letters home from camp when he was eleven, for instance; Earle Birney's thousands of archival files include a lock of blonde hair from his first haircut and his first baby shoes. For Loring and Wyle — whose families did not anticipate their future fame — I have had to rely on uneven material: the context of the arts in Canada at the time, photographs, and accounts by the handful of people still alive who knew them. The few who knew them well[xxiv] mostly report that they were not lesbian. These categorical denials — bolstered by accounts of Frances's flings with men and Florence's undying worship of Charles Mulligan, her married teacher at the Art Institute, are themselves interesting. Is there a conspiracy to protect them? Is this why Loring did not want her life written about? Or are we superimposing contemporary assumptions on another era? Do we simply say, "They *must* have been," because we project today's much freer acceptance of same-sex relationships (including, in Canada, same-sex marriage) onto the past?

Whether or not The Girls were lovers, theirs was the closest emotional relationship either of them ever had. In Platonic terms, they were soulmates, as complementary to each other as Yin and Yang. They shared the church's small vestry, closed off with peaked doors, as a bedroom. Immediately after they moved into the church in 1920, a journalist reported that the vestry served as "bedroom, living-room, kitchen and pantry."[xxv] Another journalist who interviewed The Girls in 1942 noted that "their bedrooms are in the vestry" and "their dining room, bath room and kitchen are in the crypt [the basement which was put in the second year they were there]." The main area in the nave was in "genial disarray" — "busts, torsos, heads, decorative statuettes and bas reliefs," some "swathed in cloths to keep damp" — and looked like "a movie set for European films of early 1920s."[xxvi] Qennefer Browne, daughter of Emanuel Hahn and Elizabeth Wyn Wood, recalls going as a child with her parents to The Girls' for a lunch some time around 1950. After lunch she needed a nap and was shown to Frances's bedroom in the vestry. "There was a big double bed in there covered with lots of blankets," she recalls. "I don't think I slept. It was an unfamiliar and fascinating place and I just looked around at things. After my mother came to get me up, I asked if I could see Florence's bedroom. There was an awkward moment. I gathered that Florence did not have a bedroom."[xxvii] By 1952, Frances had the vestry to herself because Wyle's new studio, bedroom, and bathroom had been added to the main building.[xxviii]

Regardless of the nature of their relationship, Loring and Wyle certainly challenged the gender stereotypes of their time. During their productive years, according to feminist art historian Fiona Carson, "to be a female sculptor was a contradiction in terms." An aura of "machismo" surrounded sculptors like Michelangelo, Bernini, Rodin, and David Smith. They were thought to be "flawed but heroic men engaged in a physically demanding struggle with durable materials and gargantuan tasks."[xxix] Before 1900, women had difficulty studying from the nude. And the tragic lives of some women sculptors, such as Camille Claudel, Suzanne Valedon, and Gwen John, gave rise to the idea that women who sculpted were doomed to disaster. Florence in particular challenged gender stereotypes. Frances kept her hair long and enjoyed dressing in feminine costume and socializing. But Florence disdained fashion.

For the last thirty years or so before her death, she appeared at social gatherings in the same grey flannel suit with a man's tie or a loose silk ascot, thick cotton stockings, and heavy men's shoes. In the early '20s she cut her hair short and kept it that way until she died. She is best described as "a not-woman, not-man," Fiona Carson's 2001 definition of a lesbian. The Girls were described variously as: co-workers, friends, a sculpture team, fellow-sculptors, partners, partner-sculptors, associates in sculpture, "this oddly matched pair,"[xxx] "intimate friends,"[xxxi] "a couple of tough old cookies,"[xxxii] and, later, "a truly outrageous couple,"[xxxiii] "intimate friends over the years,"[xxxiv] lifelong friends,[xxxv] and life-mates. They hated the term "sculptress,"[xxxvi] though it was used for them as late as 1979. Other feminine diminutives plagued them too: their Great War statues were called "statuettes"; their country property made them "farmerettes"; the park devoted to them is a "parkette."

The miracle is that the unconventional Loring and Wyle were able to function within the limits of an extremely confined society in Toronto. They were regarded with skepticism and raised eyebrows at first. But they were not marginalized or ridiculed. Even the fact that they were American (and Florence's nasal midwestern accent would have been a constant reminder of this) did not relegate them to the margins. On the contrary, they were welcomed into the art scene, in particular through friends Alex (A.Y.) Jackson and Fred Varley, before the Group of Seven formed. And — largely because of Frances's unusually cultured background and gregarious nature — they were welcomed by the staid, Victorian "society" of wealthy Toronto women into their arts organizations. The oddity of their partnership was attributed to the fact that they were artists. It lent interest, and did not result in their being outcasts, as might have been the case had they been anything else.

There may be clues to their relationship in their sculpture. Late in life, Frances Loring recognized that "a young artist is more emotional, a more mature artist has more repose."[xxxvii] She was referring specifically to her own early work *Hound of Heaven*, which depicted an anxious woman fleeing from her conscience. This work was done in 1916 at the studio-home she shared with Florence in Toronto after they left Greenwich Village. Given the heady, sexually rebellious climate of the time in the Village, and given that Florence created her most erotic work — a nude, ecstatic woman called *Sun Worshipper* — at about the same time, it may well be that the two women experimented with sexuality as so many others had openly done all around them. Later in life, interviewers described them in largely masculine terms. One wrote, "Frances Loring has a deep vibrant voice — maybe you've heard it over the radio? — a warm grip of the hand, and a ready laugh. Terse and straight-forward is Florence Wyle, the other half of a partnership that has endured."[xxxviii] So thoroughly were their lives intertwined that it would not be possible to do a biography of one without the other.

This joint biography of Loring and Wyle, like all biographies, is a study in timing. Those who emerge at the top of any field are usually found to have been in the right place at the right time. This is true of Loring and Wyle, whose move from the United States to Canada in 1911 was fortuitous. Yet their early success at the end of the Great War was eroded by timing that did not work in their favour. They hit their peak during the Depression, in the years when funding for the arts was negligible. Ironically, they were later marginalized by 1970s feminism. In their era, the "feminine" and the "feminist" would have been viewed as opposite (and "femininity" and "the cult of true womanhood" kept "feminism" under control).[xxxix] Although they had *lived* feminist lives, their age conceptualized them merely as colourful eccentrics. A 1973 article called "Feminists Challenge Male Art Values" in the *Toronto Star* mentions them only because the author quotes Rebecca Sisler, who uses their example to dismiss claims that men create art and women create children.[xl] Long before Germaine Greer, Betty Friedan, or Gloria Steinem, Loring and Wyle asserted the possibility of agency for women. Wyle's *Mother of the Race* — her best sculpture — and her obsession with female torsos suggests what feminist theoretician Linda Zerilli calls "remem-oration," in which the female body — remembered from infancy — is the site of subversive desires. French feminist theorists, Zerilli explains, ground femininity on the bedrock not of Freudian penis envy, but the body of the mother.[xli]

The Girls were notoriously casual about their records. In one interview for the *Ottawa Evening Citizen*, Florence Wyle, speaking about her teaching at Chicago, typically said, "I taught for six or seven years; I never remember details,"[XLII] and later added, "I was too lazy or something."[XLIII] In such interviews and other records, various dates for the same sculpture or event appear. I have come across three different dates for Frances's arrival at the Art Institute of Chicago (1905, 1906, 1907) — all recorded by Frances herself. I have chosen 1906 as the most probable of these from circumstantial evidence. Frances was well-known to embellish stories; indeed, she was loved by her friends for this very trait. Factual truth has been difficult — at times impossible — to pin down. Variants have usually been recorded in footnotes. But factual truth is not the only truth in biography. I have tried to convey those other essences: two separate, yet overlapping, personalities, the timbre of Toronto, and the developments in Canadian sculpture during The Girls' half-century together.

The method I have used for this biography is mainly that described by Lytton Strachey in his *Eminent Victorians*. Strachey disliked the multi-volume, all-inclusive biographies that characterized Victorian England. Instead, he attempted to "row out over that great ocean of material, and lower down into it, here and there, a little bucket, which will bring up to the light of day some characteristic specimen, from those far depths, to be examined with a careful curiosity."[XLIV] In the absence of a "great ocean of material," I have dipped into The Girls' lives in the same way, letting the single incident stand for many similar ones. I have also used techniques from film, which contemporary audiences have become used to. Readers will find that close-ups of The Girls' doings are juxtaposed with panoramas of the broader contexts in which they worked. Indeed, it seems to me that sculpture once played the role films play today: to recreate "reality." Moving around a three-dimensional figure was to experience the fluid sequence of one silhouette after another, which suggests the statue is "alive." I have also occasionally taken certain liberties with my material along lines suggested by Truman Capote's theory of "creative non-fiction." At every point such liberties are based on facts my research has discovered, as my notes will explain.

The time has come to reclaim what was a necessary and important stage in the evolution of Canadian sculpture. It is not just that the works of Loring and Wyle opened the way for the next, less inhibited generation to break free, or that they were fully aware that the fund for scholarships they left would apply to work that they would be totally unable to comprehend. There is no denying their sculpture was created with enviable talent and skill, and it still projects a powerful presence and integrity. Partly because they were women, partly because their neoclassical work eventually became outdated, partly because of the fervour for urban renewal that gripped Toronto — like many other cities — in the 1970s, Loring and Wyle were unjustly relegated to the margins of our culture. Too many of their sculptures have been moved, or destroyed, or covered, or blocked, in the name of progress. Their many fine works still stand today in and around Ontario and elsewhere, but these are often lost in the chaos of today's Toronto or tucked away in obscure places, mute testimony to the highest level of the tradition in which their creators were trained. Although many of them no longer occupy the public spaces they were created for, these works can, and should, be visited and admired.

❧ONLY CONNECT❧

Frances ⇌

I magine a dark-haired young woman climbing a broad stone stairway. It leads her up towards three round terracotta arches, suggestive of the Gothic entrance to Notre Dame at Poitiers, and into the Art Institute of Chicago. To the two huge bronze lions that flank the stairs, her arrival is a matter of indifference. They had been commissioned twelve years before by Mrs. Henry Field from famed American *animalier* Edward Kemeys. These glossy male symbols of nobility and power gaze away from the stairway in opposite directions as if scanning the horizon for possible dangers. The date is probably Monday 1 October 1906 — the day classes begin. She is determined to be a student at the Institute.

Frances Loring — thick hair coiffed with pricking hairpins, long dress blown around the low-heeled boots that sounded her entrance into the high-ceilinged circular lobby of the Institute — must have been eager to proceed to the room where her class was to be held. This is not the only art school she has attended. It is her fifth. From the first time she touched clay

— six years ago in Geneva, when she was thirteen — felt its slippery magic in her palms, the endless possibilities it posed for her fingers, the way "she first thrilled"[1] to its texture, she knew she would sculpt. A friend who was taking an art course had handed her the seductive clay. "I'll never forget it," Frances would later say. "There's something about the feel of clay in your hands. You get a sense of power and delight. Clay is so fascinating that once you start working with it you can't stop. That's when I started to be a sculptor."[2]

As a child, Frances had fooled her friends into believing her elaborate mud pies were really chocolate cakes. Now she was bound to shape clay to her imagination. It had been her strong will that had driven her mother to persuade the École des Beaux-Arts in Paris to admit her daughter directly into the modelling class, bypassing the drawing and perspective classes usually considered necessary preparation for sculpture.[3]

The Lorings — mother and two children — were stranded in Europe at the time. Frances's father, Frank Loring, an adventurous, cheery man who delighted in elaborate tales, wry twists of fate, and practical jokes — some of which he later wrote down[4] — had been caught in a twist of fate himself. As a mining engineer, he was swept into the speculations that promised sudden fortunes to anyone who was at the right mine at the right time. At Coeur d'Alene, Idaho, where silver had recently been discovered, he had met and wed Charlotte Moore. Frances Norma Loring was born in Wardner, another mining town, on 14 October 1887, a year after her brother, Ernest. When she was five, they moved from the elaborate tents that were their home in the mining outpost to a large, turreted house in Spokane, Washington — a taste of genteel stability that did not last. By 1899, after a sudden mining breakthrough in Rossland, B.C., where Frank Loring was part owner of Josie Mine (later Le Roi No. 2 Mining Company), he had become rich overnight.[5] He set himself up in Washington, D.C., to play the stock market. The following year, he treated his family to a lavish European holiday.

They had hardly begun their travels when the stock market slumped, and Frank Loring was broke. Returning abruptly to the United States, he settled for an office job that paid $80 a month. "It was enough," Frances would later recall, "to keep him alive at home and us alive in Europe."[6] In Europe,

Frank's wife, son, and daughter enjoyed the Grand Tour (their *wanderjahr*, Charlotte liked to call it). With her mother and brother, Frances soaked up bits of foreign languages, and slaked her eager curiosity about the arts. They visited museums and galleries, attended churches and cathedrals of no particular denomination, where there might be a challenging speaker, gazed up at architectural spectacles, and in the summer bicycled through the shimmering landscapes recently immortalized by the Impressionists. It would be seven happy years before the Loring family would return to the United States.

Frances would recall no sense of deprivation during those seven years. Living in modest *pensions* that cost little by American standards, they thrived; Ernest studied engineering while Frances pursued sculpture. After Geneva, she studied with Professor Güttner in Munich, marvelling at the display of Greek sculpture in the Glyptothek. Then, as the family travelled further, she took classes in Paris at the Académie Colarossi,[7] a school that — like the Royal Academy of Munich and unlike the more famous and conservative École des Beaux-Arts — admitted women and allowed them to sculpt from nude models, male and female.

By the time Frank Loring could call his family back to America, his daughter had seen many of the artistic and architectural masterpieces of Europe. It is unlikely she could have identified the building she had just entered in Chicago as Bedford limestone, but she probably would have recognized the architectural style as Italian Renaissance.

She had acquired other sophistications as well. During one short visit to his family in Paris when she was sixteen, her father had taken her to the Moulin Rouge. On looking down through the glass floor inside the infamous nightclub at the naked women below, she asked him in shocked surprise, "Is this a place ladies can come?" to which he had replied, "Certainly. A lady can go anywhere."[8]

Reunited now in Chicago with a father she had seen only occasionally since she was twelve, Frances entered the School of the Art Institute of Chicago, with some command of German, Italian, and French, with far more direct experience of sculpture than any of the other students, and with an obstinate ambition that had finally convinced her family to support her dream.

‖ 2

The World's Columbian Exposition of 1893⤚

The building into which Frances Loring walked in the fall of 1906 had been constructed thirteen years earlier on the west shore of Lake Michigan as part of a well-worked-out plan. First it would house the Congress of World Religions — which, among other things, introduced Buddhism to the United States — along with other congresses that took place as part of the World's Columbian Exposition of 1893. Such congresses had been an important part of the Paris Exposition that launched the Eiffel Tower in 1889 and were therefore thought to be essential. Afterwards, the building would house the Art Institute of Chicago, which had entered a period of rapid expansion. So ambitious were the plans for the Columbian Exposition, that they scuttled Montreal's plans to celebrate its 250th year as "the number one city in the Dominion [of Canada]." Montreal's plans never materialized because of the anticipated competition from tourists to Chicago.[1]

Fifty years earlier there was no art in Chicago, that brawling, brash commercial centre. The first glimmer of culture took the form of G.P.A. Healy, whose "overmodelled" and "photographic" paintings of "Chicago's uncouth over-dressed matrons"[2] made his fortune.

The pursuit of the visual arts began seriously in Chicago in 1866 when the Academy of Art and Design was formed and held exhibitions in Crosby's Opera House. The opera house burned down in the great fire of 1871, but the Academy of Art and Design rose phoenix-like from the flames, changing its location and its name: first to the Chicago Academy of Fine Arts in 1879, then to the Art Institute of Chicago in 1882. By this time, "Chicago's ever-generous business titans had discovered art (or their wives had) and George Armour, the meat-packer, became the Institute's first president. He was suc-ceeded by Levi Z. Leiter of Leiter and Fields Department Store, and Leiter, in turn, gave way to Charles L. Hutchinson, who didn't need his wife to get him enthused about art and who was one of the true pillars of culture in Chicago for many years." It was under Hutchinson's leadership — with archi-tect William M.R. French as director — that Frances Loring would study.[3]

No matter how quickly the Institute responded to increases in enrol-ments, acquisitions, and art events, it never seemed to have enough space. As Chicago grew apace, so did the arts. By 1885, the first skyscraper there had launched a new method of building. In 1887, after surviving various locations and manifestations, the Art Institute of Chicago building on Michigan Avenue at Van Buren Street, which Frances Loring was to enter in 1906, was opened. Wealthy Chicagoans who had made sudden fortunes in the railroads, the meat industry, and other businesses had money, leisure, conscience. The city's spirit was "violently democratic." Expecting "to ben-efit the masses of the people," Chicago money went to parks for the poor and free libraries. Classes at the Art Institute were almost free: $25 a term at the time Frances arrived.[4]

In 1889, 141,534 people visited the Institute; the income from member-ships was $20,000. Student enrolment had leapt from 100 day and evening students in 1883 to 400 in 1889.[5] By 1899, Chicago had three large public libraries, three women's cultural clubs, and over a thousand pupils attending art classes.[6] Lacking an endowment and patrons to sponsor the Institute's moves from one location to another, money somehow had to be found for expansion. Hutchinson's fundraising manoeuvres never ceased. "Devoid of all pretence, he looked up in his quick, nervous way through a pair of blue-grey eyes that invited approach ... No one would doubt [his] shrewdness, but somewhere about his face was the mark of kindliness," recalls a contemporary.[7] If he asked anyone to lunch, it was understood the topic of conversation would be money for the Institute. Those who questioned the incongruity of hog-packers sponsoring art, or the claims — mainly justified — that Chicago had too rapidly become an important art centre, were likely to hear this retort from the president of the Institute: "We have made our money in pigs, but is that any reason why we should not spend it in pictures?"[8]

A solid financial and physical base had been laid for the Art Institute before the World's Columbian Exposition of 1893 celebrated Christopher Columbus's discovery of the New World. But the exposition propelled the Institute into a new era. How could it not? The permanent building that the Institute would acquire after the event was the least of it. All World's Fairs since the Great Exhibition of 1851 in London had been spectacular, especially the 1889 Paris Exposition. But Chicago's Columbian Exposition was stupendous. Twenty-eight million visitors — close to half the total population of the U.S. and approximately seven times the population of Canada at the time — came to Jackson Park on Lake Michigan between 1 May and 1 November 1893. And what they saw there was almost beyond anyone's imagination. Architectural designs for the huge pavilions — some a third of a mile long — and the overall layout of the fair would alter American architecture and city planning forever. The most "electrical" fair ever, it used three times more electricity than the city itself and ten times the electricity used at the Paris Exposition. Replicas of Columbus's caravels, the Nina, the Pinta, and the Santa Maria, were made in Spain and sailed to the fair. The first amusement park ever to appear at a fair sprang up on Chicago's long, broad Midway, which would lend its name to the rides and games at future fairs and carnivals. At the eastern end of the Midway, the first Ferris wheel (designed by George Ferris and initially considered impossible, then outlandish) rose 264 feet and carried thirty-six cars the size of buses, each of which took forty passengers. The cost for this ride was fifty cents, a sum equivalent to the cost of admission to the whole fair. The Paris Exposition had featured a "human zoo" of blacks, but at Chicago there were displays of fifty-one foreign peoples and their cultures, many of which had never been seen in North America, as well as representative groups and exhibits from forty-seven states and territories. Canada's contribution was a 22,000-pound cheese, 3,500 samples of grain, extensive mineral specimens, and a somewhat misleading exhibit of "Esquimaux" from north Labrador, with huskies and harpoons, paddling a canoe. (When hot weather struck, ten of the twelve "tribes" threw off their fur parkas and went home.) The ethnic exhibit that attracted most attention was the *danse du ventre* (belly dance) of Little Egypt — tame by today's standards, but exotic beyond compare in 1893. In the building that would become the Art Institute, 5,978 addresses were made to audiences totalling over 700,000 for the World's Congress Auxiliary.

The sixty-one-acre "White City" was raised on a series of islands and lagoons created almost magically from the flat sandy scrubland along Lake Michigan. With water drained from the lake, a web of canals — several miles of them — interlaced land contoured with dredged soil. The Great Buildings, housing displays of everything from Queen Isabella's will to Bach's clavichord to a map of the United States made of pickles, were eclectic evocations of architectural styles from antiquity to the Renaissance. Made of staff — a white mixture of plaster, cement, and hemp trowelled onto wooden lath — the effect sought was of a pristine Venice.

This pseudo-Renaissance atmosphere, and the concurrent rave in the United States for civic monuments, dictated that heroic statues and architectural ornamentation would be an important part of the Exposition. Augustus Saint-Gaudens, the most distinguished American sculptor of the period, whose 1881 *Farragut Monument* to a Civil War Admiral had ushered in a renaissance of American sculpture, came from New York to supervise the exposition's sculpture. These works, too, were created of staff. The skilled workmen were mainly Italians; some were French; only a few were American.

Of these Americans, twenty-seven-year-old Frederick MacMonnies, known for "sheer dexterity and manipulation,"[9] created the fair's most impressive work: the largest fountain in the world, the *MacMonnies (Columbian) Fountain.*[10] Thirty-seven twelve-foot figures comprising the symbolic "Ship of State" were placed in the centre of a huge round pool with jets of water that sprayed 150 feet into the air. Eight sturdy maidens representing industry and the arts propelled the ship with long oars. At the prow stood Fame, at the stern an athletic Father Time leaning into the rudder. Crowning the ship, on a pedestal throne, sat imperious Columbia. Scattered here and there were seahorses, dolphins, outriders, nymphs, and cherubs. At night, coloured searchlights illuminated the scene. The cost of this elaborate compliment to American ingenuity was $48,000 — about $1 million in today's terms.

At the opposite end of the Grand Basin, facing the *MacMonnies Fountain*, towered the massive *Statue of the Republic* (or *Columbia*) by Daniel Chester French. French was the brother of William M.R. French, director of the Art Institute and a major American sculptor noted for his *Minute Man* (1875), a tribute to the reserve forces of the Civil War, *John Harvard* (1882), at Cambridge, Massachusetts, and the portrait heads of his Concord neighbours, writers Ralph Waldo Emerson and Louisa May Alcott.

In Jackson Park stood the original plaster versions of Edward Kemeys's pair of lions that, after the Exposition closed, were cast in bronze to guard the entrance to the Art Institute. The Palace of Fine Arts sported 200,000 square feet of paintings from many countries and housed a huge array of sculpture in every possible material from bronze to marble. Despite the suggestive gyrations of Little Egypt, Auguste Rodin's now-famous sculpture *The Kiss* was relegated to an inner chamber where it could be seen only by personal application and a fee.[11]

With hindsight, it is easy to see that the World's Columbian Exposition bridged the nineteenth and twentieth centuries. Although the temporary buildings and sculptures — even the Ferris wheel — were dismantled within a year after the fair closed, its effects were nonetheless indelible. It was there that Frederick Jackson Turner delivered the speech that set American ideology for years to come: "The Significance of the Frontier in American History." As a result of seeing the "White City," poet Katharine Lee Bates wrote "America the Beautiful" and L. Frank Baum wrote *The Wizard of Oz*. Stockholders realized a profit; visitors learned much about foreign cultures; Chicago gained prestige on the world stage.

And the movement to emancipate women took a step forward. The Women's Building, which was designed by a twenty-one-year-old female architect, Sophia Hayden from Boston, was managed and decorated entirely by women. Works (selected by all-female juries) had been submitted from numerous countries in every imaginable branch of science, industry, and art. Women's accomplishments in science, medicine, literature, invention, exploration, education, painting, and sculpture filled the building. A then-unrecognized Mary Cassatt painted an avant-garde mural, *Modern Women*, which was attacked by critics.[12] Five Canadian women painters had works — mostly sentimental Victorian landscapes, children, and still lives — on display.[13] Women leaders in manifold fields lectured on their research and offered their opinions. Sixty women's organizations from the Women's Christian Temperance Union to Susan B. Anthony's suffragettes had their say. A female doctor clad in bloomers warned an audience of long-skirted, corseted women that tight lacing caused more than fifty disorders.[14]

But rumblings against the segregation of women into their own building were in the air. According to one report, "Restricting women exhibitors to one building would have been a fatal blow, for awards received in competition only with the work of other women would have been of comparatively little actual commercial value."[15] For this reason some women's artistic works were entered in competitions with men in other great buildings. Barriers between the sexes had begun to break down.

The Modelling Class⤐

The Life Modelling class that Frances Loring walked into that fall of 1906 surged with energy. The nude male model had already struck a pose and one of the students had chalked lines around his feet so he could resume his place exactly after his breaks each half hour. Unlike the modelling classes Frances had attended in Europe, which were made up mainly of male students, seventeen of the twenty-five students in the day class were women.

After throwing on her long smock with fashionable leg-of-mutton sleeves, Frances joined the rush in and out of the classroom, down the hall to the engine room where the Institute's engineer was wheedled into parting with pieces of lead pipe. Next came a raid on the carpenter's shop, where old Casper was pressed into service helping construct the rough armatures that act as skeletons for the clay sculptures. Experienced students wedged sticks into chairs, secured them across their knees, and sawed furiously. New girls like Frances pressed Casper to use his sawhorse. Sometimes he could be persuaded to make the whole frame and stand, ingeniously securing the lead pipes with heavy wire for arms and legs and tying on bits of sticks and other debris from his floor until a primitive human shape emerged. Other students ran back to the classroom to construct their own armatures.

Amid this chaos, the model stands motionless. Soon peace falls as one by one the students take little pieces of wet clay fished from the clay box in one corner and stick them onto the armature, building up the clay figure bit by bit. One woman jokes that she feels like a child making mud pies, a thought Frances shares, remembering the ingenious mud pies she used to make.[1] Another curses the engineer, calling him a "stingy old pig,"[2] as a wire limb drops off or an armature sags lopsidedly. Complete silence is rare. Good-natured repartee, witty observations, and satiric barbs are traded back and forth. Serious topics such as political and legal opinions — thought by society at large to be unladylike — are ventured. Religion has begun to wane, but the new "sciences" of transmigration of the soul, palmistry, and hypnotism are hotly debated. So is the question of women sculptors. One student recalls the "rapt and radiant" faces of her classmates, the obvious inspiration, the disregard for financial reward. As if to defy the common view that no woman can cope with the exigencies — the sheer physical labour — of sculpting, she asserts that these are not "weak, fragile, vaporish creatures." "Did it ever occur to you," she wrote in the student magazine *Brush and Pencil*, "that Phidias [of fifth century BC Greece] has quite long enough occupied the supreme place in sculpture? Has it never occurred to you that some time in the near future a demand will be made by a woman for a share of his glory?"[3]

In fact, a few women had already succeeded as sculptors. By 1906 in France, Camille Claudel had challenged her lover Rodin, the greatest sculptor of the late nineteenth century, with her own work — including a superb bust of him executed in his style — which was exhibited in the major salons of Paris. She had ended their decade-long affair in 1892, after an unwished-for abortion, to strike out successfully on her own, before descending into madness, which by some accounts was the result of social pressure to conform. In 1913, she would be confined to a psychiatric hospital by her mother, who had always opposed her career.

Harriet Hosmer, a swashbuckling American from Massachusetts, left for Europe with her friend, Boston actress Charlotte Cushman, in 1852. There she appropriated the dress and behaviour of male artists and sculpted subjects from antiquity such as Daphne (transformed into a laurel tree to avoid rape), Medusa (who turned men to stone), Beatrice Cenci (who murdered her incestuous father), and Zenobia (queen of Palmyra, warrior, intellectual, and patron of the arts), works which anticipated contemporary lesbian feminism. Author Nathaniel Hawthorne, who visited Hosmer's studio in Rome in 1858 and disliked her on sight, describes her as a "brisk, wide-awake figure ... frank, simple, straightforward, and downright. She [wore] a sort of man's sack of purple broadcloth, into the side pockets of which her hands were thrust as she came forward to greet us ... She had on a male shirt, collar and cravat, with a brooch of Etruscan gold; and on her head was a picturesque little cap of black velvet ... There never was anything so jaunty as her movement and action; she was indeed very queer."[4] He used her as the model for the American expatriate painter Hilda in his novel *The Marble Faun*. Sculptor Thomas Crawford was shocked by the anatomical studies on Hosmer's walls and ordered his wife to "cut her dead."[5] Hosmer had exhibited works in the Chicago Academy of Design's first annual show in 1867. Her last important project was a full-scale *Queen Isabella* for the Columbian Exposition in 1893.

Other women, too, in America and elsewhere, had begun to succeed as sculptors as the nineteenth century drew to a close. Modelling classes in the leading American art academies began to admit women in the 1880s. The flurry of activity at the Chicago World's Columbian Exposition in 1893 legitimized the work of women sculptors a step further. Partly as a result of the Exposition, the National Sculpture Society (NSS) was founded later that year, and the women who had worked as assistants at the Exposition became members. By 1908, thirty women showed in the NSS; by 1910, eight more women had become members, bringing the number of women to about one-third of the total.

Frances was part of this first wave of women studying sculpture in America. Plunged into the excitement of the first American modelling classes that signalled her family's wholehearted support of her will to sculpt, the experience at the Art Institute was a heady one.

The Master ⤚

On Wednesdays and Fridays at one o'clock an expectant hush fell over the modelling class. Those were the days when instructor Lorado Taft, who insisted on being called "The Master," appeared to assess his students' progress. Behind his back the students referred to him as "Taffy," not only because of his light auburn hair and natty goatee, but also more specifically in reference to a popular comic character of the time. Taffy, the Scottish Laird, appeared in George Du Maurier's *Trilby*, published in *Harper's Monthly* (1894), as an artist in Paris used by Du Maurier to satirize the Bohemian lives of painters. If Taft were slightly late, the more outspoken students were known to comment, "I wonder what Taffy had for lunch today that keeps him so?" Taft, a slight man of medium height with penetrating pale blue eyes, would sweep into the room, toss off his elegant jacket, remove his round glasses, and throw a long white sleeveless smock over his head. As one student describing a 1898 modelling class in detail recalls, "You can feel the atmosphere around you clearing up ... the broken whispers of conversation cease, and the room puts on an air of expectancy. His presence seems to have thrown new life into everything. 'The one in most need of help shall have my attention first,' the forty-six-year-old Taft would say in his cheery voice, rolling up his sleeves, 'Now who is it today?'"[1] Though modesty prevails at first, there is soon a chorus competing for The Master's attention. He begins with the nearest.

Taft's methods are direct and interventionist. He teaches by doing. "Put on your clay loosely and fearlessly," he says to one, daubing clay onto her statue. "Look," he says to another, drawing on a precise knowledge of anatomy that the students are themselves acquiring in classes in anatomical drawing and — if they pay extra — in dissection laboratories of the University of Chicago medical school. "Take your measurements all over again to be sure the proportions are right." He calls the student's attention to a dozen things. "This curve is formed by a muscle cunningly encasing itself between these two overlapping ones," he adds. "It makes a tiny plane. All curves, you know, are made of these tiny planes." And on goes another dab of clay, which is scooped and patted with surgical precision at just the right angle. Then he steps back and cocks his head as he walks around the statue he has improved, looking back and forth at the motionless model. "Do not work long standing close to your figure," he admonishes. "Step away from it often, and compare it with the model from every angle, and from above and below. Study it closely [so] you ... bring out the action and character ... Your torso is very good," he says, swinging around to face another student, but adds, "If you succeed with the arms and legs, which are yet a little woodeny, you will have done very well."[2]

No one is left without some encouragement and the feeling that she has his sympathy and interest. As he removes his smock and throws on his jacket, smoothing the tie under his wing collar into place, he addresses the group as a whole, "Remember Carlyle's definition of genius: 'An infinite capacity for taking pains.'" There is no doubt that The Master knows he is such a genius. Pinching the bottom of the girl nearest the door, he is off.[3]

LORADO TAFT IN 1906 had the assurance of a man who knows he had entered the high point of his career. He had arrived in Chicago in 1886 fresh from training in Paris at age twenty-six to begin first as a lecturer, then as head of the Sculpture Department of the Art Institute of Chicago. With almost manic energy, he wrote endless articles on art for Chicago newspapers and produced commercial works, such as bronze relief sculptures with subjects like Learning, Love, Labor, which were mass-produced for the market in home decoration. He also crafted several portrait busts of members of the artistic, intellectual, and business community of Chicago, such as Victor Lawson, founder of Chicago's *Daily News*, novelist Hamlin Garland, and realtor Simeon B. Williams.

The Columbian Exposition in 1893 thrust him into prominence. Like so many who achieve fame, he was in the right place at the right time. He had been named Superintendent of Sculpture for the fair, a position he relished. Although the outstanding works at the fair were by Frederick MacMonnies and Daniel Chester French, Taft's elaborate group sculptures — *The Sleep of the Flowers* and *The Awakening of the Flowers*, flanking the entrance to the Horticultural Building — were close runners-up. More important, as superintendent he could hobnob with visiting sculptors at what Augustus Saint-Gaudens, the leading American sculptor from New York, called "the greatest gathering of talent since the fifteenth century."[4]

He could also enlist the help of students from his modelling classes. Taft, whose sister Zulime was a painter, considered himself forward-thinking about women artists. He made opportunities for a number of women sculptors at the fair, mainly because of pressing deadlines. When Taft asked whether he might hire women, Daniel Burnham, chief architect of the fair, responded, "Hire anyone, even white rabbits if they'll do the work."[5] So "White Rabbits" his female assistants were called, and the nickname suited them. Plaster and staff covered their long, upswept hair, ankle-length dresses, and smart leather boots with a fine white dust. Partly as a result of their experience and exposure at the fair, Taft's proteges, including Janet Scudder, Carol Brooks, Enid Yandell, Julia Bracken, and Bessie Potter Vonnoh, emerged as major American sculptors.

In the years since the Exposition of 1893, Taft had built his career shrewdly. He began as a lecturer with notes prepared for him by Mayne E. Allison, a former student.[6] These notes indicate that Taft offered his students a conventional, chronological view of the history of sculpture from the Greeks and Romans, through Michelangelo, to contemporary Americans such as Saint-Gaudens and Daniel Chester French. Taft put his lectures to good use in a lengthy history of American sculpture, which he published in 1903. In a country with almost no literature on its own sculpture beyond reviews of exhibitions and periodical articles, Taft's *History of American Sculpture* was a pioneering work that became the standard text for years and — because Taft took a biographical approach — earned him the sobriquet "the American Vasari."[7] Students studying the history of sculpture or modelling from The Master found him formidable and took his word as indisputable truth.

It was at the World's Columbian Exposition in 1893 that the thirty-three-year-old Taft first encountered the work of Rodin, including *The Kiss* and one of the figures from *The Burghers of Calais*, the powerful group sculpture that Rodin had almost finished. Later, Taft would say, "The unconventionality and emotional power of Rodin's *The Burghers of Calais* has always laid a strong grip on me ... [W]ithout precedent in the history of sculpture, they are ... Rodin's highest achievement."[8] Rodin had only recently been established as a major influence in 1889 at the Paris Exposition, partly because he had shared a show that year with Monet. It is surprising that Taft had not seen Rodin's work, since he had studied at the École des Beaux-Arts in Paris from 1880 to 1885, apart from one year back in Champaign, Illinois, where he had grown up. Now, however, seeing Rodin's burgher and outlines of the group of six in which it would play a role, set Taft on a path he would follow until his death in 1936: he would attempt group sculptures himself. It was a new direction that would alienate some of his students.

By 1906, this process was well underway. Taft had never liked portrait statues — those edifying tributes to great men that reminded Europeans, and early Americans, of the battles and political events that had imprinted history. "One pair of bronze trousers is very much like another," he used to say.[9] By 1899, as if announcing a shift to a new direction, his small study for a tentative group sculpture, *The Solitude of the Soul*, offered two men and two women still half-lodged in a circular block of plaster. This "non finito" technique, like Rodin's, emphasized mass and outline.[10] In 1904, enlarged to life-sized scale, this remarkably fluid and expressive work — the first major composition in Taft's mature style — took the gold medal at the St. Louis Exposition.[11] Just as Rodin's *Burghers* made manifest a historical text, Taft's *Solitude* dramatized a philosophical concept. Taft recorded his inspiration for *Solitude*: "The thought is the eternally present fact that however closely we may be thrown together by circumstances ... we are unknown to each other."[12] A marble reincarnation of the sculpture, commissioned by the Friends of American Art in 1913, stands today in the Sculpture Gallery of the Art Institute.

Taft had accomplished *Solitude* himself, but found the process of group sculpture too slow. As the century turned, he developed an ingenious program to speed up the process of creating large group sculptures. When class size and skill level permitted, he designed grand compositions comprised of several large figures on a small scale and assigned each figure to a different student. He guided them in the construction of one-third-size working models — or maquettes, as they were called — then assisted them in modelling the giant replicas. "A perfect beehive," he said of this activity, made up mainly of young women: "one of the merriest, prettiest scenes that I ever looked upon."[13] By the end of the year his composition would be fully realized and ready for display in public.

This first project for the Women's Life class of 1898–99 caused a scandal he did not anticipate. *Fountain of the Nymphs* is an exuberant composition of ten eight-foot nudes splashing water mischievously at each other. The central figure throws back her head laughing, while another kneels and clings to her hips, shrinking and drenched. Yet another shields herself from the spray of water directed at her from the six impish nymphs around the circular basin. The basin and figurines were erected in the Lakefront Park, between the Institute and Lake Michigan, as a temporary summer exhibit (since the figures were made of plaster, which would eventually erode).

Over a hundred newspaper articles attacking the fountain — some from as far away as New York and Oshkosh — led Taft to a final defence of his project, pleading an analogy with MacMonnies's mermen in *The Ship of State* and somewhat disingenuously using words like "jolly," "merry," "comical," "amiable," and "childlike" to describe a composition that is clearly pagan and erotic.[14]

It might have been MacMonnies's far more controversial statue *Bacchante and Infant Faun* (1894) that inspired Taft. That statue of a young mother, dancing naked in an exuberant, probably drunken, state while waving her baby and a bunch of grapes in abandon overhead has precisely the irreverent energy of what came to be called "*that* fountain."[15] The contrast between the body-shrouding clothes that women sculptors of the day wore and the brazen nudity of the "nymphs" says much about why the public were offended. Some condemned the very fact that women were drawing and modelling clay from the nude.

In 1906, a debate about nudity was raging in the art community itself. One Anthony Comstock had raided the Art Students' League in New York, taking books with nudes in them, and published an article on "the crime of the nude." Although most in the art community thought Comstock prudish, the question of *public* (i.e. unavoidable) displays of nudity in works of art was seen as a challenge to "the sound mandate of public policy" to abide by the unwritten American law: "screen your nakedness."[16] By 1906, it had only been three years since the best student anatomical drawings in the Art Institute's calendar featured fig leaves.

Taft fared better with his second class project in 1901–02. *A Primitive Funeral Procession* could hardly be accused of flagrant eroticism. Six women draped head-to-toe in hooded, heavy clothes, preceded and followed by two mourners, carry a coffin. The procession is based on a decoration from the medieval tomb of Burgundian Philippe Pot, which Taft had seen in the Louvre. As before, each figure is modelled by a different student.

His third project, accomplished by the following year's class, and fortuitously funded by the recent bequest to the Institute of $1 million from lumber merchant Benjamin Franklin Ferguson, was to result in one of his most famous works: *Fountain of the Great Lakes*. The interest from Ferguson's money was earmarked for municipal art to beautify Chicago, and Taft was the first to avail himself of this annual grant.[17] "It is glorious!" he exclaimed. "It means success on the movement to build up a school of sculpture in Chicago."[18]

Above all, it meant building up the reputation of Lorado Taft. The project had simmered in his mind since a remark made at the World's Columbian Exposition. Daniel Burnham chided the American sculptors for "not 'making anything' of the great natural resources in the west, especially the Great Lakes."[19] Taft brought his youthful fascination with the Danaïdes (forty-nine sisters doomed to carry water in sieves to atone for the deaths of their husbands) to bear on the group work. Five beautiful American Danaïdes — each sculpted from Taft's composition — pour water gracefully from one large fluted shell to another. Lake Superior holds the top shell aloft, and the overflowing water moves through shells held by Michigan, Huron, and Erie until it reaches Ontario, who gazes out along her extended arm towards an imaginary ocean as the water flows along an imagined St. Lawrence River. The students' small-scale models were later enlarged, then bronzed in 1913. The *Fountain of the Great Lakes* now adorns the west wall to the right of the entrance to the Art Institute. Few know that students modelled the original figures that were said to embody "all that was best in essentially American art, uninspired by alien ideas."[20]

By 1905, Taft had perfected the use of students to speed up his Rodin-inspired group sculptures. That year, he conducted the fourth and most ambitious of his class projects, *An Incident in the Temple* (or *The Woman Taken in Adultery*), from the New Testament parable, a subject that tempered a controversial subject with the moral condemnation of it. Ten students — eight women and two men — crafted their individual figures based on Taft's design. In the centre of the "panorama,"[21] Christ kneels and writes on the ground while a Roman centurion behind him asserts his authority in a dramatic gesture towards a crowd of twenty-five spectators of all ages and from many walks of life: scribes, Pharisees, even a child. The terrified woman herself cringes apart from the others.[22] The Institute's 1906 exhibition showed clearly the way Taft was using his students. Many exhibits were designed by Taft, but executed by his students. Two of them, *St. George and the Dragon* and *Witch Fountain*, were made by a promising student called Florence Wyle, though she also displayed a fountain, *Boy Piping to Fishes*, that she had designed herself.[23]

That same year, in keeping with the expansion of his Sculpture classes at the Art Institute, Taft realized another dream: the creation of a Renaissance *bottega* or live-in workshop for himself and his students. The University of Chicago's campus bracketed Midway Plaisance, the mile-long ribbon of green that had been the site of the Columbian Exposition's sideshows, with the Ferris wheel at its eastern end. Roughly in the middle of the south side of the grassy Midway stood a large red brick building, originally a group of stables. This was the building Taft leased for his Midway Studios, which he used for the rest of his life. Next door was a big house where Taft lived with his family. As other loosely connected buildings were added on (eventually there were thirteen), the Midway Studios not only accommodated Taft's increasingly ambitious projects, but also housed his retinue of assistants — sometimes as many as thirty. Sculptors who at one time or another worked at Taft's Midway atelier included Charles Mulligan, the marble-cutter he had invited to become his fellow teacher at the Institute; Leonard Crunelle, also recruited by Taft, whose delicate winsome garden sculptures, which reminded Taft of "the purity and simplicity of the fifteenth century Florentines,"[24] were made in 1905; Fred Torrey, who would later do low-relief decorations for the first art deco skyscraper in 1927, and his wife, Mabel Torrey; Frederick Hibbard who completed a heroic monument to Carter Henry Harrison for Union Park in 1907; and Nellie Walker, a tiny (4'10") protege of Taft with a "winning personality,"[25] whose bust of Lincoln (done when she was sixteen) had been exhibited as the "Work of an Iowa Girl" in the Iowa pavilion of the Columbian Exposition. At Midway Studios Taft quickly established an artistic community, anticipating that a constant exchange of ideas, technical know-how, and encouragement from other sculptors would stimulate creativity — especially his own.

This complex of loosely connected buildings was known as "The Barn." It accommodated studio space for Taft, his assistants, and associated sculptors; a dormitory; a kitchen (Taft called it "the only submarine kitchen in Chicago")[26] that provided food for twenty-five or so apprentices in a dining room sporting a little bower with artificial vines; a small stage on which pageants were performed; his "Dream Museum" room that contained tiny models of sculptural masterpieces and eight dioramas — an early form of "peep show" — of famous Greek, Roman and Renaissance statues, also created by students, and used by Taft in lectures across the United States; and a large inner courtyard overflowing with Taft's works-in-progress. The scale of this operation was enormous. It still stands — though it was moved a block west in 1929 to accommodate the University of Chicago's expansion — as a testament to Taft and his dreams of greatness. Only one of Taft's multitude of creations remains in the courtyard today: the *Shaler Memorial Angel* (1932), a seven-foot bronze statue cast from the original marble gravestone in a Waupon, Wisconsin cemetery. It is a seated angel that lifts its lovely head in prayer, looking up from an open book across its knee, as if expecting divine bliss — like Taft himself.[27]

TAFT'S MIDWAY STUDIOS community grew out of a less formal summer colony where he was "perpetual president"[28] — Eagle's Nest Camp, high atop the bluffs along Rock River at Oregon, Illinois, which began in 1898. Wallace Heckman, the University of Chicago's business manager, leased the fifteen acre property to eleven Chicago men engaged in the arts for one dollar a year. Taft had erected a sixty-foot Indian statue, *Black Hawk*, at the highest point on the bluffs.

In the summer of 1907 the Eagle's Nest campers performed an *al fresco* rendition of Maurice Maeterlinck's *The Blind* (*Les Aveugles*), a tragic play in which a group of blind people wander in the woods holding up a baby who can see and is their only hope of deliverance. "We acted it [one glad Sunday] in the autumn twilight under the 'immemorial oaks,'" Taft recalled, "reciting our parts in quaint French, enveloped all in weird institutional cloaks made from old tent-flys."[29]

The result was his most powerful group sculpture to date. "Winter was upon us before the enlargement began in 'The Barn' ... in Chicago," Taft recalled, "and as usual, the lecture engagements called [me] away when [I] thought I was most needed. Not a bit of it! Those girls went to work with hammer and saw, and built up the entire frame-work of wood, as beautiful art-nouveau hen-coop or Filipino residence, as you please, and had the clay all on before my return. It was done accurately, too; not a thing to do but to 'finish.'"[30] *The Blind* dominated the Institute's twelfth annual exhibition in 1908, where three hundred works of art had been culled from a thousand entries. The Art Institute *Bulletin* reported, "It is safe to say that no similar American exhibition — we mean the sculpture department of a purely local exhibition — of late years has equalled it, even in New York."[31]

The Institute had begun to see itself as rivalling art institutions in the east. As the Institute's president Charles Hutchinson commented in 1910, "Chicago is regarded as a sink hole beside the lake by the artistic cult of Europe ... I don't know how [they] got this impression of Chicago ... [T]he three foreign members of the art jury which passed [judgement] upon the pictures in the present exhibit are going away with altered ideas ... I expect them to do missionary work among the great painters with whom they come in contact."[32]

Much was being written at the time about the precise nature of American art vis-à-vis European art. Although it is difficult to separate rant and propaganda from reliable observation, American artists in the early years of the twentieth century were convinced that a new era had begun. "Neither Briton nor Frenchman would have painted with similar frankness and sensibility," ran a typical article in 1904, "one would have been true to his venerated tradition, and the other lost in his inherent passion for obtrusive spectacular effect."[33] In particular, the slavish adherence to the tradition of European art was contrasted with the fresh and vigorous work of America. "Imitation," as one critic put it, "was the curse of American Art."[34] "Freedom from affectation," "sane balance," "lack of reserve," "formalism," and "rugged strength": these were the qualities associated with the more energetic creations of the New World.[35] This energy was especially associated with artists, like Taft, from the midwest. There, youthful naivety and independence of mind, even a certain "rawness" was touted as a driving force in the arts that — potentially at least — could invigorate American art in general. A "new epoch"[36] in American art — which some equated with the Italian Renaissance[37] — was perceived as having begun. As one writer put it, "American art has emerged from the chrysalis and come at last into its own."[38] And the centre for this purest form of American rejuvenation of the arts was Chicago, a city that had invented the skyscraper, held the biggest world's fair to date, and prided itself on forward-looking brash energy: that "Stormy, husky, brawling,/City of the Big Shoulders," as poet Carl Sandburg would later describe it.[39]

In Chicago the democratic was proclaimed in art as elsewhere. Art was not for the elite alone. Just as many of Chicago's industrialists had hauled themselves up by their bootstraps, artists and the audiences for art were not intimidated by their lack of pedigrees. The Art Institute, for example, prided itself on being "as nearly free as possible" and accepted the poor as students (termed "Arabs of the street") as well as the rich.[40] Kemeys's lions were chosen to flank the Art Institute stairs partly because Kemeys "[believed] in things which appeal to the people."[41] As one critic observed, "To an artist, one of the charms of the West is that it has been only partly exploited ... The most encouraging thing about the newly developed aestheticism of Chicago is the opportunity for virile and original work which lies at hand."[42]

At the time Taft arrived in Chicago in 1886, sculpture was represented by three main types of public monument: tributes to great men, usually on horseback; markers celebrating critical events in American history; and memorials to those who could afford them in graveyards. These were usually positioned high on pedestals to inspire awe. An article on the New York sculptor Saint-Gaudens was typically subtitled "The Sculptor Who has Typified American Character and has left us Noble Memorials of Great Events in American History."[43] In Chicago, Saint-Gaudens's *Abraham Lincoln* (1887) — a work with which all Art Institute students would have been familiar — portrayed the simple, gaunt figure standing in front of a large chair, his left hand grasping the lapel of his frock coat, head bent as if listening to something important or preparing to utter something profound. Leonard Volk's *Volunteer Fire Fighters' Monument* (1864), *Our Heroes: Civil War Monument* (1869–70), and *Stephen A. Douglas Tomb and Memorial* (1881) — the first public statues in Chicago — were characteristically earnest and edifying. Their object was to commemorate, dignify, and idealize America. These larger-than-life statues monumentalized their nation. Just as their subjects had shaped the country, such sculptors shaped statues that would forever remind all citizens of its greatness. As one art critic of the time put it, "The statues and monuments that adorn our cities and towns should ... be memorials to brave men and brave deeds."[44] Another wrote, "The great monuments of the world are the mile-posts in the roll of the centuries — their production marks like a sad sweet refrain the great moments of the race ... Every monument is the last note — a personal message sent down to the people to come."[45]

Although one of his first commissions in Chicago had been a monument to the battlefield at Gettysburg, Taft disliked national anthems in stone or bronze.[46] The "academic" neoclassical style, inspired by Greek and Roman statues, which he had been trained to imitate at the École des Beaux-Arts in Paris, was not quite what he wanted either. It seemed to him too sedate, too static. Starting with *Solitude of the Soul*, he was feeling his way into a different kind of sculpture — one whose goal was Beauty. He abandoned the over-worked detail of his early monuments and commercial narrative panels in favour of naturalistic, sweeping sculptural masses that embodied huge rhythms. The sculpture he produced has a powerful feminine quality that distinguishes it from the erect heroics of his predecessors Saint-Gaudens and Volk and takes more seriously the organic nature of his materials, letting the mediums he used speak through and with his compositions in one harmonious whole.

This focus on Beauty was what — above all — he transmitted to his students. His larger and larger ideas — culminating eventually in his stupendous eighty-two-foot-long *Fountain of Time* (1922)[47] at the west end of the Midway — were often based on literary texts or fragments, words which struck him not only because they were beautiful, but also because they somehow expressed the human condition, the state of the soul. Most of his group sculptures concerned what he called "the great beyond ... veiled from humanity"[48] and the tortured agony of humanity in its struggle to pierce that veil. *Fountain of Time*, conceived in 1909, was inspired by a couplet from "The Paradox of Time" by poet Austin Dobson "expressing the wave-like surge and movement of life itself passing in review before a rock-like mysterious hooded figure"[49] twenty feet tall: Father Time. "Time goes, you say? Ah, no / Alas, time stays; we go!"[50]

It was this fragile and transitory limbo between Christian — and national — conviction and the secular abstract manipulation of form that Taft captured in his own work and impressed on his students. By the end of the first decade of the twentieth century, The Master, Taft, presided over American sculpture. He was a member of the National Sculpture Society, the Society of Western Artists, the Chicago Society of Artists, the Municipal Art League, the Municipal Art Commission of Chicago, and the Polytechnic Society. He was a force — perhaps *the* force — to be reckoned with.

Florence◦⟋

When Frances Loring entered the Life Modelling class at the Art Institute of Chicago in the fall of 1906, one of her new classmates was Florence Wyle. Florence, compact and self-contained, was well-established at the Institute. Six years older than Frances, she had spent the last three years in the sculpture program. As one of the more talented students, who had shown her works alongside those of Taft, she had been invited to teach in the Summer School that year — its seventh season — and had just finished teaching her first class in modelling before resuming her own courses. To a new, younger student like Frances, she would have seemed experienced and capable: admirable in every way. To Florence, Frances, with her wide and varied experience abroad at Europe's major art centres, would have seemed an enviable — quite exotic — creature, decidedly unlike the midwest girls who were the school's main fare. Later they would agree that they "clicked" at once.[1] "It seemed amazing how congenial [we] were, how [our] ideals merged."[2]

Florence — like Harriet Hosmer half a century earlier — had intended to become a doctor. Florence had chosen medicine after a rural Illinois childhood spent caring for "scores of creatures that she mended and befriended,"[3] and "because," as she later said, "I wanted to do something useful in this world."[4] But whereas Hosmer could not study in Boston because women were not accepted into medical school in 1850 (she went to St. Louis, Missouri, instead, where she was allowed to study anatomy), Florence set her sights on the Department of Medicine at the University of Illinois, which had just opened its medical school to women the year before she graduated from high school in 1899.

But before she could enter the medical school, she was obliged to complete a three-year pre-med program. One of the required courses at the small Urbana campus of the University of Illinois was Art and Design, oddly set amid science courses in Chemistry, Botany, Physics, Physiology, Psychology, Zoology, and one in Latin.

Florence's heroine when she was a teenager was Rosa Bonheur, an eccentric French painter of the early-to-mid nineteenth century. "I remember that I used to think Rosa Bonheur was a wonderful person (I think so still)," she recalled in 1918, "and I would have liked to do the same work, but it never occurred to me that a common mortal might be an artist. Later I learned that anyone may do anything if he cares enough about it to work hard."[5]

Rosa Bonheur's main appeal to Florence was her love of animals, the main subject of her art.[6] Bonheur "had a complete menagerie in her home: a lion and lioness, a stag, a wild sheep, a gazelle, horses, etc.," a friend recalled. "One of her pets was a young lion whom she allowed to run about and often romped with."[7] She arranged an unconventional means of studying animals. In 1852, at age thirty, she received permission from the prefecture of police in Paris to dress in men's clothing and visit butcher shops, slaughterhouses, and agricultural fairs to study animal anatomy. Photos show her, hair cropped, in men's trousers and shoes, wearing a smock, fedora in hand. She also rode horses astride instead of sidesaddle and smoked cigarettes in public: extraordinarily daring for a woman at the time. Her success as an *animalier* won her the Legion of Honour in France in 1865, an occasion on which it was said, "genius has no sex."[8]

It was Newton Wells, a painter, sculptor, and architect who had trained at the Académie Julien in Paris, who noticed Florence's artistic flair and persuaded her to give up medicine for painting and modelling.[9] She had studied anatomical drawing in her first year; in her second, painting; and in her third, sculpture. "When I got to sculpture," Florence recalls, "I knew that was for me."[10] Much later, she would remember that she responded to art because, like Rosa Bonheur, "I was interested in life — trees and animals and such things — and I watched them, and I thought about them. And now and then I'd see a drawing of a bird or something and I'd connect things together."[11] In the fall of 1903, after three years in pre-med, Florence moved from Urbana to Chicago to study sculpture at the Art Institute.

Her family — and in particular her "fiercely religious and strict"[12] father — did not approve of her career switch. On her graduation from high school (with outstanding marks), Florence's father had given her $500 "to establish herself in life." A small-town druggist from farming stock, he ran the Wyle household "with a heavy Victorian hand." Florence, who had a twin brother and three other siblings, recalls the torture of her father's supervision of their sleep: "He insisted ... that man was the only species capable of sleeping on its back ... Therefore, all five of his children were to sleep on their backs ... And he rose in the middle of the night to check that his edict was not over-looked."[13] According to Wyle's friend, sculptor Rebecca Sisler, Benjamin Solomon Wyle's rigid puritanism "may indeed have been the beginning of her deep-rooted distrust of men. By the time she had reached womanhood, she could have been taken as the prototype of a feminist."[14]

Benjamin's child rearing almost inevitably resulted in a resentment of men. She and her twin brother Frank, born in Trenton, Illinois, 24 November 1881, were treated entirely differently. To Florence, it seemed he had all the fun, playing outside while she remained inside and did the housework she hated. She recalled how her father would tell Frank to do some gardening, and how Frank would play baseball instead. While he played, Florence did his gardening, for sheer love of being outdoors. When their father came home, he would praise Frank, who knew his sister could be counted on to cover for him.[15] At school, Florence was noted for her love of physical exertion and athletic skill. She was captain of the girls' basketball team. "She was a bit on the daring side," a classmate would later recall, "and shocked some of her elders by wearing bloomers in 'skinning the cat' and other stunts. She was skilled in boxing too. Give her a pair of boxing gloves and she packed a wallop."[16]

A photo of Florence as a child shows a small tomboy, "hair spiking out in defiance of feminine tradition," a rooster cradled under one arm. She had lovingly applied a splint to the rooster's broken leg and kept it in a box outside the kitchen door until it healed. After that, she recalled, "he used to come and wait for me."[17] Like Rosa Bonheur, who began drawing animals at age ten, Florence's favourite pastime, encouraged by her artistic mother, Libbie, was copying pictures of animals.[18] When she was told at an early age that her beloved animals could not go to heaven, she rejected God.

Florence's move to the Art Institute in 1903 opened a whole new world for her — one quite unlike the rural environment she grew up in or the small-town university campus at Urbana where she had taken the pre-med program. She moved in with a relative in the respectable west-end Chicago suburb of Oak Park with its arching trees and sprawling lawns free of fences, where Ernest Hemingway was then a pampered boy of three, and thirty-six-year-old Frank Lloyd Wright had already begun designing and building his organic, earth-hugging structures — what came to be known as "The Prairie School of Architecture"[19] — in the open-concept house he had built for himself in 1895. Florence travelled to and from the Institute by train through the seedier part of Chicago. At the time it was possible to get a meal for five or ten cents. By 1906, her summer school salary of $80 for the session would have gone a long way to defray her expenses.[20]

Florence arrived at the Art Institute when it was at the height of expansion. The first generation Chicago industrialists and meat packers had begun dying off at the turn of the century, and many of them had left large amounts of money to the Institute. Soon after the Columbian Exposition, director Charles Hutchinson and associate Martin Ryerson had scooped up several art treasures at the auction of Prince Demidoff's collection in Florence, Italy, to the horror of European art lovers. They acquired works by Rembrandt, Hals, Jan Steen, Hobbemas, Van Ostades, Ted Borch, Massys, and Ruisdael. Mrs. Henry Field donated her lions, and the Fullerton family funded the

500-seat Fullerton Lecture Room. Extravagant suggestions for a menagerie, a gymnasium, and a conservatory were aired (but never realized) in 1896. In 1898, the Stickneys sponsored further acquisition of artworks, a bequest that was soon followed in 1899 by a donation from Martin Ryerson to establish the Ryerson Library, and another from Timothy B. Blackstone in 1900 to build the Great Sculpture Hall, which opened in 1903, the year Florence arrived. In 1903, too, Maria Sheldon Scammon donated money to start the annual Scammon Lectures. Prize money and travelling scholarships from civic clubs and individuals began to appear. And to crown all these donations, in 1905, pioneer lumber merchant Benjamin Franklin Ferguson bequeathed a million dollars to the Institute, to fund sculptures to beautify Chicago — a mandate perfectly suited to Lorado Taft, whose *Great Lakes* fountain was the first to be funded. Charles Hutchinson — promoting the democratic spirit of the west — commented, "In no other city are there organizations so well adapted to the peoples' needs."[21]

During 1906 — the year Florence met Frances Loring — classes were punctuated by the loud sounds of renovation. An eastern corridor on the second floor costing $11,000 was being built to accommodate new collections. That same year, Alphonse Mucha — the Czech painter, made famous by his 1894 art nouveau poster of a fairy-like young woman with long swirls of red hair meant to depict Sarah Bernhardt in her role as Gismonda — was in residence. Like Frances, he had studied at the Munich Academy of Art and the Académie Colarossi in Paris. At the Institute, he taught students the primacy of *line*, whether undulating, abstract, or geometric. "[He] said we must study everything around us carefully," one student recalls, "not only the human figure but animals, flowers, and all there is in nature around us. We must become sensitive to the smallest things, feel their full beauty before we can give others our conception of them in drawings."[22] Each year there was a flurry of exhibitions, lectures, receptions, and evening entertainments. Overall, these first few years of the century were "the unfoldment of one dream and then another."[23]

Enrolment mushroomed accordingly. Between 1883 and 1889, fees from tuition (at $25 per twelve-week term for day classes) rose from $6,588 to $10,164. During the decade that followed, enrolment increased by another sixty percent. The growth of the Institute was "a vital part of the city's evolution."[24] The Life Modelling class Florence entered in 1903 had 368 students, 267 of whom were women.

At the same time as the Institute developed, the philosophy underlying its program changed. Under the direction of architect and landscape gardener William M.R. French, the school had been founded firmly on the principles of the Düsseldorf school in Germany. This meant a diploma program in which students advanced through three classes: the elementary form, the prepatory class, and the top form. Translated into the coursework at the Institute, this meant moving from outline and perspective drawings that copied other works to drawing — especially the full figure and busts — from sculpture in the Institute's galleries then, finally, drawing, painting, and modelling from life — whether models were costumed or nude. Nude classes were in session all day, sometimes involving as many as ten models a day.[25] Live models — some probably drawn from Chicago's lively tenderloin only a few blocks south — for 1891 cost the Institute over $1,000; by 1903 that cost had increased considerably. Although no dissecting was done in the Institute, arrangements to watch dissections could be made with the University of Illinois's medical school, and French's classes in drawing anatomy (Artistic Anatomy) were mandatory. As French, who had graduated from Harvard with a degree in Classics in 1864, stated, "The study of the human figure is by universal consent the vital stem or basis of academic art study."[26]

Lorado Taft had taught sculpture since 1889 when he joined the Institute, and his department was highly rated. As the school's calendar claimed: "The department of modelling and sculpture is of unusual importance." John Vanderpoel, author of the text *The Human Body*, taught drawing meticulously — or, rather, meticulous drawing. As a student himself he had been reprimanded for putting six toes on his drawing of a model until his instructor realized that the model actually had six toes. Largely due to Vanderpoel, the School of the Art Institute acquired its reputation as a school of "severe drawing."

Just prior to Florence's arrival at the Institute, the French method had replaced the Düsseldorf philosophy. The rigid German "diploma" method gave way to ongoing student competition. From 1903 on, entering students

— except teachers in training — would not graduate with a diploma. Students attended a *concours*, or competition, at the end of each month's work; those with the highest grade would be given their choice of seating position during the posing of the next model.[27] As Lawton S. Parker, an AIC instructor who had introduced this change after a trip to Europe, argued, "The great mistake made in America [has] been the insistence that the student work at art for art's sake alone. The principal advantage in competition was that it enabled the teacher to discover his gifted pupils and at the same time gave each one something to work for besides mere success at painting."[28] Such a philosophy not only pleased students, who were now allowed to choose their teachers and the ateliers they worked in, but also dovetailed with Chicago's buoyancy.

Added to the excitement of an art school that was burgeoning in the first years of the century was the almost intoxicating freedom women were at last enjoying in all fields of education. European and American academies alike had been mainly inaccessible to women in the last quarter of the nineteenth century. Especially in fields such as medicine and sculpture — where direct viewing of the naked human body was essential — women were excluded on the grounds that such knowledge would terrify, corrupt, or ruin them. When Florence entered the Institute in 1903, it had been a mere twenty-five years since women had been first allowed in 1877 to draw from the male nude at the Pennsylvania Academy. Before that, women could only look at the Academy's collection of nude classical plaster casts at specified times on "Ladies' Days."[29] Only a few women attempted to become sculptors before 1850, and they accomplished little: "[P]reachers and ladies' magazines warned that a woman, especially a married woman, who attempted serious intellectual labour [of any kind] would bring chaos into the social order, warp the development of her children, overtax her small brain and delicate constitution, and go mad or develop 'brain fever.'"[30] Women like Rosa Bonheur or Harriet Hosmer, who succeeded in establishing careers in painting or sculpture, tended to be outrageous eccentrics who appropriated male privileges.

Controversies also continued to rage around whether or not women's classes in art and the art they produced should be conducted or exhibited separate from the classes and work of men. The Women's Pavilion at the

Columbian Exposition had been a case in point. Many articles raised and discussed this subject. One in 1905 (by a woman), about a woman sculptor, Clio Bracken, concluded, for instance, with these reassuring words: "The worker is less than thirty [in fact she was thirty-five], with a face of great beauty and a heart full of youthful enthusiasm for life. In her character there is the simplicity of true genius. And her children are dearer to her than her art."[31] Another (also by a woman) several years later, argued that because women have less freedom than men, their art will be different. "What of the mother of children, the tender, devoted, adoring mother who also has the great gift? There is much that a woman can do which is beautiful and essential and a definite part of the world's development in art conditions with her studio next to the nursery; nevertheless, these women do not eventually find seats on Olympus."[32] A third article (by a man) about an exhibition of paintings by women artists, agreed that, because women's lives differed from men's, their art would differ too; but, according to him, "a 'woman's exhibit' is something out of the past ... and belongs to the helpless days of the crinoline when ladies fainted if they were spoken to with undue harshness; when a sampler, at least in America, was the only field for feminine artistic endeavour."[33] In a follow-up article about a woman sculptor in whom he saw both masculine and feminine perception, the same writer complained about "separate standards of excellence for men and women in art," and held that galleries and juries are prejudiced against women. He defended women artists by arguing that their very difference from men is their strength: "[T]he tenderness, sensitiveness and sympathetic qualities which women give their art ... is born of motherhood, real or potential ... which is one of the compensations which women receive for a certain separateness of life which social conditions so often force upon them."[34]

Women were expected to be beautiful and inspire art, not create it. This was a time when the cult of Beauty, fostered by the nineteenth century and intensified almost into a religion (at a time when organized religion was just beginning to lose some of its force), provoked reverent awe. "Why should the world have thrust upon it, in the name of art," one art critic typically maintained in 1906, "pictures of deformity, ugliness, obliquity, inanity, mental vacuity, spiritual poverty — anything out of touch with great, righteous manhood and pure, honourable womanhood, with glorious nature, with the full life, that should be, but too often is not?"[35] Artists were male, muses were female, and the purpose of art was to create Beauty to exalt the viewer.

Even so, most sculpture students at the Art Institute when Florence was there were women. It was as if the floodgates of social restraint had opened and waves of women surged into an occupation that was previously taboo. As in other professions, such as medicine, law, and academic teaching, women now had an opportunity to become financially independent.

A vivid picture of student life for women and men is described in the student publications *Brush and Pencil* (begun in 1893), *The Sketchbook*, and *'Art Throbs*, which began the year Florence arrived. Initiation ceremonies into the Life Class were rowdy: singsongs, burlesques of faculty, duels using paintbrushes as swords and palettes as shields, and gargantuan pie-eating contests.[36] Social events were as elaborate as those of the Eagle's Nest campers. The Renaissance Pageant held in the Great Sculpture Hall, for instance, was a full-costume affair. Students borrowed costumes of royalty, artists, nuns, and monks from the storage rooms of the Costume Life Drawing Class, and danced the night away. "Once again," a student write-up goes, "Botticelli meets Simonetta, his Venus of the Sea; once again Lorenzo pleads absolution from Savonarola, while the light of the burning Vanities flickers over all."[37] A Halloween party in the anatomy room featured skeletons and jack o' lanterns; stunts and competitions, such as jumping over lighted candles, augmented the requisite dancing. The St. Patrick's Day party involved a shamrock puzzle-hunt, kissing the Blarney stone, Irish songs, and a dancer in national costume, followed by dancing for all. At one Mardi Gras party on the theme of "The Arabian Nights," a camel wandered freely around the Great Sculpture Hall. At every event, there was more dancing, which Florence — loosed from her puritan family — loved: "I danced every dance," she later recalled.[38]

Anxiety around the problems for women who wanted to be artists emerged in The Old Maid Party. The winner in 1909 sported corkscrew curls, a parrot, and horn-rimmed spectacles. One solution to this problem was jokingly voiced in "The Song of the 1907 Initiates":

We've resolved never to marry, marry,
But will turn to art again;
In our work we never tarry, tarry,
For the false, deceiving man;
Yet we know that we'll be happy, happy,
If succeed we only can,
Not to wed, but instead,
Just to draw the perfect man.[39]

‖ 6

Charley Mulligan ⟿

In the basement of the School of the Art Institute of Chicago, a young, darkly handsome marble-cutter named Charles Mulligan conducted sculpture classes three evenings a week from seven to nine-thirty. In his musical Irish accent, Charles — who went by Charley — offered instructions and encouragement amid the sharp regular blows of mallets on chisel and the irregular clip of marble chips on the floor. Some sculpted directly on stone, but others moulded clay, "each one intent on some idea peculiar to himself."[1] Most came to Charley — Mr. Mulligan — to learn how to cut statues directly from stone, watching the miracle of flesh emerge from rock.

Taft's classes were mainly made up of women, but Mulligan's were mainly made up of men. In 1903, for example, out of forty-nine students, forty were men. These men could only attend evening classes; during the day they were marble- or metal-cutters themselves, or photographers, modellers, and sculptors' assistants. They turned to Charley to "[enlarge] their usefulness ... [and acquire] more refined taste, more artistic treatment, better construction and technique, and a desire for better artistic results."[2] Charley understood these men. He himself had fit in night classes for twelve long years in his attempt to become a sculptor, and it had been a happy accident that Taft heard of the few statues he had made in his spare time at the marble-cutting factory. Taft saw and liked his work, after which he summoned the twenty-year-old to become his student at the Institute in 1887. After Charley had worked a year under Taft's tutelage, his parents, "possessing means,"[3] had sponsored him to go off to study in Paris at Taft's alma mater, the École des Beaux-Arts. On his return to Chicago, Taft made him foreman of the statue-making crew in the Horticultural building at the Columbian Exposition, where, Taft said, "Instantly all was peace and harmony."[4]

Taft ought not to have been surprised. A working-class man like Charley Mulligan knew how to roll up his sleeves and pitch in with other men — especially immigrants like his own family, who arrived in Chicago from Riverdale, Ireland, when he was six. He viewed his students as peers, not as subservient assistants the way Taft did. Charley worked hard, as his parents had. Students remember his "unusual energy," "characteristic personal force," "enterprising spirit," and the "thorough knowledge" he gleaned "from his stint in Europe and his practical experience in the trades."[5] For these students, the acquisition of sculptural skills was not an embellishment on a charmed life. It was the means by which a step up from a lifetime of hard labour might be won. After straining to finance the preliminary courses in drawing and modelling from the head and standing figure, as well as the assigned compositions, many could not even afford the clay and plaster for casting. These supplies were provided to the night students free of the charges day classes entailed.

Charley's practical approach to sculpture was forcefully and surely given: first, "breadth and simplicity — seeing the modeling in the largest masses, and treating masses by broad planes." Later came "finish and detail." "Proportion of the figure," he told them, "character, pose, and line of weight" were paramount. Constantly, he referred them back to their day trades, reminding them that they already had "minds accustomed by mechanical pursuits and conventional commercial taste to [eliminate] the unessentials to the sacrifice of the big things seen in the best work."[6] As elsewhere at the Institute,

Mulligan believed, "[T]he bedrock of study was the human figure, and it was to be shaped to the highest beauty in order to [emancipate] us from the world of ugliness that touches us on every hand."[7]

Charley's evening classes had been steadily increasing ever since he took them over, two years after his work at the Columbian Exposition was finished, from Herbert MacNeil, who had left for Rome in 1895. Chicago had reaped the benefits ever since. In the mid-1890s, manufacturers of metal work and ornamental iron and bronze, for instance, could not find men to do their work; by 1898, however, they attributed their implementation of artistic designs in industrial art throughout the city to the training at the Art Institute.[8] Without realizing it, the clean-shaven young Irishman, dressed like his students in white shirt and black bow tie, was advancing the Institute in a direction it would later emphasize: the wedding of fine arts to practical crafts through design.

Apart from his evening classes, Charley Mulligan had his own atelier — a workshop where he created his own sculptures and taught students. He also maintained a studio at his family's cottage at Bass Lake, Indiana, for the summers. Florence Wyle was one of the first entrance students under the new regulations to have free choice of teacher and atelier, and it was to Charley Mulligan — a man whose background was not far from her own down-to-earth rural family — that she turned. And it was from him, both in the Institute and at Bass Lake, that she learned to chisel direct from stone. This skill was — above all — what Mulligan brought to the Art Institute, and it was because of him that it gained a reputation as "the only Art school in the country where young sculptors were taught to chisel their creations from the marble block ... as part of their regular instruction."[9] It was mainly this innovation which led William French to claim: "[T]he department of sculpture [has] asserted itself in a manner not easily overlooked and [is] the most important department of its kind of which I [have] knowledge."[10]

FLORENCE DID NOT like Lorado Taft. Beginning in her second year, she took his day class in modelling. "I studied with him very little," she later recalled, "as I had [already] begun with Mr. Mulligan & greatly preferred his work."[11] What little contact she had with Taft did not endear him to her. She did not appreciate his familiarity with female students — those playful pats on the knee and the odd pinch on the bottom that he felt were his right.[12] Nor did she like the way he used his students — a parallel to the way her brother had used her — to do his work for him. She had soon been "promoted" to working on Taft's own large group sculptures. Hers was the "honour" of modelling hands and feet for his various works. One photograph shows her in a long dress, sleeves rolled up, her thick brown hair piled on her head, working on *The Woman Taken in Adultery*, Taft's group project for 1905–06. That same year, a student sculpture of a nude couple — probably goddesses — feeding a rabbit was appropriated by Taft in 1911[13] for an Italian marble copy renamed *Pastoral* for the Fernery greenhouse in the Garfield Park Conservatory.[14] Florence's regard for Taft finally plummeted when an Indian head she had modelled in class disappeared, then reappeared in one of The Master's monumental sculptures in Washington.[15]

At the time Florence began studying with Charley Mulligan in 1903, he was being praised by Taft in one of his many articles as "one of the men of promise in American sculpture."[16] Taft thought Mulligan's judgement was "not infallible," but he liked his "faithfulness and energy," and found him "amenable and ready to put your suggestions to good use," as he wrote in a letter of recommendation to Daniel Chester French.[17] Mulligan created the requisite public monuments. In 1900 he was the sculptor for the Civil War memorial dome (modelled on the Roman Pantheon) at Vicksburg, Mississippi. He designed and executed the allegorical figures of Justice and Goodness, Knowledge and Education, the Dignity of Labour, and Morality for the Supreme Court Building in Lincoln, Illinois. In Chicago, he created the *Fourth of July* fountain (1902); a somewhat forced piece, *Lincoln the Orator* (1903); and the *William McKinley Monument* (1905), commemorating the 1890 tariff bill that bears McKinley's name. But his real talent lay in a unique sensibility that united tender concern for animals and children with the vigorous depiction of working-class men.

He first struck this note in 1901 with his *Miner and Child* (*Home* or *The Miner's Homecoming*), a moving depiction of a father crouched down to embrace his small daughter on his return home from working in the mines. Mulligan's *Fourth of July* fountain — on its Liberty Bell–shaped base — had featured two boys and two girls celebrating the holiday with noisemakers, flares, and a drum and bugle, with one uppermost swirling a flag, but it seems conventional compared to his miner and child. For the 1903 Pan-American Exposition in Buffalo, at which his *Lincoln the Orator* was first exhibited, he showed *Digger* and four other figures of working men in the Illinois Building. It was sculpture such as this that led Taft to compare him to Constantin Meunier, the Belgian painter who had turned to sculpture at age fifty after visiting mines and factories in the 1880s. Meunier's humanitarian interest in labourers induced him to celebrate the dignity of labour in romantic, idealistic statues of miners, farmers, blacksmiths, and working-class mothers. Always Mulligan had in mind "the marvellous achievement of ... converting an ideal country into one of activity with an attitude of beauty."[18]

As a social realist, Mulligan offered no threat to Taft's dramatic vision of neoclassical beauty. Taft praised him fulsomely. Of Mulligan's works at the Pan-American Exposition, he wrote, "[they have] an individual quality, a convincing robustness and dignity, which remove them far from the usual stop-gaps of architectural sculpture. His *Miner and Child* is one of his most poetic works, and will be employed for decorative purposes at St. Louis' [Louisiana Purchase Exposition]. It offers in a simple sculptural mass a remarkable union of strength and tenderness. [He] seems to have a decided 'call' for this kind of work, and may be destined to become the prophet of hopeful, cheerful labour, an American Meunier."[19] According to Taft — who had no aspirations to sculpt like Meunier and no financial worries — Mulligan worked too hastily and never realized his potential because "he never commanded sufficient payment to permit him the luxury of careful planning and execution."[20] Mulligan's salary at the Institute for three evening classes a week during the nine months of the academic year was only $785 in 1903, raised to $1,050 in 1907. It didn't go far in supporting a wife and three sons.

Mulligan's work was closer to that of Leonard Crunelle, another budding sculptor whom Taft had recruited as an assistant, then an associate at the Midway Studios. Crunelle, born in France, but transplanted as a child to Illinois, where — after a time — he joined his father as a miner, specialized in soft, delicate works that one critic described as "caressing tributes to childhood."[21] His small, sweet fountain figures *Crane Girl*, *Fisher Boy*, *Turtle Boy*, and *Dove Girl* (1905) still grace the rose gardens in Grant Park near the Institute, as if they had been lifted from Versailles. Although Crunelle's works shared the tenderness of Mulligan's, they lacked his virile energy and homage to hard work.

By 1906, when Frances Loring arrived at the Institute, Mulligan had begun to incorporate these special qualities into his public monuments. For a commission (a mere $750) from the women's association in Lincoln, Illinois, to sculpt a drinking fountain outside the Logan County Courthouse, he created a lovely life-size Indian mother with her papoose out of pink (red) Tennessee marble. It was to be not only a fountain "of the people, by the people, and for the people," as its inscription said, but also a fountain for their pets. The spring water, pumped from a ground-level pedal through coiling iced pipes, poured from an urn in the woman's hand, fell into a basin, then ran through the base into two hollows near the ground.

Sculptures of native people such as his *Indian Mother and Papoose* (*Indian Maiden*) were one of the standbys of the time. Such subjects tended to be like Taft's *Black Hawk* — over-inflated tributes to the "noble savages" who had a "natural" dignity, but by contrast emphasized the more sophisticated "culture" of the white man. Mulligan's much gentler creation seemed to speak out of silence on a human level — a mother like all mothers, caring for her child and going about her daily work.

By 1912 he had completed another statue of Lincoln — quite unlike his 1903 monument *Lincoln the Orator* for Chicago's Garfield Park. In *Lincoln the Railsplitter*, cast in bronze for $2,905 from the original he created for the Springfield, Illinois monument in 1906, he depicted Lincoln not as a man above other men gesticulating stiffly as he gives the Gettysburg Address, but as the simple pioneer of humble beginnings, axe in hand and sleeves rolled up in a moment of relaxation — the epitome of the democratic man. Though Mulligan was paid nothing but the cost of casting, the sculpture was hailed as "one of the most intimate and human of our Lincolns,"[22] "a nation's ideal ... a free symbol of the opportunities that await the humblest in the land."[23] It became one of the most famous statues of Abraham Lincoln ever.[24] At about the same time, for $3,500, he carved his own *Miner and Child* in Georgian marble for Chicago's Humboldt Park.

Mulligan's open-hearted temperament, his devotion to animals and children, his unpretentious, passionate approach to sculpture, his forceful commitment to hard work, and his devotion to the beautiful were bound to attract Florence Wyle. Despite his wife and three sons, she fell in love with him. As Rebecca Sisler reports, "She definitely regarded her relationship with [him] as a love affair ... of some depth and duration."[25]

❧ENFLESHMENTS❧

Turbulence ⇜

It was common practice at the time for friends to exchange many letters. Frances and Florence — who had become close friends over the academic year 1906–07 — would have been no exception. When Frances left the Art Institute of Chicago in the spring of 1907 to join her family at Cobalt in northern Ontario, where her father was mining silver, she wrote to arrange for Florence to visit once her summer school teaching was finished. The next fall, when Florence returned to Chicago, Frances went to Boston, where her brother Ernest lived, to study at the Fine Arts Academy, and the letters continued. The following summer, Florence visited the Lorings again. More letters would have kept the two friends in touch over the next year while Frances's father set her up in a studio in the Atelier Building in Union Square, New York, while Florence — who was teaching at the Institute to support herself — returned to Chicago. Florence visited Frances in New York when the school year was over. In 1909, Frank Loring brought Frances to Toronto to join him at the King Edward Hotel. He paid for a studio for her across the street at 36 1/2 King Street East. Again, Florence visited. Later that year, the two young women agreed that Florence was to leave Chicago permanently and join Frances in the new studio her father had agreed to sponsor in Greenwich Village.

Some speculate that their letters were burned, either by themselves or by friends cleaning up their studio once they were hospitalized or, perhaps, after their deaths.[1] Whether this speculation is apocryphal or not, it is probable that letters were exchanged and that none of them survived. This is not surprising, since both Frances and Florence were cavalier about keeping records, and might have lost or destroyed them themselves. The anticipation of greatness that caused families and friends to keep the letters of young men usually did not apply to women. Such materials in archives or private hands are sparse indeed.

Some idea of the kind of letters typically written by educated American women who had formed friendships like that between Frances and Florence can be seen in a letter written by Jeannette Marks — an English teacher at the first American women's college, Mount Holyoke in Massachusetts — to Mary Woolley, the college's first president. In this sample letter from a biography of these two women, Jeannette Marks writes to Mary Woolley in the summer of 1905. Like Frances and Florence, Marks and Woolley would eventually spend their lives together.

Dearest,

If I say I will come next summer, will you take care of me and help give me a chance to do the work I long to do? ... If I give all to you and give up the idea that I must protect myself from you, will you really care for my work as well as loving me? ... I believe anyone seeing the dignified dependence of two people who love each other deeply is the better for it. One thing I have always admired in Miss S_____ is the simple reserved evidence she always shows of her love for Miss S_____. I despise conventionality ... I would not take a kingdom for the proof at the dinner table ... that you depend upon me; there is no gift equal to the dignity you can confer on me that way.[2]

Such a letter is likely to be construed today as lesbian. That such a relationship — despite protestations of love and devotion — was not lesbian was entirely possible. Jeannette Marks, for instance, wrote elsewhere of the dangers of unwise and unwholesome friendships between college girls, "[W]e have to be on our guard sometimes to distinguish between what is a natural expression of affection and an unnatural attraction ... to fling oneself into any intimacy is to take a great risk ... a friendship that cannot be lived in the open may become a detestable influence."[3] For those who knew Marks and Woolley, as well as for their biographer later, it was impossible to say whether their lifelong relationship was lesbian or not.

By the end of the first decade of the twentieth century in Europe, a lesbian society had begun to surface, although that would not become apparent outside a small circle for another twenty years, save for the partnership between two American expatriates, Gertrude Stein and Alice B. Toklas, which began in 1907. Loring and Wyle would, however, have known of Harriet Hosmer, the scandalous sculptor who lived in Rome with Boston actress Charlotte Cushman — both "maverick[s] in life-style and mannish costume."[4] And it would not be long before the Chicago editor of the avant-garde literary magazine *Little Review*, Margaret Anderson (described as having "a whim of iron"), and her mannish-looking partner, Jane Heaps, fled Chicago's too-tame Bohemia, which had sprung up in vacant souvenir shops and restaurants near Taft's Midway Studios, for New York, where they would publish James Joyce's *Ulysses* in instalments and be tried for obscenity.[5]

What was known of lesbianism in the early years of the twentieth century was that it was a sickness. Richard von Krafft-Ebing's *Psychopathia Sexualis* (1882) and Havelock Ellis's *Studies in the Psychology of Sex: Sexual Inversion* (1897) portrayed love between women as morbid and, at times, insane. The "disease" was believed to be hereditary. Krafft-Ebing traced lesbianism to inborn "cerebral anomalies" that manifested in nervous complaints. Ellis, who gave the world the term "inversion," was also convinced that lesbianism was congenital. The "true invert," according to Ellis, who believed that erotic love between women was common, manifests masculine qualities and exhibits an unnatural and depraved attraction to women.[6] Such ideas were beginning to acquire credence in medical and intellectual circles — such as institutions of higher education like Mount Holyoke and The Art Institute of Chicago — in the first decade of the twentieth century. These beliefs were unlikely to encourage sexual expression between women, no matter how deep their affection. And if such sexuality was expressed, they certainly discouraged any admission of it.

THE MOVE TO Greenwich Village marked the beginning of a shared life for Florence and Frances. In the few years between Frances's departure from the Institute and their move to New York, their careers had been separate. Florence had enjoyed ever-increasing success in Chicago. In addition to her summer school classes, she now taught Saturday morning children's classes. In 1908, her work had been shown in the annual exhibit of works by Chicago artists alongside such major sculptors as Taft, Mulligan, and Crunelle. In 1909, the Institute bought a marble fountain, *Boy and Grapes*, which she had sculpted in Mulligan's class the year before, and installed it in the Institute. The fountain struck a note that Florence would develop over and over again in the future: a sweet-faced infant of about eighteen months seated under a grape vine is barely able to pour water from a small urn. While Florence was enjoying her sale to the Institute, in Toronto Frances exhibited the head of a violinist she had modelled at the Ontario Society of Artists show in a building close to the old Princess Theatre. That, she later liked to recount, was her first "sale" — or rather, her first income from her work. The theatre burned down and the insurance money reimbursed her for her violinist.[7]

The Lorings did not object to Florence sharing their daughter's studio. They both liked Florence. They felt that she stabilized their unruly daughter, and they had offered their hospitality at Cobalt freely, knowing that her own parents did not approve of her career as a sculptor. And what hospitality it was! Frances's mother had set out to imitate European elegance as nearly as was possible in a northern Ontario mining camp. The Lorings enjoyed "commodious tents furnished with large carpets and traditional chairs and sofas ... amid the rough surroundings of the silver mines."[8] They dressed for dinner and ate off good china with silver cutlery. The following summer Frances and Florence built their own log cabin in Temagami, where Frances's father was temporarily working.[9]

The generally adventurous, worldly Lorings did object, however, to Greenwich Village. It was to their horror that the two young women — now twenty-nine and twenty-three — took their living space and studio together at 6 MacDougal Alley in the heart of New York's Bohemian enclave.

It was not surprising that the Lorings did not want Frances to live there. Frances would later recall that her mother wept when she learned of their plans. Her parents' reasons for disapproving were no doubt the same ones that made Frances determined to go there. In 1910, the Village was in its heyday as a Bohemian centre for the arts, something Frances would have known from her year in the Atelier Building in Union Square only a few blocks north.

What was meant by "Bohemian" was somewhat vague. Some naively thought Bohemians were nothing more than jolly, gypsy-like eccentrics, usually poor, who were interested in the arts. Others rightly believed — or, like the Lorings, feared — that Bohemians were the high-spirited few who dared, or had the means, to live exactly as they wished. And how they wished to live involved outright rebellion against tradition: unconventional dress, erratic work — if any — indifference to physical surroundings, all-night parties, sleeping wherever they happened to be, walking the streets in pyjamas, girls with unusually long or unusually short hair smoking in the streets, plenty of drink, living from moment to moment. Above all, it involved anarchist — or at best socialist — politics and free love.

The Village was a haven for the rebels of a new generation. Starting in the early years of the century, the population of the Village had increased rapidly. Italian and Irish immigrants filled the newly built tenement houses in this largely industrial area at the same time as a young, restless generation of middle Americans sought forms of self-expression that were unacceptable to their parents. Young writers and artists, like Frances, who had lived and loved in Paris — or who had read about a European artistic way of life in such novels as George Du Maurier's widely-read novel *Trilby*[10] — unerringly found their way to Greenwich Village. They came to seek "escape from their community, their families, or themselves."[11] By 1910 the Village was conspicuous for its strong whiff of artistic Bohemia. There was a kind of magic in the air.

To the outrage of the hard-working, largely Roman Catholic immigrants of the area, Greenwich Village had become New York's version of the Latin Quarter in Paris, crowded with "long-haired men and short-haired women," artists and pseudos, tea rooms, cabarets, and dubious candle-lit haunts. Side by side with Italian immigrants and their children, who made up more than half of the local population, Irish longshoremen, Jewish shop-keepers, Spanish seamen, and a remnant of staid old American and German citizens, the young rebels of a new generation of Americans flouted manners and morals.[12]

The Village exerted this magnetic force on young Americans mainly because rents were so low. Tenements, and the influx of factories that employed the immigrants who lived in them, had transformed what had once been "a liberal lesson in cleanliness, good citizenship, and self-respect"[13] into an outright slum by 1893. In what to young adventurers seemed a "glorious Maze of narrow streets — laid out over old footpaths — lined by small houses, usually red brick, some pleasantly spruce, some wildly decrepit, all bearing the cosy, slightly raffish look of the Left Bank in Paris,"[14] cold-water apartments and studios with high ceilings and large fireplaces, which had once housed servants or horses, could be had for $25 or $35 a month. Individual rooms went for $8 to $10.

Immigrants made no effort to conceal their hostility to the artists, journal-ists, professionals of small means, and hangers-on known as the Villagers. As one Irishman put it: "It's crazy, I call it, living in made-over stables. There's no other name for those people, they're nuts."[15] It was the immorality of the Villagers that was most troubling: the rowdy drinking, smoking — especially by women — and, above all, the flagrant sexuality that was linked to suffrage parades and meetings that advocated women's claim for equal rights. To the Italians and Irish, intent on raising law-abiding Catholic children, living among the Villagers was almost like living in a large-scale disorderly house. As one pious woman exclaimed, "Those nuts that call themselves artists, and not even taking the trouble to close the blinds when they entertain a girl!"[16]

Frances's studio was at the very centre of the Village on MacDougal Alley.[17] This tiny blind alley leading east from MacDougal Street was once the place where the horses and carriages of the residents of nearby elegant

Washington Square were stabled. Life there was colourful, as children ran about among the rubbish, women scolded, and vendors peddled their wares. In the past, Irish coachmen dashing in and out of the alley had taken pride in its Irish name. Once the aristocratic households of the Square moved uptown, commercial vehicles had been stored in the former stables. The area declined further to accommodate Italian peddlers (upstairs) and their wagons (downstairs). Then came thugs and gamblers, making the alley dangerous after nightfall. In choosing this cockroach-ridden studio,[18] Frances and Florence might have been reminded of Lorado Taft's Midway Studios, since they too had formerly been stables and offered low-rental space on a site that had been associated with the somewhat unsavoury sideshows of the Columbian Exposition.

It had been Frederick E. Triebel, a sculptor newly returned from Italy sometime between 1900 and 1905, just before Frances met Florence in Chicago, who first saw the alley's potential for studios.[19] Unhappy with the typical New York studio on the top of some high building, he found in the picturesque decrepitude of the MacDougal Alley stable a space that resembled the sunny first-floor studios he had used in Italy. Before long, he was joined by other sculptors — Philip Martigny, Edwin Willard Deming, Andrew O'Conner, and J.E. Fraser — who also took studios on the Alley. Photos of these studios show large open rooms with wood plank floors and brick walls beneath exposed beams and peaked roofs. Some have large fireplaces. Deming decorated his studio with the heads of moose and deer; Martigny sculpted a semicircular relief over his fireplace. In 1907, thirty-two-year-old Mrs. Gertrude Vanderbilt Whitney "brought vast prestige to a burgeoning Bohemia" by setting up a studio there behind Eighth Street, which would later become the famed Whitney Museum.[20] Although Whitney, a married socialite with an astounding $200 million, was a most unusual tenant in the Village, she was a serious sculptor (and patron of other artists), whose famous *Titanic Memorial* (1931) in Washington, D.C.'s Waterside Park later suggested the memorable windblown posture taken by Leonardo DiCaprio and Kate Winslet on the ship's prow in the 1997 film.

Frances and Florence knew Gertrude Whitney, as well as the other sculptors on MacDougal Alley. For Frances, who had sampled so many art schools in Europe and the United States, the Village would have echoed all that was stimulating and exciting in her experience. To Florence, who had known nothing but a rural upbringing and classes at the Art Institute of Chicago, the experience must have been dizzying. Together they sporadically attended classes at the Art Students' League; mostly they worked away in their studio at their own sculptures by day and thrived on Village life at night.

Artists of all kinds and their hangers-on arrived in the Village. As one wag put it, the area was full of "Inglorious Miltons by the score/And Rodins, one to every floor."[21] The tea rooms, restaurants, and casual clubs were filled with poets reading aloud, would-be playwrights and actors presenting plays, or groups of literati discussing new kinds of poetry: free verse and, after 1910, imagism. In shady dens throughout the Village the gullible or curious absorbed "art." Tea rooms advertised famous characters, such as Max Eastman, Helen Stokes, and later Eugene O'Neill and Edna St. Vincent Millay, as patrons.

Radical politics were the order of the day. By 1912, the idealistic Woodrow Wilson was elected president, an election in which one million Americans voted socialist, a political climate that spawned *The Masses*, a radical socialist periodical. Annual fancy dress balls, not unlike the student affairs at the Art Institute of Chicago, encouraged acting out even the most bizarre fantasies of the creative Villagers and cost only a dollar. Romantic rides on the uncovered tops of Fifth Avenue buses or night-long rides on the Staten Island ferry cost almost nothing. Artists and intellectuals alike frequented eating-houses. The most famous of these — Polly's Restaurant — was on MacDougal Street, just around the corner from Loring and Wyle's studio. At the time they moved in, it was the social hub of the Village.

Paula ("Polly") Holladay, an anarchist from Evanston, Illinois, just north of Chicago, offered home cooked meals for thirty cents in her cosy tea-room atmosphere to her clientele, many of whom did not have cooking facilities in their rented rooms. The walls were hung with modern art. Her handyman-cook-waiter-*maître d'*, Hippolyte Havel, also an anarchist, swaggered around the place twisting his formidable black moustache and shouting, "Bourgeois pigs!" into the faces of patrons. Photos show the compact Hippolyte in his black vest and long wraparound white apron carrying plates of food to the long tables on either side of the room for young men and women swathed in scarves and draped in the loose smocks of the day.

By 1913, the Liberal Club was established upstairs from Polly's. There, in its two large parlours and first-floor sunroom with their high ceilings, open fireplaces, magnificent mahogany doors, and sparse furnishings, "A Meeting Place for Those Interested in New Ideas" took form. An air of dusty Bohemianism, similar to that of Polly's downstairs, was enhanced with Cubist, Futurist, and other shocking new European art on the walls. On Friday nights for twenty-five cents, there were wine-and-talk parties. To the disapproving bourgeois elsewhere, "communist" was code for any secret activity; "socialist" suggested a person of low morals. The young — often more interested in finding new partners than in new ideas — danced in a daring, intimate manner to the pounding melodies of an electric upright player piano and descended the rear stairs from time to time to the grassy garden behind Polly's. In fact, every night was party night at the Liberal Club: everyone was welcome to dances, plays, poker games, and poetry readings.

THE EPITOME OF the Bohemian Villager was Henrietta Rodman, a high school teacher of English literature who believed that "to do something solely because others do it is 'the most immoral act I can conceive.'"[22] Rodman's flock of female followers — mostly teachers and high-school students — dressed like her in loose flowing meal sacks or knickers and sandals, and bobbed their hair. Men — some bearded — abandoned hats and never seemed to bother with grooming. They also sported sandals and loose shirts with gaily coloured flowing ties. They all shared "a delicious sense of being 'pioneers into the forbidden.'"[23] Rodman's dinners were put together by sending someone off with five dollars for a few loaves of bread, a couple of pounds of butter, several large cans of spaghetti, and a big tin pail full of beer. Rodman's table consisted of boards across sawhorses. "Coming up to my apartment," she declared, "is like a progress of the soul."[24] Her friends — a motley collection of abstract painters, artists, poets, social workers, journalists, and assorted feminists, who smoked on principle — would hash over such subjects as the desirability of flamboyant free love, premarital sex for women, the glories of socialism, the lesbian theories of Havelock Ellis, and psychoanalysis. In such a setting, "the virgin was a rarity."²⁵ Promiscuity and homosexuality were becoming commonplace. To be immoral, Henrietta and many others believed, was the highest form of morality.²⁶

Such ideas were reinforced by visits to the Village by such radical feminists as Emma Goldman, the magnetic crusader for women's rights, and unfettered dancer Isadora Duncan. Both women openly enjoyed lovers; Duncan frequently stated that her "body had caused her so much pain from assorted headaches, backaches, and toothaches that she felt it owed her all payment possible in sexual rapture."²⁷

In this heady brew of politics, art, and sexuality, Frances Loring and Florence Wyle made their tentative start into life as sculptors. In 1910, the first year the National Academy dedicated a whole gallery to sculpture, Florence's bronze *Dancing Boy* was chosen for their exhibition. The somewhat awkward piece depicts a faun-like boy of about five or six raising one arm and kicking out a leg in happy abandonment. A reviewer for the show called it "grotesque," but nonetheless singled it out with three other works from the one hundred and forty sculptures in the show.²⁸ The showstopper was Abastenia St. Leger Eberle's prizewinning *The Windy Doorstep*, which marked a dramatic shift in subject matter from classical and heroic subjects to the ordinary and feminist. The work showed a working-class woman, skirts flying in the wind, sweeping her stoop. The reviewer credited her with "seeing where the throng [of sculptors] has been blind."²⁹

THERE WAS AN article about Wyle in the February 1911 issue of the prestigious trade journal *Arts and Decoration*: "Miss Wyle has come into notice in art circles within the last few years as a young sculptor of whom much may reasonably be expected. She is one of the younger school who looks with disdain on the artist who permits a helper to touch his work. From the first sketch to the last polish of the marble, Miss Wyle's work is the product of her own fingers."³⁰ Wyle had learned well from Charley Mulligan, who specialized in doing his own carving; she had no intention of being like Taft. The article notes that her bronze *Dancing Boy* is on display at the National Academy of Design, where her marble *Mother and Child* was shown the previous year, and highlights an illustration of *The Water Boy* — a chubby infant pouring water out of an urn, not unlike her *Boy and Grapes* fountain at the Institute in Chicago — which had just shown at Peoria, Illinois, and in Indianapolis at the Society of Western Artists exhibition. Florence — like Charley Mulligan — is praised for her "ability to catch and portray the child spirit." Her response to this was characteristically testy: "[she] is anxious to avoid the reputation of an artist of one style and expects to undertake work ere long that will bring her additional laurels in a new field."[31]

By 1912, Florence — as if to prove a point — created a work both classical and heroic. *Angel of the Pool* (*Sprite of Spring or The Rites of Spring*) is a huge kneeling angel with wings unfurled. It struck the familiar neoclassical note fostered by the Art Institute. In the same year, Florence showed *Dancing Boy* again — this time at the sixteenth annual exhibition of the Society of Western Artists, in which Taft showed *Paducah Fountain* based on an Indian motif. She was listed as "Homer Wyle," which was either an error or, possibly, Wyle's deliberate use of a male pseudonym. Again, her sculpture was praised as "buoyant with the exuberance of youth."[32] By all accounts she was poised on the brink of an American career.

Much later, she would recount a curious incident that must have happened at about this time, an incident that — whenever it did happen — would have fuelled her anger that boys like her twin brother somehow had it better than girls. "Once a group of officials from a southern state," she said, "admired [my] pieces because they showed a knowledge of anatomy — the structure of the body. But they refused to give [me] a commission for work because, in their opinion, no woman would be able to complete a statue."[33]

Frances lagged behind. Less sure of herself, she experimented, and found a subject less orthodox than anything Florence did in the shiny rain-cape of a New York City traffic policeman as it draped the haunches of his horse while he stopped traffic. It was an almost satiric treatment of the "great men on horseback" favoured by male monumentalists. For her model, she arranged for the neighbourhood grocer's horse to pose in the alley. (Although she promised to repay the foundry that cast the statue in bronze, it was shown in several places, but never sold.) A poem by Edgar Allan Poe — who had been one of the first literary Bohemians in Greenwich Village, where he wrote his tragic "Ligeia" — inspired another work: *A Dream within a Dream.*

This literary-based sculpture (later carved in marble) echoed some of Taft's work: a young girl in tears — "while I weep, while I weep" — stands on the shore cupping the sands of time in her hands and watches them "slip away into the deep."[34]

FRANCES WAS ALSO the subject of articles in 1910 and 1911, though these appeared in local newspapers, not in art journals. The first appeared in a Spokane, Washington, newspaper when Frances worked in the Atelier Building. There she is hailed as a former Spokane resident and the "talented and successful" daughter of Frank, "a very prominent mining man." Her small maquettes, sundials, fountains, and bas-reliefs for interior decoration are praised as the work of a promising young sculptor: "There is already a demand for her work," the article continues, rather hopefully, given that her work was mainly in the planning stage, "some of which will ornament some beautiful private grounds in Toronto and perhaps Spokane also."[35] The following summer, her father — who had ulterior motives — persuaded her to visit his sister and her husband, Edwin I. Grenfells, in Denver on the way to Spokane, where she was to submit a model in a contest to create a memorial fountain. The article in the *Denver Colorado News* is more or less a society piece highlighting Frances's visit to her family and her friendship with Gertrude Vanderbilt Whitney in New York. It is illustrated with a photo of the girlish Frances in a high-necked white blouse and another of her sundial of a muscular nude woman holding a flat rock on her shoulder. It mentions other work: numerous fountains and some "splendid bronzes, including ink stands and a 'snake-charmer,'"[36] actually a representation of Keats's poem "Lamia," which describes the transformation of a woman into a snake at her wedding, copies of which were available at fashionable Tiffany's and Gorham's art rooms in New York. "Although she does not care for portraiture in bronze or marble, Miss Loring has done several ... [S]he lives and moves in the great visions which some day she hopes to see glorified in marble — the big themes which have haunted her since she was a mere child in Italy and first felt the stirrings of the art of Michelangelo."[37] Frances, too, seemed ready to become a major American sculptor.

In the meantime, money was scarce. The employment the two young women hoped to find in New York with Daniel Chester French had not materialized. In fact, French had been "mystifyingly brusque."[38] They had asked Taft for a reference, assuming it would be a strong one — especially for Florence, who had attended the Institute for six years, and taught there for five. As they later told Rebecca Sisler, "Taft, still nursing his bitterness towards Florence, self-persuaded that she had not fully appreciated all he had done for her, had written French, warning him that Florence and Frances were not only inconsequential sculptors but a couple of Lesbians to boot."[39] It would not be until much later that the reason for French's rejection of them would come to light. But given the goings-on in Greenwich Village, French would have thought such an accusation more than likely. And, in fact, it might have been true.

Had they received positions as French's assistants, their fate as American sculptors would probably have been sealed. As it was, with only a trickle of sales, they had to turn to Frances's father to pay even the modest bills on MacDougal Alley. Frank Loring who had never become reconciled to their being in Greenwich Village, and now thought that the experiment would end in failure, waited for his chance. When he persuaded Frances to visit his sister in Denver en route to the competition in Spokane, Florence went off elsewhere — possibly to a family member's — for a short stay. In their absence, Frank travelled from Toronto to New York, went straight to MacDougal Alley, put their works into storage, and closed down their studio for good.[40]

‖ 8

Casting⤸

In their Greenwich Village studio, Florence and Frances modelled portrait busts of each other. They are companion pieces, meant to be partnered. Florence looks prim, upright, girlish. Her long dark hair is braided, then wound across the top of her almost-round head. She gazes straight ahead, her grey-blue eyes candid with purpose. She seems closed in, her mouth set in what might signal severity or a defence against vulnerability. A loose tie, possibly silk, is drawn into a soft bow under a rounded collar done up firmly at the neck. Over the neat blouse is a tightly pleated smock. Frances looks sensual, romantic, handsome. Her dark-brown hair is also arranged in a braid around her long, oval head, but the effect is different. She leans forward a little, as if about to speak, and her hair, gathered into a softer arrangement than Florence's, looks as if it might fall free. Her brown eyes are heavy lidded, mysterious. Her smock is open at the neck, the flat collar framing her upper chest and neck, as if awaiting a necklace.

Are these portraits acts of love, or simply the expedient work of aspiring sculptors without funds to pay models? Certainly, they modelled for each other. Florence's sketchbook contains a nude and a head, both of which can be identified as Frances.[1] Today, the two portrait busts can be seen in the small park on the northeast corner of St. Clair Avenue and Mount Pleasant Road in Toronto, where a bronzed Frances gazes forever at a bronzed Florence, both on pedestals. The effect is haunting.

Leaving Greenwich Village to move to Toronto in 1911 could only have been a shock for Frances, twenty-four, and Florence, thirty. The severe, grid-based streets, laid out by minds that preferred mathematical purity to organic design, could not have differed more from the chaotic labyrinth of streets in the Village. Toronto's population of some 377,000 — swelled to this number by the recent annexation of the far-flung villages of North Rosedale, Deer Park, East Toronto, West Toronto, Midway (east of the Don River), Dovercourt and Earl's Court, North Toronto, and Moore Park — was severely British, conservative, and pious. The gargoyled, pink-stone city hall with its Romanesque campanile, completed only a decade before amid a "fever of construction" in the 1890s, had been hailed as "a symbol of the people's aspirations and their moral calling," by which was meant, in part, "the high imperial destiny of the British race."[2] Fifty years earlier, Charles Dickens had found "[t]he wild and rabid toryism of Toronto ... *appalling*."[3] In almost every way, the city was the opposite of Greenwich Village. Hell-bent on technological progress and moral rectitude, it was a place where the arts were handmaidens of business, industry, and good behaviour.

Torontonians took their religion — mainly puritanical forms of Presbyterianism and Methodism — seriously. Sundays marked the strict observance of sanctified inactivity and churchgoing. This was the era when a book denouncing drunkenness, *Of Toronto the Good* (1898), marked the city as a dull place of intolerant citizens for decades. When Frank Loring forcibly moved his daughter and her friend out of the Bohemian Village in New York and into a downtown Toronto studio (which he at first paid for) at 24 Adelaide Street West, above the post office, Toronto had already gained the reputation as a place of "boring Puritanism and smugness, a colonial blandness that the ultra-loyal Anglo-Saxon majority imposed on their insti-tutions and social life, and anti-Catholic bigotry."[4]

Toronto's protestant fervour was related to the steady development of trade, finance, and manufacturing. The vigour and initiative of Scotch, Irish, and English businessmen and labourers, whose religion encouraged the work ethic and a keen business sense, transformed the city from a sleepy, unattractive backwater in the early nineteenth century to a civic centre that boasted parliament buildings (1832), a governor's residence (1828), a boys' school, Upper Canada College (1830), the Law Society of Upper Canada in Osgoode Hall (1829), and numerous churches (nine by 1834), of which one — the Anglican St. James' Cathedral, patronized by the upper echelon of Toronto society — boasted that it had the tallest spire in North America.[5]

By the 1890s — just a decade before Frances and Florence arrived — a hub of railways criss-crossed a waterfront enlarged with landfill and ugly utilitarian buildings. The downtown grid of streets quickly filled with public buildings and banks. Victorian and Edwardian mansions for the wealthy sprang up along Sherbourne, Jarvis, St. George, and Davenport Streets, as well as in the exclusive Rosedale area. Architecture — unlike the skyscrapers and innovative "Prairie Architecture" of Frank Lloyd Wright in Chicago — conspired to remind Torontonians of their links with a glorious British past — a link realized by the regiments who eagerly joined Britain in the Boer War and fought for the "Highest Beliefs"[6] at the very end of the century.

Toronto architecture owed much more to H.H. Richardson — the Boston architect who had designed many buildings in Chicago — who had a genius for adapting Romanesque architecture to North America. Buildings in the Richardsonian mode, such as the City Hall (now the Old City Hall) on Queen Street at Bay Street, and the Legislative Buildings at Queen's Park,[7] might have made Frances and Florence feel somewhat at home. Sir Henry Pellatt — the epitome of Toronto's self-made man — was busy erecting his enormous architectural folly, Casa Loma, having already made the grand gesture of sponsoring the Queen's Own Rifles' bugle band to play at the Coronation of Edward VII in 1902, and in 1910, sending the whole regiment to the Imperial Army's annual manoeuvres at Aldershot, England.[8] "The tall-spired Gothic Revival churches [for the barons of industry] and the later heavily-proportioned Romanesque-style tabernacles [for the working class] that appeared in great profusion during the 19th century were endowed by the same men who controlled the banks, investment firms, insurance companies, and owned the factories and general stores that gave a soberly affluent commercial look to the main streets."⁹ On the streets, despite the recent appearance of the motorcar and sufficient numbers of men wealthy enough to own them, horse-drawn vehicles were still common. Horses drew paddy wagons, streetcars, and fire engines. Most deliveries were made by horse and cart or sleigh. A few routes were lucky enough to have electric trains that cost five cents a ride.

It is not surprising that such a city — completely unlike Greenwich Village and even unlike industrialized Chicago, where businessmen assumed patronage of the arts — should scorn creative work, except where it served to decorate businesses or glorify industry and civic progress. "Canada's great artists today," wrote a *Globe and Mail* columnist in 1910, "are not the whole busy bunch of story-tellers and verse writers," but men like "Mackenzie and Mann ... Sir William and Sir Donald, the contractor knights, who were honoured for growing rich from building an extra transcontinental railroad ... and those epic-minded workers who are writing a new kind of blank verse in townsites and railway iron."¹⁰

When Florence joined Frances in Toronto in 1912, there were only a handful of Canadian sculptors, and only one of them — Winnifred Kingsford — was a woman. She was currently in the midst of a five-year stint in Paris studying with Émile Bourdelle. Her studies had been delayed by her responsibilities as an eldest daughter at home, but at twenty she took a studio where she taught drawing, design, and pottery work. She sculpted lamps and vases — anything that would sell — until she could enrol in the Technical School where she spent two years before leaving for Paris.

For Torontonians at the time, lamps and vases were hardly sculpture. Public sculpture was monumental and nothing else. As in the United States, great men and pivotal points of history were idealized on high pedestals meant to inspire. Subjects arose not because of considered value, but because interested groups with sufficient funds commissioned them. The results were random. The few public sculptures in Toronto in 1911 — some by British sculptors — were clustered together in Queen's Park, around the pink sandstone parliament buildings of Upper Canada: Robert Reid's *Canadian Volunteer Monument* (1870), lauding the defence of Canada's frontier in 1866; a monument to Conservative journalist George Brown (1884) by British sculptor Charles Bell Birch; statues of Christian educator Egerton Ryerson (1887) and Prime Minister Sir John A. Macdonald (1894) by Hamilton M. MacCarthy. A decade later they would be joined inevitably by a bronze copy of a British sculpture of Queen Victoria (1903),[11] whose values impressed Canada — especially the city of Toronto — for decades to come (though she never troubled to visit the city or the country). Elsewhere in the city, David R. Stevenson, a Scottish sculptor, had immortalized poet Robert Burns (1902) in the Allan Gardens on Sherbourne Street.

AMONG THESE EARLY British and Canadian sculptors, the mainly self-taught Walter Allward stood out. He had garnered more commissions than MacCarthy, his nearest competitor. Four of his sculptures monumentalized important moments in Canadian history for Queen's Park: the *North-West Rebellion Memorial* (1895); his tribute to Upper Canada Governor John Graves Simcoe (1903) and Ontario's Premier, Sir Oliver Mowat (1905); and his John Sandfield MacDonald (1909), prime minister (as premiers were then known) of Ontario, 1867–71. He had also created several busts that went to the Normal School, the *War of 1812 Memorial* (1906) in Portland Square, and — just before Frances and Florence arrived in Toronto — he had won the plum commission to erect the *South African War Memorial* (1910) to the Boer War on University Avenue north of Queen Street.[12]

On arriving in Toronto, Frances stayed with her father in the Queen's Hotel, site of today's Royal York, which was built on its ruins in the 1920s. The Queen's Hotel symbolized twentieth-century progress. For $3.00 a day (a working man's salary was $20.00 weekly for sixty hours' labour), its modern amenities included the first hot air furnace, the first elevator, the first electric bells, and the first baths with hot running water in a Toronto hotel.[13] There, where "all famous Victorian visitors stayed — from Jenny Lind to General Sherman, and the Prince of Wales,"[14] Frank Loring lectured his daughter on the bright future she would enjoy in this magnificent country.

He had succeeded as part owner of the Rossland mines in B.C. and at the Cobalt mines in northern Ontario. She could succeed in sculpture here in a way she could not in the United States — or anywhere else. Echoing the sentiments Frances would have heard at the Art Institute about the raw promise of midwestern American art from Taft and Mulligan, Frank Loring held that every aspect of life in Canada was sitting in readiness, waiting to be discovered and exploited by those with enterprise and a disposition to take risks and work hard.

Something must have been said about Florence. According to a friend to whom they recounted the story, Frank was persuaded to install her in Frances's studio partly because he and his wife knew and liked Florence and still thought her a steadying influence on their impulsive Frances, and partly because Florence was ill. Without support from her disapproving father, Florence had no money for the medical expenses her bouts of bronchitis, tonsillitis, and pneumonia incurred. Mainly because of this, Frank Loring agreed to help her out along with his daughter.[15]

After a short stint in the studio on Adelaide Street West,[16] the two of them set up a studio above a carpenter's shop at 114 1/2 Lombard Street, on the corner of Church and Lombard Streets. It was one of Toronto's most disreputable neighbourhoods, but — after Greenwich Village — Florence and Frances did not care. The rampant drunkenness that sparked the diatribe against alcohol in *Of Toronto the Good*[17] was apparent everywhere. Many of the city's over three hundred taverns — and the prostitutes and hangers-on associated with them — were right nearby. Occasionally, someone would appear at the door downstairs, asking to speak with "Rose." Walking in the streets on Toronto's cedar plank sidewalks meant propositions. "You damn fool!" was Florence's usual reply.[18] They soon had two dogs.

But the studio itself charmed them. It was not unlike the studio on MacDougal Alley: light flooded in from several large, deep-set windows, a great fireplace dominated one side of the spacious room. The other walls — supported by hand-hewn rafters — had ample space for shelves of books and small sculptures. There they set to work — hard.

They had to give up any thought of retrieving their New York works, which Frank Loring had put into storage when he closed their MacDougal

Alley studio. It was an agonizing choice: either they spent what money they had on shipping them to Canada, or they spent it on the clay, plaster, and tools they would need to continue. They abandoned their early work, including Florence's magnificent *Angel of the Pool*, which was later auctioned by the storage company leaving no record. Just as Frank Loring had cut his losses in his early mining ventures, they struck out towards a future that Frances, at least, was convinced would somehow pay off. This risk-taking attitude smacked more of the Village than of stodgy, conservative Toronto. Such a venture was hardly in keeping with Toronto's business milieu, or its fledgling art scene.

Nor were Frances and Florence in tune with Toronto's religious fervour. Both of them had abandoned any pretence of Christian belief or practice. St. James Cathedral and the Methodist Church nearby were ideal places to walk their dogs, but attendance at services was out of the question. Later, on reading Winwood Reade's *The Martyrdom of Man*, they recognized a kindred spirit and urged their friends to read the book because it was "what we believe in."[19] This book regarded Christianity as but one among many world religions, deplored the hypocrisy and false morals of many practising Christians, and discussed Jesus as "a man with all the faults and imperfections of the prophetic character."[20] As students of the arts, they knew that art in the service of Christianity had long since passed its zenith. As Bohemians from the Village, they had been exposed to many exciting, radical ideas about a newly burgeoning free society in which women might appropriate a more powerful position.

Not surprisingly, their life — which was lived fully in accordance with such ideas — offended the respectable citizens of Toronto. This disapproval after the freethinking milieu of Greenwich Village was more troublesome than being accosted in the streets near their studio. "How odd," they were made aware, "to have come to Toronto for such a strange enterprise as sculpture! And two women, mark you ..." There was a distasteful implication. In Frances's words, "They thought it a peculiar thing that two young women should live together." She and Frances dismissed it all. "You can't go through life worrying about what the public's going to think of you."[21]

Elsewhere⋐

Within a year of The Girls' forced departure from the Village, the movement later called "Modernist" got underway. Harbingers of the revolution in art, literature, and architecture had recently reached New York. The Ashcan school of art there was already challenging heroic subjects. The Dadaist phenomenon and the radical ideas of the Futurists were being bandied about by the avant-garde in Polly's Restaurant and, later, upstairs at the Liberal Club. Alfred Stieglitz, who had visited and shown in the galleries of Europe and was now intent on using new photographic technology to apply theories of modern art abroad to his photography, had opened his studio, the Little Galleries of the Photo-Secession (later known as Gallery 291 for its address on 5th Avenue not far from the Village). The energetic Stieglitz mounted shows of modern European artists such as Henri Matisse and Paul Cézanne as well as drawings by Auguste Rodin. Stieglitz's studio was a landmark to Village artists. Had Frances — and Florence — stayed in New York, they would have seen Picasso's first solo show there in 1911.

But it was the Armory Show in 1913 that challenged — and in most quarters, horrified — the American art world. The Stieglitz shows had merely set the stage for the world-shaking Post-Impressionist Show at the 69th Regiment Armory on the corner of Lexington Avenue and 25th Street, which would be hailed as "[t]he first, and possibly the last, exhibition of paintings held in New York which everyone attended."[1]

Had Florence and Frances remained in Greenwich Village they would undoubtedly have seen it. Their fellow MacDougal Alley sculptor, Gertrude Vanderbilt Whitney, had backed the show financially, and another fellow sculptor in Greenwich Village, Jo Davidson, was on the selection committee for the grandiose event. Many American artists were represented in the show, such as political radical Robert Henri, leader of the Ashcan school of art, which sought out derelicts and scenes of poverty as subjects for art. There was only one Canadian painter in the show: David B. Milne.[2]

ON THE EVENING of 17 February, the Armory Show opened to over four thousand guests. The president of the committee who organized it claimed that it was "the most complete art exhibition that has been held in the world during the last quarter century." There, in the eighteen improvised rooms festooned with greenery, yellow streamers, pine trees, and flags, more than 1,300 American and European works of art, calculated to give the American public "a mental jolt,"[3] were put on view. And jolted the public was. Only a third of the exhibits were foreign; the rest were intended to demonstrate that American artists could hold their own in the world of art. But it was the foreign contributions that stirred the public to outrage or derision.

Paintings by Post-Impressionists Cézanne, Gauguin, and Van Gogh, who had already achieved status as "old masters" in Europe, were almost entirely new to American audiences. And much more radical were the modernist works by Henri Matisse, Marcel Duchamp, and Pablo Picasso. The most violent attacks were against the latest manifestations of artistic revolution: Fauvism and Cubism.

The work that attracted most attention in the Cubist Room (known as the "Chamber of Horrors") was Duchamp's painting *Nude Descending a Staircase,* and it soon became the show's focal point — a symbol of moral degeneracy or madness or outrageously funny artistic irresponsibility. It inspired endless take-offs, jibes, doggerel verse, burlesques, and even a serious attempt to chart where exactly the nude was in the painting.[4] Insulting pronouncements by those who could not understand its attempt to convey motion included: "an explosion in a shingle factory" and "an orderly heap of broken violins."[5]

Cubism appeared so odd that it could easily be ridiculed. Only a few saw it as reflecting the surge of industrialism in modern life — especially in America — with its consequent fracturing of stability and hectic pace of life. Next to Duchamp's painting, Matisse's uncompromising art made him another target. His *La Coiffeuse, Panneau Rouge*, and *Portrait of Marguerite* were seen as the epitome of something that was reviled throughout the Armory Show: a violation of Beauty, especially in female nudes. Anything that subverted the "female form divine" — pronounced as one word — was disgusting and immoral. The European modernists — especially Matisse — "seemed to take an almost sadistic pleasure in destroying any vestiges of divinity still residing in the age-old academic clichés of the female nude."[6] Though a few critics wrote positively of the show, one critic in the New York *Review* more typically dismissed the Matisses: they were widely thought to "[d]istort the human form divine until it becomes a nauseating monstrosity."[7] Another critic wrote that Matisse took "the ugliest models, pose[d] them in the most grotesque and indecent poses and [drew] them as would a savage and depraved child."[8] Matisse was seen as blatantly undermining not only the nude, but also still life, the portrait, genre painting, and lofty symbolic themes, such as those honoured by Lorado Taft. And, since he knew how to draw accurately, his fluid, distorted works were dismissed as "unaccountable" examples of "wilful impertinence."[9]

Sculptures by Bourdelle, Maillol, Lehmbruck, Archipenko, and others who had begun to alter realistic presentations of the human form were also on display. Some, like Romanian Constantin Brancusi's rough-hewn, columnal *The Kiss* (1907–08) and the fetus-like bust *Mlle. Pogany* (1912), Picasso's even rougher, hatchet-shaped *Head of a Woman* (1909), and Matisse's *The Back, I* (1909), which was a still rougher, out-of-proportion relief of a large nude woman from behind, were incomprehensible because they made no attempt to be anatomically realistic. President Theodore Roosevelt, who attended the show on his last day in office, commented that Wilhelm Lehmbruck's sculpture *Kneeling Woman* (*The Kneeling One*) (1911) had "the lyric grace of a praying mantis," and wondered "why a deformed pelvis should be called 'sincere'" or "a tibia of a giraffe-like length 'precious.'" These were, he said, questions of "pathological rather than artistic significance."[10] Such sculptures as those in the Armory Show could not have been less like Lorado Taft's polished, elegantly beautiful, neoclassical works. Not only was Taft not included in the Armory Show, he was not considered. Even Daniel Chester French, whose work Taft had described as "so noble and so original,"[11] was considered, but excluded.[12] By the end of the month-long show on 15 March, 87,620 people had attended it.[13]

A TRUNCATED VERSION of the Armory Show was sent on to Boston and Chicago, where the response was even more dramatic. There — knowing already of the reaction in New York — the press focused on the circus-like spirit of the spectacle, and its freakish aspects were highlighted even before it opened in the Art Institute of Chicago in the third week of March. Press reviews were predictably more acrimonious than those in New York. The Cliff-Dwellers club — of which both Lorado Taft and Charley Mulligan were members — produced a burlesque exhibition in its headquarters in Orchestra Hall much in the spirit of the Eagle's Nest goings-on. In a protest more vehement than anything in New York, students from the Art Institute — led by Taft — demonstrated violently against the show. They staged a mock trial of Matisse (Henri Hairmattress) who was "accused and convicted of a long list of crimes, then stabbed, pummelled, and dragged about the terrace to the edification of a large crowd on Michigan Avenue." Imitations of Matisse's *Le Luxe* and *La Femme Bleu* (*Blue Nude*) were burned and, according to one newspaper, "A sort of May frolic dance followed the ceremonies, and then a cubist song was sung, led by the [Chicago Art Students League] and accompanied by the league band."[14] An official of the Art Institute — possibly William French, the director, or Taft himself — praised the students for their "display of sanity." Nonetheless, the show attracted 188,650 visitors — over twice as many as saw it in New York. Some of the press — notably Harriet Munroe of the *Little Review* — argued in the *Chicago Sunday Tribune* for tolerance and a clear view of the facts.[15] But such defences from the new Bohemian quarters of Chicago, emerging just after Florence joined Frances in New York, were widely regarded as nonsense.

With the Armory Show, American artists had their comeuppance. While they imagined that their "vigorous" art, infused with (especially midwestern) energy was "progressing" beyond that of "decadent" Europe,[16] the revolutions in European art found in Post-Impressionism, not to mention Fauvism, Dadaism, Futurism, and Cubism, had far outdone them. For over a decade European art had "revolted against the sophistication and 'decadence' of the late nineteenth century, and was searching for 'fundamentals,' while American aesthetic thought was still naively sold on 'progress'" within nineteenth-century traditions.[17]

It was not surprising that Taft objected so violently to the Armory Show. It sounded his death knell as a mainstream sculptor. His poetic, allegorical tributes to female beauty and high ideals became almost overnight a thing of the past. Perhaps the difference between his aesthetics and those of the European modernists can best be seen in their attitudes towards children. For Taft, Mulligan, and Crunelle in Chicago, and for other major sculptors like Saint-Gaudens and Daniel Chester French, the child was a symbol of innocence best represented as a beautiful, naive creature of divine origin "trailing clouds of glory." The modernists like Matisse, the "apostle of ugliness,"[18] looked to childhood for a fresh vision uncluttered by the imposition of nineteenth-century sentimentality, a source — possibly — of techniques that were as vital as they were "unschooled." The neoclassicists created the sleek cherubic child, as if looking back nostalgically on childhood; the modernists wanted to recapture the raw amoral viewpoint of a child. Matisse especially was trying to achieve a childlike or primitive vision, in a similar way as Picasso had looked to African masks for inspiration for his *Demoiselles d'Avignon* in 1906. The whole idea was to recover the roots of art, a quest that called forth remarks like this from one critic of the Armory Show: "The childlike attitude as an *idée fixe* shows degeneration ... It is as if man, having by ages of effort learned to walk upright, should petulantly conclude ... he would better achieve his adventure on all fours."[19]

The New York *Globe* was right: after the Armory Show "American art [would] never be the same again."[20] The general sentiment was, "Men, it was a bully show, but don't do it again."[21] But sculpture — like painting — would now begin to move further and further away from representation-alism through the streamlined quasi-abstract to full abstraction. Taft was left behind by the modernists he demonstrated against. At the end he was a sad, old man who knew he was "old-fashioned."[22] At seventy-six he was attempting to find support for a monumental companion piece to *The Fountain of Time* called *The Fountain of Creation*, which would face it from the other end of the Midway Plaisance. "I guess that was a dream that went up in smoke,"[23] he admitted shortly before he died. A few years after the Armory Show launched the Poet-Impressionist school in Chicago, and Taft, "hitherto venerated by students, came into disrepute with the new admirers of Cézanne, Matisse, Van Gogh, Modigliani, Gauguin, and Seurat." He was a relic, a fuddy-duddy. "The new sculptural pied piper [in Chicago] was the Polish wild man, Stanley Szukalsi, who was the son of a Chicago blacksmith and whose sculpture, to Taft's mind, looked like something 'hammered out on an anvil with a duck-down pillow.'"[24]

As for Charley Mulligan, he died suddenly at age forty-nine only three years after the Armory Show, his loss lamented in superlatives by Taft at a memorial gathering in the Institute: "Charley Mulligan, the boy at forty-nine, the enthusiast, the optimist, the personification of eternal health and tireless vigour — dead! Charles Mulligan, the artist with dreams and ambi-tions still unfulfilled, taken away when he was just coming into his own. Never has death seemed to me more unreal, more unreasonable."[25] And elsewhere, at a distance in Toronto, he was mourned by Florence Wyle, who still kept his photo by her bed. It is possible that her poem "Let the Dead Sleep," written much later, was for him:

Let the dead sleep,
They need not rise
To walk the earth again,
Except in other guise;
Nature knows no waste,

The flower may hold the image of the child,
The strong oak, a man's virility;
There is no waste —
But that dark head will lift no more
To wonder at the stars
Or watch the light
The window throws in golden bars
Across the night.[26]

Settled as they now were in Toronto the Good, neither Florence nor Frances would know first-hand of the radical new directions American sculpture would take from then on.

1913 ⬱

The shock waves of the 1913 Armory Show did not reach Canada. That same year, *The Yearbook of Canadian Art* — the first in what was planned as an annual series — offered a synopsis of the Canadian arts that seems almost Victorian by contrast.[1] Each chapter — some of which are English on one side, French on the other — was written by a different expert. Painters are praised for the "tranquil" qualities of their works. Horatio Walker's *Milking, Evening* is "big and confident"; Homer Watson's *Evening After the Rain* is "restful"; Archibald Browne's work is "decorative." Impressionist J.W. Morrice is praised for the "shadowy suggestiveness" of his Italian scenes; William Brymner's work is "luminous"; and Maurice Cullen's glowing snowscapes are extolled.[2]

As for the sculptors, portraitist Edmond Dyonnet's chapter on "French-Canadian Painting and Sculpture" notes works by sculptors Louis-Philippe Hébert, Phimister Proctor, and Alfred Laliberté. The only English-Canadian sculptor treated — in a separate chapter — is Walter Allward. All the sculptures are examples of monumentalization or portrait tributes to great men. Dyonnet lists Hébert's public monuments to Maisonneuve, Crémazie, Mgr. Bourget, Mlle. De Vercheres, and his group sculptures of members of the Quebec parliament, before mentioning his current work on a statue of King Edward VII for a square in Montreal. His *Martine Messier* is described by painter Lawren Harris as "a red warrior, his axe raised to strike, springs upon a woman who, crazed with terror, vainly mounts guard over the body of her husband — revolting figures, but compelling in every detail."[3] Alfred Laliberté was planning a memorial to Sir George-Etienne Cartier. Proctor's relief, *Lions*, is praised for "breathing wild Life and jungle tragedies."[4] In his chapter on Walter Allward, James Mavor lists Allward's five Queen's Park sculptures and his busts for the Ontario Department of Education. Mavor highlights the three important commissions Allward was working on: the *Bell Telephone Memorial* in Brantford, the King Edward memorial, and the Baldwin-Lafontaine monument near the Houses of Parliament in Ottawa. Descriptions of Allward's plans for these monuments emphasize "their high if sombre note," his use of symbolism, and his allegiance to "masculine ... as well as feminine beauty."[5] According to Mavor, "He has no competitor in this country at the present time."[6]

Despite the varied authorship of the 1913 *Yearbook*, certain themes run through it. First, the idea that in such a young country as Canada, the arts cannot be expected to flourish. As Dyonnet puts it, "Here we are in the beginning. The men whom history will name as the pioneers of Canadian art are still living. Our artistic life began only yesterday ... [F]ew people have leisure enough to discover that besides a mere material life there are joys superior and intellectual, the development of art is bound to be slow and gradual."[7] Second, that — despite the fact that many Canadian artists either visited or trained in Europe — the modern revolutions in art abroad had no place in Canada. For the most part, contributors to the *Yearbook* seemed unaware of these revolutions, but when modernist trends are mentioned they are summarily dismissed. "[A]lthough Impressionism has had a certain influence on one of them," wrote Dyonnet, "no French-Canadian painter fortunately has dreamed of following in their folly those despisers of art who have undertaken the mission of denying beauty and proscribing truth.

Cubists and Futurists may go by. Our country is too young not to be attracted by novelty, but it has enough native good sense not to allow itself to be made a fool of, or to take the grin of a monkey for the smile of a woman."[8] S. Morgan Powell called thirty-one-year-old A.Y. Jackson, whose work was singled out as "quite as interesting as anybody who exhibited this year," an Impressionist, but added this caveat: "He knows the line where sanity ends and the kingdom of freaks begins. He pushes the Impressionist technique and theory to the limit, but he does not overstep it."[9] Third, several contributors mentioned "that perennial bone of contention,"[10] the need for a national art to express the particularities — especially historical and geographical — of a new country. Portraitist E. Wyly Grier wrote, "I believe that our art will never hold a commanding position, to use a soldier's phrase, until we are stirred by big emotions born of our landscape; braced to big, courageous efforts by our climate; and held to patient and persistent endeavour by that great pioneer spirit which animated the explorers and soldiers of early Canada ... There is something of the romantic interest of knight-errantry in our undertaking."[11]

These ideas about the arts in Canada were a heady mix, unlike the artistic milieu of any other country at the time. In contrast to Europe, there was no decadent tradition to disparage and displace. Unlike the United States, there was no midwestern exuberance to express. In 1913, Canada had been a nation for only forty-six years and — in the absence of an upheaval like the American Revolution — was still essentially colonial. The deeply held notion that evolution was preferable to revolution permeated the artistic milieu, just as it permeated the general ideology of the nation.[12] Given Canada's situation as a country beginning to move past physical pioneering and towards artistic pioneering, it is not surprising that the main thrust of artistic endeavour should have been to establish a national art that set in place the peculiar characteristics of this particular nation. As cultural historian Maria Tippett observed, "cultural activity [during these years] had a mission."[13] Painters were being directed to the unexplored, varied, and virtually indigestible Canadian landscape as *the* subject for art.

In the fall of 1912, the first harbinger of what would become the Group of Seven occurred when Tom Thomson — an untrained amateur —returned to Toronto from sketching in the Mississauga Forest Reserve. "[His] twenty-or-so sketches were awakenings," Thomson's friend Arthur Lismer commented, "and we all [Lismer, J.E.H. MacDonald, and Lawren Harris] saw ... that not only was Tom opening up as a painter, but that the north-land was a painter's country."[14] That same fall, MacDonald and Harris had seen the Scandinavian art show in Buffalo, which clinched their view that northern landscape scenes were the essential subject matter for Canadian art. James McCallum — the wealthy Toronto doctor and Sunday painter who had decided to patronize artists — financed a three-storey building with Lawren Harris at 25 Severn Street — a cul-de-sac off Rosedale Valley Road — called "The Studio Building for Canadian Art." It was at this time that J.E.H. MacDonald, Lawren Harris, Arthur Lismer, Fred Varley, and Tom Thomson made their first sketching trips to northern Ontario. In 1913, Harris persuaded A.Y. Jackson — who had already signalled his primary interest in Canadian landscapes in 1909 and first painted in Georgian Bay in 1910 — to leave Montreal and join them in Toronto.

Sculptors who had no way of sculpting the landscape — northern or otherwise — were expected instead to build upon a sparse and inadequate record of national history to establish clearly in the public consciousness whatever it was that was unique and inspirational in Canada. According to a 1898 article on sculpture by monumentalist Hamilton MacCarthy, their subjects were to be either "the *Ideal single figure*, commonly armed and emblematic, expressing some emotion, passion or attribute of Man's inner being ... [or] the *Ideal group* of two or more figures, [which] has greater human interest, if less philosophy, and larger scope for composition and for lines."[15] "[A]lready in our public places we see monuments of bronze and granite commemorating the great events of our history,"[16] wrote Dyonnet, as if to urge sculptors to continue to shape a national ideology.

What fledgling sculpture Canada had to show for itself was mainly in Quebec City, Montreal, and Ottawa. Quebec, in particular, boasted a long tradition that began with religious woodcarvings for the churches of Lower Canada. And Ottawa, as the nation's capital city, naturally attracted monuments to national heroes. Such works — like the *Queen Victoria* in the centre of the Parliamentary Library — were created at first by British sculptors.

Toronto lagged behind. "On visiting Toronto," wrote Hamilton MacCarthy in 1898, "the traveller and lover of Art expresses surprise at seeing so few public monuments and so little Statuary in its public buildings."[17] By 1913, a few more monuments graced Toronto's public spaces, but not many.

Certainly, opportunities abounded for Florence Wyle and Frances Loring, who were well trained in neoclassical sculpture, had admired numerous examples of monumentalism both in Chicago and New York (and in Frances's case, Europe), and were primed by Frank Loring to regard Canada as a land of opportunity where success was likely to fall to those who were enterprising. That Frances's father was also willing to support them at the outset solved the problem stated more than once in the 1913 *Yearbook*: the absence of wealthy families whose offspring might dabble in the arts or the disinclination of those who *were* wealthy — especially in Toronto — to become patrons of the arts. Artists in Canada often had to abandon their ambitions so they might earn a living.

Those who persisted found some solace in a society that was beginning to take the arts seriously. Arts organizations in Canada had evolved from fledgling operations that seemed forced into birth before their time in the 1870s and 1880s into more confident assemblages.[18] In 1912, Eric Brown, the new curator of Ottawa's National Gallery,[19] announced that "the time is ripe for Canada to have a national gallery worthy of its best traditions ... to aid the development of Canada's art" and mount "the best exhibitions of the world's art obtainable."[20] The provincially sponsored Ontario College of Art had just begun offering classes in Toronto; plans were completed to build a new art gallery at the Grange (former home of Goldwin Smith), which opened in 1912 with Edward Greig as its first curator, and the city had bought adjacent land and funded the upkeep of the property. Most important, Sir Edmund Walker, president of the Canadian Bank of Commerce, became director of both the new National Gallery in Ottawa and the Art Museum at the Grange in Toronto. Walker, unlike most of Canada's businessmen, had taken a personal interest in the arts since 1900. Walker's style — he had a full beard and sported a monocle — was that of the Victorian statesman accustomed to leading without challenge. He expected no input from artists in the creation of the National Gallery — a trait that infuriated

Royal Canadian Academy (RCA) members, who were just getting around to admitting women.[21] They expected to have a say in the institution they had sought since the RCA's foundation in 1882. Walker handpicked Eric Brown, a thirty-year-old Englishman at the time of his appointment as the Gallery's director in 1910. Nonetheless, unlike the Toronto industrialists whose work ethic, puritan bias against artists, and narrow focus on money making rendered them indifferent to the arts, Walker saw "the necessity for creative expression in the building of nationhood and publicly declared it."[22]

BEFORE 1913, MEMBERS of the Ontario Society of Artists (OSA), which welcomed painters, sculptors, architects, and craftsmen of all kinds, held their exhibits in a haphazard fashion at various places in and around King Street, or at the Toronto Public Library on College Street, or at the yearly shows of the Toronto Industrial Exhibition (later the Canadian National Exhibition), where an extremely small gallery resembling a railroad station had been replaced in 1905 by a building resembling a Roman temple with the word ART illuminated by light bulbs in its pediment. Although these early art exhibits had begun to emphasize Canadian work (one-third of the congested Toronto Industrial Exhibition displays were to be Canadian material, for example) and the foremost aim of the OSA was to foster Canadian art, ideas of what was meant by "Canadian" owed much to British Victorian trends. In 1905, artists were urged "to search for and record the historical, characteristic and picturesque features of this great land."[23] Such aims — particularly the wording of them, which suggests the artist's responsibility is to make photographic "records" and infuse them with "picturesque" qualities — differed essentially from the more independent aims expressed in the 1913 *Yearbook*, which at least recognized the contribution Impressionism had made to European and Canadian art.

As for students of art, aside from private classes and "academies" — patronized mainly by young ladies somewhat in the spirit of finishing schools — and the Mechanics Institute, there was only the Central Ontario School of Art and Design (later the Ontario College of Art). Located at 165 King Street West in Toronto, it was only open three days a week. Since the 1890s, the OSA had offered free lectures on such subjects as "William Morris" and

"Great Portrait Painters" — topics that elevated British and European art well above anything from North America. Typical of the pre-1913 era in Toronto, the Toronto Guild of Civic Art — an organization of artists, architects and art-loving citizens — vowed to "[stimulate and guard] civic art."[24]

THE "DISTINCT DEPARTURE" from pre-1913 cultural doings in Canada, that "great change" noted by S. Morgan Powell and others in the 1913 *Yearbook*,[25] was a reality. Although to Florence Wyle and Frances Loring the Toronto art scene must have seemed retrograde compared to Chicago — not to mention Greenwich Village. It was actually in the midst of an important step forward.

Contacts ⋍

In an article called "Women Sculptors of Canada" in the 20 June 1914 edition of *Women's Saturday Night*, Estelle M. Kerr made the following observations about Florence Wyle and Frances Loring:

> Miss Wyle has a dominant personality that overcomes difficulties and, though she is fond of fun, it is plain to be seen that nothing will be allowed to interfere with her work. She does not simply copy the figure, but uses it to interpret her own ideas and emotions, though in her passion for exquisite modelling she may sometimes forget for a time, her first conception.
>
> Miss Loring is very versatile ... Her portraits, whether in the round or [in] low relief, are always pleasing. A bronze representing a mounted policeman in the attitude of stopping the traffic shows courage and originality, while her decorative designs for everything, from a fountain to a hand-mirror, show great charm of line.[1]

Kerr's title was optimistic to say the least, for there were only three women sculptors in Canada then: Wyle, Loring, and Winnifred Kingsford, who had recently returned from Paris to her Adelaide Street studio near Wyle and Loring's: "a far cry from the Latin Quarter."[2]

Nothing even remotely like European schools existed in Toronto. Instead, Canada's three women sculptors had rolled up their sleeves two years before to throw together *The Spirit of Canada*, a temporary plaster group of lioness and cubs to decorate the new Dufferin Gates at the eastern entrance to the Toronto Industrial Exhibition. Desperate for money, Frances quickly managed to model the lioness and a generic cub whose detachable head could be set at different angles. Florence and Winnifred enlarged the models, and they were set in place within ten days. (The three were cleaning the plaster off their hands behind the scaffolding as the mayor dedicated the gates.)[3] Although Kerr singles out Kingsford because she is "made in Canada," Wyle and Loring are clearly welcomed: "[I]t is even more gratifying to think that two such talented young American sculptors should come to live amongst us." Kerr states that Florence's work is "stronger than that of the other two."[4]

Six months earlier, Wyle had done a three-hour sketch of the Hon. Robert Laird Borden for a medal to be used for prizes at the Toronto Industrial Exhibition. It was deemed "an excellent likeness." The obverse side featured an agricultural emblem. (Both Wyle and Loring did other medals that year for the Exhibition.) The medal was commissioned by the Albany Club, which had heard of Wyle through architect John Pearson. Pearson, a British immigrant in his mid-forties who worked for the Toronto firm Darling & Sproatt, had been the first vice-president of the Ontario Association of Architects in 1902. He had already designed the Royal Tower and the Grain Exchange Building in Winnipeg, and was well-known in Toronto for his Imperial Bank of Canada (1906) at King and Sherbourne Street and the University of Toronto's round Convocation Hall the same year. In 1913, he was working on Toronto's Canadian Pacific Railway Building.

Pearson and others soon became interested in the work of Wyle and Loring after seeing their sculptures in exhibits of the OSA and the RCA in Toronto. The Bank of Commerce also commissioned some enlarged coins for their display room, a commission that was possibly arranged by Sir Edmund Walker himself. (Pictures show that Wyle and Loring knew him around that time, though perhaps not quite this early, and visited him at De Grassi Point on Lake Simcoe.) Such commissions — small as they were — began a trickle of income.

The thirty-eight-year-old sculptor Walter Allward was the first to break the icy reception Torontonians gave Wyle and Loring. He and his wife invited them to his Walker Street home, but — unlike Pearson, and despite his unchallenged position as top English-Canadian sculptor — he had no intention of steering commissions their way. As Frances recalled later, "He was a very self-absorbed man. A fine man, but not interested in promoting other people."[5]

Probably at the initiative of the more adventurous Frances, the two sculptors went to the National Gallery in Ottawa where they met Eric Brown. As Brown's wife, Maud, recalls, "Those two stalwart characters, Frances Loring and Florence Wyle, the Toronto sculptors, were among our earliest friends."[6] Although Brown had recently moved to Ottawa from England, and Frances and Florence were Americans, he appreciated and supported their work from the outset.

They met Robert Flaherty, the flamboyant northern prospector for iron ore, whose attraction to — and for — the Inuit peoples he encountered while exploring the Belcher Islands in Hudson Bay diverted him into a career photographing and filming them. Like Frank Loring, who shared Flaherty's passion for adventure and prospecting, Flaherty stayed at the Queen's Hotel when in Toronto. When the handsome, blue-eyed, blond adventurer hit Toronto he would "practically buy out a whole delicatessen and flower shop and burst into Florence and Frances's studio. 'You'd feel as though a whirlwind had struck you,' Frances recalled."[7]

On one occasion, the wildly impulsive Flaherty invited the two young women to dinner at the Queen's Hotel. When they arrived, "there was no sign of their host in the unusually silent lobby." When Flaherty finally appeared, "white and very washed out," he explained: "I've been in the bathtub trying to sober up. I determined today that I was going to get the entire Queen's Hotel [including the staff] tight, and I've succeeded." Not surprisingly, the reckless adventurer left behind in the Arctic a number of blue-eyed, blond children named Flaherty. Frances, who herself seems to have had a fling with Flaherty — they shared "a warm flash of sensual fire"[8] — confessed, "He would have been hell to live with. Heaven help anyone to whom he meant a great deal — because you'd have to take him with terrific humour," which both Wyle and Loring did.[9] It was Flaherty who took the most memorable, sensitive photograph of his two friends, probably at the time he premiered his first Baffin Island film at Convocation Hall in March 1915 to a large and distinguished audience, including the Lieutenant-Governor.[10] In the photo, the two young women are seated side by side, but looking in one direction. A bond between the two women is palpable. Florence, in front, wearing a flowered, kimono-like dress, clasps her knees and looks ahead of her with determination, like a visionary. Behind her, in a dark, open-necked dress, adorned with a loosely tied silk scarf, Frances cranes her head around in an almost protective attitude to see Florence, her expressive hands one atop the other in her lap. They are both beautiful: Frances in a dark, languid, Mediterranean manner; Florence in a more austere, American midwestern way.

Another set of photos — separate ones — of Florence and Frances were taken in 1915 by another pair of friends, Toronto's top photographers, Charles Ashley and James Crippen.[11] These two men — known as "The Boys" — were partners in business and in life. Unlike Flaherty's photo, Ashley and Crippen's separate pictures of Florence and Frances emphasized their work as sculptors. In one photo, Florence is depicted in a dark blouse and light skirt, seated, her arm resting casually in front of her sculpture of a nude female torso. Her dark hair is gently swept up, her face luminous and soft. In the other, Frances, in a loose old smock covered with daubs of plaster, stands beside one of her sculptures, one arm protectively over it, a wire-end sculpting tool in her other hand. Her hair is also upswept, and her heavy-lidded eyes glance sideways away from the sculpture.

AT THIS TIME, two painters who would later become members of the Group of Seven also befriended them: Fred Varley and A.Y. Jackson. Wyle and Loring — who offered hospitality with great naturalness and skill — gave them meals regularly, and when Varley sold his first painting he took them both out to dinner to celebrate. They recalled Varley as fiery with artistic zeal. "He was burning up always with blazing talent," they said. A.Y. Jackson was his opposite. A genial, gnome-like man with a receding chin, A.Y., or Alex, who had attended The Art Institute of Chicago briefly in 1906–07[12] but had not known either of them there, was garrulous and mellow. His genius for friendship endeared him to the two women for life.[13] In 1914, he moved into a studio on the top floor of the Studio Building at 25 Severn Road.

Florence and Frances also met painters Walter R. Duff, who etched Florence's portrait in 1915, and Dorothy Stevens, a painter and etcher then active in Toronto. But none of these artists resembled the Bohemian set in Greenwich Village. "The artists in Toronto are ordinary people who go home to their families," Frances later commented in a radio interview after defining Bohemianism as "a sort of looseness of morals." "I really only knew one really outright Bohemian [in Toronto] and that was Curtis Williamson, a painter known as 'the Canadian Rembrandt.'"[14]

But social life was superseded by work. It is tempting to see in one of Florence's major works at this time a symbol of her own state of mind. *Rebirth* showed a man levelled by life struggling to get up on his feet again. "It can always be done," Florence maintained, almost as a motto. Here, indeed, was the "dominant personality that overcomes difficulties" that Estelle Kerr had noticed.

SOME IDEA OF life in the studio can be gleaned from Florence's recollection — which would have horrified her parents — that the model she used for *Rebirth* was a shapely Englishman who relaxed his aching muscles from posing by "walking around on his hands. Naked, of course."[15] By 1916, Florence's exuberance was expressed in *Sun Worshipper*, a statue that was frankly sexual. A young woman, naked, bends backward, clasps one breast in her hand, and stretches the other hand out and up in abandon.

Frances — whose varied training and peripatetic life had made her "versatile," but also uncertain of what direction she would take — made one striking sculpture based on a florid Victorian poem: Francis Thompson's "The Hound of Heaven." Perhaps it too reflected her inner state. In this poem, God is depicted as a hound tracking down the soul of the unbeliever to retrieve it for Christianity. From an excerpt (the first fifteen lines) kept by Frances,[16] her specific interest in this startling and melodramatic situation can be determined. As she claimed, "The poem simply put [me] in a certain rhythmic mood."[17] That rhythm — the fast thrusting stride of a determined escapee — resulted in *The Hound of Heaven* (1917), the emotionally powerful statuette of a woman running from her conscience. Frances gave it "a Rodinesque sinuousness of surface."[18] Though it is impossible to say with any certainty, Florence's *Sun Worshipper* and Frances's *Hound of Heaven* may have arisen from the same experience. The sexual expression of the one and the guilty conscience of the other could suggest a sexual relationship between them.

As Estelle Kerr noted, Florence was the stronger sculptor. She was well grounded in anatomy and far more established than Frances, who had sold only a few minor pieces through her father when she worked in the New York atelier.[19]

The two women thrived in their Adelaide Street studio after Florence arrived permanently in the spring of 1912.[20] But before long, they had moved to 114 1/2 Lombard Street, at the northwest corner of Church on the second floor of Hunter's Inn (properly called Kingston House). Hunter's Inn was the first stone building in Toronto — a city, which was otherwise brick and wood. It is likely that the large, open second floor was once a room for dances and gatherings, since that was a common use of such space at the time.[21]

There, with the twisting into shape of armatures, the splattering of plaster, the sharp blows of the chisel and the scraping of an array of other tools, sculptures of many sizes and shapes and kinds sprang to life. A board across two high stools served as a moulding platform under a small cloth-covered lamp suspended from the ceiling. Rudimentary shelves behind a pot-bellied wood stove held maquettes and portrait busts, including those they had made of each other in the Village. Open cans with brushes and a large bottle of water for mixing stood beside an old barrel. And, among the few drawings pinned unceremoniously on the wooden-plank wall, there is a copy of part of Michelangelo's *Creation*, focusing on Adam stretching out his hand to receive the divine spark from God.[22]

Had Florence and Frances remained in the United States, there would have been a larger market for their sculpture and more commissions to compete for. But there would also have been much greater competition for those commissions. By 1913, there were about sixty women sculptors in the United States, some of them with excellent connections, well-known for their skills in many branches of sculpture: public and private fountains, animals, public monuments, small decorative works, portrait busts, and reliefs of all kinds.[23] The work of these women had been encouraged since 1889 by the National Association of Women Artists.[24] Though there is no reason to believe that Florence and Frances would not have stood out among their American peers, they probably were — as Frances's father said — better off in Canada.

THE FACT THAT Wyle and Loring joined Winnifred Kingsford — a sculptor much their inferior — as two of only three women sculptors in Canada was greatly in their favour. Their location in Toronto was also an advantage. Only in Quebec could they have met a few male sculptors. But there they would have to have spoken French. Frances had picked up some French when she lived in France, and Florence had valiantly taken extra classes in French for two years at the Art Institute, no doubt in the hope of travelling to Europe, but had acquired only a smattering of the language.

The fact that the two of them stumbled into the first wave of excitement and change in Toronto's cultural scene in 1913 also favoured their endeavours. The United States, where there were enough artists in each field to form specific subgroups, differed significantly from Canada, where a handful of artists, patrons, and businessmen still interacted closely. In the United States, they would have been active in various sculpture associations, but they could not have met a variety of important men like Walter Allward, or John Pearson, or Robert Flaherty, or Sir Edmund Walker, or Eric Brown, or Fred Varley, Arthur Lismer, and A.Y. Jackson. Despite the meagre income she and Florence managed, Frances was convinced that sculpting in Canada was an exciting pioneer effort, a breaking of new ground.[25]

⋇ THE GREAT WAR ⋇

Positionings ⤻

High aloft on a crude scaffold consisting of a plank supported by two ladders sits Frances Loring, at work on a huge white plaster statue of Miss Canada. It is 1917, and the statue will mark the fiftieth anniversary of Confederation. Loring is wearing baggy overalls, a light smock smeared with plaster, and flat boots. Around her head is a bandana, also spattered with gobs of plaster. The ends of the bandana fall halfway down her back, giving her a raffish, Bohemian appearance. She is assisted in her work by fellow sculptor Margaret Scobie,[1] because Florence has fallen ill again with respiratory troubles and suspected tuberculosis. She is recovering at the Gravenhurst Sanatorium. The sixteen-foot figure Frances and Margaret have almost finished is "standing in an attitude of triumph ... holding proudly the [Red] [E]nsign of Canada in her right hand while in the left, posed on the pedestal, is a shield of all [nine] of the Canadian Provincial arms." She is crowned with laurels and maple leaves "*à la Canadienne.*"[2] In fact, the flag is the Union Jack, emphasizing Canada's colonial role supporting the Mother Country.

The construction of this larger-than-life statue is taking place in a huge improvised white tent. It stands in the outdoor yard of the T. Eaton Company department store, which has sponsored the work, at the corner of Louisa and Teraulay Streets in Toronto (two of the seven small streets later closed to make way for the Eaton Centre). Loring and Scobie have constructed a strong armature of lead pipe and wood framing and have wired it together before overlaying it with rough burlap. Now they are working it over and over with layers of sticky plaster. It is "a lesson in ingenuity," one journalist commented of the huge work that nevertheless had to be light enough to move and to lift to its place of honour.[3] The magnificent — almost mythical — head and shoulders and the flagbearing arm that points dramatically upward were modelled on the tent floor. But now they have been positioned on the body, and the finishing touches joining the mammoth torso to its head and limbs are being done. "I have never modelled quite so large a figure before," says Loring, "and I feel very nervous crawling around this scaffolding twelve feet above the ground."[4]

To make matters more difficult, it has been raining all week. This has not daunted either of the women. "Everyone has been so kind," Loring says. "The blacksmith has dried our clothes and we've eaten our lunch in beside the forge."[5]

Loring and her assistant have worked relentlessly, often longer than twelve hours a day. They have used over seven barrels of plaster. The whole enterprise has taken exactly one week.

On 30 June, when *Miss Canada* is mounted on the formal portico that extends from Eaton's main entrance over the sidewalk on Yonge Street, the effect is tremendous. Passersby — men in their suits and pork-pie or bowler hats, women in white stockings and shoes beneath light summer frocks and fetching straw hats — can look up to see miniature trees, bushes, and spring flowers surrounding a statue that inspires patriotic pride. Around the upper edge of the portico the nine provincial coats of arms — four on each side, with Ontario's at centre front between two Doric columns — direct the gaze upwards to Miss Canada, whose swirling Grecian drapery suggests vigorous purposeful action. "The result," one journalist commented, "outdid expectation. The figure ... suggests more of life and youth than many a laboured statue in marble ... It [gives] fitting expression to what the day stands for."[6] Another, mindful of the war in its third year that was draining the country, commented, "It is a symbol of the brave and dauntless spirit of Canada's young men and women."[7] As far as the T. Eaton Company was concerned, it was a wildly successful business enterprise: "We need not go out of Canada for any work we want done. Canadians can do anything."[8]

FRANCES LORING WAS just beginning to show that she could do anything, quickly, and on any scale. Between 1914 and 1917, she had been biding her time, positioning herself for some sort of opportunity. She and Florence Wyle had worked away on the smaller pieces they had ready to show when the Art Museum of Toronto held its first sculpture exhibit in 1915. By then the number of women sculptors had grown to nine: in addition to themselves and Winnifred Kingsford, Margaret Scobie, Bessie Muntz, Beverley Robinson, Lady G.W. Ross (Mildred Peel), and Mabel Stoodley were producing work. None of them could compare to Wyle or Loring.

Among the forty-one pieces Loring and Wyle showed at the 1915 exhibit were their companion busts of each other and a pair of busts that celebrated the nobility of those marginalized in society: Loring's *The Old One* (1914) and Wyle's *Newsboy* (1914). They were subjects similar to those chosen by sculptors and painters of the Ashcan school in New York. These two busts — similar in subject and modelled the same year — offer an ideal opportunity to compare the two sculptors, for already they had begun to show their differences. As art historian Christine Boyanoski observes, "Wyle has considered the base to be quite independent of the head, an architectural element that serves to display the head to advantage, offering a clear definition of form and contour. Loring's more vigorously modelled head emerges from a base that has been considered part of the design."[9] In other words, Florence's work was characterized by self-containment, serenity, and clarity, and differed from the more vital, out-flung, and dramatic work of Frances.

While Frances went on that summer to build on her success with *Miss Canada* by sculpting *The Spirit of Canada* lions for the Canadian National Exhibition, in the sanatorium, Florence has made a delicate medallion relief of the head of her doctor's infant son. The contrast could not have been greater. As Florence gradually recovered that year, Frances went from strength to strength. In 1911 she had confessed that she "lives and moves in the great visions which someday she hopes to see glorified in marble." *Miss Canada* — though it was only temporary plaster, not marble — offered her the first chance to undertake what she said she wanted to do all along: "the big themes which have haunted [me] since [I] was a mere child in Italy and first felt the stirrings of the art of Michelangelo."[10]

The Great War⤸

The First World War was probably the best thing that could have happened to Florence Wyle and Frances Loring, although at first glance it seemed inimical to their lives and art.

Frances would later explain the fact that neither of them had married by saying that all the young men their age had been killed off in the Great War.[1] But neither of them showed much interest in marrying anyone. Florence had long since given up hope on Charley Mulligan, who was married in any event, before she left Chicago in 1909. By 1916, he was dead. In 1912, she had a brief flirtation with a young married architect whose office was across the hall from their Adelaide Street studio. When his wife found out, she pressured him to end it. Sometime during the war, Frances had for a short time become involved with a German who wanted her to elope to the States, but her father stepped in and ended their romance, arguing that her beau was the enemy.[2]

Whether or not the war thwarted the possibility of marriage for Florence and Frances, it appeared to spell disaster for the arts, which seemed to be a luxury at a time when the world was channelling funds to gear up for battle. Worse than that, many people involved in the production, criticism, and organization of art on both sides of the Atlantic found an outlet for their hostility to modernism by blaming the international "spirit of unrest" for producing grotesque works of art.[3] Soon after the war began in the summer of 1914, one writer describing an event at the Royal Academy noted with relief the "complete absence of the young painter with flowing hair, eccentric necktie, and velvet jacket"; instead, "men of bronzed face, alert in bearing, and wearing khaki uniform ... turned aside for an hour from military duties to give final touches to pictures."[4] One official at the British Department of Information observed gladly that the Bohemian artist would be "brought into contact with reality and the hard facts of warfare, instead of doing things entirely out of his own head."[5] In fact, the more extreme schools of European modernism — such as the Vorticists and Futurists — had lost steam. By 1916, Estelle M. Kerr commented hopefully in *The Canadian Magazine* that "ultra-modern art which had its birth in Germany had been killed by the war."[6]

Soldiers were first sent overseas to serve in the Allied forces against the Germans in October 1914. For the first part of the war, Canada had no war correspondents at the front, nor did Britain. However, the thirty-nine-year-old Canadian industrialist millionaire, Max Aitken, returned to Canada from England, where he had hobnobbed with the likes of Rudyard Kipling and Lord Rothermere, bent on convincing Prime Minister Robert Borden and others that he could and should work to "maintain [Canada's] soldiers as a distinctive force" and, at the same time, assert "Imperialist solidarity [with Britain]."[7]

Aitken roamed around the Canadian lines and sent back eyewitness reports and photographs to England and Canada that were candid, uncensored, and designed to increase nationalistic fervour. He aspired to "maintain patriotism and enthusiasm and eager interest in our Army in France" and — especially with photographs — "to form a source of information of the utmost value to Canadian historians."[8] In April 1916 — partly due to the climate of Canadian nationalism fostered by Aitken — the Canadian War Records Office (CWRO) appointed its first war photographer and, in August, Canada's first war cinematographer.

By then Aitken himself had already published *Canada in Flanders* (1915), with photographs and illustrations. Aitken's goals were overarching: he wanted "a possession for all times." The sole aim of reports, photographs, films, and other documents of the war, he believed, was a legacy "to increase the repute of Canada and her soldiers."[9] The function of the CWRO was to publicize Canada's achievements in the war throughout Allied and neutral countries; to promote recruitment in Canada, where conscription would eventually become necessary[10]; to compile as complete a record as possible for historians; and to provide news of Canadian troops to British and Canadian presses. Small wonder that the director of Britain's Department of Information observed that the distribution of CWRO photographs in Britain and America "might well lead one to believe 'that Canada is running the war.'"[11] Later, in 1919, a reporter at the *Manchester Guardian* echoed this sentiment: it was "long open to doubt," he wrote sarcastically, "whether there was anybody but Canadians fighting in France."[12]

BY THE SUMMER of 1917, when Frances was sculpting *Miss Canada*, Aitken, now elevated to the British peerage as Lord Beaverbrook, headed the Canadian War Records Fund (CWRF), which had been established in November 1916 amid protests from the Royal Canadian Academy of Arts and other members of the arts community who had not been consulted. The government-run fund attracted contributions from many sources, including admissions to exhibitions of CWRO photographs. In particular, over 80,000 had seen the "monster attraction": "a photograph measuring some twenty-two by eleven feet depicting the Canadians at Vimy Ridge."[13]

It took no time for Canadian artists to get wind of the government's offer — actually a stepped-up version of Aitken's passionate mission to have a Canadian record of the war — to pay artists to record the war and paint portraits of Canada's major officers and heroes. Among the many who sought funding was A.Y. Jackson, who was recuperating from a war wound[14] in a reserve battalion at Shoreham Camp in the south of England. He was there when fellow Canadian artist Ernest Fosbery arranged an interview for him with Lord Beaverbrook. For Jackson, "camp life had been anything but pleasant: there was not enough food and too many military police; the soldiers, mostly casualties, were drilled and disciplined by men who had not been in France. Jackson left Shoreham and joined the CWRF just before a small mutiny broke out."[15] He received a temporary honorary commission as a lieutenant and with Richard Jack (who had no knowledge of fighting conditions) became one of the first two CWRF artists.[16] Arthur Lismer welcomed the chance to paint the devastation caused by the Halifax explosion[17]; Maurice Cullen accompanied Fred Varley, J.W. Beatty, and C.W. Simpson to the front because his four stepsons had enlisted.[18] Lawren Harris and Marc-Aurèle de Foy Suzor-Côté refused to take part in the CWRF, though Harris supported others who did. By 1917, forty-five artists were employed by the CWRF in Britain, half of whom were engaged in painting portraits of such notables as Sir Robert Borden, Sir George Perley, Sir Edward Kemp, many distinguished military officers, and every Canadian Victoria Cross recipient. Other works reconstructed unrecorded battles.

Canada emerged as the first country to patronize war art with public money. The British, who had made no attempt to apply public funds to military artistic purposes, accused Canada of "robb[ing] them of] every British artist of distinction."[19] Since the Americans did not enter the war until April 1917 — almost three years after it began — there was no comparable scheme in place there. (Wyle and Loring's Greenwich Village acquaintance Gertrude Vanderbilt Whitney later sculpted at least two war pieces, *Found* and *In the Trenches*.)[20] Beaverbrook, who had already raised thousands to fund Canadian war art by the end of 1917, anticipated raising yet another £100,000.[21] Finally — as if to leave no military stone unturned — Lord Beaverbrook sent a number of artists to various places in Canada to paint munitions factories, portraits, and training camps in what was known as the "home work section."

It was because of this glance homeward — and the funds Beaverbrook anticipated raising — that Florence Wyle and Frances Loring benefited from the CWRF. In the fall of 1918, Sir Edmund Walker took up the new challenge. He commissioned Frank (Franz) Johnston to draw what went on in flying schools and C.W. Jeffries to portray troops drilling on the University of Toronto campus. Prodded by Lawren Harris to follow Walker's suit, Eric Brown suggested such subjects as shipbuilding in the Toronto harbour to Robert Gagen and the recruiting of soldiers on the Boston Common to

Arthur Crisp. But it was Brown's observation of the women munitions workers in their overalls at the Canadian National Exhibition that inspired him to suggest to Florence and Frances (who had works on display at the CNE) that "they were very fine subjects for a series of small bronzes."[22] As cultural historian Maria Tippett remarked, "The home front artist ... dealt with a different, quieter type of heroism." The *Windsor Magazine* noted "the splendid patience, the pathetic devotion, the utter self-abnegation of women," which along with other evidence on the home front testified to "the raising of standards of duty; the deepening and broadening of national consciousness ... caused by the war."[23] Wyle and Loring had had modest successes already and were well positioned to take on such an assignment. In 1915, they had been singled out in the first sculpture show at Toronto's Art Museum: Wyle, first, for a war theme — *The Sacrifice* — and an "exquisite study of a child listening to the mysterious sounds of a shell"; then Loring for a style "freer" than Wyle's in *Transmutation* and her socially conscious *The Old One*.[24]

AS IF GALVANIZED into action by the confidence Brown displayed in their work and the purposefulness of their assignment — not to mention the money they would earn — the two sculptors produced an astonishing group of home workers for the CWRF. Wyle modelled nine figures; Loring, six. Eleven of the fifteen small bronzes (just over two feet high) were women. Broke as usual, Wyle and Loring had to borrow money to pay for the bronze casting of the fifteen statuettes representing industrial and agricultural war workers.

According to art critic Kristina Huneault, these statuettes, like other "home front" creations by Canadian women, "indicate a new and revolutionary attitude to early twentieth-century women. Their dress, postures, and expressions, their apparent strength and sense of physical embodiment, even the movement and modelling of the physical medium in which the women are cast,"[25] marked a radical challenge to the social status quo. This radical challenge is easy to see in Wyle's strapping *Farm Girl* in high laced boots, one hand on her hip, staring forcefully ahead, or her lithe *Munitions Worker*, or her *Noon Hour* worker in overalls, who leans back to slake her thirst from a bottle held high. And Loring's *Furnace Girl* in a worker's cap and heavy gloves, twisting sideways to manipulate long, hot tongs is vital and compelling, as are her *Two Girls with a Rail*, who from a distance look like men in overalls and caps, hoisting a heavy rail with determination. These few statuettes — cast athletically in Rodinesque disquiet — mark the transition from "perceptions of women predicated on feminine domesticity, dependence, weakness, and passivity" in a two-gendered patriarchal framework to one of independent strength. The women Loring and Wyle depicted were not half-persons. They confidently conveyed an "unyielding sense of bodily integrity ... characterized by a sort of unbroken wholeness or self-sufficiency" comprised of "a physicality which exists in and for the figures themselves" and conveying "confidence, independence and strength."[26] Women's experience in the sweatshops and factories had proven "that there is no operation on shell work that a woman cannot do ... even to the heavy operations which require great physical strain."[27] Wyle and Loring's war worker women — especially their munitions workers — are emblematic of the huge social change that had begun to occur long before the war: the entrance of women into the workforce — over 35,000 in Canada by the end of the war — and the *embodiment* among women of what had hitherto been masculine qualities.

Such works could have been disturbing, and were to some. The need to neutralize this social revolution was urgent at a time when women were campaigning for equal rights — especially the vote — and when restrictive female clothing and elaborate, time-consuming hair styles were seen as impediments to freedom. According to Huneault, this social anxiety was calmed (until the war ended and men returned to demand their jobs back) by the notion that the war offered an acceptable context for women's entry into the workforce. The self-sacrifice that had previously been an aspect of feminine domesticity was now subsumed in the sacrifices of war. Patriotism "explained" women's work outside the home, and reframed a frightening new masculinity and power into roles that could be understood as "helping" men at the front. Women's increasing independence could be reconfigured as nothing more than a new form of supportive partnership to men. Wyle and Loring's statuettes — along with Loring's relief *Noon Hour in a Munitions Plant*, of several female munitions workers who "in gesture and pose ... could be Hellenic warriors skirting a Greek vase"[28] — were hailed as the "embodiment of Canada's 'determination to win the war.'" They — along with other war creations — demonstrated beyond a doubt that "native art in Canada was equal to any demand that can be made upon it."[29]

Pleased beyond measure at the outcome of his suggestion that Wyle and Loring sculpt women war workers, Eric Brown purchased the statuettes for the National Gallery in 1918: Wyle's *Woman with Adapter, Munitions Worker, Farm Girl, On the Land, Noon Hour, A Moulder, Furnace Man, The Rimmer*, and *The Blacksmith*; and Loring's *The Rod Turner, The Shell Finisher, Furnace Girl, Two Girls with a Rail, The Oiler*, and her relief panel *Noon Hour in a Munitions Plant*. Reviewers were ecstatic. The statuettes were admired as "wonderful," "epic," "excellent," "finely executed," and "a joy to behold."[30]

AS FOR WYLE and Loring, their war art offered them the chance to justify their odd, ungendered existence. Huneault flirts with the notion of lesbianism, describing their lives as "outside the heterosexual contract of gender" and noting that their "artworks" "transgressed the boundaries of heterosexuality," but she stops short of naming their orientation.[31] Like the munitions workers they sculpted, Florence and Frances dressed in "masculine" garments (one photo shows Frances in wide canvas trousers pinned at the ankles) that were usually splattered with clay and other detritus. Florence's farm girls were reminiscent of her own girlhood mucking about in the garden among farm animals. And, like the industrial and agricultural women they portrayed, they, too, were engaged in work that called for unusual physical strength and endurance. One article in the *New York Times* by Janet Scudder, an American woman sculptor of the time, explains "Why so Few Women are Sculptors." "Once upon a time," she writes, "sculpture was declaimed as being too strenuous a profession for women and they were said to be physically unfit to meet the demands of important orders [commissions] ... In the lowest classes the scrub women are on their knees most of the working day. Higher along the shop girl stands hours at a time. No one has ever objected that they were physically unfit. The woman sculptor has to stand about and walk until she is ready to drop, but she easily adapts herself to these requirements, and I have never heard one of them complain of an abnormal tax on her strength."[32] Scudder says that so few women are sculptors, not because of the physical stress involved, but because they do not take the occupation seriously enough: those long years studying anatomy carefully, drawing and modelling from the nude, and apprenticing to practising sculptors (Scudder studied with Taft, MacMonnies, and Daniel Chester French). Female sculptors, like women in the war factories, were clearly demonstrating that they were strong enough to handle physically challenging work.

Certainly Wyle and Loring took sculpture seriously. Furthermore, they had long since developed a taste for working-class subjects and the dignity of labour in the Ashcan tradition as well as under Charley Mulligan in Chicago. The women workers on the home front could not have been better suited as subjects to their skills and temperaments. Unlike most of the Canadian war painters, who were "unreflective observers trying, frequently with little success, to adapt their style to what they ... persisted as seeing as an uninspiring subject ..." because they had "no direct experience of what they were asked to paint [and consequently] felt out of touch with their subjects,"[33] Wyle and Loring themselves were home workers in the industry of sculpture. Now, like the munitions workers, they could contribute to the war effort from behind the scenes by using their strength and talent to create memorials that would transform self-sacrifice and heroism as they were experiencing it themselves into everlasting bronze.

From Church to Church

After the Great War — and because of it — Florence Wyle and Frances Loring had made their names. Their doings of all kinds became news. The arts column in the 27 November 1920 issue of the *Toronto Daily Star*, for instance, headlined their move into a new studio with the subtitle, "Ladies Show Resource in Obtaining Place with Required Headroom":

> Miss Florence Wyle and Miss Frances Loring have been obliged to vacate their old quarters on Church Street and had difficulty in getting any new studio with ceiling sufficiently high to admit their big pieces of sculpture. They finally secured an old church not in use and are fitting it up for combined studio and dwelling.[1]

This news upstaged portraitist E. Wyly Grier's return from a painting trip to Halifax, the move of the Society of Graphic Arts to the St. George's Hall Building upstairs from the Ontario Society of Artists, the preparations of the

Society of Painter-Etchers for a travelling exhibition to cities and "towns of any size" throughout Ontario, and the opening of a show at the Women's Art Association of the watercolours, handicrafts, and statuary of Miss Katherine Wallis, recently returned from France.[2] In eight years, Loring and Wyle had become important Toronto figures.

The CWRF money for fourteen of their works enabled Florence and Frances to buy property. At a time when $3.99 bought an iron bedstead, $1.49 a down-filled pillow, $.99 a hardwood rocking chair, $.50 a silk scarf, and $.02 a book, $5,000.00 was a handsome amount — the first substantial income they had seen in over a decade of work. Even after the costs of bronze casting were deducted, there was plenty to spare. In a flurry of excitement, they had bought a rundown farm property thirty kilometres east of the city at Cherry Wood on the Kingston Road near the Rouge River where Florence could continue to recuperate from her respiratory difficulties. As if returning happily to her farming roots, she delighted in the idea of "a real garden she could dig in."[3] They planned to rent the farmhouse on Lot 1, Concession 3, Scarborough, to friends and use the little square shack up on the ridge overlooking the river as a summer studio. "We only wanted to buy ten acres," they later said, "but found it was cheaper to buy a hundred and fifty"[4] (actually forty-five acres, to which they periodically added more).[5] An idea of the cost can be surmised from the earliest tax record available, which valued the land at $900.00 in 1945.[6] Fifteen years earlier, it would have cost much less. To get back and forth, they bought a boxy old car, "the oldest Ford in Toronto."[7] Frances drove, transporting Florence, their two Airedales, "Sampson" and "Delilah," occasional friends, and bits of plaster statuary. Frances, who was a terrible driver, dubbed the car "Susan" or "The Old Flyver,"[8] an allusion to the English slang word meaning a small, cheap automobile or plane.

The idea was to escape the city air and unpleasant Church Street neighbourhood on weekends, relieve Florence's allergies, and save money by growing their own vegetables. Florence promptly installed a black cat at the property "for luck."[9] The last thing they anticipated was the transfer of their Toronto building to new management and the urgent need to find another studio — especially one they had to buy. "Rather foolish to buy [two properties] the same year," they would recall later, "but one came on top of the other."[10]

They probably caught wind of the church building from their photographer friends Charles Ashley and James Crippen, who shared a house a block south, at 110 Inglewood Drive.[11] The red board-and-batten frame building had been the Sunday schoolhouse north of the Anglican Christ Church in Deer Park. These buildings — on the Yonge Street Gore, the sharp triangle of land where Lawton Boulevard branched off from Yonge Street — served their purpose from the early 1870s until 1910. The church and its Sunday school serviced the Anglicans north of Yorkville Avenue. As Toronto grew, newly arrived Anglicans had begun to settle as far north as Davisville Avenue. By 1910, the larger congregation funded a new brick building across from the Yonge Street Gore. The original frame church was sold for $300.00 and was moved on rollers a few blocks west along Lonsdale Road. The Sunday schoolhouse was moved — also on rollers — east along St. Clair Avenue, and across the bridge that spanned the little Vale of Avoca, to 110 Glen Rose (formerly Pleasant, later Glenrose) Avenue on top of McLennan Hill,[12] where it underwent a symbolic conversion into a meeting place for the Century Baptist Church.[13] Florence and Frances thought The Church — as they called it, somewhat sardonically — was magnificent. It was thirty feet by forty, with a peaked ceiling eighteen feet high — a space that could accommodate huge sculptures, if necessary. To the two of them, the discovery of The Church was exhilarating. It seemed the perfect place for their shared life. Later, Frances would recall "the touch of the romantic in the way in which she and her lifelong friend Florence Wyle with their common interest in sculpture came across the little red church in Rosedale."[14] Their friends didn't agree: "But it's so far out," one warned. "Architects and patrons will never get out there to see you!"[15] Mortgaging both their properties, Florence and Frances bought the weathered building set on blocks on the unpaved street, its roof's tarpaper flapping in the wind, for $3,200.00.

"This was orchard land then," Frances later recalled, "We had to walk [uphill half a dozen blocks] from Walker Avenue, that was the end of the car line, and over the Avoca Bridge. There was no basement. The church was up on cedar posts. There was no plumbing. There were no drains on the street. We brought our water from a neighbour's pump. There was a big stove in the middle of the huge empty room."[16] Frances had grown up in mining camps, and Florence had lived on a farm. Hardships of daily living were no reason to miss this chance.

As they delighted in telling Rebecca Sisler later, their moving in was so dramatic it took years for their few neighbours to recover. The sight of two trousered women chopping wood, rolling stones around, hammering nails, and unloading sculptures, some of which were nude, into the building threw the area residents into a state of alarm. Children rushed home to report that religious objects were being carried into the church, and adults suddenly found it necessary to trim hedges and sweep porches to get a better look at the bizarre things that were happening.[17]

As soon as they moved in November, winter was upon them. The pot-bellied stove threw a great heat, but most of the warm air wafted up to the uninsulated peaked roof. Everything they did was close to the stove: especially sculpting during the day. The closed-off vestry was their bedroom.[18] At night the stove invariably went out; the water under it that was kept for Sampson and Delilah and the stray cats Florence insisted on rescuing would be frozen by morning.[19] They bathed near the stove too, in an old tin tub. Frances recalled the day when the door was flung open just as she was having a bath and two men — believing that the Baptist Church was still in operation — walked in. "[I felt] quite like Susanna and the Elders," she commented with a laugh, referring to the biblical account in the Apocrypha of two men who see the married Susanna bathing and threaten to expose her for adultery if she refuses to lie with them. (She refuses, they follow through, but are thwarted by a clever lawyer who separates them and elicits inconsistent testimony as to where the adultery took place, upon which the men — not Susanna — are executed.)[20] Perhaps the most significant part of this remark is the implication that Loring considered herself "married" to Florence.

The following spring — probably because they had somehow survived the winter — their friends gave them a housewarming party. Plans grew more and more fantastic, until the event developed into a costume party like those at the Art Institute. It was a hot night, the large doorway stood open exposing the sculptures inside, and the guests outdid themselves exercising their considerable creativity in making costumes. As Florence and Frances later recalled, "[T]he comings and goings ... pushed neighbourhood curiosity beyond controllable limits. The sight of a woman lounging in front of the open doorway in a rather transparent pyjama garment attracted a steady parade of passersby."[21]

That first summer, Frank Loring — not wanting them to endure another winter like the first — gave them money to excavate a partial basement (the "Crypt") and block off holes and cracks in the floor that had already left Florence and Frances with the first signs of arthritis. They moved the awkward front porch around to the back so Florence could have a chicken house. They named their chickens after the Group of Seven ("Frank (Franz) Johnson was a fat Rhode Island Red.")[22], who had held their landmark first show at the Toronto Gallery the year they moved in. To neighbours who complained of the early-morning crowing and cackling they blithely said, "It's because they're named after the Group; whenever they lay an egg they [have] to make a great to-do about it to be sure everyone [notices]." And during the following winter they built a huge fireplace that opened into a cozy, new dining room in the Crypt, as well as one that opened into the main studio above. Since the contractor happened to be employed at Christ Church Deer Park, tearing down the building to make way for the new church at Lawton and Heath, he brought the bricks from that demolition to use in the basement and fireplace on Glen Rose Avenue. He also rescued the pointed Gothic windows from the old church and incorporated them into the improved studio.

Neighbours and passersby in the streets of what was then the northern edge of Toronto must have stared in amazement as the two women appeared, doing their shopping on Yonge Street and St. Clair Avenue, or heading downtown from the Walker Street terminal of the Toronto Transit Commission (TTC) — then a small network of streetcars and buses — or walking their dogs in the Rosedale ravine. "They would [proceed] along the street, oblivious of the impression they were creating," observed Rebecca Sisler, "the one large majestic figure cruising along with the dignity of a ship under full sail, the other tiny figure following in her wake — bristly, bemused, cursing away under her breath about the noise and fumes from the wretched automobiles. Both would be wearing trousers, men's shoes, baggy coats with scarves dangling from the neckline, and moth-eaten berets pulled down over one ear."[23] They had become Toronto characters. And they remained Toronto characters from then on. In the 1930s, one young boy named Timothy Findley, who lived on Rosedale's Crescent Road not far away and would become one of Canada's top novelists, remembers having them pointed out to him by his father: "One day," his father said, "you will remember those two women, and you will understand how wonderful they are."[24]

It was at this time that Florence and Frances became known as "The Girls,"[25] an affectionate term, but also one that knowingly suggested that they were a couple, like The Boys.

Armouries⁀

The emergence of the Group of Seven into wide public consciousness with their first major show in the Art Gallery of Toronto from 7 to 27 May 1920 caused almost as much stir as the Armory Show had in New York in 1913. And for some of the same reasons. The equation of art with beauty and reverence — if not with the divine in man and nature — was almost universally accepted in Canada. According to A.Y. Jackson, "a European formula"[1] — especially as represented by the French painters of the Barbizon school (Millet and Corot) — was much in vogue.[2] In Montreal in particular, where wealthy collectors had begun to patronize the arts early in the century, the nineteenth-century French Barbizon school and the nineteenth-century Dutch masters such as the Maris brothers (Jacob and Mattias), Hendrik Mesdag, Jozef Israëls, Jan Weissenbruch, and others, who painted gentle, precise landscapes, portraits, and domestic interiors in subdued tones, were highly sought after as investments. Such collectors ignored Vincent Van Gogh and Piet Mondrian, who were probably the most important

Dutch painters of the time, because they were too revolutionary. They also tended to overlook Canadians Maurice Cullen (who returned from training in France to Canada where he painted superb Impressionist landscapes) and James Wilson Morrice (who travelled far afield and painted various locations, also in an Impressionist style).[3] According to Jackson, "The French Impressionist influence ... was regarded [in Canada] as extreme Modernism."[4] Elsewhere, Jackson asserts, "If there was a spiritual awakening as a result of the war it was not in evidence in Toronto; nor did it extend to the arts. There never had been less interest in painting."[5] In such a context, the Group of Seven's brash, rugged landscapes, in colours that owed much to the Fauves and the Post-Impressionists, were as disturbing as they were exciting.

In his 1926 volume, *A Canadian Art Movement*, F.B. Housser spoke of the "shock" of the spring exhibition at the Toronto Art Gallery (formerly the Art Museum) that launched the Group of Seven. In fact, as art historian Peter Mellon has shown, earlier shows, before the Group was known as such — notably an exhibition of A.Y. Jackson's Georgian Bay sketches at Toronto's Arts and Letters Club in December 1913 — sparked the criticism that is often associated with the 1920 exhibit.[6] It was in reaction to this show — and to the early works of other young landscape painters who would later form the Group — that H.F. Gadsby's famous "Hot Mush School" appeared in the *Toronto Star*. "All their pictures," Gadsby wrote, "look pretty much alike, the net result being more like a gargle or gob of porridge than a work of art."[7] Mellon argues convincingly that the Group of Seven deliberately used such adverse criticism to generate interest in their work. Although there were some favourable reviews of their paintings from the outset, comments such as "a spasm in green and yellow,"[8] "Post-Impressionists shock Local Art Lovers,"[9] and "an inarticulate fetish for the amusement of bad draughtsmanship ... [and] incompetent colourists"[10] drew public attention to their work. In 1919, a show of 144 works painted in Algoma, north of Sault Ste. Marie, by Lawren Harris, J.E.H. MacDonald, and Frank Harris also drew critical attacks.[11]

As if to emphasize these negative comments, the catalogue for the 1920 show provocatively announced that "the artists invite adverse criticism," and asserted that "[i]ndifference is the greatest evil they have to contend with."

And adverse criticism they received, some from people who had not even seen the show. "Products of a deranged mind," "art gone mad," and "the cult of ugliness" were typical responses.[12] Seven years after the much more radical Armory Show, which also generated fear that art was abandoning beauty, the Canadian art world still regarded Impressionism with scepticism and looked upon the relatively mild adaptation of a European art movement, which had been revolutionary over twenty years earlier, to Canadian landscapes as an insult to taste.

SUCH COMMENTS WERE shrugged off by several artists, many of whom, like Jackson, had studied abroad, but Frank Johnston took the criticism seriously. Fearing that no one would buy paintings that were so vilified, he left the Group after the 1920 show. In fact, after the show Eric Brown bought five paintings for the National Gallery. The Group was a loose affiliation of like-minded men — then in their thirties and forties — with a similar purpose: to paint "Canadian" landscapes. Despite the fact that the CWRF had supported their painting, for them the war was an interruption. Without it, the Group might have formed and developed sooner — probably in 1914. The war subjects they had been required to paint were often far from their choosing (A.Y. Jackson despaired of the portraits of war heroes he was commissioned to paint)[13] and for the most part were commissioned near the end of the war. As Jackson wrote, "After an absence of four and a half years, I set about trying to revive my interest in painting the Canadian scene, and to regain the excitement which had sustained me in the months before the war."[14] Jackson returned to the Studio Building he had left for the front. Situated on Severn Street just off the Rosedale ravine, he was now walking distance from The Church — the new studio-home of his old friends Florence and Frances.

It has become a truism that the Great War was the catalyst for the emergence of Canadian nationalism as a cohesive force. Men from widely separated regions of Canada met for the first time on the battlefields abroad, and out of this mix developed a sense of their sameness as Canadians. As Colonel Stacey, a Canadian war historian, put it, Canada became a nation largely because of the unlikely success of Canadian soldiers as a fighting force.[15] With its huge Canadian losses, the battle of Vimy Ridge was the bloodbath that horrified, then unified, a people, leaving them sceptical of the imperial mother country that had exacted such a toll. Canada entered the war a colony, but exited it a nation. From the end of the war on, Canada began to consider how to reconcile this weakened Britishness with its obvious North-Americanness.

Such issues found expression in the arts. Within a few years of the end of the war, nationalist views were being printed in *The Canadian Forum* magazine, F.B. Housser's *A Canadian Art Movement: The Story of the Group of Seven*, and W. Stewart Wallace's *The Growth of National Feeling*. Housser's book — considered a landmark work by historian Ramsay Cook[16] — urged Canadian artists to break from British and European traditions and directed them to embrace a North American perspective. This post-war assertion of nationalism in the arts could only have made the artistic environment in Canada more hospitable to Americans like Florence Wyle and Frances Loring. More important, monuments and memorials clearly celebrated *Canadian* achievements instead of colonial attachments. One scholar found Canadian war memorials more hopeful and optimistic than their European counterparts, which tended to glorify war or depict the anguish of death.[17] Typical symbols on Canadian war memorials were the poppy, laurel wreath, palm frond, and cross. These emphasized regrowth, success, and redemption. The Group of Seven painters reverted to their pre-war explorations of a northern landscape empty of people. But sculptors like Wyle and Loring, whose work by definition focused on the human body, took the same nationalism and directed it to Canada's achievements in the Great War, achievements which had fostered nationalistic feelings in the first place.

Although the course was set for a North American future, it would be decades before the break from Britain was complete. An exhibition of CWRF works opened in London, England, in 1919, then travelled to the Anderson Galleries in New York in June and July of that year.[18] The Canadian opening followed in August at the Canadian National Exhibition (CNE). It was a grand spectacle that acknowledged Canada's colonial role in the war. To the military tunes of the British Grenadier Guards band, visitors could inspect guns and planes around the grounds and look up to see German, British,

French, and Italian planes zooming about in the sky. There were 447 CWRF works on display, along with the CWRF's photographs.[19]

This CNE exhibit was not nearly as important to the three future Group of Seven painters as their Algoma show the same year. The Algoma show marked a return to the "big emotions born of our landscape ... [and] that great pioneer spirit which animated the explorers and soldiers of early Canada," which had been mentioned by E. Wyly Grier in the 1913 *Yearbook*.[20] But the CNE exhibit of war sculptures confirmed the reputations of Florence Wyle and Frances Loring. Grier had used war metaphors to describe what he thought paintings such as the Group's could accomplish: he saw the new Canadian landscape art as an endeavour of "romantic knight-errantry" headed for "a commanding position."[21] However, in a somewhat different sense of "romantic knight-errantry," the war sculptures of Wyle and Loring had gained "a commanding position" by virtue of their monumentalization of the war effort. Their work in the "home front" section of the CNE exhibit — even though it was on a small scale — was palatable to those who might have recoiled from some of the more graphic depictions of death and destruction at the front, such as *The Void* by English artist Paul Nash, a painting of a spread-eagled corpse in No Man's Land that particularly offended some viewers, or *For What?* by Fred Varley, depicting a wagon full of corpses.

In Toronto, where a second display took place at the Art Gallery of Toronto right after the CNE shut down, and in Montreal, where the show opened in October 1920, the war worker statuettes of Wyle and Loring were consistently singled out for praise. The *Globe and Mail* termed Wyle and Loring "brilliant artists" who had "excelled their own past achievements."[22] The *Mail and Empire* reported that "not the least important part of the exhibition consists of the bronzes done by Miss Florence Wyle and Miss Frances Loring which show the various types of workers who have been described as 'the women behind the men behind the gun.' ... No one could have done it better than Miss Wyle and Miss Loring."[23] The *Montreal Daily Star* also singled them out and claimed the show constituted "the largest and most diverse but at the same time the finest examples of modern war-art in the World."[24] Or, as Barker Fairley, the University of Toronto philosophy

professor who had become one of The Girls' friends, wrote, "[T]he statuettes of Frances Loring and Florence Wyle — especially the latter — are
the most interesting thing in the exhibition. The dress and attitude of the
women workers in field and factory, [far] from being the subject of 'farmerette'
jokes, has here been turned to account as the source of a beauty that is finely
nervous and supple. It is hard to select, but Miss Wyle's *Woman with Adapter*
is a joy to behold."[25] Eric Brown, who had solicited the works in the first
place, "looked upon [them] as among the most brilliant of the Canadian
sculpture."[26] Their friend A.Y. Jackson told Brown that the series of bronzes
"make him wish to knock down all the statues in Toronto and let [Florence
and Frances] replace them with anything [they] wish."[27]

Once the brouhaha over the Armory Show had died down, sculpture had
gradually become more experimental in the U.S. than it was in Canada.
Women sculptors, as well as men, were starting to incorporate some of
the more interpretive concepts of three-dimensional shaping that had been
exhibited in 1913. New York sculptor and political activist for suffrage, Alice
Morgan Wright, trained in Paris, then returned to the post-Armory Show
ferment in Greenwich Village, where she moved beyond Rodinesque work
into abstract sculpture that incorporated overlapping geometric planes similar to Marcel Duchamp's *Nude Descending a Staircase* and those of Futurism.
In 1916, she showed her work at the Marius de Zayas Modern Gallery with
two other American Modernists — Adolf Wolff and Adelheid Roosevelt —
and Europeans Amedeo Modigliani and Constantin Brancusi. Morgan's
Wind Figure (1916), for example, was "a dancing, ghostly, hooded figure,
reduced to simplified planes"[28] in black. Roosevelt's *Tennis Player — Serving*
(1915) was even further advanced in the direction of abstraction; it was
constructed entirely of geometric forms, and an upper circle suggests the
path of a racket circling to hit the ball.[29] Romanian sculptor Brancusi began
his series of elegantly streamlined birds in 1910, the first of which was *Maiastra*
in white marble.[30] (By 1912, it appeared in sleek bronze. In 1923–24, it
would become the even sleeker and more abstract *Bird in Space*.) Had they
stayed in the United States, Loring, more than Wyle, might have been
attracted to such experimental structures that tried to capture the essence of

movement, since her bronze war workers were caught in action poses, whereas Wyle's statuettes typically illustrated times of rest.[31]

Although there is no way of knowing whether Wyle and Loring would have moved into such abstractions had they stayed in Greenwich Village, their move to Canada fixed their more conservative path as creators of national memorials. This was true despite the fact that a 1922 show of the CWRF works at the Art Gallery of Toronto, including their statuettes, did not garner public favour. Nor did shows at the National Gallery in Ottawa in 1923 and 1924. By then, a backlash against women's employment at the expense of returned soldiers had set in, and "the Ottawa papers virtually ignored Wyle and Loring's sculptures. When they were mentioned at all it was as an afterthought, as part of a list of artists."[32] This backlash made no difference to Wyle and Loring; their reputations were solidly made. In an act that would have been deeply significant for her because of her father's enthusiasm for Canada, Frances Loring became a naturalized citizen in 1918. Florence — typically feisty — refused to do so. As she told Rebecca Sisler, "[A]t the time [I] happened to be disgusted with some government policy or other, and in any case, [I] would not cut the formal bond with the land of [my] birth."[33]

It seems Florence's thoughts turned homeward in 1920, whether because the war ended or because she had faced the possibility of becoming a Canadian citizen is hard to say. At that time she contacted her father's younger brother, Abraham Wyle, a shoemaker in Reading, Pennsylvania. His almost illiterate return letter answers questions she posed about her family. He says he is glad that the Wyles "are not In It when it comes to making money." As for her father, he reports, "He was a Selfmade man a carpenter by trade worked In the summer went to School In the Winter And Attended School In the summer was always a Sober Industrious Man well thot of In the Community."[34]

Frances had family matters to attend to as well. Her mother had died during the war, and her father — now centred in Toronto and a more frequent visitor than ever before — seemed to need a wife. Florence and Frances arranged a party at The Church to introduce him to a dozen spinsters and widows they knew. They narrowed the field to three, then to one — Miss Burns — whom Frank appeared to favour. As they later told Rebecca Sisler, when he said he liked a certain kind of fruitcake, and declared he "might marry the woman who could bake one," "a scurry of activity among noted cooks within their group of intimates produced a suitable cake," which Miss Burns was said to have baked. The two soon wed.[35]

Christine Boyanoski surmised that Wyle and Loring began to pursue what might be called the industry of war memorials in Canada in the summer of 1919.[36] Since Wyle was praised at the CWRF exhibits as the stronger sculptor, it was not surprising that she was commissioned to do a memorial to Edith Cavell, the English war nurse who was executed by the Germans for helping Allied soldiers during the occupation of Brussels, for the Toronto General Hospital, with funds of $4,000 raised largely from schoolchildren.[37] Perhaps because it seemed increasingly odd (and a disadvantage when seeking commissions) that an American sculptor should be creating Canadian national monuments, Florence changed her mind about becoming a Canadian citizen sometime in 1920 or 1921. Ironically, it was at this point that she entered hometown mythology in Waverly, Illinois. "Waverly Girl Chosen to Execute Memorial Statue by Canadian Government," ran the headline in the local newspaper. "I was sure glad to hear that Florence was chosen ... to do the work," Mrs. Libbie Wyle, her mother — "the happiest and proudest mother in the world" — was reported as saying. "I know she make good [sic]." Florence — who is remembered as "the bright little girl" and "a real Waverly product" — is compared to Cavell herself as being strong and tender. Florence, who was visiting a relative in Los Angeles at the time, outlined in a Los Angeles newspaper report her plans to "idealize the heroic qualities not only of Miss Cavell ... but of all the nurses who have given their life blood for their country." She added that there would be "no trace of bitterness or hatred in the portrait statue as that would not be true to the nobility of Miss Cavell's character."[38]

Wyle began work on a bronze tablet for the northeast corner of University Avenue and College Street, facing the parliament buildings. The tablet in relief symbolized the service of nursing in a group of three: a wounded man just back from the front, a comrade carrying his kit, and centred above the two, nurse Cavell. Wyle emphasized the role played by women in the war; the sacrifice of Cavell's life was equal to that of any soldier. The monument's completion — after two years' work with consulting architect Jules Wegman — on 27 August 1921 coincided happily with a visit from the Governor General, Lord Byng, and his wife Lady Byng, though Lady Byng did not unveil the memorial as hoped.[39] Upon completion of the tablet, the *Toronto Star* ran an interview with Wyle in which she claimed in her strong midwestern accent, that the recipe for success was "[a] great desire to do the thing, then real hard work ... Talent without industry won't get one very far."[40]

At the same time as Florence was sculpting her Edith Cavell memorial, Frances was working on the memorial tablet to Major-General M.S. Mercer and the officers of the 2nd Regiment, the Queen's Own Rifles of Canada (whom Sir Henry Pellatt had earlier treated to trips abroad). The Premier of Ontario, Lionel Clarke — among other dignitaries — attended the unveiling in April 1921.

A REPORTER WHO visited The Church to interview Frances for this occasion found her lively and appealing, and wrote an enthusiastic description of her and the studio, which shows what Loring was like at the time. "Tall, slight, with that look in her brown eyes usually associated with genius, the sculptress impresses you as but a merry girl to whom life is intensely and always interesting — one whom her work could at times absorb — but, on emerging from her studio, would enter into sport and enjoy everyday life with the rest."[41] The reporter notes various sculptures — the War Records panel *Noon Hour in a Munitions Plant*, *A Dream within a Dream*, Wyle's *Newsboy*, and Loring's latest project. She is working on "a Byzantine cross of mystic suggestion and rich colouring"[42] to be hung over the chancel at St. Mary Magdalen's Anglican Church for which Loring modelled the life-size Christ and Frank (Franz) Johnston did the colouring. The model for the crucified Christ — selected from the wide range of unemployed men who responded to Loring's advertisement to pose for seventy-five cents an hour — stole money and a few valuables and left through a window.[43] The interviewer was obviously relaxed with the hospitable Loring — whom she refers to as a "farmerette" because of the Rouge River retreat — and strikes a note of casual humour, observing that the dog "Delilah" appropriately lives in a church, but the black cat "Beelzebub" — who "stretched her claws lazily, blinked indifferently, but submitted to being stroked"[44] — certainly did not.

Loring's *Mercer Memorial* tablet — like *Noon Hour in a Munitions Plant* — shows walking figures in profile, which are lent dignity by the allusion to Greek friezes (such as are found in the Elgin marbles). But unlike the working clothes of the munitions workers, the female figure in the *Mercer Memorial* wears ancient Greek robes and carries a laurel wreath symbolic of victory — details that increase the nobility of the bronze tablet. The memorial was unveiled at the old City Armouries on University Avenue in 1921 by the prime minister of Canada, Arthur Meighen. (It was later moved to the new Moss Park Armouries on Queen Street.)[45]

Wyle's *Edith Cavell Memorial* and Loring's *Mercer Memorial* were only two among the many tributes to the Canadian soldiers who served in the Great War. And the two sculptors designed several others that were never realized.[46] The sculpting, murals, and stained glass windows commemorating the war dead became a virtual business in Canada. Over sixty-six percent of the 1,200 memorials in Canada were built right after the Great War.[47] For sculptors, in particular — whose enduring monuments could withstand public display outside — commissions were plentiful. However, such commissions were not challenging to the creative abilities of sculptors. As one critic wrote, "The art of the monument is not the art of innovation."[48] Several Toronto schools raised money from their students and staff to commission tributes to their own lost ones. By May 1919 Harbord Collegiate had amassed $2,000 for a bronze statue of "a private in trench outfit in action" by Montreal portrait sculptor George W. Hill, who later contributed work to Parliament Hill in Ottawa.[49] Alfred Howell, the first art director of the Central Technical School, sculpted a mother and her soldier son in the poetic French Romantic style for the school, where it can still be seen. Emanuel Hahn created a statue in 1922 for Malvern Collegiate. Hahn, who had immigrated to Canada from Germany as a boy, was unjustly vilified for his "nationality." In 1926 he lost the commission he won against forty-seven competitors for the Winnipeg cenotaph because he was German. This stigma

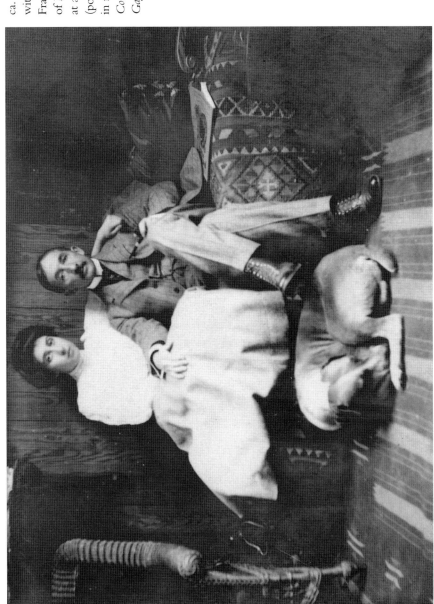

ca. 1906–07. Frances with her father, Frank Loring, "Dean of Mining Engineers," at a mining camp (possibly at Cobalt) in northern Ontario. *Courtesy of Frances Gage.*

Early 1900s. Modelling Class at the Art Institute of Chicago, where female students had only recently been permitted to work from nude models. *Courtesy of the Art Institute of Chicago Archives.*

Early 1900s. Lorado Taft
with some of his monumental
works at his Midway Studios
in Chicago. *Courtesy of the
University of Illinois Archives.*

1905. Florence Wyle (top centre) working on Lorado Taft's *The Woman Taken in Adultery*, one of the group sculptures that was formed by students working from Taft's designs. It would be these sculptures that would eventually make him famous. *Courtesy of the Art Institute of Chicago Archives.*

Early 1900s. Charles Mulligan (centre back with white sleeves) with his Evening Class at the Art Institute of Chicago, where many young tradesmen hoped to improve their skills and incomes. *Courtesy of the Art Institute of Chicago Archives.*

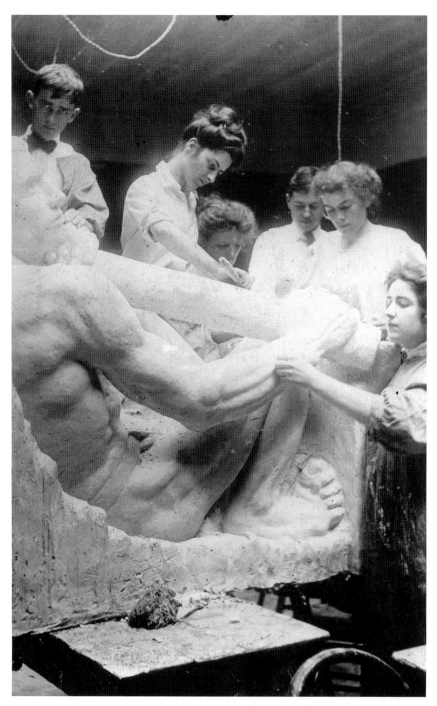

ca. 1907. Florence Wyle (second from left) working on *Spirit of the Mines* at the Art Institute of Chicago, which was famous at the time for teaching carving from stone. *Courtesy of the E.P. Taylor Research Library & Archives. Frances Loring and Florence Wyle Fonds, Art Gallery of Ontario, Toronto.*

ca. 1907–08. Florence Wyle, *Boy and Grapes Fountain*, bought by the Art Institute of Chicago and installed in one of its halls. *Courtesy of Donald F. Scalzo.*

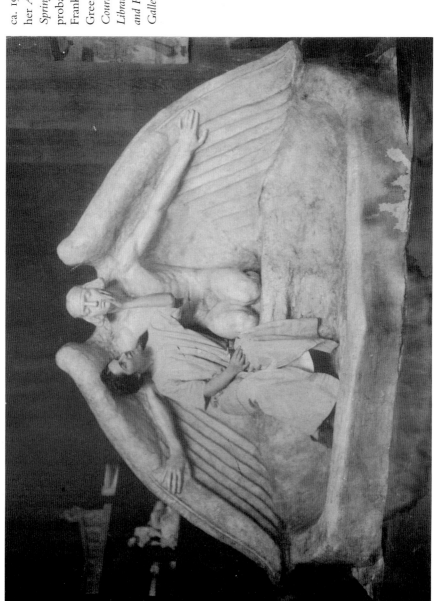

ca. 1910. Florence Wyle and her *Angel of the Pool (Sprite of Spring)*, which disappeared — probably auctioned off — after Frank Loring closed the Greenwich Village Studio. *Courtesy of the E.P.Taylor Research Library & Archives. Frances Loring and Florence Wyle Fonds, Art Gallery of Ontario, Toronto.*

ca. 1910–11. Loring and
Wyle's portrait busts of each
other: "acts of love, or the
expedient work of aspiring
sculptors without funds to pay
models?"

Florence Wyle — *Bequest of
Frances Loring, Toronto, 1968,
National Gallery of Canada.*

Frances Loring — *Bequest of
Florence Wyle, Toronto, 1968,
National Gallery of Canada.*

ca. 1916. Florence Wyle, *Sun Worshipper*, ecstatic and erotic. *Sun Worshipper* — *Purchased 1918, National Gallery of Canada*.

ca. 1915–19. Frances Loring, *Hound of Heaven*, based on the poem by Francis Thompson, depicts a woman fleeing from her conscience. *Courtesy of the E.P.Taylor Research Library & Archives. Frances Loring and Florence Wyle Fonds, Art Gallery of Ontario, Toronto.*

ca. 1912. (Left to right) Florence Wyle, musician Evelyn Pamphilon, Frances Loring, and Sir Edmund Walker at Walker's De Grassi Point retreat on Lake Simcoe. *Courtesy of the E.P. Taylor Research Library & Archives. Frances Loring and Florence Wyle Fonds, Art Gallery of Ontario, Toronto.*

ca. 1915. (Left to right) Painter Archibald Brown, etcher/painter Dorothy Stevens, Frances, Brown's wife, unknown, and Florence at the Toronto Industrial Exhibition. *Courtesy of the E.P. Taylor Research Library & Archives. Frances Loring and Florence Wyle Fonds, Art Gallery of Ontario, Toronto.*

1917. Frances Loring (on scaffold) and Margaret Scobie sculpting *Miss Canada*, which they finished in one week. *Archives of Ontario, F 229-308-0-1089, Sears Canada Inc. Fonds.*

Miss Canada, above T. Eaton Co.'s main entrance on Yonge Street, holding the Union Jack aloft as a symbol of Canada's allegiance to Britain in the Great War. *Archives of Ontario, F 229-308-0-1089, Sears Canada Inc. Fonds.*

ca. 1918–19. Florence Wyle, *Farm Girl*, and Frances Loring, *Furnace Girl*, two of the "home front" war workers statuettes that made their names as major sculptors in Canada. These two, in particular, could stand as emblematic of their two creators and were important in drawing attention to women's contribution to the Great War. *Beaverbrook Collection, Acc. # AN 19710261-0415 and AN 19710261-045-0423, Canadian War Museum.*

1920. The Church, set in the then-rural area of Moore Park, Toronto. *Courtesy of Tom Loring.*

ca. 1920s or 1930s. The Farm at Cherry Wood, "a little square shack" overlooking the Rouge River in Scarborough. *Courtesy of the E.P. Taylor Research Library & Archives. Frances Loring and Florence Wyle Fonds, Art Gallery of Ontario, Toronto.*

also attached to his Canadian wife, Elizabeth Wyn Wood, who won the second contest for the same memorial and was denied it.[50] Loring did a carving for Western Technical School.[51] Outside Toronto, Hahn also created the *Fort William Memorial* (1921), and war monuments in Springhill, Nova Scotia; Moncton, New Brunswick; Gaspé, Quebec; Meaford, Ontario; and Fernie, British Columbia. Walter Allward designed two war monuments: the *Stratford War Memorial* (1922), which featured two Rodinesque figures "Spiritual Triumph" and "Brute Force," and later the *Peterborough War Memorial* (1929), which also used an opposing pair of Taft-style allegorical figures, "Humanity" and "Aggression."[52] Over the next decade hundreds of such monuments sprang up across Canada.

A defining characteristic of these monuments was the way in which they differed from monuments elsewhere. As one historian of the Great War, Jonathan Vance, has noted, Canadian monuments did not emphasize the themes of loss, despair, aimlessness, and futility, but focused instead on "promise, certainty, and goodness."[53] Wyle's *Edith Cavell* was therefore typical. Her personal wish to avoid "bitterness" and "hatred" in order to portray "nobility of character" was completely in line with the Canadian tendency to celebrate hope instead of futility. The distinctive national voice in monuments was well exemplified in Elizabeth Wyn Wood's *Welland-Crowland Memorial*, which depicts a soldier in a Canadian uniform protecting a woman carrying a sheaf of wheat.[54]

Wyle and Loring had created their "home front" war workers — especially the women with whom they could identify — with the utmost sincerity. Wyle's approach to her *Edith Cavell* was also touched with direct authenticity. Again, identification with the subject was crucial. Wyle had empathy for a woman who was trained in medicine, was devoted to helping the helpless, and who sacrificed herself for a cause. Loring, however, began to regard war monuments with some scepticism. She had enjoyed the creation of the monumental *Miss Canada* in 1917 and the war worker statuettes, but the prospect of creating endless male soldiers in sentimental postures did not challenge her. As she complained to Eric Brown, "We have wasted a lot of time on fool monuments that we would have preferred putting on war records."[55]

WHAT WOMEN
ARE DOING

Wembley ⟞

There are two photos of the committee that met for three days in Ottawa to choose which Canadian works of art would be sent to the British Empire Exhibition at Wembley in northwest London in the spring of 1924. In the official photograph, the dozen members of the committee — some seated, some standing — look serious. In the photo taken minutes afterwards they are joking and laughing, an indication of the camaraderie the Wembley Jury of Fine Arts enjoyed. Given the situation, that camaraderie was surprising.

The Exhibition was intended to confirm the allegiance to the Empire that had bonded its eighty countries during the Great War. It was to celebrate the fact that — as John S. McKinnon, director of the exhibition's Canadian Section said to the Empire Club of Canada in Toronto two years after it was over — "the products of their countries [proved] that the British Empire was greater and mightier than any person had any previous idea of; that it was self-contained and self-supporting, and that the Empire is the greatest power in the world for good."[1] The seven leading countries in the British Empire represented there were Canada, Australia, New Zealand, South Africa, India, Ceylon, and Malaya. Among these, Canada had pride of place. Three buildings (a government building flanked by two representing the CNR and CPR railroads) displayed natural resources, manufactured products, and works of art. Canada's wealth and sophistication — a mere fifty-seven years after Confederation — was unmistakeable. The consensus of opinion after some 28 million people — including King George V and Queen Mary — had toured the grounds was that the Canadian Buildings were "the outstanding feature of the Exhibition."[2]

The lead-up to the selection of the Canadian committee that was to choose which paintings and sculptures would be displayed at Wembley was rancorous. It caused a full-blown crisis in the Canadian art world. On the one hand, the Royal Canadian Academy of the Arts, firmly established by royal charter since 1880, was convinced that it should have the authority to select — largely from its own ranks — which artists should be represented. On the other hand, Eric Brown, hand-picked from England by Sir Edmund Walker to be director of the National Gallery eight years before, believed that he should put together the committee which would choose the art that would typify Canada.

The dispute, which rankled for months,[3] centred on the revolutionary shift in Canadian painting that had begun in 1912 and saw full realization with the Group of Seven show in 1920. J.E.H. MacDonald had been a member of the RCA since 1912, Arthur Lismer and A.Y. Jackson since 1919, and Fred Varley had become a member in 1921, but those with clout in the organization — most of them older painters who were still working in the nineteenth-century realist tradition — disdained the "freak art"[4] of the Group. Eric Brown, by contrast, was enthusiastic about the new trend in Canadian landscape painting.

The question was this: would Canada be represented by painters like the sixty-nine-year-old Homer Watson, whom Oscar Wilde had dubbed "the Canadian Constable"; or were they to be represented by the younger Group of Seven's appropriation of Impressionist techniques and Fauvist colour for nationalistic purposes? To some extent, the fray was a Montreal/Toronto one. The "rebel" Group of Seven was associated with Toronto, and the "old fogeys"[5] of the RCA — some of whom frequented the Pen and Pencil Club (which did not allow female members until the 1960s) — were Montreal-based.

At first, the RCA knew nothing of the Wembley Exhibition. Eric Brown had subverted any initiative the reactionary element in the RCA might have taken. Catching wind of the exhibition in 1923, he obtained the names of the two men in charge through friends in England. In a candid letter to them he outlined the ideological rift between academics and rebels in the Canadian art scene and suggested that the management of the Canadian art section at Wembley should not be left to "some self-centred and narrow-minded organization,"[6] by which he meant the RCA.

This ploy was successful. The manager of the British Empire Exhibition at Wembley approached the Canadian government and suggested that the Board of Trustees of the National Gallery handle the exhibit. The first thing the RCA members knew of Wembley was the arrival of the entry forms and circular for the show in their mail in May 1923. They were livid.

The jury was faced with about five hundred entries from which it selected one hundred and twenty-five. Given the magnitude of the occasion, in which Canadian art was to be put on display for millions of viewers, the selection was a huge responsibility.

THE OFFICIAL PHOTO of the Wembley Jury of Fine Arts shows the jury turned towards Harry McCurry, Eric Brown's right-hand man, who holds a sheaf of papers. On a stand nearby is the only artwork in the photo: Frances Loring's statuette *Two Girls with a Rail*. Despite Brown's manipulations, this committee could not have been more judiciously chosen to heal the rift between the RCA and the National Gallery. All but one were painters, and all were either full Royal Canadian Academicians or Associates (a lesser rank) of the RCA. Two of them stood for conservatism: sixty-six-year-old Horatio Walker, who was well-represented in Canada and abroad, and portraitist E. Wyly Grier, now sixty-two, who — although he belonged to the old guard — had praised the new, young painters in the 1913 *Yearbook*, and was well-established in the Canadian art world. A.Y. Jackson called him "the little cuss."[7] The other members were thirty-nine-year-old Franklin Brownell,

one of the new wave of confident, Paris-trained academicians waiting in the wings for the old guard to lose steam; thirty-four-year-old F.S. Challener, bronze medallist in the St. Louis World's Fair of 1904; and forty-three-year-old Clarence Gagnon, silver medallist at St. Louis, famous for his Quebec winter scenes. Each had strong reputations and an individual approach to painting "which was in no way startling or unacceptable to the average gallery-goer."[8] Only two members of the committee could have been called modernist: thirty-six-year-old Montreal painter Randolph Hewton, who mainly did portraits and nudes, and Arthur Lismer. Only Lismer was a member of the Group of Seven. And only one juror — also an Associate of the RCA since 1920 — was a sculptor and a woman: Florence Wyle.

And there she sits in the official photograph of the committee — "the great man-hater,"[9] as Rebecca Sisler termed her — fully at ease among her avuncular male painter colleagues. Wearing a simple, dark, collarless dress, dark stockings, and plain black shoes with the short heel fashionable at the time, she now sports wire-rimmed glasses and has cut her long hair to a length not unlike that of the tweed-suited, pipe-smoking men around her. She has been chosen for the committee not just to represent Canadian sculpture, but more importantly, because "she was an individualist who expressed her own opinions without bias."[10]

The committee deliberated for three days, and selected from the five hundred submissions of painting and sculpture those that would be sent to England. The irrepressible Arthur Lismer — "whose pencil would never stay in his pocket"[11] — made caricature sketches of the members while they voted on entries.[12]

Armed with her United States passport — in which the picture of her in a fedora and broad-lapelled wool coat might be mistaken for that of a man — Florence Wyle headed out on a trip that was long overdue. Not only would she attend the gala opening of the British Empire Exhibition, but she would also take a few extra weeks to visit museums and galleries in London and Paris, which she had longed to see when she was an art student in Chicago. She would also take some master classes while she was there. Paris, which she had so longed to see, was a disappointment, according to Rebecca Sisler;[13] at forty-two Wyle was too old to realize her youthful dream of delightful and instructive travel abroad. London, however, charmed her completely — despite her American background.

The Fine Art Pavilion in the Canadian Buildings at the British Empire Exhibition was a remarkable success — largely because of the Group of Seven paintings. According to Maud Brown:

> The art critics, thirty or more of them, had seen the British rooms hung with pictures they knew so well and had written about so often. They had seen contributions from India, Australia, New Zealand and South Africa, and finally, looking more than a little bored, they trouped silently in and looked around [at Lawren Harris's *Shacks*, Walker's *Oxen Drinking*, Lismer's *September Gale*, Brownell's *Beach St. Kitt's*, and [C.W.] Jeffreys's *Western Sunlight* ... and many, many more]. There was colour, force, individual attack and deep sincerity. We waited. You could almost hear the gasp of surprise; notebooks and pencils came out. There was a buzz of conversation. Here was something new. We were inundated with questions. Was Canada like this? Could shadows on snow possibly be as blue as Albert Robinson had painted them? Surely MacDonald had exaggerated the reds and yellows of autumn? Who were all these painters and why had their work never been seen before?"[14]

Some viewers were convinced that such colourful paintings must have been done by Indians. The British press was ecstatic. "We feel as we look at these pictures," wrote J.M. Millman, "the rush of the mighty winds as they sweep the prairies, the swirl and roar of the swollen river torrents, and the awful silent majesty of her snows. And such is Canada's art — the 'pourings out' of men and women whose souls reflect the expansiveness of their wide horizons ..."[15] J. Lewis Hind concurred: "These Canadian landscapes ... are the most vital group of paintings produced since the war — indeed this century."[16]

Eric Brown was present when the Royal Family — King George V, Queen Mary and their two sons, the Prince of Wales (later Edward VII) and the Duke of York (later King George VI) then in their early thirties — came to see the exhibit. It was a "trying experience."[17] The building was closed for the occasion. "[A]n alcoholic fog accompanied the royal party, with one royal temper on edge and an appreciation of modern art ... in very slight evidence."

The King expressed himself "with warm sincerity" and asked to have "the wilder Canadian works explained." Eric Brown was more than obliging.[18] In a coup for A.Y. Jackson, the Tate Gallery in London bought one of his paintings from the exhibit, although it was a war work and not specifically a landscape: *Entrance to Halifax Harbour.*[19]

The Canadian sculpture at Wembley was not mentioned in the press. Wyle and Loring had both submitted some of their "home front" statuettes; Wyle had included her *Dancing Boy* and exuberant bronze *Sun Worshipper*, and Loring had her bronze *Grief* and the marble *A Dream within a Dream.*

While Florence was abroad, Loring was hard at work on her war memorial for St. Stephen, New Brunswick. She had lost the commission for a Sault Ste. Marie memorial to Alfred Howell the year before. But now she acted with typical ingenuity and aplomb. Knowing that sculptors often lost out on war commissions because tombstone manufacturers beat them to the draw with hideous statues at lower prices, she packed a maquette of a young soldier holding a rifle, a cross at his feet, sorrowing for his lost companions, into a cereal box and boarded a train to St. Stephen. There she presented her maquette to Arthur Gagnon and his committee. Her competition was a carver of granite tombstones with a gift for making people weep. Frances's charm — and the grace of her maquette — won the commission.[20]

Despite the rave reviews of the Fine Arts Pavilion, Wembley almost cost Eric Brown his job. An article in the *Toronto Star* ran the headline, "Painters Demand the Head of the Art Dictator of Canada." The "painters" remained anonymous. Lismer and Hewton protested that they had no regrets about sitting on the Wembley Jury of Fine Arts, as the article implied they had. Letters — in a campaign spearheaded by Florence Wyle — defended Brown. In the end, all went on as before. Brown had tricked the RCA at the outset of the Wembley affair, but was right to observe that in Canada, "[a]rt is becoming more individual and less reproductive [realist, as in a photograph], whether it is music, poetry, painting or sculpture."[21]

‖ 17

What Women Are Doing

The enormous breakthrough for women represented by Florence Wyle's selection for the Wembley Jury of Fine Arts must be seen in the context of Toronto's art world — and women's place in that art world — at the time. From the beginning of the Great War, women had played an important role in the arts, but one that had little to do with creating art and much to do with patronizing it. An item from a 1914 "Social and Personal" column in the *Toronto Daily Star* shows what arts events were like at the time:

> The private view of the Royal Canadian Academy [art exhibit] drew a large and fashionable gathering to the Art Gallery, College [S]treet [Toronto], last night when his Honour the Lieutenant-Governor and Mrs. Hendrie with Miss Enid Hendrie and Major Caldwell were received by the president Mr. William Brymner. Mrs. Hendrie was wearing a handsome gown of black satin with steel embroidery and diamond ornaments and she carried a magnificent bouquet of pink

roses and ferns. Miss Hendrie was in black satin and net, with a rope of pearls.[1]

The column goes on to list many of the four hundred guests who attended, including Miss Wyle and Miss Loring, drawn from the artistic, military, and social ranks of Toronto and Montreal.

THE ARTICLE IS typical, for there is a blurring of boundaries between the artistic and the social. Apart from art institutions themselves, the wealthy members of Canada's elite were the only ones who could afford to commission portraits and portrait busts or buy works of art. It followed that they were invited to gallery openings. Socialites, in turn, needed grand events to attend at which they could show off their finery as well as make contacts with each other and with the artists who might someday create portraits of them. Few were educated — or even interested — in the principles or history of art. On the other hand, many of those who were artists or were informed about art could not afford to take part in such social gatherings. Despite the Great War, such occasions for the urban elite continued and even gathered force after 1918. It was wishful thinking to assume — as a speaker opening the 1923 War Memorials show in Ottawa had — that art gallery exhibits "did more to cultivate a love of the fine arts [in the population at large] than any other medium."[2] It was not the population at large whose taste was being cultivated; it was mainly that of a wealthy elite.

The positioning of such notices of art exhibitions in the women's pages of all the Toronto newspapers — the *Globe and Mail* called their column "What Women are Doing" — continued through the 1920s. They invariably emphasized social status at the expense of the art itself. Descriptions of women's clothes and decorations upstaged comments on the paintings and sculpture. Reports of gallery openings ran side by side with announcements of debutantes' comings-out, engagements and weddings, or visits of socialites and their families in and out of the city. On the same pages were fashion, health, and family-centred advertisements like these: "Auction Sale of Jewellery," "Baker's Cocoa is for Robust Men," "Day and Night Creams," "Mark These Fine Corset Values," "Spats are Absolutely the 'RIGHT

THING' for Fall," "Frocks for Wee Lassies, Half-Price and Less," and "When He's Seven or More He Must Have an Eton Suit."[3] Women, it is clear, were in charge of the arts, as they were of domestic life and fashion. Serious and more important matters such as the war, business, and politics were men's concerns, and were found headlined on the front page or strategically placed in the front section.

This assignation of the serious to men and the frivolous to women characterized early twentieth-century life in Toronto as elsewhere. Women would not get the vote in Canada until the end of the Great War on 24 May, Victoria Day, 1918. And it would be some time after that before the assumption of political authority and the comfortable expression of opinion in what had been a thoroughly "man's world" became widespread and felt natural. In the meantime, as Montreal social observer Stephen Leacock — who fiercely opposed suffrage — wrote, "It is quite impossible for women ... to go in for having a career ... *they can't do it.*"[4]

It followed that women's organizations would foster the arts. Most men had no time to do so. Men of means had their clubs — why shouldn't women? In Toronto, the York Club, the Hunt Club, the Yacht Club, the Toronto Golf Club, and the Arts and Letters Club, as well as the military messes that sprang up during the war — among many others — offered lunches and dinners to businessmen who gathered to discuss the events of the day while their wives dealt with domestic matters at home. But at the beginning of the century — later in Canada than in the United States — various branches of education had opened their doors to women. Emily Jennings Stowe, the first Canadian woman authorized to practice medicine, got her licence in 1880; women were first admitted to the University of Toronto in 1886; and Clara Brett Martin became the first Canadian woman — the first in the British Empire, in fact — to be admitted to the law court in 1897. It followed that women would eventually want their own clubs, and, in most cases, when they succeeded in getting them, such clubs focused on the arts.

The most important of these in Toronto were the Women's Art Association of Canada (WAAC) and the Heliconian Club. The Women's Art Association had started in 1886 when a group of women in the city organized a self-governing art society. By 1912, it was incorporated federally and had branches in other parts of Canada, all under the official patronage of the wife of the Governor General. In 1916, the association bought a pair of semi-detached two-and-a-half-storey houses at 23 Prince Arthur Avenue, a block north of Bloor Street, adapted two upstairs rooms as galleries and made the downstairs rooms suitable for the teas and receptions associated with exhibits. The Heliconian Club had begun in 1909 when a singing teacher at Toronto's Royal Conservatory of Music brought together a group of women working in the arts and letters to "end women's isolation by giving them an opportunity to meet and exchange ideas."⁵ In 1923, the club bought Heliconian Hall, a former church building in the Yorkville district, also just north of Bloor, where numerous musical concerts, literary readings, and art exhibits took place.

Frances Loring became a member of the Women's Art Association in 1918, though Florence — possibly because she had far less experience of "society" or was simply more curmudgeonly — did not join the club until a few years later. Frances, who had a canny sense of business, no doubt saw that if she and Florence were to survive as sculptors they must take advantage of every possible outlet for their work. They were already associate members of the RCA and had memberships in the OSA, the two most important organizations for their work. The regular exhibitions of work offered by these two organizations were key outlets. The CNE was also an important venue for their work. Despite the fact that it was essentially an agricultural fair that sported a midway and catered to a pleasure-seeking crowd more interested in being dazzled by industrial displays and pyrotechnic spectacles than art of any kind, the chance to decorate buildings and display such sculptures as their bronze war statuettes offered a chance to reach the masses, not just the elite. Frances's creation of the temporary *Miss Canada* for the T. Eaton Company had proven to be an important contact too. For the month of April 1923 the department store held an exhibit of Wyle and Loring's work in which, alongside their larger sculptures, a number of their smaller works such as candlesticks and bookends were for sale. Eaton's would continue to hold exhibitions of their work. In addition, the Hart House Gallery at the University of Toronto, where they had acquired a number of academic friends, such as German philosophy professor and painter Barker

Fairley,[6] philosopher Fulton H. Anderson,[7] and Dr. Frederick Banting (who the same year Wyle and Loring bought their Church studio had begun the experiments that would lead to the discovery of insulin in 1922), occasionally showed their work.[8]

Apart from the professional organizations, the Women's Art Association was by far the most important organization for Wyle and Loring's purposes, and there are many references to shows and social events held at 23 Prince Arthur Avenue in which their names appear, usually together. Here they could make contacts with the wealthy wives of Toronto businessmen, women who might steer them in the direction of commissions or who might want a portrait bust or bas-relief medallion done of themselves or a family member. Every bit of exposure — no matter where or to whom — kept their names before a public unaccustomed to thinking about sculpture.

As Toronto boomed in the post-war years of the '20s, and the number of families with wealth increased, sculpted fountains for lavish gardens also became a potential source of income. Fountain sculpture suited Florence Wyle much more than the war memorials that appealed to Frances's love of large-scale works. Florence's first sale — to the Art Institute of Chicago in 1908 — had been a fountain sculpture, *Boy with Grapes*. She had since done several others, notably variations on an infant pouring water from an urn. Fountain sculptures had been popular in the United States since early in the century.[9] At a time when the western world was recovering from the Great War and making rapid industrial advances — in particular the motorcar, which was speeding up the pace of life — there arose in reaction a longing for a never-never land of pastoral certainty. As one 1916 article about an exhibit of garden sculpture at the Gorham Galleries in New York (where Loring had offered her early sculpture for sale) put it, "Alas, were it not for the artists, the sculptors and poets we would forget even the tinkling names of the pleasant woodland and garden folk ... We must not let them fade out of our lives ... nor must we grow so high and heavy that we cannot have them for companions in our walks and quiet times."[10] The positioning of nymphs, cherubic children, fauns, animals, birds, fish, and other amphibian creatures amidst foliage and beside pools reminded viewers of the mysterious, organic animation of nature. And — more importantly in an age that was threatened by modernism's disregard for beauty — such works were "innocent" and "beautiful": "Children playing with animals, little boys with shells, children with butterflies and rabbits, women, primitive mothers, with children on their backs, water animals and water babies were in evidence; everything that was beautiful, light and joyous ... We are all indebted to the sculptors who make images of the lovely things we have almost lost the power to see for ourselves and who give us laughing children who never grow old."[11]

The last point was an important one. Sculpture had the power to make eternal what was ephemeral in life. It arrested change. In an article called "Children that will Never Grow Old," the "unpretentious, unconscious, loveable, everyday youngsters" of more than one American sculptor — all of them women — are praised for being "so beautiful, so idealized."[12] One of these sculptors was Janet Scudder, "a trendsetter since 1901 ... for bronze fountain figures of small children and elfin sprites to serve as focal points in the gardens of the wealthy."[13] Scudder rejected monumental sculpture commemorating great men in favour of her whimsical fountains: "I won't do it!" she declared in 1912 when she was working on a grotto fountain of a small boy playing with a crab for John D. Rockefeller's estate near Tarrytown, New York. "I won't add to this obsession of male egotism that is ruining every city in the United States with rows of hideous statues of men-men-men-men-men each one uglier than the others ... Banish the thought that I was going to teach anyone anything ... My work was going to make people feel cheerful and gay, nothing more!"[14] Perhaps something of the same sentiment — along with her training in neoclassicism at the Art Institute — convinced Florence to pursue this type of sculpture. Perhaps it was her empathy with Charley Mulligan, whose tender depiction of children was remarkable and unusual in its time. Perhaps it was the death of her mother in 1926. Or, perhaps it was one way for a woman at the peak of her childbearing years to give birth to children who would remain ideal forever: children who would never grow old, never disappoint. Children for a woman who knew she would never marry.

The vogue for garden sculpture took longer to appear in Canada than it did in the United States — probably because of the war. When it did take hold, Florence Wyle was its primary practitioner. An article in the March 1927 issue of *Canadian Homes and Gardens*, called "Sculpture as a Garden Decoration," featured a headline photo of Wyle's *Salome* — a "spectacular and beautiful piece ... which calls for a setting or screen of shrubbery."[15] In it a fluidly draped, nude Salome, emerging from the rock, tenderly cradles the severed head of the Baptist. This powerful, unsettling image — an odd one for a woman who was not Christian — suggested the brutal abandonment of the male, the decapitation a symbol of castration. It echoed an earlier sculpture of hers based on Keats's poem "Pot of Basil," in which a woman digs up the corpse of her murdered lover, decapitates it, and hides the head in a pot of basil that she waters with her tears. There are also photos of Wyle's wall fountain of a baby holding an urn aloft and one by Loring called *Mermaid and Child*: a windblown mermaid — in the back yard of The Church — gazing at the standing infant on her knee. Since all the other photos in the article are of garden urns, Wyle first and foremost, then Loring, represented garden sculpture in Canada. Later, Loring would write a "how-to" article on garden sculpture, using Wyle's fountains as illustration.[16]

Had Florence and Frances been men, the Women's Art Association would have been off limits. As women they could take part in the social life of the club as well as exhibit their work in the upstairs galleries. The *Globe*'s "What Women Are Doing" and the *Star*'s "Social and Personal" columns record many such occasions. In November 1920, the WAAC held a show of Wyle's war memorials, a bust of Dr. Monash, and two models for fountains and other work, as well as Loring's war memorials and a decorative panel.[17] Typically, Wyle and Loring would show works they hoped might sell to WAAC members in one gallery while another show was exhibited in the next room. On one occasion in 1922, they shared an exhibit with painter Louise Brown: "Book ends by Miss Wyle of two children nestling against each other, and a number of portraits in relief have to do with the things of daily life. Surely no child's portrait could be more appealing than the little sculptured head. A charming bit of fancy is Miss Loring's relief panel 'The Mermaid and Nippocambus [sic]' which being translated means that the little mermaid is conversing with sea horse, as we call him, way down in the sea."[18]

By 1928, although both sculptors had done war memorials and more intimate works — especially fountains — differences between the two had clearly emerged. Loring was drawn to large-scale, dynamic, monumental works and Wyle preferred more intimate sculptures of women and children. A 1928 notice of their work on exhibit at the Toronto Art Gallery's first autumn show notes the distinction: "Although Miss Frances Loring has several later reliefs, heads and fountains, much interest still attaches to her great work in rendering in bronze some of the types connected with war work at home, such as *Girl with Shells* and *The Rod Turner*, with grace combined with realism. Two decorations for the Memorial Chamber at Ottawa [*Recording Angel* and *War Widow* (1928) and *Memorial Tablet to Dr. Alpheus Todd*, parliamentary librarian (1928)] are also striking in their refined treatment of figures. Miss Florence Wyle is also represented by some of her earlier bronzes of war workers, several portrait busts, and by some new figures and reliefs. Garden sculpture is one of Miss Wyle's happiest forms of expression."[19] Since Wyle's no-nonsense, brittle manner struck people as more "masculine" than Loring's penchant for the social graces and feminine dress, it was remarkable that Wyle created the more "feminine" sculpture.

"What Women Are Doing" in the *Globe* implied that Toronto women were dressing for display at arts events; visiting and being visited for teas, receptions, and dinners; engaging in the business of getting married; and shopping carefully for their children and husbands.

Meanwhile, Florence and Frances were working hard. Shaping spiky armatures with odds and ends of pipe and wire; patting and shaping and modelling the cold slippery clay onto those armatures; creating maquettes that might win commissions, or at least serve as the basis for enlargements; finding time between commissions for the realization of their own sculptural dreams; mixing the icing-like plaster in the messy casting room downstairs in the Crypt to slather onto hardened clay which, when set, could be split in half to make moulds for casting; overseeing the business of sending off models to be cast in bronze at the Roman Bronze Works foundry in New York (since Canada had no foundries); hauling sculptures in and out to their Rouge River farm in summer, as well as to and from various exhibitions in the fall, winter, and spring — all this in addition to the demands of daily living.

The Loring-Wyles ⤳

According to *Saturday Night*, 9 January 1926 was to be a "red letter day."[1] On that day, Vincent Massey, then a trustee of the National Gallery of Canada and a Liberal cabinet minister, opened an expanded Toronto Art Gallery of "metropolitan dimensions" to the public. Three new courts surrounded by galleries on all sides were to be built over the summer. The central axis of the addition, which was entered directly from the main Dundas Street doors and was fittingly named the Sir Edmund Walker Memorial Court, was to be devoted entirely to sculpture. A portrait of Sir Edmund, the first president of the Art Gallery of Toronto, and a plaque outlining his accomplishments was to form a permanent memorial to the man who had not only done so much for the arts in Canada up to his sudden death in 1924, but had also fostered the work of Florence Wyle and Frances Loring.

The sculpture court, with its large ceiling skylights and blue glass "day-light" lamps for evening, was calculated to give an illumination as close as possible to natural light. Plans were already in place for doubling the size of the sculpture court through its temporary north wall at the same time as building a driveway that would lead to a new main entrance off Dundas Street.[2] In the end, only one of the proposed three courts — the Walker Court — was completed.

Wyle and Loring had been important in establishing the need to treat sculpture in Toronto as a pursuit serious enough to warrant a permanent sculpture court, but they were by no means the only ones. Their acquaintance Walter Allward had not usually shown his works in the Toronto art exhibits on the grounds that they were too large.[3] In 1923, he had won the plum government commission for the Vimy Memorial to be erected above the Douai Plain in France. In 1925, Florence Wyle wrote a letter to the editor of the *Mail and Empire* to say she regretted that Allward's memorial would be in France, not in Canada, since his work has always been "inspired not by tradition but by a man's love of his country and faith in her growth and standing among nations ... This memorial marks a new era in art ... and embodies the highest and noblest type of beauty."[4] In undertaking the Vimy Memorial, Allward — until then Canada's main sculptor — effectively removed himself from the Toronto art scene; he would not return to Canada until 1938. Then, at age fifty-two, exhausted by the thirteen-year-long struggle to finance and complete his massive tribute to the Great War, he sank into a state of mental distress and obscurity, a situation movingly described by Jane Urquhart in her 2001 novel *The Stone Carvers*.

At the Ontario College of Art, Emanuel Hahn headed the sculpture program and, apart from the controversy stirred up about the appropriateness of someone with his German background for sculpting Canadian war memorials, successfully exhibited at various shows. His wife Elizabeth Wyn Wood headed the sculpture department at Central Technical School, and also exhibited frequently. This couple was more strategically placed than Wyle or Loring to influence the next generation of sculptors. On the other hand, they had to spend hours teaching twice weekly that Wyle and Loring could spend sculpting. Hahn in particular had other reasons to resent the two women. Before their arrival in Toronto, he was positioned as next in line after Allward as Canada's pre-eminent sculptor. With Wyle and Loring in Toronto, he suddenly had to share commissions with them. This partly explains why he and Loring often quarrelled.[5] Alfred Howell sculpted several Canadian war monuments in the French Romantic style — even more outdated than the neoclassic tradition in which Wyle and Loring worked.

Nonetheless, the centrality of Wyle and Loring in the sculpture of English Canada during the 1920s was unassailable. Eric Brown, director of the National Gallery of Canada, who visited them whenever he was in Toronto,[6] described several examples of their work in his gallery as "among the most brilliant of the Canadian sculpture."[7]

THIS WAS NOT to say that the Loring-Wyles did not experience failures. Christine Boyanoski speculates that they both probably competed for the Canadian Battlefields Memorials Competition won by Allward's Vimy Memorial. If so, Florence's letter to the editor of the *Mail* asking the Canadian government to install a copy of the Vimy Memorial somewhere in Canada is generous. In 1923, both Wyle and Loring — the only women who submitted designs — had competed against seven others for the Sault Ste. Marie War Memorial (1924) won by Alfred Howell. Neither of them won the more important 1922 competition — complete with precise regulations[8] — open to architects (with a sculptor), artists, and sculptors (with an architect) in the British Empire, for a federally funded war memorial in Ottawa. Loring (the only woman), together with Toronto architect W.L. Somerville (who had designed the Shakespeare Memorial Theatre in London, England), were among the seven finalists out of 127 original submissions from Canada, Britain, the U.S., France, Belgium, and Italy. The English sculptors Vernon and Sydney March[9] won the commission for the *Great Response*, a work Loring later described as "a cheap melodrama."[10] (The March brothers, known for their statue of Champlain in Orillia, also won the federal commission for the Halifax *Sailor's Memorial*, and George Clemshaw did the federally sponsored *St. Julien*, in Belgium.) Loring resubmitted her design — a three-quarter round monumental relief of oversize figures emerging dramatically from the three-part architectural wall (but without its side figures representing the sacrifice of mothers, since they were too expensive) — successfully to the competition for the *Galt War Memorial* (1930) in 1928.[11]

In addition to the Galt Memorial, Loring undertook so many memorials at the end of the 1920s that it seems impossible she could have managed them all. In 1928, during three months in Italy, she completed her finest memorial in Carrara marble for the Great Library at Osgoode Hall, commissioned by the Law Society of Upper Canada. Based on a phrase from the English war poet Rupert Brooke — "These laid the world away" — Loring's seven-foot statue depicts a draped, nude young man standing with eyes upturned and arms extended with palms upward before a marble panel of the names of those from the Law Society who lost their lives in the Great War. The allegorical marble statue is neoclassic, eloquent, and noble. The cost of marble, materials, and carving was $954. The ceremony to unveil it on Armistice Day was a grand Toronto affair. It was conducted by Bishop Sweeney and Canon Baynes-Head, after a grand procession led by the choir of St. James followed by the Lieutenant-Governor, Hon. W.D. Ross, the justices of the Supreme Court, benchers, and members of the bar — all in robes and medals — followed by the relatives of those who fell in battle. Col. G.R. Geary read the roll.

At the same time as she sculpted the Osgoode Hall War Memorial, Loring also undertook a strongly stylized central group of three figures — a mother and two children — entitled *The War Widow* (1928), and a tympanum figure panel, *The Recording Angel* (1928). Both were done in collaboration with friend and architect John Pearson for the memorial chamber of the Parliament Buildings in Ottawa. She also carved the memorial tablet to Dr. Alpheus Todd, former librarian of Parliament. *The War Widow* and *The Recording Angel*, which was not modelled but imaginatively created, allowed Loring to confirm her love of working on the monumental scale that had excited her since *Miss Canada*.

Meanwhile, Florence was working on an animal figure for Guelph's Agricultural College and a deer panel for the library at Baron Byng High School in Montreal.

The following year, Loring adapted her *St. Stephen War Memorial* (1925) for another war memorial in Augusta, Maine. It is unlikely that the citizens of Augusta realized that their war memorial was an approximation of a Canadian statue that had been in place for four years when they looked at the "pictures of the model which she [had] executed from ideas furnished her by the local committee."[12] Once she was chosen in competition, Loring visited Augusta in June 1929 to select a site and negotiate the base of pink granite to be built by the Lewiston Monumental Company. She was then off to Antwerp, Belgium, to make sure that the American uniform and rifle she had sent over to replace the St. Stephen Canadian version were accurately cast in bronze. (Later, she would comment wryly, "If we [sculptors] had our way, all the military uniforms in the world would be the same design. Then it would be so easy to do war memorials. Now they're all different and such a bother.")[13]

She was also present as a house guest of Hon. and Mrs. George E. Macomber, who had sponsored the memorial, for its unveiling on Armistice Day, Monday, 11 November 1929. During the week she stayed at the "charming State Street residence" of the Macombers, Frances made a strong impression. "[She] has been met very pleasantly by a number of Augusta people," a local newspaper reported. "Miss Loring is most gracious and with a delightful and friendly personality that at once wins for her a warm place in the hearts of those who are privileged to meet her." The *Augusta Portland Star* noted that "When Mr. and Mrs. Macomber and Miss Loring were introduced at the supper session ... the entire assembly rose and accorded them a splendid ovation" before launching into singing several old army favourites such as "Long, Long Trail," "Keep the Home Fires Burning," and "Pack Up Your Troubles in Your Old Kit Bag."[14] A long illustrated profile of "the young Canadian sculptor" (she was forty-two) in the *Portland Sunday Telegram and Sunday Press Herald* the day before the celebrations presented Loring as a fully established Canadian sculptor from Toronto, emphasized her war memorials, but also listed her many works such as *Grief* and *The Derelicts*, which had more to do with the socially oppressed than the war. The accompanying photographs showed a close-up of Loring in profile in front of her bust *The Old One* (1914), a full-length photo of her in smock, trousers, and scarf at work with chisel and hammer on her fountain statue *Girl with Squirrel* (ca. 1922) — possibly inspired by Crunelle's *Squirrel Boy* in Chicago[15] — for the Oshawa garden of Colonel R.S. "Sam" McLaughlin (the head of McLaughlin Motors, later General Motors), her Greenwich Village traffic policeman on his horse, her "Gault [sic]" war memorial, and her fountain statue *Mermaid and Child* (ca. 1923) adorning "the gardens of a fine estate in Toronto."[16] There is no mention of Florence Wyle, who was following a different path.

Unlike Frances, who was attracted to the strong, large-scale, monumental pieces that the war called forth, Florence returned to the smaller, more serene works for which she had all along exhibited a special talent. "All those lovely tender babies and girls"[17] now came to the fore. First was the plump bronze cherub holding aloft an urn pouring water into the *W.D. Young Memorial Garden Fountain* (1920) in Toronto's Kew Beach Gardens. Florence collaborated with architect Maurice Klein, who designed the formal stone arbour — enhanced with reliefs by Florence — in which the infant stood. So appealing was the stone baby that he was stolen soon after the fountain was installed. (He was replaced much later with a replica cast by a friend, sculptor Frances Gage, in 1978.) In 1923, Wyle created another fountain figure, *Boy with Dolphin*, a traditional subject for fountain sculptures and one her old Chicago teacher Lorado Taft had used in his *Great Lakes Fountain* (1913). In 1926, the first of Wyle's many sweet, demure young women appeared with *Study of a Girl*, a partly draped nude with eyes downcast, which would serve as the maquette for a full realization in bronze in 1931. In 1928, she completed the marble *Mother and Child* for the Mothercraft Society; this incarnation of maternal tenderness still stands outside the entrance to the Mothercraft building at 32 Heath Street West, Toronto. And in 1928 she created *Baby Fountain, Girl* and *Baby Fountain, Boy* for the Marjorie Gibbons Counsell Garden in Gibbons Park, London, Ontario. These whimsical infants in short drapes — as in so many of Wyle's fountains — pour water from urns. The same year she created two fountain figures for the King City estate of Sir John Eaton, who had been on the advisory committee for the Kew Beach Gardens fountain: *Dancing Baby* (1928) and *Child with Flute* (1929). She also sculpted *Young Mother* (1928) in bronze — a quiet nude who is modestly draped by the cloth in which her baby is wrapped.

These sculptures of women, mothers with children, and animals — often in fountain form — now began to define Wyle's work not only in subject but also in style. Starting in 1926 with *Study of a Girl*, she honed her style — found her voice — in sculpture. More responsive than Frances to the simplified stylization that characterized the art deco aspect of the modernist movement, the anatomically precise work she favoured at first evolved into sleek, smooth forms that suggested the art deco fashions of the day. Her work was certainly far from the experimental abstractions of some American women sculptors, but it was nonetheless what Christine Boyanoski calls "a gradual distillation"[18] in her treatment of human forms. She mastered a satisfying tranquility and a delicious sense of soul, such as was found in the Greek sculpture she admired above all. Her work had become recognizably Hellenistic — in a word, beautiful.

Wyle's prolific output in the 1920s included a number of portrait busts and reliefs, including many of personal friends and some of Toronto's wealthy citizens. Three portrait busts were of their Group of Seven friends: *F.H. Varley* (1921), *Lawren Harris* (1928), and *A.Y. Jackson* (1929). "Florence made a bust of me for the O.S.A.," Jackson wrote a friend good-humouredly. "I look as though I was solving some weighty problem. Frances was doing Florence as she did me."[19] Three reliefs were of Ethel Ely (of whom Loring had already done a portrait bust in 1921) and her husband Alan Ely, Frances's father Frank, and Montreal painter and educator Anne (Annie) Savage.

Annie Savage — a member of the loose association of Montreal artists known as the Beaver Hall Hill Group — had become a friend through an assignment given to both Wyle and Savage by the National Gallery of Canada. French-Canadian anthropologist Marius Barbeau, who had been conserving Indian and Quebec folklore since he wrote his thesis at the Sorbonne in Paris on "Social Organization and 'Totemism' among the Northwest Coast Indians of British Columbia,"[20] had recently turned his attention again to the culture of the west coast native people. As part of his project for the National Museum (now the Canadian Museum of Civilization) where he was employed to build their collection, he collaborated with his friend J. Murray Gibbon of the Canadian Pacific Railway who provided free transportation for Barbeau and others to tiny, remote communities along the Upper Skeena River. He prodded the National Gallery to sponsor artists to ride what Emily Carr called the "meek trains" that "[s]lithered travellers through the forests."[21] These artists visited the B.C. location of Hazelton (formerly Kitenmaks, the northernmost stop of the railway), and en route stopped to see the lovely, peaceful villages Kispiox, Kitwanga ("The Place of the Rabbit People"), Hagwilgel, and others, to record in painting and sculpture the totem poles that were rapidly deteriorating. (Emily Carr, whom Wyle would not meet until later that year, had been painting totems since 1908, but even by 1913 the B.C. government was uninterested in purchasing her work, and Carr gave up painting then for over a decade.)[22]

It is possible that Eric Brown or A.Y. Jackson — who had already gone on one of Barbeau's excursions to the Skeena River area with Montreal painter Edwin Holgate the year before — suggested Wyle's name to him. However the introduction happened, Barbeau was added to the ever-growing list of friends who found a hospitable welcome at The Church.

After their return, the "most interesting examples of this Indian craft work procurable" by Savage and Wyle, along with "as much as possible of the best work done by our modern Canadian artists in the same region,"[23] was displayed in an exhibition of Canadian west coast art at the National Gallery in November and December of 1927. Annie had sketched the village that was once the site of Temlaham, a legendary paradise lost, while Florence made models of the totem poles.[24]

Articles in the Toronto newspapers about Wyle's trip to the west coast reveal much about the naivety of Wyle and the Canadian population on ethnic matters in the mid-1920s. "Daring Canadian Girl in an Indian Village: Meets Queer Tribe," ran the headline in the *Toronto Star*, above an article that outlined the "odd custom" in the tribe at Kitwancool of having a woman, the daughter of a previous chieftain, govern.[25] Wyle, typically, praised the orderliness and thrift of the "forbidden village," so called because the natives did not want whites to exploit them. She also noted — no doubt as directed by Barbeau who was later proven wrong — the "Mongolian features and traditions" of the Indians, spoke of their hospitality and marriage customs (no intermarriage within the same tribe), and admired greatly their totem poles. Because colour did not distract from their sculptural qualities, she preferred the unpainted ones. "Some of the poles are two hundred years old," she remarked. "The best ones are those which are unpainted. They are a lovely silver gray in colour and where they have not been restored [by the government] lean in picturesque angles along the streets of the village. There is no other race in the world," she added ingenuously, "that has erected monuments such as these."[26]

As Emily Carr's biographer, Susan Crean, observed, Barbeau's well-intentioned collection of Native artifacts was unwittingly detrimental.[27] He perpetuated the myth of the "disappearing Indian," considered Native society primitive and uncivilized, and did nothing to accept and further contemporary aboriginal artists. In sending off white mainstream artists like Jackson, Holgate, Savage, and Wyle to copy Indian creations such as the totem poles, he encouraged what today is disdained as "appropriation of voice": the theft of creations from marginal cultures which interprets them for a mainstream audience.[28]

On her return to Toronto, Wyle made six plaster totem poles, some small sculptured owls (one of which — a little black iron one with the inside beak painted red and the eyes white — was copied from a Kispiox drawing by A.Y. Jackson the year before),[29] along with iron owl bookends, paperweights, and totem lamp stands. These were on sale in December 1927 at the Grange craft shop,[30] a co-op run by OCA students, and at Eaton's gift shop where their exotic nature was emphasized.[31] That same year she created four angels for the altar at Bishop Bethune College Chapel in Oshawa.[32] She also wrote a poem, "The Owl" — one of many she had begun to write in her spare time — based on clichés about the "noble savage," which are as simplified as the ceremonies of Lorado Taft's Eagle's Nest colony in Oregon.

FLORENCE'S FRIENDSHIP WITH Annie Savage, which had begun with their west coast adventure, resulted in a 1927 commission from Baron Byng High School in Montreal, where Savage was head of the art program. Wyle created a large panel of five deer before a mountain forest of conifers — highly stylized and radiating peacefulness — for the school library.

As if Loring's memorials and Wyle's fountains and other works were not enough, the two of them collaborated in 1923 with some of the Group of Seven painters to decorate the interior of St. Anne's Church on Gladstone Avenue in Toronto. According to Eric Arthur, historian of Toronto architecture, this "labour of love," sponsored by a $5,000 bequest of a parishioner, resulted in "one of the most colourful church interiors in Toronto."[33]

J.E.H. MacDonald supervised the decoration program, and Fred Varley and Frank Carmichael painted gilded frescoes of religious figures in the church's Byzantine dome between the spandrels. Loring and Wyle did the heads of four Old Testament prophets, and plaques symbolizing the Evangelists. Loring's *Madonna and Child* (1923) medallion was probably an offshoot of her work with Wyle on the four medallion plaques.[34]

By the end of the 1920s, Loring and Wyle — or "the Loring-Wyles" as they were often called now, even by themselves — had consolidated their careers and had established their own separate identities within a partnership that was as intimate and personal as it was public. Gradually — through hard work, talent, and the acumen needed to build social connections within the artistic community — they had become famous. They continued to appear frequently in the social pages of all the Toronto newspapers at events such as the Heliconian Club's resumption after the summer of 1919, where Mrs. Healey Willan poured tea, and the "new and very charming little President, Miss Lina Adamson, took over the reins."[35] Or at the Home Musical Club, also at the Heliconian, where "a crackling fire in the grate, rose-shaded lights and a supper table decked with narcissus, tulle and silver summed up a concert of Haydn, Debussy and Dvorak."[36] In the list of guests at such social events, their names were now always linked, unlike the early days when their individual names were randomly mentioned. Increasingly, the other names in the guest lists were friends and acquaintances. They were now usually discussed first in notices of art exhibits and referred to as "well-known Toronto sculptors." The strong-minded, peppery Florence lectured friends on the glories of Greek sculpture, and Frances, with her outgoing friendliness, deep vibrant voice, warm smile, and penchant for inventive cooking and relaxed entertaining, had been welcomed into the wider community of Toronto's intellectual, academic, and social elite. She was asked to be a judge — the only woman of five — for the first Miss Toronto beauty contest in 1926 at Sunnyside, the lakeside amusement park known as "the poor man's Riviera."[37] Both the Loring-Wyles were judges in 1929 for the statuettes and garden ornaments contest for the students of the Technical School at the Royal Winter Fair.[38] Towards the end of 1929, the Heliconian Club held a luncheon in their honour.[39]

The Church — now a comfortable home where they entertained their ever-increasing number of friends for tea in their blue Spanish pottery, or at fairly regular Saturday night gatherings to which friends contributed food and drink — had captured the popular imagination. As one interviewer put it, their fireplace, "the biggest ever," drew to its warm bosom "the keenest and brightest of the city's artists and college people."[40] One guest recalls that "Florence used to crawl right into the fireplace to light a fire."[41] Being surrounded by statues appealed to everyone's sense of the dramatic. If guests were lucky, it might be a night on which Florence gave her ear-splitting rendition of hog calling on the farm. When artists such as Australian tenor Percy Grainger came to Toronto (in this case to Massey Hall), they not only attended performances, but also held receptions at The Church afterwards that resulted in fast friendships.[42] In 1926 they hosted freethinking women's activist and anarchist Emma Goldman, whom they had met in Greenwich Village. It was the year Goldman took refuge in Toronto from the U.S., where she was banned, and from England and most of Europe, where she was unwelcome, and lectured on such scandalous subjects as birth control. Goldman found Toronto a repressed, puritanical city, largely due to religion: "Both Catholic and Anglican hold the city by the throat." A librarian told her, "No, we do not censor books, we simply do not get them."[43] Neighbourhood children dropped by to see what animals Florence had rescued or to get a lesson in modelling from the Clay Ladies, as they called them.[44] Douglas Phibbs, who was taken to The Church as a ten-year-old boy, recalls being amazed at Loring's *Goal Keeper*: "I couldn't understand how a woman could make that huge hockey player. As far as I was concerned, hockey was for men."[45] (A 1999 children's book — *The Clay Ladies* — described another such experience with the two eccentric women.) Even their dog Delilah was eccentric, now that Sampson had died. She was treated as "the daughter of the house,"[46] occupied the best chair, and was never disciplined. She was inclined to snap, and on one occasion rushed out the door to attack the new fur coat of a neighbour walking by. "Serves her right," The Girls said. "No one should wear a coat made out of all those dead animals!"[47] When tours of artists' studios were initiated by the WAAC, theirs, along with the Studio Building nearby where A.Y. Jackson lived, was highlighted. Reporters who interviewed them caught at once the romantic vision of the little red church peopled by statues, busts, and maquettes, and littered with candlesticks, bookends, and paperweights. Nowhere else in Toronto could the Bohemian life of the artist — such as had existed in Europe for decades and in Greenwich Village since the early years of the century — be found. Probably Florence and Frances were part of what Robert Fulford meant by "the city's small community of anarchists" when he described Emma Goldman's Toronto friends.[48] The Girls did arrange a fundraising lecture for her. Although she praised the artists in her autobiography, she told a correspondent, "Their intentions were certainly admirable, but the result was poor."[49] The Girls and The Church had come to symbolize something important at the centre of Toronto the Good. The whiff of lesbianism that made "The Girls" a euphemism with a decided subtext gave an exotic and vital air to their existence and their magnificent creations.

The Sculptors' Society
of Canada ⇒

E arly in the fall of 1928, Frances Loring — now forty-two years old — boarded a train at Toronto's Union Station with fellow sculptor forty-seven-year-old Emanuel Hahn. They were headed to Montreal to meet with French-Canadian sculptor, the forty-four-year-old Henri Hébert, to discuss the formation of a national society for sculpture. The irascible — even belligerent — Mani Hahn (as he was known to his friends) had come to Canada from Germany in 1892 at the age of seven and was now head of sculpture at the Ontario School of Art. Hahn — with his unfashionable European goatee — was a blustery, prickly man. He and Frances — both of them "alpha" personalities — had often locked horns in arguments that some remember as so turbulent that Mani would slam out of The Church and sit in his car until he calmed down or Florence went out to placate him.[1] Hahn was best known by then for his sculpture of Canadian *Ned Hanlan* (1925), world-champion rower from 1876 to 1886, which was at Hanlan's Point on the Toronto Islands.

For the moment, unified by a common purpose, their grievances were probably set aside. It had been agreed by the other two Toronto sculptors linked in this venture — Florence Wyle and Elizabeth Wyn Wood (who as a child made "clay" with soda crackers, talcum powder, and water)[2] — that Frances and Emanuel should undertake this important mission because they both spoke French.

They were all aggrieved — frustrated beyond measure — that art exhibits treated sculpture like a poor cousin to painting. Many gallery visitors thought the sculpture was something you bumped into when you were backing up to see a painting. The Ontario Society of Artists was especially negligent. Too often they parked sculptures in obscure back corners or along hallways where they stood unnoticed or were passed by en route to rooms full of paintings. With their backs to the wall, three-dimensional sculptures lacked the space needed to be appreciated. As for the RCA, their quota of five academician sculptors in a membership of forty — to be replaced only on the death of a member — indicated the academy's view of sculpture's relative unimportance.[3] There seemed no hope of fostering the particular interests of sculptors in either of these organizations. Neither Loring nor Wyle, nor either of the Hahns, was a full member of the academy, though Emanuel Hahn would be within three years.

Now that the huge upsurge of war memorials had quieted somewhat, it was time to focus on other types of sculpture. Part of the problem was a widespread ignorance of sculpture, even on the part of experts and reviewers. Painting was fully accepted as a "fine art," but sculpture too often was confused with crafts like gravestone-cutting and architectural decoration. Painters signed their paintings, boldly declaring their pride in creation, expecting acknowledgement and recognition. But people walked right by sculpture without the least interest in knowing who the sculptor was, a situation exacerbated by the fact that many sculptors did not bother to sign their work.[4] If passersby were interested at all, it was in the subject, not the artist. Henri Hébert surmised that "colour had more general appeal than form," which made painted portraits more attractive than busts. He also believed that sculptures suggested unpleasant thoughts about death masks and tombstones.[5] Especially in Toronto, those of a religious bent might have recalled the biblical commandment against making graven images. Newspaper reviewers had little space to expand on artistic techniques, even those of painters; when they did, they seemed to lack the vocabulary to point out styles and features of particular sculptures. As art historian Joyce Millar rightly points out, writers on Canadian art in the 1920s and later, like Newton MacTavish, M.O. Hammond, C. Graham McInnes, and William Colgate, "provided only chronological surveys and factual documentation on public monuments, with little stylistic or structural analysis that would provide the viewer with an understanding of the medium [which could vary enormously in sculpture], the artist, or the climate in which the work was produced."[6] This view is confirmed by Maria Tippett, who noted that critics were "reluctant — and for that matter, perhaps not able — to apply critical analytical tools to the works."[7] All told, sculpture suffered from "public apathy" and was regarded as "the Cinderella of the arts."[8]

Apart from the fifteen "home work" statuettes of Wyle and Loring, the National Gallery had bought only a few Canadian sculptures for its permanent collection: Alfred Laliberté's *Bust de Louvigny de Montigny* (1909); Tait McKenzie's *The Competitor* (1911); Wyle's *Dancing Boy* (1915); Laliberté's *La Muse* (1916); Hahn's *The Indian Scout* (1917); Wyle's *Sun Worshipper* (1918); Katherine Wallis's *Son Meilleur Jouet* (1920); Elizabeth Wyn Wood's *Head of a Negress* (1927); and Hahn's *Head of Elizabeth Wyn Wood* (1928).[9]

As if these drawbacks were not enough, Canada had no foundries specializing in the bronze casting of artistic works. The Robert Mitchell Company in Montreal and — by the 1920s — in Toronto did a few works, but cast them poorly.[10] Most sculptors — certainly Loring and Wyle — used the Roman Bronze Works foundry in New York or the Gorham Company in Providence, Rhode Island, or else they turned to European foundries like the William A. Rogers Company in Paris and Brussels. When a branch of the Gorham foundry opened in Toronto, Loring and Wyle used it for their war records statuettes, but the results were not as good as expected, and they located foundries outside Canada for future works, despite the costs of shipping and import duties.

The situation for stone carving was no better. There were a few stone carvers — notably Georges-Edouard Tremblay in Iberville, Quebec, who opened a studio for carving marble copies of plaster models in 1907. The rest were essentially grave monument carvers like Louis Temporale, who occasionally did carving — and did it well — for sculptors. Such carvers used pointing machines with huge callipers to enlarge plaster maquettes to scale within 1/4 inch, then returned works to sculptors for the final cut and surface treatment. More often, sculptors had their plaster models shipped to Italy — as Loring had done with her *Osgoode Hall Memorial* (1928) — or Belgium, where a better job of carving could be done.[11]

Now that Toronto had a new sculpture court at the Art Gallery (though Loring thought "sculpture does not display well there"[12]), Loring in particular believed something must be done to raise the awareness of the public at large that sculpture was as important as painting — that Cinderella was at least the equal of, if not superior to, her stepsisters. Wyle, who lacked Loring's keen business sense and hated meetings, doggedly held to her philosophy of hard work and the creation of as many worthy sculptures as possible as the key to success.[13]

The fact that both the Art Association of Montreal and the Art Gallery of Toronto occasionally brought in travelling exhibitions of European and American sculpture was hopeful. In 1927 an important exhibit called the "Selected Group of Modern European Sculpture" featured the passionately political works of Yugoslavian nationalist Ivan Meštrović; the rough-hewn — at times shocking — nudes of American-born British sculptor Jacob Epstein; the soft, fluid beauty of French sculptor Aristide Maillol's chunky female bodies (his work had already been exhibited in Toronto in 1926);[14] and the grotesquely playful works of Sweden's most famous sculptor, Carl Milles, among others.[15] It was a huge success. As was the display of American sculptor Paul Manship's work in 1928. These exhibits resulted in the purchase of several modern sculptures for the gallery — notably Rodin's *Study for a Head* (1886) and *Eve* (1881), Meštrović's *Mother at Prayer* (1926),[16] and Paul Manship's sensuously fluid *Dancer and Gazelles* (1916). This seemed, at least, to indicate that sculpture mattered. What remained was to assert the importance of Canadian work by sculptors of the same age as these Europeans and Americans: sculptors like Wyle and Loring, or Hahn and Wyn Wood.

By 1928, Frances had already made several inquiries to the federal government's Secretary of State about how to incorporate a group of sculptors.[17] She had a copy of Chapter 27 of the Act Respecting Companies,[18] and quite likely she and Mani went over it as they travelled east, trying to plan how one organization might include both English and French sculptors for national clout. She had also obtained a copy of the charter of the National Sculpture Society (NSS) in the United States, which had been formed thirty-five years earlier in 1893. Its terms, "to foster ... encourage ... [and] promote sculpture ... [and] to improve the quality of the sculptor's art,"[19] might also have been hashed over with Hahn as they approached Montreal.

The gregarious Frances had already tried her hand at founding organizations. In 1919, the Ontario Advisory Committee on War Memorials had been set up to develop ground rules for the many war memorials that were anticipated. The committee, chaired by George A. Reid, principal of the Ontario College of Art, with representatives from the OSA, the Society of Graphic Art, and the Ontario Society of Architects, had proved to be almost useless, partly because no advertising was done, but largely because they had not one sculptor on it, despite the fact that war memorials were created by sculptors.

Loring stepped in. She proposed a national committee that would be made up of disinterested members drawn from the RCA, the Association of Architects, possibly Eric Brown of the National Gallery, and a "newspaper man for publicity purposes."[20] Her idea was that such a committee would suggest suitable locations for war memorials, provide referrals to sculptors suited for them, or act as judges for competitions.[21] There is no evidence that Loring's proposal was realized. However, she pursued her goals elsewhere by convening a War Memorial Committee within the OSA, and tried to initiate a Royal Architectural Institute of Canada conference focused on clarifying war memorial competitions. (Such competitions had already been discouraged by the American NSS because making maquettes — or sketches — to enter them was so costly, and "artistic qualities" were no guarantee of success, since they were often overlooked when they did not correspond to the "tastes of layman juries.")[22] It was probably her frustrations in these failed attempts to organize the world of Canadian sculpture — along with the experience she picked up on various women's committees — that fuelled Loring's determination to bring into existence a national society for sculptors alone.

Both Loring and Hahn knew Henri Hébert, who had been a full member of the RCA since 1922, taught modelling at the Monument National and the Architecture School of McGill University, and was considered the best sculptor in French Canada.[23] Although he usually exhibited with the RCA, the Art Association of Montreal (later the Montreal Museum of Fine Arts), and the Arts Club of Montreal, he had shown his work occasionally in Toronto shows. The son of the famous monumentalist Louis-Philippe Hébert — premier sculptor of Confederation who created the first public memorials on Parliament Hill to Sir George-Etienne Cartier and Sir John A. Macdonald representing the two-nation Canada — Henri was completely familiar with the exigencies of life as a sculptor. He had turned at the outset of the Great War to more emotional subjects than his father's, combining traditional with modern forms. His *1914* (1918) personified the war as a huge brutal man wielding a sword over a large hunk of wood. In 1919 — more in the tradition of his father's tributes to history — he created *Evangeline* for Grande Pré. A few years later, he summed up his artistic credo: "Let us be Canadians, conserving and respecting the picturesque ways of the past, but let us be of our own times, and put art on the level of present day activities."[24] In his *Monument aux Morts de la Guerre (Monument to the Dead of Outremont)* (1925), a grieving woman covers her face, but the fluid lines of her garments and the flag she carries suggest vitality and hope. Hébert — like Florence Wyle — had responded to the simple lines of the international art deco movement that arose from the Exhibition of Decorative Arts in Paris in 1925.

The stocky, outgoing Hébert, with his round open face and thick moustache, welcomed Loring and Hahn to his studio at 34 LaBelle Street[25] in Montreal, and the three of them hammered out the terms for a charter for the Sculptors' Society of Canada (SSC).

Although it would be a few years before the Charter and Letters patent for the SSC were in place, the Society took shape almost immediately. For some reason, Hébert's name does not appear on the formal papers of application for the SSC Charter and Letters patent, but he was the representative who brought Alfred Laliberté (also a full RCA member since 1922) and Marc-Aurèle de Foy Suzor-Côté into an organization that depended on representation from French Canada as well as English Canada if it was to speak for Canada as a whole. In addition to the four original Toronto sculptors, a fifth — Alfred Howell, already one of Canada's main war memorial sculptors — was included in the original application.

On 5 October 1928 — only weeks after Loring and Hahn's Montreal meeting with Hébert and four full years before the SSC was an official organization — the inaugural exhibition opened at the Art Gallery of Toronto, soon to be followed by two other exhibitions in Ottawa in February 1929, and in Montreal in April. Statues were no longer pushed into back corners or jammed into corridors. All three galleries at the Art Gallery of Ontario — the East, West, and Cox galleries — were used to display 170 works in such a way that people could walk around them and view the myriad of silhouettes sculpture is meant to offer, each a fluid aspect of the whole.

Since the SSC exhibitions were to be open to all sculptors, a few who had not yet joined the new organization exhibited their work. In all nine sculptors were represented: Loring and Wyle, Emanuel Hahn and Elizabeth Wyn Wood, and Alfred Howell from Toronto; Henri Hébert, Alfred Laliberté, and Marc-Aurèle de Foy Suzor-Côté from Quebec; and Lionel Fosbery from Ottawa. Of these, Florence Wyle was most prolific, exhibiting fifty-three works. Frances Loring, whose output had been slowed down somewhat by the time spent in setting up the SSC, showed over thirty. As if to announce that the age of monuments was over, potentially large pieces were represented by maquettes, and the sculptures for the most part were decorative.

Hopes that having a society for sculptors would increase public awareness were realized, and newspapers gave extensive coverage to the "dazzling collection."[26] "Few of us knew that Canada had enough moveable sculpture to fill one room, let alone three," wrote Augustus Bridle in the *Toronto Daily Star*, validating Loring's concerns that sculpture was often overlooked.[27] (As did a French review of the Montreal inaugural show which observed that "partout la sculpture cede à la peinture et à l'architecture," everywhere sculpture bows to painting and architecture.)[28] "But the new society," Bridle went on, "had twenty years' work to gather and so by periods here it is, from two provinces in all styles, subjects, shapes, moods and suggestions." Bridle ranks the works by price, rather than merit: Fosbery's head of Sir Robert Borden has a price tag of $2,250 (Bridle prefers his *Dr. Saunders* at $125), and Hahn's *Music* costs $4,000. Bridle sees Hahn as having taken over Walter Allward's place in Toronto sculpture because his creations (maquettes of war memorials and vivid portrait busts — especially the one of his wife) are "allegorical" and "broad-angled." Loring and Wyle — "these gifted workers" — are compared: "I think Miss Loring inclines more to the action pose than does Miss Wyle ... but [they are on] similar planes of development." He finds "the prodigal variety" of Loring's work to be "inspiringly beautiful and full of strength" — her munitions workers a "sharp contrast to the fanciful, allegorical, classic and portrait pieces." From Loring's works, he singles out *Two Girls with Rail*, *Girl with Jug*, *Ashman*, *The Old One* (*Old Jew*), *Knife Grinder*, *Hounds [sic] of Heaven*, *Grief*, *Lamia*, and repliques [sic] of the decorations for the memorial chamber in Ottawa. He finds the best of Wyle's work to be: *Girl with Sickle* ("no finer poised figure in the whole gallery"), *Girl with Grapes*, *Woman with Key*, *Kneeling Man*, and *Consolation*. He notes especially Wyn Wood's experiments ("modern but not too expressionistic") with form and material in *Cedars* (1928), which was made of tin, and her plaster relief *Passing Rain* (1928), as well as Hahn's stylized *Flight* (1926). Alfred Howell's pieces are considered last, but found "delicate," "dramatic," or "strong."

Bridle thought the French sculptors distinct from the English. "They have more humour and ... a little more freedom." Hébert's plaques *Love* (blind) and *The Woman* are "admirably flippant," in contrast with his rugged portrait bust of painter Alphonse Jongers. *The Calf Feeding at the Pail* is "bucolically humorous," though his head *Le Fleur* and *La Croix Rouge* are "vividly expressive." Laliberté's work he finds "poetic." He does not comment on the works of the other French-Canadians — Mme Montigny-Giguère, Cyril le Peloquin, Mlle M.J. Antoine Roy, and Charles Fainmel — who were discussed following the Montreal inauguration.[29] The *Montreal Herald* critic fell back on Wyle and Loring's "home front" works: "Miss Loring has moulded with her clever hands, figures in bronze to commemorate the work of those who remained at home during the war ... [The] works show tremendous life in her conception of the patriotic Canadian girl who stayed at home and worked ... Miss Wyle has moulded many wonderful figures of both men and women in the pursuit of their home work during the war."[30]

OVERALL, BRIDLE — LIKE other reviewers — was struck by "the fine balance between progressiveness and traditional reserve, without flamboyant radicalism" in the show. The point was important. As the "Selected Group of Modern European Sculpture" the year before had clearly demonstrated, some of the modernist trends in sculpture by Matisse, Picasso, and Duchamp that had seemed so outrageous at the 1913 Armory Show in New York were now beginning to be incorporated into the work of major sculptors throughout the world. The Art Gallery of Toronto had purchased a few works from that show for good reason: such works no longer seemed outrageous, but were part of the mainstream of international sculpture as it developed away from the neoclassical styles of the late nineteenth and early twentieth centuries. The tradition that Wyle and Loring had been trained in at the Art Institute of Chicago was becoming passé. Even Lorado Taft, who had been in the height of his glory in the first decades of the twentieth century, had gone into decline after finishing his tour de force, *The Fountain of Time*, in 1922.

The international acclaim accorded Constantin Brancusi's sleek, aero-dynamic *Bird* had ushered in a new era for sculpture in 1925 at the same time as revolutionary literary works, such as T.S. Eliot's *The Waste Land* and James Joyce's *Ulysses* appeared. Brancusi's *Bird* signalled a change in sculpture all over the western world. From that point on, anatomically correct sculptures, such as were customary for memorial work and portraits, or graceful allegories like Taft's *Solitude of the Soul* or his *Great Lakes* fountain — which emphasized beauty over all else — were losing ground to *interpretations* of the human condition in an industrialized world through experimental techniques that would — before long — lead to abstract creations.

In Canada, however, conservatism was deeply entrenched. The Great War had ensured that conventional monumentalism with its typically Canadian overtones of optimism would prevail. Now that the age of memorials was over, the general ignorance of the public and art critics alike — despite the European sculpture show in Toronto in 1927 — about the new paths sculpture had taken elsewhere, limited the expression of modern trends. Augustus Bridle (who rightly admitted that his was only an "average eye") was not alone in deploring "flamboyant radicalism," and praising "balance between progressivism and traditional reserve."[31] *Saturday Night* critic Hector Charlesworth had been attacked for years (especially for his denunciation of the Group of Seven) on grounds that his taste in the arts was too conservative.

There had been some attempt to incorporate modern trends into the work of two sculptors in the ssc's inaugural show:[32] Wyn Wood and Hahn. Elizabeth Wyn Wood's use of tin for her plaque *Cedars* was itself experimental. In this work and in her plaster relief *Passing Rain*, Wyn Wood experimented also with form, nudging the kind of stylization in Wyle's 1927 *Deer Panel* for Baron Byng High School a few notches further in the direction of modernism. Most experimental was Emanuel Hahn's "stylized bird-like form"[33] *Flight* (for the Canadian Aviation Museum in Winnipeg), "a psychic study of line and proportion,"[34] which was understood as a response to the aviators of the Great War, but which might have been equally a response to Brancusi's *Bird*. Yet these few works were a far cry from the intense and powerfully personalized works of Meštrović, Epstein, Maillol, and Milles.

THE PROBLEM THAT faced Canadian sculptors at the end of the 1920s was not so much the unification of English and French sculpture into a society that would promote national and international exposure, teach appreciation of sculpture, advise on public memorials, organize exhibits, and foster professional standards: all goals of the ssc. The problem was this: would Canadian sculptors join the international community of sculptors in embracing changes that incorporated discoveries in science, industry, psychology, anthropology, and cultural history — as well as new materials — into their work? French-Canadians needed sculptures that glorified famous French-Canadians and the nostalgia of a Catholic rural past to shore up a culture that was threatened with assimilation. On the other hand, English-Canadians in Toronto the Good were surrounded by traces of a puritanism that decried art generally — and art depicting "immoral" subjects in particular — and by a philistinism that could easily see the point of glorifying statesmen and soldiers, but was unsure about art for art's sake. Would either the French or the English settle for sculpture that "competes with the arts and crafts of older nations"[35] in traditional ways, or could they join the ranks of modernism?

In this situation, amid people isolated from and resistant to the international trends they certainly would have encountered frequently had they stayed in Greenwich Village, Wyle and Loring stood largely for traditionalism. Wyle, in particular, had long since pledged allegiance to the Greeks and saw no reason to veer from the artistic values she had learned at Chicago. Loring — much bolder than Wyle — had become associated with grand public memorials and was disinclined — despite the variety of her work — to experiment with modernist techniques, even as much as Hahn and Wyn Wood had done.

THE CLOSEST LORING came to modernism at the time can be seen in a lecture she gave to the Women's Art Association called "Modernism in Sculpture" in 1919. She had a large audience — including the Alfred Howells — and she illustrated the lectures with slides. She used illustrations from her favourite, Michelangelo — hardly a "Modern," but probably included as a model against which modern trends could be measured. Her main point — as recorded in the *Globe and Mail* with almost all the sculptors' names misspelled[36] — was that "the few outstanding masterpieces of all ages have been enjoyed and appreciated by all classes."[37] It was probably in relation to this comment that she referred to Charley Mulligan's favourite, Constantin Meunier, the social-realist Belgian sculptor of the late nineteenth century whose work focused on the dignity of labour, but was not in any way modernist. It is not surprising that she included Rodin — the French sculptor who revolutionized sculpture at the turn of the century, transforming it from smooth-surfaced beauty to dynamic, impressionistic, sometimes tortured, representations of psychological truths. Some of Loring's own works, such as *Lamia, The Old One, Hound of Heaven* — even her "home front" munitions workers to a lesser degree — are clearly influenced by Rodin's fondness for agitated surfaces and contorted postures. Her inclusion in her lecture of Gutzon Borglum — who had been on the committee for the Armory Show (and resigned because he objected to the avant-garde entries) — suggested that she saw her topic as "Contemporary Sculpture" rather than "Modernism in Sculpture." Borglum was an American monumentalist without a trace of modernist influence (though he studied with Rodin) who was to undertake the staggering Mount Rushmore tribute to four American presidents in 1927. Loring also mentioned George Grey Barnard, an American who had studied at the Art Institute of Chicago, whose 1917 statue of Lincoln provoked controversy because it had rough-hewn features (à la Rodin) and a slouching stance. It was hardly a modernist work. The only real modernist Loring presented that evening was Henri Gaudier-Brzeska, the French Cubist sculptor, colleague of Jacob Epstein, and friend of Ezra Pound, a pioneer in the exploratory transitional era in Europe when sculpture was being redefined. But Gaudier-Brzeska, who showed enormous promise, never realized his potential because he died tragically in the Great War at age twenty-three.

If we are to take this lecture as Frances Loring's views on modernism in sculpture, we can only conclude that she knew very little about the major practitioners in the field. Any sense that the modernist movement involved a radical departure from the traditional, that it recorded a particular attitude to the present — one that saw life not as eternal and immutable, but as ephemeral and fleeting, that it was as interested in treatment and new techniques as it was in its subjects, that its most common message was one of anxious tension or irreverent playfulness, not repose, that it considered art as an end in itself, not a representation of something "real," and concerned itself with social, gender, and aesthetic issues peculiar to the twentieth century — all these tenets of modernism[38] were missing from Loring's presentation.

Nonetheless, it was Loring's drive that led to the creation of Canada's first sculpture society, and at least with such an organization in place there was a possibility that sculptors in Canada would have a base from which to redefine the role of sculpture. The whole enterprise certainly accomplished one thing. To that point, Florence Wyle had been the dominant one in their personal and professional relationship. But after the creation of the Sculptors' Society of Canada Frances Loring was uppermost. Now it was the Loring-Wyles indeed.

THE GREAT DEPRESSION

The Thirties ⪬

The first sculpture of Frances Loring's that was purchased by the National
Gallery of Canada seems symbolic. The year was 1929, and the sculpture was *The Derelicts*, one of the works first seen at the inaugural exhibition
of the Sculptors' Society of Canada. This work — which depicted a thin,
dejected mother trudging barefoot down a country road over rocky ground,
body thrust against wind and rain, clasping her young child to her breast[1] —
followed firmly in a series of subjects now well-established by Loring (and,
to a much lesser extent, by Wyle). It was apt and poignant in the year of
the stock market crash that ushered in the Great Depression and the derelicts that crowded the streets. One critic would later say, "It conveys much
of the pathos and appeal of one of the world's great problems."[2] Loring had
already sculpted busts of *Ashman* and *The Old One*, and reliefs of the *Old
Toe Dancer* and *Knife Grinder* — all socially conscious variants on the poor
and needy. This series of subjects, chosen by Loring herself in the New York

tradition of the Ashcan school, formed the obverse side of the portrait busts
of the famous or wealthy that were necessary for income.

The Great Depression hit Toronto hard. In 1930, the city established a
Civic Unemployment Relief Committee to look into relief jobs, and a Central
Bureau for Unemployment Relief was set up with money from federal,
provincial, and civic sources. By 1931, seventeen percent of Torontonians
were jobless; by 1933, that figure had risen to thirty percent in Toronto, as
elsewhere. Two years later in 1935, twenty-five percent of the population
was still on relief. Even Toronto's commercial and industrial prowess could
not withstand the crisis: construction almost ceased, and manufacturing
was cut back, declining to an all-time low in 1933–34, the worst year of the
Depression throughout North America. That year, relief funds hit $10 mil-
lion, and the number of strikes was greater than in any other year.[3]

It stood to reason that sculpture would suffer in this context. In fact, it
was one of the Depression's first victims. Almost overnight, contrary to the
post-war boom in monuments and public memorials that had boosted the
reputations of Loring, Wyle, and other sculptors during the 1920s, sculpture
became a luxury. That this should happen at the very moment the Sculptors'
Society of Canada was established was a cruel twist of fate. Rebecca Sisler
recalls that even though government funding for monuments and commissions for fountains, portrait busts or panels, and knick-knacks dried up, "The
Girls, probably because of their established reputations, were assumed to be
immune from the cares of struggling for professional survival."[4] Not so. There
were long periods when they were on relief, and their already frugal lifestyle
became even more austere. They never went hungry, they would later recall,
but they became bored with the limited selection of foods they could afford.[5]

As if the expensive supplies to create sculpture were not enough of a
drain, financial questions around the export of plaster casts to stonecutters or
bronze casters and the import of finished works of art were vexed. The issue
was how to distinguish works of art from the import and export of other
plaster, marble, or bronze items. Tariff regulation #348a of Canadian
Customs regulations provided for the "duty free entry of works of art in
bronze, cast from models made in Canada and designed by sculptors domi-
ciled therein."[6] But to prove that an object was a work of art, each shipment

required a letter of verification from the National Gallery. Marble statues were subject to a sales tax and an import tax: statues were taxed at 27.5% and "manufactures of marble" (i.e., marble objects that were not works of art) at 32.5%. In addition to these high customs duties, there was a four percent sales tax. The situation was further muddied by a regulation that plaster casts could travel duty free only if they had not increased in value while out of Canada. Who was to say whether their value had increased or not after the weeks or months it took to transform and enlarge plaster models to stone? Customs also required specific letters of authorization from either the National Gallery of Canada or the RCA. Elizabeth Wyn Wood, who took over from her husband as president of the SSC in 1935, tried to remedy the matter with what now fell within the jurisdiction of the Department of Finance. Eventually she concluded that, although the government's intention was clearly to encourage art and sculpture, tax and tariff restrictions "actually [protect] no Canadian industry but [do] hamper the artist."[7]

EVEN DEFINITE ASSIGNMENTS, when they came, were a kind of financial torture. In February 1931 the National Gallery approached Florence for what amounted to an unofficial commission. "The Trustees showed great interest in your woman's torso shown at the Sculptors' Society exhibition here and expressed their desire to have first opportunity of considering it again in the event of its being cut in stone or marble of a colour not unlike the plaster, which seems to suit it very well."[8]

The torso was splendid — quite the most impressive work Wyle had yet created. It was sturdy, somewhat in the style of Maillol's strong female forms, which Wyle had seen in the 1926 exhibition at the Art Gallery and read about in Maurice Denis's 1925 book, which she owned. Its neck, thighs, and arms ruggedly terminated close to the trunk. The posture was not at all soft or passive, like so many of Wyle's female forms to date, such as *Study of a Girl* (1926, 1931) and *Young Mother* (1928). It was assertive, chest raised, back slightly arched, as if to suggest a readiness to take on the world. Wyle called it *Mother of the Race*.

This statue marked an astonishing development in Wyle's work. The National Gallery had already bought her bronze *Sun Worshipper* in 1918, recognizing in Wyle a special affinity for the female form. But with *Mother of the Race*, it was as if that erotic young woman had matured into full womanhood and now unequivocally asserted her enduring primitive power. "Inspired by the moderns and in emulation of the ancient Greeks,"[9] wrote Christine Boyanoski, "[it] throbbed with life force — like a plant unfolding itself irresistibly and triumphantly to the world."[10] Eric Brown thought it "quite one of the most outstanding things of its kind done so far in Canada."[11] No one could doubt that the female form was Wyle's essential subject, and her rendering of it now rivalled the best sculpture anywhere. *Mother of the Race* is archetypal woman.

Had the Great Depression never occurred, Wyle might have created with ease a much greater number of outstanding works. She had hit her peak as a sculptor when the times were least conducive to her success. As A.Y. Jackson wrote to a friend in 1932, "The Girls are hard up. I don't know how they manage at all. They never say anything."[12] The aging Frank Loring, who had remarried, now needed his savings for himself and could not bail them out as he had in the past. The National Gallery's inquiry about *Mother of the Race* did not mention any money to carry out the permanent carving of the statue. Even though Eric Brown warned her that "the estimates ... are harrowing," Wyle decided to go ahead anyway, since he and the gallery trustees liked the statue.[13] She sent off the torso to a stonecutter who agreed to use his pointing machine to make the usual mechanical copy on the basis of the official letter alone. She then finished the rough-cut piece, which had been carved to within a 1/4 inch of its actual surface, with chisel, adze, and rasp during the summer of 1932 in the ramshackle studio of old boards and tarpaper she and Loring had built themselves at their farm. "Florence is working day and night to finish the torso for Ottawa," A.Y. Jackson wrote to Anne Savage in Montreal. "They are full of hope that it will replenish their empty coffers."[14]

On seeing the magnificent marble, the National Gallery agreed to buy it, but they could not pay the full $2,000 Wyle asked for, and they delayed payment for almost a year until the following spring. This despite a letter from Florence in January 1932: "We are awfully broke — even worse than usual." When she was finally paid for *Mother of the Race*, Florence wrote Eric

Brown, "It has taken me this long to recover from the shock (but not to cash the cheque). It was very welcome indeed. I'm in the midst of an orgy of bill-paying. You wouldn't think there would be that many 'please remits' in the world."[15]

Loring and Wyle were loath to admit the terrible poverty they were enduring. Rebecca Sisler recalls that they were too proud to ask for help or even to say that they needed it. "It was absolutely taboo to mention or even pretend to notice the state of their finances."[16] Wealthy patrons who had become friends tried asking for sculpting lessons, but The Girls refused a fee, and the "lessons" tended to turn into social visits. Some students seemed like a waste of precious time: "Great Scott!" Florence wrote on one occasion to Harry McCurry, who had taken over as Director of the National Gallery after Eric Brown's untimely death in 1939, "I am weary — two unruly, nice, self-willed, pampered young ladies studying sculpture with me every morning."[17] As a compromise, "students" such as Elizabeth Gordon, and Sophia Buckingham brought generous quantities of food for suppers after lessons, and a hat was put out for voluntary donations. Despite their acute poverty, and the tiresome starchy foods they ate daily, The Girls were not interested in teaching posts. Emanuel Hahn had been Director of Sculpture at the Ontario College of Art since 1922. Elizabeth Wyn Wood was almost denied the position she wanted at Toronto's Central Technical School in 1930 because of rules established during the Depression that prevented women whose husbands could earn a living from taking jobs. She got the job only because she was "particularly qualified for the position" and because the only two other sculptors so qualified — Loring and Wyle — "would not be available."[18] Like their friend A.Y. Jackson, who resigned once and for all after teaching at OCA for a year,[19] Loring and Wyle did not want teaching to drain away the energies needed to produce art.

Even the manipulations of friends to help support them were fruitless. The money in the hat sometimes went to "charity cases" known to The Girls. One of these — Hardy, a down-and-outer who did janitorial work for The Girls once a week — would shuffle up to the door every morning for his breakfast of oatmeal porridge, and, on the days he worked there, was treated to one of Frances's creative dinners. Their neighbourhood was the last stop for the Italian grocer with his pushcart, and he sold them cheaply whatever was left over from his day's sales in exchange for a home cooked meal. They once gave a Christmas dinner for forty needy mothers and their children, which was a disaster; the gifts were too practical, the mothers uneasy, and the children shy.[20] They paid for Italian lessons from their friend the Italian consul, to help him survive his starvation allowance. And, of course, there were the animals to feed — not only their bad-tempered dog Delilah and their own cats — but also the usual series of neighbourhood strays. The cash necessary to buy the expensive supplies needed to build sculpture and send it out of the country for bronze casting or marble-cutting was gone.

Oddly, art exhibitions in Toronto went on through the 1930s, although the ssc dropped its membership fee from $10 to $5 in 1931. Frances Loring, "the most dynamic member of the group,"[21] remained centre stage at the ssc. Her "extroverted nature, coupled with a steadfast integrity and dedication to the cause of sculpture, made her the undisputed force behind the new association,"[22] and she navigated the final stages of obtaining a formal charter for the ssc, which was delayed until August 1932 because of a misunderstanding about the fee. Loring understood from W.P. O'Meara at the Department of Secretary of State that the fee would be $15, but was assessed $100, a sum beyond the means of the few original members. When she challenged the amount and found it unchanged, she reluctantly withdrew the application. O'Meara was able to reduce the fee, and on 20 August Loring wrote to him, "We are very grateful that you have found a means of our getting a charter without so great an outlet of money."[23] By September 1932, the Letters patent finally arrived, and the ssc was official.[24] Hahn, Wyn Wood, Loring, and Wyle immediately resigned from the Ontario Society of Art,[25] indicating — perhaps too politely — that "this move is prompted by no ill will ... [H]owever ... our contribution and our needs are different from the majority."[26] Meetings of the ssc were usually informal gatherings at The Church — sometimes part of The Girls' Saturday night get-togethers.[27] Although Emanuel Hahn was the inaugural president — probably because he was male,[28] and Loring the secretary — because she could type — Harry McCurry, Eric Brown's assistant at the National Gallery, wrote to her, "I had an impression all along that you were the president anyway!"[29]

Meetings at The Church were typically run by Frances. She would be "puffing away like a smoke stack, hammering out contract outlines and drafting letters of protest to this or that organization." In the days before she developed severe allergies to smoke, Florence would roll cigarettes for Frances and pass them over. Her contribution to meetings consisted of "the odd incisive comment that set matters squarely in place." There was much squabbling with the irascible Mani Hahn, and "bursts of invective between Mani and his wife Betty, whose cool intellect could slice through trivia like a knife through wet clay."[30]

On one occasion, Frances and Mani had a terrible fight, which Frances won. "Hahn got up in a towering rage, retrieved his coat, and stomped out to the door. 'Good-bye beloved!' Frances called gaily after him, with devilish glee. Hahn turned, spat out, 'God damn you to Hell!' and slammed the door resoundingly behind him."[31] Yet, somehow, despite such interruptions, the work of the SSC soldiered on. They were so few they needed each other if anything were to be accomplished.

Despite the Depression, there were alternating exhibitions of the SSC at the National Gallery and the Art Gallery of Toronto in 1931 and 1932, and in 1935 the SSC exhibition succeeded in drawing a crowd of 1,000 visitors in one afternoon at the National Gallery.[32] The SSC's main achievement in their first decade was the travelling exhibit for the National Gallery. Again, this was organized by Frances, who wrote in June 1935 to ask Eric Brown to ensure that sculpture be included in its extensive program of travelling exhibits.[33] Loring's request was successful. The first exhibition of Canadian sculpture — featuring forty-seven works by Hahn, Wyn Wood, Loring, Wyle, Hébert, Loring's student Alvin Hilts (with whom she compiled a four-teen-page list of resources for sculptors), Jacobine Jones, an *animalier* from England who had moved to Canada in 1932[34] and joined the SSC in 1939, and two younger sculptors, Stephen Trenka and Orson Wheeler — travelled across Canada after opening in Ottawa in October: first to Montreal, then to Winnipeg, Edmonton, Vancouver, and finally Calgary in June 1937.

The show was welcomed everywhere. The *Winnipeg Free Press* reported on the exhibit — where 101 catalogues were sold — typically noting that it was a "splendid exhibition."[35] Nonetheless, the exhibit generated no sales.

(Because of budget cuts, the National Gallery bought only three sculptures that decade: Wyle's *Mother of the Race*, Jacobine Jones's *Equestrian Figure* in 1934, and Wyle's bust *A.Y. Jackson* in 1936.) Even sculptors like Henri Hébert, who had enjoyed secure commissions for years, pleaded with Eric Brown in 1933 to purchase one of the bas-reliefs from his *Lafontaine Monument* as a way of helping him out of "dire financial straits."[36] And, despite the indisputable fact that the efforts and exhibitions of the ssc raised public awareness of sculpture in Canada, the society had only eight members by 1937 — almost a decade after its genesis.[37]

Eric Brown, who fiercely wanted to help sculptors and painters, was forced to give the same reply to everyone: "Needless to say, the National Gallery would like to help everyone in similar circumstances but it is restricted as much or more as [sic] private people ..."[38] In the absence of anything like the American Works Projects Administration (wPA), which supported artists in the Federal Arts Project Building program by allocating one percent of construction funds for art in all United States federal buildings built during the Depression, Canadian artists had no recourse to public money, apart from relief.[39] Had Loring and Wyle stayed in the United States, they might have profited from the wPA program during the period when their creative powers were at their peak.

More unfortunate yet, the first stirrings of modernism could not take hold in Canada. Elizabeth Wyn Wood, twenty years younger than Loring and Wyle, had begun to experiment with landscape sculpture. Her unusual tin relief *Passing Rain* had won the first Willingdon Art Competition, established in 1929 by the Governor General Lord Willingdon,[40] sharing the award with Quebec's Sylvia D'Aoust's (later Daoust) more conventional *Bronze Head*. *Passing Rain* attempted to do in sculpture what the Group of Seven had done in painting: create a stylized representation of the Canadian wilderness — especially in its turbulent moods — that conveyed its power in broad strokes. (Wyn Wood planned to make an even more dramatic black marble copy of this sculpture, but never did.) Wyn Wood continued in this vein, especially with her abstract *Reef and Rainbow* (1929–30), an intricate, stylized linking of rainbow arch and jagged rocks constructed again of cast tin on a black marble base to suggest water. But the exigencies of the

Depression ensured that her energies after 1933 would be channelled into teaching and, after 1935, into her role as president and spokesperson for the ssc. As Joyce Millar observes, her production of sculpture — already undermined by her role as a mother once her daughter was born in 1937 — diminished almost in proportion to these other activities.[41]

THE GLOWING, OPTIMISTIC article written in 1929 by modernist painter Bertram Brooker called "Sculpture's New Mood" in the second *Yearbook of the Arts in Canada*, sixteen years after the first yearbook, expressed views that were doomed to obscurity by the Depression. Brooker singled out Wyn Wood's inventive *Island* and *Passing Rain* — "landscape rhythms treated in 'abstract' fashion" — as Canada's outstanding example of a new direction. She was "a grand-daughter of the Sumerians and a sister of Brancusi," he claimed, with some exaggeration. Brooker also tips his hat to her husband Emanuel Hahn — particularly to his non-representational, streamlined creation *Flight* — claiming that it "combines the precision and sleekness of the modern manner with a motif that by its freedom of movement suggests the great spaces and the freed consciousness of this continent." Elsewhere, Brooker says that Hahn is "a 'modern' in the sense that in spite of academic training and his duties as a teacher, he is 'open' to the fresh gusts of a new kind of consciousness peculiar to this country, while at the same time being alive to the whole new crystallization of design, which has rather suddenly evolved in almost every country as a result of the shift from the slow-poke and stuffy and over-formal civilization of the eighteenth and nineteenth centuries to a faster and freer and more mechanized life today."[42] Though these aspects of modernism had been available to North American artists since the Armory Show in 1913, Brooker's message was clear: Canada now had a new — more modern — sculpture for a new country. Modernism in Canada was subsumed in nationalism. In 1929, Brooker could write confidently of "the forces in this country, which are encouraging a new and untrammelled expression, characteristic of our environment here and growing out of it, without servile submission to the academic aims of older countries,"[43] but the Depression made it impossible to realize such a dream. Even those — like Hahn and Wyn Wood — inclined to try modernist techniques were timid by international standards. Henri Hébert seemed to speak for a whole generation when he "advised against taking up modernistic art unless one was sure of understanding it, for this was something in process of development and it was necessary to be able to discriminate between what was good and what was bad."[44] By 1936, *Saturday Night* art critic Graham McInnes noted that "sculptors last season were singularly silent" and "sculpture seems to be passing through a sterile period."[45]

In a 1937 article in *Canadian Forum* called "Art and the Pre-Cambrian Shield," Elizabeth Wyn Wood struggled to define the subject matter appropriate for Canadian painting and sculpture. She dispensed with "world-shaking events" such as the Depression, feeling that these — along with class issues — were subjects for European countries, not North America. She noted that Canadians are "hesitant" about Surrealism, and dismissed "nationalism" as a binding force in Canada. In the end, after much confused reasoning, she came down on the side of "natural life" as the source of any great art that is likely to be produced in Canada: "I proclaim the long stride, the far vision, the free spirit," she concluded, somewhat vaguely.[46]

As it was, with Wyle just over fifty and Loring just under that mid-century mark (and neither of them inclined to attempt such radical creations as those of either Hahn or Wyn Wood), the works that ought to have built up their reputations were no doubt fewer because they were sculpted with inadequate funds, and could not easily sell because no one had enough money to buy them — even the art institutions. "We could do far more and better work," Wyle complained, "if we were not always cramped by lack of money."[47] According to Sisler, they never lost their sense of humour. "From time to time, when the going was particularly difficult, they would declare that they were contemplating suicide. But then, they reasoned, their demise would not be of great value unless they took along a few others with them. They would proceed to draw up a list of the dozen people the world would well be rid of. Mackenzie King always headed the list."[48]

Penury did not stop them from sculpting some of their best works to date. There was probably some truth to Frances's assertion, "I don't think anyone can really do great sculpture until they're past forty. Maybe poets are better when they are young, but not sculptors."[49] In 1934, Loring produced

her magnificent portrait bust of The Girls' friend Frederick Banting —
discoverer of insulin and amateur sidekick painter of the Group of Seven.
Loring herself believed that *Sir Frederick Banting* was one of her best works
to date, despite the fact that "he was very shy and reserved."[50] She pitched
out her first effort, based on hours of sittings. The second "I did quickly, and
caught the impression I wanted all of a sudden,"[51] she later said. Using
techniques perfected by Rodin that gave a dynamic animated surface to the
work and its rugged base, Loring worked on the principle of "two heads,
one from the sitter and one from [my] head."[52] By informing the literal with
her imaginative grasp of her subject — she turned her subject's head to one
side as if he were inquiring into something — she was able to convey
Banting's strength, curiosity, intelligence, and sensitivity. "It is a splendid
likeness and technically excellent, among the finest ever sculpted in this
country," Rebecca Sisler wrote. "[S]he has caught in it the questing pioneer
spirit of the man himself. Strength and character thrust out through the
bronze, with the rugged simplicity of the brilliant doctor accented in the
surface modelling treatment. The bust is alive."[53] So great was Loring's
involvement in this portrait bust that she later commented, "Anyone you
have sculpted belongs to you in a sense after that. Part of them belongs to
you always."[54] (Five replicas were made in 1949 and three sold at $2,000 each
to the National Gallery, the Art Gallery of Toronto, and the University of
Toronto. A sixth was made in 1966 for the medical library of UBC.)[55]

In 1935, Loring combined her love of colossal monuments with the
Canadian nationalism touted by the Group of Seven, Bertram Brooker,
Hahn, and Wyn Wood. She created an archetypal *Goal Keeper* seven and a
half feet tall in full hockey gear (lent to Loring by Maple Leaf Gardens, which
was "unofficially interested" in the work).[56] It was as if she transformed the
experimental work of Wyn Wood — itself related to the vast landscapes of
Canada in the manner of the Group of Seven's paintings — into something
uniquely her own. Instead of using a large canvas, she created a monument.
Instead of focusing on a vast landscape, she identified a larger-than-life person.
Instead of finding national consciousness in the intimidating wilderness of
the north, she chose the national "hero": the goalkeeper in the icy sport of
hockey. (Later she would remark that she wished Canadians would "pursue

sculpture as vigorously as they do sports.")[57] The principles were similar to those that motivated Wyn Wood; the result was completely different. It suited the vision of great Michelangelo-like works she had always dreamed of creating by identifying in Canadian life a figure worthy of such treatment.

In 1936, she was commissioned to sculpt a statue of St. Michael over the Bond Street entrance to St. Michael's Hospital in Toronto. When it was pointed out that the saint's big toe extended beyond hospital boundaries onto city property, the Mother Superior quipped, "No need to trouble, Miss Loring. We'll just have the Chief Surgeon look into the matter!"[58] More typical of her work during the '30s was *Miner* (*Moose River*), done the same year. The bust of a dishevelled draegerman was inspired by the mining disaster at Moose River when three miners were trapped for three days, which — recalling her early days at the mines — Loring followed closely on the radio.[59]

But it was her *Eskimo Mother and Child* (1938) — also a quintessential Canadian subject — that crowned all her sculptural endeavours so far. Again the sculpture was large, and again it was "northern": a monument to the Arctic peoples who were strong enough to survive one of the globe's harshest climates. But this time, her subject was a woman, a woman with her baby on her back. Loring had never been up north, but she had certainly seen Robert Flaherty's groundbreaking photographs of people from his 1912–13 expeditions to the Belcher Islands in Hudson Bay. She had also probably seen his first film of the natives of Baffin Island, screened at the University of Toronto's Convocation Hall in April 1915, and later his box office success *Nanook of the North* (1921).[60] As with her Banting bust, she had an inner and outer view of her subject. She based her statue on her imaginative recall of the images she had already seen, but more precisely she used a photograph topographer J.R. Cox had taken in May 1916 of an Inuit woman, Manigurin, and her baby Itayuk, in coat and hood.[61] Loring probably saw the photo in Diamond Jenness's book *The People of the Twilight*, though the image had already appeared in an American journal in 1925. But she had access to it from Jenness himself, since he was at the time an ethnologist at the National Museum of Man (now the Museum of Civilization) in Ottawa where The Girls' friend Marius Barbeau also worked.[62] Although her sculpture was generally true to the details of dress, Loring simplified the lines, omitting creases and tassels, and anything that detracted from the strong rhythms she established in the sculpture's powerful, fluid lines. By changing the tilt of the woman's head from a direct gaze to an angled downward-looking position and replacing her smile with a serious expression, Loring dignified the work and rendered it more powerful. Although Wyle had done a relief of an *Indian Mother and Child* after her trip to the Skeena River in 1927, that relief was gentle, even patronizing, because Wyle concentrated on the tender relation between the mother and the child on her back, a tenderness echoed in the small size of the panel itself. (Wyle may have been influenced in this work — including its sentimentality — by Charley Mulligan's 1906 *Indian Mother*.[63])

As Christine Boyanoski points out, the use of aboriginal people as a subject for art was well-established in Canada by this time. The subject was a popular one often taken up by sculptors, not only because of the inherent drama of exotic lifestyles, but because the sculptor was challenged in creating what were thought of as different racial anatomies. Certainly Loring and Wyle would have been familiar with some examples in the United States. But in Canada there were a number of examples well-known to the sculpture community: Phimister Proctor's Indian heads and warriors in the early twentieth century; their ssc colleague Alfred Laliberté's *Jeunes Indiens Chassant* (1906) in the National Gallery; Emanuel Hahn's *Chief Thundercloud* — also owned by the National Gallery — which they would have seen at the first exhibition of the ssc; de Foy Suzor-Côté's *Caughnawaga Women* (1925) in the Art Gallery of Toronto; and Louis-Philippe Hébert's monument *Pecheur à la Nigogue* in front of the Quebec legislature. Such sculptures were, to a greater or lesser degree, in the tradition of the "noble savage." In ways that today seem condescending — not to mention appropriative — these images of native peoples by white sculptors were often done to preserve the history of what was presumed to be a dying race, or they were created to present dramatic, interesting images. In somewhat the same way Indian names and "customs" were appropriated for summer camps and cars, native images in art suggested the white fantasy of living close to nature and at the same time asserted the dominance of white civilization.[64]

Loring's *Eskimo Mother and Child* moved Canadian aboriginal imagery away from this tradition. Perhaps because of her early life in mining camps, she was closer to the real experience of native life herself. Or, perhaps, the flexibility she had acquired travelling in Europe and moving around in North America made her more receptive to otherness. Perhaps her interest in monumentalism played a role, too, for she was drawn to dignifying her subjects through large-scale works. It could also have been that times were changing, and thanks to early anthropologists, Eurocentric views were being challenged. In the United States, for instance, sculptor Malvina Hoffman had undertaken the enormous project in 1931 of travelling around the world to document all the races in sculpture. (She did 104 sculptures in this project.)[65] For whatever reasons, Loring's powerful *Eskimo Mother and Child* stands today as an unsentimental, dignified tribute to motherhood and a people strong enough to survive in extremely difficult circumstances — a subject that must have resonated deeply, given that she and her partner Florence Wyle were enduring such hardships in their own daily lives.

THOSE HARDSHIPS BEGAN to lighten late in the decade. Much-needed income appeared in the form of commissions — one from the Niagara Parks Commission in 1938, the other from the unlikely source of O'Keefe Brewery the following year.

It was the architect W.L. Somerville who set them up to work for the Niagara Parks Commission.[66] The parks commission, under the direction of Liberal minister M.A. McQueston, wanted decorations for the Harry Oakes Pavilion at the summit of the small rise that overlooked the Oakes Garden Theatre at Niagara Falls. Those medallions were exercises in nationalism, celebrating Canadian flora and fauna; Wyle did four birds (*Seagulls, Bluejays, Wrens,* and *Orioles*) and Loring did three (*Pigeons, Canada Goose,* and *Owl*) against typically Canadian trees or shrubs. They were also commissioned to do a series of reliefs at the Rainbow Bridge in the garden, bus stop, and service station (now demolished). Travellers from the United States could not miss the large Canadian coat of arms on the Customs House directly facing the bridge — the only work both women sculpted together (possibly because it involved no inventiveness, but simply copied a motif). Somewhat in the stylized "landscape" mode of Elizabeth Wyn Wood (who had three sculptures in the same park: a stylized fountain relief of three Canada Geese rising vertically into flight, one of three squat owls back to back, and another of four salmon leaping),[67] Florence Wyle created the small reliefs *North Country*, *Rainbow*, and *Farm* on the garden walls, and several reliefs of Canadian wildflowers over the shops in the arcade (now demolished). On a south-facing wall next to what used to be the service station is a large relief — also by Wyle — of Johnny Canuck shaking hands with Uncle Sam, a tribute to the increasing cooperation of Canadians and Americans across the nearby border. Loring — typically — contributed larger, more muscular reliefs: *The Invention of the Wheel* (also demolished with the service station) and *Deer Panel*, a huge stylised work on the south-facing wall at the north end of the garden. It is similar to the deer panel Wyle had already done for Baron Byng High School in 1927, but it is larger and more ambitious in its treatment of the caribou (or deer) and a flock of Canada geese. As Loring later observed in her typically wry fashion, these works in Niagara Falls — which brought desperately needed income to The Girls in 1939, just after the Second World War broke out — were "sneaked in sort of as construction work" because "[the government officials] are so scared that the opposition should realize that art is being indulged in during war times."[68] The art critic for the *Globe and Mail* was enthusiastic about the nationalistic Rainbow Bridge project, as much for its "Canadianness" as for any aesthetic consideration. "The very best that could be desired has been procured at minimum cost," he wrote, "with the result that the people of Canada actually own what costs each citizen a small fraction of a cent ... We own inspiring art for ourselves and coming Canadians. That is good business, good art, and good pride for Canada."[69]

Almost as an afterthought, after twenty years as an associate member, Florence Wyle was finally made a full member of the RCA, the first female sculptor (and fourth woman)[70] in Canada to attain a position now rendered almost redundant by the SSC. "I have been an associate member 20 years, and you kind of look forward to becoming an Academician," she commented acerbically to an interviewer, rubbing clay from her hands on an apron over a blue sports sweater.[71] Her diploma piece was *Harvester* — a farm worker stripped to the waist leaning back to slake his thirst from a large jug — a sculpture very much in the tradition of her "home works" war memorial pieces almost twenty years before. It would be another decade before Loring received the same honour in 1947.

The opening of the new Queen Elizabeth Way west of Toronto also occasioned a source of income for Loring and Wyle. M.A. McQueston was in charge of this project too. Again, W.L. Somerville was instrumental in getting them both involved in the decoration of a monumental pillar he designed, that would be placed where the new highway began near the Humber River, just west of Toronto's waterfront. Loring and Wyle tried to get Indiana limestone, but were told it was "filthy American stone" and instead used "patriotic" Queenston limestone. Wyle did a circular, medallion-like relief of King George VI and Elizabeth in profile, part way up the base of the pillar. On the steps leading up to the base, Loring created a huge stylized "pugnacious" lion, rising to his feet and roaring splendidly — the traditional symbol of England rising from slumber to meet the challenge of the Second World War. They secretly hired a German stonecutter, who was replaced by an Englishman who disliked taking orders from a woman. When he made a change to the line of the lion's neck, Loring fired him, and finished the job herself.[72] "I often stopped and said hello to [the lion] and asked how he was getting along," she later said.[73] During their visit to Canada that year,[74] the royal couple dedicated the QEW at its southwestern end in Niagara — a ceremony that probably amused the two American sculptors who had no particular interest in Canada's ties to Britain.

IN 1939, THE year after work began on the Niagara Falls commissions, The Girls were asked to do four plaster wall reliefs for the boardroom of the new Canadian Breweries Limited building (called O'Keefe Brewery) established by business tycoon E.P. Taylor at 297 Victoria Street, Toronto. The panels were to represent sowing, reaping, brewing, and drinking. How Florence, who abhorred drinking, reacted to this commission can only be surmised, but Loring, who liked Canadian Club rye, would have welcomed the challenge. Perhaps because of Wyle's need to distance herself from alcohol, The Girls devised bas-reliefs that elevated the whole business of beer making to a mythic level by copying Greek sculptural styles in much the same way as Loring had in her *Noon Hour in a Munitions Plant* in 1919. One panel by Loring inside the elegant art deco stone-faced building (now part of Ryerson University)[75] — *Beer Making in Greece: The Brewing* — shows two women in classical drapery and sandals smashing hops with their mortars in a large pestle while a man, also in long robes and sandals, holds a sheaf of wheat over his shoulder. Beside these figures in profile a sheep grazes in pastoral bliss. Nothing further from riotous debauchery — that might have offended Toronto the Good, which still had stringent liquor control laws — could have been imagined.

The Oakes project, the QEW lion monument, and the O'Keefe commission more or less saved The Girls from destitution. Then a real financial break came completely unexpectedly. Later the same year, when gravel was discovered on their farm, they sold sections of it to a gravel company. "[They] have just about joined the capitalist class," A.Y. Jackson wrote, with a touch of envy. "They won't have to worry about finances for some time."[76]

Though The Girls were once again solvent, the opportunities they might have had in more prosperous times to display and sell their free-standing sculpture were lost forever. Towards the end of 1938, in a climate more prosperous than it had been for a decade, several Canadian sculptures were sent to an exhibition called "A Century of Canadian Art" at the Tate Gallery in London, England, where according to one critic — who singled out Loring's *Eskimo Mother and Child* — "behind all [the free, forceful and vigorous] work is the consciousness of a new land which must be treated in a new way. If [Canadian art] has not attained to a universal stature, it has made a genuine and original contribution to the world of art; and its future lies ahead of it."[77]

This tentative success in England was followed by unqualified success in the United States. In the summer of 1939 the New York World's Fair at the Pan-American Building marked the first recognition of Canadian sculpture since the War Memorials show in 1919. In a flurry of national pride, *Saturday Night* announced (inaccurately): "Canadian Sculpture Makes its First Bow in the U.S."[78] This mainly photographic report singled out nine of the sculptures selected by the SSC and sponsored for travel by the National Gallery. (Due to customs complexities, Harry McCurry advised that all the works be shipped together under the auspices of the gallery.)[79] Loring and Wyle are the only two sculptors with two works each; the others are by Hahn,

Wyn Wood, Hébert, and a new younger sculptor, Donald Stewart. Stewart's sculpture *Confusion of Mind* is truly modernist — a featureless female twisted into a sinuous abstracted posture that suggests anguish. Wyn Wood's *Woman with Skein* is less abstract, but also is modernist in its almost monolithic simplicity, emphasizing rhythmic lines and drawing attention to the textured, pocked surface. The other works, including Loring's and Wyle's are much more traditional. Hahn's quasi-Etruscan horse head *Equestrian Fragment* and Hébert's bust of Jongers, first seen at the ssc inaugural show, are fine examples. Wyle's demure *Study of a Girl* (1928, 1931), seen from the back, and her mahogany-carved female bust *The Cellist* (1937) both exude serenity and tenderness. Not so Loring's two works — *Eskimo Mother and Child* and her small fountain statue *Girl with Fish* (1932). Just as Wyle has staked out her primary territory as a sculptor of the eternal female form ("I prefer figure work to portrait work because it is better sculpture as a rule."),[80] so Loring has declared her engagement with down-to-earth women and men whose daily work renders them noble and heroic. Wyle's techniques — smooth patinas and softly dappled surfaces — enhance her subjects' paradoxical strength and gentleness. Loring reveals a penchant for strong, vigorous moulding, especially where geometrical patterning occurs. In *Girl with Fish* the scales of the fish slung over the Mediterranean girl's shoulders are echoed in the sharp, repeating semicircles of the several folds of drapery in the sarong-like garment encircling the hips of the otherwise naked girl. *Goal Keeper* lent itself to the same treatment: the leg pads and thick gloves run in strong ridges that mirror the strips of tape lashing the hockey stick. In *Eskimo Mother and Child*, the split sides of the trousers open in clearly defined ridges like an opened peapod and close in a pronounced inverted V-shape across the stomach. This design is repeated in the V where the sleeves meet the neck. This basic pattern is duplicated in the energetic cross-hatching on the cloth, the rounded toque, and the baby's cup-like papoose. Even the woman's crossed hands, her fingers like a larger form of cross-hatching, echo this powerful pattern and convey the woman's strength. As Loring said in a 1939 speech to the Toronto University Women's Club, "The lines [in a sculpture] should lead in to create harmony and concentration of interest: and there must be dignity of theme if a monument is to last through the years."[81] That same year, in a CBC Radio program on sculpture (one of a series of six), she said, "A straight horizontal line in a landscape causes a melancholy reaction. A perpendicular line, as in the Gothic churches, lifts one up to the unknown and the spiritual. Diagonal lines give a feeling of movement. The principles are as old as art itself."[82] By 1946 she claimed to get "artistic satisfaction" from such repetitious shapes as "the draping of a gown, the scales on a fish, the links in St. Michael's armour."[83]

Compared to her sinuous *Eskimo Mother and Child*, Loring's stiff, unathletic *Goal Keeper* is inferior. As one critic would later note, "her most epical and imaginative creations are of women, not as models, but as allegorical types."[84]

Both the *New York Times* and the *Herald-Tribune* praised the Canadian sculpture show extravagantly, linking its success (and the success of the Canadian Society of Painters in Watercolour show that accompanied it) to a strong Canadian artistic scene. "Canada has so much that one show fails to do it justice," the *Herald-Tribune* reported. "For the first time in history, Canadian art gets more newspaper space in review than Canada's big cheese did from Chicago at the first World's Fair in 1893," and on display was "sound work which would hold its own with the big American group shows."[85] The Canadian Pavilion at the fair was the only place where changing exhibitions were sponsored by another country. Next to show would be the Canadian Group of Painters, the more inclusive association that replaced both the Group of Seven and the Beaver Hall Hill Group. American critics noted, as well, the Mendelssohn Choir, the Hart House String Quartet, Edward Johnson, "a whole roster of singers," an opera conductor (Pelletier), several composers, a number of actors (including Raymond Massey), and "a small host of novelists, poets and playwrights" — all "in the front rank of the March of Time across the border."[86] Painters as diverse as Alexandre Bercovitch, André Biéler, Fritz Brandtner, Charles Comfort, David Milne, Pegi Nichol, Carl Schaefer, Arthur Lismer, Leonard Brooks, and Will Ogilvie (all predicted to be "future trends" in Canadian painting)[87] are mentioned. As for the sculptors, Loring's bust of Banting and Wyle's *Study of a Girl* are singled out — along with Hahn's *Equestrian Fragment*, his bust of Wyn Wood, and her *Man and Woman*, a fluid merging of male and female.[88] With the Tate Gallery show in 1938 and the New York World's Fair in 1939, Canadian sculpture was finally recognized on the international scene.

‖ 21

What Depression?

While it was true that the Depression of the 1930s had an impact on Toronto, and posed special hardships for artists like Florence Wyle and Frances Loring, some aspects of life in Toronto belied this fact. The Girls' success with their war memorials in the 1920s, the consolidation of sculpture in Canada with the formation of the Sculptors' Society of Canada in 1928, in which Loring played the key role, and the emergence of the Loring-Wyle church-studio as a *salon* where artists, intellectuals, and wealthy patrons gathered, made The Girls the darlings of Toronto cultural life. Since the formation of the ssc, their studio had become "a national home for sculptors,"[1] "a centre where one wave after another of Canadian talent has been encouraged,"[2] a place where "no weary artist or stray cat ever failed to receive hospitality."[3] Newspaper coverage of their doings increased during the 1930s. In the absence of husbands and children — or any other family — they devised a sort of Bohemian Christmas for themselves, gathering as many painters, sculptors, intellectuals, and musicians as they could pry loose from other, more conventional celebrations to join them for a dinner that would be partly supplied by their guests, but mainly cooked by Frances, sipping on a glass of Canadian Club. Their close friend, the avuncular A.Y. Jackson, painted and cut out a fabulous Christmas tree on bristol board that could be used year after year.[4] One of these occasions was described in a 1931 *Toronto Daily Star* column, "Women's Daily Interests at Home and Abroad." Nothing in it would suggest that the Depression had hit Toronto:

> With Yuletide logs blazing, and an abundance of Christmas decorations, Miss Frances Loring's and Miss Florence Wyle's Christmas party promises to be a gay affair in their old church studio tomorrow evening. A few of the guests will arrive just before the dinner hour, a number of others arriving later augmenting the numbers to 40 or more for supper. Dancing will provide part of the entertainment. Miss Loring will wear a gown of burnt orange and gold lamé, and Miss Wyle will be in midnight blue velvet.[5]

On such an occasion, Florence, who insisted on having a piano player,[6] danced gracefully and sang to her heart's content in her midnight blue velvet jacket, even though her idea of a strong drink was a glass of ginger ale cut with water.[7] Frances would have designed Florence's jacket — and her own burnt orange and lamé gown — from her well-thumbed copy of *Dress Design: An Account of Costume for Artists & Dressmakers*,[8] usually used to check details for statues and reliefs, but now taken to a seamstress to save money in the creation of flamboyant apparel for herself, and the darker, tailored clothes Florence preferred. Downstairs in the Crypt people would help themselves to Christmas turkey, a Dutch loaf on a bread board, an assortment of vegetables concocted creatively by Frances, bowls of puddings, and fruit served from the long refectory table that The Girls' friend Keith McIver had fashioned from an old door from The Boys' renovated house nearby. Light from the gargoyle lamp, augmented by candles in old wax-encrusted wine bottles and lanterns, would reflect off the raw brick walls.[9] Upstairs the scene would be an odd one: guests animated and chatting before the huge fireplace, or whirling around in the space cleared for dancing, while the silent statues, some of them swathed with cats, looked on — stony-faced — from the side-lines. Perhaps later in the evening, Florence would be persuaded to give one of her astonishing demonstrations of hog calling on the farm.

There is little in the social notes of the Toronto newspapers to indicate that there was a Depression at all. This was probably because the women featured in those notes were married to men whose lives were not devastated during the 1930s. It was true that the working class was hard hit by unemployment, and that construction and manufacturing were decimated. But because saving — even among the middle classes — replaced investment in industry, Toronto's financial institutions, and the men who ran them, were financially stable. In addition, affluent businessmen refused to pay higher taxes and continued to buy new houses, especially in York, Forest Hill, Leaside, and Etobicoke. The combining of Toronto stock exchanges in 1934 and the tight auditing of the Ontario Securities Board helped prevent bankruptcies. Ironically in Toronto the Good, it was especially because of liquor and beer production that Toronto's stock markets took precedence over Montreal's.[10] "In other words, the financial sector suffered little in comparison to wage workers"[11] and artists. Beyond that, as the modernization of the 1920s continued into the 1930s, white-collar jobs proliferated, and, although civil servants, school teachers, and professors were paid less, their dollars were worth more because prices had declined substantially. The number of radios, automobiles, and refrigerators manufactured and sold jumped dramatically during the decade.[12]

For this reason, one of the main venues for art remained the Women's Art Association, which had in 1930 become affiliated with the international Lyceum Club, an elite women's art club established in London, England, in 1904. Throughout the 1930s, the luncheons, garden fetes, teas, suppers, receptions, and exhibitions at 23 Prince Arthur seemed even more extravagant than they had been in the 1920s. One garden fete in June 1930 featured sculptures by Loring and Wyle (and Merle Foster and Elizabeth Wyn Wood), sales of cut flowers, a homemade cake and candy booth run by "a bevy of attractive girls," a presentation of fairy and folk tales by a children's Little Theatre Group, and a performance of Haydn's "Toy Symphony" — all before tea at "interesting little tables."[13] Another gathering for tea in

February 1935 featured "some fine exhibits in sculpturing by Miss Florence Wyle and Miss Frances Loring," drawings by Carl Schaefer, special music by Healey Willan, a violin performance by Miss Isabel Ericson,[14] and tea readings.[15] In January 1937, Frances chaired the association's annual luncheon, attended by over 200 women,[16] and in September she presided over a fashion show.[17] In January 1939, "Miss Frances Loring — gowned in fuschia crepe — and her party," with a group of "smart matrons" from the Lyceum Woman's Art Association, were among those who celebrated the end of the year at a lavish supper dance and bridge party in the Royal York Hotel's Palm Court, decorated "with tall green palms and softly-shaded lamps."[18] In June 1939, she was deeply involved in the Country Fair and Dance put on by the Lyceum WAAC. And, as usual, she "received" the guests and presided over the baked beans supper.[19] This gala event was opened by Mrs. R.S. McLaughlin, wife of the wealthy Oshawa motorcar manufacturer and mother of Isabel McLaughlin, a painter who was a friend of the Beaver Hall Hill painters. (Through John Pearson's arrangement for a commission, Frances had created her *Girl with Squirrel* (1922) as a fountain for Colonel Sam McLaughlin's magnificent estate Parkwood.)[20] Apart from round and square dancing on the lawn behind 23 Prince Arthur, there were madrigal singers, the Kiwanis Boys' Band, fortune-telling, a delicatessen, and a stall selling "accessories for every woman and her boudoir."[21]

Quite often, the Lyceum WAAC featured artists from Montreal — notably the women in the Beaver Hall Hill group, to which A.Y. Jackson also belonged. The connections — begun through art shows and consolidated with Florence's 1927 trip to the Skeena River with Annie Savage, the Beaver Hall Hill artist who had commissioned her to do the *Deer Panel* for Baron Byng High School in Montreal — had developed through shows in both cities. There were visits back and forth, especially by Florence, who visited portraitist Lilias Torrance Newton[22] for a week in June 1930 and travelled by car with singer Mme Jeanne Dusseau to Montreal where Dusseau gave a concert at Moyse Hall, McGill University, in March 1931. In February 1931, Frances in "an embroidered cerise gown" and Florence "in black velvet" entertained Prudence Heward, "in rose crepe — the clever young Montreal painter," and Isabel McLaughlin at a tea in front of an open fire in the "cozy setting" of their studio decorated with spring flowers.[23] In 1937, the Lyceum WAAC hosted an exhibit of women painters from Montreal at which Frances Loring — vice president since 1932 — "received" the guests with long-time president and founding member of the association, painter Mary Ella Dignam. Special guests were Arthur Lismer and his wife, recently returned from eighteen months in South Africa, and playwright John Coulter and his wife.[24]

Frances and Florence appear frequently in the social notes of the Toronto papers at other events as well. In March 1932, shortly after Florence had returned from her twin brother's funeral,[25] they attended a lunch given by the Heliconian Club for their old friend Eric Brown from the National Gallery. "Artistic people usually wear interesting clothes," ran a *Toronto Daily Star* account of this occasion, "and they certainly know their colours. Eric Brown ... wore a light tweed suit that bordered on mauve, a green tie and a cream silk hankie tucked in his sleeve. He also wore a monocle, which dropped from his eye each time he looked down at his notes in a way that uniquely punctuated his speech. On his right sat Miss Frances Loring who was very Romney-looking, as one of the guests said, in her vivid green-silk frock, brick-coloured scarf and dark tam."[26] The Loring-Wyles were among the guests listed for a concert by violinist Harry Adaskin in November 1932,[27] and at a second concert of his at Massey Hall in 1933, where Frances was singled out for her "brown satin [gown] over which she wore a wide circular cape of brown velvet."[28] In August 1935, they entertained the musicians from the Promenade Symphony and other guests at a supper in The Church where "cheery log fires, tall red candles and large bouquets of black-eyed golden daisies lent a colourful note to the attractive studio."[29] In June 1939, Frances attended a lecture at the University Women's Club by philosopher Dr. W. Jarvis McCurdy.[30]

"Frances *loved* all those social gatherings," recalled Rebecca Sisler.[31] Florence, who was increasingly given to crusty opinions that distanced people, was not nearly as enthusiastic. It was not surprising that Frances was elected President of the Lyceum Women's Art Association in October 1938, at almost the same time Florence so belatedly became the first woman sculptor elected to the Royal Canadian Academy of the Arts. Nor was it surprising that Florence attended fewer and fewer of Toronto's social and cultural events with her partner as the decade wore on. By the end of the 1930s, Florence's name is missing from the newspapers' lists of guests at such events more often than it appears. Frances, on the other hand, attended them all.

Florence was more comfortable with the informal entertaining they offered at Cherry Wood, their country place. Some of these occasions were also reported in the social notes of the papers. One such announcement in 1932 read:

> Miss Frances Loring and Miss Florence Wyle are having their usual busy season at their summer cottage near Cherry Wood, Pickering. They entertained Alan Burt there before he left for Ottawa to sing at the Imperial Conference concert tour, Mme. Jeanne Dusseau, Mr. A.Y. Jackson and Mrs. De Bruno Austin [Dorothy Stevens], among other well-known members of Toronto's musical and artistic circles.[32]

IF ENTERTAINMENTS AT The Church were Bohemian, gatherings at Cherry Wood — for weekends, or picnics — were even more so. For Frances, who had grown up in mining camps, and Florence, who came from farming people, living without life's comforts was not difficult; it was fun. How some of their more sophisticated guests reacted to the farm can only be conjectured. "The shack had been a dilapidated tumbledown place when The Girls bought it," Rebecca Sisler recalls, "and it never was much better. A porch was added, the floor propped up and the roof patched, to make it liveable, but it always exuded an air of very dubious stability. Its charm rested in the general atmosphere of unquestioned relaxation. Inside, the furniture was unmentionable. Boards had been put together for benches and bedsteads, bits and pieces had been added from friends' attics. At one point an acquaintance kindly donated a lovely formal dinner set ... but of course they were terribly out of place. The Girls sat around hating them for a time and then went back to using their chipped pie plates."[33]

Inside the shack, there were many beds "in varying stages of decrepitude — enough to sleep about a dozen people who did not object to mouse holes in the blankets. Frances herself was awakened one night by an insistent tugging on her long braid that trailed from her cot onto the floor. A mouse was intent on dragging the prize home to his nest. House guests were safer from rodents on hot nights, for then the beds were hauled onto the roof of the porch."[34]

Sisler recalls that "Saturday picknickers would wander about, doing as they wished — sketching, dawdling, collecting firewood, whatever they felt like. Then, toward evening, they would be drawn together by a heady aroma ... Frances working her miracles over what must have been one of the original outdoor barbecues ... an iron grill scrounged by a second-hand dealer from a street drain set on stones. Florence, in her role as assistant, would have earlier broken up a big hubbard squash with an axe ... The mouthwatering results [typically thick steaks, squash, and fruit] became legendary."[35]

Florence had an ongoing campaign to root out poison ivy, which thrived on the property. Unfortunately, not much else did. There were some scraggly asparagus and a few wild quince, despite Florence's efforts to have a vegetable patch. "Those who knew her," Sisler recalls, "laughingly pronounced her [energetic rooting out and burning of poison ivy] as symbolic of Florence — the rooting out of evil." At night, her efforts to save moths were as tireless as her daytime compulsion to destroy the ivy. "A tumbler was placed over each moth that came to rest on the screen, a piece of paper slapped over the mouth of the glass, and the creature carried to the door and carefully released into the night."[36] It seems Florence's need to perform good works accelerated during the 1930s. Hers was the first signature on a petition to exonerate friend Eric Brown from a boycott of the National Gallery by 118 artists who were enraged "because of alleged discrimination in favour of modernism." ("If our artists would leave amateur politics alone and paint, they might have less cause for complaint.")[37] She defended women's abandonment of stockings in favour of bare legs ("Bare legs? I think they're great! You bet your life that saves money. Where would sculptors be if everybody was afraid to go with bare legs? In fact, I don't approve of clothes at all.").[38] And she wrote an eloquent letter with an imprint of her signature on behalf of the *Toronto Daily Star*'s Fresh Air Fund for underprivileged children to spend two weeks at camp in the summer of 1937 ("Why should fathers and mothers be forced to bring up their children amid squalid surroundings when there is so much beautiful country?").[39]

While Florence busied herself with good works, Frances leaned back and entertained guests, in a style exactly like that of her father,[40] with "fascinating gossip and salacious tales" that, as their close friend, Keith McIver, said, "[e]nlarge so at each telling ... it's impossible to remember the original story."[41] It was as if Frances became even more like her father — that "colourful Mine Figure who put Rossland on the map," as one of his obituaries said[42] — after his death in 1938, a passing away that was a relief to The Girls as they did not know how they would meet the winter's expenses.[43] The only material things she inherited were some books — though he had earlier given her the rights to some mining claims in Temiskaming,[44] — but she inherited his looks and to a great extent his personality, including his faith in Canada.

All these entertainments at the farm were subjected to the excitements of Delilah the dog. Her "contribution to these idyllic outings was to sit on the back stoop and bark incessantly throughout the entire weekend. Everyone but The Girls could cheerfully have poisoned her," recalls Sisler.[45] And when the dog finally died after a dotage in which The Girls carried her outside in a blanket sling to lie in the sun, The Girls' friends were so thankful there was a flurry of phone calls: "Did you hear the good news? Delilah's dead!"[46]

ON ONE HOT Sunday, The Girls took their guests at the farm for a beer at the Rouge Valley Inn nearby, a place patronized by local farmers and their wives after church. The plan was to cool off in the pond in front of the terrace. One of their guests — a young reporter with the *Daily Star* who had downed too many beers — decided to join the swimmers already enjoying the water. He wore one of the ancient bathing suits kept at the shack for guests. He dove in, circled back, and climbed out of the water to dive again, quite unaware that he had lost the bathing suit in the water. Onlookers gasped with shock, but "the Loring-Wyle group were in hysterics. Three or four men ... surrounded him" and shuffled him out of sight.[47]

The Girls' social activities — whether they were the gala events of Toronto's wealthy matrons in various societies, parties at The Church, or the eccentric Bohemian gatherings at the farm — helped to offset the misery and deprivations of the Depression. A modest economic upswing, the loosening of art institution purse strings, and the gradual reassertion of normal life as the decade drew to a close seemed to hold a promise of better days to come.

The Second World War ⮑

It was natural that Canadian artists hoped for government sponsorship to create records of the Second World War, along the same lines as the Canadian War Records Office initiated by Lord Beaverbrook had done in the Great War. Loring and Wyle in particular had good reason to expect that funds might come their way in this war, since the bronze statuettes they had created for the "home work" section of the CWRF in 1918–19 had been such a success — artistically and financially.

Frances had picked up a little extra money at the outset of the Second World War by writing a booklet called *How to Get Started: Woodcarving for Pleasure* for the Canadian Armed Forces and the Merchant Marines. The idea for this project came from A.Y. Jackson and Arthur Lismer, who had written the first two booklets in this series on arts as pastimes for soldiers and sailors.[1] She and Florence had also recently managed to cash in on the decorative reliefs at the Harry Oakes Pavilion and various other embellishments near the Rainbow Bridge in Niagara Falls. Loring regarded her large *Deer*

Panel (1939) on the south-facing wall of the Oakes Garden as one of her best
works and complained when plantings partly obscured it. "They've let vines
grow all over the wall," she said in 1965, "and now they've planted a row of
trees right in front of it. You can't see it at all. I mentioned it to them once,
but they've never done anything about it."² Her massive British lion on the
QEW — unveiled just before the outbreak of the war (and commemorating
the "courage and resolution of their majesties in undertaking the Royal
Visit in the face of imminent war")³ — attracted wide public attention to her
work. It had become a Toronto landmark. Children passing it in cars greeted
it as the "lucky lion." The fifty-three-year-old Loring had endured the chill
November winds off Lake Ontario from her favourite spot high on scaffolding. There she had used power tools for the first time to make sure
the finishing touches on her lion were just as she wanted them. She had had
to borrow a pointing machine from Allward, who had by now finished his
Vimy Memorial and returned to Canada in 1938. Because of these highly
visible public works, Loring especially had reason to hope for further government commissions; her reputation for monumental national works in Canada
exceeded all others, except Allward's.

But the Canadian government did not immediately involve artists in the
Second World War as it had less than two years into the Great War. And it
was largely to address this question that the Kingston Conference of the Arts
was held at Queen's University. There in late June 1941, artists, museum and
gallery directors, art historians, and others interested in the arts — including
almost every important Canadian artist at the time — met to discuss the role
of the artist in Canada.⁴ It was the first time that artists from all over Canada
had met. Among the 150 people who took part in the conference were
Frances Loring and Florence Wyle.

The conference was arranged by André Biéler, a Swiss-born professor of
art at Queen's since 1936, who was also a painter, watercolourist, printmaker,
muralist, and sculptor. Money for the conference, including travel expenses
for everyone attending, came from the Canadian Committee of the American
Carnegie Corporation of New York and from the National Gallery, where
Harry McCurry had replaced Eric Brown after Brown's death in 1939.
(Frances wrote of Brown's passing, "Art in Canada has lost its greatest cham-

pion. It would have had a hard struggle without his courage and help.")⁵
Biéler invited American painter Thomas Hart Benton and Edward Rowan
from the U.S. Treasury Board's Public Works of Art Project as special guests.
The presence of these two men — especially Rowan — set the conference
firmly on the path of using American expertise to obtain support for artists
in wartime from the Canadian government. It was the Treasury Board's
Public Works of Art Project and the Works Progress Administration's (WPA's)
Federal Art Project under President F.D. Roosevelt (who had received an
honorary degree from Queen's University in 1938) that had employed
American artists during the Depression. Biéler no doubt hoped that Rowan
would offer practical advice to Canadian artists who aspired to receive
government support. Also attending the conference were representatives of
the Boston Workshop Group (funded by the WPA), who were expected to
explain how the U.S. government helped ensure the quality of their materials.
To spur national pride, the delegates were to be sent to Ottawa on the last
day of the conference for a tour of National Gallery works led by Marius
Barbeau, a viewing of H.W. Southam's collection of Group of Seven paintings, and a fine lunch at the Chateau Laurier.

The broad assumptions behind the conference were that in the 1920s
"networks of intellectuals, writers, artists and public servants had forged an
elite vision of the country, of 'nation,' that informed public policy and provided the foundations for the achievement of the Statute of Westminster
(1931): Canada had moved from colony to nation."⁶ On that basis of nationhood (i.e., Canada's increased autonomy), it was understood that during the
Depression a national interest in art had emerged. That being the case, the
argument for government support of the arts was far stronger than it had
been in the Great War.

Part of the proceedings also had to do with ideas that had emerged during
the 1930s: a suspicion of elites — especially capitalist elites — and strong
endorsements of democracy, if not of socialism and communism. In this
context, elite institutions, such as conventional art museums catering to the
wealthy, came under attack. The idea of the wealthy patron of the arts, such
as H.W. Southam, now seemed distasteful. Most participants at the conference agreed that art should speak to all people. Benton, who had launched

the conference with a nationwide broadcast about the role of the artist in wartime on Queen's radio station CFRC, went so far as to say that "pictures should be in the homes of people, or anywhere but in museums."[7] Frances Loring was also outspoken: something had to be done, she maintained, "to counteract the feeling, which is rather general, that it is a disgrace to in any way patronize art until the war is over." Recalling her own experience creating war works at the tail end of the Great War, she continued, "I do not mean that the artists should perhaps be just kept alive until after the war, and then used during the reconstruction period. I mean that during the war the artists really have something to say, and towards the life of our community." Indicating her interest in taking practical steps to make this a reality, she added, "Could we perhaps organize some publicity campaign, or something, that would really try to impress upon the public the fact that they need art now? I feel that we want to do our bit for the war, but we have been crushed ... Could we have a committee whose job it would be to work along those lines? I just leave that thought with you."[8]

Oddly enough, given that Loring had just created her stunning *Eskimo Mother and Child*, the Inuit artist was touted at the conference as a model of the integration of the artist into society. The idea was that daily life, practical implements, and artistic creation were interdependent. Rowan spoke of the commissions his program had given to aboriginal peoples. (There were no aboriginal artists at the conference.) Other models were the Mexican muralists Diego Rivera and José Clemente Orozco, whose work addressed "fiercely intense social questions."[9] Such models acquired urgent relevance at a conference held only four days after Germany's renunciation of the Nazi-Soviet pact with Hitler's invasion of Russia, for there was a general consensus that artists in a democracy ought to be able to "combat" fascism through public assertions of the values democracy enshrined. In other words, art — even in Canada — could be politically useful.

Not surprisingly, some participants thought that an artists' union — formed along lines of trades unions — was in order. Others favoured a suggestion first articulated in a letter from Lawren Harris (who was teaching in Vancouver and did not attend the conference), which proposed "forming a nation-wide and inclusive organization ... [and] working through that organization to serve the cultural needs of the Canadian people."[10] Since all the arts societies were exclusive at the time, the word "inclusive" was key.

To sort out the various issues raised at the conference, a Continuation Committee was struck under the chair André Biéler. The committee's members were Walter Abell, a young academic and critic from Acadia University, Nova Scotia, where *Maritime Art* (later *Canadian Art*), the only art magazine in the country, was published; A.Y. Jackson; Arthur Lismer, now in the Fine Art Department at McGill University; and one woman, Frances Loring. With her long history of committee work, her experience as president of the Lyceum Women's Art Association in Toronto, and her initiative in founding the SSC, Loring was well-suited to this work. Although the Continuation Committee eventually established the Federation of Canadian Artists (FCA), their job was made almost impossible. Wartime regulations specified that annual meetings could not take place, and communications by mail were sorry substitutes for discussions. Despite this, the committee managed to set up some energetic regional groups, an achievement that proved somewhat at odds with the national goals of war records proposals and post-war reconstruction plans.

WHEN THE FCA did meet, the results could be frustrating — especially to Florence, who, although she thought meetings were a waste of time, had high hopes for the FCA. At one meeting held at the museum in Toronto, "several long-winded extroverts [dominated the meeting]. The morning droned on with every indication that the garrulous participants would go on forever without moving any closer to decisive action. Finally, an adjournment for lunch was announced, leaving all business suspended for further discussion in the afternoon. As the delegates stretched their cramped muscles, a voice rang out from the back of the auditorium. 'You people may be going out for lunch, but I'm going home!'" Florence — who, in her early fifties, had become even more eccentric with her man's tie and wiry greying hair still cut like a man's — had had it.[11]

It seems that Florence did not fully grasp the shift in perception around the arts that the Kingston Conference gathered to discuss, though Frances certainly did. Emanuel Hahn had kindly suggested to *Canadian Art* that

Florence contribute an article called "Sculpture and the People." Walter Abell, the journal's editor returned her draft as unpublishable. In it she outlines the history of sculpture from the Egyptians, through the Greeks, Romans, Renaissance Italians, and so forth, in much the same way as Lorado Taft had done in his lectures at the Art Institute of Chicago years before. If the piece has a theme, it is that the high point of world sculpture was Greek sculpture, a position she had always held and would continue to hold. "This experience is unfortunate for all of us," Abell wrote back to her. "I assumed that the subject would be treated in relation to modern democracy and the progress made or problems involved in bringing sculpture into closer touch with the people of the modern world."[12] He invited her to submit another article, but she let the matter drop. The closest Florence came to adapting to new perceptions of the arts was a shift of interest to handicrafts, which had assumed an important role in the war effort, since knitted garments and other practical items were being sent — often through the Canadian Red Cross — to soldiers overseas. There are many references to Florence's ceramic exhibits — including a lovely terracotta *Torso*[13] — at shows of the ssc (which by 1944 had fourteen members) or the Canadian Guild of Potters, of which she was president in 1944.

Frances, meanwhile, threw herself into public education. Education to undercut elitism in the arts and connect them with the general public had been one of the themes at the Kingston Conference. How could artists give flesh to democracy? How could they educate ordinary people so that they understood, cared about, and bought art? Florence had attempted a couple of lectures, but she had no talent for public projection. In a presentation at the Sunday School Sketch Club in London's Williams Memorial Art Museum about how to model in clay and soap, she launched into a spirited sermon on the importance of school: "If I had young people to train as artists," she said on that occasion, "I would send them to university. General knowledge is a good thing, and particularly that of science. There you put down the bedrock, you find out about the earth beneath your feet and when you come to discovering yourself in art, this knowledge helps you."[14] As Rebecca Sisler recalls, it was "not that [Florence] was mute on issues — anything but. She was a constant defender of the faith as it applied to artists, but preferred her confrontations face to face. Her small stature and gentle appearance were absolutely deceptive. Let anyone give her an ideal to defend and, as one friend said, 'God help you!' Another friend once cut into one of her dissertations with an exasperated, 'Florence we love you in spite of your virtues!' Florence stopped immediately to laugh heartily at herself."[15] As always, Florence believed that hard work was the one essential. She was more comfortable donating thirty-two works (twenty-four hers, the rest Loring's) to her hometown of Waverly. For this occasion, the town designated 13 December 1945 "Florence Wyle Day," and Florence was there to take part in the ceremonies.[16]

It was Frances, with her warm smile, welcoming handshake, and attractive deep voice, who was charismatic in front of a crowd. By 1944, in her late fifties, she had matured into a beauty of person and character that would inspire a number of portraits by painters and sculptors alike. A splendid portrait of her at that time by Montreal friend Lilias Torrance Newton, which eventually went to the National Gallery,[17] shows her as an exotic, regal figure in vivid green with a scarlet cape thrown over her shoulders. Her long, dark hair is parted in the middle and pulled back, giving her the air of a Spanish dancer or Italian countess.[18] This portrait — in which, one art critic said, "her red shawl could be played on cymbals"[19] — shows why Florence began to nickname her "Queenie." She gave many lectures — most illustrated with a slide lantern — on the history of art, the importance of sculpture, modernism in sculpture, or the Vimy Memorial, and also gave a "Great Sculptors" series of lectures for CBC Radio on Epstein, Rodin, Allward, Meštrović, and Saint-Gaudens. These were her old standbys, but she seems to have moved slightly in the direction of modernism: "Experiments must go on," she said in her program on the history of sculpture. "Do not condemn too quickly the searchings of a newcomer in any creative field."[20] These were new ideas for Frances, but, although she refers to the Vorticists, the Cubists, the Futurists, and the Surrealists, there is no evidence that she understood these modern movements in art. She gave regular demonstrations at the Art Gallery of Toronto on modelling and sculpting. In 1939, she gave a series of evening classes at Northern Vocational School. Many of her lectures differed little from standard art school fare, but in one lecture she gave for the University Women's Club, "The Present and Future Development of Sculpture in Canada," she spoke candidly about the problems facing sculptors in Canada. "The last generation of sculptors found it easier to begin their careers," she said, clearly recalling her own case and Wyle's, "because so many were employed in making war memorials. Younger sculptors of today [are] finding difficulty in beginning a career, because even older sculptors [have] no more work than they can handle. Most drop out before they reach the professional stage because the years of training are longer and the time needed for production longer than in any other art." Loring had in mind the younger sculptors, some of whom had begun studying with her and with Florence, not the frivolous daughters of wealthy patrons, but dedicated young artists who already included, or would soon include, Elford Cox, Stephen Trenka, Alvin Hilts, Dora de Pédery Hunt, Donald Stewart, Frances Gage, and Rebecca Sisler. Loring reiterated an observation made frequently by others: "Canada [has] the inferiority complex of a new country, and Canadians [are] afraid to trust their own judgment in matters of art." Again, with her own experience in mind, she added, "A work of art [has] to be endorsed by London, Paris, or New York before Canadians would accept it." She concluded by urging her audience to go to exhibits and teach their children to respect sculpture.[21]

Ultimately, the FCA failed. Prime Minister Mackenzie King did not meet with representatives to sign a petition, signed by a thousand artists, asking that artists be enlisted in the war effort. (The petition was mailed to him instead, to little effect, in February 1943.)[22] Their plan to decentralize the National Gallery by having regional galleries share national shows was scotched by Harry McCurry, who did not want to see his National Gallery undermined, and, in fact, had plans which proved successful to enlarge it. The final blow came from Quebec, where Maurice Duplessis had just been elected on a French-Canadian nationalist/provincial rights platform. French organizations in Quebec were suspicious of the FCA recommendations for education — so important to Loring — and withheld their support for the regional network plan on grounds that it would interfere with their church-based education policies, despite Elizabeth Wyn Wood's persistent attempts to draw them into the FCA plan.[23] What Wyn Wood, Hahn, Loring, and Wyle had been able to do when they enlisted French-Canadian sculptors into the SSC in 1928 proved impossible for the FCA to achieve.

Most of all, the ideological climate in Canada during the Second World War was different from that in the Great War. In 1914–18, idealistic views about "the war to end all wars" were possible. Canada could and did develop a nationalism that arose from its sense of becoming a great nation instead of a provincial backwater. By the end of the Depression, a sullen cynicism had developed in Canada, as elsewhere, that was unsure about what degree of democracy was desirable. With a larger population, and in the absence of a driving force such as Lord Beaverbrook provided at the outset of the Great War, political and social issues were not clear enough to gel into any single ideology. Artists lacked a common conviction and direction.

Wyn Wood — with assistance from Loring — did succeed in presenting the FCA brief, which largely consisted of the ideas of Lawren Harris, the new president of the FCA, to the Commons Committee on Reconstruction and Re-establishment (the Turgeon Committee) in 1944. The brief asked that the government construct war memorials in community centres across Canada. That same year, in a move that signalled anticapitalist sentiments, Canada sent an exhibit of seventy-five paintings and sixty sculptures, including Loring's *Goal Keeper* and *Eskimo Mother and Child*, to Russia under the auspices of the National Council for Canadian-Soviet Friendship.[24] The FCA plan was far-reaching; it represented a huge step towards national recognition of and support for the arts. The goal was to topple elitism in the arts and bring art to the people.

In addition to Harris's suggestion that a network of twenty-five community centres be built across Canada, which would be serviced by the National Gallery, the Film Board, and the CBC at a cost of $10 million (and run by further operating grants), the FCA brief recommended that a government body be set up to supervise all cultural activities and that a survey be made of "The Arts in National Life." The brief also recommended a National Orchestra Training Centre, a State Theatre, a National Library, National Archives, and a National Film Board. The idea was that "original thought and creative activity are major national resources,"[25] and that the government should support them for its own sake. The matter was an urgent one for Loring and Wyle. Even their gravel money from the farm was running out. "Frances and Florence may have to close up unless they get more [commissions]," A.Y. Jackson wrote to a mutual friend.[26]

THE FCA EVENTUALLY gave up its position of national leadership to a coalition of artists' associations called the Canadian Artists' Liaison Committee, though it remained representative of regional arts organizations. Out of this new coalition, in December 1945, came the Canadian Arts Council, which maintained national leadership. However, the FCA was the organization that presented the brief in 1949 to the Royal Commission on the National Development in the Arts, Letters and Sciences (the Massey-Lévesque Commission) which finally positioned the arts in Canada in the place hoped for by the participants at the Kingston Conference eight years before. Artists had gathered in Kingston to explore the role they might play in wartime, but the long-term results of their deliberations far surpassed this goal. Discussions in the arts community that outlasted the war itself confirmed the notion that the artist has an essential role to play in society, whether there is a war or not. It was the FCA brief to the Massey-Lévesque Commission, which was based on the FCA's original brief to the 1944 Turgeon Committee, that in 1957 successfully recommended the establishment of the Canada Council.[27]

23

How to Carve Soap ⤳

The radio played a crucial role in the Second World War. This technology — advanced for its time — enabled listeners around the world
to hear news from the front much more quickly than newspaper reports.
Families gathered around the radio to hear Hitler speak, to hear Edward VIII
give his abdication speech, to hear George VI hesitantly offer encouragement to members of the British Empire, to hear Prime Minister Mackenzie
King comment on the conscription plebiscite.

It was probably in imitation of Roosevelt's fireside chats that the Canadian Broadcasting Corporation in Canada began a series of programs during
the war called "Fireside Fun." People switching on their radios at 4:00 p.m.
one winter Friday in 1942 — the third year of Canada's participation in the
war — would have been arrested by the warm, deep, resonant voice of Frances
Loring: "Let me first warn you," she began, "that you are being deceived if
you think I am just going to tell you how to spend a pleasant evening by
your fireside. I thoroughly agree with your desire to stay at home instead of

wasting gasoline on the highways, but my ambition goes away beyond the passing of an agreeable evening."[1]

Frances is about to describe the process of sculpting in terms that the general public can understand. It is part of her drive to bring sculpture to the people — to educate Canadians in the art that is so often overlooked. The type of sculpting she describes is not modelling with clay, which involves building up a figure with clay on an armature. It is that other, more difficult type of sculpting, the type taught by Charley Mulligan at the Art Institute of Chicago: the art of cutting and chipping away from a block of material like marble.

"I want to make you carve," she continues, "I want to make sculpture seem less strange to you, to have you look at it with less awe." She is convinced that anyone can carve, if they just put their minds to it. The thought that it might be a rare talent requiring years of training and practice does not seem to cross her mind. The description that follows offers insight into the way *she* carves and the way her partner Florence carves — as if it is easy.

"I want to give you an itch in your fingers," she says, "that will never leave you at peace until you humour it — an itch to carve. I would like to start a contagion of carving that will spread through the whole family, from grandmother to baby. I would like to unearth that smothered creative urge that lies buried in almost everyone. I want to instill into it a spirit of adventure. I would like to hear you say, 'It would be wonderful to carve if only I knew where to begin.'"

In choosing an inexpensive bar of soap as her material, Frances recognizes wartime privation, but also expects that its malleability and availability will engage her listeners in trying sculpture for themselves. It will be easy, she promises, and exciting. "The thrill is just as great if you are expressing your urge to create in a small piece of soap as it is for the sculptor who is hewing the creature of his imagination out of stone.

"Come, try it. You can do it," she urges as if she is speaking directly to her listener. "If you have eyes to see the things around you, and hands that might peel a potato, you can carve soap." She tells the listeners what's needed, expecting them to fetch these items before she goes on: the bar of soap and a paring knife or penknife. She fills the next few minutes with a thrifty reminder that chips from the soap can be saved and used.

Frances suggests carving a cat. Her first instruction is to look at the shape of the bar of soap, as if this will somehow trigger a concept of "cat." "The shape of the material is the first problem of the sculptor in his heroic conception, just as much as it is yours," she says. Then she suggests visualizing the cat as curled into "an oblong ball ... without the ears protruding: it is always best to eliminate projections."

There is more to sculpting a cat than to peeling a potato. But on she goes to the next step: "Find the highest point of the highest mass — the hump of the back. Mark its location on your cake of soap with a pencil. Outline its shape ... Do the same with the other masses, marking the highest point of each ... Now cut. Don't be afraid, just cut from one high point to another ... and define the hollows around each mass ... Do not put in the divisions of the paws or the nostrils in the nose, or the hairs. This is ... the difference ... between just making an exact copy of a cat and creating a work of art."

Frances echoes what Lorado Taft and Charley Mulligan taught at the Art Institute of Chicago: the whole aim of sculpture is *beauty*. "The difference between good sculpture and bad [is that] it presents a pleasant shape as a whole, [because] your detail [is] subservient to the balance and flow of bigger forms." Like most neoclassicists, she singles out the *Venus de Milo* as a prime example of good sculpture. "The first long distance view is of an agreeably shaped piece of white marble. When you approach more closely, you are pleased with the sense of ease and balance, a beautiful arrangement of masses and forms. Nowhere has the sculptor cut so deeply that the harmonious flow of light and shade is disturbed."

As an example of bad sculpture, she chooses *The Laocoön* from the Vatican Gallery. This example, too, could have come from Taft's lectures or Mulligan's carving instructions in Chicago. In this tortured group scene a father and his two sons struggle with huge serpents. "It is full of holes, some cut clear through," Frances points out to an audience of listeners who had probably never considered Laocoön or even heard of him. "The detail is beautifully modelled, but you get lost in it ... It is an exhausting piece of sculpture, like a person who talks so much that you forget what he is talking about."

In her radio talks and her many lectures elsewhere, Frances never veered from the principles and methods she had learned as a student: sculpture must be beautiful; sculpture must combine masses in a way that is "pleasant" and "agreeable"; too much detail and too many openings ruined the necessary "harmony" of light and shade. Florence, whose prickly personality and Illinois twang were unsuited to radio, was even more conservative in her approach, touting the necessity of accurate anatomy and the incarnation of beauty in all that she created. Unfortunately, by 1942, at a time when Canada had had a sculptors' society for a mere fifteen years, the world of sculpture outside Canada had moved into new aesthetic philosophies that owed more to modernism than to neoclassicism.

24

Art for the People⁥

The northwest corner of King and Bay Streets, in the heart of Toronto's financial district, was the site for the new Bank of Montreal Building. Construction of the building had been stopped on the outbreak of the Second World War — leaving only the concrete walls, the vaults in the basement and sub-basement, and the steel structure up to the third floor. Most of the rest of the steel for the sixteen-storey building, first designed by Chapman & Oxley, had been fabricated and was stored awaiting the resumption of building. It was not until 1946 that building started again under a new architectural firm.

There were already three other banks at this corner,[1] but the Bank of Montreal was to be different. The new architect — F.H. Marani of the architectural firm Marani and Morris — had agreed to work with a team of six sculptors under the direction of Walter Allward to produce a building that would showcase the theme "Spirit of the Provinces."[2] Such a concept was completely in keeping with the discussions at the Kingston Conference and those of the committees that later articulated a new relationship between the artist and Canadian society. From the outset, Frances expressed reservations about "this collaborative idea."[3] She agreed, however, that if art was now to come down from its elitist pedestal, stop relying primarily on wealthy patrons, and create works that spoke to the general population in terms they could understand and enjoy, what better place to begin than the workplace. People had to go to banks; then let this public building where everyday business was transacted offer examples of art that ordinary people would notice and appreciate.

The concept for the sculptures was a simple one — "contemporary classical."[4] It specified Canadian content in much the same way that the designs at the Harry Oakes Pavilion and Garden had required Canadian flora and fauna. There would be large relief panels with allegorical human figures on ledges high up on the reveals of the entrances on both streets representing each of the nine provinces, as well as Newfoundland, the Arctic, and the Northwest Territories. The name of the province or territory would be carved into the relief, and each figure representing the province would be accompanied by symbols of the main pursuits of the people in that province. The gender of each allegorical figure was decided beforehand.

Not surprisingly, Frances Loring created the two most important panels on either side of the main entrance off King Street: Ontario and Quebec. Ontario — a nude male figure in sandals and a cape — would hold a scroll suggesting science and the arts and stand in front of machine parts symbolizing industry and science; Quebec — a sturdy female nude, also in sandals and a cape — was to be accompanied by the lyre and the spool representing the province's folk-music tradition and textile industry. To prepare for these bas-reliefs, Frances has laid thin layers of clay on sheets of brown paper or pieces of linoleum or glass to create sketches.[5] Florence Wyle — who commented tartly, "too bad to have to please a committee but we get paid for it"[6] — chose New Brunswick and Prince Edward Island, both female. Her New Brunswick is a female archer, much like Diana of the hunt in classical mythology. In fact, all the figures suggest Greek mythological allegories. In the interests of consistency among six sculptors, some agreement about the style was necessary. It seems that Loring and Wyle — who had done the wall

reliefs at the Harry Oakes Pavilion and Garden and the O'Keefe Brewery —
prevailed. These new panels in the allegorical neoclassical tradition with some
stylization in the art deco mode were shared among six sculptors: Loring and
Wyle, Emanuel Hahn, Elizabeth Wyn Wood, Donald Stewart, and Jacobine
Jones. In addition, Jacobine Jones was to use her special talent as an *animalier*
to create a series of Canadian animals — beaver, howling wolves, walrus,
polar bear, buffalo, and skunk — on the large curved lintels over the front
and side doors, giving rise to endless "jokes about the wolves and skunks of
Bay Street." To emphasize the Canadian theme, Scott Carter, a heraldic
designer, was to create a war memorial plaque to sit underneath the Canadian coat of arms over the revolving doors.

Inside, Frances Loring was to add two large plaster panels: *Dawn* (in which
a kneeling woman releases three doves from her open hands into the azure)
and *Dusk* (in which a reclining man rests one arm on the setting sun and
shakes the clouds from his shoulders). At the preview reception one moonlit
evening on the 15th floor terrace of the offices of John S.D. Tory, KC, after
the work was finished in 1949, Mani Hahn livened the party by looking up
and commenting, "Who designed the moon?"

Overall, it was clearly recognized that the team effort to decorate the Bank
of Montreal was aimed at bringing art to the community. "The design ...
doesn't any longer belong to Marani and Morris," commented arts journalist
Pearl McCarthy in the *Globe and Mail*. "Already people are beginning to say,
'This panel is mine,' or 'You can have that one; I don't like it as well.' This
adopting of the brain-children of designers is the very basis of community art
... and is so very different from being awed by magnificence ... [T]he use of
six leading Canadian sculptors in a type of decoration which is new, makes
Canadian art history."[7]

But some people in Toronto the Good objected to the nudity. "There are
[war] shortages, admittedly, but not as short as that," said one. "[The public]
will point to the façade of the Stock Exchange," one writer speculated,
"where art is wedded to architecture in dress suited to the occasion in
surroundings where people can definitely lose their shirt — the miner is in
overalls, the broker in a business suit, and the financier spreads confidence
beneath a top hat. The climate is certainly changing, such people argue, but

is it meteorologically correct and constitutionally advisable to show a woman as 'Arctic' wearing nothing but a knee-length cape without even a *collar*?"[8]

For some time in Canada the lines between architecture and sculpture had been blurred. It was easy to see that a free-standing sculpture, such as Florence Wyle's *Sun Worshipper* and *Mother of the Race* torso, or Frances Loring's portrait bust of Frederick Banting, had nothing to do with buildings, but what about Loring's war memorial in Galt? And what about plaques, like Loring's *Mercer Memorial* inside the Toronto Armouries or Wyle's relief, *Edith Cavell*, outside the Toronto General Hospital? And what about fountains? The sculptures dominated, but they needed structures around them: pools, basins, rivulets, or, in the case of wall fountains, walls to which the semicircular basins were attached. The sculptures were designed by sculptors, but the structures in or on or against which they were placed were often created by architects. Even gardens were designed by landscape specialists to highlight the placement of sculpture. Since the early 1920s, Loring and Wyle had worked with architects or landscape designers. John Pearson and W.L. Somerville, in particular, had been essential in the design of several of their works. Even Loring's *Miss Canada* had depended upon the portico at Eaton's for its impressive setting in 1917. And, most recently, the relief murals they had done to decorate the boardroom walls of the O'Keefe Brewery and the medallions and wall panels they had done for the Harry Oakes Pavilion and Garden were intended to enhance architectural structures already in place.

In 1927, the first exhibition of Architecture and the Allied Arts mounted by the Ontario Association of Architects was held at the Art Gallery of Toronto. In it, a model of the altar designed by William Rae for Bishop Bethune College, Oshawa, was displayed, including the four plaster angel candlestick holders created by Florence Wyle. William Rae was also the designer of the Byzantine rood in St. Mary Magdalene Church on Ulster Street, Toronto, for which Frances Loring had sculpted the life-size Christ. Loring and Wyle exhibited regularly with the Allied Arts Association in their biannual shows from 1927–39. In them, Loring displayed models and photos for the Osgoode Hall War Memorial, and the model for her Galt war memorial. Wyle exhibited a shield for the Canadian Bank of Commerce, and a model of the *Deer Panel* for Baron Byng High School in the 1931 show and her art deco relief *The Cellist* in 1933. On one occasion she showed a typical beaux-arts sculpture of a drum decorated by reliefs of dancing children for the Gage Memorial Fountain, designed by architect John Lyle for Hamilton.[9] In 1942, in cooperation with the landscape designers Howard and Lorrie-Alfreda Dunington-Grubb, Florence Wyle created the most splendid fountain she would ever sculpt for the grounds of H.R. Bain in north Toronto. A timeless art deco beauty, draped simply, looks demurely down and kneels on one knee over a wide basin set in a pool. She holds aloft a smooth shallow bowl at one shoulder from which water overflows in a steady shimmer over her and into the large basin. The effect is one of medieval serenity: the essence of peace.

Such collaborations between architects or landscape designers and sculptors increased in Canada in the late 1930s and 1940s. According to Stephen Vickers, in an article for *The Journal of the Royal Architectural Institute of Canada* in 1949, "The architecture of the 1920s [in Canada] was as barren as architecture ever has been of sculpture."[10] But by 1938, an editorial in the same journal stated, "[F]or the first time in Canada, architects' conversation is likely to turn to the subject of sculpture on building."[11] While Vickers and others clearly wanted architects to work with sculptors in the creation of modern buildings, certain problems had begun to emerge. For sculptor Cleeve Horne, one problem was the ignorance of architects: "Few architects today, very few, exhibit the knowledge, judgment or taste required to utilize sculpture in its true aesthetic role on a modern building."[12] For Vickers, despite the similarities between modern sculpture and modern architecture (an interest in materials and textures, and an ability to use three dimensions to create an ever-changing image as the spectator moves), the effects of sculptural low reliefs on a building were usually marred because the screen (or front) wall is meant to present one flat surface interrupted only by openings of doors and windows. A relief sculpture, on the other hand, was intended to give an illusion of considerable — even unlimited — depth. The screen wall and the reliefs on it were, in other words, visually at odds with each other.

Both architectural critics disliked the Bank of Montreal sculptures. Vickers put the blame squarely on the sculptors, especially on Donald Stewart's Nova Scotia, which he found "lamentable" and "disturbing" because the shallow illusion of depth in the relief caused the screen wall "to vanish into space!"[13] Horne is more forgiving. He acknowledges that the sculpture gives "a very human, almost feminine touch to otherwise stark architecture" and that "the work as a whole radiates something that is unique, complete, absolute." But he also feels that "two or three panels ... have failed to maintain the original concept."[14] He says the project would have been better assigned to two sculptors, not six. He hopes that the architects have gained more appreciation of sculptors and will work with them again; if not, he predicts, "within the next decade we will witness a dearth of sculpture, and a consequent period of refrigerated architecture."[15] Loring had been right; collaboration among so many sculptors had not been a good idea.

Although some questioned the appropriateness of nude figures as bank decorations in downtown Toronto,[16] no one appears to have considered how appropriate the allusions to classical Greece were. Certainly, Jacobine Jones's Canadian animals were suitable for a project that, like the Oakes Pavilion and Garden reliefs, was commissioned to be "Canadian." But, in the same year that saw Paul-Émile Borduas's revolutionary manifesto of modernist art in Quebec, the *Refus Globale*,[17] nudes draped in capes wearing sandals, the women with their long hair bound up on their heads, were hardly the stuff of 1940s Toronto. Even the *Globe and Mail* art critic Pearl McCarthy — devoted to the arts though she was — observed, "there may be debate as to whether the ideas might have been treated differently."[18]

If this was art for the people, it retained enough aesthetic elitism to place it far from anything the ordinary bank patron could identify with. Furthermore, the almost double life-size figures were placed high above ground level. For a pedestrian gazing up at the panels, the impression was of gods and goddesses of the provinces in a mythological world of timeless symbols, not a down-to-earth representation of ordinariness transformed into art. In concept and execution, the Bank of Montreal reliefs — all in profile — were only a short step from the O'Keefe reliefs. And those O'Keefe reliefs, in turn, were not far from Loring's war relief *Noon Hour in a Munitions Plant* in which the weary women's work clothes look like nothing so much as classical drapery.

⚜ WHO IS SCULPTURE? ⚜
WHAT IS SHE?

Who is Sculpture?
What is She?

Frances Loring and Florence Wyle believed that they were bringing sculpture to the people when they created their neoclassical *Beer Making in Greece* reliefs for O'Keefe Brewery at 297 Victoria Street (now a Heritage Building) in Toronto in 1939. They also thought that their "contemporary classical" reliefs on the "Spirit of the Provinces" theme for Toronto's Bank of Montreal on King Street seven years later brought sculpture even closer to ordinary citizens. Loring and Wyle were too busy creating sculpture to attend international sculpture shows, even close by in New York. Nor could they afford to travel further than their farm or, occasionally, to Montreal or Ottawa by train. They did not even have time or energy to read much about sculpture elsewhere. The list of their books, which was filed with their papers at the Art Gallery of Ontario, indicates that by the 1940s they had, among other items, books on Egyptian sculpture and Greek sculpture (possibly textbooks from their student days), some on design and form, and a 1914 treatise called *The Beginnings of Art*. They owned a 1919 book on Ivan Meštrović, which emphasized his nationalist work. Their main holdings in modernist sculpture were Eric Newton's tribute to sculpture in the British Empire, *British Sculpture 1944–46*, which included works by Henry Moore and Loring's bust of Dr. Frederick Banting, Jacques Schnier's *Sculpture in Modern America* (1948), two books about José de Creeft (1949 and 1960), and a book on William Zorach (1959).[1] This library was not sufficient to keep them up to date on changes in the theory and practice of sculpture, especially given that Henry Moore and Barbara Hepworth had emerged in England as young sculptors carving abstract forms in the 1930s. Loring had picked up some information on new trends, probably in preparation for her various lectures, but friends of The Girls remember that they read in the evenings after a hard day's work, although that was usually detective novels for relaxation.

OUTSIDE CANADA, THE international sculpture scene had been changing rapidly during and after the Second World War, largely because the technologies derived from war industries transformed life and increased the pace at which it was lived. The theme of the 1939 New York World's Fair, at which Canadian sculpture sent by the SSC made its American debut, was "Building the World of Tomorrow." As its centrepiece stood the huge round Perisphere and tall, spiked Trylon — white buildings whose stark, futuristic simplicity was in complete contrast to the two central images at the Chicago World's Columbian Exposition almost half a century before, in 1893: the elaborate beaux-arts sculptures *Republic* by Daniel Chester French and Frederick MacMonnies's *Ship of State*. The world had changed from one that cherished European tradition to one that anxiously anticipated a streamlined North American future.

By 1939, both French and MacMonnies were dead. Although the figurative tradition they embraced remained a part of the 1939 World's Fair, the beaux-arts style was no longer dominant. The simple, utilitarian architecture was Bauhaus inspired, and design elements everywhere were now closely aligned with the aesthetic of the all-powerful machine. One of the first televisions and a keyboard-operated speech synthesizer were among the fair's exhibits. Power had begun to replace Beauty.

The limbo in which sculpture languished in 1939 could be seen symbolically in two works at the World's Fair that stood for the extreme diversion of styles. James Fraser's *George Washington* proclaimed the heroic, the historic, the monumental. But elsewhere on the grounds, Isamu Noguchi's *Chassis Fountain*, an eighteen-foot-high work that combined forms based on automobile parts for the Ford Motor Company Building, declared the supremacy of industry and the hypnotic beauty of the machine.[2] Although there were more academic works than modernistic ones at the World's Fair, these hardly seemed congruent with "the world of tomorrow." The fair coincided with the emergence of so-called radical sculpture — "abstract, non-objective art, which was represented in the show by five examples, including a welded steel construction by David Smith."[3]

Such "radical" artists were not untrained. By the mid-1940s, the sculptors who came to prominence in the United States deliberately abandoned traditional figurative work in favour of individualized, modernistic explorations. Many had been trained in traditional techniques at the usual beaux-arts institutions. Isamu Noguchi, for example, had apprenticed with Gutzon Borglum (of Mount Rushmore fame) and studied at the Leonardo da Vinci School of Art before deciding to create nonrepresentational art. Others like Ibram Lassaw, Jacques Lipchitz, and Alexander Calder had followed similar paths. Lassaw went to New York's Beaux-Arts Institute of Design before developing an abstract style in his architectonic structures; Lipchitz — like Frances Loring — attended the École des Beaux-Arts, Académie Julien, and Académie Colarossi in Paris before becoming a leading member of the American avant-garde; Calder ignored the academic sculpture of his father and grandfather and created whimsical, bright mobiles and stabiles.[4] By the end of the 1940s in America, the modernist movement — or abstract expressionism — had become an established school and was accorded respect by galleries, museums, and critics alike. There was "a sense that much of the sculpture produced in the previous half century was passé and was considered in extreme instances invalid as art. It was not uncommon for museums to move figurative sculpture to storage or even to deaccession (sell or remove from lists of holding) works no longer in fashion by the 1950s."[5]

The emphasis in sculpture had shifted from an absorption in the subject to an absorption with materials and with the self, at least in part because the advent of psychology and anthropology in the early twentieth century was radically changing the way man viewed his world. Sculptors, and their critics, were no longer interested in rhapsodizing about "the soul" or "beauty" or "perfection." They were more likely to say things about the texture of their materials or their personal interpretation of their subjects. "Everyone with the feeling for sculpture," observed American sculptor Concetta Scaravaglione, "expects his work to have the character of the material in which it is made. He also expects it to express himself ... to be insistently personal."[6] "I would define sculpture as the *art* of creating and organizing significant forms or shapes (representational or non-representational, natural or geometric), the goal being to enrich one's experience in regard to form and form relationships," wrote another.[7] "Suppose several different materials — a dark wood, a light wood with a colourful grain, marble or granite — were given to me with an order to make a figure from each," a third wrote. "The result would not be the same figure. In each case I would be concerned not only with synthesizing in a pleasing manner the forms of the figure, but also with the character of the material — its texture, grain, color and hardness."[8] Yet another commented, "[T]o obtain a real work of art the *sine qua non* is an inner impulse. A work of art should be the result of an artist's own intense interest, something which he receives or perceives through his senses, develops in his own mind and heart during a real gestation period, usually of years."[9]

The British sculptor who had emerged in the mid-1920s and would dominate modern sculpture from then on — Henry Moore — was articulate about his approach to the art. He rejected the beaux-arts ideals: "Beauty, in the later Greek or Renaissance sense, is not the aim of my sculpture," he stated categorically.[10] His early *North Wind* relief on the wall of the Underground Building at St. James's in London makes a telling contrast to the elegant Hellenic personifications of Canada's provinces and territories on Toronto's Bank of Montreal Building. *North Wind* was Moore's first commission in 1928 — two decades earlier than the Toronto Bank building. It portrayed a dynamic, sturdy figure reclining on its side that, as one Canadian critic observed, managed to convey its full volume without suggesting weight. ("Here is a figure which is both man buffeted by the gale and the force of the gale itself ... without any tiresome references to bellows, billowing cloaks, or puffing cheeks.")[11] Compared to Moore's relief work, the placid, flattened Bank of Montreal allegories seem outdated and static, including their billowing cloaks. Moore fully understood the new path his sculpture was taking: "Because a work does not aim at reproducing material appearances it is not, therefore, an escape from life — but may be a penetration into reality, not a sedative or drug, not just the exercise of good taste, the provision of pleasant shapes and colours in a pleasing combination, not a decoration to life, but an expression of the significance of life, a stimulation to greater effort in living." Later, as his sculpture became more and more abstract, Moore commented, "My sculpture is becoming less representational, less an outward visual copy, and so what some people would call abstract; but only because I believe in this way I can present the human psychological content of my work with the greatest directness and intensity."[12] As one of Moore's critics put it, "This removal of the Greek spectacles from the eyes of the modern sculptor ... helped him to realize again the intrinsic emotional significance of shapes instead of seeing mainly a representational value, and freed him to recognize again the importance of the material in which he works ... to know that sculpture in stone should look like stone, that to make it look like flesh and blood, hair and dimples is coming down to the level of the stage conjurer."[13]

Compared to this shift in the direction of sculpture at the end of the 1930s, the figurative pieces sent by the ssc to the New York World's Fair must have seemed decidedly tame, if not entirely passé. Only the work of Elizabeth Wyn Wood and Emanuel Hahn would have appeared the least bit innovative. But compared to something like Isamu Noguchi's *Chassis Fountain* or David Smith's welded work, Wyn Wood's *Passing Rain* and Hahn's *Flight* would have looked like timid explorations at best.

A 1945 article entitled "Sculpture," by Canadian critic Walter Abell, makes clear what contemporary sculpture in Canada was like a few years later. His point of departure is the 1920s — "that epoch in which a growing national consciousness and an intense experience of native landscape culminated in the painting of the Group of Seven."[14] In Wyn Wood he sees the attempt "to translate Canadian landscape into sculpture." "Out of such seemingly unsculptural subjects as wind-blown trees, clouds, rainbows, and the wild goose poised with outspread wings, [she] created compositions which are as rhythmic as fine abstractions and which, at the same time, are significant interpretations of reality."[15] The article is headed by a photo of Wyn Wood's *Reef and Rainbow*, a piece that could be described as only semi-abstract, since the reef, the rainbow, and a cloud are easily distinguished. The new bust by Emanuel Hahn, *Madame X in Mood Y*, is strongly reminiscent of Brancusi's *Mlle. Pogany*, a portrait Brancusi created and reworked from 1912 on. However, Hahn's *Madame X* (who also bears an uncanny resemblance to Elizabeth Wyn Wood) is not nearly as streamlined or stylized as Brancusi's much earlier work. Donald Stewart's *War Widow* — a simply draped woman with exaggeratedly large hands and feet whose scarf shrouds her face as she kneels before an empty upturned helmet — is somewhat similar (in concept and dress, not posture) to Ivan Meštrović's *Mother at Prayer* (1926). Again, Stewart — and for that matter Meštrović — could hardly be called a modernist. Works by Sybil Kennedy — a Canadian expatriate returned from the U.S. — (*Standing Woman*) and Stephen Trenka (*Mother and Child*) are distorted and stylized in the modernistic vein, though they do not lose their representational aspect. Dora Wechsler strikes a new note by introducing humour and satire into sculpture with her "folk-art" group of three on a bench, *Railroad Station, Between Trains*; Elford Cox shows a male torso cleverly carved to take maximum advantage of the wood's grain; Quebec sculptor Sylvia Daoust's elegant elongated *Madonna* stands in a long liturgical tradition. Byllee Lang's three *Coal Miners* riding a coal car are thoroughly representational, although they achieve what the Bank of Montreal relief panels failed to do: they offer down-to-earth art for the people. (This work was proposed for the Wartime Information Board of Canada, but was never carried out; instead, the Canadian National Railways commissioned it — and a series based on it — to show varied personnel in their railway system.)

And what of Loring and Wyle? It is Loring's *Sir Frederick Banting* and Wyle's art deco *Bain Fountain* that are featured. In no way is either of these works modernist. Abell rightly relegates Emanuel Hahn, Walter Allward, Frances Loring, and Florence Wyle to "the older generation" of Canadian sculptors. The others, he says, form "the middle generation."[16] Perhaps the most important information in Abell's report on "contemporary Canadian sculpture" — information which he delivers in an offhand way — is that the Society for the Furtherance of British Columbian Arts and Crafts has been formed and that Canadians can look ahead to sculpture from West Coast Indians as well as carvings, dance masks, and ivory miniatures from the Eskimos in the Arctic.[17] It is around this time that the sculptor Sing Hoo appears as an exhibitor — the first major ethnic artist in the field.

SMALL WONDER THAT one critic of the ssc exhibit in the spring of 1949 deplores "the 'feel' of the show," calling it "dull and depressing."[18] "There were too many mediocre heads," Andrew Bell complained, "and there were no large works. Our sculptors sometimes complain that theirs is the Cinderella of the Canadian arts. Reflecting about this show there is a nasty temptation to retort that if *this* is what Cinderella looks like, it would be best if she stayed at home."[19]

Bell singles out two works, one by Frances Loring — a strong female "non finito" *Head* that only barely emerges from the creamy butternut surround she has carved. But he finds her plaster models of the Bank of Montreal reliefs merely "competent": "for me, [they are] lifeless and uninteresting. The large butternut head, on the other hand, is something quite different. With [this strong and sensitive essay in character] Miss Loring shows herself as one of the best of our sculptors." He also singles out Elford Cox — "clearly one of the most promising of the younger sculptors" — whose evocative *Abstraction* is the only truly modernist work in the show. "Despite its non-objective character, this remains very much sculpture 'in the round' with the eye of one's mind carried on, and around, and about."[20]

In her 1948 glance backward over the last decade,[21] Elizabeth Wyn Wood also singled out Cox, showcasing his Henry Moore-like *Carving* and comparing his technique in handling wood to that of Brancusi or Moore's contemporary, Barbara Hepworth, both of whom had been prominent in England since the 1930s. She notes Cox's unique interest in having viewers handle his sculptures ("Let them *feel* them.") — something most sculptors would have abhorred. Although her article is somewhat unfocused, she too notes that some important shift has occurred in the field of sculpture. She identifies the decade from 1928, when the ssc was formed, to 1938 bitterly as one of "Salon Sculpture": "[T]he bulk of the work was shown in galleries and three or four public art museums even purchased a few pieces ... Canadian galleries put together have purchased scarcely a handful of sculpture in the past fifteen years, practically none by Canadians, and in the last ten it has become increasingly difficult to arrange for contemporary exhibitions except in private and commercial galleries."

Probably as a result of the scathing condemnations of the "elitism" of museums and galleries at the Kingston Conference, art institutions had begun programs to involve a wider public directly. As Elizabeth Wyn Wood understood it, galleries had "unconsciously rejected" the art of sculpture in their pursuit of other activities: "concerts, lectures, puppet-shows, festivals and try-it-yourself parties."[22] The "old dilettante atmosphere of the 'Spring Salon' and the self-styled 'critics'" had had their day.[23] Given the lack of sophistication of some of the "self-styled 'critics,'" this could only be an improvement. One such critic actually stated in 1948, "Fifty years ago in all Canada [there was] not one sculptress, nor pianiste, nor woman violinist, except Nora Clench ... no, only poets, novelists, actors and 'femmes' of patchwork quilts."[24]

Wyn Wood does not look to new trends to explain the shift in sculpture. She seems unaware of the scope of modernism apart from Brancusi and Hepworth. Nothing in her article indicates that she or any other Canadian sculptor was aware of mechanical forms or techniques involving welding, such as were touted at the New York World's Fair in 1939. Instead, she identifies "the most vigorous Canadian sculpture" opening up in two areas in the late 1930s. Not surprisingly, since she had done some of the reliefs and fountains at the Rainbow Bridge in 1939 and, with her husband, was currently involved in the Bank of Canada relief panels, one of these is "permanent installation on buildings or in parks."[25] (Henry Moore was sceptical of reliefs and avoided doing them because "they forego the full power of expression in sculpture.")[26] The other area identified by Wyn Wood is sculpture for the home. "I think *millions* of small sculptures must have been absorbed into Canadian homes," she writes, speculating that "war ... produces a sense of insecurity which finds compensation in contemplating the eternal values and is symbolised by the most solid of the arts."[27] Small works, such as those by Sybil Kennedy, portraits of animals and children by Eugenia Berlin, Jarko Zavi's small ceramic animals, and Pauline Redsell's works seem to Wyn Wood to be harbingers of the future for sculpture in Canada. Even Florence Wyle had begun to do "limited editions" of works such as her pink biscuit *Torso* and reliefs of children and animals. Hahn's designs for coins and medals, such as the Leacock Memorial Medal for humour in literature, also promised work for sculptors. Similarly, opportunities could be found in display departments and industrial design.

At least Wyn Wood struggled to grasp what was going on in sculpture, what trends were occurring, and where the future path of sculpture might be headed — especially for Canadians. No doubt her time and energy in this pursuit were severely limited by the demands of motherhood, her teaching, and her responsibilities as president of the ssc, not to mention dealing with her irascible husband. As for The Girls, according to Christine Boyanoski, they "clung to a romantic definition of sculpture," as if the explorations of Brancusi and Moore had never happened. As late as 1957, Wyle was still maintaining that "[a] sculptor is one who sees and understands the beauty and dignity of natural form — in man and in all life even in the growth of a plant and whose interest has led him to study and acquire the technique necessary to portray these harmonious forms in clay and wood and in the more enduring mediums of stone and bronze."[28] Loring remains firmly grounded in neoclassicism when she describes sculpture as "the artist's analysis of life in terms of three dimensions and in terms of silence."[29] It was a definition so vague as to be almost meaningless. More typically in her talks on sculpture (which she herself did not like because she thought she sounded "vaguely pompous"),[30] Frances relied on the old standbys of her training decades before.

THE FIRST FILM on Canadian sculpture, *Third Dimension*, was released in February 1948. It was one of the seventy films chosen from the 170 films made by the National Film Board that year for the library circuit. The program was distributed in the most unlikely manner as part of the Physical Fitness Division of the National Health and Welfare Department. The reasoning was that this department was responsible for "recreation and cultural interests." The eighteen-minute black-and-white film opened with a shot of Florence Wyle's elegant *Bain Fountain* illuminated at night. At first we see the sculpture on its own, then the water begins to bubble out of the upheld bowl, into the larger basin, and finally flows shimmering into the pond. The effect is spectacular. After that, the film takes the form of a studio tour of eight sculptors. "To see sculptors at work with every material," one review read, "with skilful fingers and sharp chisel manipulating wood, clay, plaster, and hacking a magnificent charger [Hahn's *Equestrian Fragment*] out of solid stone, was enough to rouse the latent artists in any young soul — and it looked like fun too. There was a real thrill in watching people like Jacobine Jones, Frances Loring, Florence Wyle, Donald Stewart, Dora Wechsler, Louis Parent, Elizabeth Wyn Wood, and Emanuel Hahn in their studios — an experience few people have in real life."[31]

Given the new international climate in sculpture, *Third Dimension* was far behind the times. The film is a hodgepodge that seems unsure of its aims. Attempts to link French-Canadian work to English-Canadian sculpture seem disjointed and odd. Homage is paid to the early religious woodcarvings in Quebec (jarringly juxtaposed to West Coast totem poles), and the only French-Canadian contemporary sculptor in the film is Louis Parent, shown at work on one of his huge figures for the Stations of the Cross on the grounds of St. Joseph's Oratory in Montreal. Such Christian themes are completely absent in the work of English-Canadian sculptors. Emanuel Hahn is singled out for his coin designs (the 1935 silver dollar with voyageurs in a canoe, the 1937 caribou quarter, and the Bluenose dime). Dora Wechsler's satirical sketches are offered for variety. Donald Stewart in his black beret and clipped moustache demonstrates how plaster moulds are made from clay models — though his portrait bust is conventional. Jacobine Jones demonstrates carving one of her horses from stone with hammer and chisel ("most successful when most simple"). Student Jean Ross shows how an armature and sculpture are built up using a live model. Elizabeth Wyn Wood's innovative Canadian "landscape" sculptures like *Reef and Rainbow* are shown. Frances Loring's *Eskimo Mother and Child* is offered as an example of her "sympathy with human character"; Florence Wyle shows how a clay maquette serves as a model for stone carving. Walter Allward's Vimy

Memorial is given pride of place ("Canadian memorial sculpture reaches its supreme execution").

The film pays lip service to "the love of sculpture born in us all," and refers to the fun children have working with plasticine; it extols the "practical use of great art" when sculpture is "applied to architecture" and "made a part of everyday life." The only indication that Canadians have any idea about the direction sculpture has been taking since the mid-1920s is the introduction of Elford Cox. "Today in Canada woodcarvers like Elford Cox discover a new motive for art in the work of native Indians inspired by its basic almost abstract form. If these carvings are close to native art they are just as close to modern European design."[32]

The Next Generation ⬳

I n 1948, Elizabeth Wyn Wood cast a backward glance over the past decade in Canadian sculpture. Her own experiments in landscape sculpture had not caught on — for her or for others. The time had come to pass the torch to the next generation. "What of the younger sculptors?" she asked in her article, "Observations on a Decade." She noted that most aspiring young sculptors fell by the wayside, and she speculated that this was perhaps because they could not cope with the stern discipline of the profession, or perhaps because there were too few opportunities for them in Canada. "Today," she concluded, "the schools are teaching the techniques of sculpture to many more thousands of art students, and ... graduating fewer with intensive training. With increasing opportunities opening today it may well be that more will develop into practising sculptors than was the case in the past. But at this moment those who are masters of all the sciences of the art are still those who were most noted ten years ago."[1]

Loring and Wyle were aware of this situation. Although it had been extremely difficult for them to get started as sculptors, they had had the financial support of Frances's father for the first few years. They had been ideally positioned to make important contacts in the small arts community in early Toronto, and there had been so few sculptors in Canada then that there were enough commissions to go around. Now that art schools were well-established and classes much larger, aspiring sculptors needed help more than ever, certainly more than Loring, Wyle, Wyn Wood, and Hahn had. The obvious way for this to happen was to find a mentor who could advise and guide students, as well as help them make contacts. Unlike Wyn Wood, who taught at Central Technical School, and Emanuel Hahn, who had a direct influence on the many students who passed through his classes at the Ontario College of Art, Loring and Wyle encountered only the few younger sculptors whose work they admired at shows, others who sought them out, and a few whom they rescued in some way or other. What they looked for was talent and hard work. To foster the new wave of sculptors who had these attributes took a special temperament, one that was caring. After all, younger sculptors were possible competitors for commissions — public and private — and could potentially do their mentors out of future jobs. It was for this reason that Walter Allward had not steered commissions their way when they first arrived in Toronto. Aware that many young sculptors "find it difficult to earn a living on sculpture alone,"[2] The Girls were extremely generous with time and the little money they had. As Frances Gage — one of the young students they launched — recalls, "They gave away what they didn't have."[3]

During the '30s Loring and Wyle had accepted students (usually wealthy friends or their daughters) who helped them financially, but were not especially talented. Now, after the Second World War, and even once Canada Council grants became available after 1960, they felt a duty to foster whatever sculptural talent they could in the next generation. Though some, like Alvin Hilts and Elford Cox, are no longer alive, others still remember or have recorded their debt to The Girls.

One of these is Dora de Pédery Hunt, now in her nineties. She lives in a small apartment on Carlton Street in downtown Toronto amid an astonishing clutter of supplies, sculptures, drawings, photos, and old papers. She still works at a window table overlooking the street on the kind of medallions that made her famous. She is welcoming, clears a small stool of odds and ends as a place to sit. Her pale blue eyes look candidly from a round face that must once have been beautiful. She searches for the right English words, eager to tell her story.

She was trained at the Fine Arts Academy of Budapest, Hungary, graduating in 1943. Five years later, she left Hungary for Canada. Her arrival in Canada takes different versions, according to which interview she took part in. The way she tells it now in her strong Hungarian accent,[4] she was born in Budapest in 1913, the daughter of an Austrian mother and a Hungarian father, who was a physicist. The family moved to their summer place in 1944 when the Germans entered Budapest and the Allies began bombing the city. The following year, when the Russians moved in and began shooting indiscriminately, her father took a job with the British Admiralty in England. (In a 1955 interview, she said that the family escaped to Germany.)[5] One of her sisters went to South Africa, the other to South America. Dora worked for a time, not on sculpture, but with her father — who was often in hospital — as his assistant in England. The British were interested in German scientists, and her mother travelled to German factories to talk to scientists there — about what Dora is not clear or prefers not to say. Dora — by then married — left her husband, expecting him to join her later, and moved to Canada in 1948, just as Loring and Wyle were working on the Bank of Montreal reliefs, "The Spirit of the Provinces."

Her immigration to Canada was managed in a devious manner that was probably not uncommon. Someone who worked with her father at the British Admiralty had a Canadian wife and two sons who were already living in Canada. One son arranged for Dora to enter Canada as his wife (she claims she had no idea of this), despite the fact that — at thirty-five — she was "ten or fifteen" years older than him and had left behind her husband in Hungary. He had some paperwork, she recalls, and picked her up at the airport with some idea that she might be a spy. Knowing she was an artist, he had arranged a meeting for her with Alan Jarvis, by then the director of the National Gallery of Canada.

Dora showed Jarvis five or six photos of her work, and she recalls that he said, "Okay, you stay in Canada." Then he gave her the phone number of

The Girls. Dora knew almost nothing about Canada, "except that Frances Loring and Florence Wyle lived there." She claims that she had read about their studio in a book on Canada written by a German.[6]

Before she made any contact with The Girls, Dora decided to get settled and find some kind of job. She refused to go to the farm that had been pre-arranged as a place for her to work, and insisted on remaining instead in Toronto. There she found employment with a family named Olsen, house-keeping and looking after the children in exchange for room and board. "I had not five cents and only homemade shoes on my feet,"[7] she recalls, "but they were lovely people."[8] During that year, she also picked up weekend jobs in factories in her time off to begin to save some money. After a year, her husband — a painter — arrived from Hungary. They both got jobs at the CNE. "We painted animal stalls, gates, lettering, that sort of thing for $2 an hour," she recalls. "My husband was impossible. I was delighted with the job, but he was angry. He didn't want to do that." He not only left the job, but also left Dora.

After that, Dora phoned The Girls. "There are some moments," she says now, "that you never forget. Mrs. Olsen drove me there to the old church. I walked in. It was a beautiful place. They had a lot of stuff, large pieces of sculpture. I am very sensitive to smell, and I knew the moment I sniffed that this is a place where I would be happy. They were wonderful. I knew they were my friends. They took me in. They were fantastic."

The feeling was mutual: "Dora de Pédery has arrived," Frances wrote to Harry McCurry at the National Gallery. "We like her very much — and think she will be a great acquisition to Canada. We have been listening our-selves for a job for her — Think something will develop."[9]

When she left the Olsens, The Girls set Dora up in A.Y. Jackson's room in the Studio Building. He was going to be away sketching, and had agreed to this arrangement. "He was very nice to me, so sweet," she recalls. "He never slept on linen. He just used the bare mattress. But he went to Eaton's and got linen for me because I was a woman. He left a basket full of fruit. I was lucky to have Miss Loring and Miss Wyle. They knew other wonderful people and very important people."

THE GIRLS LOOKED after Dora well until she could get established. "I used to go there for beautiful dinners, which Miss Loring cooked on Sundays," Dora recalls. "They used to call me 'our little darling so-and-so,' and ask 'what can we do for you?' 'Have some eggs,' they would say, 'Have some bread,' or 'Here, take this brush,' and so on. Every Sunday that summer Miss Loring — usually wearing old shorts — would pick me up in that huge, old, dark red car and we would go to their farm. She was the *worst* driver. She could have had a very, very big accident. One time she was driving in the wrong direction on the QEW and she was stopped. She told the policeman she had no idea how she got there."

In anecdotes that strain credibility, Dora remembers The Girls' generosity. As Dora tells it, one day, when they were driving to the farm, Florence noticed that she was upset and asked her what was wrong. Dora replied, "I should be able to make more money. Then I would be able to bring my parents to Canada permanently." According to Dora, Florence didn't say a thing. Then she asked, "How much is it?" Dora just shook her head. She didn't know. Dora recalls that Florence reached into her pocket and pulled out a crumpled cheque and made it out for $700. (Dora did not need to cash the cheque; her parents came over on a government-assisted plan in 1950.) "So," says Dora, "Miss Loring said, 'Okay. We'll go to Ottawa right now. Maybe we can find something for you.' Miss Loring had a great name in Ottawa. So we went to Ottawa and she took me to see Alan Jarvis again. He remembered me and arranged to come and see my work in Toronto. My apartment was a mess, full of stuff and plaster casts all over the bed. (I used to make money doing plaster casts for other sculptors who hated doing them.) There was no table or chair. He liked a little plasticine head I had made. He took it and made six copies. He bought one for the National Gallery, gave me one, and sold the rest for me. Later, he got me a $700 grant to go to Europe for six months. It got me started."

She remembers her first success in Canada, "an over-life-size head of Frances, which I exhibited at the CNE in 1958. I borrowed tools from The Girls to make it, and I invented a mix of material that cost less than wood or plaster. Miss Loring called me to offer to take me and the sculpted head to the opening. I had it wrapped in a towel. When I unwrapped it to show her, she said, 'It's terrible! I look like *that*?'" The head — a copy of which Dora still has in her apartment — depicted Loring in an unattractive carica-ture with her eyebrows quizzically lifted up in the middle. Frances held no grudge, however, and later helped Dora get a job teaching sculpture at Toronto's Northern Vocational School.

Dora was not accepted into the SSC for a long time. "Naturally, the new-comer was not entirely welcome. I was refused membership ... for several years. But once in, one could be assured of the goodwill and helping hand of The Girls and others. For me, it proved to be the only place where I could talk about sculpture, sculptor's materials, acquire new tools, learn new casting methods, have access to reference books, and in general be among people of 'my trade.'"[10] Dora de Pédery Hunt eventually served a term as president of the society.

Dora remembers The Girls as two distinctly different characters. "Miss Loring was the strong one. She had a beautiful Spanish face, and a beautiful voice, resonant like a fine organ. Everyone who talked to her noticed it. She was like a queen. Miss Wyle always called her 'Queenie.' Miss Wyle was the poetic one. She wrote poetry, but whether she was writing or not, she was a poet. Her hair was so awful — like a boy. Her family didn't want to talk to her. They were so straitlaced; 'You can't sing. You can't dance,' they had told her. She loved animals. One time when her old black-and-white cat Benjie (Benjamin Franklin) got stuck high up in a tree in their garden, she was con-vinced he was dying there. Finally, Miss Loring called the fire people. They came with big ladders. Miss Wyle was saying, 'Be careful! Be careful!' Then Benjie turned around and came down just like that. They had to pay $5 for the fire department. They were wonderful. I loved every moment of them."

Without prompting, Dora addresses the question of whether or not The Girls were lesbian. Her face becomes distorted with anger and her accent thickens. "I could kill anybody who is telling they are lesbians. No. Nowadays nobody cares. At that time it was impossible to talk. Miss Loring talked to me about this. She said, 'I know so many lesbians, but we are not.' Besides, Miss Wyle had a professor at Chicago who fell in love with her, or maybe she loved him. It was a bad thing, didn't work out. That man left her and it was very hard on her."

Alan Jarvis got Dora started on her main career as a medallist. He commissioned her to create a Canada Council medal to present to people who had contributed to the country's cultural life. Among many others, she designed the Canadian Centennial Medal in 1967 (8 million copies distributed), the Commemorative Medal for the Montreal Olympics in 1976 (350,000 copies), and a medal with an endearing ark-load of animals for the Metro Toronto Zoo. She also made the portrait medal of Dr. Norman Bethune presented by Prime Minister Pierre Elliott Trudeau to Chairman Mao Tse-Tung in 1973.

At ninety-three she is still sculpting medals. She is almost finished one of Hungarian-Canadian poet George Faludi. Asked how she feels now about Loring and Wyle, she becomes tearful. "They are still with me," she says quietly.

FRANCES GAGE — AN aspiring young sculptor — met Frances and Florence ten years after Dora de Pédery Hunt. She, too, remembers The Girls with deep affection and gratitude.

Today, she lives with her dog and two cats in Cobourg, Ontario, in a small house with a large garden in which she has set a few sculptures — some hers, some by friends. The garage has become a cluttered studio where she stores much of her work and continues to create sculptures. Right now she's doing a bust of a neighbourhood boy. Inside the house, the rooms are filled with paper, photos, sculptures, and paintings. In the living room, there is nowhere to sit; the chairs are covered with papers, photos, and other odds and ends. On the table is a recent article about her in the local paper.[11] The photos show a young woman with blonde curls and a face like Grace Kelly. Even now, in her late eighties, she is still beautiful, though she has trouble getting up from her chair. "My knees are shot," she says in a wry, matter-of-fact way. Despite this, she still rides her adult tricycle, with her dog in the basket behind the seat, back and forth to the local market. She points out several sculptures by The Girls in her house — things they gave her, or works she had made from their casts after they died.

Asked how she decided to become a sculptor, Frances Gage tells a story that duplicates Loring's recollection of the moment she knew what her future career would be. "My parents didn't approve of art. I didn't know what art was. But one day in Hamilton when I was a girl someone gave me some clay and I knew at once what I wanted to do."[12]

The Second World War was an interruption. Gage joined the Women's Royal Navy Service (WRENS) where she was part of a team of sixteen women who eavesdropped on Japanese radio transmissions and were trained to break their code. "[Our] job was so secret, [we] didn't really know *how* secret until we were discharged."[13] After the war in 1946, Gage served on Mackenzie King's Flag Committee: "He was a dictator. It was awful. He came in and told us what he wanted: a Union Jack in the corner and a multicoloured maple leaf." Because she liked drawing and had skill in portraiture, she then studied art at the Ontario College of Art. "In first year, it was sculpture that turned me on," she recalls. So she specialized in sculpture for the next three years. She avoided Emanuel Hahn, who was in charge of sculpture. "He hated women," she said. "It must have been difficult for Elizabeth Wyn Wood living with him. She thought marrying him would improve her career. I don't think it did. But that portrait of her he did in Carrara marble; you can see the love in it. I took refuge in Will Ogilvie's class. He wasn't a sculptor like Hahn; he was a watercolourist. But he was a lovely man."[14]

It was a female couple that introduced Frances Gage to The Girls. Dr. Freda Fraser, a University of Toronto professor of medicine, and Edith Williams, who — as their veterinarian — was extremely well-acquainted with Florence and Frances, lived together and had quickly become part of the Loring-Wyle's extensive social circle. "You haven't met The Girls?" Edith asked Frances Gage in surprise. On learning she hadn't, Edith invited them all to dinner.[15]

Frances Gage remembers well her first sight of The Girls in Freda and Edith's garden. "Frances Loring, always in the vanguard, appeared ... sporting a pair of elephant-sized green trousers. Despite dieting she had become immense. She was walking with the support of one cane, while her other hand was holding her old brown coat, which trailed along on the ground behind her. A tacky green beret was pulled rakishly down on one side of her head. Florence brought up the rear, tottering along, dressed for the dinner outing in her old grey suit. Neat enough, except for the heavy stockings which drooped in wrinkles around her ankles." Frances Gage realized immediately that she was in the presence of "two very great personalities." "That was 1951 or '52," Gage recalls today. "I was twenty-seven or twenty-eight. I didn't know such people existed. I was bowled over. I'd never seen anything like it."[16]

The Girls invited Gage to tea at The Church. "It was just jammed, crammed full of sculptures, full of cats, full of dirt," she remembers. "They were so encouraging. They were so generous. They didn't have much, but what they didn't have they gave away. I was just back from a summer job at a camp in Algonquin Park. The teaching position I had arranged at Mount Allison for the fall fell through. When I told her this, Florence said, 'Come and work for us, then.' They couldn't afford it really, but they paid me to do some of their casting. I cleaned for them and washed dishes. I painted their floor and did other odd jobs." Because of the confusion that resulted from having two Franceses in The Church, Frances Gage became known as "Frances Junior," then simply as "Junior." As a result of a few additional odd jobs around Toronto and letters of introduction from Loring, she was able to go to the Art Students' League in New York where Frances and Florence had attended occasional classes when they lived in Greenwich Village. Eventually, through a combination of money from the Department of Veterans' Affairs and a Royal Society scholarship, Frances Junior had enough money to spend eight months in Paris at the École des Beaux-Arts.

In 1957, after she returned to Canada, The Girls helped Frances Junior get set up in Tom Thomson's shack behind the Studio Building. Keith McIver and his wife Edith had been living there, but had decided to move to the Albion Hills. So, for $10 a month, Frances had the use of the shack which had a Lawren Harris iceberg on one wall, a painting by A.Y. Jackson of a Quebec landscape on another wall, and a portrait of Keith McIver — all painted in a "painting bee" in 1933. There had also been another painting by Florence on the wall over Keith's bed before he married, but Edith McIver — a notoriously jealous wife — had insisted on having the "large, very pink, red-headed female nude"[17] painted out.

Once she settled into the shack, Frances Gage pursued her career relentlessly. Beautiful as she was, she had no intention of marrying. "I knew at about age four that any woman who married was a damned fool," she says acerbically. She spent plenty of time with The Girls. She remembers with delight the parties at The Church that by this time had become legendary. "The place was known for its wild parties. Once they got in Blake Mackenzie — a bagpiper — to get rid of the rats. Everyone plugged their ears and he played and played. That was the end of the rats! There was lots of drinking — except by Florence, of course, who never drank. Sometimes she'd have ginger ale cut half with water; that meant she was really living! I remember Dorothy Stevens, the painter, being quite high and saying things such as, 'I like people like you to like people like us.' There was a core group who were usually there: Alex Jackson, Keith and Edith McIver, Dick Hungerford and his wife, the sculptor Sophia, Walter and Elizabeth Gordon, Freda (who also didn't drink) and Edith Williams, their vet, Eleanor and Sam Sniderman. Robert Flaherty would show up if he was in Toronto, and so would any artist or musician who happened to be passing through town.[18] If it was winter, we drank 'slotch' — scotch poured over clean snow. We'd all get gorgeously drunk."

Frances Gage also met the few members of The Girls' families who visited. Tom Loring, Frances's nephew, lived with them briefly while he was studying forestry. And Florence had a nephew who paid a short visit once. But they saw very little of their families. Frances Junior observed first-hand the difference in The Girls' backgrounds and felt this influenced their work. "Frances — who was a much-loved, well-travelled child from a privileged background — went on developing," says Gage. "She came to like modern sculpture. But Florence — who didn't enjoy Europe on her one trip there, and whose people were unsophisticated farm people — stopped developing as an artist at some point, probably after the 'home front' War Records statuettes. She just kept doing the same thing: all those lovely female torsos, babies, and animals. Frances used to get Florence to do the children in her group statues; she said her babies and children were too tough. For Florence, it was simple: it all started and ended with the Greeks."[19]

Like Dora de Pédery Hunt, Frances Junior offers unasked her opinion on whether or not The Girls were lesbian. "They were not lesbian. I cleared up this allegation on CBC Radio. Peter Gzowski asked me about it in [his program *Morningside*] and I said 'No.' I once overheard Frances saying 'Hello, darling' at the top of the stairs. When I said something about it when she came down, she said, 'No, I'm not that kind of girl. I was talking to the cat.' Some of their friends — Keith and Jean Horne, for instance — used to spread gossip about them. In fact Frances had lovers — before and after she began living with Florence. She had a few male lovers, but kept herself free of husbands. Had it both ways, I suspect. Pretty canny! She used to say to me, 'Go to Europe. Have as many affairs as you want. Just don't bring back any Italian men.' She told me she was chased once by an Italian. She laughed and added, 'You have no idea how hard it is for a man to run with his pants down around his knees.' She used to tell me in private of some of her escapades like that. Whenever she did, she always added, '*And Florence never knew.*' As for Florence, she had an old teacher she had been in love with. She kept his photo on the table by her bed."

Frances Gage would go on to create many sculptures, notably her war memorial *Jenny the WREN* (1972) for the Cambridge Public Library in Galt, and a twice life-size reclining nude, *Rosamund* (1968), in front of the apartment building at 50 Prince Arthur Avenue, Toronto, as well as her large semi-abstracts, *The Discovery of the Hands* and *Kaspar the Cat*. She has also done portrait busts of Fred Varley and Keith McIver, among others. And several portrait heads — notably *Colonel Sam McLaughlin* (1992) for the Royal College of Physicians and Surgeons, Ottawa; *Elmer Iseler* (1991), for Roy Thomson Hall; copies of *Douglas Duncan* (1957), in several universities; and copies of *Dr. Jason Hannah*, for five Canadian universities. She is probably best known for *Woman* (1971), a seven-foot Carrara marble carving at the Women's College Hospital in Toronto. Without The Girls' help in the beginning, these works might never have existed.

IN 1957, HALF a dozen years after Frances Gage met Loring and Wyle, another young aspiring sculptor, Rebecca Sisler, met The Girls. Not only did Sisler face the formidable challenges of sculpting, she also was a single mother with a year-old son, Adam. Sisler had met her husband in Europe while she was studying there; as she puts it, "our ill-starred marriage was over almost before it began." She and the baby moved in with her mother who lived on a small rural property at Unionville, northeast of Toronto. Her studio was the slowly crumbling barn. It was a difficult time, she recalls, but Sisler was determined. "Caring for my son, and making sculpture and exhibiting it wherever I could was what I did."[20]

Now Rebecca Sisler lives with her grown son in a tiny house on the east side of Calgary, Alberta. She is a slight, neat woman, whose home and minis- cule garden are meticulously kept. She dresses stylishly and looks youthful for someone in her mid-seventies, even though she has carefully groomed white hair. She no longer sculpts much. Her talent has always been split between sculpture and writing. Her first book, in 1972, was *The Girls*, a per- sonal recollection and anecdotal biography of Loring and Wyle. In 1980, she published *Passionate Spirits*, a carefully researched, illustrated history of the RCA, and in 1986 she produced a history of the Watercolour Society of Canada called *Aquarelle!* In 1993, she wrote a history of art in the Toronto schools: *Art for Enlightenment*.

Rebecca Sisler was twenty-four when she met The Girls. They had noticed her work at a show and admired it, as had other members of the SSC. Unsure whether they should welcome her into the SSC or not, Elford Cox was dis- patched to meet her in Unionville and see more of her work.

Cox himself had had a difficult time getting into the SSC. The Girls — who could not fathom his abstract work — opposed his entry for three years on the grounds that he had no training, and worse, no wish for training. "The reason we kept you out," they candidly explained later, "was that you didn't know a bloody thing about anatomy."[21] Eventually, they softened, realizing that this young teacher at Upper Canada College was serious and wanted to define good sculpture for himself. He was included in their Saturday night gatherings at The Church, admitted to the SSC, and was soon exhibiting his remarkable abstract and semi-abstract work alongside their own.

Cox's reaction to Sisler's work was positive, but she soon realized he held a grudge towards Loring. "As we relaxed over a cup of tea in the kitchen after he looked at my work," she recalls, "we discussed the SSC and Loring's name came up. 'Loring needs her wings clipped,' Cox declared, 'And I'm just the one to do it!'"[22]

Sisler met Frances first, at a meeting of the SSC in sculptor Pauline

Redsell's studio in the old "Village" on Gerrard Street. Florence was not there, having given up all meetings some years earlier. Sisler remembers well this first encounter with Frances. "I was sitting among my new colleagues feeling distinctly humble even before Frances's startling figure loomed in the doorway, leaning heavily on her cane. She was ungainly and untidy. When she lowered herself down on the couch she took up room for two. She looked tired. Could this be the celebrated sculptor so feted for her success?"[23]

Any doubt was dispelled when Frances spoke. She greeted Rebecca warmly when she was introduced. As Sisler recalls, "She was certainly not shy; she radiated acute intelligence, common sense — and utter charm. 'Miss Wyle and I know your work well,' she said to me. 'It's the real thing.' She made me feel one among equals. I was able to thaw out enough to enjoy the rest of the meeting, even to crack an inward smile when I saw that El Cox was treating her with both affection and deference just like everyone else."[24]

A business matter at the ssc led to Sisler meeting Florence, not long after. The ssc's battered sculpture stands, used as platforms for sculpting and for displays, had been replaced by Frances on the understanding that members would reimburse her when they could. When Sisler called at The Church to pay for her stand, Florence answered the door. "She was a diminutive figure with metal-rimmed glasses and spiking hair, which gave her the appearance of a suspicious, aging owl," recalls Sisler. When Rebecca explained why she was there, Florence's demeanour changed into that of "a welcoming, beautiful, warmly human sprite," and she invited her in. "'Frances!' Florence called. 'It's young Sisler come to give us twenty dollars!' A cane could then be heard thumping on the floor from somewhere in the depths of the building. 'It takes Miss Loring a while to get where she's going,' Florence said matter-of-factly. When she finally appeared, Frances urged me to call in my mother and small son who were waiting in the car. My son felt more comfortable with Florence," says Sisler. "Frances was overwhelming to him." Their friendship went on from there.

Rebecca Sisler recalls that Frances loved social gatherings, even though she could hardly hobble around. She would phone Rebecca to ask for a drive to operas or concerts. On such occasions, she'd set up a bed in the studio and invite Rebecca for supper. "We'd have a drink of Canadian Club before supper," she recalls, "while Florence, who hardly ever went out, sat nearby reading some scientific treatise or a detective mystery. After dinner, I'd somehow get Frances into the car." As for Frances's clothes, Sisler recalls they were "awful." Her dramatic evening gowns were a thing of the past. She had become so large, she had to have things made. "She had a large bosom and things would fall onto it. So her clothes were very dirty with splotches of food. On the rare occasions when Florence did go out, she never wore anything but her gray suit and a black velvet tie, and brogues with cotton stockings." One friend told Sisler that Florence once wore an old velvet window curtain to a formal opening.[25]

Sisler visited their farm too, an experience she describes vividly in *The Girls*. Though it sounded charming, the reality was anything but. As Sisler recalls, "It was a shack really, ready to tumble down at any minute." Until she heard about the sale of gravel that had kept The Girls alive at the end of the Depression, she had no idea how poor they were. "Once I naively said to them that if I could earn $2,000 a year from my sculpture, I'd be satisfied. They laughed and said, 'My dear, there have been many years we did not make $2,000!'"

Like Frances Gage, Rebecca Sisler met the various family members who showed up at The Church from time to time. She heard a great deal about Loring's father, Frank. People were always saying that he was "a legend in the north." She also read about him in the papers. One article, shortly before his death at seventy-nine in 1938, called him "A Dean among Canadian Mining Engineers." One of his obituaries recalling his pioneering exploits at Rossland, Cobalt, and Kirkland Lake, noted that he was founder of the Canadian Institute of Mining and Metallurgy, and said he was "known for his unbounded faith in Canada's north and her resources."[26] Sisler met Frances's nephews Bill and Tom, sent to Toronto for several occasions and over holidays by her brother Ernest, who worked as a mining engineer in Fisher, Quebec. Ernest had a daughter, Alice, but she had shocked the family by becoming a nun at a convent on Bayview Avenue in Toronto.

Like Frances Gage, Sisler noticed the difference between Frances and Florence and their work, and attributed it to their different backgrounds. "Frances — whose family carried culture with them wherever they went —

was full of life in a joyous kind of way," she recalls. "Florence — who came from puritanical farming people — was quieter, until you got to know her. Her family had little to do with her. They thought it was appalling that she had taken up sculpture." As for their work, within the bounds of neoclassicism (which they said they were too old to change), Frances was suited to the public, monumental statue. Florence was not. As Sisler sees it, these differences were subsumed in their "fierce loyalty to their work." In that they were totally one: dedicated and professional. Even the stresses that accompanied competition with each other as they submitted maquettes for the same commissions did not divide them. "I never saw any hard feelings expressed between them," Sisler — like many others — observes. "They were delighted when the other one got an assignment."[27] Frances always maintained that Florence was the better sculptor.

Rebecca Sisler is clear on the lesbian question in her book *The Girls*. Today, she still holds that they were not lesbian. It was a question she asked the fifty or more people she interviewed for her book. "Some were aghast at the question," she recalls. "But all of them said 'No.' These were people, in some cases, who did have lesbian friends. Gwen Williams, for example, said that she played [piano accompaniment] for a famous singer who had a long-time partner, and there was a feeling between them that was totally missing between Loring and Wyle. A.Y. Jackson told me that Frances had a pretty active sex life with men. Actually the rumours of lesbianism upset Frances enormously. She was very protective of Florence and tried to make sure nothing was said to her. They brought the subject up with me. Frances thought the idea hilarious that anyone should bother to think such a thing. Once she said to a friend, 'Could you possibly imagine the fastidious Florence?'"[28]

Thanks in part to The Girls' acceptance of her as an equal from the start, Rebecca Sisler became a full-fledged sculptor in her own right. In 1957 she carved the walnut *Crucifix* for St. Paul's United Church in Lindsay, Ontario and sculpted *The Exile* in Indiana limestone. In 1959, the Art Gallery of Ontario bought her walnut carving *Tree of Life*. *The Minstrels*, done in Praedes marble, was installed in Centennial Park, St. Thomas, Ontario, in 1966. Her red cedar *Continuum* is in the Toronto Board of Education's Sesquicentennial

Museum. Her *Dancer* in Indiana limestone was acquired by an Ottawa collector in 1977. In 2005, she completed *Unfurling* in black walnut.[29]

Today Sisler has turned back to writing. Having made a strong contribution to Canada's art history, she is now trying her hand at a novel.

Unlike Dora de Pédery Hunt, Frances Gage, and Rebecca Sisler, Eleanor Milne was only briefly acquainted with Loring and Wyle. But Milne owes her successful career as Dominion Sculptor for three decades, 1961–93, partly to The Girls — especially Frances Loring. Of the more than twenty applicants for this position, Milne was the only woman. It is doubtful that she would have been selected for the position if The Girls had not paved the way by showing that women were capable of monumental sculpture. It is even doubtful that such a position as Dominion Sculptor would have been created in Canada (the only country in the world to have it) if Wyle and — particularly — Loring had not played a major role in consolidating Canada's national identity through their public statues after the Great War.

According to Sandra Alfoldy, who interviewed Milne in 1998, Milne met The Girls in the 1940s on a trip to Toronto when Montreal was a "very separate sphere." She had studied with Arthur Lismer for two years (1944–46) at the Montreal Museum of Fine Arts School of Design, and went to Toronto to learn more about the art scene there. The Girls befriended her, invited her to stay with them, and gave her meals. They advised her to make her casts from agar (isinglass, like gelatin). "They were nice to young artists and helped them as much as they could," Milne recalls.[30]

Milne also studied with Ivan Meštrović at the University of Syracuse in classes that were very small: "We were allowed to use the studio at any time at all — late at night, weekends," one of Milne's fellow students recalls. "And most of us did. Meštrović brought to us in the autumn of his life a quality of spirit, a way of seeing light, and a total commitment to hard work."[31] In this, too, Loring played an important role. Loring herself had made the pilgrimage to Syracuse in 1947 to meet the great man whose sculpture she admired beyond all other living sculptors — a pilgrimage that gave her common ground with Milne. There is a direct line from the Yugoslavian monumentalist Meštrović, to the Canadian monumentalist Loring, to the Dominion Sculptor Eleanor Milne.

In her years as Dominion Sculptor, Milne, like Wyle and especially Loring before her, rendered in stone the history and values of Canada. She contributed many elements to the Centre Block of Parliament in Ottawa where Loring had done her *War Widow* and *Recording Angel* after the Great War. Like Loring, Milne adapted Meštrović's "modern Gothic" style to the Gothic architecture of Parliament Hill. She created stone carvings of the *History of Canada*, the *British North America Act*, and the *Origin of Life in Canada* for the House of Commons. Her inclusion of First Nations peoples in her *History of Canada* frieze may owe something to works like Loring's *Eskimo Mother and Child* and Wyle's Haida productions and to their early struggle to include Inuit sculptors in the Sculptors' Society of Canada.

Through their support and encouragement of younger sculptors, and through the example they set, Frances Loring and Florence Wyle were an essential part of the establishment and continuation of Canadian sculpture through these and other young sculptors.

The Fall of 1952 ⤏

"This mid-century date, 1950, is a good time for self-examination," wrote Andrew Bell in his review[1] of a remarkable art show in March at the Art Gallery of Toronto. The show celebrated the gallery's Golden Jubilee, but, more importantly, it was intended to be a visual correlative to the formal briefs of the Royal Commission on the Arts, Letters and Sciences (the Massey-Lévesque Commission, 1949–51) that would eventually result in the establishment of the Canada Council. If the commission were investigating the state of the arts in Canada at mid-century, it made sense to display artistic works the public could see and judge for themselves.

In this show — for the first time — nearly all of the important artistic organizations in the country merged their usually separate annual shows into one huge display. These organizations included the RCA, the Canadian Group of Painters (which had amalgamated the Group of Seven, the Beaver Hall Hill Group, and others), the OSA, the Canadian Society of Painters in Water Colour, the SSC, the Canadian Society of Graphic Art, the Royal Architectural Institute, the Canadian Handicrafts Guild, the Canadian Guild of Potters, and the Spinners and Weavers of Ontario, among others. Anyone in Canada could submit entries; more than 2,000 were received, and 816 were selected. The gallery's rooms could not hold all of these, and some spilled into the hallways. Crowds were much larger than normal for the first week of the exhibition. Sales of works were unusually high.

But Andrew Bell found the exhibition disappointing. To him, the artist should be someone with "spark" and "sparkle": "The artists who endure," he wrote, "are those with a particular bite or passion to their stuff, men who acknowledge the joys and sorrows and problems of their period and depict them according to their own burning lights — straight." Such artists were not to be found in this exhibition. Instead, Bell found example after example of Canada's "national reserve." "Canadians are an inhibited people. We find it infernally difficult to say adequately what we think or feel. Nor do we like bringing out into the open unpleasant things ... We are disciples of a gentle compromise which aims to please as many as possible of the people all the time. It has been so in our politics and our private lives and this exhibition was a startling demonstration that it is equally true in our arts."

Bell found the so-called "differences" between various painting "movements" "exceedingly small." As for the room devoted to sculpture, he thought it "resembled exactly a cemetery. Works were ranged about on pedestals like so many ill-placed tombstones. There were a few pleasant works, yes, and it is important to acknowledge how hard it is in Canada to be a sculptor; yet here, too, the work was blemished by tightness and compromise." Bell not only blamed the "inhibited" disposition of Canadian artists for the insipid display, he also blamed the general public: "We still think of our artists as luxuries, and deny them scandalously the adrenalin of basic encouragement."

Bell's mid-century assessment could be seen as a statement about the necessity for government support of the arts. But it could also be seen as a challenge to artists to take risks, experiment according to their own impulses, and abandon the need to please a public that was more comfortable with well-established — even out-worn — traditions in the arts than with anything revolutionary.

Bell was not the only one to note this situation. Another *Canadian Art* article in 1950 was fittingly titled "Contemporary Canadian Sculpture Shows More Caution than Experiment," and Canadian sculptors were criticized as "too unassumingly naturalist to be regarded as 'contemporary.'"[2] Christine Boyanoski confirms that "the 1950s represented a period of hiatus in sculpture."[3] According to her, Loring and Wyle — and others like them — "were soon to be eclipsed ... by a new generation rooted in Surrealist sculpture of the 1930s, whose use of the 'found object' took sculpture into the realms of conceptual art." Loring and Wyle had become old-fashioned. Even their health, after years of strain, was beginning to wane. Frances had a gallstone operation in 1949; that same year Florence had a heart condition for which she was given injections of vitamin E.

Though Frances — described as "a friendly, dynamic woman who is 63 and looks 50" — bravely tried to move forward in her public lectures to include both "primitive" sculpture (a focal point of modernism ever since Braque and Picasso used African masks to challenge three-dimensional space in Cubism) and contemporary abstract work, it is clear she is only touching the surface. In one major well-attended lecture, "A Sculptor Looks at Sculpture," at the National Gallery in Ottawa amid seventy-two pieces of sculpture, she moved from Rodin's *Thinker* — "not the intellectual thinker, but the powerful primitive man to whom thought has come. It's like the birth of the first thought. The first questioning and the first Why?" — to the "urgency" in Canada to "encourage" the "sculptural talent of the Indian race." She deplored the use of Canada's primitive peoples for making tourist knick-knacks: "We must stop shoving them into the past. This race, especially endowed to be sculptors, should find expression in the life of today." Though Loring can be seen here to argue for the development of Native and Inuit sculpture which was to play such an important role in the Canadian arts, she is — from her own perspective — reiterating her father's great conviction in the artistic potential of an undiscovered pioneer country — a belief she profoundly endorsed.

Frances Loring recognized that her career — along with Canadian sculpture generally — was flagging in the early 1950s. The taste for war monuments after the Second World War had been nothing like the enthusiasm for them that followed the Great War. "I do very much need to get away and brush off some cobwebs," she wrote to Harry McCurry in response to his invitation that she and A.Y. Jackson should make a two-week tour of northern Alberta in October 1952 as an educational venture for the Canadian arts.[4]

This tour — sponsored by the National Gallery of Canada, the Fine Arts Department of the University of Alberta, the Cultural Relations Board of Alberta's Department of Provincial Economic Affairs, as well as a few local organizations such as the Rotary Club — was widely covered by the media. A photo in the *Edmonton Journal* shows Loring — sporting a voluminous jacket with aboriginal designs and a black beret roguishly drawn over one ear — holding one of Florence's woodcarvings in each hand.[5] She and A.Y. departed Toronto on 17 October. Their strenuous itinerary of towns and villages in the Peace River district included Dawson Creek (at the beginning of the Alaska Highway), Beaverlodge, Grande Prairie, Spirit River, Fairview, Berwyn, Peace River, McLennan, and High Prairie. Later, on 4 November, they lectured at Coste House in Calgary. Blake MacKenzie, Alberta's representative for cultural affairs, accompanied them as they drove by car from place to place. They ended up at Winnipeg on 5 November, where Jackson stayed with painter L.L. Fitzgerald and Loring visited an old friend, Florence Brigden, and her husband. In all, they covered 1,900 kilometres.

The format included talks by both artists, using slides, followed by films. These were the NFB films *Third Dimension* (1947), which featured Loring among other Canadian sculptors, and *Portrait of a Painter* (1941), a short film showing Jackson (assisted by Keith McIver) in canoe and on snowshoes — pitching tents or spending jolly evenings playing cards with French-Canadian hosts. Jackson ("Père Raquette," Father Snowshoe, to the French-Canadians) is seen making sketches in the wilderness, discussing techniques, and then enlarging the sketches in the Studio Building in Toronto later. Admission to some of the lectures was free; others took a collection at the door. Before or after the presentations — or the following day — Jackson was available to offer suggestions to local painters of all ages who brought in their work.

Grande Prairie, where the event was held on 22 October in the high school auditorium, was typical. Jackson reviewed and criticized work done by the Grande Prairie Art Group in the hour before the lecture ("[M]ost constructive and much appreciated," the local paper reported). Then Frances gave her illustrated lecture on Egyptian and Greek sculpture, Michelangelo, some French compositions, and modern Canadian work. Blake MacKenzie introduced Jackson as "a revolutionary who became respectable."[6] Jackson spoke, then showed films and pictures of Canadian scenes. "Miss Loring and Dr. Jackson were warmly applauded by the audience which was regrettably small, considering that this was an opportunity which will scarcely repeat itself for the people of this town to see and hear these two artists, who are so famous in their own achievements and so distinctively Canadian."[7]

According to Rebecca Sisler, "Frances grumbled laughingly for years afterwards that A.Y. ... always managed to upstage her by taking the platform first. Since he was a fascinating but garrulous talker, the audience would be restive by the time Frances got up to speak. At the end of one evening [probably at Grande Prairie], A.Y. warmly congratulated her on her talk, saying that he had never heard her speak so well. 'No wonder!' Frances said when she repeated the story later. 'It was the first chance I'd had to speak first and with enough time to develop my theme properly!'"

Near the end of the Peace River tour, on 28 October, things went awry. Night had fallen as they drove, and they hit a large bump in the road. Not until many miles had passed did they realize that the trunk had sprung open and Jackson's suitcase, MacKenzie's dunnage bag, and Frances's sculpture photos were gone. Back they went, but after hundreds of kilometres in the dark without seeing a trace of their things, they gave up and turned back to High River. "A.Y. was quite concerned, as it meant that he was left with only the clothes on his back. They rolled into High Prairie and their hotel, empty-handed, at 6:45 in the morning."[8] "The frail ones are still sleeping," Frances wrote an Edmonton friend, Mrs. H.A. (Bobby) Dyde, "but I have had my breakfast — my tummy says breakfast at nine no matter what. Such a beautiful night it was, though — I really am not a bit tired."[9]

Back at The Church in Toronto, Florence was having adventures of her own. She had lost interest in travel. "Frances cannot get Florence to go anywhere," A.Y. Jackson wrote to a friend. "She is tired and listless, and then I think she is so attached to her cats she won't leave them."[10] In the spring, The Girls had decided to use the balance of their gravel money from the farm at Cherry Wood to build a separate studio wing for Florence that would include her own bedroom and bathroom. The old stationmaster's stove, which had rendered guests too hot on one side and too cold on the other for forty years, was finally replaced by an oil furnace. Trees had been cleared by late June. By August, the studio was in complete chaos. Workmen had temporarily closed both entrances. Frances complained, "I haven't reduced quite enough for the window we have to use to get in and out."[11] The prospect of a trip west that fall was a welcome escape.

Florence, the expert craftsman, "could hardly bear to watch the [workmen's] slipshod methods and disorganized movements. 'They climb over a pile of concrete blocks sixty-two times a day rather than move them. It would only take two minutes to move the silly things,' she wrote to Bobby Dyde ... 'Well, well. I guess I am too orderly.'"[12]

Perhaps Florence *wasn't* too orderly. Against her explicit advice, the workmen had piled scrap material in her new wing's fireplace and decided to burn it. The scrap blazed up and set fire to the wall between the new and the old studios. Frances Gage happened to be on her way to The Church at the time, and arrived to find firefighters swarming all over the roof with axes. "They had broken through the skylight and smoke was billowing out in a cloud."[13] All Florence could think of was her black-and-white cat "Petey" (Peter the Great). Firefighters were forcibly holding her back from trying to get into The Church to find him. She was distraught.

Before the fire was out, the fire chief sent men with large tarpaulins into the studio to cover all the sculpture. "In spite of soaking the whole place with water, no major works were seriously harmed."[14] And eventually "Petey" was found hiding safely under the table in the Crypt.

This event did nothing to assuage the apprehensions of local residents. There had already been strong objections when the new wing was proposed. The flocks of pigeons The Girls encouraged to nest everywhere had raised the ire of one neighbour who had reshingled his roof with dark blue asphalt tile (The Girls airily suggested, "You should just paint your roof all white!").[15] Avian control was a concept they wanted no part of. The neighbours seemed to expect that the eyesore Church would "dilapidate itself out of existence."[16] The fact that new sewers and a new wing were going in dashed that hope. Only the new coat of respectable pale-grey paint (no doubt intended to minimize the effect of the pigeon droppings) covering the peeling and disfigured original red paint reassured them for the time being.[17]

It was hard to say which of The Girls had endured more over the past two weeks when Florence and some friends met Frances and Jackson at the airport. Frances was exhausted and had a bad cold. Jackson was uncharacteristically silent. He admitted later "to having talked more out West than he ever had in his life." Frances wrote wryly to Bobby Dyde, "Florence seems to have had a good time — which indicates she needs more excitement. Hope she doesn't realize it and start more excitement."[18]

In the end, Florence was delighted with her studio, bathroom, new bedroom, and casting room. The north-facing wall of windows bathed her studio in a greenish light reflected from the trees, and soon she was hard at work again filling the room with a maze of works in various stages of completion. "No one entered that maze," Rebecca Sisler recalls, "without being touched by the tranquility of spirit that permeated the area. It was like a quiet refuge from the tumult of the world, from which one came away strangely renewed."[19]

Frances — who enjoyed the tumult of the world — took over the main studio as a space to conduct committee work and business related to sculpture. She sat on the Art Gallery of Toronto's Canadian Collection Committee from 1950–55, where she fought regularly with Martin Baldwin, the new director. (On one occasion, she snapped, "It would take more than either a Martin or a Baldwin to put down a Loring!")[20] She also took an active role in organizing an exhibition of the work of Ivan Meštrović in 1951–52. (She and Florence and Donald Stewart — who had become president of the SSC in 1947 — visited the great monumentalist in Syracuse, where he was teaching at the University of Syracuse. She invited him and his wife to stay with them when the exhibition opened in Toronto, but his wife's health prevented him from attending.)[21] In addition, she kept her hand in the SSC, the RCA, and the OSA. But her disabilities forced her into prolonged periods of physical inactivity, and she conducted her "meetings" about sculpture from a comfortable chair by telephone.

The wild parties at The Church had inevitably come to an end, though the Loring-Wyles's attendance at Art Gallery openings continued. As Rebecca Sisler recalls, "The Girls were still showstoppers at such events. As one artist recalled, many of these rather conservative gatherings would not have been particularly memorable without the presence of The Girls. Frances was decked out [at one opening] in some sort of green satin cape, topped by a turban. She was splendid. Or, as one artist described her, 'enough to terrify God.' Florence, deaf to the call of fashion, had ceased making concessions to formal dress. For the next twenty years she found her ancient grey flannel suit quite adequate to any occasion. 'They must be very wealthy,' people concluded."[22] Instead of coming for Saturday night parties, friends from all walks of life dropped in to visit. "It was not unusual for a friend happening by at tea time to find himself sitting down around the fireplace with anyone from the latest casualty with a hard luck story to a diplomat or Cabinet minister. Frances would sit on the couch, vivid with charm, intelligence, and sometimes wicked humour. Florence, alternatively pithy or warmly earthy ... clumped about in her heavy shoes, doing the tea honours."[23]

Frances was just as pleased about her western tour with A.Y. Jackson as Florence was with her new quarters. For years to come she would refer to the great experience it was to speak to busloads of students who responded so positively to sculpture and painting. "There were far more questions from the young people of that remote area than from the informed and well-off audiences that [I] was used to encountering at home," she told Rebecca Sisler.[24] "The school children were wonderful," she told one reporter on her return. "They were so thrilled and excited to hear about art and sculpture and to talk about it, and they all wanted to know how they could begin." Her only worry was how their enthusiasm could be sustained. "It's all very well to stir up their interest, but where do they go from here?" she asked.[25] But above all, her experience in the Peace River district confirmed the long-held conviction she had adopted from her father: that the Canadian wilderness was a place of vast potential, whether that potential was in geological resources or the arts. "The great sculptors in Canada's future," she predicted, "would come from the frontier country ... They can discard tradition and start fresh."[26]

Rivers and Trophies ⤸

It is not clear exactly when Florence Wyle seriously began to carve female torsos in wood for her *Rivers of America* series. Both Girls were used to turning to woodcarving when they were tired of working hard on clay, plaster, and stone. "When I want to relax, I do a bit of wood-carving," Frances once told a reporter.[1] Apart from woodcarving, their only relaxation was a little gardening and reading.

But Florence's carved torsos were hardly tossed off as relaxation; they were works of art in their own right. As early as 1935, she had carved an elegant female *Torso* in soft pine, one truncated arm uplifted, which was bought by the Winnipeg Art Gallery. And in 1944 she created another *Nude* with a short drape over one shoulder in wood for the National Gallery of Canada. But these smooth, neoclassical works were bland compared to the series of torsos she began carving in the late 1940s.

Cost was probably a factor in this new direction for Florence. One critic commented after the ssc's seventh exhibition at the Art Gallery of Toronto from 18 March to 9 April 1944 (later re-shown at the London Art Museum), "wartime conditions probably accounted ... for the lack of variety in architectural sculpture which was evident in the show."[2] The work of the fourteen members of the ssc no doubt did suffer from wartime conditions. Commissions for memorials were far fewer than they had been after the Great War. Many communities simply added lists of names of casualties from the Second World War to monuments already in place from the Great War. The very materials used by sculptors — such as wire, wood, pipes of all shapes and sizes, metals and metallic materials, rubber, burlap, linen, lath, plaster, paints, lacquers, and other finishes for their armatures — were those most needed for the war effort. In fact, sculptors were the first artists to suffer shortages of supplies and tools once the war industry got underway. They had to scrounge antimonious lead, sticks, stones, rags, cement, wire from newspaper bundles, twigs, and odd leavings in garbage dumps. Elizabeth Wyn Wood, who had planned to use imported materials for two of the fountains she created for the Oakes Garden in Niagara Falls, was forced to resort to native limestone. "[The fountains] were originally designed for cast glass, white marble and mosaic ..." Making the best of the situation, she rationalized, "Probably this sterner drab stone, rather than more luxurious, fragile and happier imported materials, have given them more enduring and honest form, even if they have less dramatic value, than electrically lit glass and coloured mosaic."[3]

Though cost was probably a factor in Florence's decision to sculpt from wood in the late 1940s, it could also have been that here she found another, challenging outlet for her favourite subject: the female form. In 1938 she had told an interviewer, "I prefer figure work to portrait work because it is better sculpture as a rule. I do most of my own stone carving and a lot of woodcarving, which is very interesting and," she added crustily with reference to the pressure on women to turn to crafts to help soldiers, "more so than knitting."[4]

Whatever her reasons, Florence now began to produce female torsos that drew on the neoclassic tradition without slavishly imitating it. For her, these carvings were experimental. Though they did not take woodcarving into the semi-abstract or the abstract, as Elford Cox had done for ten years or more, they pushed the limits within which she had so far worked. The series of ten[5] torsos carved from Canadian sumac was called *Rivers of America* — a name that suggested Florence perceived herself as North-American, rather than Canadian. Although she is more likely to have been influenced by Cox (who had done at least one male torso to display the grain of cedar in 1942[6] and would do a semi-abstract female torso in marble in 1953[7]) than by early sculpture, there existed a precedent for her concept in the work of the early American sculptor William Rush, who created a pine life-size *Allegory of the Schuylkill River* in 1809.[8] As Christine Boyanoski describes Wyle's new works — which were not life-size like Rush's, but just over a foot high — "She went beyond earlier works and exploited the wood to its fullest by using the strong [purple] grain of the sumac to define individual forms, the concentric rings around the breasts and belly in *The Platte* and *The Hudson*, for example, and by allowing an element of 'non finito' with some of the outer bark untouched, as in *The Illinois*, [where] the figure appears to emerge from its woody sheath, a sort of Daphne in reverse. Of all the rivers, *The Hudson* most strongly maintains the cylindrical shape of the tree."[9]

One *Saturday Night* interviewer who visited The Church in November 1944 singled out Florence's wood sculptures for extravagant praise. Obviously taken by The Girls, who were now 62 and 57 and appeared as a longstanding couple, Lyn Harrington wrote, "Not least in charm, are the beautiful wood-carvings done by Florence Wyle. Her torsos in wood are breathtaking."[10] After the summer 1949 Exhibition of Canadian Sculpture, critics again singled out Florence's *Rivers of America* series. "The *Rivers of America*, eight [sic] modest woodcarvings in sumac, by Florence Wyle, are hard to describe. Each is a feminine form (or a part thereof!) and is intended to symbolize a large American river. The symbolism to me was rather far-fetched, but not so the delicacy and beauty of treatment. Every one in its own way is a gem, and Miss Wyle achieves a real *tour de force* in the manner in which she squeezes every ounce of nuance out of the wood graining."[11]

Florence explained her method as follows: "[I do not usually model directly from nature] although I have done so in the past, and constantly observe nature. Take the human body, the oldest symbol for the expression of thoughts and feelings in the history of art. You copy different models for years and eventually gain an instinctive knowledge of anatomy. It then becomes fatally easy to make your statue a copy of the model, rather than a symbol for your ideas. Generally, I design the statue first, get the idea and the movement, then compare the statue with a model to avoid anatomical errors."[12]

Florence hoped to sell the *Rivers of America* as a series to a single buyer or gallery. (One price list indicates she wanted $250 for each.)[13] This was not to be, and the series went one by one to individual buyers, as did three later works in the same vein: *Spring* (1951), *Summer* (1952), and *Autumn* (1953), as well as a female *Atlas* holding up the world (ca. 1953).[14] In 1951, she earned some money on a commission in Calgary to do two painted plaster reliefs, *Little Boy Blue* and *Innocence*, for the Alberta Red Cross Crippled Children's Hospital. And in 1953 for $2,000,[15] she completed a thirteen-foot-wide, five-foot-high low-relief panel of typical Ontario farm animals for the MacNabb Memorial Library in the Ontario Veterinary College at Guelph.[16] With the confidence of one who knows something about farming, she said, "[They are] not thoroughbred but good stock, horse, cows, chickens, dog, ducks, barn, trees, gulls — good earthy creatures."[17] The panel was inspired by an illustration used by Master Feeds of Toronto on calendars and feed bags during the 1950s. At the same time, Frances did a portrait bust of A.L. MacNabb, principal of the college from 1945–50.[18]

THE DISPLAY OF Florence's *Rivers of America* at the new Laing Gallery on Bloor Street West led to a far more important commission. Blair Laing had transformed the Laing Gallery, which had been established by his father twenty-five years earlier, into what he claimed somewhat extravagantly was "the first commercial art show-room in America." Its opening show featured paintings of Mexico by York Wilson; Frank (Franz) Johnston's "wooded, watery landscapes"; Varley's paintings of the Inuit; Jackson's depictions of boreal forest; and Lawren Harris's dark mountain peaks, which one critic found "infinitely more fetching than his ice-cream cones of snowclad mountains."[19] Florence's spectacular *Rivers of America* series were the only sculptures.

It was during this time that Calvert Distillers took over as sponsors of the expanded Dominion Drama Festival. The new sponsors decided that trophies should be made as annual awards for winners from the various regions of Canada. This shift of sponsorship in the arts from an elite government institution to a wealthy business enterprise spoke of dramatic changes in the positioning of the arts in society. After one attempt to procure a design had failed, The Girls' friend, painter A.J. Casson, advised David Ongley, QC and president of the festival, and Pauline McGibbon, the other committee member (later Lieutenant-Governor of Ontario, 1974–80), to visit the Laing Gallery and have a look at Florence's small carvings. They decided at once that carvings of a similar nature — though not in the "non finito" style, but in a more traditional finished style — would make striking trophies for the festival. As Rebecca Sisler recalls, Mrs. McGibbon visited The Girls for tea, and "joined the ranks of those who found themselves not altogether prepared for the Church and its occupants. She could not help but notice that cleanliness was not one of the prime requisites ... But, as usual, The Girls' diverting personalities soon drew attention away from chips of wood in the teacups and bits of plaster on the cake."[20]

A commission for several trophies was offered in 1953. Florence was to carve the top festival award — the Calvert Trophy, *Drama*, at thirty inches, a piece somewhat larger than the rest of the trophies. True to form, Florence drew from the solemn, draped Greek tradition for this trophy. Because there were to be fourteen trophies representing "the Influences on the Theatre,"[21] the commission was shared among Florence, Frances, and the Quebec sculptor, Sylvia Daoust.

The Girls had known and admired the fifty-one-year-old Sylvia Daoust for years; she had shown her lovely, slightly elongated woodcarvings — often on religious themes — frequently in Toronto. Walter Abell praised her tender, haloed *Madonna* in wild cherry wood: "Rarely did the more baroque Madonnas of earlier French Canada equal this modern one either in depth of feeling or in unity of design."[22] The inclusion of Sylvia Daoust as the third sculptor — rather than Elizabeth Wyn Wood, for example — indicated the committee's interest in representing both French and English Canada in the creation of national drama trophies — a principle clearly established by Frances Loring at the time the SSC was founded in 1928.

In addition to the main trophy in white wood, Wyle created *Poetry* (appropriate, since she continued to write her own poetry), *Wisdom, Humility,* and *Truth*. In preparation for these allegorical carvings, Florence wrote out definitions that not only indicate her sculptural aims, but also reveal her spiritual, moral, and aesthetic philosophy of life: "Poetry — a crystallization of man's natural love of life and growth and beauty; Wisdom — knowledge that enables man to see and judge the way of life and make the road more bright for those who follow after; Humility — an instructive understanding of the immensity and glory of the universal and man's place therein; Truth — the life force, that moves the universe."[23] When asked by a journalist if the rewards of sculpture are worth it, she replied crisply, "Depends what you want from life. If you want to make a lot of money — well few sculptors have ever become rich. And only a few are permanently famous. But if you want to create beauty in lasting form, then sculpture is worthwhile. Most of the rewards are likely to be spiritual."[24] The media seized on the occasion almost before the trophies were begun. One photo shows Florence's cat Peter the Great on the worktable, "as usual superintend[ing]" as she works on *Drama*.[25]

Frances Loring undertook the figures for *Invocation* (a close reworking of her early plaster of the same title), *Dance*, *Mystery*, and *Nature*. (These were later renamed *Dance*, *Silence*, and *Faun*.) Sylvia created *Charity*, *Music*, *Love*, *Meditation*, and *Tragedy*.

The woods each sculptor wanted to use were not available in Canada. White wood, tulip wood, and mahogany had to be ordered from a hardwood outlet in New York. After a long wait, The Girls sent letters of inquiry. The wood had been shipped. Another long wait, then a tracer was put on the shipment through border customs. "Finally an extensive search unearthed the wood in the corner of a customs shed — packed in old onion bags. They had been set aside for fumigation ... [O]nions had suffered a blight that year, and nothing connected with them was allowed across the border without being decontaminated."[26]

Soon Florence and Frances were hard at work, chipping the various woods into rough shape, then following the grain with hammer and chisel. "F. and I have been pretty busy for elderly ladies (ha! ha!)," Florence wrote a friend.[27] David Ongley and Pauline McGibbon dropped in perhaps more than was necessary to supervise the progress of the trophies, bearing gifts of vanilla ice cream for Florence and rye whiskey for Frances.

The trophies were superb. Florence had done *Wisdom* in mahogany, and *Truth*, *Poetry*, and *Humility* (also called *Dedication*) in the strong-grained sumac she had used for her *Rivers of America* series. Frances had used white wood for *Dance*, and mahogany for *Invocation*, *Silence*, and — by far the most unusual of the trophies — *Faun*, a hoofed satyr musing atop a stump. Sylvia Daoust used maple for her *Charity*, red birch for *Music* (she had already done a lovely Ste. Cécile, patron saint of music),[28] mahogany for *Love*, and tulip wood for *Tragedy* and *Meditation*. The trophies — fifteen in all — are in the Canadian Museum of Civilization.

Sylvia was "a guest of Miss Frances Loring" when the exhibition of the Calvert Drama Festival Trophies opened at the Art Gallery of Toronto on 10 June 1953[29] — an event duly reported in the *Globe and Mail*'s "Social and Personal Notes."

The trophies — excellent though they were — caused a political brouhaha. How could such refined arts trophies in honour of the dignified cause of drama be sponsored — even *named* — after a liquor company? The very idea of replacing an award that originated with Lord Bessborough, the Governor General, with the name of a liquor company was scandalous. It took another Governor General — Vincent Massey — to quiet the brouhaha. Massey took it upon himself to attend the final festival in May of that year in Victoria, B.C., and on the night of the awards ceremony, he himself presented the controversial awards to the winners.

THAT SAME YEAR, Florence was honoured officially for her years of devotion to sculpture. Ironically it mentioned the art societies of which Florence had never been fond. She received the announcement from Buckingham Palace that she had been awarded a Coronation Medal "to be worn in commemoration of Her Majesty's Coronation" on the occasion of Queen Elizabeth II's coronation on 2 June 1953 for her "distinguished place as a member of Canadian Art societies."[30] She could no longer quip that the only award she had won was "a ten dollar prize for a wallpaper design" at the Art Institute of Chicago.[31]

In a neatly handwritten letter she replied on 20 August 1953,

To Her Majesty, Elizabeth II, Queen of England.

With deep gratitude I thank you for the honour conferred upon me by the unexpected and inspiring presentation of the Coronation medal.

May my future sculpture justify the faith in my work shown by this act.

I venture to think that all Canadian artists will join with me in thanking you. [32]

Florence Wyle, RCA, SSC

29

The Great Coat

Sculpture in Canada hovered uneasily between the traditional and the contemporary in the early 1950s, as Andrew Bell had noted in his mid-century assessment. Passersby viewing such works as the Bank of Montreal bas-reliefs were likely to make comments like, "I'm wondering why [a skunk] is on a bank?" and receive the reply, "Who knows? Sculptors are such queer, Bohemian people."[1] Much as they were both respected, Frances Loring and Florence Wyle — who were indeed "queer, Bohemian people" — clearly belonged to the old school, though they supported work unlike their own. In 1950, Frances had been instrumental in getting the Art Gallery of Ontario to purchase Elizabeth Wyn Wood's *Reef and Rainbow*,[2] which — though it was experimental in attempting Group of Seven style landscape in sculpture — was hardly part of the advancement of sculpture into the new areas represented by Henry Moore, Jacob Epstein, or welder David Smith. New arrangements for sculpture display were attempted by the SSC (now grown to twenty-five members): works by Emanuel Hahn, Elizabeth Wyn Wood,

Cleeve Horne, Arthur Tracy, Elford Cox, and Loring and Wyle were on display on a vacant lot next to the Laing Galleries on Bloor Street for a month in late August and early September 1950 in attractive, garden-like settings. Florence did not have high expectations: "Frances and I have both been too busy since we came home [from the farm] getting things ready for the CNE & Laing's open air show," she wrote to friend Norah de Pencier in the third week of August. "Frances is down there now repainting her sea horse fountain. It's a nice idea but a lot of hard work and exhibits never seem to accomplish much. However it is all in the days work."[3] The aim of this "glamorous" and "intelligent" show was to bring sculpture out of the musty museums "to the man in the street."[4] In this it succeeded. More than two thousand paid the twenty-five cent admission fee, and more sculpture was sold than at all the previous SSC exhibitions combined. However, the sculpture on display was largely traditional. (The CNE copied this idea with an outdoor display of sculpture — a mixture of representational and semi-abstract works — in the summer of 1953.)[5] At about the same time, Florence tried her hand — unsuccessfully — at a sculpture that was to be her last. *Sea and Shore* (1950) was a fluid female torso with a Grecian drape over one shoulder that leaned back at a precarious angle and melded quite awkwardly with the rounded rock and sand-like forms at its base. Far more successful was her elegant, streamlined *Sleeping Cat* (1949–50), finished with gelva, a new acrylic multipolymer, into which she poured her profound appreciation of her favourite animal (she now had three: Benjamin Franklin, Peter the Great, and Yellow, an orange Persian). Also in gelva was Frances's saucy, whimsical bas-relief wooden plaque *Rooster* (1952), which Pearl McCarthy observed "exemplifies as no words can what experienced mastery is."[6] But these were minor works, and as Christine Boyanoski noted, during the 1950s "there had been few new ideas in their work for a number of years," and "they now [tended] to fall back on earlier solutions to aesthetic problems, reworking old themes in a new context."[7]

Ottawa was attempting to free things up for the arts on another front. In 1953 the Robertson Galleries opened with the initiative of J.K.B. Robertson and his wife. Robertson had been associated for some time with the National Gallery, and he hoped to remedy the problem that art patrons in Ottawa had to go to Toronto or Montreal to find any wide choice.[8] The Robertson Galleries exhibited the work of contemporary Canadian artists, starting off with seventy-five painters and thirteen sculptors. In March 1953, Loring sent four works: her plaster *Pigeons* from the Oakes Pavilion ($50); her wooden *Rooster* plaque ($400); *Aurora*, also wood, ($275); and *Martha* cut from Indiana limestone ($1,500). Wyle sent sixteen pieces: her plaster *Wrens*, *Orioles*, and *Gulls* ($50 each) from the Oakes Pavilion; three of her fine wood torsos: *Spring* ($250), *Summer* ($250), and *Autumn* ($225); her wood *Dancer* ($300); the plaster bust *Justice* ($50); a plaster *Madonna* mounted on chestnut ($75); a plaster plaque *Violin* ($30); a gelva *Cat* ($75) and gelva *Turtle* ($45); a number of pottery items — *Duck* ($45), *Indian Baby* ($75), *Penelope* ($60); and a magnificent bronze casting of *Rebirth* ($1,500).[9]

CANADIAN SCULPTORS WERE now competing on the international scene. Canada's response to a call for entries for a 1952 competition in Britain for a monument to The Unknown Political Prisoner was not impressive. Of forty-one submissions, only three were chosen for the international competition: "a thorny, lattice-like figure"[10] by the young Montreal sculptor Anne Kahane which won a prize of £25 in the final judging, a reclining Moore-like abstraction by Julien Hébert of Montreal, and an Epstein-inspired *Sampson* by Robert Norgate of Ottawa. Of the rest, one or two undoubtedly had some merit, but the bulk of them were mediocre and even grotesque both in conception and execution.[11]

The confusion about what made good art affected Canadian painters as well as sculptors. They also seemed to inhabit a limbo somewhere between the old and the new. Although Toronto painting moved into the era of Abstract Expressionism during the early 1950s, it did not find immediate success. According to one critic, "Toronto [was coming] to think of itself as some sort of Paris of the North (it was to learn quickly of New York) ... [The] young artist ... as public figure [was invading] the consciousness of a city that had suffered too long its image as Hogtown, City of Churches, the home of the CNE, and the world's largest Orangemen's Parade."[12] It was not until 1955, with the formation of Painters Eleven, that English-speaking artists "first successfully approached the problems presented by the most advanced painting of their time."[13] The group included William Ronald, Kazuo Nakamura, Alexandra Luke, Ray Mead, Tom Hodgson, Oscar Cahen, Jack Bush, Jock MacDonald, Hortense Gordon, Walter Yarwood, and Harold Town. Their first exhibition, almost twenty years after the formation of the American Abstract Artists in New York in 1936, was held in the Roberts Gallery in Toronto. Large crowds attended, but there were no sales and little critical attention. According to Harold Town, probably the most outspoken of the Painters Eleven, "the Establishment harumphed, swatted at a random moth and promptly went back to sleep in its leather chair."[14]

IT WAS IN this tenuous and somewhat retrograde artistic climate that the Federal Parliament in Ottawa decided in February 1953 to commission a tenth portrait statue for Parliament Hill. In April, Prime Minister Louis St. Laurent announced that a competition would be held to create a sculpture of Sir Robert Borden. It would be administered by the National Gallery of Canada, and the commission fee would be $50,000, with $300 each to the six runners-up. The monument was to reflect the Victorian style of Parliament Hill; in particular, it was to complement the Laurier monument, which graced the Parliament Buildings on the opposite side of the hill.[15] Such a work would certainly harken back to traditional monumentalism, and it was hardly surprising that it would appeal to The Girls. They had both met Borden in 1912 when Florence sketched him for a prize medal at the Toronto Industrial Exhibition. Frances, as always, was galvanized into enthusiasm at the prospect of a monumental work. They both submitted maquettes to compete with thirty-one other sketches by twenty-four contestants. The judges were John Bland, head of the Department of Architecture at McGill University; W.G. Constable, former assistant director of the National Gallery of London and currently curator of the Department of Painting at the Boston Museum of Fine Arts; and Sylvia Daoust.[16]

Although the terms of the competition seemed reasonable, they encouraged a step backwards into sculptural styles of the past. As one critic put it, "[I]t is too often decided by a committee to have a man in a frock coat with a scroll in one hand and very little left to the sculptural perception of the artist."[17]

This condescension towards portrait statues held some truth. At this time there were ten portrait statues on Parliament Hill: Queen Victoria, seven prime ministers, and two Fathers of Confederation. The earliest four — *Sir George-Étienne Cartier* (1885), *Sir John A. Macdonald* (1895), *Queen Victoria* (1901), and *Alexander Mackenzie* (1901) — were all created by Louis-Philippe Hébert. Typically, his statues were lofty creations embellished with meticulous detail, emphasizing the dignity and responsibility of nation building. His Cartier points to the text of his speech advocating Confederation at the Quebec Conference of 1864; his Macdonald is also portrayed as an orator with a stack of books at his feet, the text of a speech in hand, and the inscription "Consolidation of British America" on the back; Queen Victoria is in the full heroic mode, standing erect in regal splendour and gazing upwards, while a young woman representing Canada at the statue's base extends the gift of Peace; and Alexander Mackenzie, also depicted as an orator, has one arm raised while in the other he holds the documents that suggest the changes he made to election laws that included the right to a secret ballot and universal male suffrage.

The next phase of portrait statues on Parliament Hill twelve years later was accomplished by George William Hill, who — like Hébert — had won competitions to gain the commissions. Hill's portraits *George Brown* (1913), founder of the *Globe and Mail* newspaper, and *Thomas D'Arcy McGee* (1913), the Father of Confederation who was assassinated in 1868, emphasized the heroism of the two men. Both of them are depicted speaking out vigorously. The next year, Walter Allward unanimously won the competition to memorialize Robert Baldwin and Sir Louis-Hippolyte Lafontaine, who together played a major role in the peaceful negotiation of responsible government in pre-Confederation Canada. In this joint statue, the two men face each other at an angle, clearly discussing serious matters.

Thirteen years later Sir Wilfrid Laurier was honoured in the statue at the southeast corner of Parliament Hill. Laurier is portrayed with one hand on his hip, a man who means business, a suitable stance for a prime minister who fostered national growth and prosperity, oversaw the entry of Saskatchewan and Alberta into Confederation, facilitated the withdrawal of the last British troops from Canada, and encouraged the founding of the Royal Canadian Navy.[18]

BY 1953, IT had been a full thirty years since a Canadian man of politics or public service had been honoured with a statue on Parliament Hill. To create a portrait-statue of Sir Robert Borden that would complement that of Laurier *and* fit in with the Victorian ambiance of Parliament Hill and the other seven statues was no easy matter. How could it be possible to avoid bland, formulaic solutions to such a problem?

One critic who saw the thirty-odd submissions for the competition was appalled, "The entries for Sir Robert Borden were even cruder ... than most of the entries for the competition for The Unknown Political Prisoner the year before ... Thirty-two ... models were for the most part stodgy variations on the familiar Parliament Hill theme, and at least one or two reverted to the Roman toga and parchment scroll."[19]

Sir Robert Laird Borden, Canada's prime minister from 1911–20, had already been the subject of two portrait busts and one painting. Famous as the Conservative leader who introduced the divisive policy of conscription during the Great War, Borden eventually achieved Canadian autonomy within the Empire-Commonwealth. In 1915, the same year that he visited the battlefields in Europe and the hospitals in Britain, he concluded — partly because he was disillusioned with the British High Command — that Canada must play a more active role in the Great War through conscription of Canadian soldiers. That same year, Alfred Laliberté sculpted a portrait bust. (Laliberté had earlier carved a full-length wooden statue of Sir Wilfrid Laurier.)[20] In 1925, Dorothy E. Vlenjt, an English painter, created "a speaking likeness ... in which the Canadian war Premier has cast off some of his office worries, and, reclining easily, suggests a latent twinkle such as his friends know in his off moments."[21] And in 1928, Ottawa sculptor Lionel Fosbery created another portrait bust, which, according to Hector Charlesworth of *Saturday Night*, was "one of the best representations of Canada's War Premier that one has seen in any medium."[22]

Frances Loring and Florence Wyle would have seen all three of these portrayals of Borden.[23] Laliberté was one of the group that founded the Sculptors' Society of Canada; both Loring and Wyle had sculptures in the same annual OSA exhibition at the Art Gallery of Toronto where Vlenjt showed her portrait of Borden; and they also exhibited several pieces at the huge assemblage of seven shows — including the newly formed ssc — that reopened the Toronto Art Gallery in October 1928. Fosbery's head, which asked the highest price of any sculpture ($2,250), would scarcely have escaped their notice.

The very thought of a prime monumental commission galvanized Frances into action, and blew the "cobwebs"[24] she had complained about six months earlier — before heading west to the Peace River district with A.Y. Jackson — right out of her mind. She submitted two fourteen-inch maquettes, just in case. Her health was precarious — she now weighed over two hundred pounds and suffered, like Florence, from arthritis after years of handling wet clay and plaster in their frequently cold studio — but her preparations were voracious. According to Rebecca Sisler, "[S]he set about assimilating everything there was to know about Robert Borden: the public statesman, the private individual, his physical characteristics, his ideals."[25] She studied all the photos she could find of him, and assiduously read his two-volume memoir, edited by his nephew, Toronto lawyer Henry Borden, and introduced by Arthur Meighen.[26] Immersing herself in this took her back to those heady times when she and Florence had enjoyed their first nationwide success. Despite the fact that she and Florence could never have called themselves politically conservative, the opportunity to celebrate the prime minister whose regime had encouraged the arts — and their sculpture specifically — at the end of the Great War was irresistible. As Sisler puts it, "[a] common chord had been struck," and as she absorbed Borden's image and ideals "[s]he began to feel a certain affinity with Borden."[27]

This feeling of affinity was not new to Frances. She had felt it with Banting, whose portrait bust is hauntingly reminiscent of Frances's own strong face. As Christine Boyanoski observes, "[T]he strong physiognomy of the sculptor is a match for that of Banting."[28] This observation is borne out in the 1950 photo of Frances next to her portrait bust of Banting. The two might be siblings. Even Frances's description of the way in which she really does "two heads in one," infusing the physical details with the "spirit within" by "selectively emphasiz[ing] certain forms as a means of interpretation" suggested empathy. That "spirit within" was as much Frances as her subject. As Boyanoski concludes, "It is those elements drawn 'from her head' that create the resemblance among the heads [she sculpted], whether portraits or otherwise. Many share a square jaw, long chin, and full lips — unmistakable Loring trade marks."[29]

As usual, Frances was clear from the outset about her proposal for a Borden memorial. "Almost every statesman on Parliament Hill is standing with his weight on one foot and his hand in the air, his first finger pointing upwards," she said. "I was determined that Borden was not going to stand on one hip, and he was not going to have his hand up in the air."[30] Moreover, Frances had for some time expressed the view that sculpture should not be frenetic. When the Canadian war memorial *The Response*, by English sculptor Vernon March, was erected in 1932 on Parliament Hill, it became her favourite example of such sculpture. "Cheap melodrama," she called it, "which means that when a person looks at it, they want to rush away and never look at it again."[31] She had said in a lecture at the Williams Memorial Gallery in London in 1942 that monuments in Canada's parks "too often show[ed] statesmen beginning actions they don't finish. If you pass one of them every day for a week, you become exhausted."[32] As for some of the other statues on Parliament Hill, "unfortunately" they were "atrocities," in her opinion,[33] especially the National War Memorial which she said "disgraces the country."[34] It was essential, she believed, that sculpture not agitate the viewer. "A restless piece of statuary quickly becomes tedious," she said in 1946.[35] "The representation of full action is not desirable in sculpture," she theorized in an address as president of the ssc. "[T]he movement of the famous disc[us] thrower is [ideal. It conveys ar]rested action and balanced serenity."[36] The statue to which she referred, known as *Discobolus*, by the fifth-century Greek sculptor Myron — in which the nude athlete is poised with the discus thrust back about to swing it forward into the throw — is an example of "contraposito" form, in which the work's vitality arises from the figure's inherent muscularity and concentration rather than from the overt, off-balance action that would follow when the discus is thrown.

THE CHALLENGE WAS enormous. How to create a suitably Victorian statue that complemented Laurier — who did have one hand on his hip — *and* meet her own personal standards of what good monumental sculpture should be?

Her first attempts did not please her. Borden was certainly "standing firmly on two feet,"[37] but he was wearing a Prince Albert (a long, double-breasted frock coat that falls just above the knee), typically worn by politicians of the day and also typically found on the statues already on Parliament Hill.[38] She found it too dull. The almost effeminate garment "constricted the possibilities for sculptural design and toned down the effect of dignity and intellectual force"[39] she wanted to convey. She got a lawyer friend, Vera Parsons — who knew Parliament Hill well — to come to The Church and walk round and round this first model. It was Vera who suggested that the Prince Albert frock coat could be replaced by a great coat (also double-breasted, but falling halfway between knee and ankle). Sir Wilfrid Laurier was wearing a great coat; possibly Vera knew this and felt the same garment on Borden would create a symmetry of mass between the two statues. As she told Sisler, Frances "grabbed up a heavy cloth and began arranging it over the shoulders of the model. It worked. The solid silhouette effect of the improvised great coat," not only gave a "sense of drama" and "vitality"[40] to the design, but also echoed the broad outline of the statue of Sir Wilfrid Laurier. The next day she developed a second model in a great coat, holding the Seals of Autonomy.

The judges pondered the entries for five long months. In March 1954, two sculptors were notified that they were finalists and should submit larger versions of their maquettes: young Montreal sculptor Jean Meroz, who had studied in France on a Canadian government scholarship from 1934–38, and Frances Loring. Meroz's Borden was everything Loring's was not. Predictably dressed in a double-breasted frock coat, the lean and elegant figure with an elongated head stands with his weight on one leg, scrolls in one hand, the other pointing out at an imaginary audience. He is poised gracefully, as if he were a dancer about to move into a pirouette. Loring's Borden was a stocky figure with a large, squarish head, upright and firm in his great coat, not pointing at all. Like Loring's somewhat masculine *Girl with Fish* (ca. 1932), he stands firmly on both feet. The two larger maquettes were off to the National Gallery in June. It would be four more months before the committee viewed the finalists' work; and another two months before they chose a winner.

Life for Loring and Wyle had gone on much as usual in the months of the competition. Loring had given one of her many demonstrations of bust and figure work to the Brantford Art League on Monday, 8 March 1954. Perhaps emboldened by her re-engagement with traditional monumentalism, she commented on that occasion that "the abstractionist fad seemed to be disappearing" and that "[t]his was not strange since it was actually not much more than experimental work that often strayed from the path of good sculpture."[41] Later that month, both Loring and Wyle displayed work in the new Eglinton Gallery on Eglinton Avenue West in Toronto, along with Professor Karl May's "readily intelligible paintings" and abstract works by William Ronald, which one reviewer described as "high-powered doodling," while conceding sarcastically that "more imaginative 'moderns' find hidden meanings in the free style of painting."[42] On Saturday, 1 May, they were among those Toronto artists[43] who opened their studios for the annual tour by members of the Art Gallery and their friends to raise money for the art purchasing fund. A photo in the *Globe and Mail* shows Loring "explaining details" of her *Eskimo Mother and Child* to a member of the Women's Committee; another shows Florence in front of her bust of A.Y. Jackson with one of the event's organizers, "stoutly maintaining she liked talking to people."[44] In early June they hauled some of their works to Stratford in station wagons to take part in the 28 June opening of the city's Shakespeare Festival, which had begun productions in its famous tent the year before. Sponsored by the Ontario branch of the ssc, which now had forty-two members and was chaired by Elford Cox, the sculptures were to be displayed in rotation (since there were so many)[45] on the first floor of a three-storey house next to the fire hall. The second floor offered a display of Canadian paintings on loan from the National Gallery and was supervised by Robert Norgate of Ottawa.

Their visits with friends continued too. "One of the nicest things that has ever happened to me," wrote Bobby Dyde, "was lunch with Frances, Florence and Alex ... Florence crawled about like a chimp replacing bits of Sculp., Frances was utter happiness, Alex was utter grump ... We all ended up by hugging everyone. What wonderful people those three are. Of all the many good and gifted people I have known I put these three very much at the top."[46]

Loring had just sent off her enlarged maquette of Borden in his great coat to Ottawa, and dispatched some works to Stratford when she heard from the University of Alberta that she had been given its 1954 national award "for long and conspicuous service to the arts."[47] No doubt Loring's trip west in the fall of 1952 and her talk about the untapped artistic potential of Canada's northwest at the University of Alberta made the university aware of her unique talents, but there is no reason they might not have given the award to the more famous A.Y. Jackson instead.[48] She was the first sculptor and the first woman to win this award. The announcement in the *Globe and Mail* was accompanied by the stunning portrait of her by Lilias Torrance Newton that by now was on display in the National Gallery of Canada.[49] The article summed up Loring's distinguished work, her backing of art societies, her lecturing to the public, and her service on committees supporting sculpture and the arts. It singled out the lion at the entrance to the Queen Elizabeth Way as one of her finest works and the one best known by the public — a sentiment expressed elsewhere in the press.[50] Her greatest contribution, the article maintained, "has been one for which no specific statistics can be given ... the fact that people who have never been in Canada nor seen Canadian sculpture have heard of the studio of Loring and Wyle. Through the years, the lofty old building on Glenrose has been the real heart of Toronto artist[ic] life, where narrowness or disparagement of other sincere artists' work was frowned on, and where generosity to younger artists has been as secret as it has been large. Birds and hurt animals have also found sanctuary in the tangled garden ... and visitors have become accustomed to ... the cats sitting high on the shoulders of finished statues. This studio life, affecting the spirit of the community, would in itself have made Loring and Wyle an institution."[51] Loring — delighted — planned to go to Banff in August to receive the medal. Bobby Dyde met her there and later wrote to a friend, "[I went] to Banff to hold Frances Loring's hand while she got her award at the Banff school. She was magnificent. These people mean so well, but they are so shy and difficult that they appear to be ill-mannered. Of course, Frances had the most difficult eating out of her hand in two days. She could melt the ICE FIELDS if necessary."[52]

Nothing was said about the Borden competition in the media reports of Loring's University of Alberta medal, and it was not until four months later, at the end of December 1954, that Frances Loring heard — finally — that she had won the competition. Sylvia Daoust was ill (or perhaps felt a conflict of interest) for the final judging. Unfortunately, Jean Meroz was not informed that he had lost. He read about it in the newspapers. On 4 January, an article in the *Montreal Gazette* gave him the opportunity to vent. "I naturally assumed I would win first or second prize," he said, "since Miss Loring and I were the only ones asked to submit enlarged models. Last week I read in the newspapers that Miss Loring had won. I still haven't heard anything. This may sound like sour grapes, but the contest seems to have been a hodge-podge of confusion from beginning to end."[53] Harry McCurry responded curtly from the National Gallery: "The jury has said that they are not in favour of the cash grants [for runners-up]. So many of the entries were so bad."[54] Eventually, after much toing and froing, McCurry awarded the $300 grants to Meroz, Lionel Fosbery, Jacobine Jones, Emanuel Hahn, and Elizabeth Wyn Wood, and Leo Mol. Jean Meroz was given an additional $300 as a finalist for his enlargement of Borden. The Sculptors' Society of Canada pushed the matter even further, demanding that — in compliance with the terms of the competition — all the models by the competitors be on display for the public at the National Gallery. In March 1955, McCurry put the models on display in the Thomson Room on the second floor of the Gallery.

"I have modelled the fighting Borden," Loring said when interviewed about her success in the competition, "the Borden not only of the war years but of the post-war period when under his leadership Canada took her position as a nation in the peace conference. Therefore, he stands firmly on both feet."[55] The nine-foot bronze statue was to be in place on its granite pedestal by the summer of 1956. It was a formidable task for a woman of sixty-nine, who now weighed at least 200 pounds, and had arthritis so badly she needed two canes to drag her heavy legs along. When the officials discovered her physical condition, they insisted on taking out an insurance policy of $10,000 on her life, and paid the premium of $1,125 per year for the duration of the project.

Frances was "galled"[56] by this slur on her capabilities. But she was no doubt buoyed by receiving an honorary degree from the University of Toronto in May. Her name was probably suggested by The Girls' friend, the

Hon. Pauline McGibbon, who had become the first woman on the university's Board of Governors. Loring was one of six to receive honorary degrees from Toronto that spring, and the only woman. The list contained a politician, two businessmen, two professors, and one artist. Loring was the second sculptor to receive an honorary degree from Toronto; Walter Allward had also been honoured for his Vimy memorial. On this occasion, Loring was not the speaker, but Professor G.W. Paton — who spoke on behalf of the group — began by paying tribute to her: "I should like not only to thank the university but also to congratulate it for its wisdom in honouring a creative artist. The first thing I would like to do with my new academic cap is to take it off to a great lady and a great Canadian, Dr. Frances Loring."[57]

In his presentation speech to Loring, after some general remarks about the place of sculpture in society, Professor Moffat Woodside turned to Loring:

Today we honour a woman who adopted Canada as her home, and whom Canada gladly accepted as her daughter. Her contribution to Canada has been vast, ranging from the work of organization and administration and even of committees — without which, apparently, the best of causes may not today be born and fostered — to the encouragement of young artists at home and from abroad, and to that rare and priceless activity of which only an infinitely small minority is capable — the creation of works of art. From the rock-bound coast of Maine to the lobby of Simcoe Hall [at this university] you will find examples of her art. You will find them in art galleries and in schools, in cities large and small, in buildings devoted to economic enterprise and to the healing of the sick. You will find them, if you look, on highways and on bridges. Some of them commemorate the achievement of those whose individual deeds are written in our history; some of them preserve the memory of those whose greatness lies in sacrifice; all of them adorn our land.[58]

The Lyceum Women's Art Association, which had been so important to Loring, especially in her early days in Toronto, made her an honorary life member not long after. In her speech at their annual luncheon (with musical entertainment)[59] in the association's galleries on Prince Arthur Avenue where she had so often exhibited her work, hosted fundraising events, served on committees and as president, and poured at teas, Loring continued her mission to forge a connection between sculpture and the public. "For goodness sake, notice sculpture," she urged forcefully. "If you like it, say so. If you don't, say so ... When you see a new building with sculpture, pay attention. If you like it, speak out, write to the papers. If you do not, do the same. In that way interest is whetted ... Do not buy just anything. Be discriminating and so help us to keep up the standards." She referred to the fact that the water pool designed to reflect Allward's statue of William Lyon Mackenzie King in Queen's Park had had to be filled up with gravel because children waded in it and hung their wet clothes on it, making it "a grotesque clothes horse." "Children certainly should have places to wade," she conceded, "but the little brats would eventually be happier and more respected if they had been taught to respect sculpture." Eager — as always — to educate children, seeing them as future adults who might support the arts, or themselves become artists, she referred to her trip west: "[They] knew of Dr. Jackson because the Group of Seven was in their textbooks. But there was nothing in these books to suggest sculpture. The boys were excited when I told them of Meštrović, showing pictures of his work, and reminded them that this greatest living sculptor had been a country boy like themselves."[60]

As an article in the *Globe and Mail* put it, "Miss Loring is not only a distinguished sculptor but one who has participated in spreading among her Canadian countrymen a realization of their own resources of intelligence. She has been artist and citizen. At the moment," the article closed as if to signify Loring's patriotic dedication, "Miss Loring is busy on the statue of Sir Robert Borden for Ottawa."[61]

And busy indeed she was. She first built up a half-size model of Sir Robert Borden in the nude, as Rodin had done with his famous *Balzac* and as many sculptors had done, as the most reliable method in preparing portrait statues. (Later she would say, chuckling, "perhaps I'd better not say that. Now people will visualize Sir Robert [nude] — who had anything but a pleasant figure.")[62] Sisler explains the point of enlarging the figure as follows: "Details, brought into focus by the larger scale, would have to be balanced and integrated with the larger forms. For once work on the massive bulk of the figure had started, it would be technically almost impossible to adjust the design except in superficial areas ... The half-size model was the battleground in which masses and forms were pushed and shoved and forced into place until they harmonized."[63] Almost immediately two problems confronted Loring. Borden had an unusually large head that — if represented accurately — would have made the statue seem out of proportion. For Loring, who believed that "the smaller the head, the more heroic the statue,"[64] this posed a serious difficulty. She simply added height to his legs for balance. Then the great coat that had been so essential to her design conflicted with her idea of his holding the Seals of Autonomy; no one dressed for the outdoors would be carrying such important papers. She easily solved this problem by substituting a small scroll to represent the brief he carried to the 1919 Peace Conference at Versailles — the very moment when she and Florence were completing their war workers statuettes. The half-size plaster was sent to New York, to be enlarged by expert technicians in a studio near the bronze foundry. But the plaster would be headless; she did not intend to risk this crucial part of her statue. She modelled the huge head herself, intending to incorporate it later into the full-sized statue.

These were the problems she recognized and resolved, but the judges challenged her proposed statue on a number of other points — most of which she defended right back. They, too, thought the Seals of Autonomy out of place. But Bland and Constable (in Sylvia Daoust's absence) had a long list of other suggestions. Most of these focused on making Borden more rugged, since Borden's private secretary, who had been consulted, thought Loring's model was not "rugged" enough.[65] (What the private secretary thought of Jean Meroz's more delicate, effete rendition of Borden can only be guessed.) Borden's "shoulders should be squared ... the boots and trousers given more character and refinement ... the back view be made more interesting; and ... the lettering of the inscription on the base be in Roman capitals such as those used on the arches of Titus and Constantine, which were characterized by an 'incised V'"; and "a large pair of fur gloves would be more appropriate [than the Seals of Autonomy]!"[66]

For the most part Frances got her way. She kept her "simpler style of lettering, which she felt was appropriate for carving in granite"[67]; she kept the scroll in its lesser form; she disregarded the fur gloves. She might have augmented the "ruggedness" of the statue, but her original maquettes were already characteristically vital and powerful.

As the work progressed, visitors to the studio gasped when they walked in. Frances had set up the scaffolding she had used for years — since her work on *Miss Canada* for Eaton's in 1917 — "two rickety step-ladders, spanned across their tops by a frail-looking plank."[68] She balanced on the plank putting fistfuls of clay from a dishpan[69] onto the armature she had constructed. A.J. Casson recalls dropping by one day to be "confronted by Frances, her two-hundred pound bulk swathed in a coverall, standing suspended in mid-air on the frail plank. The plank sagged in terrifying fashion." Casson "appealed in subdued alarm to Florence who was poking about nearby," possibly working on her own lovely fountain of a draped child pouring water from an urn for the Marjorie Gibbons Counsell Garden in Gibbons Park in London, Ontario.[70] "'Florence!' he whispered in agitation. 'If she's going to fall she'll bounce!' Florence assured him matter-of-factly."[71] A.Y. Jackson reported to a friend, "Florence looks tired, but Frances is busy on another commission so they will have no worry about finances."[72]

Something of the spirit Frances had in mind for her memorial to Borden can be heard in a speech she gave mid-project on 9 December 1955, at a public meeting in the Hamilton Art Gallery. Probably because the Hamilton Gallery had a copy of her bust of Banting on display, she compared him to Borden. She linked the two by emphasizing the fact that she had done her Banting bust shortly before the Second World War, in which he lost his life in an RCAF plane crash. To her, they were both "fighters" — a characteristic she herself shared. "It was that powerful driving force that made Banting. I suppose to succeed you have to have a little of the fanatic in you. You have to be able to get on one track and stay there. That's Banting." As for Borden, "Once I got started on those Memoirs I couldn't put it down. You have no idea what an interesting man he is. In one way, he is just like Banting. They have one thing in common. They're both fighters." She contrasted Banting and Borden to the prime minister she detested: Mackenzie King. "I would never want to have to do Mackenzie King," she said, in a statement that reveals much about the importance to her of engagement and admiration in her work. "I can't get any impression there. Undoubtedly there's a strong personality, but it doesn't come through. You can't feel it."[73]

She saw the Borden project as the culmination of her pioneering work in Canada as a sculptor. Her father's myth had become even more deeply entrenched: "Working in this country," she said, is "a stimulating experience. Here [I] can create something of [my] own and use [my] inherited pioneer instincts."[74] "Canadian sculpture has undergone great changes since I came here in 1912 [sic] and it has a wonderful future," she said, "but we still have to do things we wouldn't have to do in other countries. For instance, I do my own plaster casting, and act as plumber and carpenter too!"[75]

Frances expressed supreme confidence in the project whose sponsors were worried she might not live to complete. "As you grow older," she told her audience, "you find your work getting better all the time. And you enjoy it more. I don't think anyone can do great sculpture until they're past forty. Maybe poets are better when they're young, but not sculptors."[76]

By April 1956, the official committee — headed by Alan Jarvis who became director of the National Gallery after Harry McCurry's death — gave the go-ahead to Frances's clay models, and the Department of Public Works — confident now that Frances could finish the monument — cancelled the "humiliating" insurance policy. The casting was done by Willie Fediow, an expert and the husband of Pauline Redsell, the painter and sculptor who had shown her work along with The Girls'. Willie complained about conflicting directions from Florence and Frances, at which they both "roared with laughter," saying, "Thank heavens! We were hoping you'd shut us up. We would never have managed to do it on our own."[77]

Soon Frances was off to New York to supervise the headless enlargement. "Mr. Borden is progressing," she reported to Alan Jarvis, "I have put his head three inches higher and his feet one inch lower. Helps him."[78] But when the time came for her to work on the figure herself, "filling in the important details, pulling the whole together, she was struck by a painful eye ailment, which signalled the decline of her eyesight from then on. There was nothing for it but to retire to bed in her hotel room and wait for the inflammation to subside. As time was pressing, she put in an urgent call for help from Florence ... Would she come down to carry on with the modelling of the detail? The buttons, the coat lapels, the shoes."[79] Florence rushed to New York and took over. Later, Frances had to redo some of Florence's understated, softly curved modelling to restore the drama to her dashing statue.

That summer of 1956, when the statue was supposed to have been finished, it was not nearly ready. However, CBC Television did a profile of Loring, interviewed by Elspeth Chisholm, for *Telescope* on Sunday, 22 July.[80] Television had appeared in Canada only four years earlier, but Frances's extensive experience on radio and in public lectures made her a natural for this early public program. The program touched on many of her best-known works — the QEW lion, the Rainbow Bridge work, the Banting bust, even *Miner*, inspired by the Moose River disaster in 1936 — but highlighted the work she was doing on Borden. Florence is described in the introduction as "her long-time sculptor colleague," and Loring mentions that she was her "student-teacher" in Chicago and their Greenwich Village studio together, but she is otherwise invisible. The program is really about Loring: Loring the pioneer like her father, Loring the major Canadian and international sculptor, Loring the war monumentalist, Loring the creator of portrait busts, Loring the co-creator with architects, Loring the woodcarver of drama trophies, and, of course, Loring the missionary ("the future of sculpture depends on you, the watchers").[81] One CBC employee who worked on the program with Chisholm commented: "[I]t [is] odd that Miss Wyle, so manly in her walk, so gruff, should do these smooth, feminine madonnas — while Loring, less assertive, slower, quieter, should do the great big tough ones."[82]

As the figure — now well past the anticipated date of completion — reached the final stage when molten bronze would be poured into a mould taken from the plaster model, Frances had yet one more battle. Ottawa wanted the lettering on the panels of the granite base to conform with that of other monuments on Parliament Hill. Frances ceded the back and side panels, but insisted on her simpler script for the front.

Finally, in late December, after the finished one-ton bronze, nine-foot six-inch statue, artificially aged with acids and a hot blow-pipe,[83] caused a furor by arriving in Ottawa four weeks ahead of time (it was stored in a basement), it was erected on the pink Laurentian granite pedestal carved by Italian-born Louis Temporale, by then Canada's leading stone carver.[84] On Tuesday 8 January 1957 at twelve noon, six months later than planned, Robert Borden's nephew, Henry Borden, pulled the cord which released the flags draping the stern-faced bronze figure before an array of dignitaries, including Prime Minister Louis St. Laurent and the new leader of the Progressive Conservatives, John Diefenbaker. St. Laurent, probably unwilling to give entirely fulsome praise to Borden, said in his speech, "Whatever opinions might be advanced on the policies which he pursued, his personal qualities and particularly his honesty and sincerity of purpose in seeking to serve his country well were outstanding."[85] Frances Loring posed for photographers from the *Ottawa Journal*, a jaunty hat with a rolled brim at a fetching angle on her head, her own double-breasted great coat — which echoed Borden's — straining at the two buttons around what used to be her waist. "[I] had 'the jitters,'" she confessed, "and felt like a singer at her first concert."[86] Now a patriot to the core, she leaned on her cane beside her last monumental creation, as the crowd joined in to sing "O Canada."

Ironically, the report of this momentous occasion in the *Kingston Whig-Standard* the next day described the statue of Sir Robert Borden as dressed "in a frock coat."[87]

Taking Art Into Account⤳

The 1951 Massey-Lévesque Report had encouraged sculptors to increase their cooperation with architects, "to follow in the path of architecture, to be a consequence of architecture and to be, so to speak, a part of an edifice."[1] The aim was to achieve "the sense of intimacy given [to a community] by great decorative groups of former times; their power to inspire, their abundant life and their unity." (The excerpt on Canadian architecture in the report admitted that the public "largely ignored" architecture and that builders across Canada were creating "architectural monstrosities.")[2] The Massey-Lévesque Commission members had been informed, however, that "although sculptors welcome the revival of interest in architectural sculpture for public buildings which has been particularly marked in the last decade, at the same time they would like a wider field for purely individual single productions. They suffer as do artists in other fields from the dearth of private patrons."[3]

The question of patronage for sculpture was vexed. The number of wealthy individuals such as W.D. Young, R.S. McLaughlin, Sir John Eaton,

Alan Ely, and Marjorie Gibbons Counsell, whose commissions had helped support Loring and Wyle, had all but disappeared. Commissions from public money never regained their wide role in sponsoring monuments and other public sculptures after the Great War. Loring's commission for her sculpture of Sir Robert Borden had been an exception. In 1958, the Canada Council began to issue grants for artists, but it would be some time before these offered substantial support for sculptors. The commissions from Catholic churches and schools for ecclesiastical works that came to Quebec sculptors like Henri Hébert and Sylvia Daoust were almost unheard of in largely protestant Ontario.

The pinch was also being felt at art institutions, which had long been a significant source of income for artists. In the fall of 1955, the Art Gallery of Toronto, still under the direction of Loring's *bête noire* Martin Baldwin, elected a new president — R.W. Finlayson — with the express purpose of raising money. "This year," an article about his appointment in the *Globe and Mail* asserted, "a minimum of $50,000 will be sought from individuals and corporations,"[4] twenty-five percent of which was to go to purchases for the gallery's permanent collection. The rest would sponsor expanded services for the gallery in the form of exhibitions, educational programs, an administration building, the return of the Grange building to its intended purpose, a cafeteria, and an enlarged staff to execute these new services. Wealthy Torontonians E.P. Taylor and A.Y. Eaton were elected two of three vice-presidents. The third vice-president was A.J. Casson. Frances Loring was one of ten councillors on the committee, which also included a number of Torontonians with money,[5] who could be expected to draw on a large network of acquaintances and companies for contributions to realize the gallery's plans.

The key target for funds was no longer individuals, but corporations. This was not new, but its range was wider than ever before. As the number of wealthy patrons dwindled and the costs of mounting exhibitions and materials — especially for sculpture — rose, the corporations began to assume a much more important place in the sponsorship of art. The mid-1950s saw the proliferation of advertising everywhere — especially on the new medium of television. The importance of advertising was the subject of Torontonian Marshall McLuhan's first book, *The Mechanical Bride: Folklore of Industrial Man*

(1951), which explored the power of manipulative advertising by corporations. Something had to be done to convince Canadians that art and business were not at odds with each other, that businesses could enhance their reputation and markets by using the talents of artists to "advertise" their companies — or at the very least to impress potential clients that they had superior taste. Ironically, this turning to corporations echoed Toronto's initial turn-of-the-century view that art should mainly be useful in forwarding business interests.

In an "experiment" that could be seen as the turning point from the old-fashioned patronage that had emerged between the wars to the corporate sponsorship that would increasingly dominate the marketing of goods, office supplier Grand and Toy, Ltd. installed a permanent exhibition of oil and watercolour painting, graphic arts, and sculpture at their office showroom at 8 Wellington Street West in the heart of Toronto's downtown business district. The idea was the brainchild of Ross Helwig, Grand and Toy's office furniture department manager, who convinced the owners "to bridge the gulf between artist's studio and businessman's office."[6] The enterprise had "no intention of advancing any particular school of art. They [tried], within the limitations of space, to present a collection which has variety but quality in each type. Breadth of taste and freedom of choice will be principles." A hundred and fifty businessmen and artists gathered at the opening to view the 107 works by fifty-six artists on an occasion that was lent serious encouragement by Ontario Premier Leslie Frost, who officially launched the collection on the evening of 27 November 1956. "[This is] more than an art exhibit," Frost said.

> It is a combination of things material and things cultural. Sponsored as it is by two of the oldest institutions in Canada, there should be no doubt as to its success. It is a mark of our advancement, our maturity as a country that this should take place. You can't add up Canada's greatness in columns of figures or in bricks and mortar. The aesthetic and the cultural — the things of the spirit — have to be taken into account. It is a mile-stone in artists' achievement that increasing recognition is now being given to those who have laboured to enhance the cultural side of Canadian life.[7]

OF THE MANY artists (most of whom lived in or near Toronto) who attended that night, only Florence Wyle and Frances Loring — by then distinctly in the old guard — were quoted the next day. "I think it is an excellent idea," Florence said curtly, "to bring the work of the artist where those who wouldn't ordinarily go into a Gallery — because it's considered sissy or high-brow — can see it. They're just as highbrow as anyone else, really, but they won't admit it." Loring (now Dr. Frances Loring and soon given to calling herself "a big fish in a small [Canadian] pool")[8], leaned on her cane and added, "It should be noted that this type of exhibition provides a special opportunity for the artist: he can show works which otherwise he might not be able to display publicly."

The president of the Architectural Institute of Canada, Douglas Kertland, summed it up precisely: "[T]he exhibition was good for the businessman and good for the artist."[9] Toronto the Good had again found a way to reconcile business and the arts.

THE COMPLETION OF Borden's statue, along with her awards from the Universities of Alberta and Toronto, had thrust Frances Loring into the position of top sculptor in Canada. For at least a decade she and Florence had been referred to as "distinguished," but now, at age seventy-one, Loring had become the "Grande Dame of Canadian Sculpture,"[10] a sculptor (or sculptress — a term she and Wyle both hated) "now in the rank of senior Canadian sculptors,"[11] an artist "at the peak of her powers."[12] One article referred to her as the "Dean of Canadian Sculptors"[13]; another called her the "Grand-mother"[14] of Canadian sculpture. In 1958, she and Jean Horne were the first women to be called as judges — the sole judges — for sculpture for the Ontario Society of Artists.[15]

The arts were also opening up to aboriginal artists. It is ironic that Loring and Wyle encouraged the inclusion of Charlie Sheguapit in the SSC — a move that not only testified to their broadmindedness in admitting sculptors whose work was so unlike theirs, but also spelled the beginning of the end for sculptors like themselves. No longer would works like Wyle's Haida owls and totems and *Indian Mother and Child*, or even Loring's powerful *Eskimo Mother and Child*, speak on behalf of aboriginal peoples once artists from those communities were given the opportunity to speak authentically for themselves.[16]

AS IF THE energy she had somehow mustered for the formidable Borden project were still in motion as she ended the work,[17] Loring plunged into another large project: a ten foot by ten foot panel in low relief to be used for the south wall of the new Women's Building (soon renamed The Queen Elizabeth Building) at the CNE, where it can be seen today. It depicted a subject that had always been to her liking: a mother with windblown hair wearing swirling long skirts — such as she herself had once worn — with her two children. "There is a handsome poetic sweep in the arrangement of the various shapes," wrote Pearl McCarthy. "The diagonal and curving dash of the pine [tree and branches in the background], and the tall but slender masses of the main figure, make a treat for the eyes. At the same time, it is not so stylized [i.e. abstract] that the general public may not enjoy it." Of special interest was the fact that Loring had used a "weather-resistant polyester, which was half the cost of bronze"[18] — one of the many changes in technique that were finally penetrating the Canadian scene. Certainly, the cost of bronze, as McCarthy explained, "except when repeat forms can be used, has become almost prohibitive in Canada, one reason being that most sculpture has to be sent abroad for bronze casting. Therefore this large piece represents a major development in finding artistic embellishment for architecture at more reasonable cost."[19] Its weather-resistance was just as important. "Stone, or other mediums for such work, [are subject to] spotting from chemicals in the city air [which can] deface monuments and decorations."[20] Loring was quick to give credit where credit was due: "While this is a large work in a material not used before, I think note should be taken of experiments in various new materials carried on for some time by Dora de Pédery Hunt and Jack de Maria," Dr. Loring said. "Otherwise I might not have had the courage to try it."[21] She found it "interesting to work with."[22]

Loring's most famous sculpture was still the British lion on the QEW. Pearl McCarthy expressed what many thought: "[Loring's lion] with 'its gallant attitude' is one of the finest pieces of outdoor sculpture in Canada."[23] In 1957, as a tribute to Canada's "Grande Dame of Sculpture," the Sculptors'

Society issued a postcard of the lion — the first in a series they planned to use to market Canadian sculpture to a wider public. The postcard included the patriotic inscription below the lion that linked Canada to the British Empire, but excluded W.L. Somerville's column and Florence's bas-relief medallion with the profiles of the King and Queen. Loring herself liked the lion that had become synonymous with her name enormously, but preferred her *Deer Panel* at the Oakes Pavilion.[24]

BUT THE WINDS of artistic change were already apparent, though they had come so late upon the Canadian scene. Loring and her lion had become of less interest to the general public, as the ties between Canada and Britain continued to loosen following the Second World War. A harbinger of the future of Canada's art could be seen on the same page as Pearl McCarthy's celebration of Loring's lion. Right beside it was a review of "younger artist" Dennis Burton, whose paintings were on display at the Gallery of Contemporary Art on Gerrard Street East. The reviewer finds in Burton's *Company House Window* and *Prairie Aurora No. 2* "proofs [that] in his work he has a place among the more freely exploring abstractionists."[25]

Burton's exhibit was typical of the new wave of younger artists who were moving away from representational work. No longer was abstract work disdained as "high-powered doodling." The Massey-Lévesque Report, and the intense scrutiny of Canada's cultural scene in the decade that had led up to it, had alerted Canadians to the importance of the arts and the importance — in particular — of establishing a Canadian culture that could compete internationally. Even the Stratford Festival's preponderance of English actors — who were still being imported from England four years after the festival needed them to launch the endeavour — was being challenged. Herbert Whittaker, drama critic for the *Globe and Mail* warned, "The Canadian actor, after that first dewy-eyed year, has taken Stratford for granted, perhaps, and his place in it. The Canadian actor may lose out more and more as more and more willing and experienced actors arrive from England."[26]

The Massey-Lévesque Commission had signalled the need to encourage Canadian culture and to ensure that the already meagre funds supporting the arts would go into the pockets of Canadian artists. Frances's $50,000 commission for *Sir Robert Borden* seemed to promise financial support for The Girls for the rest of their lives, but — once expenses for her maquettes, materials, plaster moulds, bronze castings, special surface finishing, carved lettering for the granite base, shipping, and her travel[27] were taken into account — she realized only $12,500 for three years' work, or $4,166 a year.[28] And then there were taxes. Louis Temporale sent an invoice to her on 14 January for the full Ontario sales tax she owed for his work carving the granite base, reminding her that she could apply to Ottawa for a reduced tax, at which time they would invoice her on the lesser amount.[29] Loring was irritated, as always, that Ontario — unlike the federal government and Quebec — charged a three percent education tax on creative work.[30]

Even while she worked on Borden, Frances was a guest teacher at OCA.[31] And she would soon seize the opportunity to profit from the new interest business was showing in the arts by sculpting a bust of John William Billes, the founder and late president of Canadian Tire Corporation, in 1959.[32] Fortunately for both The Girls, Florence, who had now often become a mere footnote to media accounts of Loring's accomplishments (her "portrait relief, also fine work" an afterthought to the description of Loring's lion), continued to bring in money.[33] She had been paid her commission for the Counsell Fountain in 1957, and had also received payment in 1956 from the National Gallery in Ottawa for her portrait busts of A.Y. Jackson and Fred Varley: $2,000 for Jackson and $1,800 for Varley.[34] In 1958, the Art Gallery of Toronto finally commissioned an Aur-Italian marble of her *Draped Torso*, the plaster model of which had appeared in the New York World's Fair of 1939.[35] That same year, she was commissioned to do a portrait medallion of Pauline McGibbon.[36] Florence's efforts in the 1950s to pursue ethnic sculpture (as other Canadian sculptors also did) had not been especially successful. Her head of black tenor *Roland Hayes* (1953) was displayed at an RCA show in December 1953.[37] And her large wood statue of a black girl, *Negress*, elicited lukewarm comments from critics who were puzzled at this "new departure in style ... She has preferred in the past the child figure or the young girl and her works have always been characterized by a femininity, a sweetness — without mawkish sentimentality. In the study of the Negro girl there is a characteristic gracefulness, but it is the gracefulness of a lithe primitive girl rather than that of a child of civilization. And there are a strength and a natural heaviness that are new to Wyle sculpture."[38]

In fact, such creations had long since served their purpose as a transition. Although younger sculptors were drawing effectively on influences from "primitive" cultures for their semi-abstract or abstract creations, the time had come when ethnic sculptors themselves would depict their culture and values in ways far different from mainstream white artists. As early as 1951, fine works in argillite by Haida artists from the Queen Charlotte Islands, and stone and ivory carvings by the Inuit at Cape Dorset, such as Tikketuk's *Seal Hunter*, were being displayed and highly praised.[39] Such works — which soon established their ongoing value as art — made the attempts of outsiders like Loring and Wyle obsolete.

The 1951 article about Canadian sculpture in *Canadian Geographical* stands as typical of the transition that tilted sculpture away from the old-fashioned, British or European representational and monumental, towards the abstract, semi-abstract or primitive, industrial and contemporary works — often in new materials — that would soon dominate. Loring's bust, *Sir Frederick Banting*, and Elizabeth Wyn Wood's bust, *Stephen Leacock*, represented one end of the spectrum. A.B. Zoltany's carvings of saints on the pulpit of Notre Dame Cathedral in Montreal were typical of the "new and increasing activity in ecclesiastical woodcarving"[40] that represented the current trend in Quebec. The bas-relief frieze in Montreal's Central Railway Station by Charles F. Comfort depicted activities of family, farm, and commerce, and Montrealer Fritz Brandtner's plaque *Neptune*, one of three on the station's exterior, represented the alliance between architecture and sculpture which the Massey-Lévesque Report encouraged. A semi-abstract half-figure — part owl, part man — indicated the trend of young Canadian sculptors to adapt primitive motifs to their contemporary works; and Haida and Inuit carvings indicated the entry of these marginalized ethnic groups into the mainstream of Canadian sculpture.

A similar spectrum of sculptural styles and subjects appeared in 1958 in *The Arts in Canada: A Stocktaking at Mid-Century*, edited by Malcolm Ross. William S.A. Dale, who contributed the section on sculpture, wrote that Loring's *Lion, Queen Elizabeth Way* and Wyle's sumac carving *Summer* represented the "competent conservatives" (Loring is singled out as "a traditional sculptor of great power"),[41] and Sylvia Daoust's pine *Madonna* is described as "a streamlined version of the earlier French-Canadian style."[42] *Blackboard*, the wall decoration for Blackburn Corners Public School made by Arthur Price from slate, bronze, and aluminum, typifies the semi-abstract, as does Louis Archambault's welded steel *L'Oiseau de fer*. The abstract is represented by Archambault's wall decorations for the Canadian Pavilion at the Brussels World Fair, 1958;[43] the maquette of Anne Kahane's winner of the competition for The Unknown Political Prisoner; another of her abstracts, the carved wood *Air Show*; and a phallic marble abstract, *Groundhog*, by Elford Cox. Aboriginal work is seen in the jolly, squat *Woman Holding a Fish*, an Inuit carving of serpentine by Johnny Innukpuk. Although Dale mentions Inuit sculptors Innukpuk, Akeeaktashook, and Munamee, he dismisses their work and fails to foresee the huge industry in excellent Inuit sculpture that their work heralded. "Launched ten years ago," he writes, "the vogue in Eskimo carvings in soapstone and serpentine" — despite "exceptional pieces" — "show little understanding of design and material, and whatever charm and vitality they may once have had as naive art has already given way to smooth sophistication."[44]

Loring and Wyle had been instrumental in getting Charlie Sheguapit into the ssc in 1958, and "promptly made him president." Sheguapit expressed his thanks in Inuit script, saying he would sculpt his best so as not to "dishonour the society."[45] However, they, too, expressed concern about Inuit sculptors' lack of training, and thought Canada's Indians were more skilled in "creating form."[46]

Florence even attempted to educate Canadian children about sculpture (and to raise money) by putting together a small booklet for elementary school children called "Sculpture Appreciation," with suggestions for different grade levels from Kindergarten through Grade Eight.[47] The ideas it contains — such as her inclusion of the old 1948 NFB film *Third Dimension* for Grades Five through Eight, which would probably have seemed almost incomprehensible to children, and her insistence that sculpture have "a quiet, serene feeling" — were already passé. Florence must have had in mind at least some school visits to The Church, for her text describes The

Church's studio, and she invents a story for children, "Tarzan the Cat," which is obviously meant to be accompanied by her own *Sleeping Cat* (1949–50): "Don't you have the feeling that at any moment Tarzan (so-named by her because of his 'beloved personality' since he 'swoops' from one sculpture to another) will wake up and rub his paw across his ears and face, quite satisfied with his 'Cat-nap'?"[48]

Ironically, Loring and Wyle's determination to educate the public and bring sculpture to the people ultimately spelled their own relegation to the sidelines as the new trends which were so startling and unpalatable at the Armory Show in 1913 finally took hold in Canada.

At its completion, Loring saw the Borden project as the culmination of her "pioneering work" in Canada. This myth — which she now believed was a genetic trait inherited from her father — had become even more deeply entrenched in her self-image. "Working in this country," she said, "[is] a stimulating experience. Here [I] can create something of [my] own and use [my] inherited pioneer instincts."[49]

⚜DEATH MASQUE⚜

Wills⤳

The completion of Frances's *Sir Robert Borden* statue seems to have marked a turning point for the Loring-Wyles. Or perhaps it was the awards each had won — Florence's Coronation Medal, then Loring's two university awards — or simply their failing health, which gave them the sense that their time was running out.

Frances became more and more lethargic, as if she were giving in to the inevitable. "I'm having a lot of eye trouble so I'm trying to slow down," she wrote to a friend in 1958. "One can expect a variety of decrepitudes as old age creeps upon one — Anyway I can still climb a scaffolding."[1] Florence typically resisted the inroads of age. When she was interviewed "in the studio where many Canadian art movements began," just after her eightieth birthday in November, she boasted that she was still shovelling snow. "I've got a lot of muscle," she claimed proudly, as if she were still competing with her twin brother. To a teasing question about whether she planned to retire, she erupted, "Never! I hope to die standing at work!"[2] To this typically blunt response, she added the same statement of moral purpose she set out with as a medical student in Urbana, Illinois, over sixty years earlier: "Work is life; and I hope to leave work of some use to people."[3]

The commission Florence was working on at the time was scaled-down copies of the Dominion Drama Festival awards. These were to be kept permanently by the winners, who until then had had to return the original large woodcarvings in time for the next competition. This — like so much of what The Girls were working on — was not original work. As Christine Boyanoski points out, Wyle worked within "very narrow limits" and believed that "innovations could be made only in terms of subject matter."[4] Her description of her work in a questionnaire for the Vocational Guidance Centre made plain the fact that the new materials and new techniques that were informing contemporary sculpture had eluded her. "The practical work," she wrote, "varies little within its limits, but the subject matter which is the essence of any art work, changes with each new piece of work."[5] Although Loring was more venturesome in such works as her *Mother and Children* panel for the Women's Building at the CNE, and was willing to explain in her lectures some of the new techniques used by contemporary sculptors, such as the holes in Henry Moore's colossal abstract and semi-abstract creations, as Boyanoski points out, "it is evident from [Loring and Wyle's] tendency to fall back on earlier solutions to aesthetic problems, reworking old themes in a new context, that there had been few new ideas in their work for a number of years."[6]

IN 1958, THE Girls began to take stock of their works as if they sensed time might be short. In 1959, Florence wrote old friend Norah de Pencier — who had sent money for their 1958 Christmas party — that they had given up parties and had diverted the money "towards casting some of their work."[7] They had never been thorough at cataloguing and often forgot when specific works had been completed. But now on 21 November 1958, they carefully typed up a list of their works, the materials they were made from, the number of copies they were prepared to produce for sale, and the price of each work. This list did not include all their sculpture by any means; it focused on the works that they were taking to the Pollock Gallery at 599 Markham Street, which had agreed to represent their work for public sale. The busts they had made of each other as young women in Greenwich Village in 1910 were available in bronze for $1,500 each. Wyle included seven fountains, in stone or bronze, of which she could make from three to seven copies. The prices for these works ranged from $1,800 to $6,000. She also listed her *Mother of the Race* torso ($4,500). All told, she had over forty-eight works to go. Loring had twenty-three pieces, including the bronze head of Sir Robert Borden ($2,500), the two remaining copies of the five she had made of Dr. Frederick Banting ($2,000), her *Eskimo Mother and Child* ($7,500), and her *Goal Keeper* ($10,000).

The *Goal Keeper* had already almost sold. Conn Smythe, who had named the Toronto Maple Leafs when he bought the hockey team in 1927, was now managing director and president of Maple Leaf Gardens, and Loring, who knew nothing about hockey, appealed to "anyone at the Gardens" to cast her statue in bronze as a display piece for Smythe's hockey arena on Carlton Street. The directors agreed to install the plaster model so they could see what it looked like. At seven and a half feet, it had to be cut in two pieces to get it out of the studio and into the rink. "A man telephoned the next day," Loring recalled, "a Mr. Smythe. All he said was 'Get your statue out of here. It's too big. No room for it.'"[8]

In another gesture that implied that their time might be limited, Florence collected the poems she had been neatly printing in old date books and scribblers and reading aloud to Frances and their friends for years, and with the editing assistance of Vancouverite Ira Dilworth published them in 1959 with Ryerson Press. The year was propitious for Canadian literature, for it was that year that Hugh MacLennan launched his landmark novel *The Watch That Ends the Night*, which, along with the earlier, less-successful *Two Solitudes*, made him the pre-eminent Canadian nationalist novelist. Florence Wyle's sixteen-page *Poems* was the sixty-first in the Ryerson Poetry Chap-Book Series brought out under the general editorship of Lorne Pierce, had a modest print run of 250 copies, and sold for a dollar a copy. The other sixty included names that had already begun to form the central canon of Canadian poetry: Sir Charles G.D. Roberts, Bliss Carman, Dorothy Livesay, Elizabeth Brewster, Raymond Souster, Louis Dudek, and Al Purdy. In his foreword, Dilworth does his best to find merit in Florence's poetry. He calls her "an accomplished and arresting artist," but admits, "there is little in her verse which can be properly described as modern or experimental." Since signs of modernism in Canadian poetry began to appear as early as the mid-1930s in the work of Patrick Anderson, A.J.M. Smith, Frank Scott, P.K. Page, Dorothy Livesay, Robert Finch, and Irving Layton, the implication is that Florence was as outdated in her poetry as she was in her sculpture. One reviewer's first impression was that "poetic form does not interest her as much as her expression of an artist's love of beauty and a sculptor's desire to reduce a thought to its simplest and most direct expression."[9] She does not sink to sentimental verses about cats, however; there are felicitous lines ("Your hands are swift and sure") and sensitive phrases ("the unhurrying snow") in the descriptive poems she writes about nature and the human condition that reveal how keenly she observed physical and emotional states of being. More often she lapses into cliché: "Thin leaves a-droop on the bough" or "little streams come singing down."[10] Purged of their nineteenth-century Romantic excesses, there are echoes of the simple, homespun Robert Frost. It is not surprising that the Canada Council refused her a grant to publish more of her poetry six years later.

As the new decade of the 1960s opened — a decade that would see a revolution in the arts that would spin Canada's artistic community headlong into a space Loring and Wyle could hardly imagine — a major piece on them by John R. Lewis appeared in *Star Weekly Magazine*. Despite all the years of media coverage — mainly in Toronto, and the rest of Ontario — that had steadily documented their careers since 1912, and despite the fact that three years earlier Loring's *Sir Robert Borden* had created a media stir, Lewis claimed, "Frances Loring ... despite her years, and the contribution she has made to Canadian art, is probably the only major artist in the country whom practically nobody knows. Her work is seen daily by passersby in Ottawa, Toronto, Galt, St. Stephen, N.B., and Augusta, Maine. Thousands have seen her face and heard her speak on CBC television [and radio] programs, but the recognition is fleeting."[11] Partly, Lewis is reflecting Loring's own disillusionment, for he goes on to report her view that "the best a good Canadian sculptor can hope for is recognition by the small circle of art patrons and devotees who know and appreciate outstanding talent. To the great mass of Canadian people, he remains a virtual non-entity. He may feed their souls with beauty and inspiration, but he's happy if, in the process, he can earn a bricklayer's wages. [This] can be doubled in spades if the sculptor should happen to be a woman."[12]

Loring and Wyle had good reason to feel disillusioned. Lewis cites D.W. Buchanan, associate director of the National Gallery in Ottawa: "Frances Loring is a great Canadian sculptor — in the traditional vein, of course, but the best sculptor in that vein."[13] It was faint praise, a far cry from the hearty enthusiasms of Sir Edmund Walker and Eric Brown long ago. Lewis goes on to quote an unnamed member of Toronto's Arts and Letters Club as saying, "[She's] one of the best sculptors Canada has produced. In her day, that is." Worse, Lewis quotes a representative of "the younger generation," Robert Fulford, art critic of the *Toronto Daily Star*. "Dr. Loring is inarticulate in the language of form," Fulford said. "There is nothing either beautiful or stimulating in her work. Her contribution to art is about on a par with President Eisenhower's contribution to political oratory."[14]

Although Lewis explains in detail the enormous effort — the "ton of clay" needed for a life-size statue, "two tons of plaster" for modelling, the "astronomic energy" it takes to create sculpture, especially monumental works like so many of Loring's — he settles for a portrait of them as a pair of old ladies "in their sunset years" pottering about with "the only members of the general public who know them well, the bevy of children who visit them regularly [for cookies and milk], to watch them at work and to bring them wounded birds for first-aid and sympathetic care ... The children do not even know their names," he adds. "To them, Dr. Loring and Miss Wyle are 'the clay ladies.'"

It was true that The Girls had slowed down and become crotchety in their "sunset years." Florence was less tactful than ever, though Frances was — in public at least — moderate about her views on contemporary sculpture. Rebecca Sisler recalls that when wealthy collectors did call, intending to see and perhaps buy some of their work, "Florence managed to scuttle their hopes."[15]

As Sisler recounts the anecdote, Frances cautioned Florence on one occasion, before the arrival of a wealthy collector and his wife. "Try not to mention Henry Moore," she said. "Henry Moore! Hmph!" Florence answered.

"Why should I mention him and those distortions that pass for sculptures nowadays?" When the couple arrived, Florence let them in. She was "the sweet, agreeable, vague self that she usually was with strangers." She showed them around the studio while Frances reclined regally among pillows on the sagging sofa. After some preliminary chit-chat, one of their guests said, "We are so fond of the work of Henry Moore." Florence exploded, "Rubbish!" The collectors were stunned. Frances intervened, hoping to salvage the occasion. "I don't agree with what Henry Moore says particularly, but I agree with his right to say it. Miss Wyle prefers the classics." At which Florence, unable to contain her indignation, expostulated. "I could never forgive him for boring holes in through a figure!" The flustered couple rose to Moore's defence, hoping to convince Florence. "But Moore weds the technical skill of the best classical traditions with new basic concepts. Surely you agree?" "Not at all!" maintained Florence, now thoroughly incensed. Then she launched into a stern lecture on the merits of classic sculpture as opposed to the decadent modern trends.[16] At this, the collectors stood up and left.[17]

Loring and Wyle had been cast aside, as the ineluctable development of sculptural styles moved relentlessly on. Welded sculpture, especially — which could be traced back to about 1930 when Julio Gonzales and Pablo Picasso attempted to render Cubism into three dimensions[18] — seemed like nonsense to The Girls. Even Frances, who was more open to new developments than Florence, doubted its authenticity. "Some of it is research work that may lead somewhere," she said, "But most of it is adult kindergarten work. They're having an awfully good time, and it's fun and it's humorous. But people in a hundred years from now aren't going to see any humour in rusted automobile fenders." Naturally Florence dismissed it with exasperation. "They bring in a heap of rubbish from the street, and set it up and call it modern sculpture. Doesn't sound very interesting to me."[19]

AN ISSUE OF *Canadian Art* in the summer of 1962 was devoted entirely to sculpture, with 126 pages of illustrated sections on painter-sculptors, welders, carvers, and modellers.[20] There was not one representational statue or portrait bust of the type Loring and Wyle had created to be seen among the fifty-four illustrations, and certainly nothing by either of them. The majority —

especially those that were welded — were completely abstract and had titles like Walter Yarwood's *Solar Device*, or Armand Vaillancourt's *Disponible* ("Available"), or Kazuo Nakamura's *Block Structure*, or David Partridge's *Standing Configuration No. 9*, or Morton Rosengarten's *Composition*. Some were semi-abstract, verging on abstract, like Harold Town's *Baroque Tree*, or Anne Kahane's *Beach Figure*, or Ted Bieler's *Bouquet*. Others drew consciously on primitive art for powerful abstract or semi-abstract creations, like Gord Smith's *A People*, or Walter Yarwood's *Small Totem*, or Yosef Drenters's *Prehistoric Drawing*.[21]

Elizabeth Kilbourn, writing of the painter-sculptors, emphasizes the "very rapid disintegration of the formal distinctions between space and time" that can be seen in contemporary sculpture. This perceptual shift was a direct result of the space race between the U.S. and the U.S.S.R., which resulted in the launching of *Sputnik*, the first Soviet satellite, followed by *Sputnik 2* a month later, and the U.S. launch of *Explorer* two months after that. "We are obsessed with the space between galaxies," Kilbourn observed, "or between protons and electrons ... Not since the end of the Middle Ages have artists in western society been confronted with the need to come to terms with new concepts of space." Acknowledging Marcel Duchamp's *Nude Descending a Staircase* as a point of departure, she claimed that Boccioni's sculpture *Unique Forms of Continuity in Space* (1913) was a translation into bronze of Duchamp's famous painting.[22] These were the antecedents of Canada's sculpture in the early 1960s.

The concept of beauty, which had been so important to neoclassic figurative sculptors, no longer held. In the face of rapid advances in the sciences, which challenged absolutes of all kinds, with the influx of media that revealed a world lacking in the ideals that had seduced the western populace into the Great War, the pursuit of beauty in the arts seemed archaic and effete, almost laughable. Torontonian woodcarver Irving Burman, thirty-four, spoke for the generation that had known Hiroshima and Auschwitz when he said, "What I see is not a pleasant thing." And, as David P. Silcox commented, "[Burman's] work is opposed to an over-assuming idealization. It conveys a powerful sense of scepticism and unnaturalness. His figures are blasted, distorted by agony, twisted in pain or standing in contemptuous arrogance against ideals of kindness, generosity and love ..."[23] The found object sculpture

which — a century later — was voted by 500 art experts "the most influen-
tial work of all time," was a work representative of the modernist movement:
Marcel Duchamp's *Fountain*.²⁴ The Girls would have been horrified.

The new generation of Canadian sculptors seemed dismissive of — even
oblivious to — the sculptors like Loring and Wyle, or Allward, Hahn and
Wyn Wood, who had preceded them. No one seemed to notice that
Loring's *Eskimo Mother and Child* had been the only Canadian sculpture sent
to the Canadian pavilion of the Venice Biennale in 1959. This was not surprising, since the notice in the *Toronto Daily Star* was headed "Our Men in
Venice."²⁵ The thirty-three-year-old Torontonian Gerald Gladstone, who
had spent the previous year in England on a Canada Council grant that
would not have been possible had artists like Loring not fought for recognition of the arts, said, "Canadian sculpture as an individual statement does not
exist. It relates directly to Europe or the USA ... My work relates directly to
the uneasy shift of values that is taking place now in modern society from
naive religious views to new scientific fact."²⁶ Thirty-one-year-old Croatian
immigrant Augustin Filipovic, who had been in Canada only three years,
said, "It is very obvious that the sculpture of Canada has not shown enough
maturity to be compared with the high achievement of contemporary European sculpture ... I am not happy with the state of sculpture here."²⁷ Not
surprisingly, Filipovic's work is influenced by Impressionism, Cubism, and
Abstraction, ideas he was passing on to his students at the Ontario College
of Art. Montrealer Morton Rosengarten, twenty-nine, asked, "Who else
[but us] is there?" referring to his generation of sculptors. He points to the
issue of *Canadian Art* itself, and accuses it of "imply[ing] that there is a large
group of senior sculptors of achievement — well-known and respected —
and in doing so betrays the fact that they (and this is typical of the Canadian
attitude towards sculpture) have not been able to distinguish between something that approaches sculpture and bullshit."²⁸

One of the excitements these younger, mostly male, sculptors claimed
as their own was the element of chance. This is especially true of welders,
who created works with metals and found objects as they went. But even
other modes of sculpting lent themselves to a process of discovery: "The
casting process itself can be used as a very direct creative medium," said

Rosengarten, words that would have chilled The Girls with their careful observance of anatomy, the delicate procedures of plaster casting and bronze moulds, and the calculated pointing procedure by which their maquettes were enlarged into marble and stone before being honed to beauty. All agreed, however, that the time had come when a sculptor in Canada could support himself.

The sculpture that, with hindsight, stands out in the 1962 sculpture issue of *Canadian Art* because it had become so popular in Toronto and elsewhere, is thirty-three-year-old painter-sculptor Michael Snow's *Walking Woman*, which was first displayed at his one-man show in the Isaacs Gallery on Yonge St. on the edge of Yorkville. "Michael Snow took a pattern of a female figure," writes Elizabeth Kilbourn, "in spirit very close to Matisse's 1952 Venus collage, and used it to explore the two-dimensional space of the canvas. But he also used the pattern to build up, with wooden strips and hammer and nails, a piece of sculpture, or at least a three-dimensional figure, a woman made from the inside out, building up her planes and forms more literally than is possible in modelling."[29] Such a concept — especially in sculpting the female form — would have been incomprehensible to Loring and Wyle.

AT THE CHURCH, which like its owners, was slowly falling into disrepair, Frances and Florence undertook more sculpture. "Florence was not well, but she had the self-discipline to pace herself." She could will herself to go on. But Frances — who had relied on bursts of energy and stamina to carry her through — was failing rapidly. Her arthritis and bursitis had almost crippled her, and her eyesight was worse. "It became almost a major engineering feat to get her dressed, out of the Church, and into a waiting car, in order to attend the meetings that meant so much to her. The time came when she was no longer part of the functioning machinery of art politics. Her impotent body could not rise to her will and she resented it bitterly."[30]

In 1962, the same year that *Canadian Art* celebrated Canada's new generation of sculptors, a small commission — Frances's last — came from Mrs. Herbert Bruce, the wife of a Toronto surgeon. Her husband's hands had worked skilfully for many years, and now that he was ninety-two, she wanted a sculpture of them.

Frances's own arthritic hands were barely capable of completing the sculpture, which took most of the long, hot summer. She could barely see, and her aged model could not sustain for long the pose she insisted on, with the right index finger raised as if to probe sensitively. Even when she cast the work her eyesight betrayed her, for she accidentally included her best metal rasp in the base of the plaster. It was the last work she was to complete.[31]

She was distracted from facing this hard truth by an invitation from Clare Bice, curator at the London (Ontario) Library and Art Gallery, who wanted to mount a retrospective of The Girls' major works from 2 to 27 November 1962. A.Y. Jackson called it "their last big effort."[32] Somehow, the two of them scrubbed up, mended, and transported their works to London. By the opening night, seventy pieces of their work — including Frances's *Goal Keeper*, *Miner*, *Sir Frederick Banting*, *Girl with Fish*, and Florence's *Justice*, *Negress*, *A.Y. Jackson*, *F. H. Varley*, and *Chicago* — had been transported to London.

AND THERE THE Loring-Wyles stood on the opening night of "Fifty Years of Sculpture in Canada," which would tour London, Hamilton, and Windsor. Frances, her thinning hair still pulled back like a Spanish dancer's, now leaned on two canes, and Florence stood slightly behind her, as if in deference to her "Queenie," surrounded by the many old friends and patrons they had known over the years and by the works that now seemed like old friends themselves. Frances was dramatically wrapped in black velvet, "her bulk regally draped in a scarlet Chinese silk stole." Florence was turned out in the "frayed dignity" of her old double-breasted grey suit with an artist's soft black bow tie under the collar of her man's shirt.[33] Dr. Charles Comfort, with his trim goatee, himself a painter and now director of the National Gallery, came from Ottawa to open the exhibition. "The man or woman who carves idealistically in the tradition of cultural heritage is rare," he said. "Loring and Wyle belong among these rare artists ... Together they contributed greatly to the early decades of art in Toronto in the 20th century when the Canadian art movement was becoming a lively force." He went on, and his remarks expressed his lively admiration for the Loring-Wyles, even if they weren't entirely accurate, "They have received all the honors Canada can give ... [This] is an exhibition which I think is long overdue to recognize the contribution made by these great artists."[34] One of the show's reviewers called them "unflagging zealots."[35] The show attracted more viewers than had been seen at the London gallery for over ten years.[36] It was the first time Florence had attended such an occasion in a long while. It was to be the last time, after fifty years of living and working together, that they appeared in public as a couple.

Inspired by the high of the London retrospective, Florence was determined to go on working. "I haven't time," she declared, when pressed to take part in some event away from the studio. "I'm senile, you know. My days are numbered and I have a lot of work to do."[37] She continued a sculpture that she had been evolving in her mind for years and for which she had made a small plaster maquette. She wanted to represent in smooth Carrara marble the idea — now more pertinent than ever as the years before her dwindled — that "the tide comes in and the tide goes out but the sea and shore remain."[38] As so often before, the symbol took the form of a woman whose arched loveliness would "evoke the feeling of a sea-wave falling on the shore."[39] The concept was derivative, hearkening back to Elizabeth Wyn Wood's *Reef and Rainbow* (1931). It was to be called *Sea and Shore*.

Louis Temporale, the Port Credit carver who had known The Girls "long before the war" and had roughed out Loring's *Eskimo Mother and Child* and her head of Borden, as well as assisting with the Bank of Montreal reliefs, for the first time found Florence difficult to work with. "Desperate to condense the whole lifetime of her commitment into this work," she could not be satisfied with anything Temporale did.[40]

When Temporale had done his best, and she had the piece back in the studio, she moved her stand to the middle of the main studio so the full light from the skylight could illuminate it. There she continued to chip away at it with her chisel and smooth its sparkling beauty with the rasp, while keeping an eye on Frances reclining on her couch looking through a sheaf of papers. "Oh Florence! Do leave it alone!" Frances would remonstrate as Florence worked feverishly away. "You're completely ruining it — you're polishing it too much!"[41] "Well," Florence would say, standing back and craning her neck to assess the statue's lines, "Just a slight bit more here that has to be ..."[42] And — since its beauty did not seem quite perfect — back she would go.

She stopped working on *Sea and Shore* only because the deadline was imminent for submissions for the annual OSA show where she had not exhibited anything for several years. Down it went — as so many of her works had gone before — to the Art Gallery of Toronto. In a few weeks, she received the customary letter from the OSA jurors. When she opened it, "she froze." *Sea and Shore* — the last sculpture she would create — had been rejected. "Why?" she asked, bewildered.[43]

A FEW MONTHS later, in June 1963, The Girls drew up wills that were identical in every way except for a few family details. No doubt it was Florence's idea that they willed their bodies to the University of Toronto for medical research.[44] Overall their wills carried forward — beyond their imagined deaths — the commitment to sculpture that had bonded them from their first meeting at the Art Institute of Chicago, through their Greenwich Village time, and on into half a century of establishing sculpture as an important fine art in Canada. It was their "mutual wish and desire to assist and encourage Canadian Sculpture," their wills read, "and by means of gifts to public institutions of learning across Canada, to afford to the people of Canada particularly, the opportunity of seeing, appreciating and enjoying the work of Canadian sculptors."[45] They intended their studio to go to the Royal Canadian Academy of Art, with no bitterness that Florence had had to wait so long to become a full member — and that Frances waited even longer. (Frances was not made a full member of the academy until 1947.) They hoped the academy would use The Church as a gallery and would continue to welcome guests, "especially neighbourhood children." If the academy could not accomplish this, the studio was to be sold, the proceeds going to a sculpture fund, which would also include any money the sale of their works might bring in. To administer this fund, a "Sculptor Advisory Committee" — made up of a sculptor from the RCA and the OSA, the president of the SSC, and "from time to time" the directors of the National Gallery of Canada and the Art Gallery of Toronto — were to advise the trustees, David Ongley and Frances Gage.[46] This fund was to be used "to purchase works of sculpture ... whether in completed form or by commission, produced by Canadian sculptors ordinarily resident in Canada."[47]

To help The Girls financially in their last years, a group organized by Guelph sculptor Sophia Hungerford, with Keith McIver and Elizabeth Gordon, in 1962, called the Friends of Loring and Wyle — including long-time friends A.Y. Jackson, W.L. Somerville, Charles S. Band, Pearl McCarthy, Eleanor Sniderman, Mary Jackman, Pauline McGibbon, and Norah de Pencier — raised a substantial amount of money ($6,657.07 before the end of the year)[48] in secret.[49] Ostensibly, the fund supported the cause of sculpture, but indirectly it offered financial assistance to the Loring-Wyles (who had sold only one piece of Florence's at the London retrospective for $35) by purchasing their sculptures and donating them to smaller regional galleries, including Windsor, London, Kitchener, Guelph, and Sarnia.[50] By 1964, The Girls were aware of this project, and had begun sending off various works for casting into bronze to the Roman Bronze Works in Corona, New York, the firm that had been casting their works since their Greenwich Village days. (The specially discounted price for casting Florence's head of A.Y. Jackson was $275 instead of $325, and other prices varied according to size; she offered such bronzes in 1964 for between $2,000 and $3,500.)[51] The "Friends" purchased a bronze casting of Loring's *Eskimo Mother and Child* for the Edmonton Art Gallery, and tried without success to persuade Philip Givens, mayor of Toronto, to have Loring's *Goal Keeper* cast in bronze and erected in front of the Hockey Hall of Fame at the Canadian National Exhibition grounds. They also approached Ryerson Press (which had published Florence's *Poems* in 1959) and the Macmillan Company of Canada to publish a book about Loring and Wyle — mainly photographs of their work and a short biography. Though The Girls supported this project, and both publishers — especially Ryerson Press — were interested, no book appeared.[52]

The Friends of Loring and Wyle stepped in to supplement any other source of income The Girls might have had. Then, finally, on 12 December 1963, Frances sold the mining claims in the Larder Lake Mining Division in Temiskaming for $4,000.[53] Mischievous as usual, Frances — who knew she had this nest egg — told journalist John Lewis, tongue-in-cheek, "Miss Wyle and I are looking for a millionaire who won't mind spending a few thousand dollars a month on bronze castings or stone so we can make our best pieces permanent."[54]

Disintegrations ⬱

Frances's sale of her mining stocks in 1963 ought to have ensured a life of relative comfort for The Girls. But years of stringent living and their declining health inhibited them. Florence, in particular, was constitutionally unable to indulge in luxuries, and arthritis had seized her joints. "Ouchie, ouchie" was her constant refrain. In the early '60s, The Girls had become more eccentric than ever, and it was only a matter of time until their eccentricities became debilitating. Conversations between the two of them — even in the presence of interviewers — were crustier and more outspoken than ever. In these exchanges, they were almost caricatures of their earlier selves, repeating anecdotes they had told often before and expressing opinions that were no longer cheeky and charming, but downright reactionary. They attacked the "silly lace tablecloths" used by Women's Committees to whom they owed so much and — of course — modern art, which had passed them by. "You don't find beauty in welding," Florence would stoutly maintain. Gallery committees, they maintained flatly, "know nothing about art." So close had they drawn after almost half a century together that in interviews they spoke almost as one. Like an old married couple, the Loring-Wyles interrupted each other, finished each other's sentences, and veered off onto trivial tangents understood only by themselves. Compared to the incisive verve Frances had displayed in earlier interviews, she was now likely to ramble on about how much she liked climbing a scaffold — something she actually could no longer do — or about the way the neighbourhood children escorted her as she walked with her canes down the block. Florence was likely to add to this that she went along and gave the children talks on kindness to animals and encouraged them to bring her dead birds to be buried. She would talk endlessly about the Greeks, the beauty of their art, the necessity of exposing children to "good sculpture." To which Loring — miffed by the failure of her *Goal Keeper* to find a place of honour — was likely to add with disgust, "Canadians are only interested in sports, in football."[1]

As early as 1961, close friends like A.Y. Jackson noticed that they were unstable. "Saw Frances and Florence," he wrote to a mutual friend, "having a tough time — both cracked up."[2] By 1963, he reported that Sophia Hungerford had written him to say, "It may be necessary to have someone look after Frances and Florence. They can not take care of themselves much longer."[3]

Frances was increasingly angry at the deterioration of her body. The realization that she could not curb her weight or climb a scaffold again infuriated her, and she was given to bursts of temper that became more and more violent. "When I depart from this world, and want to come back to haunt you," she began announcing to Florence, with the authority of a queen, "listen for my canes. When you hear them you'll know it's me with a message for you."

And with that she would hurl her canes from the studio down the stairwell ahead of her before descending laboriously down the walled-in staircase to the dining room in the Crypt for dinner. The loathed canes — symbols of her loss of independence — and would "dance and clatter from step to step" and against the walls before crashing into the room below. It had become a common occurrence, a harrowing experience for the few guests who still shared The Girls' generosity at dinner.[4]

Not only had the boundaries between the two of them begun to dissolve, their grasp of reality was slowly becoming tenuous. By early 1963, Frances Gage, who was the most energetic of the Friends of Loring and Wyle, began letting people know how bad The Girls — especially Frances — actually were. They no longer had a car, and Frances Gage now did their shopping for them, always including Canadian Club rye for Frances and vanilla ice cream for Florence.

Florence's niece, Helen Von Drache in Sarasota, Florida, responded to a letter from Gage in early February 1963: "Your letter of the 28th [January] came as quite a shock. Jean Irving wrote during the [Christmas Holidays] that both Aunt Florence and Frances were better in health than for several years. In talking with Aunt Florence while we were there this summer and in former correspondence we understand that the Art Society, to whom Aunt Florence & Frances are leaving their property, would have someone staying with them as required."[5] Helen coolly kept Florence's situation at arms' length. She is almost seventy herself, she writes; it is out of the question that she come to take care of Florence. Florence would be welcome there (but not Frances), but only if her medical expenses were covered. Besides, Florence refused to visit there in the past and she has told her "she would not be happy away from her work and she doesn't like warm weather." Helen could only "help out a little" financially. Frances Gage, appalled at Helen's lack of concern for her aunt,[6] wrote back even more coolly assuring her that she need not come to Toronto, that Florence would be looked after financially, and that "whatever is done for Miss Wyle & Miss Loring should be done as long as possible in their own home."[7] Helen did come up later, and removed Frances from the hospital after her "coronary" — in reality a severe bout of dementia. "The niece got her out," Frances Gage recalls, "then left her with David and me to deal with. We then had to find round-the-clock help, as the dementia was very bad."[8] Another concerned relative of Florence's (who called Frances "Minty") wrote from Los Angeles, California, to ask if it was true that "Minty" had been in hospital with a coronary. "Who is looking after you chaps, or coming in to see you?"[9] Even Florence admitted openly that she was "getting hazy" that summer of 1962 when her niece visited.[10]

It is ironic that Miss Briault — a stranger — wrote to Frances in November 1962 asking her advice about the possibility that sculpture might be helpful to someone she knew who was mentally ill. In one of her more lucid moments, Frances wrote back to say that she didn't know enough about mental conditions to say "whether sculpture might be beneficial or merely frustrating" to such a patient. But she added, "I have always felt that the mere act of handling clay could be very soothing."[11] Clay was not soothing enough to prevent Frances from having periods of hallucinations — usually that she was being persecuted in some way. "She thought people were coming after her. When she had such spells, she shouted, and so on."[12]

The *Hound of Heaven* Frances had created in the Church Street studio when she and Florence had moved to Toronto all those years ago, and which was one of the statues on display in the London retrospective, had become an intermittent reality for her — though, in Frances's case it was entirely devoid of religious meaning. At those times she was like the guilty woman in flight, one hand to her contorted face, cringing and looking over her shoulder. Like the lines from Francis Thompson's poem, she "fled down the labyrinthine ways / Of [her] own mind," hearing the warning, "All things betray thee, who betrayest Me."[13] Her *A Dream within a Dream* — which spoke of the desire to prevent the passage of time[14] — was becoming a nightmare.

On the occasions when she lapsed into that nightmare, her conversations became urgent and incoherent. What had been the wry statements of an opinionated eccentric were now rants of persecution. Her canes became weapons. She began to destroy things, swinging the canes wildly at anything in her path. "Once she broke a window with her cane," Frances Gage recalls, "then she started attacking Florence. We were afraid she would harm her. She was convinced that Florence was an imposter. When she shouted, 'You are an imposter! An imposter!' Florence would indignantly say, 'No, I am the *real* Florence Wyle.' Then Frances would scream furiously, 'No, you aren't. You're an *imposter!*' Florence gradually became sweetly demented, but Frances really went mad."[15]

Celluloid ⤳

There is only one visual record of Frances Loring interacting with Florence Wyle — a videotape of the weekly CBC Television program *Telescope*. It is a documentary profile produced by Peter Kelly and directed by Christopher Chapman. The program aired at 9:30 p.m. on 7 May 1965 when The Girls were long past their prime: Loring was seventy-seven, and Wyle was eighty-three. The CBC is paying tribute to the "two charming women ... in their large rambling studio."[1] The host, Fletcher Markle, an unctuous man with hair slicked neatly back and wearing a dark jacket and tie, introduces the evening's guests. He has the mid-Atlantic accent favoured at the time. His introduction touches on most of the points that have gelled into Toronto mythology over the years: the initial friendship of "two marvellous young ladies," Loring's European "sojourn," the founding of the Sculptors' Society of Canada, Loring's *Eskimo Mother and Child* right there on display, her "great stone lion" and Sir Robert Borden, Wyle's bust of *A. Y. Jackson*, also on display, their salon in the romantic Church, their early hardships there, even the chickens. It has been, Markle says, a "prolific part-nership that has enriched Canadian sculpture with scores of radiant works."[2]

There is a poignant disjunction between Markle's praise of The Girls and their physical presence. He has just finished saying that "their creative spirit is as enduring as the bronze and stone of their work to be found in our art galleries and public buildings, on Parliament Hill, and the unique studio we visit this evening," and there is Frances in a large, loose dark bouclé top over pants, hobbling on her two canes past statues on either side of her to the easy chair into which she slowly lowers her bulky body. Behind her on her left is a bowl of fruit. On her right is one of Florence's fountain cherubs. If the tilted urn were full, it would pour water over her shoulder.

The camera moves outside to the garden, showing The Church — not as a buzzing centre of activity, but as a dilapidated semi-ruin. The garden is full of odds and ends: old sawhorses, a few wooden boards, a weathered bird feeder aslant on a clothesline.

In response to a question about how she got started, Loring takes up a piece of clay and begins shaping it in her strong, graceful fingers. "Once you touch clay, you know, that's what you want to do. I'm amazed that the whole world isn't modelling because clay is so attractive," she says, reiter-ating lines she has fed interviewers for almost half a century. And she explains how she uses maquettes to remind her of an idea — could be "a coin" or "a child around the street" she will later build up into a permanent work. Sadly, she doesn't look equal to any such task.

Asked about her lion, she says, "He was cut into stone, enlarged from the half-size model right on the spot by what they call a pointing machine that takes a measure on the model, repeats it twice that size on the piece of stone, and the carver cuts between those points." She adds almost wearily, "And it's very interesting." She speaks slowly, her resonant voice falling at the end of each sentence as if she is exhausted.

The camera switches to Florence who is wearing a white apron over a man's shirt with the sleeves rolled up. She is chiselling away at her marble statue, *Sea and Shore*, using a small mallet. Asked if she is satisfied that it is complete, she peers like an inquisitive bright-eyed bird through her glasses around the side of the statue and replies curtly, "Oh no. I never would be, likely. But I might." She falters, and her words don't entirely make sense. "Much, much better than it was and better than I hoped I could get it so quickly." She has been working on it for fifteen years. In her American midwestern accent she recounts a time in Chicago when someone suggested she try carving and she picked up the hammer. She chuckles. "It was terribly heavy, I used it and did what they told me to, what they asked me to, and then when I got through with it, one of the men said, 'Do you know, madam, that's a sixteen-pound hammer you're using?'" She laughs. "I didn't know it." She laughs again, "*Now*, if it was half a pound I'd know it."

Only a careful observer would see that Florence moves in and out of vagueness, that she doesn't finish sentences, that she hesitates, uncertain what to do or say next, that Frances is the one in charge, telling her what to do, as she does now: "Florence, come over here and sit here." Florence obeys, taking a seat on a chair beside her. Asked what inspired the statue she was just working on, Florence scowls and says brusquely, "Something in my head." Asked if it was a memory, she looks off into space and says, "I think so." This might be funny if it weren't so sad.

After eliciting, finally, Florence's description of the statue — "I just had the idea of having a waterfall and a sea and a shore" — Markle tries another tack. "You worked a great deal with the female form," he says, to which Florence replies the way she has since she was a student in Chicago: "Well the female is the mother of the race. That's the reason I used it, and the Greeks used it, and they used it well."

Markle then says, "Mmhmm. So it's certainly more graceful and attractive than the male figure." Florence emphatically agrees. "Well I think so, maybe ..." But before she can finish, Loring interrupts — as if worried about what Florence might say next. She says, even more emphatically, "I don't," and they all laugh. "I like men too, you know," Florence continues, oblivious to the fact that Frances might be being careful not to give the impression that they could be lesbian, "but I had a twin brother. We used to try and do things together with ... I could do anything he could do, and it annoyed him awfully."

Asked to comment on a photo of herself as a child, Florence says, "That's me. I think I was about five or six years old, and the chicken was found with a broken leg, and I ..." Frances leans towards her and prompts her, "Rooster wasn't he?" Florence says indignantly, "It's a rooster, yes, but a rooster is a chicken, and I put a splint on his leg and kept him in a box near the outside door of the house so I could go to him if he needed help and he survived and his leg was healed." When asked how she first became interested in sculpture, her voice softens: "I was interested in life, trees, and animals and such things and I watched them and fell in love and now and then you'll see a drawing or something of a bird that I was very much interested in." She pauses, "I think that's what started me off ... likely."

Asked if they ever collaborated on the same work, Loring replies, "Just one piece together; it was a coat of arms." A close-up of her face shows wisps of thin grey hair that have escaped from a bun, and dark circles around her eyes. She does not look well. Markle says, "I would presume though there are certain ways in which you influenced each other's work." Frances jumps in quickly: "Contrary ways, I think," and she laughs. "I mean we ... I'd come in and suggest Miss Wyle do this or that, and she always does the opposite." They all laugh. Florence adds, "Maybe that's why she suggests it, I wouldn't know."

Asked what her best work is, Florence pauses, then says, "Well I'm not sure at all. What did I do?" she asks, turning to Frances. "I can't remember everything. There's the girl ..." Frances gives her a cue: "In the other room." "Well, yes, Frances, the girl in the other room ..." Loring steps in again to say, "And the torso that's in the National Gallery." Florence responds, "Well, yes, that's the torso there." Loring contradicts her outright, "No, oh no." "This torso here," Florence continues, "is in our gallery in town ... It's the female torso that interests me the most."

Unlike Florence who can't even remember her own works, Frances responds clearly when asked about her favourites. She's canny, doesn't want to be pinned down to one "best" work. She is accustomed to marketing her work according to the situation and the interviewer. "I think ... it's hard to say ... different periods you have different favourites. I'm very fond of this large *Eskimo Mother and Child* ... then, my lion on the Queen Elizabeth Highway ... and that relief that's over on the wall." She points to a panel of a nude woman in profile, her long hair swirled back in simple art deco lines, her index finger pointing down at her side, "and the head of Doctor Banting."

Markle then asks Loring a question that's obviously been scripted in advance. "Would you tell us something about your feeling in arresting movement for the purposes of sculpture?" Her reply is lengthy, part of a message she's been trying to get across to the public in numerous lectures, newspaper interviews, radio programs, and workshops for years; educating the public in what good sculpture should be. "In all movements, from one movement to another movement, there's one period where it changes. That's the moment of arrested action. And that's why the Ottawa war memorial is so bad, 'cause it's full of action. That's why statesmen jumping off a pedestal in a park would exhaust you so that you'd always go home the other way. Walter Allward's *Vimy Ridge* monument, Canada's national war memorial at Vimy Ridge, is one of the greatest monuments that have happened since the Egyptians, and it is a combination of sculpture and architecture, and it is serene."

Asked for an example of arrested action, she starts to describe *Discobolus*, then suddenly turns to Florence, taps her on the arm, wiggles her fingers as if to move her up off the chair, and orders, "Florence, get up, and show them how the discus thrower throws." Florence gets up, then asks, confused, "How you would naturally throw it you mean?" "No, the arrested ... no, the moment of arrested action," Loring replies, as if directing a small child. And Florence bends over, swings one outstretched arm backwards until it can go no further, then holds the pose, saying, "Discus back here, all ready to throw." Then she swings it forward. "But doesn't do *that* because they're opposed to the figure being in action." It's the same point Loring has been making for years, about her lion on the QEW, for instance "Holding the head back was extremely important."[3]

LORING IS NOW in full lecture mode. She picks up a small bronze abstract sculpture mounted on a plain pedestal. Markle observes that it looks like a Henry Moore or a Barbara Hepworth. "I don't approve of the Henry Moore-Barbara Hepworth connections," Frances says. Florence, who has either been coached *not* to comment on Henry Moore or doesn't understand what has been said, offers the non-sequitur, "She did it herself." Loring ignores

ca. 1912. Frances Loring, one of the first subjects of Toronto photographers Ashley & Crippen, who were among their earliest Toronto friends. *Courtesy of Ashley & Crippen, Toronto.*

ca. 1915. Florence Wyle, *Baby*, one of her many "children who never grow old." *Gift of Mr. Jack Brunke, Toronto, 1999, Acc. # 99/42, Art Gallery of Ontario, Toronto.*

ca. 1919. Florence Wyle and her relief of Ethel Ely, one of the wealthy Torontonians whose commissions supported the two sculptors. *Courtesy of Toronto Star Newspapers, Ltd., Torstar Syndications Services.*

1924. Selection jury for the Canadian Fine Arts Section of the British Empire Exhibitions at Wembley, England. The jury contained such artistic luminaries as Clarence Gagnon, George Harbour, Florence Wyle, F.S. Challener, R.S. Hewton, Horatio Walker, Eric Brown, E. Wyly Grier, Lawren Harris, and Arthur Lismer. Florence Wyle was the only sculptor and the only woman on this important jury. *Library and Archives Canada, Harry Orr McCurry Collection/Acc. # 1979-232.*

ca. 1919–21. Florence Wyle's memorial to Edith Cavell, the nurse who gave her life in the Great War. As a former medical student, Wyle probably identified with Cavell. *On the grounds of Toronto General Hospital, James Chambers, Art Gallery of Ontario, Toronto.*

1924. Florence Wyle's passport photo from the year she served on the Wembley Jury, travelling to England and France. She enjoyed England, but was disappointed in France. *Courtesy of the E.P. Taylor Research Library & Archives. Frances Loring and Florence Wyle Fonds, Art Gallery of Ontario, Toronto.*

ca. 1925. Frances stuffed this clay model into a cereal box and travelled to St. Stephen, New Brunswick, so she could present it to the committee selecting a war memorial. She won the competition. *Pringle and Booth Ltd., Courtesy of the E.P. Taylor Research Library & Archives. Frances Loring and Florence Wyle Fonds, Art Gallery of Ontario, Toronto.*

1929. Frances Loring, *The Derelicts*, a sculpture created on the eve of the Great Depression that now seems prophetic. *Gift of the Canadian National Exhibition, 1966, Acc. # 1686, Art Gallery of Ontario, Toronto.*

1950s. Loring beside her 1934 portrait bust of friend Dr. Frederick Banting; the resemblance is uncanny. *Courtesy of the E.P. Taylor Research Library & Archive. Frances Loring and Florence Wyle Fonds, Art Gallery of Ontario, Toronto.*

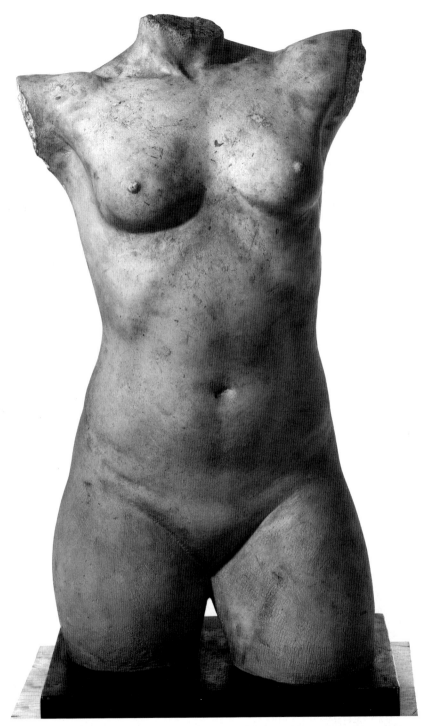

ca. 1935–37. Florence Wyle, *Torso (Mother of the Race)*, "archetypal woman." *Torso —*
Purchased 1933, National Gallery of Canada.

1930s. Frances and Florence entertaining at The Church, with friend Keith McIver (far right). *Courtesy of the E.P. Taylor Research Library & Archive. Frances Loring and Florence Wyle Fonds, Art Gallery of Ontario, Toronto.*

1935. Frances Loring, *Goal Keeper*, almost (but never) sold several times. *Goal Keeper* — *Gift of the Estates of Frances Loring and Florence Wyle, Art Gallery of Ontario, Toronto.*

1938. Frances Loring, *Eskimo Mother and Child*, a subject that would become passé once the carvings of First Nations Canadians entered mainstream markets. *Eskimo Mother and Child* — *Gift of the Estates of Frances Loring and Florence Wyle, Art Gallery of Ontario, Toronto.*

1939–40. *The Queen Elizabeth Monument* with pillar by W.L. Somerville, "Loring's British lion" rising from slumber to the challenge of World War II, and Wyle's medallion profile reliefs of King George VI and Elizabeth (later the Queen Mother), in its original location at the eastern entrance to the Queen Elizabeth Way. *Jean Gainfort Merrill, Courtesy of the E.P. Taylor Research Library & Archives. Frances Loring and Florence Wyle Fonds, Art Gallery of Ontario, Toronto.*

1971. *The Queen Elizabeth Monument*, after it was moved to Sir Casimir Gzowski Park on Lakeshore Boulevard West, Toronto. *James Chambers, Art Gallery of Ontario, Toronto.*

June 1941. The Kingston Conference for the Arts, the largest gathering of Canadian artists ever, here gathered on the lawn at H.S. Southam's Ottawa home after the meetings in Kingston. Loring stands on the far left; Wyle, wearing white, is in the middle row just to the right of centre. *Library and Archives Canada, Hazen Size Collection / Acc. # 1974-266.*

1942. Florence Wyle, *Bain Fountain*, an exquisite art nouveau piece, located in North Toronto. *Bain Fountain, Herb Nott — Courtesy of the E.P.Taylor Research Library & Archives. Frances Loring and Florence Wyle Fonds, Art Gallery of Ontario, Toronto.*

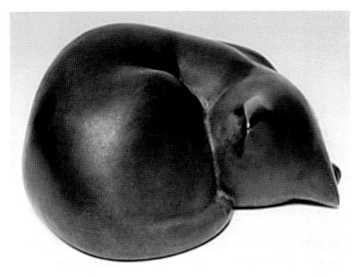

1949–50. Florence Wyle, *Sleeping Cat*, one of the many animal sculptures she did. *Sleeping Cat — Courtesy of the E.P.Taylor Research Library & Archives. Frances Loring and Florence Wyle Fonds, Art Gallery of Ontario, Toronto.*

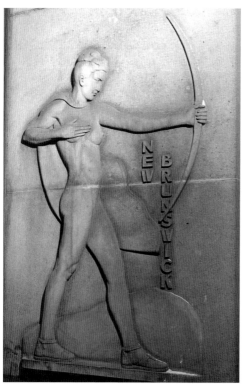

1948. Bank of Montreal relief panels at King and Bay Streets, Toronto, done in the "classical contemporary" mode. *New Brunswick and Ontario, Gilbert Milne — Courtesy of the E.P. Taylor Research Library & Archives. Frances Loring and Florence Wyle Fonds, Art Gallery of Ontario, Toronto.*

Florence Wyle, *New Brunswick.*

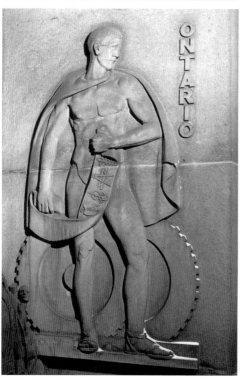

Frances Loring, *Ontario.*

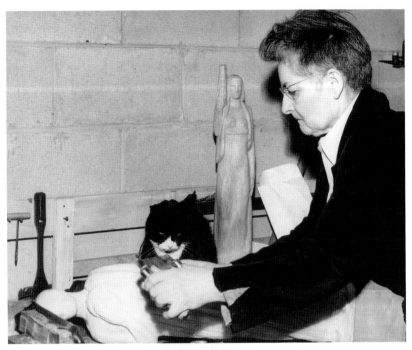

1948. Florence and Peter the Great working on Dominion Drama trophies. *Globe and Mail — Courtesy of the E.P. Taylor Research Library & Archives. Frances Loring and Florence Wyle Fonds, Art Gallery of Ontario, Toronto.*

ca. 1950s. "The Clay Ladies" with neighbourhood children. *Clay Ladies — Courtesy of the E.P. Taylor Research Library & Archives. Frances Loring and Florence Wyle Fonds, Art Gallery of Ontario, Toronto.*

1956. Frances Loring's maquettes for *Sir Robert Borden. Courtesy of the E. P. Taylor Research Library & Archives. Frances Loring and Florence Wyle Fonds, Art Gallery of Ontario, Toronto.*

ca. 1955. Jean Meroz, the other finalist, with his maquette of Robert Borden. *Jean Meroz, Mac Juster, The Gazette (Montréal).*

1957. (Left to right in foreground) Opposition Leader John Diefenbaker, Prime Minister Louis St. Laurent and Frances Loring at the unveiling of her *Sir Robert Borden* monument at Parliament Hill. *Library and Archives Canada, Malak/Malak Collection/PA-145822.*

1957. Frances Loring, *Sir Robert Borden*, on Parliament Hill, Ottawa, 1957. *Sir Robert Borden on Parliament Hill, Larry Ostrom — Art Gallery of Ontario.*

ca. 1960.
Frances Loring
conducting busi-
ness. Behind her
is her *Girl with a
Squirrel* and on
the left is one
of Florence's
fountain sculp-
tures. *Courtesy of
the E.P. Taylor
Research Library &
Archives. Frances
Loring and Florence
Wyle Fonds, Art
Gallery of Ontario,
Toronto.*

Mid-1960s. Frances and Florence
at a time when their health had
begun to fail. *Courtesy of the E.P.
Taylor Research Library & Archives.
Frances Loring and Florence Wyle
Fonds, Art Gallery of Ontario, Toronto.*

this and proceeds, "It's a lamb's hipbone, pelvis bone. It is so perfect in design ... Henry Moore introduced the hole into sculpture, and in every art school all over the world, students are making holes in the middle of their women's chests."

THE SCENE THEN changes to a tea at the big table downstairs at The Church. Loring is now wearing an ample wraparound dress in a small dark pattern; Wyle has removed the apron, but is still wearing the man's shirt over a skirt. She absent-mindedly drags crumbs across her plate with one finger. Around the table are A.Y. Jackson, A.J. Casson, Frances Gage, and Keith McIver. Jackson is in the middle of a joke about the provincialism of Canadians towards art as Frances pours tea and Florence sits quietly beside her. The conversation seems intended to offer a glimpse of a typical discussion of the arts in Canada, but it doesn't ring true. They are all — apart from Frances Gage — elderly. The men wear jackets and ties that are reminiscent of the '50s — hardly the flamboyant dress of artists of the mid-1960s. Florence says nothing; Frances offers tea.

All of them voice reactionary views about contemporary art, except Frances Gage, who states gently another point of view, trying tactfully to defend her own semi-abstract work. But her defence of sculpture that has moved beyond the neoclassical seems to make no impression on the older artists gathered there. As a write-up of the television program later stated, "[Loring and Wyle's] sculpture is hardly the current vogue."[4]

What went unsaid was that this program was a heart-wrenching look at two artists whose ideas and work had scarcely changed in the over fifty years they had lived together, and that Loring now dominates Wyle, partly because it was her nature to exercise power, partly because Wyle was scarcely able to function.

Centennial '67

By the mid-1960s, sculpture was no longer the "Cinderella" of the fine arts in Canada. "This year, with an intensity reminiscent of first love, the Canadian public found itself singing the praises of the nation's younger sculptors," wrote Hugo McPherson, an English professor at the University of Toronto, in an article for *Canadian Art* called, "The Scope of Sculpture in '64." "The 'real thing' had come along," he added. Sculptors were no longer "the orphans of the art scene." They were "shining more brightly than [Canada's] painters. The new sculpture was charged with vitality and power and the public was responding with ardour."[1]

McPherson was referring in particular to a large, two-part exhibition of fourteen sculptors called "Canadian Sculpture Today" at the new Dorothy Cameron Gallery on Yonge Street in Toronto, held in March and April of that year. Three other galleries — the Isaacs, the Moos, and the Jerrold Morris, all in Toronto's hippie Yorkville area nearby — cooperated in this "landmark" event.

"The real thing" did not include even one member of the Sculptors' Society of Canada, where meetings had grown "duller and duller, the average age of the members higher and higher, and in the late 1960s anybody under forty was considered an adolescent."[2] That year the society called off its own annual show in the face of competition from the private galleries. "The SSC (which had kept going largely out of respect for The Girls)," McPherson wrote, "offers less and less to the genuine professional." In a direct slap at Loring, Wyle, and the other sculptors of their generation, he went on, "The bad old days when Canadian sculptors carved polite lions or created thin allegorical reliefs on office buildings are almost over; and so, apparently, is the need for a society whose members exhibit together annually and bemoan the plight of their art."[3]

Even the Second Canadian Sculpture Exhibition at the National Gallery in Ottawa in June of that same year, did not have the "richness" and "splendour" — or the verve and sophistication — of "Canadian Sculpture Today." That old-fashioned exhibition of seventeen works by eleven sculptors (selected from more than two hundred entries) did not "serve well either the National Gallery or the artists involved," lacked commercial savvy, and did not elicit those "gasps of surprise"[4] that the Toronto show did. McPherson singled out David Partridge, Yves Trudeau, and Jack Harmon, but clearly the Toronto show outdid the Ottawa exhibition.

Compared to "Canadian Sculpture Today," the exhibition of painting and sculpture that accompanied the presentation of *King Lear* and *Richard II* at Stratford that summer was also behind the times. "Faces of Canada" included Loring's *Sir Frederick Banting*, Wyle's *F.H. Varley*, and Hahn's *Elizabeth Wyn Wood*, as well as Charles Comfort's portrait *Louise* and Paraskeva Clark's *Portrait of A.Y. Jackson*. Other portrait busts included Frances Gage's *Douglas Duncan*, Elizabeth Holbrook's *Harry Somers* (whose musical compositions like *North Country Suite* were attempts to render Group of Seven landscapes into music) and — most appropriately — Ursula Haynes's head of the young Stratford actress *Frances Hyland*.[5]

The sculptors McPherson heralded in the Toronto show were not interested in "the philistine demand for decorative and representational objects; each is intent on exploring a personal vision." Unlike Loring and Wyle, they were "ill at ease in their major 'public' commissions." Instead they produced works that were "fresh in conception and boldly experimental in technique."

An example of what McPherson meant appears in an interview with Walter Yarwood, a self-taught painter-turned-sculptor whose works had already been acquired by the National Gallery, the Montreal Museum of Fine Arts, the Art Gallery of Toronto, and the Winnipeg International Airport. Now in his late forties, Yarwood was at work on two pieces for the University of Toronto: *Forest*, his impression of being inside a clump of cedars, to stand outside the Faculty of Pharmacy, and a series of plaques to be mounted on the *Mo-sai* panel next to the entrance to Sidney Smith Hall.

Yarwood, who had briefly been one of the Toronto Painters Eleven, began by taking a welding course. "After working with a welding torch on plate steel," he explained, "the metal [becomes] blue-black ... *Pine Tree* has been covered with a red lead primer coat and then painted with flat black enamel" to "slow down the rusting process." He used a new plastic paint to protect from rust. Yarwood also welded bronze, and described a fountain he created that is very far indeed from the neoclassical decorative fountains created by Florence Wyle. It consisted of a group of tall spikes topped with a number of shapes. "I use a solution of ammonium chloride and copper sulphate to get a green patina," he says. "An aerated jet of water comes up in the centre to form another column in the sculpture. The dark [abstract] shapes would contrast with the white water. Then there was to be a ring of mist around the bottom. Without water it could be used as a garden piece by separating the elements and putting them in the ground in some other arrangement. A sort of 'do-it-yourself' garden piece."[6] Yarwood also carved directly from heavy bars of steel, and developed a technique of carving or imprinting objects on plasticine. The "found objects" he used might be gears, ink bottles, doorknobs, bolts — even a circular saw or "a tin can run over by a truck ... any crazy thing you pick up and think you can use." Yarwood would take his plasticine imprints to a foundry for casting into bronze. Although, while they were coherent, Loring and Wyle had viewed such antics as the ridiculous — even reprehensible — elevation of the ugly to art, Yarwood found such work beautiful: "I've no social comment to make," he said, "but I'd like to produce works of beauty out of things I've seen and felt in my lifetime."⁷

This shift in Canadian sculpture, which redefined beauty, was entirely in keeping with the shift in all the arts throughout the western world in the early and mid-1960s. Radical changes — such as women's liberation, civil rights movements, secularization, and alternatives to the nuclear family — were occurring throughout the western world. In the United States, Pop Art, such as Andy Warhol's *Small Torn Campbell's Soup Can* (1962) was now "with it," as was Op Art (Optical Art and Perceptual Abstraction), such as Victor Vasarely's vibrating, dizzying geometric paintings or M.C. Escher's visual tricks and paradoxes, such as *Drawing Hands*, which showed a hand drawing a hand, drawing a hand. American composer John Cage had begun parallel experiments that questioned the very definition of music. Best-known for his *Black Mountain, 4'33"* (1952) comprised of three movements without a single note, he espoused what he called "purposeless play" and "chance music" (in which some elements were left to chance), and he was a pioneer in electronic music.⁸ The stream-of-consciousness writing of James Joyce and Virginia Woolf and the quirky modernism of Gertrude Stein, which had been so controversial in the 1920s and '30s had become commonplace in Canada with works such as Sheila Watson's high modernist *The Double Hook* (1959) and Leonard Cohen's postmodern rhapsody *Beautiful Losers* (1966) — both published by Canadian nationalist Jack McClelland.⁹ In Canada, changes to the Immigration Act in 1962 had begun the transformation that would result in a multicultural society and the inclusion of many ethnic voices in the artistic mainstream.¹⁰

Sculptors like Walter Yarwood, whom McPherson — and the public — so admired, included many who had appeared in John Lewis's assessment of sculpture two years before: such as Ted Bieler, Anne Kahane, Robert Murray, Harold Town, Yosef Drenters, Armand Vaillancourt, and John Ivor Smith. Viewers were likely to encounter Harold Town's *Gaudi on Television*, made of plywood and buttons, or his "visceral, phallic" *Penetralia*; or *Cerberus*, directly carved in compound stone, by Elza Mayhew, who also did carvings in Styrofoam for metal castings; or one of Ted Bieler's fibreglass figures; or one of Les Levine's "strange environmental constructions" with kitchen chairs for bones and plastic coated canvas as skin stretched over them, the "bones jutting out wilfully." McPherson laments the absence of Michael Snow from the Toronto exhibition, explaining that he is currently in New York.

Even R.H. Hubbard's sedate book *The Development of Canadian Art* (1964), published by the National Gallery of Canada, recognized that the "scope of Canadian art has broadened perceptibly. The century-old dominance of painting has at last been challenged ... Sculpture and the graphic arts have some distinguished exponents."[11] The only illustration of sculpture in the book was Elizabeth Wyn Wood's 1930 *Reef and Rainbow*.

These years of the early and mid-1960s saw radical changes in all the arts throughout the western world, and Canada was no exception. But Canadian artists were spurred to even greater creative activity as the nation prepared to celebrate its Centennial. The international world's fair Expo '67 in Montreal was the focus of these events, but towns and cities across the country also manifested their patriotic feelings in various ways. In Toronto, Dorothy Cameron, whose gallery on Yonge Street had hosted the "Canadian Sculpture Today" exhibit in 1964, was commissioned by the National Gallery of Canada (now under the direction of Dr. William S.A. Dale) to select and coordinate a major Centennial exhibition of outdoor Canadian sculpture. From the beginning of April 1966 until the show opened in Nathan Phillips Square, the expansive mall in front of the Toronto's new City Hall, on 1 June 1967, Cameron traversed the country twice and visited Canadian sculptors working in American and British cities to select the best sculptures. Sculpture had blossomed in Canada from the handful of Toronto and Montreal sculptors who founded the Sculptors' Society of Canada in 1928 to 225 professional sculptors — some well-known on the international scene — by 1966. And, as Dora de Pédery Hunt observed, "the humiliating poverty is gone."[12] Cameron did not intend regional representation, but selected sixty-eight works by fifty-four of the country's sculptors on the basis of quality alone. The works of Frances Loring and Florence Wyle were not even considered.

Of the fifty-one sculptors whose works finally appeared in Nathan Phillips Square, three-fifths were "avant-garde" sculptors and two-fifths were "traditional." "In *Sculpture '67* you find neither dogmatism nor uniformity: you participate in an effervescence," commented Françoise Sullivan, one of the "avant-garde" sculptors.[13]

The interviews that Dorothy Cameron conducted with each sculptor reveal a wide range of approaches to the creation of three-dimensional works, but almost all of them — even the "traditionalists" — speak of their work in ways that would have been incomprehensible to Frances Loring and Florence Wyle. "I delight in the 'art scene' of the electronic revolution," said "traditionalist" John Ivor Smith, "but not all of it that pleases is art."[14] Anne Kahane, another "traditionalist," confessed somewhat apologetically that she needed "the crutch of the human form," but her work *Runners*, carved from cedar, looks like three quasi-geometrical shapes fashioned only vaguely into human forms.[15] Avant-garde Vancouver sculptor Iain Baxter — whose large inflated vinyl flower, *VSI-Pool Flower*, electrically illuminated, floated on the pond in front of City Hall — spoke of his work as the exploration of found objects: "Because an object is labelled 'glass,' people see simply g-l-a-s-s. They do not see all the intrinsic potentials of 'glass-ness': how the glass is a bubble; how it's a container that captures space; how it's a clear window into some other little world."[16] Michael Snow, whose work *First, Last* was a 6'10" plywood, aluminum, and glass square with small slits and openings to peer through, tried to convey the concept of "framing." This interactive work influenced by the camera and film "frames things that are fortuitous, (like clouds passing in the sky)," he said.[17] An International Sculpture Symposium — also held on various sites in Toronto that year — featured the same kinds of works.

Loring and Wyle would not have understood such concepts and would have dismissed them as rubbish or child's play unworthy of their discipline. The fact that almost half of the fifty-one sculptures chosen for the Centennial exhibit were by Toronto sculptors indicated that Toronto was the Canadian centre for sculpture — a position the city would not have enjoyed if Loring and Wyle, with only a few others, had not worked since 1912 at producing sculpture, establishing the SSC, and lecturing about how to create and appreciate sculpture. A few, such as Walter Yarwood and Ted Bieler, had exhibited in the 1964 "Canadian Sculpture Today" show at Dorothy

Cameron's gallery. But there were several new sculptors — many of them immigrants to Canada from the United States, the United Kingdom, Czechoslovakia, Hungary, Romania, the U.S.S.R., and Guyana, or second generation immigrants — who had made Toronto a part of "the global village" Marshall McLuhan had described.[18] And though Michael Snow was currently working in New York, and William Featherstone was currently in England on his second Canada Council grant, they were both Toronto-born.

Within a year, however, The Girls' friend Alan Jarvis would write in a new arts journal called *Canadian Collector*, "The art of sculpture in Canada has been something of a poor cousin compared to painting. That it has survived at all, much is owed to two distinguished sculptors, who are also two great women, Frances Loring and Florence Wyle."[19]

Death Masque

Frances did not attend the Loring and Wyle retrospective mounted by Jack Pollack at his two-storey gallery with fashionable black walls early in 1966. She was in hospital. It was less than a year since the *Telescope* profile documentary, but, although she was coherent and good-natured on television, she had become unmanageable. Florence had pneumonia and was barely able to attend. A news photo with the caption "Half a Team of Sculptors" shows her on the Sunday evening of the gallery opening on 9 January, gaunt and rumpled in her ancient grey suit, a dark ascot tie loosely tied inside the open collar of her white shirt, looking up at her statue *Young Girl* (1930).[1]

The Girls had become so passé in the Toronto art scene that their retrospective — the first ever in Toronto to focus only on the works of Loring and Wyle — was considered an act of courage. "Unlike many galleries in Yorkville which insist on Op and Pop exhibits," wrote a reviewer for the University of Toronto newspaper *The Varsity*, "The Pollack Gallery in Markham Street has dared to produce a retrospective show of Canadian sculpture by Frances Loring and Florence Wyle."[2] Jack Pollack had devoted a whole wall to photos of The Girls and several of their bronze, plaster, and wooden plaques. But most of the show consisted of the statues that had surrounded The Girls in their studio and been available to galleries, museums, and the buying public for years: Florence's many powerful female torsos in various materials, her sweet mothers and children, those delicate creatures from her Greenwich Village days, including *Rebirth*, which in the interim had acquired the subtitle *Man Falls to Rise Again*. Loring's *Eskimo Mother and Child*, *Grief*, *Ashman*, and her fountain piece *Girl with Fish* stood by like old familiars. The war worker statuettes that had made their names in 1919 were there, on loan from the National Gallery. Art reviews had become much more sophisticated over time (even the University of Toronto *Varsity* reviewer offers astute insights),[3] and the Toronto galleries themselves had proliferated and diversified into a significant aspect of the city's cultural life, as they had in all of Canada's major cities.

And there was now a buying public. By the end of the show, $12,000 worth of sculpture had been sold, including the sale to McMaster University of a bronze head — the last of five copies — of Loring's *Sir Frederick Banting*,[4] Wyle's bronze head of Vincent Massey to Massey College at the University of Toronto, and her portrait bust of Fred Varley to a private collector.[5] Several of Wyle's smaller animal sculptures and various plaques also sold, including a bronze which sold to Loring's nephew Bill, who attended the show and wrote back, "I was delighted to see some old pieces which I have loved for years. We purchased your bronze cat and can hardly wait until it arrives."[6] Loring sold two copies of her cocky rooster and two woodcarvings. It was by far the highest income either of them had made from any show. The immediate income Wyle made was $3,257.50; Loring made $3,700 after the fee of $87.50 each for use of the gallery and a twenty-five percent agent's fee to Jack Pollack. The rest would come later from buyers who had postdated their purchases.

Pollack was elated and no wonder, since he probably foresaw he would sell even more: $30,000 worth of Loring and Wyle sculptures over the next year and a half to collectors across Canada.[7] "The interest was fantastic," he said of the show. "In one day we would have as many as 400 visitors. Viewers

came here by the busload and every day I did guided tours. I'm keeping many
of the pieces for display in the gallery from now on. They'll be available for
viewing at any time. You can't beat solid excellence — despite passing
trends."[8] Elated though he was, Pollack's next show included Pop Art
collages by Ron Martin. And the Women's Committee of the Art Gallery
of Toronto had moved on from the elegant afternoon teas The Girls once
attended to events like a Manner-of-Mondrian luncheon for men only, which
included a fashion show of bathing suits influenced by the Dutch neoplasti-
cist painter Piet Mondrian.[9]

Frances was completely unaware of the success of the Pollack retrospective. In mid-September she had been hospitalized, first at the Lakeside Long
Term Care Centre at 150 Dunn Avenue, then at the Queen Elizabeth Hospital
on University Avenue. There she lay in a bed of the psychiatric wing —
sometimes under restraint — flailing about at times and shouting at others
that people were coming after her.[10] The Girls' doctor, T. Ormiston Smith,
who had only charged The Girls $5.00 per house call for a decade — visited
her without charge (The Girls occasionally gave him a sculpture, and his
wife bought a woodcarving and a bronze *Spring* of Wyle's for $200 each).[11]
Frances Gage and David Ongley, their neighbourhood lawyer (who also
received sculptures in lieu of payments), were executors of their estates and
visited Frances twice a week. One friend wrote from Los Angeles, "I was
knocked out by hearing what had happened to Frances, for she was her same
self, humorous and looking after Florence, when we saw them at Christmas.
One goes to pieces fast, past seventy ... It's an irony too hard, that this financial success and recognition should come when neither of them have wits to
realize it."[12] Another friend from Ottawa, who wanted to buy a copy of
Loring's *Sea Horses and Mermaid* and visited Frances in hospital, wrote, "I saw
Frances Sunday — a shattering experience. It was one of her bad days,
shouting to get out & very disoriented, though she knew me from time
to time. Florence must *certainly* not go."[13] Rebecca Sisler recalled, "I used to
visit [her] in hospital ... She was senile, but her mind was still creative. She
would talk to me in that wonderful voice, telling me incredible and quite
romantic stories ... with all the same old vitality coming out in her tales."[14]
"The only pity," David Ongley wrote later, "is their health was such they

were not able to fully appreciate [the retrospective's] success."[15] Another friend, writer Jean Bannerman, who had just published *Leading Ladies, Canada*,[16] a Centennial project book that included "major sketches"[17] of Loring and Wyle, wrote Frances Gage to say, "I am so very sorry that they will not be able to enjoy [my book] themselves."[18]

Florence's bout of pneumonia in the middle of January[19] during the retrospective at Pollack's gallery dragged her down, and she was unable to cope on her own by the middle of March. When she waved and walked out of the Pollack Gallery, it was the end.[20] Bewildered by Frances's six month absence, her own health shaky, she was admitted to the geriatric wing of Queen Elizabeth Hospital. Rebecca Sisler recalls that when she visited Florence once, she was still indulging in acts of mercy: "A woman patient whose leg was in traction kept complaining so much that Florence's old medical training and her inability to let anything — cat, dog, bird, human — suffer came to the fore. She went over and lowered the pulleys for the woman."[21]

FRANCES GAGE AND David Ongley now took over Loring and Wyle's affairs, which they handled meticulously. Over the next three decades they initiated and assisted in a series of exhibits[22] and in any endeavour that might help sales of The Girls' works. The first matter of business was writing to all the many friends and few relatives listed in The Girls' well-worn address book. Frances Gage received a "whining"[23] letter from Helen Von Drache, who did not want to be involved. Then they had to negotiate The Girls' finances — paying their bills to Dr. Ormiston Smith and others, ordering a bronze casting of Loring's *Hound of Heaven* — the first of several Frances Gage would order from a foundry in Norway over the next few years,[24] and responding to a request from the University of British Columbia's medical school for a sixth bust of Sir Frederick Banting.

On 17 March 1967, an article in the *Toronto Telegram* with headshots of both artists in their younger days asked the question, "Whatever Happened to Frances Loring and Florence Wyle?" The answer was that these "two Toronto women, who are among Canada's most distinguished sculptors, have quietly brought their working days to a halt ... Ill health has forced both sculptors, who are now in their 80s, into retirement. Both have been in hospital for the past year." Despite the misinformation about their ages (Florence was eighty-six, but Frances was seventy-nine), and the misleading connotation of "into retirement," the article is a tribute — a short tribute — to Loring and Wyle. Loring is still preferred: "Miss Loring is the better-known sculptor," the article states.

In fact, Loring was no longer in hospital by March 1967. The Queen Elizabeth Hospital had informed David Ongley in January that "Miss Loring has to be moved within a month," and he began negotiating her transfer to one of the Metro Toronto homes for the aged. "Miss Loring is not an indigent case," he wrote to the Commissioner, Department of Welfare, at City Hall; "funds are available at this time for her upkeep."[25] It is apparent from Ongley's letter that Florence Wyle had already been transferred from Queen Elizabeth Hospital to a home for the aged, where Loring soon joined her at Greenacres in Newmarket, just north of the city.

The next month, Ongley arranged to have The Church evaluated. It would have been impossible to put a price on the place that A.Y. Jackson (who had just told an audience of painters at Bells Corners near Ottawa that "abstract art was doomed")[26] had once called "the hub of culture in Toronto," a place remembered by so many for the hospitality, help, and creativity they found there over five decades. The Canada Permanent Company's real estate office assessed the land to be worth $2,750 and the building worth $4,000. The 1967 taxes — still outstanding — were $598.05. Given its historical value, the property might fetch approximately $15,000 at most. However, because "the interior of the building is in rather rough or unfinished condition," the assessment read, "it may be difficult to obtain a purchaser to continue the present conforming use and, due to the condition and layout of the building, the cost of converting it to a single family dwelling would possibly be prohibitive."[27]

In August, the executors raised a little money by allowing the CBC to film the sculptures inside The Church for a TV program called "Patrons of Canadian Art."[28] But something had to be done to maintain the building. Just before Christmas, Ongley wrote Bert Wreford — who with his wife had provided live-in help for The Girls over their last few years — to settle matters. "It now becomes obvious that Miss Loring and Miss Wyle will not be returning to the studio," he wrote. To "make the house self-sustaining," the executors offered to pay the $110 a month for taxes, heating, hydro, and water until the end of 1967, leaving the Wrefords to pay only their telephone. As of 1 January 1968, however, the Wrefords would pay a monthly rent of $100, much less than a normal rental would have been.[29]

Meanwhile Frances and Florence existed in their separate limbos in separate rooms on separate floors at Greenacres. The soulmates who had lived in such closeness for fifty-seven years were split apart. Their main means of communication were messages carried back and forth by the staff. "It was very pleasant there, but the situation was very sad," recalled Frances Gage, whose labours of love on their behalf went on for years. "The rooms were double-locked at night. The keys were visible, but the patients couldn't find them or comprehend it. David and I used to visit them regularly. Florence was usually leading some little old lady about by the hand."[30] "The nurse on Florence's floor was deeply impressed by her kindness," wrote a friend after visiting Greenacres, "& I'm sure Frances was a bright spot to many of them ... I think these two had gathered so much dignity & humanity within their lives that there was plenty for them to carry past life."[31] Frances Gage recalls, "They didn't know who we were. David would get drunk after we went there."[32] Lawrence Hayward, a neighbour who for some time attempted — without success — to publish a book about Loring and Wyle and to establish a centre for sculpture in Ontario[33] — recalls visiting The Girls at Greenacres. "It was an awful place," he recalls. "Loring was confined in a wheel chair and treated like nothing. She lost her teeth and glasses at the end. I even went and took some photos of her works to let them know WHO SHE WAS. They said she talked about all the people she knew who were her friends. They dismissed it all as untruths. I told them she did have an audience with the Queen of England they were no reply [sic] on that account. I went one day and she called me doctor Hayward. She made motion that she was going to walk and stood up for me to prove she could do it. I took them both to the local café for a cup of coffee and ice cream. They talked normal [sic] to each other. Loring asked Florence did she get all her messages. Frances Gage never knew I went so often."[34]

Even before they died, a number of people wanted to honour The Girls in different ways. Hayward claimed that Frances Gage told him The Girls were as good as dead and that he needn't bother visiting them. "I know it was on a Monday Loring was put in and by Wednesday Frances was in the studio burning everything and throwing stuff in the garbage, the fireplace was just hopping. The neighbour called me to find out what all the noise was about. She was in there with the 'Cahr woman' helping to destroy all of the clay models and plaster moulds.[35] I never was allowed in the studio after that."[36] Rebecca Sisler, who interviewed Hayward for *The Girls*, found him uncooperative. "When I interviewed him for my book," she said, "he had a great file on them — a hodge-podge of stuff — which he wouldn't let me see. I could see a photo of their first studio on Lombard Street — rare things like that."[37]

ON 14 JANUARY 1968, Florence Wyle died. "One of Canada's Great Sculptors Dies," read the special obituary in the *Toronto Telegram*;[38] "Human Anatomy Classes Turned her from Medicine to Sculpture," ran the obituary headline in the *Globe and Mail*.[39]

Frances Gage and David Ongley arranged a memorial to be held in The Church on the evening of 1 February at 8 p.m.[40] There — surrounded by the statues, busts, and plaques that had kept The Girls company and blindly gazed down on so many parties and celebrations — the friends, relatives, and neighbours of Florence Wyle gathered to pay her tribute. "I am only sorry there are going to be people there who were not intimate friends of The Girls," Sophia Hungerford wrote from Guelph to Edith McIver, Keith's widow. "If only their closest friends could gather around the fire and go downstairs and spread into Florence's studio for a visit — it should be like that ... I'm taking forsythia, daffodils & tulips from the Lorings[41] and a few sprigs of white lilac & freesias from us."[42]

"The sack of seeds which she used to keep at the front step for the winter birds was missing," wrote Kay Kritzwiser in the *Globe and Mail* the next day.

Only one pampered cat sneaked through the door, instead of the mangy alley cats forever seeking her handouts. And in the window where she used to sit and carve torsos (and mutter about the young people of today who knew nothing of anatomy) the servers in white aprons dispensed drinks and coffee and sandwiches. But the aura of Florence Wyle ... was vivid last night in the old studio–church.⁴³

Lady Banting, Sir Frederick's widow, and Cecilia Long, with whom she shared a home, Loring and Wyle's former students — now sculptors in their own right — Rebecca Sisler and Dora de Pédery Hunt, painter Paraskeva Clark, the Gordons, the McGibbons, and many others were there to pay tribute. Most of the guests, including Frances Gage, David Ongley, Jack Pollack, Sophia Hungerford, Norah de Pencier, and Frances's nephew Tom Loring, sat on backless benches. A.Y. Jackson and A.J. Casson stood at the enormous brick fireplace that had warmed their hearts so many times before to hear the speeches. The host, William Withrow, who did not know Wyle or Loring well and preferred modernist art to representational work,⁴⁴ was director of what had been renamed the Art Gallery of Ontario two years before.⁴⁵

Though Loring was still alive, it was impossible to contemplate Florence without Frances. Not only were they two halves of one whole, neither of them could have achieved what she did without the other. "It is almost 50 years since Florence Wyle and her partner Frances Loring (affectionately known in the Toronto art world as *The Girls*) began to make their studio the unofficial centre of the creative arts," Withrow said. He went on to acknowledge Florence's roots in the U.S., but added, "For many years, particularly of course in the twenties and early thirties, Miss Wyle has been so much a part of Canadian art history that we easily forget [this]. [Her] work was identified with the emergence of National pride in Canadian art. Indeed, we have come to think of her work in almost exclusively national terms, consequently narrowing our appreciation of its nature. Her simplicity of form and line, her honest use of stone and wood, and her choice of subject matter clearly remove her from the provincialism of Toronto in the twenties. Her contribution to Canadian art in both her life and the body of works which she created gains a longer and more accurate dimension if we remember that she was a part of a chapter in the history of Canadian art."⁴⁶

Charles Band recalled, "Florence would have disliked a eulogy because she was essentially a very modest person who always minimized her own talents and tried to give credit to others." This was true. Florence had been happy to give way to Frances, whose reputation had overtaken her own, just as Frances was sure Florence was the better sculptor. In their later years she had answered the door to interviewers with the words, "Come in and meet Miss Loring."[47] "When she spoke she always looked one clearly in the eye," Band said, "and did not shrink from declaring criticism when she felt it necessary. But for all her frankness, Miss Wyle was generous in her praise and unstinting in her help to other artists, especially those who were young."

He too could not separate Wyle from Loring. "They gave to Toronto and to Canada all they had to give, and this was a rich offering. Their sculptures adorn the streets and highways of this city and of the nation's capital. Virtually every museum in Canada and countless private collections treasure their work."

A.J. Casson recalled crowding around the pot-bellied stove with winter coats on. Yvonne Housser spoke of "the wonderful Christmas Eves." "They took in all the poor young artists and fed and warmed us." John Murphy spoke with pride of carting their sculptures to shows for fifty years. To conclude the memorial, Jack Pollack[48] read one of Florence's poems, "Death":

> It is not ugliness that kills
> But lack of beauty —
> If man's soul is not enraptured
> Warmed and pulsed by beauty's fire
> He dies — slowly, but as surely
> As forgotten unsunned flowers
> In winter die.[49]

DURING THE MEMORIAL service "word came that the death of Miss Loring was expected momentarily."[50] It was electrifying, as if Frances were there in spirit. Frances seemed to have been wrenched from life by some sense of the permanent absence of Florence at Greenacres, as if she were somehow so connected to her that she must follow quickly.

Frances Loring died on 5 February, only three days after the memorial service, three weeks and a day after Florence. The obituaries poured out in Toronto, Ottawa, and Quebec: "Frances Loring, 80, Famed Sculptor, Dies,"[51] "Sculptor Frances Loring Did Stone Lion on QEW,"[52] "Canadian Sculptor Frances Loring Dies,"[53] "Miss Loring a Laissé un Oeuvre Considerable."[54] The *Globe and Mail* showed a photo of Frances in her seventies, smiling her small enigmatic smile and looking up at her *Hound of Heaven*.

Frances — true to her sense of high drama — had added a codicil to her will in 1961 to say, "I hereby direct that my body shall be cremated and the ashes scattered to the four winds."[55] Yet her body, too, went to the University of Toronto medical school, and there was no funeral. "The school called us when their searches were done," Frances Gage wrote, "and there was a private ceremony and a final burial in the school's plot."[56]

Urban Renewal: Toronto ⌣

On 27 October 1966 — a month after Frances was hospitalized — a crowd of 10,000 people watched the unveiling of Henry Moore's huge abstract bronze sculpture *Three-Way Piece No. 2* (*The Archer*) in front of Toronto's new City Hall. After some dickering over the price, Moore was paid $123,410.[1] It was a sum that would have supported Loring and Wyle for roughly thirty years.

Before illness overtook her, Loring had been a member of the committee choosing the design for the new City Hall. At first, three of Toronto's largest architectural firms were selected to collaborate on the design, but the result was "an extremely conservative structure that was rejected."[2] She would have known that Finnish architect Viljo Revell had won the international competition for its design in 1958, and that construction had begun on the modernistic streamlined semicircular high-rise. She might have known — no doubt to her displeasure — that Revell himself wanted to commission Henry Moore to create a sculpture for the open square in front of the hall that would be imaginatively embraced by his building.[3] Like Moore — who declined commissions to do relief sculptures like those that Loring, Wyle, and others had done for the Bank of Montreal because it seemed to him "the humiliating subservience of the sculptor to the architect"[4] — Revell "believed strongly that sculpture should not be merely an appendage to a building."[5] It was probably just as well that by the time the unveiling took place, Frances could not have comprehended anything.

Not everyone liked the new City Hall. Some found it too modernistic, and many disagreed that Moore's sculpture should grace Nathan Phillips Square. But there was only one dissenter on the selection committee — Controller William Denison. One letter to the editor of the *Toronto Daily Star* thought Loring's *Goal Keeper* should be the statue that stood in front of Toronto's City Hall: "We have two of the best sculptors in the world right here in Toronto in Frances Loring and Florence Wyle ... [Loring's] hockey player in action is a superb piece of work and would have been a much more appropriate and fitting tribute to the city that gave birth to the world's greatest hockey team, the Toronto Maple Leafs [than] the two-ton formless hunk of abstract that the mayor and his avant-garde followers [chose]."[6] In his speech at the unveiling, Mayor Givens said pointedly, "What has been brought here is a work of public art that Toronto people will learn to cherish."[7]

Eight years later, Toronto became Moore's Canadian city. The Royal Canadian Academy of Arts honoured him with their RCA Medal in 1972. In 1974 Moore donated 200 of his works to the new Henry Moore Centre at the Art Gallery of Ontario, one of which — a massive, smooth, bronze abstract with holes — stands outside the gallery on the corner of Dundas Street West and McCaul Street.

CLARE BICE, PRESIDENT of the Royal Canadian Academy of Arts, which by that point had sixty full academicians and 100 associates, wrote to Frances Gage in December 1968 to say that "the Academy does not intend to renounce the gift [of 110 Glenrose Avenue]," but needed time "to investigate the condition, the zoning regulations etc. of the building." The RCA appointed a committee: Mr. Arbuckle, Hugh Allward (son of Walter

Allward and also a sculptor), and Cleeve Horne to look into the matter.[8] They also approached Montreal art critic Robert Ayre to do a book on The Girls, but Ayre declined.[9]

A week after John Lennon and Yoko Ono stayed at the Windsor Arms Hotel in Toronto following their week-long "Bed-in" in Montreal, Jack Pollack organized an open house for the public at the Loring and Wyle studio. There, on the weekend of 14–15 June 1969, his mother, "smart as any Rosedale matron in blue lace dress and flowered bonnet, [and] with [a] white fox fur" poured tea.[10] Hoping to raise money to fund the scholarships to younger sculptors mentioned in the Loring and Wyle wills, Jack Pollack and Frances Gage had "combed the studio for works to sell at his Gallery" in an exhibit to follow — the largest of which, a bronze version of the *Goal Keeper*, could be cast for $30,000.[11]

The failure of the postal system to deliver the invitations to the weekend Open House at The Church seemed like an omen at first. But sales of The Girls' works in Pollack's 1969 exhibit were far greater than anything they had known in their lifetimes: Wyle's totalled $37, 000 and Loring's $15,000, after Pollack's new gallery fee of 33.3% was deducted.[12] But it was too late to benefit Loring or Wyle.

It was only a year after The Girls had died when an article by Sid Adilman about The Girls and their studio appeared in the *Toronto Telegram*: "It was the Salon of Canada's Art World, but Time seems to have Passed it By."[13] For the first time, the respect that had consistently been paid by the Canadian media to Loring and Wyle since 1912 had disappeared. No longer was the public to think they had "retired" — if the public thought of them at all. Adilman quotes "a close associate of theirs"[14] as saying, "Wyle was quite doty [sic] for the last 10 years of her life. She just went quietly and happily senile. There were times when she didn't even know that Loring had been moved to the hospital. Loring in her later years became infirm and she got arthritis and it made her too heavy to work. And she went partially blind and couldn't work any more. By the end she didn't know people. She, too, went mad."[15] "Loring made enemies," Adilman went on. "She was a dominant personality. In later years, Wyle, always the quiet one, withdrew, almost becoming a recluse. Loring adopted masculine dress and she cropped off her gorgeous hair. She was a terrible feminist but she went out of her way to make herself unattractive. Wyle got belligerent in later years. I guess she was disappointed that Loring all their lives got the lion's share of the publicity and the honors."[16]

Like so many, Adilman confused Loring and Wyle. It was Wyle who cut her hair — long before, in the early 1920s. And it was Wyle who adopted masculine dress, though Loring usually went about in baggy pants and an old sweater when she was working. It was Loring who became belligerent, not Florence, who never begrudged Loring's honours, just as Loring did not begrudge hers. Lawrence Hayward — who hoped to use the photos and materials he had collected from The Girls to write a book about them — wrote an angry letter to Adilman in their defence.[17]

By 1977, an Ottawa show of contemporary sculpture at the National Gallery had moved even further away from neoclassicism than the Centennial '67 exhibits. "Traditionally, sculpture occupies three dimensions," wrote Mayo Graham in the catalogue introduction to *Another Dimension*. "It is a measurable mass or spatial extent having length, width, and depth. However, in the twentieth century, and especially the last decade or two, new dimensions have been integrated into the sculptural vocabulary: light, sound, movement, and time are now as much a part of that vocabulary as are volume, weight, and area."[18] Tracing these "new dimensions" back to Marcel Duchamp's 1913 *Mobile* — a bicycle wheel mounted on a stool — Graham explains that three types of motion are represented in the sixteen works by four sculptors in the show: sound, light, and physical movement. Norman White's *Splish Splash One* used incandescent bulbs "electronically activated to form changing congruent figures which simulate water ripples." And Michael Snow's *Two Sides to Every Story* used light projected through film in such a way that "the actual movement of the film as it passes frame by frame through the projector, and the light — each stresses the activity of the other. And within the film itself, the recorded imagery on projection reconstructs real movement (a woman walking, waves rolling)."[19] Ever since Duchamp's attempt to capture motion, the stolid immobility of beautiful neoclassical statues had increasingly failed to reflect the acceleration and mechanized power of the industrialized world.

The Church no longer hosted the arts world of Toronto. "Privately, the trustees have asked the [Royal Canadian] academy to renounce its gift," Adilman reported. "Privately, there is talk in the Academy of demolition."[20] Adilman hoped the politicians in Toronto would save the building from the wreckers (as did the writer of a letter to the editor of the *Globe and Mail* six months later, who suggested it become a "national monument"),[21] but the fate of The Church stood undecided. (Frances's nephew Frank wrote unsuccessfully to the trustees from B.C. to say, "I don't think Frances would mind if part of her estate goes to mining engineers.")[22] The Royal Canadian Academy would have to apply to have the city rezone the area to allow a meeting hall or collective artists' studio.[23] By 1970, two years after The Girls died, the academy had still not made up its mind what to do about the property that had been left to them by their "beloved benefactors."[24]

RELOCATION OF LION MONUMENT
Q.E.W. AT HUMBER
CONTRACT NO. IB-3-73

On behalf of the Ministry of Transportation and Communications, we wish to advise [the Friends of Loring and Wyle] that Alden Contracting Ltd. has been awarded the contract to relocate the Lion Monument from the west side of the Humber River to the new location on the east side of the Humber River in the City of Toronto Park, Sir Casimir Gzowski Park ...

We have been advised that the Contractor will dismantle the Monument stone by stone, transport them to the new site via Lakeshore Boulevard and re-erect the Monument· complete with a new concrete core. The Lion, Crown, and Crown Base will each be moved in one piece ...

The Contractor will be on the site on or about June 1, 1974, and will complete the project by September 1, 1974.[25]

THIS LETTER FROM R.S. Adachi, Assistant Chief Engineer of Transportation for Toronto, spelled the end of public familiarity with Loring's lion. The

1939 monument that had proudly stood on an island between eastbound and westbound lanes of traffic would now stand lower and out of sight of QEW traffic, near Lake Ontario.

Even this "stone by stone" demotion of the Lion Monument was a compromise. At first, the Ministry of Transportation had scheduled it for demolition to make way for the widening of the QEW from two to four lanes each way. Letters of protest to the ministry and to the newspaper persuaded the ministry to undertake the cost of moving the monument down over the hill into the small park accessible only by a tortuous route of one-way streets off the QEW and across Lakeshore Boulevard. An editorial in the *Globe and Mail* expressed the hope that The Monument (as it was commonly known in Toronto) would be given "a place of prominence by the Queen Elizabeth Way, or another place of equal prominence." The editorial warns, "A country which sweeps aside its past and its art for ribbons of concrete is going nowhere of any importance."[26]

Rebecca Sisler, who had just outdone Lawrence Hayward by finishing her book on The Girls,[27] wrote to the *Globe and Mail*: "Surely The Monument represents something rare in the annals of Canadian achievement: a synthesis of artistic excellence, historic significance, and public affection. Is this province so poverty-stricken, spiritually and financially, that funds cannot be allocated to preserve our best-known monument? ... Are there no sites in the core of Ontario's capital where the column and its splendid Lion could be re-erected in the mainstream of everyday life where it can continue to stir public imagination?"[28] There were not.

At the same time as The Monument was being disassembled, the *Toronto Star* ran an article called "Sculptors Hope Toronto will be Known for its Art." But what they had in mind were sculptures like Sorel Etrog's mammoth hand or Henry Moore's *The Archer* in front of City Hall.[29]

With no understanding of how sculpture is enlarged from maquettes by trained stonecutters, the ministry even questioned Loring's right to claim the lion. The Sculptors' Society set them right: "It is the practice of sculptors the world over," wrote an indignant Andrew Boszin on 6 September 1972, "to hire professional carvers to work from the models which the sculptors have provided. We know this to be the case with the late Frances

Loring. We know, also, that the piece was completed by Miss Loring herself, working on the site, on a scaffolding, in the howling winds of a southern Ontario autumn."[30]

Loring and Wyle had only been dead for four years when the decision was made to remove the limestone monument that for Loring had become — along with *Sir Robert Borden* — the work that defined her to the Canadian public. She dated the beginning of her serious arthritis from those raw November weeks high on the scaffolding in 1939.[31] But the patriotic monument that celebrated Canada's ties to Britain seemed hopelessly outdated — not to mention offensive to Quebec — at a time when Canada was quickly moving towards severing colonial ties and feared that Quebec might separate. The final stage in the slow evolution of Canadian autonomy, which would be realized within ten years of the relocation of Loring's lion, was Prime Minister Pierre Elliott Trudeau's repatriation of the Constitution in 1982.

An editorial in the *Globe and Mail* damned the monument with faint praise as "a handsome piece and a good example of the work of one of our most distinguished sculptors."[32] It didn't matter any longer that less than forty years before it had seemed "an inspiring symbol of the democratic great Empire on which the welfare of all decent men and women depends."[33] At first, the ministry proposed moving the monument to Ontario Place. The height of the column would have to be reduced, of course.[34] But on reconsideration, the ministry decided that it would be "out of place" in that "honky-tonk atmosphere."[35] And besides, it would obstruct "the rapid transit experiment at the Exhibition Grounds." It should go — the ministry thought, as if the lion were an elderly retiree — somewhere with "pleasant surroundings."[36]

On an August Sunday in 1975, "an eclectic crowd"[37] gathered at noon to see The Girls' friend the Hon. Pauline McGibbon unveil Loring's lion monument. The military were represented by a colonel, who was McGibbon's aide. Loring's nephew, Tom, and his wife had come from New Mexico for the occasion. Dr. Freda Fraser and Edith Williams were there to witness the inconspicuous site. Frances Gage, Charles Band, and David Ongley were present — sad, no doubt, to see the literal decline of The Monument. "I remember when I was a kid always looking for the lion," Dennis Reid, now chief curator of the AGO, recalled of family drives on the QEW. After 1974, drivers and children would no longer say, "Hello, lucky lion," and "Good-bye, lucky lion," as they drove in and out of Toronto.[38]

THE HEAD BRANCH of the Bank of Montreal at King and Bay Streets in Toronto was demolished in 1972 — only twenty-five years after Loring and Wyle and others had sculpted their Canadian bas-relief panels and animal motifs on its walls — to make way for larger commercial buildings.

Had it not been for the efforts of engineer and philanthropist Spencer Clark and his pianist wife, Rosa Breithaupt, who rescued fragments of many Toronto buildings as they were razed in the name of progress, the panels that had caused such controversy would have disappeared forever. Today the provincial nudes, and the skunks, wolves, and bears that shocked Torontonians and irritated architects in 1948 are propped up where anyone can see them on the grounds of Clark and Breithaupt's Guild Inn at 191 Guildwood Parkway. Since the Guild Inn is at the extreme eastern edge of Toronto, on the Scarborough bluffs, it is unlikely that many people will bother.[39] The carvings that were meant to be seen daily in downtown Toronto and bring art to the people have been relegated to the margin.

IN 1983 THERE was an announcement that a small Toronto park was to be dedicated to Frances Loring and Florence Wyle. The park was to be located at the corner of St. Clair Avenue East and Mount Pleasant Road — the noisy throughway that was anything but pleasant to The Girls when it was built in the early 1950s right past the west side of their property. It was this announce-ment that revived the notion of finding a home for Loring's monumental *Goal Keeper*. An editorial in the *Toronto Star* on 27 May 1983 argued, "Here's an opportunity for Harold Ballard of the Toronto Maple Leafs and John Ziegler of the National Hockey League to become patrons of the arts and to salute Toronto's fervent hockey fans at the same time." The larger-than-life statue which Loring had hoped — in vain — would greet hockey fans in the lobby of Maple Leaf Gardens, was now "gathering dust in the vaults of the Art Gallery of Ontario." It was one of the 190 Loring-Wyle statues that had been donated to the gallery by the executors of the Loring-Wyle estate that year because their many efforts to sell them to raise more money for younger sculptors had failed. Conn Smythe had promptly dismissed the sculpture as "too big," for Maple Leaf Gardens in 1937. In 1948, it seemed that the Gardens would take it after all: "I am about to sell my *Goal Keeper* to Maple Leaf Gardens ... for $3,000.00 in stone. My profit is to be about $1,600.00," Loring wrote Harry McCurry.[40] But that too fell through. In 1964, Charles Band had unsuccessfully tried, through Mayor Philip Givens, to have it cast in bronze and erected in front of the Hockey Hall of Fame at the CNE as a memorial to Donald D. Summerville.[41] A decade later, the Centre for Sports and Recreation approached Loring's estate to see if the statue could be incorporated into the Centre's Canadian Sport Art Collection. Frances Gage got an estimate from The Morris Singer Foundry in London, England, but the Centre decided against spending the $9,500 it would have cost to cast it in bronze.[42]

But why not put it in the new Loring and Wyle park? "There could hardly be a more fitting spot as a permanent site for the *Goalkeeper* [sic]," the editorial argued. "How about it, Messrs. Ballard and Ziegler?"[43]

Donald Jones, in his *Toronto Star* column "Historical Toronto," reported in 1983 that Toronto alderman John Sewell had proposed that Loring's *Goal Keeper* be displayed at the Canadian Sports Hall of Fame. This proposal failed. Curator Tom West said, "Thanks, but the hall honors heroes, not an unknown goaltender."[44] Besides, the cost — now $40,000 — to cast the work in bronze was exorbitant. Jones suggested the Hockey Hall of Fame, where it could serve as "a towering, identifying symbol." This too failed. Another possibility, Jones suggested, was to put it in the College Street subway station across from Maple Leaf Gardens, where fans could see it as they headed for the games. Already the College Street TTC station was slated for an enormous mural (31 1/2' x 8') on a hockey theme (later completed by Toronto artist Charles Pachter). "If Paris can line its Louvre subway station with sculpture to symbolize Paris as a City of Art, committees in Toronto should be considering placing Loring's *Goal Keeper* at the subway station that most Torontonians would agree has made Toronto the centre of the Hockey World in Canada."[45] No luck. So the "gloomy goalkeeper" was stored at the Art Gallery of Ontario.

Four years later, Robert Fulford, who had never liked The Girls' work and had given them short shrift in his 1977 book *An Introduction to the Arts in Canada*,[46] wrote an article for the *Toronto Star* in 1987 to explain why the "generation gap" between sculptors in Canada was "too far to bridge."[47] He focused on the "saddest incident" in Loring's career — the "pathetic story of unfulfilled ambition" represented by the fate of the *Goal Keeper*, who still languished in the vaults of the AGO. Fulford argued that many of the Loring-Wyle sculptures currently on display in a large retrospective show of their work curated by Christine Boyanoski at the AGO "have a place in local history but no interesting place in art. Certainly if these sculptures were to arrive here from Frankfurt or Los Angeles or Melbourne and be booked into the AGO, they would evoke puzzlement at best, derision at worst."[48] As for the *Goal Keeper* — who had been displayed at the CNE four times, as well as at the Pollack Gallery retrospective, the Queen's Park Macdonald Gallery, and Windsor's Willingdon Museum — "It's not a work of power or originality; it's a minor artist's failed attempt to deal with a popular subject she didn't understand." Later critics were even more blunt. A sportswriter in 2001 comparing Loring's *Goal Keeper* to Ken Danby's classic Canadian painting *At the Crease* (1972), wrote, "Loring's giant brooding statue is anything but a celebration of Canada's game. Though a relic of hockey's golden age, the huge work has a dumb, lumpen quality that seems to put players only a few evolutionary steps above ungulates."[49]

As for the park, which replaced an old streetcar loop[50] and had been suggested by the Moore Park Residents' Association (who loved their Clay Ladies), it was opened by Mayor Art Eggleton on 5 June 1986. There were four statues in the park — along with a plaque commemorating Loring and Wyle. Wyle's RCA diploma piece *The Harvester*, hoists his jug above his head, and her *Young Girl*, draped in the Grecian mode, stands naked and serene. It seems odd that the busts The Girls did of each other in their Greenwich Village days are not facing each other. Although *Frances Loring* looks towards Florence, an indifferent *Florence Wyle* gazes northward up Mount Pleasant.[51] There are few passersby on foot, and the park — so small most drivers on the busy streets of Mount Pleasant and St. Clair would not even glimpse it — has been called a "parkette."

Echoes ⤳

It's almost cause for despair. If you drive into Toronto on the QEW from the west, there is nothing left of Loring's noble lion monument that celebrated the opening of that very highway in 1939. The highway blasts straight through, as if there had never been an oblong island displaying the sculpture. Even the wrought iron streetlights with the initials "E R" entwined near their tops that signified *Elizabeth Regina* have disappeared, except for a few further west on the bridge over the Credit River near Mississauga, and much further west at the entrance to St. Catharines and Niagara Falls.

If you glance sharply to the right where the QEW ends and the Gardiner Expressway begins, you can just glimpse the top quarter of the pillar designed by W.L. Somerville and a bit of the crown that Florence added to the top of Somerville's magnificent column, provided it is not summer and there are no leaves on the trees. In summer, you can only see the top of the crown.

Leaving the highway to drive north up Bay Street, you soon come to King Street West, the intersection where the old Bank of Montreal once stood on the northwest corner. Now it is gone. There is nothing left of the bank with its "contemporary classic" reliefs of the provinces and territories and its motifs of Canadian animals, meant to bring art to the people in 1948. As Europe counts history, that's an eye-blink back to the past — almost modern. If the traffic lights are in your favour, you might have time to see briefly what replaced that handsome building with its elegant personified provinces. Now there's a bigger Bank of Montreal in squared, streamlined concrete and glass — a commercial improvement, no doubt — and next to it, the Toronto Stock Exchange, the hub of Canada's financial life.

If you cross west to University Avenue and drive north to Toronto General Hospital in the hope of seeing Wyle's relief of Edith Cavell, just before the corner of College Street, you can't. Only if you turn in to the semi-circular driveway that leads to the Robert R. McEwen Atrium, built in 2003, can you pause for a minute, jump out of your car and take a quick look at the large monument. It is now imbedded in free-standing concrete just to the right of the doors at 585 University Avenue. Soon after it was unveiled, it mysteriously acquired a metal wreath from Toronto's patriotic Italian society, a gesture which Wyle would never have agreed to, but at which she laughed acceptance.

If you continue north around Queen's Park and up Avenue Road to turn right at St. Clair Avenue, you will go over the Vale of Avoca across which the Deer Park Sunday School building was dragged on rollers in 1910 to its rural setting among the apple trees on Glen Rose Avenue long before Mount Pleasant Road existed. If you continue east in the clogged traffic along St. Clair to the Mount Pleasant throughway that encourages more and more cars at faster speeds to arrive downtown, you will only be able to take a quick look at the Loring-Wyle Parkette on the northeast corner if the light is red. If you want to get out to see it, you will have to search for a parking spot some distance away. Once you do this, you can enter the parkette, read the plaque of dedication and sit on the bench. It's unlikely you will want to stay to contemplate what The Girls did for each other, for this city and for their chosen country. The park is tiny and its shape — a narrow north-south rectangle along Mount Pleasant — is not conducive to reflection. There is no fence or hedge to protect you from the noisy traffic and fumes from the two major roads that intersect here. Besides, the park is full of litter, the shrubs untrimmed. The place does not speak of respect for anyone or anything. The park is otherwise empty. It's hard to imagine anyone coming here on purpose.

A block to the south is Glenrose Avenue, and you can easily find The Church at number 110. It is the house on the north side, closest to Mount Pleasant. The front garden shadowed by a huge maple is rampant with weeds and ivy. The blue Ontario Historical Plaque dedicated to Loring and Wyle on 25 October 1976 — the same year the second volume of Wyle's poems was posthumously published — is overgrown with weeds, honeysuckle, and vines. Raised only slightly above ground level, it is almost invisible. I clear the overgrowth from it, though I have no expectation that anyone else will bother to visit and read it.

LORING-WYLE STUDIO
This board-and-batten building, originally the schoolhouse for Christ Church, Deer Park, was acquired in 1920 by Frances Loring and Florence Wyle. Sculpting in the classical tradition, they achieved national prominence and executed many impressive public works, among which are Loring's Sir Robert Borden on Parliament Hill and Wyle's Edith Cavell in Toronto. They were founding members of the Sculptors' Society of Canada, and their studio was an important artistic centre where musicians, writers, sculptors, painters, and patrons of the arts congregated. When Frances Loring and Florence Wyle died in 1968 they bequeathed their studio to the Royal Academy of Arts. The sale of the building allowed the Academy to establish a trust for the development of Canadian artists.[1]

I try to imagine The Church as it was when Loring and Wyle bought it in 1920. Then it had a flapping tarpaper roof and stood on cedar blocks at the four corners. The road was dirt. There was no water. It was red then — romantic, Loring used to say. It is still romantic. Now it is still the light grey The Girls chose in 1948 to disguise the pigeon droppings. The pointed Gothic windows are as they were from the beginning, and I can just see the three skylights they put in to improve the light for working. On the right is the addition they added — almost too late — for Florence. There's the garage where many "old flyvers" resided.

I am apprehensive as I knock on the door. I expect that all will be changed inside, now that it's a private home. I recall that when journalist Lyn Harrington interviewed The Girls at their studio in 1944, she remarked, "It's rather a ghostly world peopled by figures in stone, in clay, in plaster and bronze. Sheeted figures, partly finished, rest on the modelling stands, with smoothly-running castors."[2] Another interviewer visiting The Church in the late '50s, on seeing many of The Girls' early works asked Loring, "Isn't it odd having all these people around every day?" To which Loring replied with her small smile, "It's appalling. That's why the trivial and the transient have no place in sculpture."[3] All this will probably have disappeared.

WHEN MARLIE SNIDERMAN — who, with her husband and son, has been the only one to live in The Church since The Girls died in 1968 — answers the door, I feel a wave of something. As Marlie and I shake hands, I can see just beyond her Loring's huge panel *Dawn*, kneeling, loosing her three doves to the rising sun. And beyond that, statues and busts I recognize silhouetted against the green filtered light streaming in from the wall of windows in what was once Florence's studio. It still looks peaceful, serene.

As Marlie tells me about how they came to be there, I realize it's just as well that the terms of The Girls' wills were not observed. The Church was to have been turned into "The Academy House," a museum-studio for visitors, especially from their neighbourhood, by the Royal Canadian Academy of the Arts. That never came to pass. The RCA waffled for two years, then decided that the expense of upgrading the building, including public wash-rooms and a sprinkler system, was too great. Frances Gage believes otherwise: "Academicians John Parkin and Cleeve Horne did not think it grand enough."[4] Finally, the academy decided to sell it.

Eleanor Sniderman, a long-time friend of The Girls who had once com-missioned a sculpted portrait bust of herself from Florence that would later appear on the label of her classical record company Aquitaine,[5] heard that the old Church she had so enjoyed visiting with her son Bobby was for sale. Worse, that it might be turned into a condominium.[6] Worse yet, that it might be demolished. She begged her husband, Sam Sniderman of Sam the Record Man fame, to buy it for her. "She'd never ask for another thing if he'd buy it," she was reported as saying. "She felt it must be preserved as something important to Toronto, and to Canada." So — in 1970 — he bought it for $144,000.[7]

Sam and Eleanor's son Bobby — one of the neighbourhood children who had visited The Girls, been given cookies and milk, shown the glories of muddy malleable clay, and marvelled at the Clay Ladies themselves — was to live there. "All Canada should be grateful," a friend of The Girls wrote Frances Gage when she heard, "that there are people like the Snidermans who care."[8]

A new generation of parties began in The Church with the wedding of Bobby Sniderman and Marlaina Sacks. They had already started to restore The Church, but had not changed its essentials.

MARLIE SNIDERMAN — AN attractive woman in dark pants and a loose rust-coloured top wearing a turquoise bracelet, her dark hair pulled back simply — leads me into the main room. It is as bright and open as it was when The Girls lived and worked here. The first thing I see is the busts they did of each other in Greenwich Village. Unlike their alienated positioning in the parkette, they face each other from either side of the mantle of the huge fireplace they built themselves. Looking around the room, I see some of their other works: there's *The Old One*, one of Florence's cats, the torso of a young girl. It takes no effort to imagine the way it was: the old station-master's stove, the hodgepodge of sculpture, the cats. The dark wood doors of the vestry that rise to a peak still shut on a bedroom, as they did for almost thirty years when Loring and Wyle slept there, and as they remained later when Loring installed an electric buzzer by her bed so she could call Florence from the new wing for help. Marlie opens them. Now it's her bedroom, and Bobby's. In what was the main studio, only a large yellow sofa and an easy chair around a table on an area rug in the middle of an otherwise bare hardwood floor indicates that a family now lives here.

The Snidermans have added a layer to the bookshelves on the left of the huge fireplace, which otherwise remains as it was. Some of The Girls' books are still there: Frances's books on sculptors José de Creeft,[9] William Zorach,[10] and Ivan Meštrović,[11] a study of British sculpture from 1944–46;[12] and one on Greek sculpture[13] — Florence's favourite. Marlie hands it to me, and I open it as if it were a religious relic.

Marlie is remembering her wedding on 26 May 1974: "We walked to the front of the fireplace," she says. "where [Rabbi David Monson][14] waited for us. The reception — prepared for by The Girls' old housekeeper Agnes — was in Florence's studio ... and throughout the house." As social columnist Zena Cherry reported in the *Globe and Mail* at the time, "The Studio was garlanded gorgeously right up to its very high ceiling with garden flowers and lilacs." Marlie, a McGill graduate, would pass Wyle's *Edith Cavell* relief at Toronto General Hospital on her way to work there as a psychiatric social worker. Bobby, a University of Toronto graduate, became franchise manager for his father's Canada-wide record firm.[15]

Marlie takes me past *Dawn* and through Florence's studio, out her back door to the garden. We stand on the porch for a minute, where she and Bobby have done nothing much but put up a couple of antique carved arches on columns they found in Quebec. The garden is an impenetrable wilderness of trees rising from a thick floor of oak leaves that must have been left there year after year. With difficulty we make our way to the middle of the half-acre garden where Florence once tended a tangle of lilac, forsythia, and lily of the valley, to one of her fountains. There, a small boy wearing a hat and holding a bowl can catch rainwater forever. "A child who will never grow old," I think. "It was among some Montgomery & Ward stuff," Marlie explains. "I have my name on the web as an interested purchaser if anything by Loring or Wyle shows up." We stand silent for a moment, then return slowly to the house.

"I can't tell you how much work we've put into this house," Marlie says once we're inside. "The drains were flooding. The roof needed fixing. There were birds in here. Things were dripping. There were noises everywhere ... and all those dusty statues. The house owned the statues. It was a matter of copyright law. The executors — Frances Gage and David Ongley — trusted us to live with them, and we lived with them for ten years. The place was like a teenage horror movie: feet, hands, maquettes, plaster moulds, a lot of rubber casing, pieces of nests all over. It had a lot of Miss Havisham in it."

I shiver. I know what she means: "ghostly presences." Marlie goes on to recount their restoration of The Church. She is careful to make a distinction between "restoration" and "renovation," which she abhors. The Snidermans laid the hardwood, replaced the old skylights and a couple of windows, searching a long time to find old leaded windows with patterned frosted glass like the originals. A new furnace replaced the "octopus" that took up half the basement. A mirror covering the east wall of Florence's studio doubles the size of the room, reflects the quiet green light she loved. The upstairs bedroom — where Florence loyally kept Charley Mulligan's photo by her bed — and its adjoining bathroom are now the domain of the Sniderman's eighteen-year-old son Zachary. "We're so grateful to be living in this place," she says, "the atmosphere, the colour of it. It's been wonderful to have a child grow up in this house. It's worthless," she shrugs and pauses. "... And it's worth a lot. This house is not let-goable."

MARLIE LEADS ME down to the Crypt, down the same stairs where Loring used to hurl her canes in frustration. I can almost hear the clatter. It is just as it appeared in the many photos I have seen. The refectory table Keith McIver made from The Boys' old door still stands in the bricked and tiled kitchen, just as it did when it was laden with food at The Girls' Christmas parties, just as I saw it in the CBC video, set for tea. On the wall above the table some sculptors' tools hang as if ready for use.

Marlie tells me that after years unravelling the technicalities of the ownership of The Girls' statues, there was a competition for them in 1983 between the Art Gallery of Ontario, the University of Guelph, and the new McMichael Gallery in Kleinberg, which, since it opened in 1966, specialized in Canadian art. The Art Gallery of Ontario succeeded in acquiring most of the remaining works. There were over two hundred pieces, only part of the 500-or-so creations The Girls left behind.[16] With a grant of $10,000 from the

Canada Council[17] that Loring helped establish, Frances Gage supervised the cataloguing of their works for the AGO. Recently a few statues have been professionally restored. The breasts and stomach of Wyle's magnificent *Torso*, "blackened by handling," have been cleaned up. A large chip in the front of the base of Loring's *Eskimo Mother and Child* has been repaired.[18]

Frances and Florence are still very much alive for Marlie, who values meditation and feels she shares The Church now with The Girls. It's not just the small boy in a hat who will live forever in the garden; nor is it the *Sleeping Cat* who will never take his folded paws from his eyes, or the *Mother and Child* with one toe missing; nor is it *The Old One*, who looks as disreputable as he did in the 1930s, or *Dawn*, which will never fade. It's not even the bronze busts of The Girls — copies that were made and given to the Snidermans in 1986 when the Loring-Wyle Parkette opened. "We feel presences here," says Marlie. "This house has a lot of presences. There are noises: clicking, ticking sounds. The sounds settled down a bit after we got the busts." I look to the fireplace. It seems natural that Florence and Frances are gazing at each other here. Marlie looks around the room, regards the other sculptures as if they are presences too. "The *Goal Keeper* is in a separate room from the rest of their things at the AGO. He's all alone. It feels bad," she says, shaking her head as if he were someone she knew and loved. She leads me back into Florence's studio. "Look!" she says pointing to an empty, black, wooden box about three feet square on the floor. It is the sculpture stand that had once supported Loring's *Eskimo Mother and Child* while she created it. In worn red paint on its top is printed unevenly the word "ESKIMO" and the initials F.L.

Acknowledgements

This book could not have been written without the generous help and encouragement of many scholars, librarians, archivists, sculptors, and friends — more than I can possibly acknowledge here. To all of them I express my gratitude.

First and foremost, I thank the Social Sciences and Humanities Federation of Canada, Brock University, and the Ontario Arts Council for the grants that enabled me to research and write this book and to assemble the photographs to illustrate it. In my preparations for these grants, I was greatly helped by Michael Owen, Fran Chandler, and Maureen Murphy in Brock University's Office of Research Services.

Marc Côté, my editor at Cormorant Books Inc., invited me to write this book in 2004. Since then he has been encouraging, helpful, and accessible. I thank him for his support in the grant application process. I could not have wished for a better editor. I am also grateful to copy editor, Steven Beattie.

I have been fortunate in having Bradley Walchuk as my research assistant.

He has worked hard and carefully on this project, including the compilation of the list of Loring and Wyle's works and independent research trips. I am grateful for his help and look forward to the day he publishes research of his own.

Antonio Jones, president of the Art Institute of Chicago, kindly arranged a viewing of the rooms where Loring and Wyle studied sculpture, gave me an interview, and provided me with photographs. The two most important interviewees were sculptors Frances Gage and Rebecca Sisler, both of whom were available in person and by email to answer a host of questions. Among other things, these two women are stellar examples of the importance of friendship. What they have done on behalf of Loring and Wyle is immeasurable. Sculptor Dora de Pédery Hunt also shared her recollections, and architect Qennefer Browne, daughter of sculptors Emanuel Hahn and Elizabeth Wyn Wood, offered her unique perspective on Loring and Wyle from a child's point of view. I am especially grateful to Dr. Marlaina Sniderman for allowing me to visit The Church where she now lives with her family and several Loring and Wyle sculptures.

I thank former colleagues Dr. Lynne Viola and Dr. Donald Wright for drawing my attention to the importance of monumentalism to my project. Dr. Charlotte Streifer Rubenstein and Dr. Sandra Alfoldy generously shared their research pertinent to Loring and Wyle. Doris McCarthy, Dr. Patricia Smart, and Lawrence Hayward gave me interesting perspectives on this project. I am grateful to Eva Tihanyi for suggesting the book's title. Dennis Reid, Lynne Viola, Rosalind Went, and Terry Murray kindly read my manuscript and made helpful comments. Any errors in the book are mine, not theirs.

My research was largely conducted at the Brock University Library, using their excellent Interlibrary loan system and databases. I found the staff at the James Gibson Library cooperative, friendly, and efficient. Those who helped me particularly were the Interlibrary loan staff: Annie Relic, Sue Moskal, Mary Little, and Jan Milligan. Justine Alsop, Brock Reference Librarian, was always helpful, as were Fran Dube, Diane Bateman, Sue Sykeman, and Maureen McCart. I am also indebted to Sally Gibson, Manager of Heritage Services of the Toronto Distillery District; Bart Rychbosch,

Archivist, Art Institute of Chicago; Randall Speller, Sylvia Lassam, Larry Pfaff, and Amy Marshall at the E.P. Taylor Research Library and Archives, Art Gallery of Ontario; Jane Rhodes and Tanya Zhilinsky, Photographic Resources, Art Gallery of Ontario; Barbara Brown and Roy MacGregor, Canadian Broadcasting Corporation; Barbara Mitchell, Women's Art Association of Canada; Mary Johnston-Miller and Catherine Butler, Library and Archives Canada; Laura Brandon, Canadian War Museum; Wendy Watts, Torstar Syndication Services; Patricia Desjardins, *Montreal Gazette*; Harold Averill, University of Toronto Archives; Cyndie Campbell, National Gallery of Canada; and numerous staff at Library and Archives Canada, National Gallery of Canada, Canadian War Museum, CNE Archives, Canadian Lesbian and Gay Archives, the Metropolitan Toronto Library, and the Archives of Ontario.

I am especially indebted to Eric Knoespel who showed me in detail how bronze sculpture is cast using the "lost wax" process at his company *Artcast Inc.* in Georgetown, Ontario.

Photographs were obtained from a wide variety of sources with the help of many different people: Art Gallery of Ontario, National Gallery of Canada, Canadian War Museum, Library and Archives Canada, Ashley and Crippen, *The Montreal Gazette*, *The Toronto Star*, Frances Gage, and Dale Fehr. The staff at CBC kindly tracked down and gave me a videotape of the 1965 TV documentary on Loring and Wyle. I owe a special debt to Don Foley, St. David's, Ontario, who took professional photos of Loring and Wyle works in the Niagara region. He and Rosalind Went also helped in the preparation of a DVD on Loring and Wyle for lecture and conference presentations.

I am grateful to Sylvia Barlow and Janet Sackfie, Brock University, for their assistance and interest throughout this project.

Finally, I want to thank all the colleagues, students, and friends who showed enthusiasm for this project during the years I was working on it. They were too many to name individually, but their encouragement meant a great deal to me.

Notes ⁘

INTRODUCTION

I   James Purdie, "Scouts Who Cleared the Underbrush," *Globe and Mail* (23 July 1977), p. 31.

II   Linda Munk, "A Talk with Miss Loring and Miss Wyle," *Women's Globe and Mail* [clipping, 6 May 1965], AGO Archives. Here and elsewhere, see the extensive and detailed "Inventory of Archival Materials from the Loring and Wyle Estates," by Susan Lowe (Oct. 1984) for specific files in the E.P. Taylor Research Library and Archives, AGO, Toronto.

III   "Frances Loring," *Canadian Cancer Society Newsletter*, [clipping, 1960], p. 10 AGO Archives.

IV   See correspondence between and among Clare Bice, Charles Band, and Sophia Hungerford, 27 Feb. 1964, AGO Archives.

V   Lawrence Hayward, emails to Elspeth Cameron, 27 Apr. 2005 and 11 May 2005, Kingston, ON.

VI   Clare Bice, letter to Robert (Bob) Ayre, 7 Feb. 1968, and Robert Ayre, letter to Frances Gage, 8 Mar. 1968, AGO Archives.

VII J.G. McClelland, letter to Frances Gage, 4 Dec. 1969, AGO Archives.

VIII Lois Milani, letter to Frances Gage, 6 June 1969. Milani had written several literary and historical articles and a full-length biography of Robert Gourlay (1778–1863) called *The Banished Briton*.

IX Arthur E. McFarlane, "Art Awakes in a Forgotten Church," *Toronto Star Weekly* (1 Aug. 1925), p. 59.

X "Survey of Canadian Sculpture Given in Art Gallery Lecture," *Globe* (13 Mar. 1928), p. 14.

XI See E.K. Brown, *On Canadian Poetry* (Toronto: Ryerson Press, 1943) for a good sense of the obstacles to Canadian art generally and a formulation of its early ideology.

XII Fiona Carson, "Sculpture and Installations," *Feminist Visual Culture* (New York: Routledge, 2001), p. 57. This philosophy of art predominated from the late 1880s to the early 1900s.

XIII Frances Loring, as cited in Roger P. Parr, "A Woman of Value: The Uses of Simplicity," *Country Beautiful* (May 1963), pp. 58–59.

XIV At the memorial service for Florence Wyle, William Withrow (with notes from Charles Band) referred to Wyle and Loring as, "these two inseparable spirits." AGO Archives. Christine Boyanoski said, "It's a nice romantic notion that one died and the other couldn't carry on but I don't think it's true." See Marilyn Linton, "AGO Celebrates the 'Odd Couple,'" *Leaside Town Crier*, (Aug. 1987).

XV Some of the subjects Ashley and Crippen photographed were: Marilyn Bell, Barbara Ann Scott, Sir Edmund Walker, the Rt. Hon. Louis St. Laurent, Mrs. Timothy Eaton, E.P. Taylor, Arthur Lismer, Drs. Frederick Banting and Charles Best, the Rt. Hon. John Diefenbaker, C.D. Howe, Hon. Jean Lesage, and HRH Queen Elizabeth II. Frances Loring wrote an introduction to *Fifty Years of Photography by Ashley & Crippen* (1965), in which she claimed she was "one of their first clients."

XVI "Women with Mallets," *The New World (Illustrated)* (Feb. 1942), p. 27.

XVII Donald Jones, "The Story of the Queen, the Lion and the Old Church Schoolhouse," *Toronto Star* [clipping, 30 June 1979], AGO Archives.

XVIII Donald Jones, "Loring-Wyle Memorial Park Honors Odd-Couple Sculptors," *Toronto Star* (18 June 1983).

XIX Robertson Davies, letter to the editor, *Globe and Mail* (14 Oct. 1995), p. D7. Davies disingenuously lists the dissimilarities between his Ladies and The Girls as proof that he did not base his Ladies on The Girls. The similarities are as follows: two women artists living together in a church building which is their studio as a couple; they are life-long partners; their weekly salons (held on Sundays, not Saturdays) are legendary gatherings of artists; the two women have run off together to live together, and one — like Florence — is cut off by her family. It is probably true that Davies never knew or saw The Girls, as he claims. But as an artistic Torontonian himself, he would certainly have heard of them.

xx   See Brian Busby, *Character Parts: Who's Really Who in Canadian Literature* (Toronto: Alfred A. Knopf Canada, 2003), pp. 144–45. Davies's disclaimer does not ring true; given his characteristic display of knowledge, it is unlikely he would refrain from mentioning the names of these "two women artists," as he does. He would have had no need to fear a libel suit from England.

xxi   Claude J. Summers, *The Queer Encyclopedia of the Visual Arts* (San Francisco: Cleis Press, Inc., 2004). Listings are alphabetical by surname.

xxii   Diana Moon, "Francis [sic] & Florence: A Love Story," *Siren* 6.2 (June/July 2001), pp. 16–17.

xxiii   The 1989 film was John Greyson's first feature film. It was shown at the Berlin Film Festival. It used The Church as the place where an unlikely historical group, including Russian filmmaker Sergei Eisenstein, Mexican painter Frida Kahlo, Yukio Mishima, and Oscar Wilde's Dorian Gray, meet to attack homophobic Toronto. See "Film Challenges 'Gay-Bashers,'" *Toronto Star* (27 Apr. 1989), p. C6.

xxiv   This includes Frances Gage, Rebecca Sisler, Dora de Pédery Hunt, Lawrence Hayward, and Doris McCarthy; as well as the fifty or so people interviewed by Rebecca Sisler for her book *The Girls*.

xxv   "Novel Studio for Sculptors," *Mail and Empire* [clipping, 20 Nov. 1920], AGO Archives.

xxvi   "Women with Mallets," *op. cit.*, p. 27.

xxvii   Qennefer Browne to Elspeth Cameron, interview 3 Dec. 2006, Orillia, ON.

xxviii   Sheila Moodie, "Noted Toronto Sculptress Finds Canada a Challenge," *Ottawa Citizen* (10 Jan. 1957). Loring said, "My bedroom is in the vestry." See also *The New World Illustrated* (Feb. 1942): "They regard the word sculptress with well founded disfavor."

xix   Fiona Carson, "Sculpture and Installations," *Feminist Visual Culture*, ed. Fiona Carson and Claire Pajaczkowska (New York: Routledge, 2001), pp. 57, 13.

xxx   John R. Lewis, "Why Would a Woman Want to be a Sculptor," *Star Weekly Magazine* (2 Jan. 1960), p. 37.

xxxi   Blodwen Davies, "Canadian Women of Brush and Chisel," *The Chatelaine* (June 1930), p. 42.

XXXII   John Bentley Mays, "AGO Tells Girls' Story with Care and Spirit," *Globe and Mail* [clipping, 31 July 1987], AGO Archives.

XXXIII   "Girls were Conservative — and Outrageous," *Toronto Star* (24 July 1987), p. E3.

XXXIV   Quebec newspaper [clipping, ca. 1964], AGO Archives.

XXXV   *Ibid.*

XXXVI   Sheila Moodie, *op. cit.*

XXXVII   Frances Loring to Elspeth Chisholm, CBC TV script interview (July 1956), p. iii, AGO Archives.

XXXVIII Lyn Harrington, "Unique Church-Studio is Home and Workshop for Loring and Wyle," *Saturday Night* (18 Nov. 1944), p. 5.

XXXIX   Norma Broude, "Modern Woman or the Cult of True Womanhood?" ed. Norma Broude and Mary D. Garrard, *Reclaiming Female Agency* (Berkeley: University of California Press, 2005), p. 273.

XL   Sol Littman, "Feminists Challenge Male Art Values," *Toronto Star* (2 June 1973), p. 79.

XLI   Mary Jacobus, as cited by Linda Zerilli, "Rememoration or War? French Feminist Narrative and the Politics of Self-Representation," *differences: A Journal of Feminist Cultural Studies* 3.1 (1991), p. 15.

XLII   Louise V. Hunter, "New Woman Academician Has Her Studio in an Abandoned Church," *Ottawa Evening Citizen* (24 Nov. 1938).

XLIII   Wyle, CBC Radio interview [n.d.], CBC Archives.

XLIV   Lytton Strachey, "Introduction," *Eminent Victorians* (London: Penguin Books, 1986), p. 8.

CHAPTER 1

1   Frances Loring to Sheila Moodie, cited in "Noted Toronto Sculptress Finds Canada a Challenge," *Ottawa Citizen* [clipping, 10 Jan. 1957], AGO Archives.

2   This is a combination of two quotations from Frances Loring: Frances Loring to Kingsley Brown, "Sculptress Finds Banting, Borden Strong Personalities, 'Fighters,'" *Hamilton Spectator* [clipping, 10 Dec. 1955], AGO Archives, and Frances Loring to Linda Munk, "A Talk with Miss Loring and Miss Wyle," *Women's Globe and Mail* (6 May 1965), p. 27.

3   Rebecca Sisler, *The Girls* (Toronto: Clarke, Irwin & Co., 1972), pp. 19–20.

4   E.P. Taylor Research Library and Archives, Art Gallery of Ontario.

5   Sydney Norman, "A Dean Among Mining Engineers Pays Tribute to the Prospectors," *Globe and Mail* (22 Apr. 1938).

6   Rebecca Sisler, *op. cit.*, p.21.

7   A few years later, in 1910, Emily Carr studied at the Académie Colarossi.

8   Rebecca Sisler to Elspeth Cameron, interview, 19 July 2005, Calgary, AB.

CHAPTER 2

1   Jonathan F. Vance, *Death So Noble: Memory, Meaning and the First World War* (Vancouver: UBC Press, 1997), p. 50.

2   Elia W. Peattie, "The Artistic Side of Chicago," *The Atlantic Monthly* 84 (Dec. 1899), p. 829.

3   Alson J. Smith, *Chicago's Left Bank* (Chicago: Henry Regnery Co., 1953), p. 162.

4   Elia W. Peattie, *op. cit.*, p. 829.

5   Anne Felicia Cierpik, "History of the Art Institute of Chicago," M.A. Dissertation, De Paul University, Chicago (1957), pp. 60–64.

6   Elia W. Peattie, *op. cit.*, p. 829.

7   Anne Felicia Cierpik, interview with Robert Daley, 14 May 1956, *op. cit.*

8   Quoted in Elia W. Peattie, *op. cit.*, p. 833.

9   Lorado Taft, *The History of American Sculpture* (New York: Macmillan, 1903), p. 332.

10 The fountain was also known as *The Ship of State* and *The Triumph of Columbia*.

11 William Harlan Hale, *The World of Rodin, 1840–1917* (New York: Time-Life Books, 1969), p. 7.

12 Norman Bolotin and Christine Laing, *The World's Columbian Exposition* (Chicago: The Preservation Press, 1992), p. 43.

13 These painters were: Mary Ella Dignam, who would later found the Women's Art Association in Toronto; Mary Alexandra Eastlake; Laura Muntz Lyall; Mary Hiester Reid; and Gertrude Spurr Cutts.

14 Norman Bolotin and Christine Laing, *op. cit.*, pp. 42–43.

15 *Ibid.*, p. 43.

CHAPTER 3

1   Rebecca Sisler, *The Girls* (Toronto: Clarke, Irwin & Co., 1972), p. 19.

2   Verdé V. Dundas, "The Modelling Class at the Art Institute," *Brush and Pencil* 2.4 (July 1898), p.173.

3   *Ibid.*, p. 167.

4   Nathaniel Hawthorne, *The French and Italian Notebooks*, ed. Thomas Woodson, 14, The Centenary Edition of the Works of Nathaniel Hawthorne (Columbus:

Ohio State University Press, 1980), p. 158. Cited by Charlotte Streifer Rubenstein in *American Women Sculptors* (Boston: G.K. Hall & Co., 1990), p. 32.

5   Charlotte Streifer Rubenstein, *op. cit.*, p. 25.

CHAPTER 4

1   Verdé V. Dundas, "The Modelling Class at the Art Institute," *Brush and Pencil* 2.4 (July 1898), pp. 167–76.

2   *Ibid.*

3   Calendar, School of the Art Institute of Chicago, 1906–07. See also Rebecca Sisler, *The Girls* (Toronto: Clarke, Irwin & Co., 1972), pp. 17–18.

4   Cited by Charlotte Streifer Rubenstein in *American Women Sculptors* (Boston: G.K. Hall & Co., 1990), p. 100.

5   Janet Scudder, *Modeling My Life*, (New York: Harcourt, Brace and Co., 1925), p. 58.

6   These handwritten lecture notes are located in the AIC Archives.

7   Allen S. Weller, "Lorado Taft, 1860–1936," in "Lorado Taft: A Retrospective Exhibition: January 16 to February 20, 1983," *Bulletin*, Krannert Art Museum, 8.2 (Urbana-Champaign: University of Illinois, 1983), p. 3.

8   Allen S. Weller, *op. cit.*, pp. 9, 5.

9   *Ibid.*, p.13.

10   Cited beside the sculpture in the Sculpture Gallery of The Art Institute of Chicago.

11   Allen S. Weller, *op. cit.*, p. 22.

12   Cited beside the sculpture in the Sculpture Gallery of The Art Institute of Chicago.

13   Lorado Taft, "That Fountain," *Brush and Pencil* 3.5 (Aug. 1899), p. 252.

14   *Ibid.*, pp. 249–54.

15   *Ibid.*

16   "Comstock's Fight for the Fig Leaf," *Brush and Pencil* 18.4 (Oct. 1906), p. 168.

17   See Robert H. Moulton, "Chicago's Dream of Civic Beauty Realized in the Symbolic Marble of Lorado Taft," *The Craftsman* 25 (1904), pp. 123–24.

18   Anne Felicia Cierpik, "History of the Art Institute of Chicago," M.A. Dissertation, De Paul University, Chicago (1957), p. 50.

19   Ira J. Bach and Mary Lackritz Gray, *A Guide to Chicago's Public Sculpture* (Chicago; The University of Chicago Press, 1983), p. 30.

20   Allen S. Weller, *op. cit.*, p. 6; and *Chicago Record Herald*, 12 Oct. 1907, Art Institute Scrapbook, 23, microfilm, AIC Archives.

21 Lorado Taft, "Exhibition of Statuary, Art Institute, Chicago," *Sketchbook* 5.10 (Aug. 1906), p. 450.

22 Taft left a detailed account; see "A New Testament Incident in Sculpture," *Current Literature* 39 (Nov. 1905), pp. 522–23. See also "A Woman Taken in Adultery," *Brush and Pencil* 18.1 (July–Dec. 1906), p. 23.

23 Lorado Taft, "Exhibition," *op. cit.*

24 "Lorado Taft and the Western School of Sculptors," *The Craftsman* (Apr. 1908), p. 22.

25 *Ibid.*, p. 14.

26 Lorado Taft, as cited by Alson J. Smith, *Chicago's Left Bank* (Chicago: Henry Regnery Company, 1953), p. 159.

27 Allen S. Weller, *op. cit.*, p. 2.

28 *Ibid.*, p. 3.

29 *Ibid.*, p. 10.

30 Cited in *Ibid.*, pp. 4, 10. The "finishing" took nine months.

31 "The Recent Exhibition of Chicago Artists," *The Bulletin of the Art Institute of Chicago* 1 (Apr. 1908), pp. 35–36.

32 Charles Hutchinson as cited in the *Chicago Tribune*, 20 Oct. 1910, Art Institute Scrapbook, 27, microfilm, AIC Archives.

33 Lena M. McCauley, "An Epoch in National Art," *Brush and Pencil* 14.5 (Dec. 1904), p. 302.

34 Gutzon Borglum "Imitation the Curse of American Art," *Brush and Pencil* 19.2 (Feb. 1907), p. 6.

35 Lena M. McCauley, *op. cit.*, p. 305.

36 *Ibid.*, p. 299.

37 Gutzon Borglum, *op. cit.*, p. 53.

38 Lena M. McCauley, *op. cit.*, p. 306.

39 Carl Sandburg, *Chicago Poems* (New York: Henry Holt and Co., 1916), pp. 3–4.

40 Elia Peattie, "The Artistic Side of Chicago," *The Atlantic Monthly* 84 (Dec. 1899), p. 839.

41 Ira J. Bach and Mary Lackritz Gray, *op. cit.*, p. 32.

42 Elia Peattie, *op. cit.*, pp. 833–34.

43 "Augustus Saint-Gaudens: The Sculptor Who Has Typified American Character and Has Left Us Noble Memorials of Great Events in American History," *The Craftsman* 13 (Oct. 1907), pp. 59–67.

44 Cyrus Edwin Dallin, "American Sculpture: Its Present Aspects and Tendencies," *Brush and Pencil* 2.6 (Mar. 1903), p. 423.

45 "Imitation the Curse," *op. cit.*, pp. 52–53.

46 Taft also did a dozen or so such monuments for towns in Illinois, Indiana, Michigan, and New York, as well as at Vicksburg and Chickamauga.

47 This sculpture is the one for which Taft is best remembered. It was restored at a cost of $1.2 million between 1998–2002. The rectangular pond separating Father Time from the linear pageant of mankind remains to be restored.

48 "Lorado Taft and the Western School of Sculptors," *op. cit.*, p. 13.

49 Allen S. Weller, *op. cit.*, p. 4.

50 Austin Dobson, "The Paradox of Time," [clipping, n.d.], AIC Archives.

CHAPTER 5

1   Rebecca Sisler, *The Girls* (Toronto: Clarke, Irwin & Co., 1972), p. 20.

·2 Frances Loring to Lyn Harrington, cited in "Unique Church-Studio is Home and Workshop for Loring and Wyle," *Saturday Night* (18 Nov. 1944), p. 4.

3   *Ibid.*, p. 16.

4   Florence Wyle, letter to Carl Stephens, University of Illinois Alumni Association, Urbana, Illinois, 9 May 1918, University of Illinois Archives.

5   *Ibid.*

6   Mariann Smith, "Rosa Bonheur, French, 1822–1899," *Albright-Knox Art Gallery*, 25 Oct. 2005 (access), Art Index A–L, http://www.albrightknox.org/ArtStart/Bonheur.html and Mariann Smith, "Rosa Bonheur, French, 1822–1899," *National Museum of Women in the Arts*, 2007, 23 Sept. 2007 (access), http://www.nmwa.org/collection/Profile.asp?LinkID=95

7   Whitney Chadwick, *Women, Art, and Society* (New York: Thames and Hudson, 1992), p. 167.

8   Empress Eugenie, wife of Emperor Napoleon III, as cited by Mariann Smith, "Rosa Bonheur, French, 1822–1899," *Albright-Knox Art Gallery, op. cit.*

·9 Rebecca Sisler, *op. cit.*, p. 16.

10 *Ibid.*, p. 17.

11 *Ibid.*, p. 16.

12 "Pioneer Canadian Sculptor Was Also a Published Poet," *Toronto Star* (11 June 1973), p. C5.

13 Rebecca Sisler, *op. cit.*, p. 15.

14 *Ibid.*

15 *Ibid.*, p. 16.

16 Mrs. Roy McCracken, cited in "The Story of a Waverly Artist," *Waverly Journal* [clipping, 21 Dec. 1945], AGO Archives. The occasion was "Florence

Wyle Day" in Waverly, which honoured her contribution of several works to the town library.

17   *Ibid.*

18   Florence Wyle, letter to Carl Stephens, 9 May 1918, University of Illinois Archives.

19   "Frank Lloyd Wright in Oak Park, Illinois (1889–1909)," *Oak Park Tourist*, updated Oct. 2003, 23 Sept. 2007 (access), http://www.oprf.com/flw/

20   Alson J. Smith, *Chicago's Left Bank* (Chicago: Henry Regnery Company, 1953), p. 63.

21   Charles Hutchinson, *Chicago Inter Ocean*, cited by Anne Felicia Cierpik, "History of the Art Institute of Chicago," M.A. Dissertation, De Paul University, Chicago (1957), p. 50.

22   As cited by Roger Gillmore, *Over a Century: A History of the School of the Art Institute of Chicago, 1866–1981* (Chicago: The School of the Art Institute of Chicago, 1982), p. 78.

23   Anne Felicia Cierpik, *op. cit.*, p. 45.

24   Details of the Art Institute's expansion can be found throughout Anne Felicia Cierpik, *op. cit.*, pp. 62–65.

25   Anne Felicia Cierpik, *op. cit.*, pp. 66–67.

26   William M.R. French, *Chicago Tribune*, cited in Anne Felicia Cierpik, *op. cit.*, p. 64.

27   Anne Felicia Cierpik, *op. cit.*, p. 81.

28   Lawton S. Parker, *Chicago Herald Record*, cited by Anne Felicia Cierpik, *op.cit.*, pp. 79–80.

29   Charlotte Streifer Rubenstein, *American Women Sculptors* (Boston: G.K. Hall & Co., 1990), p. 18.

30   *Ibid.*, pp. 25–26.

31   Mary Annable Fanton, "Clio Hinton Bracken, Woman Sculptor and Symbolist of the New Art," *The Craftsman* 8 (July 1905), p. 481.

32   Lucretia D. Clapp, "The Quality of Women's Achievement," *The Craftsman* (1908), p. 298.

33   Giles Edgerton, "Is There a Sex Distinction in Art? The Attitude of the Critic Toward Women's Exhibits," *The Craftsman* 12.2 (June 1908), p. 240.

34   Giles Edgerton, "The Quality of Women's Art Achievement: A Young Austrian Sculptor Who Possesses Both Masculine and Feminine Perception," *The Craftsman* 17.1 (Dec. 1908), p. 300.

35   "The Cult of the Unworthy," *Brush and Pencil*, 17.5 (May 1906), pp. 211–12.

36   Roger Gillmore, *op. cit.*, p. 78.

37 Sis Hopkins, "Song of the 1907 Initiates," *'Art Throbs: An Annual by the Normal Students of The Art Institute of Chicago*, 1908–09, p. 44.

38 Rebecca Sisler to Elspeth Cameron, interview, 19 July 2005, Calgary, AB.

39 Sis Hopkins, *op.cit.*, p. 45.

CHAPTER 6

1 A Sculptor's Scullion, "The School of The Art Institute of Chicago, Il., The Evening Modelling Classes," *Brush and Pencil* 1.6 (Mar. 1898), p. 204.

2 *Ibid.*, p. 205.

3 "Designer of the Centennial Monument is Dead at Chicago," *Chicago Illinois Examiner* [clipping, 31 Mar. 1916], AIC Archives.

4 Ira J. Bach and Mary Lackritz Gray, *A Guide to Chicago's Public Sculpture* (Chicago: University of Chicago Press, 1983), p. 306.

5 A Sculptor's Scullion, *op. cit.*, pp. 204–05.

6 *Ibid.*, pp. 205–06.

7 *Ibid.*, p. 208.

8 *Ibid.*, p. 206.

9 Anne Felicia Cierpik, "History of The Art Institute of Chicago," M.A. Dissertation, De Paul University, Chicago (1957), p. 68.

10 *Ibid.*, p. 69.

11 Florence Wyle, letter to Carl Stephens, 13 July 1937, Archives, University of Illinois Archives.

12 Rebecca Sisler, *The Girls* (Toronto: Clarke, Irwin & Co.), pp. 17–18.

13 One astute journalist noted that it was "so different from Mr. Taft's usual style" (Clyde G. Chandler, "Sculpture Exhibit in Humboldt Park, typescript, 1911, 4 pp., AIC Archives). Another described it as a variant on student work (Ira J. Bach and Mary Lackritz Gray, *op. cit.*, p. 316.).

14 The student original can be seen in Maude I.G. Oliver, "Recent Work at The Art Institute of Chicago," *The International Studio* 29.113–16 (July, Aug., Sept. & Oct., 1906); Taft's later version can be seen in Ira J. Bach and Mary Lackritz Gray, *op. cit.*, p. 316.

15 Rebecca Sisler, *op. cit.*, p. 18.

16 Lorado Taft, "Sculptors of The World's Fair," *Brush and Pencil* 13.3 (1903), p. 199.

17 Lorado Taft, letter to Daniel Chester French, 4 Sept. 1907, AIC Archives.

18 "Designer of the Centennial Monument is Dead at Chicago," *op. cit.*

19 Lorado Taft, "Sculptors of the World's Fair," *op. cit.*, pp. 227–28.

20   Lorado Taft as cited in Ira J. Bach and Mary Lackritz Gray, *op. cit.*, p. 308.

21   Ira J. Bach and Mary Lackritz Gray, *op. cit.*, p. 24.

22   "Chicago's Newer Sculptured Park Memorials," *Park and Cemetery* 22 (Feb. 1913) pp. 290–91.

23   "Untitled" [clipping, n.d., after 1949], p. 101, AIC Archives.

24   *Ibid.*, p. 315.

25   Rebecca Sisler, *op. cit.*, p. 18.

CHAPTER 7

1   Frances Gage wrote in an email to Elspeth Cameron, 24 Oct. 2005, "I recall no letters between the Girls. Perhaps they were destroyed."

2   Jeannette Marks to Mary Woolley, as cited by Anna Mary Wells, *Miss Marks and Miss Woolley* (Boston: Houghton Mifflin Co., 1978), p. 93.

3   *Ibid.*, p. 113.

4   Charlotte Streifer Rubenstein, *American Women Sculptors* (Boston: G.K. Hall & Co., 1990), p. 34.

5   Finding Chicago too prudish, they moved to New York in 1917. They were fined $200 for the publication of Joyce's work. See Caroline F. Ware, *Greenwich Village, 1920–1930* (Boston: Houghton Mifflin Company, The Riverside Press, 1935), p. 181.

6   See Lillian Faderman, *Surpassing the Love of Men* (New York: Quill William Morrow, 1981), pp. 241–50.

7   See "Swift Fire in the Ontario Art Gallery," *Toronto Evening Star* [clipping, 19 Apr. 1909], AGO Archives. The only other sculpture in the show — also burned — was a bust by Quebec sculptor Alfred Laliberté.

8   Rebecca Sisler, *The Girls* (Toronto: Clarke, Irwin & Co., 1972), p. 20.

9   Estelle M. Kerr, "Peace and Victory to Guard Memory of Galt's War Dead," *Toronto Star Weekly*, [clipping, Oct. ca. 1930], AGO Archives.

10   Allen Churchill, *The Improper Bohemians* (New York: E.P. Dutton & Co., 1959), p. 25.

11   *Ibid.*, p. 6.

12   Caroline F. Ware, *Greenwich Village, 1920–1930* (Boston: Houghton Mifflin Company, The Riverside Press, 1935), p. 3.

13   T. Janvier, "Greenwich Village," *Harper's Magazine* 87 (1893), pp. 356–57.

14   Allen Churchill, *op. cit.*, p. 21.

15   Caroline F. Ware, *op. cit.*, p. 4.

16   Allen Churchill, *op. cit.*, p. 61.

17   "Washington Mews and MacDougal Alley, hitherto deemed suitable only for horses, rose to eminence among the desirable locations in the Village," *Ibid.*

18   Rebecca Sisler to Elspeth Cameron, interview, 19 July 2005, Calgary, AB.

19   P.T. Farnsworth, "The Artists' Colony in MacDougal Alley, Where Some of Our Best-known American Painters and Sculptors Live and Work," *The Craftsman* 11.1 (Oct. 1906), pp. 57–69.

20   Allen Churchill, *op. cit.*, p. 162.

21   *Ibid.*, p. 61.

22   *Ibid.*, p. 66.

23   *Ibid.*, p. 159.

24   *Ibid.*, p. 67.

25   *Ibid.*, p. 160.

26   *Ibid.*, p. 160.

27   *Ibid.*, p. 24.

28   "Sculpture Important in the National Academy Exhibition for the Winter of Nineteen Hundred and Ten," *The Craftsman* 19.5 (Feb. 1911), p. 452.

29   *Ibid.*

30   Helen Christine Bennett, "Child Figures in Fountains: Good Modelling and Faithful Portrayal of Child Spirit Characteristic of Florence Wyle's Work," *Art and Decoration* (Feb. 1911), p. 174.

31   *Ibid.*

32   Ernest Bruce Haswell, "The Sixteenth Annual Exhibition of the Society of Western Artists," *The International Studio* 57.186 (Aug. 1912), pp. 18–19.

33   "Pioneer Canadian Sculptor was also a Published Poet," *Toronto Star* (13 June 1973), p. C5.

34   Rebecca Sisler, *op. cit.*, p. 22.

35   "Miss Loring Succeeds," [clipping, ca. 1910], AGO Archives.

36   "Girl Depicts Dreams in Marble and Bronze; Gotham Sculptor Enters the Spokane Contest," *Denver Colorado News* [clipping, 22 Aug. 1911], AGO Archives.

37   "Miss Loring Succeeds," *op. cit.*

38   Rebecca Sisler, *op. cit.*, p. 21.

39   *Ibid.*, p. 21.

40   *Ibid.*, p. 22.

CHAPTER 8

1   Florence Wyle, "Sketchbook," NGC Archives.

2   William Kilbourn, *The Toronto Book* (Toronto: Macmillan of Canada, 1976), p. 52.

3 Charles Dickens, letter to John Foster, 1868, as cited by William Kilbourn, *Ibid.*, p. 37.

4 William Toye, "Introduction," to John de Visser, *Toronto* (Toronto: Oxford University Press, 1975), p. 7.

5 William Kilbourn, *op. cit.,* p. 53.

6 William Kilbourn, *op. cit.,* p. 57.

7 Eric Arthur, *Toronto: No Mean City* (Toronto: University of Toronto Press, 1964), pp. 166–201.

8 *Ibid.*, p. 55.

9 William Toye, *op. cit.*, p. 6.

10 William Kilbourn, *op. cit.*, p. 56.

11 June Ardiel, *Sculpture/Toronto* (Toronto: Leidra Books, 1994), p. 70.

12 Details concerning all these sculptures can be found in June Ardiel, *op. cit.*

13 *Ibid.*, p. 53.

14 *Ibid.*

15 Dora de Pédery Hunt to Elspeth Cameron, interview, 20 October 2005, Toronto, ON.

16 Linda Munk, "A Talk with Miss Loring and Miss Wyle," *Woman's Globe and Mail* [clipping, 6 May 1965], AGO Archives.

17 C.S. Clark, *Of Toronto the Good: A Social Study* (Montreal: Toronto Publishing Co., 1898).

18 Rebecca Sisler, *The Girls* (Toronto: Clarke, Irwin & Co. Ltd., 1972), p. 26.

19 Rebecca Sisler to Elspeth Cameron, interview, 19 July 2005, Calgary, AB.

20 Winwood Reade, *The Martyrdom of Man* (London: Jonathan Cape, 1927), p. 431.

21 Rebecca Sisler, *op. cit.*, p. 26.

CHAPTER 9

1 Allen Churchill, *The Improper Bohemians: A Recreation of Greenwich Village in its Heyday* (New York: E.P. Dutton & Co., 1959), p. 45.

2 Milne had five paintings in the show. There were a few Canadian-born artists also represented: Bessie Marsh Brewer, Edith Haworth, Cecil De B. Howard, Edward Middleton Manigault, Maurice B. Prendergast, Boardman Robinson, and Ernest Lawson. See Edward H. Dwight, "The Armory Show — New York 1913," *Canadian Art* 20.2 (March.–Apr. 1963), pp. 118–19.

3 Milton W. Brown, *The Story of the Armory Show* (New York: Abbeville Press, 1988), p. 43.

4   *Ibid.*, p. 136.

5   *Ibid.*, p. 137.

6   *Ibid.*, p. 164.

7   *Ibid.*

8   *Ibid.*, p. 170.

9   *Ibid.*, p. 168.

10   *Ibid.*, p. 146.

11   Lorado Taft, *The History of American Sculpture, rev.* (New York: Arno Press, 1969), p. 331.

12   Milton W. Brown, *op. cit.*, p. 100.

13   *Ibid.*, p. 118.

14   *Ibid.*, p. 210.

15   *Ibid.*, p. 211.

16   See Ida M. Tarbell, "Lorado Taft and the Western School of Sculpture," *The Craftsman* 13.1 (Apr. 1908), pp. 12–26.

17   Milton W. Brown, *op. cit.*, p. 170.

18   *Ibid.*, p. 171.

19   Adeline Adams, "The Secret of Life," *Art and Progress* (April 1913), as cited by Milton W. Brown, *op. cit.*, p. 170.

20   Milton W. Brown, *op. cit.*, p. 109.

21   Edward. H. Dwight, "The Armory Show — New York 1913," *Canadian Art* 20.2 (Mar.–Apr. 1963), p. 119.

22   Antonio Jones to Elspeth Cameron, interview, 18 May 2005, Chicago, IL.

23   Lorado Taft, as cited by John Drury in "Lorado Taft 76: Devotes the Entire Day to His Art," *Chicago Illinois Tribune* [clipping, 28 Apr. 1936], AIC Archives.

24   Alson J. Smith, *Chicago's Left Bank* (Chicago: Henry Regnery Company, 1953), p. 171.

25   Albrecht Monteglas, "Tribute Paid to Mulligan by Taft," *Chicago Illinois Examiner* [clipping, 31 Mar. 1916], AIC Archives.

26   Florence Wyle, "Let the Dead Sleep," *Poems* (Toronto: The Ryerson Press, 1959), p. 16. The handwritten manuscript of this poem is dated 26 Feb. 1955, AGO Archives.

CHAPTER 10

1   *The Yearbook of Canadian Art*, compiled by The Arts & Letters Club of Toronto (Toronto: J.M. Dent & Sons, Ltd., 1913).

2   Lawren S. Harris, "The Canadian Art Club," *Ibid.*, pp. 214–15.

3 *Ibid.*, p. 216.

4 *Ibid.*, p. 215.

5 James Mavor, "Walter Allward, Sculptor," *Ibid.*, pp. 252–53.

6 *Ibid.*

7 Edmond Dyonnet, "French-Canadian Painting and Sculpture," *Ibid.*, p. 221.

8 *Ibid.*, p. 229.

9 S. Morgan Powell, "The Montreal Art Association," *Ibid.*, p. 235.

10 E. Wyly Grier, "Canadian Art: A Resumé," *Ibid.*, p. 247.

11 *Ibid.*, p. 246–47.

12 See Carl Berger, "The True North Strong and Free," *Nationalism in Canada*, ed. Peter Russell (Montreal: McGraw-Hill Ryerson, 1966), and Carl Berger, *The Sense of Power: Studies in the Ideas of Imperialism, 1867–1914* (Toronto: University of Toronto Press, 1970).

13 Maria Tippett, *The Making of English-Canadian Culture, 1900–1939: The External Influences* (Toronto: ECW Press, 1987), p. 3.

14 Cited by F.B. Housser, *A Canadian Art Movement: The Story of the Group of Seven* (Toronto: The Macmillan Co. Of Canada Ltd., 1926), pp. 60–61.

15 Hamilton MacCarthy, "The Development of Sculpture in Canada," *Canada: An Encyclopedia of the Country*, ed. J. Castell Hopkins, vol. 5 (Toronto: Linscott Publishing Co., 1898), p. 381.

16 Edmund Dyonnet, *The Yearbook, op. cit.*, p. 221.

17 Hamilton MacCarthy, *op. cit.*, p. 378.

18 Detailed accounts of the origin and development of Canada's art organizations can be found in the following: Joan Murray, *Ontario Society of Artists: 100 Years, 1872–1972* (Toronto: Art Gallery of Ontario, 1972); Anne McDougall, *Anne Savage: The Story of a Canadian Painter* (Montreal: Harvest House, 1977); John Robinson, ed., *Once Upon a Century: 100 Year History of the 'Ex,'* (Toronto: J.H. Robinson Publishing Ltd., 1978); Rebecca Sisler, *Passionate Spirits: A History of the Royal Canadian Academy of the Arts, 1880–1980* (Toronto: Clarke, Irwin & Co., 1980); Maria Tippett, *Making Culture: English-Canadian Institutions and the Arts before the Massey Commission* (Toronto: University of Toronto Press, 1990).

19 See R.H. Hubbard, ed. *The National Gallery of Canada: Catalogue of Paintings and Sculpture*, vol. 1 "Older Schools" (Toronto: University of Toronto Press, 1961), p. vii. Brown hoped to add new works to the gallery's collection, which consisted mainly of diploma works deposited by the Royal Canadian Academy of the Arts (RCA).

20 Eric Brown, as cited in *The Yearbook, op. cit.*, and F.B. Housser, p. 58.

21 The RCA began admitting women in 1913, twenty-six years after its beginning.

22 F.B. Housser, *The Yearbook, op. cit.*, p. 59.

23 Cited by Joan Murray, *op. cit.*, p. 5.

24 *Ibid.*, p. 12.

25 S. Morgan Powell, *The Yearbook, op. cit.*, p. 233.

CHAPTER 11

1 Estelle M. Kerr, "Women Sculptors of Canada," *Women's Saturday Night* [clipping, 20 June 1914], AGO Archives.

2 Winnifred Kingsford, as cited by Estelle Kerr, *Ibid.*

3 Rebecca Sisler, *The Girls* (Toronto: Clarke, Irwin & Co., 1972), p. 32.

4 Estelle Kerr, *op. cit.*

5 Cited by Rebecca Sisler, *op. cit.*, p. 27.

6 F. Maud Brown, *Breaking Barriers: Eric Brown and the National Gallery* (Ottawa: The Society for Art Publications, 1964), p. 66.

7 Cited in Rebecca Sisler, *op. cit.*, p. 28.

8 Rebecca Sisler to Elspeth Cameron, email 8 Dec. 2005, "I would strongly suspect a Loring/Flaherty affair. They were best of friends, and both seem to have been touched with a warm flash of sensual fire."

9 Rebecca Sisler, *The Girls, op. cit.*, p. 28.

10 Robert Flaherty, *Robert Flaherty: Photographer/Filmmaker: The Inuit 1910–1922* (Vancouver: The Vancouver Art Gallery, 1980), pp. 113–14. See also, Arthur Calder-Marshall, *The Innocent Eye: The Life of Robert J. Flaherty* (New York: Harcourt, Brace & World, Inc., 1963).

11 Dan Gibson, ed., *Fifty Years of Photography by Ashley & Crippen* (Toronto: Ashley & Crippen, 1965). By 1914 Ashley & Crippen had won numerous awards for their black and white portraits in Canada and the U.S. They would eventually photograph such luminaries as Sir Edmund Walker, skater Barbara Ann Scott, swimmer Marilyn Bell, Queen Elizabeth II, Princess Margaret, Louis St. Laurent, John Diefenbaker, Jean Lesage, Dr. Charles Best, and E.P. Taylor.

12 A.Y. Jackson hated Chicago, though he enjoyed the Art Institute itself. In a letter to his brother, Ernest, in Montreal, 28 Apr. 1907, he wrote, "I will tear back to God's country, and trust that I will never come back to Chic. again on anything but a visit." A.Y. Jackson papers, LAC.

13 Rebecca Sisler, *op. cit.*, p. 27.

14 CBC Radio interview, [n.d.], CBC Archives.

15 Rebecca Sisler, *op. cit.*, p. 25.

16 AGO Archives.

17 Rebecca Sisler, *op. cit.*, p. 25.

18 *Ibid.*

19 "Miss Loring Succeeds," [clipping, ca. 1910], AGO Archives.

20 "In the Studios of Toronto Artists," *Toronto Daily Star* [clipping, 8 June 1912], AGO Archives.

21 James Hunter built the house in 1820, and part of the main floor housed his tailor's shop. After its time as a hotel, it housed Rev. Thomas Phillips, vice-principal of Upper Canada College. Dr. James Daly occupied the house later. In 1894, it was an auctioneer's headquarters. By the time Wyle and Loring rented the large upstairs, a shoemaker had a shop downstairs. See Lucy Booth Martyn, *The Face of Early Toronto: An Archival Record 1797–1936* (Sutton West & Santa Barbara: The Paget Press, 1982), pp. 28–29, where a painting of the building in 1912, at the time Wyle and Loring moved into it, can be seen.

22 A photo of the studio interior on Lombard Street can be seen in Christine Boyanoski's *Loring and Wyle: Sculptors' Legacy* (Toronto: Art Gallery of Ontario, 1987), p. 14.

23 For a thorough treatment of these women sculptors, see Charlotte Streifer Rubenstein, *American Women Sculptors* (Boston: G.K. Hall & Co., 1990), pp. 97–257.

24 *Ibid.*, pp. 98–99.

25 Rebecca Sisler, *op. cit.*, p. 24.

CHAPTER 12

1 Margaret Scobie does not appear in Canadian Encyclopedias or Who's Who collections. However, her sculpture of herself and her infant son, John, can be seen in the Annual Report of the Toronto Public Libraries, 2000, http://www.tpl.toronto.ca/pdfs/AnnualReport_2000.pdf, p. 6. The bronze sculpture was donated by Elliott and Ann Alycin Hayes to the John Sullivan Collection in 1993.

2 "Miss Canada in Yonge St.: Heroic Figure of Lady of Confederation in Front of T. Eaton Co. Store," *Globe and Mail* [clipping, 20 June 1917] AGO Archives.

3 *Ibid.*

4 Frances Loring, as cited in *Ibid.*

5 "Canadian Girl Sculptors Do Unique Work," *Toronto Evening Star* [clipping, June 1917], AGO Archives.

6 "Miss Canada in Yonge St.," *op. cit.*

7   "Canadian Girl Sculptors Do Unique Work," *op. cit.*

8   *Ibid.*

9   Christine Boyanoski, *Loring and Wyle: Sculptors' Legacy* (Toronto: Art Gallery of Ontario, 1987), p. 18.

10   "Miss Loring Succeeds," [clipping, ca. 1910], AGO Archives.

CHAPTER 13

1   Frances Loring to John R. Lewis, "Why Would a Woman Want to be a Sculptor?" *Star Weekly Magazine* (2 Jan. 1960), p. 37. When asked "Have you ever thought seriously of marriage?" Loring replied, "Of course I have. More than once. But you must remember, I lived through two world wars."

2   Rebecca Sisler, *The Girls* (Toronto: Clarke, Irwin & Co., 1972), pp. 31–32.

3   Maria Tippett, *Art at the Service of War: Canada, Art, and the Great War* (Toronto: University of Toronto Press, 1984), p. 6.

4   *Ibid.*, p. 7.

5   *Ibid.*, p. 6.

6   Estelle M. Kerr, "The Etcher's Point of View," *The Canadian Magazine* (Dec. 1916), p. 158.

7   Maria Tippett, *op. cit.*, pp. 17–18.

8   *Ibid.*, p. 19.

9   *Ibid.*, p. 20.

10   *Ibid.*

11   *Ibid.*, p. 21.

12   *Ibid.*

13   *Ibid.*, p. 27.

14   Jackson, a private in the 60th Battalion, was wounded in the shoulder by a shell at Sanctuary Wood in June 1916. See F.B. Housser, *A Canadian Art Movement: The Story of the Group of Seven* (Toronto: The Macmillan Co. of Canada Ltd., 1926), pp. 126–129.

15   *Ibid.*, p. 14.

16   Lord Beaverbrook also hired Canadian artists Cyril Barraud and James Kerr-Lawson, and British artists Augustus John, David Cameron, and Gyeth Russell. The British, Belgian, and Australian forces lent Percy Wyndham Lewis, Alfred Bastein, and James Quinn, who were soon joined by British artists Laura Knight, Clare Atwood, Anna Airy, and Charles Shannon, among others. (See Maria Tippett, *op. cit.*, p. 30.)

17   An account of Lismer's work and that of other Canadian war artists who got

underway near the end of the war can be found in A.Y. Jackson, *A Painter's Country* (Toronto: Clarke, Irwin & Co., Ltd., 1958), pp. 35–43.

18 Maria Tippett., *op. cit.*, p. 15.

19 *Ibid.*, p. 34.

20 Guy Pène du Bois, "Mrs. Whitney's Journal in Art," *The International Studio* 76 (Jan. 1923), p. 354.

21 Maria Tippett, *op. cit.*, p. 35.

22 *Ibid.*, p. 49 and Rebecca Sisler, *op. cit.*, p. 28. Tippett writes that Brown made the suggestion to Loring, but Sisler says he approached both sculptors. Since Sisler's information came direct from Wyle and Loring, I have followed her version. In fact, Brown wrote to Loring, but included Wyle in his invitation to do war sculptures.

23 A.B. Cooper, "War Themes in Modern Art," *The Windsor Magazine* 41 (Jan. 1915), p. 259; cited in Maria Tippett, *op. cit.,* p. 72.

24 "Toronto Sculptors Spring a Surprise," *Globe and Mail* (15 Nov. 1915), p. S7.

25 Kristina Huneault, "Heroes of a Different Sort: Gender and Patriotism in the War Workers of Frances Loring and Florence Wyle," *The Journal of Canadian Art History* 15.2 (1993), p. 41.

26 *Ibid.*, pp. 31, 29.

27 Imperial Munitions Board, *Women in the Production of Munitions in Canada* (Ottawa: Imperial Munitions Board booklet, 1916), p. 32; cited by Kristina Huneault, *op. cit.*, p. 29.

28 Maria Tippett, *op. cit.*, p. 72.

29 Note 47 MT 92, Cited by Maria Tippett, *op. cit.*, p. 92.

30 "Canadian War Art Exhibition," *Montreal Herald* (25 Sept. 1920), p. 3; "Art and Artists," p. 10; "Women Artists' Work Exhibited," *Montreal Daily Star* (2 Oct. 1920), p. 30; Hector Charlesworth, "Reflections," *Saturday Night* (18 Sept. 1920), p. 2; Barker Fairley, "At the Art Gallery," *The Rebel* 4.3 (Dec. 1919), p. 125.

31 Kristina Huneault, *op. cit.*, p. 34. She also cites Adrienne Rich, "Compulsory Heterosexuality and Lesbian Experience," *Blood, Bread, and Poetry, Selected Prose, 1979–1985* (New York: W.W. Norton, 1986).

32 Janet Scudder, "Why so Few Women are Sculptors," *New York Times* (18 Feb. 1912), p. SM13.

33 Maria Tippett, *op. cit.*, p. 72. Wyle and Loring's sculptures were frequently praised in newspaper accounts of the several shows in which they were displayed between 1919 and 1924, whereas Montreal painter Mabel May's *Women Making Shells* was not written up in the press. They were still being mentioned

as creators of war works as late as 1964. See Kay Kritzwiser, "The 'Terrible Beauty' of Women in Wartime," *Globe and Mail* [clipping, 21 Nov. 1964], AGO Archives.

CHAPTER 14

1   "Turn Unused Church into Sculptor's Studio — Ladies Show Resource in Obtaining Place with Required Headroom," *Toronto Daily Star* (27 Nov. 1920), p. 22.

2   *Ibid.,* and Anne Merrill, "Sculptor from Paris," *Mail and Empire* (4 Sept. 1920), p. 23.

3   Rebecca Sisler, *The Girls* (Toronto: Clarke, Irwin & Co., 1972), p. 33.

4   *Ibid.*

5   "Assessment Roll for the Municipality of Scarborough, for the year 1945," p. 1528, City of Toronto Archives. My thanks to librarian Sally Gibson, for locating this information.

6   *Ibid.* By 1945, they had also acquired twenty adjacent acres at Lot 2, Concession 3, Scarborough, which was worth a total of $550 ($400 for the land and $150 for the buildings).

7   Frances Loring to Arthur E. McFarlane, "Two Toronto Sculptors," *Toronto Star Weekly* (19 Aug. 1923), p. 4. There is a photo of Frances at the wheel in this article.

8   "Novel Studio for Sculptors," *Mail and Empire* [clipping, 20 Nov. 1920], AGO Archives.

9   *Ibid.*

10 Rebecca Sisler, *op. cit.*, p. 33.

11 I am indebted to Sally Gibson, Manager of Heritage Services of the Toronto Distillery District, for drawing this information to my attention.

12 Eva-Lis Wuorio, "Sculpture a Lifetime Job, View of Frances Loring," *Globe and Mail* (1 June 1946), p. 13.

13 Jeanne Hopkins, "Looking Back: Deer Park's Christ Church was Established by a Group of Neighbours," *Post Newspapers* (June 1993), p. 30. An article in *Mail and Empire* (20 Nov. 1920) claims that it was "a meeting house for Methodists and Presbyterians." ("Novel Studio for Sculptors.") Earlier (1910) the Century Baptist Church was at 12–15 Macpherson Ave., City of Toronto Archives.

14 Frances Loring, lecture at the Women's Association of Hamilton [clipping, Nov. 1954], AGO Archives.

15 Rebecca Sisler, *op. cit.*, p. 6.

16 Linda Munk, "A Talk with Miss Loring and Miss Wyle," *Woman's Globe and Mail* [clipping, 6 May 1965], AGO Archives.

17 *Ibid.*, p. 7.

18 "Novel Studio for Sculptors," *op. cit.*

19 Frances Loring to Linda Munk, as cited in "A Talk with Miss Loring and Miss Wyle," *op. cit.*, p. 27–28.

20 Rebecca Sisler, *op. cit.*, p. 8.

21 *Ibid.*, p. 7.

22 Frances Loring to Linda Munk, as cited in "A Talk with Miss Loring and Miss Wyle," *op. cit.,* p. 27. Francis Hans Johnson, first known as Frank, then as Franz, was fat.

23 Rebecca Sisler, *op. cit.*, p. 3.

24 Timothy Findley, "Introduction," Rebecca Sisler, *Art for Enlightenment* (Toronto: Fitzhenry & Whiteside, the Learnxs Foundation, and the Board of Education for the City of Toronto, 1993), p. 4.

25 Rebecca Sisler to Elspeth Cameron, email 8 Dec. 2005. Calgary, AB. "It just happened. Someone referred to them affectionately as The Girls, and it seemed so right that it caught on. ... It [probably] took at least full root during the early church studio days."

CHAPTER 15

1 A.Y. Jackson, *A Painter's Country: The Autobiography of A.Y. Jackson* (Toronto: Clarke, Irwin & Co., Ltd., 1958), p. 54.

2 *Ibid.*, p. 15.

3 *Ibid.*, p. 16.

4 *Ibid.*, p. 20.

5 *Ibid.*, p. 47.

6 Peter Mellon, *The Group of Seven* (Toronto: McClelland and Stewart, 1970), p. 53.

7 H.F. Gadsby, "The Hot Mush School," *Toronto Evening Star* [clipping, 12 Dec. 1913], AGO Archives.

8 Moyer, [cartoon] "I Can't Get It School," *Toronto Star* [clipping 12 Dec. 1913], AGO Archives.

9 Cited in F.B. Housser, *A Canadian Art Movement: The Story of the Group of Seven* (Toronto: The Macmillan Co. of Canada, Ltd., 1926), p. 72.

10 S. Morgan Powell, cited in *John Lyman* (Montreal: Montreal Museum of Fine Arts), [clipping, 1963], AGO Archives.

11   Peter Mellon, *op. cit.*, p. 82.

12   A.Y. Jackson, *op. cit.*, p. 54.

13   A.Y. Jackson, *op. cit.*, p. 40.

14   A.Y. Jackson, *op. cit.*, p. 43.

15   Col. C.P. Stacey, "Nationality: The Experience of Canada," *Historical Papers* (Canadian Historical Association, 1967).

16   See Susan Crean, *The Laughing One: A Journey to Emily Carr* (Toronto: Harper Flamingo Canada, 2001), p. 213.

17   Robert Shipley, *To Mark Our Place: A History of Canadian War Memorials* (Toronto: NC Press, 1987), p. 144.

18   "Canada at War Shown in Pictures," *Daily Mail and Empire* (19 June 1919), p. 10.

19   *Ibid.*

20   E. Wyly Grier, "Conclusion," *The Yearbook of Canadian Art*, compiled by the Arts & Letters Club of Toronto (Toronto: J.M. Dent and Sons Ltd., 1913), pp. 246–47.

21   *Ibid.*

22   "Art and Artists," *Globe and Mail* (21 Oct. 1919), p. 10.

23   "More Paintings of War Activities," *Daily Mail and Empire* [clipping, 20 Oct. 1919], AGO Archives.

24   "Women Artists' Work Exhibited," *Montreal Daily Star* (2 Oct. 1920), p. 30.

25   Barker Fairley, "At the Art Gallery," *The Rebel* 4.3 (Dec. 1919), p. 125.

26   Eric Brown to M.K. Turner, Office of the City Clerk, Fort William, Ontario, 8 Feb. 1922, NGC Archives, File 05.1. As cited by Christine Boyanoski, *Loring and Wyle: Sculptors' Legacy* (Toronto: Art Gallery of Ontario, 1987), p. 29.

27   Eric Brown to Florence Wyle, letter, 3 Nov. 1919, 5.42.W, NGC Archives.

28   Charlotte Streifer Rubenstein, *American Women Sculptors* (Boston: G.K. Hall & Co., 1990), p. 221. For a more thorough treatment of women avant-garde sculptors, see pp. 220–33.

29   *Ibid.*, p. 224.

30   Eric Shanes, *Constantin Brancusi* (New York: Abbeville Press, 1989), pp. 28–29.

31   I am indebted to Christine Boyanoski for this idea. See *Loring and Wyle: Sculptors' Legacy* (Toronto: Art Gallery of Ontario, 1987), p. 23.

32   Kristina Huneault, "Heroes of a Different Sort: Gender and Patriotism in the War Workers of Frances Loring and Florence Wyle," *The Journal of Canadian Art History* 15.2 (1993), p. 40.

33   Rebecca Sisler, *The Girls,* (Toronto: Clarke, Irwin & Co., 1972) p. 29.

34   Abraham J. Wyle to Florence Wyle, n.d. 1920, AGO Archives.

35 Rebecca Sisler, *op. cit.*, p. 37.

36 Christine Boyanoski gives a full account of the "home front" sculptures in *Loring and Wyle: Sculptors' Legacy* (Toronto: Art Gallery of Ontario, 1987), pp. 21–25.

37 *Ibid.*, n. 29, p. 27.

38 "Waverly Girl Chosen to Execute Memorial Statue by Canadian Government," Canadian Artists file, Metropolitan Toronto Library Board.

39 According to Christine Boyanoski, this information was provided by the architect for the memorial, Jules Wegman, to M.O. Hammond, who recorded it in his notes on Canadian monuments, now in the Archives of Ontario. An article in the 25 Aug. 1921 *Globe and Mail* indicated that the memorial was being "rushed" so that the Governor General's wife could unveil it.

40 "'Can't Get Very Far without Hard Work,'" *Toronto Star Weekly* [clipping, 27 Aug. 1921], AGO Archives.

41 "Waverly Girl Chosen to Execute Memorial Statue by Canadian Government," *op. cit.*; "Sculptress at Home is Merry Girl," [clipping, 1921], AGO Archives.

42 "The Rood at St. Mary Magdalen's Anglican Church, Toronto" *Saturday Night* (11 Mar. 1922), p. 11. This article features an illustration and says that the huge crucifix was designed by William Rae.

43 Arthur E. McFarlane, "Art Awakes in a Forgotten Church," *Toronto Star Weekly* (1 Aug. 1925), p. 59.

44 *Ibid.*

45 Christine Boyanoski, *op. cit.*, p. 25.

46 Illustrations of some of these unrealized designs can be seen in Christine Boyanoski, *op. cit.*, pp. 88–89.

47 Robert Shipley, *op. cit.*, n. 2, p. 88.

48 Joyce Millar, "The Sculptors' Society of Canada: The First Fifty Years, 1928–1978," M.A. Thesis, Art History Dept., Concordia University, Montreal, Quebec, Canada, 1992, n. 12.

49 Rebecca Sisler, "The Schools Remember," *Art for Enlightenment: A History of Art in Toronto Schools* (Toronto: Fitzhenry & Whiteside, the Learnxs Foundation, and the Board of Education for the City of Toronto, 1993), pp. 155–77.

50 *Ibid.*, pp. 159–60. See also Betty Jane Wylie, "Winnipeg's Cenotaph," *The Manitoba Pageant* 8.2 (Jan. 1963), http://www.mhs.mb.ca/docs/pageant/08/winnipegcenotaph.shtml

51 John Sewell, *Doors Open Toronto: Illuminating the City's Great Spaces* (Toronto: Alfred A. Knopf, 2002), p. 120.

52   *Ibid.*, p. 31.

53   See Ian Hugh Maclean Miller, *Our Glory and Our Grief: Torontonians and the Great War* (Toronto: University of Toronto Press, 2002), p. 6. See Jonathan F. Vance, *Death So Noble: Memory, Meaning, and the First World War* (Vancouver, UBC Press, 1997).

54   Shipley, *op. cit.*, p. 93.

55   Cited by Christine Boyanoski, *op. cit.*, n. 11, p. 54.

CHAPTER 16

1   John S. MacKinnon, "A Canadian's View of the Empire as Seen from London," Empire Club speech, Toronto (18 Mar. 1926), p. 12.

2   *Ibid.*, p. 3.

3   For a full blow-by-blow description of the crisis that preceded the Wembley Exhibition, see Rebecca Sisler, "The Wembley Controversy," *Passionate Spirits: A History of the Royal Canadian Academy of the Arts* (Toronto: Clarke, Irwin, & Co., Ltd., 1980), pp. 101–10. A personal view from Eric Brown's wife can be seen in F. Maud Brown, "The Wembley Exhibition and After," *Breaking Barriers: Eric Brown and the National Gallery* (Ottawa: The Society for Art Publications, 1964), pp. 69–75, and F. Maud Brown, "I Remember Wembley," *Canadian Art* 21.4 (July/Aug. 1964), pp. 210–12.

4   Hector Charlesworth, as cited by Rebecca Sisler, *op. cit.*, pp. 94, 98.

5   As cited in Rebecca Sisler, *op. cit.*, p. 107.

6   *Ibid.*, p. 102.

7   A.Y. Jackson to Norah de Pencier, 10 June 1935, Norah de Pencier Correspondence, LAC.

8   F. Maud Brown, *Breaking Barriers*, *op. cit.* p. 70.

9   Rebecca Sisler, *The Girls* (Toronto: Clarke, Irwin & Co., Ltd.), p. 38.

10   F. Maud Brown, "I Remember Wembley," *op. cit.*, p. 211.

11   *Ibid.*, p. 12.

12   See these in *Ibid.*, pp. 210–12.

13   Rebecca Sisler to Elspeth Cameron, interview, 19 July 2005, Calgary, AB.

14   F. Maud Brown, "Eric Brown: His Contribution to the National Gallery," *Canadian Art*, 4.1 (Nov. 1946), pp. 13–14.

15   *Press Comments on the Canadian Section of Fine Arts, British Empire Exhibition, 1924–25*, as cited by J. Russell Harper in *Painting in Canada: A History*, 2nd ed. (Toronto: University of Toronto Press, 1977), p. 288.

16   Rebecca Sisler, *Passionate Spirits, op. cit.*, pp. 108–09.

17 *Ibid.*, pp. 108–09.

18 *Ibid.*

19 The painting was repatriated in 2005.

20 Rebecca Sisler, *The Girls*, *op. cit.*, p. 30; and Irene B. Hare, "Close-ups of Toronto's Women Artists, No. 1: Miss Frances Loring and Miss Florence Wyle," *Sunday World* [clipping, 25 May 1924], AGO Archives.

21 Cited from the *Ottawa Journal* by F. Maud Brown in *Breaking Barriers*, *op.cit.*, p. 75.

CHAPTER 17

1 "Social and Personal," *Toronto Daily Star* (20 Nov. 1914), p. 11.

2 "Hon. H.S. Beland Officially Opens Exhibit of War Memorials," *Ottawa Citizen* [clipping, 6 Jan. 1923], AGO Archives.

3 *Ibid.*, *Globe and Mail* (6 Nov. 1920), (7 Jan. 1922), (30 Sept. 1918), (25 Apr. 1919), (6 Apr. 1923) [clippings], AGO Archives.

4 Stephen Leacock, "The Woman Question" (1915), *The Social Criticism of Stephen Leacock*, ed. Alan Bowker (Toronto: University of Toronto Press, 1973), pp. 57–58.

5 "Toronto Heliconian Club (1909–)," *Music Division Archival Guide*, National Library of Canada, created 14 May 2001, updated 15 Mar. 2006, http://www.collectionscanada.ca/4/7/m15-503-e.html

6 It was probably Fairley's interest in the arts — and in the human figure as opposed to landscape — that endeared him to Wyle and Loring. He wrote, "What is needed then ... is to set the whole subject matter of art free and not just the landscape part of it. It is the human subject, the human face, the human figure whether alone or in groups or in crowds, in town and country, in war in peace, in life and death, that is the real and central subject of art ..." See Barker Fairley, "What is Wrong with Canadian Art," *Canadian Art* (Autumn 1948).

7 Anderson was from Prince Edward Island. He taught in Colorado for four years before his appointment at the University of Toronto. He became Acting Head, then Head, of the Philosophy Department in 1924.

8 See, for example, "Vigor and Fine Taste Seen in Work of Local Sculptors: Exhibition by Florence Wyle and Frances Loring at Hart House, Sketch Club Reveals Marked Progress of Delicate Art in Canada," *Globe and Mail* (23 Mar. 1926), p. 11.

9 See Charlotte Streifer Rubenstein, "Fauns and Fountains — Traditional

Women Sculptors: 1905–1929," *American Women Sculptors* (Boston: G.K. Hall & Co., 1990).

10   "The Sculptor and the Garden: Another Chance for the Fairies," *The Craftsman* 30 (June 1916), p. 240.

11   *Ibid.*, pp. 246, 249.

12   "Children that will Never Grow Old," *The Craftsman* 30 (July 1916), p. 548.

13   Charlotte Streifer Rubenstein, *op. cit.*, p. 148. See also Janet Scudder, *Modeling My Life* (New York: Harcourt Brace & Co., 1925).

14   Janet Scudder, *op. cit.*, 292–93.

15   H.B. Dunington-Grubb, "Sculpture as Garden Decoration," *Canadian Homes and Gardens* (Mar. 1927), p. 17.

16   Frances Loring, "Sculpture in the Garden," *Canadian Art* 1.2 (Dec.–Jan. 1943–44), pp. 64–67. Loring also used one fountain by Elizabeth Wyn Wood.

17   "What Women Are Doing," *Globe and Mail* [clipping, 6 Nov. 1920], AGO Archives.

18   "Sale of Canvasses Put Toronto on the Map," *Toronto Daily Star* [clipping, 25 Mar. 1922], AGO Archives.

19   "Art and Artists," *Globe and Mail* [clipping, 6 Oct. 1928], AGO Archives.

CHAPTER 18

1   "The Toronto Art Gallery: New Extensions to be Opened Shortly Bring it to Metropolitan Dimensions," *Saturday Night* (9 Jan. 1926), p. 5.

2   *Ibid.*

3   See, for example, "Local Artists Show Sculptory," *Mail and Empire* (27 Nov. 1915), p. 10. "The only addition one could wish … would be something by Mr. Walter Allward, but his studies in recent years have been too large for such intimate exhibits."

4   "An Inspiring Memorial that is Needed at Home," *Mail and Empire* [clipping, 2 Apr. 1925], AGO Archives.

5   Qennefer Browne to Elspeth Cameron, interview, 2 Dec. 2006, Orillia, ON.

6   See F. Maud Brown, "Eric Brown: His Contribution to the National Gallery," *Canadian Art* 4.1 (Nov. 1946), p. 13. She writes, "When in Toronto we were sure to see Frances Loring and Florence Wyle in their converted church studio and would spend whole evenings with them."

7   Eric Brown to M.K. Turner, Office of the City Clerk, Fort William, ON., 8 Feb. 1922. NGC Archives File 05.1, as cited by Christine Boyanoski, *Loring and Wyle: Sculptors' Legacy* (Toronto: Art Gallery of Ontario, 1987), p. 29.

8   *General Conditions for the Guidance of Architects, Artists, Sculptors in Preparing Com-*
    memorative Designs for the Proposed National War Monument for the Dominion of
    Canada in Ottawa (Ottawa: 12 Feb. 1925), File 9238-1-A. RG II Vol. 4004, LAC.

9   Vernon March, who was the main sculptor, died before the project was com-
    plete. It was completed by his three brothers: Sydney, Walter, and Percival:
    mainly Sydney. See *Toronto Star* [clipping, 11 Apr. 1946], AGO Archives.

10 Christine Boyanoski, *op. cit.*, p. 34.

11 *Ibid.*, p. 35.

12 "Toronto Woman to Design Augusta War Memorial Gift of the Macombers,"
    Augusta Portland Star [clipping, 10 Nov. 1929], AGO Archives.

13 Wesley Hicks, "Skunks are Pretty," *Toronto Telegram* [clipping, 3 Feb. 1950],
    AGO Archives.

14 "Donors and Sculptor of War Memorial Guests at Rotary," *Augusta Portland*
    Star [clipping, 12 Nov. 1929], AGO Archives.

15 The two statues are almost exactly similar, and Crunelle's statue was illustrated
    in the same article that illustrated Florence Wyle's *Boy with Grapes* fountain,
    bought by the Art Institute of Chicago. See Henry Charles Payne, "Fine
    Work in Chicago Sculpture Exhibit," *Monumental News* 20 (Mar. 1908), pp.
    196–99.

16 "Dedication of War Memorial Feature at Augusta Monday," *Portland Sunday*
    Telegram and Sunday Press Herald [clipping, 10 Nov. 1929], AGO Archives.

17 Frances Gage to Elspeth Cameron, interview, 30 June 2005, Cobourg, ON.

18 Christine Boyanoski, *op. cit.*, p. 37.

19 A.Y. Jackson to Norah de Pencier, 1 Mar. 1944, Norah de Pencier Corres-
    pondence, LAC.

20 Naomi Jackson Groves, *A.Y.'s Canada* (Toronto: Clarke, Irwin & Co. Ltd.,
    1968), p. 152.

21 Emily Carr, "Eagles of Skeena River," as cited by Naomi Jackson Groves, *op.*
    cit., p. 156.

22 "Emily Carr," http://emily-carr.biography.ms/ Emily Carr met Varley in
    Vancouver on 10 Nov. 1927, and she met A.Y. Jackson, Lismer, Harris, Wyle,
    and Loring in Toronto sometime between 14 Nov. and 14 Dec. 1927 when
    she came east to attend the Canadian West Coast Art exhibit at the National
    Gallery of Canada. See Emily Carr, *Hundreds & Thousands* (Toronto: Clarke,
    Irwin, 1966), pp. 3–18.

23 Director, National Gallery of Canada, to Dr. Charles Camsell, deputy min-
    ister, Department of Mines, Ottawa, letter, 21 Nov. 1926, NGC Archives, as
    cited by Christine Boyanoski, *op. cit.*, p. 51.

24 Barbara Meadowcroft, *Painting Friends: The Beaver Hall Women Painters* (Montréal: Véhicule Press, 1999), p. 64.

25 "Daring Canadian Girl in an Indian Village," *Toronto Star* [clipping, 10 Sept. 1927], AGO Archives.

26 *Ibid.*

27 Susan Crean offers a thoughtful discussion of this matter and the career of Barbeau in *The Laughing One: A Journey to Emily Carr* (Toronto: Harper Flamingo Canada, 2001), pp. 210–232.

28 For a thorough discussion of this issue, see Rosemary J. Coombe, "The Properties of Culture and the Possession of Identity: Postcolonial Struggle and the Legal Imagination," *The Canadian Journal of Law and Jurisprudence* 6.2 (1994).

29 Naomi Jackson Groves, *op. cit.*, p. 164. Groves describes fully Marius Barbeau's involvement with the Skeena project and the villages her uncle, A.Y. Jackson visited in 1926, which Wyle and Savage also visited in 1927, on pp. 152–171. This section also includes A.Y. Jackson's sketches of the area. Jackson himself wrote an article about his 1926 trip for *Maclean's* magazine in 1927.

30 Unidentified clipping, Art Gallery of Ontario scrapbook (6 Oct.–31 Dec. 1929), as cited by Christine Boyanoski, *op. cit.*, p. 51.

31 "Eaton's Daily Store News," *Globe and Mail* [clipping, 20 Dec. 1929], AGO Archives.

32 John M. Lyle, "The Allied Arts at the Recent Toronto Chapter Exhibition," *The Journal of the Royal Architectural Institute of Canada* (May 1927).

33 Eric Arthur, *Toronto: No Mean City* (Toronto: University of Toronto Press, 1964), p. 231. There is an illustration of this interior on this page.

34 John Bentley Mays, "Singing the Praises of St. Anne's Interior," *Globe and Mail* (15 Apr. 1995); Val Ross, "Artistic Heritage Feared Crumbling along with Church Ceiling," *Globe and Mail* (23 July 1998); Edward Regan, "Group of Seven's Angel at Work," *Globe and Mail* (19 Feb. 1999). To see the head of St. Matthew by Wyle and the lion symbol for St. Mark, see John Sewell, *Doors Open Toronto: Illuminating the City's Great Spaces* (Toronto: Alfred A. Knopf, 2002), p. 184.

35 "What Women Are Doing," *Globe and Mail* [clipping, 30 Sept. 1918], AGO Archives.

36 "What Women Are Doing," *Globe and Mail* [clipping, 25 Mar. 1919], AGO Archives.

37 See *Globe and Mail* (7 Aug. 1926) and (11 Aug. 1926). [clippings], AGO Archives. These articles use words like "maidens" and "pulchritude." Sculptor Alfred

Howell was also one of the judges. Loring, for some reason, was unable to attend the occasion — which drew a crowd of 25,000 — and was replaced by Mrs. Dorothy Blaness Austin (née Stevens). Miss Ellis Fitzgerald won the contest and her ringlets were praised in light of the fact that "bobbed hair is passé."

38 "Technical School Students Compete in Statuettes," *Toronto Star* [clipping, 21 Nov. 1929], AGO Archives.

39 *Toronto Star* [clipping, 19 Nov. 1929], AGO Archives.

40 Arthur McFarlane, "Two Toronto Sculptors," *Toronto Star Weekly* (19 Aug 1923), p. 4.

41 Rebecca Sisler to Karen Wells, "Arts National," CBC Radio (12 July 1978), CBC Archives.

42 "What Women Are Doing," *Globe and Mail* [clipping, 25 Apr. 1919], AGO Archives.

43 Robert Fulford, "Emma Goldman saw Toronto Harshly," *Toronto Star Weekly* (19 Feb. 1983), p. F5.

44 Arthur McFarlane, *op. cit.*

45 Douglas Phibbs to Elspeth Cameron, 12 Dec. 2006, Toronto, ON.

46 Rebecca Sisler, *The Girls* (Toronto: Clarke, Irwin & Co., 1972), p. 12.

47 *Ibid.*

48 Robert Fulford, *op. cit.*

49 Cited by Theresa Moritz and Albert Moritz, *The World's Most Dangerous Woman: A New Biography of Emma Goldman* (Toronto: Subway Books, 2001), p. 88.

CHAPTER 19

1 Dora de Pédery Hunt to Joyce Millar, see Joyce Millar, "The Sculptors' Society of Canada: The First Fifty Years, 1928–1978," M.A. Thesis, Concordia University, Montreal (1992), n. 67, p. 35.

2 Jehanne Bietry Salinger, "Elizabeth Wyn Wood Hahn," *The Canadian Forum* III.128 (1931), p. 302.

3 Joyce Millar, *op. cit.*

4 Emanuel Hahn, for example, signed only one of his five war memorial sculptures, the one in Westville, NS. The others were in Springhill, NS; Moncton, NB; Gaspé, Quebec; Meaford, ON; and Fernie, BC. See Robert Shipley, *To Mark Our Place: A History of Canadian War Memorials* (Toronto: NC Press, 1987), pp. 94–95.

5 Henri Hébert, "Sculptor Gives Discourse on Art," *Montreal Gazette* [clipping, 17 Feb. 1932], AGO Archives.

6 Joyce Millar, *op. cit.,* p. 17. See also Newton MacTavish, *The Fine Arts in Canada* (Toronto: Macmillan Co. of Canada, Ltd., 1925); M.O. Hammond, *Painting and Sculpture in Canada* (Toronto: Ryerson Press, 1930); C. Graham McInnes, *A Short History of Canadian Art* (Toronto: Macmillan Co. of Canada, Ltd., 1939); and William Colgate, *Canadian Art: its Origin and Development* (Toronto: McGraw-Hill Ryerson, Ltd., 1943).

7 Maria Tippett, as cited by Joyce Millar, *op. cit.*, n. 44, p. 32.

8 *Ibid.*, n. 46, 47, p. 32.

9 William Colgate, *op. cit.*, p. 194; and M.O. Hammond, *op. cit.,* p. 56.

10 Joyce Millar, *op. cit.*, n. 28, p. 31.

11 *Ibid.*

12 *Ibid.*, as cited from Alvin Hilts Papers, courtesy of Barbara Hilts Graham, Peterborough, ON.

13 Rebecca Sisler, *The Girls* (Toronto: Clarke, Irwin & Co., 1972), p. 46.

14 The exhibition at the Art Gallery of Toronto was called "Sculpture and Drawings by Aristide Maillol" (22 June–31 August 1926).

15 Other sculptors were Frank Dobson, Herman Haller, and Georg Kolbe.

16 Joyce Millar, *op. cit.*, n. 39, p. 32.

17 Joyce Millar, *op. cit.*, n. 57, p. 34. Correspondence between Loring and W.P. O'Meara of the Department of the Secretary of State regarding the incorporation of the SSC occurred between Oct. 1928 and Aug. 1932 when the final charter was granted. SSC papers, LAC.

18 "An Act Respecting Companies from the Federal Government" Chapter 27 (1927), SSC papers, LAC.

19 Joyce Millar, *op. cit.*, n. 53, p. 33.

20 Letter from Frances Loring to Eric Brown, 17 Oct. 1922, Loring papers, LAC. As cited by Christine Boyanoski, *Loring and Wyle: Sculptors' Legacy* (Toronto: Art Gallery of Ontario, 1987), p. 33.

21 *Ibid.*

22 Joyce Millar, *op. cit.*, p. 13.

23 J.C., "Chronique D'Art: La Société des Sculpteurs du Canada," *La Revue Populaire* (June 1929), p. 9.

24 As cited in "Sculptor Gives Discourse on Art," *Montreal Gazette* [clipping, 17 Feb. 1932], AGO Archives..

25 A photo in Janet M. Brooke's *Henri Hébert, 1884–1950, Un Sculpteur Moderne* (Quebec: Musée du Québec, 2000), p. 34, shows Hébert entering his studio.

26 R.H. Choate, "Canadian Sculptors Strike Sure Note," *Daily Mail and Empire* [clipping, 8 Oct. 1928], AGO Archives.

27 Augustus Bridle, "Big Crowds, Seven Shows as Art Gallery Reopens," *Toronto Daily Star* [clipping, 6 Oct. 1928], AGO Archives.

28 J.C., *op. cit.*, p. 7.

29 *Ibid.*, p. 9–10. See also "Sculpture Show at Art Gallery," *Montreal Gazette* (or *Herald*) [clipping, 1929], AGO Archives. The show was held in the lecture hall of the Art Association.

30 "Canadian War Art Exhibition," *Montreal Herald* (25 Sept. 1920), p. 3.

31 Augustus Bridle, *op. cit.*

32 Joyce Millar points out that these works by Hahn and Wyn Wood "showed that the Canadian sculptors were aware of modernist trends." *op. cit.*, p. 25.

33 Hector Charlesworth, "Contemporary Canadian Sculpture," *Saturday Night* [clipping, 27 Oct. 1928], AGO Archives.

34 Augustus Bridle, *op. cit.*

35 Katharine Clive, "The Canadian Galatea Comes to Life," *Canadian Homes and Gardens* (Feb. 1931), p. 17.

36 The names were spelled as follows: Michelangelo, Meilier, Rodin, Gutzon Borglum, George Roy Barnnard, Gaudier, Breschika, Paul Morishuf.

37 Frances Loring, as cited in "What Women Are Doing," *Globe and Mail* (28 Apr. 1919), p. 10.

38 See "What is Modern?" *Modernity and Modernism: French Painting in the Nineteenth Century*, ed. Nigel Blake, et al. (New Haven: Yale University Press, 1993), pp. 6–15.

CHAPTER 20

1 See description in Andrew Nurse, "Sculpting Canada: The Art of Frances Loring," *Woman* (Spring, 2000), p. 35.

2 "Sculptor Issues Call for Support," *Kitchener-Waterloo Record* [clipping, 16 Jan. 1960], AGO Archives.

3 James Lemon, *Toronto Since 1918: An Illustrated History* (Toronto: James Lorimer & Co. and National Museum of Man, 1985), pp. 59–79.

4 Rebecca Sisler, *The Girls* (Toronto: Clarke, Irwin & Co., Ltd., 1972), p. 46.

5 *Ibid.*

6 J.A. Watson, for the Commissioner of Customs, Department of Customs and Excise, Ottawa, to Frances Loring, 25 Apr. 1924, Loring papers, 1924–1939, LAC.

7   See full discussion of the details in Joyce Millar, "The Sculptors' Society of Canada: The First Fifty Years, 1928–1978," M.A. Thesis, Art History Dept., Concordia University, 1992, pp. 49–54.

8   *Ibid.*

9   Christine Boyanoski, *Loring and Wyle: Sculptors' Legacy* (Toronto: Art Gallery of Ontario, 1987), p. 41.

10 Joyce Millar, *op. cit.*, p. 47.

11 Eric Brown, letter to J.O. Marchand, 13 Apr. 1932, Curatorial Files, *Torso* 4087, NGC Archives.

12 A.Y. Jackson, letter to Norah de Pencier, 21 June 1932, Norah de Pencier Correspondence, LAC.

13 Eric Brown, letter to Florence Wyle, 17 Feb. 1932, Florence Wyle fonds, NGC Archives..

14 A.Y. Jackson, letter to Anne Savage, 6 June 1932, Anne Savage Papers, LAC.

15 Christine Boyanoski, *op. cit.*, pp. 41, 49.

16 Rebecca Sisler, *op. cit.*, p. 55.

17 *Ibid.*, p. 54.

18 *Ibid.*, p. 45. See also, "Favour Breaking of Rule," *Toronto Telegram* [clipping, 28 May 1930], AGO Archives.

19 A.Y. Jackson, *A Painter's Country* (Toronto: Clarke Irwin & Co. Ltd., 1958), pp. 68, 78.

20 Rebecca Sisler, *op. cit.,* p. 62.

21 *Ibid.*, p. 44.

22 *Ibid.*, pp. 37–38.

23 Frances Loring, to Thomas McMulvey, Under Secretary of State, 20 Aug. 1932, File: Charter 1928–1932, 1974. SSC papers, LAC, cited by Joyce Millar, *op. cit.*, p. 60.

24 Joyce Millar, *op. cit.*, pp. 37–40.

25 *Ibid.*, pp. 40–41.

26 OSA Minutes, 4 Apr. 1933. MU 2257, Archives of Ontario, Toronto.

27 Joyce Millar, *op. cit.*, p. 42.

28 This is Joyce Millar's speculation, *op. cit.*, p. 45.

29 *Ibid.*

30 Rebecca Sisler, *op. cit.*, p. 72.

31 *Ibid.*

32 *Ibid.*, p. 68.

33 Frances Loring, letter to Eric Brown, 29 June 1935, File: 5.5-S, SSC Travelling Exhibition 1936–37, LAC.

34   Jacobine Jones was trained at the Regent Street Polytechnic under Harold Brownsword.

35   Alex J. Musgrove, "Sculpture Show Fine Attraction at Art Gallery, Works of Canadian Artists Show Deft Craftsmanship and Artistic Expressiveness," *Winnipeg Free Press* (6 Feb. 1937), p. 4.

36   Hébert to Eric Brown, 22 Feb. 1933, Correspondence file: 7.1H, NGC Archives, as cited by Joyce Millar, *op. cit.*, p. 47.

37   Joyce Millar attributes this low number of members to the fact that a secret vote to accept new members might have led to the society's accepting only members who were known to the core group. See Joyce Millar, *op. cit.*, pp. 39–40.

38   Eric Brown to Henri Hébert, letter, 23 Feb. 1933, correspondence file: 7.1-H NGC Archives, as cited by Millar, *op. cit.*, p. 47.

39   Holger Cahill, "Art Goes to the People in the United States," *Canadian Art* 1.5 (Feb./Mar. 1944), pp. 106–07. See also Joyce Millar, *op. cit.*, n. 55, p. 65.

40   This competition built on the Lord Grey Competition for Music and Drama, including new awards for painting and sculpture. Lord Willingdon was Governor General from 1926–31.

41   Joyce Millar, *op. cit.*, p. 58.

42   *Ibid.*

43   Bertram Brooker, *Yearbook of the Arts in Canada 1928–1929* (Toronto: The Macmillan Co. of Canada, Ltd., 1929), pp. 99–104, 102.

44   "Sculptor Gives Discourse on Art," *Montreal Gazette* [clipping, 17 Feb. 1932], AGO Archives.

45   G. Campbell McInnes, "Thoughts on Canadian Art," *Saturday Night* [clipping, 1 Aug. 1936], AGO Archives.

46   Elizabeth Wyn Wood, "Art and the Pre-Cambrian Shield," *The Canadian Forum* 16.193 (Feb. 1937), pp. 13–15.

47   Florence Wyle, letter to Eric Brown, 19 Apr. 1932, Curatorial files, *Torso* 4087 NGC Archives, as cited by Christine Boyanoski, *op. cit.*, p. 41.

48   Rebecca Sisler, *op. cit.*, p. 69.

49   Frances Loring to Kingsley Brown, "Sculptress Finds Banting, Borden Strong Personalities, 'Fighters,'" *Hamilton Spectator* [clipping, 10 Dec. 1955], AGO Archives.

50   *Ibid.*

51   *Ibid.*

52   Frances Loring to Elspeth Chisholm, CBC broadcast interview, 1956, [typescript], AGO Archives.

53   Rebecca Sisler, *op. cit.*, p. 53.

54   *Ibid.*, p. 55.

55   Frances Loring, letter to A.Y. Jackson, Chairman, Canadian Purchase Committee (9 Feb. 1949), AGO Archives.

56   Rebecca Sisler, *op. cit.*, p. 56.

57   "Urges Canadians Pursue Sculpture with Sports Spirit," *Sarnia Observer* [clipping, ca. 1959], AGO Archives.

58   Cited by Lyn Harrington, "Unique Church-Studio is Home and Workshop for Loring and Wyle," *Saturday Night* 60.1 (18 Nov. 1944), p. 4.

59   *Toronto Star* [clipping, 1936], AGO Archives.

60   See *Robert Flaherty: Photographer/Filmmaker: The Inuit 1910–1922* (Vancouver: The Vancouver Art Gallery, 1980).

61   See photo in Christine Boyanoski, *op. cit.*, p. 51. The original photo appeared first in *Art and Archeology*, 20.2 (1925), then in Diamond Jenness's *The People of the Twilight* (New York: Macmillan, 1928), and then in Rev. C.E. Whittaker's *Arctic Eskimo: A Record of Fifty Years Experience and Observation Among the Eskimo* (London: Seeley, Service and Co., 1937).

62   Christine Boyanoski, *op. cit.*, p. 51. Loring later commented, "Dr. Jenness ... would not permit me to work from models or photographs when I did some Indian figures for him." As cited by Lyn Harrington, *op. cit.*, p. 5.

63   Leigh Henson, "The Logan County Courthouse, Past and Present," *Mr. Lincoln, Route 66, and Other Highlights of Lincoln, Illinois* http://www.geocities.com/findinglincolnillinois/logancocourthousehistoricarea.html

64   This phenomenon in attitudes to aboriginal peoples as expressed in the arts in Canada is analyzed in Daniel Francis, *The Imaginary Indian* (Vancouver: Arsenal Pulp Press, 1993).

65   Malvina Hoffman, *Heads and Tales* (New York: Garden City Publishing Co. Inc., 1943).

66   For a more detailed description of this set of projects at the Rainbow Bridge in Niagara Falls, see Elspeth Cameron, "Deck the Walls with Wyle and Loring," *Niagara Current* (Summer, 2003), pp. 50–55.

67   Josephine Hambleton, "Canadian Women Sculptors," *The Dalhousie Review* 29.3 (Oct. 1949), p. 335.

68   Frances Loring, letter to H.O. McCurry, 28 Feb. 1941, 7.1 Loring, NGC Archives.

69   Pearl McCarthy, "Art and Artists," *Globe and Mail* [clipping, 13 Aug. 1942], AGO Archives.

70 Charlotte Schrieber was appointed soon after the RCA was founded in 1880; and painters Marion Long and Lilias Torrance Newton had been elected within the previous three years.

71 Florence Wyle to Louis V. Hunter, "New Woman Academician has her Studio in an Abandoned Church," *Ottawa Evening Citizen* [clipping, 24 Nov. 1938], AGO Archives.

72 Margaret McKelvey and Merilyn McKelvey, *Toronto: Carved in Stone* (Toronto: Fitzhenry and Whiteside, 1984), p. 84.

73 Frances Loring, CBC Radio interview, [n.d.] CBC Archives.

74 See a partial account of this visit, especially the Winnipeg portion, in Robert M. Stamp, *Kings, Queens and Canadians* (Toronto: Fitzhenry & Whiteside, 1987), pp. 215–29.

75 "Renovations Elevate CE to New Heights," *The Forum/Ryerson Polytechnic University* 28.4 [clipping, Mar. 2003], AGO Archives.

76 A.Y. Jackson, letter to Anne Savage, 14 Mar. 1940, Anne Savage Correspondence, LAC.

77 Graham McInnes, "A Century of Canadian Art: Exhibition at the Tate Gallery, London," *The Studio* (Dec. 1938), p. 295.

78 "Canadian Sculpture Makes its First Bow in the U.S.," *Saturday Night* (15 July 1939).

79 Joyce Millar, *op. cit.*, p. 52.

80 Florence Wyle, as cited in Louise V. Hunter, *op. cit.*

81 Frances Loring, as cited in "Budding Canadian Artists Work Under Disadvantages Born of Lack of Confidence," *Globe and Mail* (21 Feb. 1939), p. 11.

82 Frances Loring, "Experiments in Sculpture Must Go On," [clipping, write-up of CBC Radio program, 1939], AGO Archives.

83 Frances Loring to Lyn Harrington, as cited in "Church, Now a Studio, Gives Elbow Room to Two Industrious Sculptors," *The Christian Science Monitor* [clipping, 30 Jan. 1946], AGO Archives.

84 Augustus Bridle, "Work of 4 Women in Sculpture Show," *Toronto Daily Star* [clipping, 13 Mar. 1942], AGO Archives.

85 Cited in "New York Critics Praise Canadian Art at the Fair," *Toronto Daily Star* (30 June 1939), p. 24.

86 *Ibid.*

87 G. Campbell McInnes, "Thoughts on Canadian Art," *Saturday Night* [clipping, 1 Aug. 1936], AGO Archives.

88 *Ibid.*

CHAPTER 21

1   Rebecca Sisler, *The Girls* (Toronto: Clarke, Irwin & Co., 1972), p. 72.

2   Pearl McCarthy, "Florence Wyle's Sculpture Excels in the Counsell Garden," *Globe and Mail* (10 Aug. 1957), p. 15.

3   *Ibid.*

4   Rebecca Sisler to Elspeth Cameron, interview, 19 July 2005, Calgary, AB.

5   "Women's Daily Interests at Home and Abroad," *Toronto Daily Star* (24 Dec. 1930), p. 16.

6   Frances Loring to Linda Munk, as cited in "A Talk with Miss Loring and Miss Wyle," *Women's Globe and Mail* (6 May 1965), p. 27.

7   *Ibid.*

8   Talbot Hughes, *Dress Design: An Account of Costume for Artists & Dressmakers* (London: Sir Isaac Pitman & Sons, Ltd., 1920). This book is one of the books owned by Loring and Wyle and listed when their books were sold after their death. Information from Frances Gage, email to Elspeth Cameron, 4 July 2005, Cobourg, ON.

9   Details from Kay Kritzwiser, "Hands that Mold Beauty," *Globe Magazine* (7 Apr. 1962), p. 11.

10 James Lemon, *Toronto Since 1918: An Illustrated History* (Toronto: James Lorimer & Co. and National Museum of Man, 1985), p. 64.

11 *Ibid.*

12 Robert Bothwell, Ian Drummond, and John English, *Canada 1900–1945* (Toronto: University of Toronto Press, 1987), p. 258.

13 "Women's Art Group Holds Garden Fete," *Toronto Daily Star* (19 June 1930), p. 28.

14 This is possibly Isabel Erichsen, who later, as Isabel LeBourdais, wrote a book defending Stephen Truscott. Her sister was Gwethalyn Graham, award-winning novelist.

15 "Plan Tea Entertainment," *Toronto Daily Star* [clipping, 5 Feb. 1935], AGO Archives.

16 "200 Guests Attend Lunch of Lyceum Art Association," *Toronto Daily Star* [clipping, 13 Jan. 1937], AGO Archives.

17 "Plan Fashion Show," *Toronto Daily Star* [clipping, 27 Sept. 1937], AGO Archives.

18 "Supper Dance and Bridge by Lyceum, Women's Art Club an Event of Monday Evening," *Globe and Mail* [clipping, 27 Jan. 1939], AGO Archives.

19 "Dancing on Green at Lyceum Lawns," *Globe and Mail* [clipping, 2 June 1939], AGO Archives.

20 Christine Boyanoski, *Loring and Wyle: Sculptors' Legacy* (Toronto: Art Gallery of Ontario, 1987), p. 46.

21 "Dancing on Green," *op. cit.*

22 Florence Wyle shared a show with Lilias Torrance Newton in Montreal at the Watson Art Galleries in Nov. 1931. "Three Artists Join in Exhibit of Recent Work," *Montreal Gazette* [clipping, 18 Nov. 1931], AGO Archives.

23 "Social Events," *Globe* (9 Feb. 1931), p. 14.

24 "Village Chapter I.O.D.E. Completes Dance Details," *Toronto Daily Star* [clipping, 2 Nov. 1937], AGO Archives.

25 A.Y. Jackson, letter to Norah de Pencier, [n.d. 1932], Norah de Pencier Correspondence, LAC.

26 "Upside-Down Party — Mr. Meighan Said — What Artists Wore at Lunch," *Toronto Daily Star* [clipping, 11 Mar. 1932], AGO Archives.

27 "Uplands Lady Golfers Elect Officers at Dinner-Bridge," *Toronto Daily Star* [clipping, 28 Nov. 1932], AGO Archives.

28 "Symphony Concert Massey Hall," *Toronto Daily Star* [clipping, 22 Nov. 1933], AGO Archives.

29 "Social Notes," *Toronto Daily Star* [clipping, 30 Aug. 1935], AGO Archives.

30 "University Women Hear Dr. McCurdy," *Toronto Daily Star* [clipping, 25 Nov. 1939], AGO Archives.

31 Rebecca Sisler to Elspeth Cameron, interview, 19 July 2005, Calgary, AB.

32 "Social Notes," *Toronto Daily Star* [clipping, 2 Aug. 1932], AGO Archives.

33 Rebecca Sisler, *op. cit.*, p. 49.

34 *Ibid.*

35 *Ibid.*, pp. 49–50.

36 *Ibid.*

37 "Paint, not Politics, Stuff for Artists," *Toronto Daily Star* (10 Dec. 1932), p. 1. Lawren Harris found that only 5.6% of the paintings on display were "modernist." Florence believed the real issue was dropping sales of paintings.

38 Claire Wallace, "Stockingless Limbs Scorned as Ridiculous, Hideous," *Toronto Daily Star* (15 May 1934), p. 26.

39 "Appalled at Poverty, Sculptress Praises Fund," *Toronto Daily Star* [clipping, 17 Aug. 1937], AGO Archives.

40 Frank Loring recorded a few of his "tall tales" from the mining frontiers. These stories can be found at the AGO Archives.

41 Rebecca Sisler, *op. cit.*, pp. 49–50.

42 *Globe and Mail* [clipping, 6 Feb. 1939], AGO Archives.

43 A.Y. Jackson, letter to Norah de Pencier, [n.d. 1938], LAC.

44 Transaction Papers, signed by Optimers, a geologist and landbroker, 12 Dec. 1963; Frank Loring's will, AGO Archives.

45 Rebecca Sisler, *op. cit.*, pp. 49–50.

46 *Ibid.*, p. 56.

47 *Ibid.*, p. 51.

CHAPTER 22

1 Frances Loring, *How to Get Started: Wood Carving for Pleasure* (Ottawa: Canadian YMCA War Services and Canadian Legion Educational Services, 1939), 16 pp.

2 Frances Loring, cited in Kingsley Brown, "Sculptress Finds Banting, Borden Strong Personalities, 'Fighters,'" *Hamilton Spectator* [clipping, 10 Dec. 1955], AGO Archives.

3 Inscription on the QEW Lion monument.

4 A full description of this event and the conference proceedings can be found in *The Kingston Conference: June 26, 27, 28, 29, 1941,* ed. André Biéler and Elizabeth Harrison (Kingston: Queen's University, 1941).

5 Frances Loring, as cited by F. Maud Brown in "Eric Brown: His Contribution to the National Gallery," *Canadian Art* 4.1 (Nov. 1946), p. 13.

6 Michael Bell, "The Welfare of the Arts in Canada," *The Kingston Conference: June 26, 27, 28, 29, 1941,* ed. André Biéler and Elizabeth Harrison (Kingston: Queen's University, 1941), p. iii.

7 *Ibid.*, p. viii.

8 Reginald G. Trotter, et al., *Proceedings: Conference on Canadian-American Affairs* (Montreal: Ginn and Co., 1937), p. 35.

9 André Biéler, "Informal Session in Connection with a Loan Exhibition of Canadian Paintings," Reginald G. Trotter et al., *Proceedings: Conference on Canadian-American Affairs* (Montreal: Ginn and Co., 1937).

10 Cited by Michael Bell, *op. cit.*, p. viii.

11 Rebecca Sisler, *The Girls* (Toronto: Clarke, Irwin & Co., 1972), p. 72.

12 Walter Abell, letter to Florence Wyle, 28 Feb. 1944, AGO Archives.

13 See illustration in Page Toles, "Sculptors' Society Exhibition," *Canadian Art* 1.5 (June/July 1944), p. 191.

14 "Says Good Education is Important for Artists," *London Evening Free Press* [clipping, 14 Apr. 1943], AGO Archives.

15 Rebecca Sisler, *op. cit.*, p. 71.

16 "The Story of a Waverly Artist," *Waverly Journal* [clipping, 21 Dec. 1945], AGO Archives.

17 Lilias Torrance Newton also did a portrait of Florence Wyle, which was given to the National Gallery of Canada on 18 Dec. 1974 by Frances Gage on behalf of the Estate of Florence Wyle. See Dr. George Ignatieff to Frances Gage, letter, 18 Dec. 1974, AGO Archives.

18 See illustration in Paul Duval, "Artists Portray Fellow-Artists in O.S.A. Show," *Saturday Night* (8 Apr. 1944), p. 4.

19 Augustus Bridle, "Canadian Art Tops Music, Plays, Poems," *Toronto Daily Star* (22 March 1944), p. 10.

20 Frances Loring, "Experiments In Sculpture Must Go On," [clipping, write-up of CBC Radio program, 1939], AGO Archives.

21 "Hard to Begin Sculpting Frances Loring Admits," *Toronto Daily Star* (21 Feb. 1939), p. 20.

22 *Proceedings, op. cit.*, p. xi.

23 *Ibid.*, pp. xvi–xix. Elizabeth Wyn Wood wrote two articles for *Canadian Art* related to these activities: "A National Program for the Arts in Canada," 1.3 (1943–44), pp. 93–95 and "Art Goes to Parliament," 2.1 (1944–45), pp. 3–5; 41–42.

24 "Pictures by Canadian Artists to be Sent to the Soviet Union," *Toronto Daily Star* (6 Sept. 1944), p. 7.

25 Queen's University Archives, 2049, Box 2.

26 A.Y. Jackson, letter to Norah de Pencier, 26 Jan. 1946, Norah de Pencier Correspondence, LAC.

27 For a summary of the Massey Report, see Robert Ayre, "Report of the Royal Commission on National Development in the Arts, Letters and Sciences," *Canadian Art* 8.4 (1951), pp. 145–80. For an overview of how the Canada Council was established, see D. Paul Schafer and André Fortier, *Review of Federal Policies for the Arts in Canada (1944–1988)* (Ottawa: Canadian Conference of the Arts, 1989).

CHAPTER 23

1 Frances Loring, "How to Carve Soap," *The Canadian Red Cross Junior* 21.6 (June 1942), pp. 9–10.

CHAPTER 24

1   These were definitely the Bank of Toronto and the Bank of Nova Scotia, and possibly the Bank of Commerce.

2   Christine Boyanoski, *Loring and Wyle: Sculptors' Legacy* (Toronto: Art Gallery of Ontario, 1987), pp. 49–50.

3   Frances Loring, letter to Kathleen [no last name], [ca. 1946], Frances Loring fonds, NGC Archives.

4   "Contemporary Classical Art Decorates a Bank Building," [clipping, ca. 1948], AGO Archives.

5   Eva-Lis Wuorio, "Sculpture a Lifetime Job, View of Frances Loring," *Globe and Mail* (1 June 1946), p. 13.

6   Florence Wyle, letter to William J. Wood, 9 June 1947, as cited by Christine Boyanoski, *op. cit.*, p. 50.

7   Pearl McCarthy, "Bank of Montreal Panels Soon Adopted by Citizens," *Globe and Mail* (3 Sept. 1949), p. 12.

8   "Contemporary Classical Art Decorates a Bank Building," [clipping, ca. 1948], AGO Archives.

9   Christine Boyanoski, *op. cit.*, p. 46.

10 G. Stephen Vickers, "The Architecture in Sculpture," *The Journal of the Royal Architectural Institute of Canada* 26.1 (Jan. 1949), p. 30.

11 Eric Arthur, "Sculpture in Building," *The Journal of the Royal Architectural Institute of Canada* 15.6 (June 1938), p. 130.

12 Cleeve Horne, "Bank of Montreal Building, Toronto ... and Sculpture," *The Journal of the Royal Architectural Institute of Canada* 26.11 (Nov. 1949), p. 377.

13 G. Stephen Vickers, *op. cit.*, p. 31.

14 Cleeve Horne, *op. cit.*, p. 377.

15 *Ibid.*, p. 378.

16 Cited by Pearl McCarthy, *op. cit.*

17 The *Refus Globale*, signed by sixteen of Borduas's friends and students, announced a new era in society and the arts and revolutionized the art scene in Quebec. A history of the currents that laid the foundation for this cultural revolution can be found in Jean-René Ostiguy, *Modernism in Quebec Art, 1916–1946* (Ottawa: National Gallery of Canada, 1982).

18 Pearl McCarthy, "Sculpture to Enhance Busy Street," *Globe and Mail* [clipping, 22 May 1948], AGO Archives.

CHAPTER 25

1   Margaret Alice Murray, *Egyptian Sculpture* (Westport, Connecticut: Green-wood Press, 1930); John Warrack, *Greek Sculpture* (London: Simpkin, Marshall, Hamilton, Kent & Co Ltd., printed by Turnbull & Spears, Edinburgh, n.d.); Percy E. Nobbs, *Design: A Treatise on the Discovery of Form* (London: Oxford University Press, 1937); Ernest Grosse, *The Beginnings of Art* (New York & London: D. Appleton and Co., 1914); ed. M. Curcin, *Ivan Meštrović: A Monograph* (London: Williams and Norgate, 1919); Eric Newton, *British Sculpture 1944–46* (London: John Tiranti Ltd., 1947); Jacques Schnier, *Sculpture in Modern America* (Berkeley: University of California Press, 1948); John J. Cunningham, ed., *José de Creeft*, American Sculptors Series (Georgia: University of Georgia Press, 1950); Charlotte Devree, *José de Creeft* (The American Federation of the Arts, 1960); John I.H. Baur, *William Zorach* (New York: Frederick A. Praeger, and the Whitney Museum of American Art, 1959).

2   Janis Conner and Joel Rosenkranz "Introduction," *Rediscoveries in American Sculpture*, (Austin, Texas: University of Texas Press, 1989), pp. 1–7.

3   *Ibid.*, p. 7.

4   *Ibid.* A stabile is a free-standing abstract sculpture or structure, typically of wire or sheet metal, in the style of a mobile, but rigid and stationary.

5   *Ibid.*

6   Concetta Scaravaglione, *Painters and Sculptors of Modern America*, ed. Monroe Wheeler (New York: Thomas Y. Crowell Co., 1942), p. 110.

7   Richard Davis, *Painters and Sculptors of Modern America*, *op. cit.*, p. 143.

8   Chaim Gross, *Painters and Sculptors of Modern America*, *op. cit.*, p. 142.

9   Heinz Warneke, *Painters and Sculptors of Modern America*, *op. cit.*, p. 118.

10 Henry Moore, *Unit One*, ed. Herbert Read (London: 1934), as cited by David Sylvester, ed., *Henry Moore, Complete Sculpture, vol. 1, Sculpture 1921–1948* (London: Lund, Humphries, 1944/1988), p. xxxi.

11 G. Stephen Vickers, "The Architecture in Sculpture," *The Journal of the Royal Architectural Institute of Canada* 26.1 (Jan. 1949), p. 31.

12 Henry Moore, as cited in *Henry Moore, op. cit.*, pp. xxxi, xxxv.

13 Henry Moore, "A View of Sculpture," *The Architectural Association Journal* (May 1930), as cited in *Henry Moore, op. cit.*, p. xxx.

14 Walter Abell, "Sculpture," *The Studio* 119.625 (Apr. 1945), pp. 132–38.

15 *Ibid.*, p. 132.

16 *Ibid.*, p. 133.

17   *Ibid.*, p. 137.

18   Andrew Bell, "An Exhibition of Canadian Sculpture," *Canadian Art* 6.4 (Summer 1949), p. 155.

19   *Ibid.*

20   *Ibid.*

21   Elizabeth Wyn Wood, "Observations on a Decade, 1938–48: Ten Years of Canadian Sculpture," *The Journal of the Royal Architectural Institute of Canada* 25.1 (Jan. 1948), p. 15.

22   *Ibid.*, p. 15.

23   *Ibid.*, p. 16.

24   Augustus Bridle, "Sculptures at Gallery," *Toronto Daily Star* (4 Dec. 1948), p. 15.

25   Wyn Wood lists several such public works involving sculpture: the Hamilton Rock Garden (Elizabeth Bradford); Montreal's Botanical Gardens (Henri Hébert); the Mission house of the Society of Saint John the Evangelist in Bracebridge (Emanuel Hahn); the Ontario Hospital at Saint Thomas (Jacobine Jones); Our Lady of Mercy Hospital in Toronto (Jacobine Jones); the Toronto Stock Exchange (Charles Comfort); the CNR Station in Montreal (Charles Comfort); the McLaughlin Family Mausoleum in Oshawa (Donald Stewart); the Wallberg Memorial Chemistry Building at the University of Toronto; and the Stations of the Cross outside St. Joseph's Oratory in Montreal (Louis Parent).

26   Henry Moore, as cited in *Henry Moore, op. cit.*, p. xxxv.

27   Elizabeth Wyn Wood, *op. cit.*, p. 19.

28   Completed form for Vocational Guidance Centre, 1957, as cited by Christine Boyanoski, *Loring and Wyle: Sculptors' Legacy* (Toronto: Art Gallery of Ontario, 1987), p. 59.

29   "Frances Loring, Sculptor, Gives Interesting Talk on Art," *Ottawa Evening Journal* [clipping, 8 Feb. 1950], AGO Archives.

30   Rebecca Sisler, *The Girls* (Clarke, Irwin & Co., Ltd., 1972), p. 62.

31   Mona Purser, "Films of Cultural Arts Bring Thrill to Viewer," *Globe and Mail* (10 Feb. 1948), p. 11.

32   *Third Dimension*, Director Laurence Hyde, National Film Board of Canada, 1948.

CHAPTER 26

1   Elizabeth Wyn Wood, "Observations on a Decade, 1938–48: Ten Years of Canadian Sculpture," *The Journal of the Royal Architectural Institute of Canada* 25.1 (Jan. 1948), p. 30.

2   Florence Wyle, letter to Alan Jarvis, 27 July 1958, Florence Wyle fonds, NGA Archives.

3   Frances Gage to Elspeth Cameron, phone interview, 30 May 2005, Cobourg, ON.

4   Dora de Pédery Hunt to Elspeth Cameron, interview, 12 Oct. 2005, Toronto, ON.

5   Margaret Aitken, "Between You and Me," *Toronto Telegram* [clipping, 28 Oct. 1955], AGO Archives.

6   Dora is most likely the post–World War II "refugee" Pearl McCarthy refers to in "Her Hope: to Die Standing," *Globe and Mail* [clipping, 16 Dec. 1961], AGO Archives. McCarthy had interviewed and written about Dora de Pédery Hunt, and Dora spoke German as well as her native Hungarian.

7   Margaret Aitken, *op. cit.*

8   Dora de Pédery Hunt, interview, *op. cit.*

9   Frances Loring, letter to Harry McCurry, 31 Aug. 1948, Loring fonds, NGC Archives.

10 Dora de Pédery Hunt, "The Sculptor's Lot: The Humiliating Poverty is Gone," *Globe and Mail* (1 Aug. 1970), p. 24.

11 Cecilia Naismith, "Frances Gage: Creator of the WREN Memorial," *Cobourg Daily Star* (11 Nov. 2005), p. 32.

12 Frances Gage to Elspeth Cameron, phone interview, *op. cit.*

13 Cecilia Naismith, *op. cit.*, p. 32.

14 Frances Gage to Elspeth Cameron, phone interview, *op. cit.*

15 Rebecca Sisler, *The Girls* (Toronto: Clarke, Irwin & Co., 1972), p. 88.

16 Frances Gage to Elspeth Cameron, phone interview, *op. cit.*

17 A.Y. Jackson, letter to Anne Savage, [n.d.] 1933, Anne Savage correspondence, LAC.

18 Vancouver painter Joseph Plaskett, for example, recalls meeting The Girls on a visit to Toronto. See Joseph Plaskett, *A Speaking Likeness* (Vancouver: Ronsdale Press, 1999).

19 Frances Gage to Elspeth Cameron, phone interview, *op. cit.*

20 Rebecca Sisler to Elspeth Cameron, interview, 19 July 2005, Calgary, AB.

21 *Ibid.*

22 *Ibid.*

23 *Ibid.*

24 *Ibid.*

25 Frances Gage to Karen Wells, "Arts National," CBC Radio, 12 July 1978.

26 Norman Sydney "A Dean Among Mining Engineers Pays Tribute to the Prospectors," *Globe and Mail* [clipping, 22 Apr. 1938], AGO Archives. Frances

and her brother Ernest inherited only some books at her father's death. His estate went to his wife.

27 Rebecca Sisler to Elspeth Cameron, interview, *op. cit.*

28 Rebecca Sisler, as cited by Kay Kritzwiser, "Different Labor of Love for Sculptor," *Globe and Mail* (21 July 1973), p. 24.

29 Rebecca Sisler to Elspeth Cameron, email, 23 Mar. 2006, Calgary, AB.

30 Eleanor Milne to Sandra Alfoldy, interview, 19 Nov. 1998, Ottawa, ON.

31 Luise Kaish, cited by Charlotte Streifer Rubenstein, *American Women Sculptors* (Boston: G.K. Hall, 1990), p. 360. See also, Sandra Alfoldy, "Eleanor Milne: The Making of an Artist in Canada," http://collections.ic.gc.ca/milne/essay.html

CHAPTER 27

1   Andrew Bell, "An Exhibition of Contemporary Canadian Art," *Canadian Art* 5.4 (Summer 1950), pp. 153–57, 177.

2   "Contemporary Canadian Sculpture Shows More Caution than Experiment," *Canadian Art* 7.3 (Spring 1950), p. 116.

3   Christine Boyanoski, *Loring and Wyle: Sculptors' Legacy* (Toronto: Art Gallery of Ontario, 1987), p. 59. Boyanoski cites Andrew Bell and William S.A. Dale, "Sculpture," *The Arts in Canada: A Stocktaking at Mid-Century* (Toronto: MacMillan Co. Of Canada Ltd., 1958) and "Contemporary Canadian Sculpture Shows more Caution than Experiment," *op. cit.*

4   Frances Loring, letter to H.O. McCurry, 8 Oct. 1952, 7.4 Jackson/Loring, NGC Archives.

5   "Distinguished Woman Sculptor Here," *Edmonton Journal* [clipping, 16 Oct. 1952], AGO Archives.

6   "Famous Canadian Artists Lecture in School Auditorium," *Grande Prairie Herald Tribune* [clipping, 13 Nov. 1952], AGO Archives.

7   *Ibid.*

8   Rebecca Sisler, *The Girls* (Toronto: Clarke, Irwin & Co., 1972), p. 90.

9   *Ibid.*, p. 91.

10 A.Y. Jackson, letter to Norah de Pencier, 3 July 1949, Norah de Pencier Correspondence, LAC.

11 Rebecca Sisler, *op. cit.*, p. 88.

12 Florence Wyle, letter to Mrs. H.A. (Bobby) Dyde, n.d., 1952, Wyle fonds, NGC Archives.

13 Rebecca Sisler, *op.cit.*, p. 88.

14 *Ibid.*

15 *Ibid.*, p. 94.

16 *Ibid.*, p. 93.

17 *Ibid.*

18 Frances Loring, letter to Mrs. H.A. (Bobby) Dyde, n.d., 1953, Loring fonds, NGC Archives.

19 Rebecca Sisler, *op. cit.*, p. 92.

20 *Ibid.*, p. 95.

21 See letters to and from Frances Loring and Ivan Meštrović, 13 Nov., 28 Nov. 1950, and 22 Jan., 26 Jan., and 30 Jan. 1952, AGO Archives.

22 Rebecca Sisler, *op. cit.*, p. 75.

23 *Ibid.*, p. 93.

24 *Ibid.*, p. 90.

25 *Ibid.*, p. 91.

26 Frances Loring to Kingsley Brown, "Sculptress Finds Banting, Borden Strong Personalities, 'Fighters,'" *Hamilton Spectator* [clipping, 10 Dec. 1955], AGO Archives.

CHAPTER 28

1 Frances Loring to Kingsley Brown, "Sculptress Finds Banting, Borden Strong Personalities, 'Fighters,'" *Hamilton Spectator* [clipping, 10 Dec. 1955] AGO Archives.

2 Page Toles, "Sculptors' Society Exhibition," *Canadian Art* 1.5 (June/July 1944), p. 191.

3 Elizabeth Wyn Wood, "Observations on a Decade, 1938–48, Ten Years of Canadian Sculpture," *The Journal of the Royal Architectural Institute of Canada* 25.1 (Jan. 1948), p. 17.

4 Florence Wyle to Louise V. Hunter, "New Woman Academician has her Studio in an Abandoned Church," *Ottawa Evening Citizen* [clipping, 24 Nov. 1938]. AGO Archives.

5 Some sources say there were ten *Rivers* sculptures; others say there were twelve. Only ten appear in photos.

6 See *Torso* by Elford Cox, in Walter Abell, "Sculpture," *The Studio* 119.625 (Apr. 1945), p. 135.

7 "Statues for the Garden Exhibited Outdoors at CNE," *Globe and Mail* (2 Sept. 1953), p. 13.

8 See Christine Boyanoski, *Loring and Wyle: Sculptors' Legacy* (Toronto: Art Gallery of Ontario, 1987), p. 60.

9   *Ibid.*

10   Lyn Harrington, "Unique Church-Studio is Home and Workshop for Loring and Wyle," *Saturday Night* 60.11(18 Nov. 1944), p. 5.

11   Andrew Bell, "An Exhibition of Canadian Sculpture," *Canadian Art* 6.4 (Summer 1949), p. 156.

12   Florence Wyle to Josephine Hambleton, "Canadian Women Sculptors," *The Dalhousie Review* 29.3 (Oct. 1949), p. 331.

13   "Sculpture from 110 Glenrose Ave., to Robertson Gallery, Ottawa," type-script (March 1953), AGO Archives.

14   L.J. Groome, "Florence Wyle, Sculptor," *The Modern Instructor*, Canadian Artist Series [n.d.], AGO Archives.

15   T. Lloyd Jones, Principal, Ontario Veterinary College, Guelph, Ontario, letter to Florence Wyle, 27 July 1953, AGO Archives.

16   See illustration *Farm Animals* in Judith M. Nasby, *The University of Guelph Art Collection: A Catalogue of Paintings, Drawings, Prints and Sculpture* (Guelph: University of Guelph, et al., 1980), p. 388. See p. ix for photos of entire wall in library with panel installed, and Wyle and Loring assembling the relief. The Ontario Veterinary College also acquired a bronze sculpture by Florence Wyle, *Shepherd Boy Holding a Lamb* (1928) in 1974. See p. 389.

17   Florence Wyle, cited in Pearl McCarthy's "Florence Wyle's Sculpture Excels in the Counsell Garden," *Globe and Mail* (10 Aug. 1957), p. 15.

18   See also Pearl McCarthy, "New Sculpture at the OVC Sets an Example of Service," *Globe and Mail* (5 Dec. 1953), p. 32.

19   Augustus Bridle, "Toscanini has 40 Shirts Precede him by Plane," *Toronto Daily Star* (3 June 1950), p. 5.

20   Rebecca Sisler, *The Girls* (Toronto: Clarke, Irwin & Co., 1972), p. 95–96.

21   Lyn Harrington and Richard Harrington, "Living With Sculpture," *Montreal Family Herald and Weekly Star* (18 June 1953), p. 2.

22   Walter Abell, "Sculpture," *The Studio* 119.625 (Apr. 1945), p. 132; illustration p. 133.

23   Florence Wyle, handwritten notes, AGO Archives.

24   Lyn Harrington, *op. cit.,* p. 2.

25   Pearl McCarthy, "Festival Trophies — A Cause for Rejoicing," *Globe and Mail* [clipping, 21 Mar. 1953], AGO Archives.

26   Rebecca Sisler, *op. cit.,* p. 96.

27   *Ibid.*

28   Albert Cloutier, "Sylvia Daoust, Sculptor," *Canadian Art* 8.4 (1941), pp. 154–55.

29   "Social and Personal Notes," *Globe and Mail* (9 June 1953), p. 18.

30   Announcement from Queen Elizabeth II, AGO Archives.

31   Rebecca Sisler, *op. cit.*, p. 97.

32   Florence Wyle, letter to Queen Elizabeth II, AGO Archives.

CHAPTER 29

1   Remarks overheard and reported by Wesley Hicks in "Skunks are Pretty," *Toronto Telegram* [clipping, 3 Feb. 1950], AGO Archives.

2   Minutes of the Canadian Collection Committee, Art Gallery of Ontario, AGO Archives.

3   Florence Wyle, letter to Norah de Pencier, Norah de Pencier Correspondence, LAC.

4   Andrew Bell, "Sculpture in Trees — A Successful Innovation," *Canadian Art* 8.2 (Christmas 1950), pp. 66–67; and Pearl McCarthy, "Sculptors Find Public Designers Score Well," *Globe and Mail* (2 Sept. 1950), p. 8.

5   See "Statues for the Garden Exhibited Outdoors at CNE," *Globe and Mail* (2 Sept. 1953), AGO Archives. This exhibition of works mounted on cement blocks covered with ferns and flowers typified the transition underway from representational to abstract sculpture. Loring's *Turkey* and, especially, Wyle's fountain in the classical style had become old-fashioned, whereas E.B. Cox's semi-abstract marble torso and Jean Horne's semi-abstract dejected reclining figure were difficult for the public to accept.

6   Pearl McCarthy, "Art and Artists," *Globe and Mail* [clipping, 15 March 1952], AGO Archives.

7   Christine Boyanoski, *Loring and Wyle: Sculptors' Legacy* (Toronto: Art Gallery of Ontario, 1987), p. 62.

8   "Ottawa Scene," *Globe and Mail* (28 Mar. 1953), p. 32.

9   "Sculpture from 110 Glenrose Ave., to Robertson Art Gallery, Ottawa" typescript (Mar. 1953), AGO Archives.

10   This sculpture can be seen in *The Arts in Canada: A Stocktaking at Mid-Century*, ed. Malcolm Ross (Toronto: The Macmillan Company of Canada, Ltd., 1959), p. 38.

11   William S.A. Dale, "Sculpture," in *The Arts in Canada*, *op. cit.*, pp. 36–37.

12   Barry Hale, Exhibition Catalogue. *Toronto Painting: 1953–1965* (Ottawa: National Gallery of Canada, 1972), p. 6.

13   Dennis Reid, in *Toronto Painting: 1953–1965*, *op. cit.*, p. 10.

14   *Canadian Art Today*, ed. W. Townsend (London: Studio International, 1970), p. 43.

15   Rebecca Sisler, *The Girls* (Toronto: Clarke, Irwin & Co., 1972), p. 99.

16   Christine Boyanoski, *op. cit.*, pp. 60–61.

17   "Sculpture in Canada," *Canadian Life* 1.4 (Spring 1950), pp. 13–14.

18   For a full history of the main Canadian sculptors — French and English — and their main works before the Borden statue was commissioned, see William Colgate, *Canadian Art: Its Origin & Development* (Toronto: McGraw-Hill Ryerson, Ltd., 1943), pp. 194–208.

19   William S.A. Dale, *op. cit.*, pp. 36–37.

20   See "Sculptor of the Rural Tradition: Alfred Laliberté," *About Sculpture*, Sculptors' Society of Canada, 2 June 2005 (access), http://collections.ic.gc.ca/sculpture/text/laliberte.html

21   "Art and Artists," *Globe and Mail* (18 Mar. 1925), p. 15.

22   Hector Charlesworth, "Contemporary Canadian Sculpture," *Saturday Night* (27 Oct. 1928), p. 3; and Augustus Bridle, "Big Crowds, Seven Shows as Art Gallery Reopens," *Toronto Daily Star* [clipping, 6 Oct. 1928], AGO Archives.

23   Frances Loring, as cited by Kingsley Brown, "Sculptress Finds Banting, Borden Strong Personalities, 'Fighters,'" *Hamilton Spectator* [clipping, 10 Dec. 1955], AGO Archives.

24   Frances Loring, letter to H.O. McCurry, 8 Oct. 1952, 7.4 Jackson/Loring, NGC Archives.

25   Rebecca Sisler, *op. cit.*, p. 98.

26   Henry Borden, ed., *Robert Borden: His Memoirs* (Toronto: Macmillan and Co., 1938).

27   Rebecca Sisler, *op. cit.*, p. 98.

28   Christine Boyanoski, *op. cit.*, p. 52.

29   *Ibid.*

30   Rebecca Sisler, *op. cit.*, p. 99.

31   Frances Loring to Rebecca Sisler, *op. cit.*, p. 98.

32   "Lecture Given by Sculptress," *London Evening Free Press* [clipping, 11 May 1942], AGO Archives.

33   *Ibid.*

34   Loring as cited in "Sculptress Says Memorial of War 'Cheap Melodrama,'" *Toronto Star* (11 Apr. 1946), p. 19.

35   Lyn Harrington, "Church, Now a Studio, Gives Elbow Room to Two Industrious Sculptors," *The Science Christian Monitor* [clipping, 30 Jan. 1946], AGO Archives.

36 "Sculptor Gives Lecture on Sculpture at Gallery," *Ottawa Evening Citizen* (8 Feb. 1950), p. 18.

37 Rebecca Sisler, *op. cit.*, p. 99.

38 Double-breasted frock coats appear on the statues of Sir John A. Macdonald, Alexander Mackenzie, George Brown, Thomas D'Arcy McGee, Robert Baldwin, and Sir Louis-Hippolyte Lafontaine.

39 Rebecca Sisler, *op. cit.*, p. 99.

40 *Ibid.*, pp. 99–100.

41 "Famed Canadian Sculptress at Brantford Art League," *Brantford Expositor* (9 Mar. 1954), p. 11.

42 Hugh Thomson, "Eglinton Gallery Holds First Show," *Toronto Daily Star* (13 Mar. 1954), p. 12.

43 The other artists included: A.Y. Jackson, Jack Nichols, Etienne Petitjean, Gordon MacNamara, Charles Redfern, and Charles Comfort.

44 "Social and Personal Notes," *Globe and Mail* [clipping, 3 May 1954], AGO Archives.

45 Sculptors with work on display also included: Emanuel Hahn, Elizabeth Wyn Wood, Jean Horne, Sing Hoo, Sheila Wherry, Alvin Hilts, Elizabeth Holbrook, Helen Robinson, Robert Norgate, and Pauline Redsell.

46 Mrs. H.A. Dyde, letter to Harry McCurry, 6 Jan. 1955, Loring fonds, NGC Archives.

47 Pearl McCarthy, "Sculptor Offered Award for Service to Arts," *Globe and Mail* (21 June 1954), p. 19.

48 A.Y. Jackson received an LL.D. from Carleton University, Ottawa, in 1957.

49 This portrait mistakenly went to the AGO, although Loring left it to the National Gallery. It was finally de-accessioned from the AGO in 1974 and sent to the National Gallery.

50 In the article "Art is Everywhere," *Globe and Mail* (4 May 1957), the lion, "much less sedate than the British lion as usually conceived," is referred to as "one of the finest pieces of outdoor sculpture in Canada."

51 *Ibid.*

52 Mrs. H.A. Dyde, letter to Harry McCurry, 24 Aug. 1954, Loring fonds, NGC Archives.

53 "Entries So Bad Prizes Cancelled, But Sculptor 'May' Get $600," *Montreal Gazette* [clipping, 4 Jan. 1955], AGO Archives.

54 *Ibid.*

55 Pearl McCarthy, "Contest-Winning Sculptor to Model Borden," *Globe and Mail* [clipping, 29 Dec. 1954], AGO Archives.

56 Rebecca Sisler, *op. cit.*, p. 101.

57 "Sculptress Awarded LL.D at Varsity Graduation," *Toronto Star* (28 May 1955), p. 5.

58 "Remarks made by Prof. Woodside — Convocation — University of Toronto," (27 May 1955), AGO Archives.

59 Irene Looseberg, mezzo-soprano, sang, accompanied by Mary Rezza.

60 Pearl McCarthy, "Art Association Honours Noted Sculptor," *Globe and Mail* (13 Oct. 1955), p. 18.

61 *Globe and Mail* [clipping, 23 (month illegible) 1955], AGO Archives.

62 "Sir Robert Comes Back to Parliament Hill," *Weekend Magazine* (supplement to the *Montreal Star*), 7.11 (1957), p. 44.

63 Rebecca Sisler, *op. cit.*, p. 101.

64 "Sir Robert Comes Back to Parliament Hill," *op. cit.,* p. 46.

65 H.O. McCurry, letter to Frances Loring, (containing comments of the judges), 10 Dec. 1954, NGC Archives 7.5 Borden, as cited by Christine Boyanoski, *op. cit.*, p. 61.

66 *Ibid.*

67 Frances Loring, letter to H.O. McCurry, 22 Dec. 1954, NGC Archives 7.5 Borden, as cited by Christine Boyanoski, *op. cit.*, p. 61.

68 Rebecca Sisler, *op. cit.*, p. 102.

69 Frances Loring to John R. Lewis, "Why Would a Woman Want to be a Sculptor?" *Star Weekly Magazine* (2 Jan. 1960), p. 19.

70 See Pearl McCarthy "Florence Wyle's Sculpture Excels in the Counsell Garden," *Globe and Mail* (10 Aug. 1957), p. 15. The article explains that the fountain was sponsored by Marjorie Gibbons Counsell to honour her parents, Sir George and Lady Gibbons. Marjorie and her sisters had donated the forty-five-acre Gibbons Park in which the "new hedged" Counsell Garden with Wyle's fountain as a "focal point" was situated because it would be "an amiable thing if adults had somewhere quiet to go and sit with a book, or just sit and look."

71 Rebecca Sisler, *op. cit.*, p. 102.

72 A.Y. Jackson, letter to Norah de Pencier, 26 Jan. 1957, Norah de Pencier correspondence, LAC.

73 Kingsley Brown, "Sculptress Finds Banting, Borden Strong Personalities, 'Fighters,'" *Hamilton Spectator* [clipping, 10 Dec. 1955], AGO Archives.

74 *Kitchener-Waterloo Record* [clipping, 16 May 1957], AGO Archives.

75 *Ibid.*

76 *Ibid.*

77 Rebecca Sisler, *op. cit.*, pp. 102–103.

78 *Ibid.*, p. 103.

79 *Ibid.*

80 Elspeth Chisholm, 2nd draft of partial script and working notes for "profile-Frances Loring," CBC TV (22 July 1956), as sent to Christine Boyanoski, AGO Archives.

81 Frances Loring to Elspeth Chisholm, interview, *Telescope*, CBC TV (22 July 1956), p. vi.

82 Elizabeth Long, as cited by Elspeth Chisholm in a letter to Christine Boyanoski, 22 Nov. 1985, AGO Archives.

83 "Sir Robert Comes Back to Parliament Hill," *op. cit.*, pp. 44, 46.

84 Louis Temporale, whose firm was in Port Credit where The Girls used to holiday before owning their farm at Cherry Wood, carved many works for Loring and Wyle and for Emanuel Hahn. He died in 1994 at age eighty-four. His son, Louis Temporale, Jr. carried on the business. See "Stone Carvings on Expressway to Ruin," *Toronto Star* (19 Aug. 2000), p. N9.

85 "Sir Robert Comes Back to Parliament Hill," *op. cit.*, p. 46.

86 Frances Loring to Sheila Moodie, as cited in "Noted Toronto Sculptress Finds Canada a Challenge," *Ottawa Citizen* [clipping, 10 Jan. 1957], AGO Archives.

87 "Unveil Statue of Former War Leader," *Kingston Whig-Standard* [clipping, 9 Jan. 1957], AGO Archives.

CHAPTER 30

1 Robert Ayre, "Some Extracts," in "Report of the Royal Commission on National Developments in the Arts, Letters and Sciences," *Canadian Art* 8.4 (1951), p. 177.

2 *Ibid.*

3 *Ibid.*

4 Pearl McCarthy, "Gallery to Seek Extra $50,000 for Year's Work," *Globe and Mail* (25 Oct. 1955), p. 10.

5 *Ibid.* The Committee Chairmen were G.T. Heintzman, Gen. Beverley Matthews, A.Y. Eaton, C.S. Band, and Mark Napier.

6 "Link Between Business, Art Seen by Premier as Exhibition Opens," *Globe and Mail* (28 Nov. 1956), p. 5.

7 *Ibid.*

8 Frances Loring to Edna Usher, as cited in "We're All in Debt to These Women," *Toronto Telegram* (25 Apr. 1959), p. 29.

9 "Link Between Business, Art Seen by Premier as Exhibition Opens," *op. cit.*

10 "Frances Loring: Canada's Grand Dame of Sculpture," *Kitchener-Waterloo Record* [clipping, 16 May 1959], AGO Archives.

11 Pearl McCarthy, "New Plastic Material in a Loring Sculpture," *Globe and Mail* (29 June 1957), p. 22.

12 "Frances Loring: Canada's Grand Dame of Sculpture," *op. cit.*

13 Everrett Roseborough, "Frances Loring, Dean of Canadian Sculptors," *The Canadian Scene* 607 (30 Nov. 1962), p. 30.

14 "'Grandma': Frances Loring," *Toronto Telegram* [clipping, 25 Apr. 1959], AGO Archives.

15 Caption, photo insert, *Globe and Mail* (27 Jan. 1958), p.19.

16 Pearl McCarthy, "Eskimo Sculptress is Honoured by Sculptors' Group," *Globe and Mail* [clipping, 5 May 1958], AGO Archives.

17 Sheila Moodie, "Noted Toronto Sculptress Finds Canada a Challenge," *Ottawa Citizen* [clipping, 10 Jan. 1957], AGO Archives.

18 Christine Boyanoski, *Loring and Wyle: Sculptors' Legacy* (Toronto: Art Gallery of Toronto, 1987), p. 62.

19 Pearl McCarthy, "New Plastic Material in a Loring Sculpture," *op. cit.*

20 "Frances Loring," *Canadian Cancer Society Newsletter* (1960), AGO Archives.

21 Pearl McCarthy, "New Plastic Material in a Loring Sculpture," *op. cit.*

22 "Frances Loring," *op. cit.*

23 Pearl McCarthy, "Art is Everywhere," *Globe and Mail* [clipping, 4 May 1957], AGO Archives.

24 *Ibid.*

25 "Dennis Burton: Refinement, Often Delight," *Globe and Mail* [clipping, 4 May 1957], AGO Archives.

26 Herbert Whittaker, "Is Stratford Too English?" *Globe and Mail Weekly* (4 May 1957), p. 65.

27 Loring particularly resented the trip she had to make to Ottawa, which cost $600, during the time her statue was stored. See Linda Munk, "A Talk with Miss Loring and Miss Wyle," *Women's Globe and Mail* [clipping, 6 May 1965], AGO Archives.

28 Frances Loring to John R. Lewis, as cited in "Why Would a Woman Want to be a Sculptor?" *Star Weekly Magazine* (2 Jan. 1960), p. 19.

29 Peter Temporale, letter to Frances Loring, 14 Jan. 1957, 2 pp., AGO Archives.

30 Kay Kritzwiser, "Hands that Mold Beauty," *Globe Magazine* (7 Apr. 1962), p. 16.

31 Sheila Moodie, *op. cit.*

32 *Toronto Star* [clipping, 28 Apr. 1959], AGO Archives.

33 Pearl McCarthy, "Art is Everywhere," *op. cit.*

34 George Hulme, Business Administrator, The National Gallery of Canada, Ottawa, letter to Florence Wyle, 26 Mar. 1956, AGO Archives.

35 Pearl McCarthy, "Watch the Youngsters Among the Sculptors," *Globe and Mail* (10 May 1958), p. 15. See illustration of the plaster model in *The New World Illustrated* (Feb. 1942), p. 28.

36 See illustration, Christine Boyanoski, *op. cit.,* p. 126.

37 Hugh Thomson, "Many Interesting Works on View at RCA Show," *Toronto Daily Star* (3 Dec. 1953), p. 16.

38 L.C., "Sculptures Form Fine Exhibition," *London Free Press* (13 Jan. 1953), p. 26.

39 See illustrations in "Sculpture in Canada," *Canadian Geographical* 43 (Dec. 1951), pp. 268–70.

40 *Ibid.*, p. 269.

41 *The Arts in Canada: A Stocktaking at Mid-Century*, ed. Malcolm Ross (Toronto: The Macmillan Company of Canada, Ltd., 1958), p. 41.

42 *Ibid.*, p. 39.

43 *Ibid.*, pp. 36–37.

44 *Ibid.*, p. 35.

45 Kay Kritzwiser, *op. cit.*, p. 17.

46 *Ibid.*

47 Florence Wyle, "Sculpture Appreciation," ms., AGO Archives.

48 Florence Wyle, "Tarzan," ms. attached to *Ibid.*

49 *Kitchener-Waterloo Record* (16 May 1957), *op. cit.*

CHAPTER 31

1 Frances Loring, letter to Harold [no surname], 13 Apr. 1958, Loring fonds LAC.

2 Pearl McCarthy, "Her Hope: to Die Standing," *Globe and Mail* [clipping, 16 Dec. 1961], AGO Archives.

3 *Ibid.* In 1918, Florence wrote in a letter to Carl Stephens, University of Illinois Alumni Association, Urbana, Illinois, 9 May 1918, that when she entered the three-year Course Preliminary to Medicine in 1899, "I wanted to do something useful in this world."

4 Christine Boyanoski, *Loring and Wyle: Sculptors' Legacy* (Toronto: Art Gallery of Ontario, 1987), p. 62.

5 "Questionnaire, Vocational Guidance Centre," AGO Archives, cited by Christine Boyanoski, *op. cit.*, n. 15, p. 66.

6   *Ibid.*, p. 62.

7   Florence Wyle, letter to Norah de Pencier, 14 Jan. 1959, Norah de Pencier correspondence, LAC, as cited by Christine Boyanoski, *op. cit.*, n.16, p. 66.

8   John R. Lewis, "Why Would a Woman Want to be a Sculptor?" *Star Weekly Magazine* (2 Jan. 1960), p. 37.

9   E.L., "Sculpture and Poetry," *Winnipeg Free Press* [clipping, 5 Nov. 1959], AGO Archives.

10   Poems cited from Florence Wyle's *Poems* are: "Your Hands," p. 11; "April Snow," p. 15; "Nights Are Still Now," p. 14; and "Spring Comes Up the Land," p. 6.

11   John R. Lewis, *op. cit.*, p. 19.

12   Frances Loring to John R. Lewis, as cited in "Why Would a Woman Want to be a Sculptor?" *op. cit.*, p. 19. Loring said much the same thing in a lecture she gave in Sarnia in 1959: "I would like to see it possible for a sculptor to earn as much as a bricklayer." "Urges Canadians Pursue Sculpture with Sports Spirit," *Sarnia Observer* [clipping, 29 Nov. 1959], AGO Archives.

13   D.W. Buchanan, as cited in John R. Lewis, *op. cit.*, p. 19.

14   Robert Fulford, as cited by John R. Lewis, *op. cit.*, p. 19.

15   Rebecca Sisler, *The Girls* (Toronto: Clarke, Irwin & Co., 1972), p. 110.

16   *Ibid.* Rebecca Sisler, intended "decadent trends," not "decent trends," which was a typographical error. Rebecca Sisler to Elspeth Cameron, email, 10 May 2006, Calgary, AB.

17   *Ibid.*, p. 106.

18   Evan H. Turner, "Welders," *Canadian Art* 19.80 (July/Aug. 1962), p. 278.

19   Rebecca Sisler, *op. cit.*, p. 106.

20   *Canadian Art*, Alan Jarvis, ed., 19.80 (July/Aug. 1962), pp. 269–95. Painter-Sculptors include: Ulysse Comtois, Kazuo Nakamura, Jean-Paul Riopelle, Harold Town, Robert Hedrick, Graham Coughtry, Michael Snow, and David Partridge. Welders include: Walter Yarwood, Gord Smith, Marcel Braitstein, Armand Vaillancourt, and Gerald Gladstone. Carvers include Anne Kahane, Yosef Drenters, Irving Burman, and Audrey Taylor. Modellers include: John Ivor Smith, Augustin Filipovic, Morton Rosengarten, and Ted Bieler.

21   Lawrence Sabbath, "Painter-Sculptors," *Canadian Art*, *op. cit.*, pp. 273–291.

22   Elizabeth Kilbourn, "Painters-Sculptors," *Canadian Art*, *op. cit.*, p. 272.

23   Irving Burman, as cited by David P. Silcox, "Carvers," *Canadian Art*, *op. cit.*, p. 288.

24   *Art News Blog* (1 Dec. 2004), AGO Archives.

25   Graham Coughtry, "Our Men in Venice," *The Toronto Daily Star* (21 May 1960), p. 36.

26 Gerald Gladstone, as cited in Evan H. Turner, "Welders," *Canadian Art* 19.80 (July/Aug. 1962), p. 278.

27 Augustin Filipovic, as cited in Lawrence Sabbath, "Modellers," *Canadian Art* 19.80 (July/Aug. 1962), p. 290.

28 Morton Rosengarten, as cited in Lawrence Sabbath, *op. cit.*, p. 291.

29 Elizabeth Kilbourn, *op. cit.*, p. 275.

30 Rebecca Sisler, *op. cit.*, 109.

31 *Ibid.*, p. 110.

32 A.Y. Jackson, letter to Norah de Pencier, 14 Sept. 1962, Norah de Pencier correspondence, NGC Archives.

33 Rebecca Sisler, *op. cit.,* p. 110.

34 Charles Comfort, as cited by Lenore Crawford, "Dr. Comfort Opens 2-Sculpture Show," *London Free Press* [clipping, 10 Nov. 1962], AGO Archives. This article has a photo of Florence and Dr. Comfort.

35 Lenore Crawford, "Fifty Years of Sculpture: Loring and Wyle at the London Public Library and Art Museum," *Canadian Art* 20.2 (Mar./Apr. 1963), p. 79.

36 Rebecca Sisler, *op. cit.*, p. 111.

37 *Ibid.*, p. 109.

38 *Ibid.*, p. 111.

39 *Ibid.*

40 *Ibid.*

41 *Ibid.*, p. 112.

42 *Ibid.*

43 *Ibid.*

44 Christine Boyanoski, *op. cit.*, p. 65.

45 Letters probate of the last will and testament and one codicil of Florence Wyle (11 July 1974), cited by Christine Boyanoski, *op. cit.*, n. 22, p. 67. The date of Florence Wyle's codicil in Boyanoski's footnote must contain a typographical error. It would have been 1964, not 1974, when Florence signed this codicil.

46 *Ibid.*, p. 64.

47 Letters probate, H (c) (ii), as cited by Christine Boyanoski, *op. cit.*, n. 25, p. 67.

48 "List of Fund Contributors," 1962, AGO Archives. Mrs. Charles Band, Mrs. H.R. Bruce, and Mrs. Bernard Radley were also listed.

49 Sophia Hungerford, letter to Mr. [Charles] Band, 11 July 1963, AGO Archives. By the fall of 1963, the fund was a secret no longer. The *Globe and Mail* wrote it up in "Fund for Sculptors Who Helped Others," (25 Sept. 1963), p. 15.

50 Christine Boyanoski, *op. cit.*, p. 64.

51 See S.P. Schiavo, letters to Florence Wyle, 20 Oct. and 6 Nov. 1964, AGO Archives. For example. See "Price List — Florence Wyle," (12 May 1964), AGO Archives.

52 "Mother and Child Find Gallery Home," *Edmonton Journal* [clipping, 2 Feb. 1964], AGO Archives; Mayor Philip M. Givens, letter to Charles S. Band, 15 Apr. 1964, AGO Archives; Clare Bice, letter to Charles Band, 27 Feb. 1964; and Clare Bice, letter to Sophia Hungerford, 27 Feb. 1964, AGO Archives.

53 "Transaction Papers," signed by Optimers, a geologist and land broker, 12 Dec. 1963, AGO Archives.

54 John R. Lewis, *op. cit.*, p. 37.

CHAPTER 32

1 Linda Munk, "A Talk with Miss Loring and Miss Wyle," *Women's Globe and Mail* (6 May 1965) and Kay Kritzwiser, "Hands that Mold Beauty," *Globe Magazine* (7 Apr. 1962).

2 A.Y. Jackson, letter to Norah de Pencier, 22 Sept. 1961, Norah de Pencier correspondence, LAC.

3 As cited by A.Y. Jackson to Norah de Pencier, letter, 27 Aug. 1963, Norah de Pencier correspondence, LAC.

4 As cited and described by Rebecca Sisler, *The Girls* (Toronto: Clarke, Irwin & Co., 1972), p. 113.

5 Mrs. Helen R. Von Drache, letter to Frances Gage, 4 Feb. 1963, AGO Archives.

6 Frances Gage to Elspeth Cameron, interview, 30 June 2005, Cobourg, ON.

7 Frances Gage, letter to Mrs. Von Drache, 10 Feb. 1963, AGO Archives.

8 Frances Gage to Elspeth Cameron, email, 17 May 2006.

9 Glad [no surname] to Minty and Florence, Los Angeles, CA, 28 Feb. 1962, AGO Archives. These relatives were English. Glad's husband Davy appears to have been an academic.

10 Florence Wyle, letter to Edith McIver, 23 June 1962, AGO Archives.

11 Frances Loring, letter to Miss Briault, 29 Nov. 1962, AGO Archives.

12 Frances Gage to Elspeth Cameron, interview, 30 June 2005, Cobourg, ON.

13 Francis Thompson, *The Hound of Heaven*, written in 1891 (published first in 1895). See *The Hound of Heaven* (Philadelphia: Peter Reilly, 1916). Frances Loring's favourite lines were the first ten lines. AGO typescript by Frances Loring, AGO Archives.

14 The poem "A Dream within a Dream," by Edgar Allan Poe, is itself full of anguish and asks whether "all that we see or seem" is no more than "a dream within a dream." These lines were typed by Frances onto her personal stationery, AGO Archives.

15 Frances Gage to Elspeth Cameron, email, 17 May 2006, Cobourg, ON.

CHAPTER 33

1 Roy Shields, "Did You See?" *CBC Times*, [clipping, 8 May 1965], AGO Archives.

2 Typescript of the CBC TV *Telescope* program by Bradley Walchuk. This is an edited version of the show to about one-third its length. Video kindly given to Elspeth Cameron by CBC Archive Sales.

3 Frances Loring, CBC Radio (interview, [n.d.]), CBC Archives.

4 Roy Shields, *op. cit.*

CHAPTER 34

1 Hugo McPherson, "The Scope of Sculpture in '64," *Canadian Art* 21 (1964), pp. 224–25.

2 Dora de Pédery Hunt, "The Sculptors' Lot: The Humiliating Poverty is Gone," *Globe and Mail* (1 Aug. 1970), p. 24.

3 *Ibid.*

4 The following year an outdoor sculpture show at Stratford of some of the same pieces elicited giggles as well; see "Sculpture Exhibition at Stratford Festival Draws Gazes, Giggles," *Globe and Mail* (15 June 1965), p. 10.

5 Alan Jarvis, "*Faces of Canada* Exhibit a Modest Social History," *Canadian Art* 21.5 (Sept./Oct. 1964), pp. 302–303.

6 Walter Yarwood, interview with Joy Carroll, *Canadian Art* 21 (1964), pp. 236–38.

7 *Ibid.*

8 "John Cage," *Wikipedia*, http://en.wikipedia.org/wiki/John_Cage

9 Sheila Watson, *The Double Hook* (Toronto: McClelland & Stewart, 1959) and Leonard Cohen, *Beautiful Losers* (Toronto: McClelland & Stewart, 1966). Jack McClelland encouraged a new wave of writers in the early and mid-1960s — and afterward — who brought Canadian literature (notably Margaret Atwood's work) into the international scene.

10 In 1962, the first version of the "points system" ranking immigrants according

to their skills, which replaced the earlier ranking of immigrants by "preferred" and "non-preferred" countries of origin, was put in place. Pierre Elliott Trudeau made the first announcement that Canada was to be "multicultural within a bilingual framework" on 8 Oct. 1971 in the House of Commons, and The Multicultural Act was passed in 1985.

11   R.H. Hubbard, *The Development of Canadian Art* (Ottawa: The National Gallery of Canada, 1964), p. 18.

12   Dora de Pédery Hunt, *op. cit.*, p. 24.

13   Françoise Sullivan, as cited by Dorothy Cameron in "Preface," *Sculpture '67: An Open-Air Exhibition of Canadian Sculpture Presented by the National Gallery of Canada as Part of its Centennial Program* (Ottawa: Queen's Printer, 1968), p. 6.

14   John Ivor Smith to Dorothy Cameron, *op. cit.*, p. 20.

15   Anne Kahane to Dorothy Cameron, *op. cit.*, pp. 44–45.

16   Iain Baxter to Dorothy Cameron, *op. cit.*, pp. 84–85.

17   Michael Snow to Dorothy Cameron, *op. cit.*, p. 91.

18   Kazuo Nakamura, Wallace French, Catherine Boureau, Julius Damasdy, Raymond Speirs, Patricia Fulford, Robert Hedrick, Sorel Etrog, Zbigniew Blazeje, Michael Cooke, Robert Kaiser, Bruce Watson, Michael Hayden, Nobua Kubota, Arthur Handy, John Fillion, and Robert James Downing.

19   Alan Jarvis, as cited by Marie Fleming, "Sculpture: Florence Wyle & Frances Loring," *The Canadian Collector* 1.1 (Apr. 1966), p. 23.

CHAPTER 35

1   "Half a Team of Sculptors," *Globe and Mail*, [clipping, 11 Jan. 1966], AGO Archives.

2   Pamela Brook, "Sculpture in Retrospect," *The Varsity* [clipping, 28 Jan. 1966], AGO Archives.

3   *Ibid.* She describes Loring's *Eskimo Mother and Child* as "sentimental" and her *Girl with Fish* as "bold" and "classical." She rightly comments that Wyle's *Rebirth* is influenced by Rodin.

4   In 1949 Loring had said that no more than five copies of her Banting bust should be made and that no price less than $2,000 should be accepted for any of them. Florence's letter was used by Frances Gage in negotiations with the University of British Columbia which wanted a copy of the bust for the Woodward Library of the Faculty of Medicine. Frances set out to get permissions from the current owners of copies of the bust for a sixth. These were

the National Gallery, the Art Gallery of Toronto, the Toronto Academy of Medicine, Mr. Charles P. Fell, and another unidentified private owner. Meanwhile the private owner of a copy in Montreal put it on the market, then withdrew it. Eventually, a sixth casting was done for UBC and sold to them for $2,700. See correspondence, Charles P. Fell, Frances Gage, and William C. Gibson, Head, Faculty of Medicine, UBC, 4 Mar.–14 Dec. 1966, AGO Archives.

5   "Wyle, Florence: Works Sold as of Feb. 22, 1966," The Pollack Gallery, AGO Archives.

6   Bill Loring, letter to Aunt Florence, 22 Jan. 1966, AGO Archives.

7   Hugh Thomson, "Loring, Wyle Influence Lives on in Sculpture," *Globe and Mail* (8 Apr. 1967), p. 28.

8   Kay Kritzwiser, "Sold: $12,000 Worth of Wyle and Loring," *Globe and Mail* (29 Jan. 1966), p. 15; and Hugh Thomson, "Loring, Wyle Influence Lives on in Sculpture," *Globe and Mail* (8 Apr. 1967), p. 28.

9   *Ibid.*

10 Frances Gage to Elspeth Cameron, phone interview, 30 May 2005, Cobourg, ON.

11 T. Ormiston Smith, letter to David Ongley, 14 July 1966, and Ongley, letter to T. Ormiston Smith, 26 July 1966, AGO Archives.

12 Gladys Davis, letter to Frances Gage, 6 Mar. 1966, AGO Archives. This could be a relative of Florence's, but Frances Gage did not recall the name.

13 Patricia Godfrey, letter to Frances Gage, 27 Feb. 1966, AGO Archives.

14 Rebecca Sisler to Kay Kritzwiser, as cited in "Different Labour of Love for Sculptor," *Globe and Mail* (21 July 1973), p. 24.

15 David J. Ongley, letter to S.P. Schiavo, Roman Bronze Works, Corona, NY, letter, 17 June 1966, AGO Archives.

16 Jean Bannerman, *Leading Ladies, Canada, 1639–1967* (Dundas, ON: Carrswood, 1967), pp. 206–207.

17 These were actually minor sketches of half a page each, since Bannerman covered hundreds of women in her book.

18 Jean Bannerman, letter to Frances Gage, 7 May 1967, AGO Archives.

19 T. Ormiston Smith, invoice for medical services from 9 Dec. 1965 to 7 July 1966 for Florence Wyle, AGO Archives.

20 Kay Kritzwiser, "Valedictory in Studio-Church," *Globe and Mail* [clipping, 2 Feb. 1968], AGO Archives.

21 Rebecca Sisler to Kay Kritzwiser, as cited in "Different Labour of Love for Sculptor," *op. cit.*, p. 24.

22 These exhibits included: a Loring-Wyle retrospective 11 July–7 August 1977 at the Macdonald Gallery of the Province of Ontario building at 900 Bay Street; another 17 June–4 September 1978 at the McLaughlin Library, University of Guelph; an owl by Loring donated by the IODE to the new Pauline McGibbon Cultural Centre, which opened 5 May 1980; an exhibit "Visions and Victories: Ten Canadian Women Artists, 1914–1945," curated by Natalie Luckyj of the London Regional Art Gallery, May 1983–10 June 1984 at the AGO. See catalogue *Visions and Victories: Ten Canadian Women Artists May 1983–June 1984* (London: Regional Art Gallery, 1983). And the most extensive show ever, Christine Boyanoski's "Loring and Wyle: Sculptors' Legacy," at the AGO 4 July–18 Oct. 1987. See catalogue *Loring and Wyle: Sculptors' Legacy* (Toronto: Art Gallery of Ontario, 1987).

23 Frances Gage to Elspeth Cameron, phone interview, *op. cit.*

24 Correspondence between Frances Gage and Kristiana Kunst and Metalstøberi in Norway, June 1967, 1968, and 1969, AGO Archives. The casting of *Hound of Heaven* cost $3,000, and the duty was $605 (letter, 9 June 1967).

25 David J. Ongley, letter to John G. Anderson, 20 Jan. 1967, AGO Archives.

26 "Local Art Examined," *Ottawa Citizen* (22 Mar. 1967), p. 22.

27 Property Assessment of 110 Glenrose Avenue, 26 Feb. 1967, AGO Archives.

28 See David J. Ongley, letter to David Gardner, producer-director, CBC TV Drama Dept., 28 Aug. 1967, and Mrs. R.J. Roberts, president, Patrons of Canadian Art, letter to Frances Gage, 21 Oct. 1969, AGO Archives.

29 David J. Ongley, letter to Bert Wreford, 20 Dec. 1967, AGO Archives.

30 Frances Gage to Elspeth Cameron, phone interview, 30 May 2005, Cobourg, ON.

31 S. John F., (Sister John Francis, Frances Loring's niece who had become a nun), letter to "Junior" (Frances Gage), [ca. Mar. 1968], AGO Archives.

32 Frances Gage to Elspeth Cameron, phone interview, *op. cit.*

33 Joyce Millar "Lawrence Hayward," ca. 1992 [based on a 1992 essay by Millar], 22 Apr. 2005 (access), http://collections.ic.gc.ca/sculpture/text /hay.html

34 Lawrence Hayward to Elspeth Cameron, email, 27 Apr. 2005, Kingston, ON.

35 These moulds would have been Wyle's. She kept her plaster moulds, but Frances did not. Kay Kritzwiser, "The Girls' Show to Foster Young Talent," *Globe and Mail* (2 June 1969), p. 15.

36 Lawrence Hayward to Elspeth Cameron, email, *op. cit.*

37 Rebecca Sisler to Elspeth Cameron, interview, 19 July 2005, Calgary, AB.

38 "Florence Wyle: One of Canada's Great Sculptors Dies," *Toronto Telegram* [clipping, 15 Jan. 1968], AGO Archives.

39 "Florence Wyle: Human Anatomy Classes Turned her from Medicine to Sculpture," *Globe and Mail* (15 Jan. 1968), p. 15.

40 "Invitation to Memorial Service for Florence Wyle," AGO Archives.

41 This could refer to either of Frances's nephews: Bill Loring or Tom Loring and his wife Beth.

42 Sophia Hungerford, letter to Edith McIver, 26 Jan. 1968, AGO Archives.

43 Kay Kritzwiser, "Valedictory in Studio-Church," *Globe and Mail* [clipping, 2 Feb. 1968], AGO Archives.

44 William Withrow was working on his book *Contemporary Canadian Painting* (Toronto: McClelland & Stewart, 1972) at the time. Later, in 1977, Withrow offended the SSC by refusing to hold an exhibit for their fiftieth anniversary. They claimed he had "contempt" for the work of Loring, Wyle, Hahn, Wyn Wood, and others because he was ambitious to be "on the cutting edge" of art. See "Art Gallery Shouldn't Cater to Elite," *Toronto Star* (12 Apr. 1977), p. B4.

45 The Art Gallery of Toronto became the Art Gallery of Ontario in 1966 under William Withrow's directorship.

46 William Withrow, "Miss Florence Wyle," speech, 2 pp., AGO Archives.

47 Linda Munk, "A Talk with Miss Loring and Miss Wyle," *Women's Globe and Mail* [clipping, 6 May 1965], AGO Archives.

48 Sophia Hungerford hoped A.Y. Jackson would read the poem. See letter to Edith McIver, 26 Jan. 1968, AGO Archives.

49 Florence Wyle, "Death," *Poems* (Toronto: Ryerson Press, 1959), p. 12.

50 "Frances Loring: A Constant Contributor to Sculpture," *Globe and Mail* [clipping, 6 Feb. 1968], AGO Archives.

51 "Francis [sic] Loring, 80, Famed Sculptress, Dies," [clipping, 6 Feb. 1968], AGO Archives.

52 "Dies at 80: Sculptor Frances Loring Did Stone Lion on QEW," *Toronto Star* [clipping, 6 Feb. 1968], AGO Archives.

53 "Canadian Sculptor Frances Loring Dies," *Ottawa Journal* [clipping, 6 Feb. 1968], AGO Archives.

54 Hugh Thomson, "Miss Loring a Laissé un Oeuvre Considerable," *La Presse* [clipping, 8 Feb. 1968], AGO Archives.

55 Codicil to Last Will and Testament of Frances Loring, 12 Dec. 1961, AGO Archives.

56 Frances Gage to Elspeth Cameron, email, 12 May 2006, Cobourg, ON.

CHAPTER 36

1   Alan G. Wilkinson, *Henry Moore Remembered* (Toronto: Key Porter Books and The Art Gallery of Ontario, 1987), pp. 8–9.

2   "Toronto City Hall," *Wikipedia*, 23 Sept. 2007 (access), http://en.wikipedia.org/wiki/Toronto_ City_Hall

3   Philip James, ed., *Henry Moore on Sculpture* (London: Macdonald, 1966), p. 4.

4   Alan G. Wilkinson, *op. cit.*, p. 4.

5   *Ibid.*

6   Bruce Hewlett, "Put Hockey Player, not Henry Moore, in City Hall Square," letter to the editor, *Toronto Daily Star* [clipping, 9 Sept. 1966], AGO Archives.

7   Mayor Philip Givens, as cited in Alan J. Wilkinson, *op. cit.*, p. 8.

8   Clare Bice, letter to Frances Gage, 19 Dec. 1968, AGO Archives.

9   Clare Bice, letter to John Ayre, 7 Feb. 1968, and Robert Ayre, letter to Frances Gage, 8 Mar. 1969, AGO Archives.

10 Lotta Dempsey, "She's 'Mother' to a Colony of Artists," *Toronto Star* [clipping, 12 July 1969], AGO Archives.

11 Kay Kritzwiser, "The Girls' Show to Foster Young Talent," *Globe and Mail* (2 June 1969) p. 15. See also Bernadette Andrews, "Classic Bronze, Weird Drawings, Mammoth Fields," *Toronto Telegram* (4 June 1969), p. 80.

12 By April 1970, Pollack had sold an additional $950 for Wyle's work and $11,000 for Loring's work. See the Pollack Gallery accounts for 3 Apr. 1970, AGO Archives.

13 Sid Adilman, "It was the Salon of Canada's Art World, but Time Seems to Have Passed it by," *Toronto Telegram* [clipping, 1 Feb. 1969], AGO Archives.

14 This is probably Frances Gage.

15 Sid Adilman, *op. cit.*

16 *Ibid.*

17 Lawrence Hayward wrote an angry letter to Adilman, claiming Frances was never mad or insane, demanding that he not "poison the public" and pointing out his errors, though he makes several grammatical and factual errors himself in the process. See Lawrence Hayward, letter to Sid Adilman, 12 Feb. 1969, AGO Archives.

18 Mayo Graham, "Introduction," *Another Dimension*, (Ottawa: The National Gallery of Canada, 1977), pp. 9–11.

19 *Ibid.*

20 Sid Adilman, *op. cit.*

21 Joseph McCulley, letter to editor, *Globe and Mail*, 23 August 1969.

22 Frank Loring, Qualicum Beach, BC, letter to Frances Gage, 5 Oct. 1968, AGO Archives.

23 Clare Bice, as cited in Sid Adilman, *op. cit.* The area was only zoned for single-family dwellings that could include a studio.

24 RCA *Report, 1969–70*, AGO Archives.

25 R.S. Adachi, Assistant Chief Engineer, Ministry of Transportation, letter to Frances Gage, 23 May 1974, AGO Archives.

26 "Vandals and a Treasure," "Different Labour of Love for Sculptor," *Globe and Mail* [clipping, 4 May 1972], AGO Archives.

27 Sisler's book was suggested at a Woman's Day luncheon at the CNE where several of The Girls' friends talked of them. One of them said it was a shame that "all that chapter of sculptural history is going to be gone." See Kay Kritzwiser, "Different Labour of Love for Sculptor," *Globe and Mail* (21 July 1973), p. 24.

28 Rebecca Sisler, letter to the editor, *Globe and Mail* [clipping, 16 Dec. 1972], AGO Archives.

29 Helen Worthington, "Sculptors Hope Toronto will be Known for its Art," *Toronto Star* [clipping, 6 Oct. 1972], AGO Archives.

30 Andrew Boszin, letter to The Honorable Gordon Carter, Minister of Transportation and Communication, Queen's Park, 6 Sept. 1972, AGO Archives.

31 Donald Jones, "The Story of the Queen, the Lion and the Old Church Schoolhouse," *Toronto Star* [clipping, 30 June 1979], AGO Archives.

32 "New Home for Landmark," *Globe and Mail* [clipping, 21 Nov. 1972], AGO Archives.

33 Pearl McCarthy, "Art and Artists," *Globe and Mail* [clipping, 13 Aug. 1942], AGO Archives.

34 "New Home for Landmark," *op. cit.*

35 "Vandals and a Treasure," *op. cit.*

36 *Ibid.*

37 Zena Cherry, "Parked Lion," *Globe and Mail* (5 Aug. 1972), p. 12.

38 *Ibid.* See also Rick McGinnis, "Historic Statue Stands Forgotten," *National Post* [undated clipping], AGO Archives.

39 John Sewell, "Preface," *Doors Open Toronto: Illuminating Toronto's Great Spaces* (Toronto: Alfred A. Knopf, 2002), pp. 216–17.

40 Frances Loring, letter to Harry McCurry, 5 Mar. 1945, Frances Loring fonds, NGC Archives.

41 Mayor Philip Givens, letter to Charles S. Band, 15 Apr. 1964, AGO Archives.

42 See correspondence, Carol Erb, Planning and Development Officer, Centre for Sports and Recreation, Frances Gage, and D.B. Ball, The Morris Singer

Foundry Ltd., Mar.–July 1974, AGO Archives.

43 "'Goalie' Statue Merits Display," *Toronto Star* (27 May 1983), p. A22.

44 "No Takers for Sculpture so Goalkeeper's on Ice," *Toronto Star* [clipping, 26 May 1983], AGO Archives.

45 Donald Jones, "Loring-Wyle Memorial Park Honors Odd-couple Sculptors," *Toronto Star* (18 June 1983), p. F10.

46 Robert Fulford, *An Introduction to the Arts in Canada* (Citizenship Branch, Dept. of the Secretary of State of Canada), (Toronto: Copp Clark Publishing, 1977). Fulford goes directly from early aboriginal carving to sculpture of the 1960s, omitting the careers of Loring and Wyle and others of their generation.

47 Robert Fulford, "A Generation Gap Too Far to Bridge," *Toronto Star* (12 Sept. 1987), p. M6.

48 *Ibid.*

49 "Athletes as Heroes a Former Staple of the Art World," *Toronto Star* (1 July 2001), p. E8. Even thirty years after creating his painting, Danby was selling between 3,000 and 4,000 copies annually.

50 See Eric Nelson, "How a Streetcar Loop Became an Art Park," *Leaside Town Crier* [clipping, Aug. 1987], AGO Archives.

51 This positioning is deplored as being "sad" by Gary Michael Dault, "This City: Artists-in-Residence," *Toronto Life* (Aug. 1985), p. 13.

CHAPTER 37

1 News Release, Ontario Heritage Foundation, "Historical Plaque to Commemorate Loring-Wyle Studio," 22 Oct. 1976, 4 pp., AGO Archives.

2 Lyn Harrington, "Unique Church-Studio Is Home and Workshop for Loring and Wyle," *Saturday Night* 60.11 (18 Nov. 1944), p. 5.

3 Frances Loring to Elspeth Chisholm, *Telescope*, CBC TV script (July 1956), p. iv, AGO Archives.

4 Frances Gage to Elspeth Cameron, interview, 30 June 2005, Cobourg, ON.

5 The company, which began in 1976, was called "Eleanor of Acquitane." Eleanor Sniderman is described as "a soft-spoken holy terror." See William Littler, "Canadian Classics Take Off: Eleanor Sniderman Becomes a One-Woman Music Industry," *Toronto Star* (28 Aug. 1976), p. H3.

6 Zena Cherry, "After a Fashion," *Globe and Mail* (27 May 1974), p. 12.

7 Frances Gage to Elspeth Cameron, interview, *op. cit.*

8 Beverly Matheson, letter to Frances Gage, 24 Apr. 1973, AGO Archives.

9 Charlotte Devree, *José de Creeft* (The American Federation of the Arts, 1960), inscribed "Dora de Pédery Hunt."

10 *William Zorach*, Whitney Museum of American Art Catalogue (Frederick A. Prager, Inc., n.d.)

11 M. Curcin, ed., *Ivan Meštrović: A Monograph* (London: Williams and Norgate, 1919).

12 Eric Newton, *British Sculpture, 1944–46* (London: John Tiranti Ltd., 1947).

13 John Warrack, *Greek Sculpture* (London: Simpkin, Marshall, Hamilton, Kent & Co. Ltd., printed by Turnbull & Spears, Edinburgh, n.d.).

14 This detail is from Zena Cherry, "After a Fashion," *op. cit.*

15 *Ibid.*

16 Frances Gage, undated one-page posthumous biographical sketch, 'Frances Loring and Florence Wyle," AGO Archives.

17 Frances Gage received an Explorations Grant in 1974. See J.T. Band, Explorations Program, Canada Council, letter to Frances Gage, 24 July 1974, AGO Archives.

18 Sandra G. Lawrence, Chief Conservator, to Doris Couture-Ligert, Restoration and Conservation Lab., NGC; and File #7790 (1995), NGC Archives.

List of Works ⤚

BY BRADLEY WALCHUK

The following list was completed using information from a variety of sources: art history textbooks, gallery exhibition programs, newspaper articles, and archival materials. While every effort was made to create as complete a list as possible for each sculpture, including the year, material, size, and note of any duplicates, there were many instances in which such information was nonexistent and could not be included in the list. Despite this, the list remains a valuable contribution to the study of the life and work of Frances Loring and Florence Wyle. Some idea of the number of works each produced can be obtained. A general idea of the subjects each of them undertook and their chronological moves from subject to subject is clear.

FRANCES LORING

Date	Name	Material	Size	Copy (Date)
1908	Fountain	Plaster[1]		
1908	Sundial	Plaster		
Early 1910s	Dancing Girl with Piper			
Early 1910s	Head of Billy Bernstein			
Early/mid-1910s	Enlarged Coins			
1910	New York Traffic Policeman			
1910	The Dancing Faun			
1910	Mother's Kiss	White Marble	30.5 x 48.6 x 33.0 cm	
1910–11	The Arresting Hand			
1911	Lamia	Bronze	30.7 cm (height)	
1911[2]	Florence Wyle	Painted Plaster	53.0 x 25.5 x 21.0 cm	1969, 1984
1913	CNE Medal[3]			
1914[4]	The Old One (The Old Jew)	Painted Plaster	62.5 x 43.0 cm	1914
1914	Old Toe Dancer (Relief)	Plaster		
1914	Portrait			
1914	Mother and Child			
1914	Man with Draped Head			
1914	Transmutation			
1915	Dancing Boy			
1915	Peacock Clock	Bronze	35.8 cm x 54.6 cm	1969
1915	Book Ends	Bronze		
1915	CNE Medal	Struck Bronze	5.4 cm x 4.2 cm	

FRANCES LORING

Date	Name	Material	Size	Copy (Date)
1916	Daughter of Israel			
1916–17	Hound of Heaven	Bronze[5]	70.0 cm (h)	1969
1917	Miss Canada[6]	Staff		
1917	Grief	Bronze	51.0 x 50.0 x 26.5 cm	1917, 1966, 1969
1917	(A) Dream Within a Dream (Pity)	Bronze	62.0 cm (h)	1938–39 (marble)
1918	Grinder (Relief)	Plaster	89.5 x 67.0 cm	
1918	La Misère du Siècle			
1918	Church Lombard			
1918–19	(The) Furnace Girl	Bronze	61.0 cm (h)	
1918–19	Noon Hour at/in a Munitions Plant	Bronze relief	88.9 x 106.7 x 15.0 cm	
1918–19	The Rod Turner	Bronze	27.5 cm (h)	
1918–19	The Oiler	Bronze	29.0 cm (h)	
1918–19	The Shell Finisher	Bronze	27.0 cm (h)	
1918–19	(Two) Girls with a Rail	Bronze	71.1 x 60.0 x 30.0 cm	
1919	St. Stephen War Memorial (model)	Clay		
1919	Queen's Own Regiment, Toronto Armories			
1919	Lioness and Cubs[8] ("Spirit of Canada")	Plaster		1920 (5 cubs made available)
1920	Female Head			
1921	The Mercer Memorial	Bronze relief	155.4 cm (h)	
1921	Ethel Ely (Mrs. E)	Painted Plaster	67.0 x 51.5 cm	
1921	The Derelicts	Bronze	57.6 x 19.3 x 28.2 cm	1929

FRANCES LORING

Date	Name	Material	Size	Copy (Date)
1921	Mermaid and Hippocampus	Plaster		1969
1921	Train Conductor (Relief)	Plaster relief		
1922	Marion Lang	Bronze	56.0 cm x 30.6 cm	
1922	Marion	Plaster/Indiana	157.0 cm (h)	
1922	Girl with Squirrel (Fountain Piece)	Limestone		
1922	Portrait of a Child			
1922	Christ[9]		life size	
1922	St. Mary Magdalene (Rood)			
1922	Circular Reliefs			
1923	Madonna and Child	Painted Plaster	25.7 cm (diameter)	
1923	Head of Woman[10]	Painted Plaster	30.3 cm (height w/out base)	1969
1923	Mermaid Fountain			
1923	Female Head (lotus base)	Painted Plaster	49.7 cm (h)	1969
1923	Evangelists (Reliefs)[11]			
1923	St. John (Eagle)[12]			
1923	St. Mark (Lion)			
1923	St. Matthew (Angel)			
1923	St. Luke (Ox)			
1923	Jeanett Gibson (Relief)			
1925	Figural Grouping[13]	Painted Plaster	24.5 cm (h)	
1925	Sketch for a War Memorial	Plaster		

FRANCES LORING

Date	Name	Material	Size	Copy (Date)
1925	Model for War Memorial[14]	Plaster		
1925	Fountain Head (Rond Bas)	Plaster		
1925–28?	Knife Grinder (Relief)	Bronze		
1926	St. Stephen War Memorial	Plaster		
1926	Ashman (Ash Man)	Plaster	71.8 cm (h)[15]	1926 (h=75.0 cm)
1926	Mermaid & Water Baby	Plaster		
1926–28	Memorial Tablet to Dr. Alpheus Todd	Bronze relief		
1927	Sketches for Osgoode Hall War Memorial	Plaster	20.5 cm (h)	
1927	Prof. Charles A. Lazenby	Plaster		
1927	Study of a Woman	Plaster		
1927	Angel Candlesticks (four)	Plaster		
1927–28	War Widow and Children[16]	Painted Plaster	62.0 cm (h)	
1927–28	Recording Angel	Stone		
1928	The Cloud	Plaster relief	184.5 x 112.0 cm	
1928	The Osgoode Hall War Memorial	Marble	213.2 cm (h)	
1928	The Galt War Memorial[17]	Indiana Limestone		
1928	Girls with Shells			
1928	Girl with Jug	Plaster		
1928	Dr. Meyer	Plaster		
1928	Huntley Gordon	Plaster		
1928	Decorative Panel (Nude) (Relief)	Plaster	182.0 cm (h)	
1928	Alice (Relief)	Plaster		

FRANCES LORING

Date	Name	Material	Size	Copy (Date)
1928	The Derelict Mother (Derelicts)	Bronze		
1928–30	Old Woman (Eskimo)	Walnut		
1929	Augusta War Memorial	Bronze		
1929	Miss Wookey			
1929	Emanuel Hahn: Contemplation			
1929–31	Enlarged Coins for CIBC			
1930s	Ryerson University			
1930	Invocation	Painted Plaster	84.0 x 27.0 x 10.0 cm	
1930	Frank Arnoldi, K.C., National Club	Plaster		
1930	Woman with Herons (maquette)		28.0 cm (h)	
1930	Three Fountain Figures (maquette)[18]		27.0/27.5 cm (h)	1930
1932	Girl with Fish	Painted Plaster/ Terracotta	97.5 x 45.0 x 27.5 cm	1950 (ceramic, stone), 1958 (ceramic)
1932	John Pearson, Esq.	Plaster[19]	66.0 x 50.0 cm	1940
1932	R.H. Greer, K.C.			
1932	Turkey	Plaster	87.5 x 66.5 cm	1969 (bronze)
1934	(Sir Frederick) Banting	Bronze[20]	62.5 x 31.2 x 31.4 cm	
1935	Goal Keeper	Painted Plaster	242.0 x 50.0 x 92.5 cm	
1935	The Cloak			
1935	Buffalo (Relief)			
1936	The Miner (Moose River)	Painted Plaster	81.0 x 41.0 cm	1960s (bronze x2)
1937	Mask			

FRANCES LORING

Date	Name	Material	Size	Copy (Date)
1938	Pigeons	Painted Plaster	64.0 cm (d)	
1938	Sea Horse Fountain	Indiana Limestone	168.0 cm (h)	
1938	Eskimo (Inuit) Mother (and Child)	Painted Plaster/ Indiana Limestone	193.0 x 53.3 x 73.7 cm[21]	
1938	Owl[22]	Painted Plaster	64.4 cm (d)	
1938	Goose	Painted Plaster	64.4 cm (d)	
1938	Pigeons	Painted Plaster	64.4 cm (d)	
1938	Electric Lineman			
1938	Mrs. Mary Dignam			
1938–39	Girl with Torch			
1939	Head, Kim (Kimbark)	Plaster relief	45.8 cm (h)	
1939	Study for The Brewing		25.5 x 27.0 cm	
1939	Four Panels for O'Keefe Brewery			
1939	Beer Making in Greece: The Brewing	Painted Plaster	81.0 x 100.2 cm	
1939	Eskimo Woman	White Wood		
late 1930s	Various 'Indian' and 'Eskimo' heads[23]			
1939	The Queen Elizabeth Monument[24]	Indiana Limestone	362.4 cm (h)	
1940	Aurora	Walnut		1950
1940	St. Michael			
1940–41	Canadian Coat of Arms[25]	Limestone	121.4 x 254.0 cm	
1940–41	The Invention of the Wheel	Limestone	99.1 cm x 117.0 cm	
1940–41	Deer Panel	Limestone		

FRANCES LORING

Date	Name	Material	Size	Copy (Date)
1941	*Bison relief*	Limestone	31.0 x 105.0 cm	1969
1941	*Margot (McCurry)*			
1942	*Eskimo Mother*	Wood		
1943	*Soldier*			
1944	*Young Soldier*			
1946	*War Memorial Tablet*[26]	Stone		
1946	*Mother and Child*	Plaster		
1947	*Dr. C.H. Best*		75.7 x 50.0 cm	
1947	*War Memorial Peterborough Collegiate*	Indiana Limestone		
1948	*Dawn*[27]	Painted Plaster	100.7 x 142.5 cm	
1948	*Dusk*	Painted Plaster		
1948	*Quebec*	Queenston Limestone		
1948	*Ontario*	Queenston Limestone		
1948	*War Memorial, Western Technical*			
1948–49	*Head*	Butternut Wood	71.0 cm (h)	
1950	*Mask of a Woman*		34.5 cm (h)	
1950	*The Cloak*	Gelvized Plaster	33.0 cm (h)	1950 (h= 37.0 cm)
1950	*Refugees (Mother and Child)*	Plaster	94.0 x 67.0 cm[28]	
1950–51	*Luna*	Poplar	57.2 x 26 x 35.6 cm	1966
1951	*Martha*	Stone	99.1 x 25.0 x 35.0 cm	1955
1951	*Woman*	Mahogany		
1952	*Rooster*	Wood		1966 (x2)

FRANCES LORING

Date	Name	Material	Size	Copy (Date)
1952	*Faun*[29]	Mahogany	63.4 cm (height w/base)	
1952	*Invocation*	Mahogany	64.0 cm (h)	
1952	*The Dance*	Mahogany		
1952	*Silence*	Mahogany		
1952	*Laidlaw Memorial, Roches Point (Arnold Matthew Mem.)*			
1953	*Study for Sir Robert Borden (a)*	Painted Plaster	38.0 x 26.0 cm	
1953	*Study for Sir Robert Borden (b)*	Painted Plaster	38.0 x 26.0 cm	
1953	*Profile Relief of a Woman*		189.5 x 65.7 cm	
1954	*Study for Sir Robert Borden*	Painted Plaster	76.0 x 51.5 cm	
1954	*Head*	Walnut		
1954	*Head of Woman*	Poplar		
1955	*Study for head of Sir Robert Borden*	Painted Plaster	79.0 x 43.0 cm	
1957	*Sir Robert Borden*	Bronze figure on granite base	287.5 cm (h)	
1957	*Mother and Children*[30]	Polyester/Plastic material	full-scale	
1958	*Eskimo Mother*	Stone		
1959	*A.J. Billes*	Bronze		
early 1960s	*E.B. Barber*			
1962	*Dr. Herbert Bruce*	Plaster	life size hands	

FRANCES LORING

Date	Name	Material	Size	Copy (Date)
undated	Garbageman			
	Widow	Wood		
	Profile of Woman (Relief)			1969
	Dr. Pierson			1969
	Maquette Fountain			1969
	Standing Woman (Relief)	Bronze		
	John Godfrey Memorial			
	Decorative Panel (Girl)	Plaster		
	Decorative Panel (Mother and Children)			
	Mr. Buller (Algoma Central R.R.)			
	Woman's Art Association	Wood		
	Head of Sarah	Wood	38.5 cm (h)	
	Indian Child	Plaster	23.0 cm (h)	
	Female Torso	Plaster	36.0 x 11.0 cm	

FLORENCE WYLE

Date	Name	Material	Size	Copy (Date)
1906	St. George and the Dragon			
1906	Witch Fountain			
1906	Boy Piping to Fishes			
1907–08	Marble Fountain (Boy and Grapes)	Marble	71.0 x 94.0 x 29.0 cm	
1910	Mother and Child			
1910	The Water Boy			
Early/mid-1910s	Robert Borden (medal relief)			
Early/mid-1910s	Enlarged Coins			
1910	Dancing Boy	Bronze	45.7 x 27.2 x 27.3 cm	
1910	Angel of the Pool (Spirit of the Spring/Angel—Memorial Fountain)	Plaster[31]		
1910	Mother and Child	Marble		
1910	Mrs. Fanny Bloomfield Zeisler	Bronze		
1911[32]	Frances Loring	Painted Plaster	55.5 x 35.5 x 24.0 cm	1969, 1984
1911	Rebirth (Man Falls to Rise Again)	Bronze	53.3 x 58.4 x 38.1 cm	1958 (3 made available)
1911	Angel	Plaster		
1912	Candlesticks	Painted Plaster	28.0 cm and 26.7 cm (h)	
1912	Sprite of Spring	Plaster		
1912	Puppy with Frog			1969
1913	CNE Medal[33]			
1914[34]	Newsboy	Painted Plaster	47.0 cm (h)	
1914	Woman with Dead Child		54.7 cm (h)	

FLORENCE WYLE

Date	Name	Material	Size	Copy (Date)
1915	The Sacrifice	Plaster		
1915	Child Listening to Shell			
1915	Letter Opener	Bronze	23.4 cm (length)	
1915	Baby (Beatrice)	Painted Plaster	46.5 x 34.0 cm	
1915	Dean Ricker		39.5 x 31.4 cm	
1915	Boy with Macaw			
1915	The Belgian Peasant			
1916	CNE Medal	Struck Gilt	5.5 cm x 4.5 cm	
1916	Sun Worshipper	Bronze	67.6 x 23.9 x 33.2 cm	
1916	Pot of Basil	Plaster/Bronze	49.0 x 40.0 cm	1958 (5 made available, bronze)
1917	Rose	Plaster	48.6 cm (h)	
1917	Frog	Plaster	life size	
1917	Turtle		life size	
1918	Edward Kendall	Painted Plaster relief	21.7 cm (d)	
1918	Winter Landscape, Gravenhurst	Oil Painting	14.0 x 20.6 cm	
1918	Landscape with Barn	Oil Painting	23.5 x 31.0 cm	
1918	Miss Jean B. Smith		23.4 cm (h)	
1918–19	The Rimmer	Bronze	88.9 cm (h)	
1918–19	Farm Girl	Bronze	69.8 cm (h)	
1918–19	Woman with Adapter	Bronze	25.75 cm (h)	
1918–19	Munitions Worker	Bronze	26.25 cm (h)	

FLORENCE WYLE

Date	Name	Material	Size	Copy (Date)
1918–19	On the Land	Bronze	21.0 cm (h)	
1918–19	A Moulder	Bronze	26.5 cm (h)	
1918–19	Furnace Man	Bronze	29.5 cm (h)	
1918–19	The Blacksmith	Bronze	35.5 cm (h)	
1918–19	War Worker	Rama Marble	45.7 x 30.5 x 25.4 cm	
1919	Noon Hour	Bronze	64.7 cm (h)	
1919–21	Memorial to Nurse Edith Cavell[35]	Bronze relief	213.0 cm (h)	1958 (5 made available)
Early 1920s	The Key			
1920	Dr. Monash			
1920	Furnace Feeder			
1920	Fountain—Chubby Child			
1920	Mother and Child (Maquette)		15.5 cm (h)	
1920	Baby (Maquette)		10.5 cm (h)	
1920	Standing Child (Maquette)		20.5 cm (h)	
1920	Seated Child (Maquette)		17.0 cm (h)	
1920	Resting Dog			
1920	W.D. Young Memorial Fountain			
1921	F.H. Varley	Plaster	36.7 cm (h)	1956, 1 in early 1960s (bronze)
1921	Head of F.H. (Frederick) Varley	Bronze	49.5 cm (h)[36]	1958 (3 made available), 1969
1922	Nuzzling Children (bookends)			

FLORENCE WYLE

Date	Name	Material	Size	Copy (Date)
1923	Mrs. Ernest (Ethel) Ely	Painted Plaster relief	59.0 x 37.8 cm	
1923	Mr. Ely	Painted Plaster relief	59.0 x 40.4 cm	
1923	Carlos Buhler	Bronze	34.0 cm (h)	
1923	Fountain, Baby with Dolphin	Painted Plaster	106.2 cm (height w/ base)	1958 (3 made available, bronze)
1923	Girl with Ducks			
1923	Evangelists (Relief)[37]	Painter Plaster		
1925	Figural Grouping[38]	Plaster	14.0 cm (h)	1925 (h= 18.0 cm)
1925	Sketch for a war memorial	Plaster		
1925	Young Geary Girl		32.2 x 33.2 cm	
1925	Blanche (Relief)		35.2 cm (h)	
1925	The Spring		29.0 x 29.0 cm	
1926	Study of a (Young) Girl[39]	Painted Plaster	55.2 cm (h)	
1926	Shepherd Boy Holding a Lamb	Bronze	86.7 x 24.8 x 26.2 cm	
1927	Totem lamp stand	Painted wood	23.2 cm (h)	Many[40]
1927	Totem lamp stand (III)	Wood	33.7 cm (h)	
1927	Raven book-ends (two)	Cast iron with paint	16.8 cm (h)	
1927	Owl book-ends (two)	Cast iron with paint	17.1 x 7.0 cm	
1927	Small Owl book-end	Cast iron with paint	11.7 cm (h)	
1927	Indian Mother and Child (Indian Mother and Babe)	Painted Plaster relief	80.3 x 60.0 cm	1969
1927	Girl with Jug		51.5 cm (h)	

FLORENCE WYLE

Date	Name	Material	Size	Copy (Date)
1927	Child with Jug, Boy		84.0 cm (h)	
1927	Totem Poles (I and II)		33.5 cm (h)	
1927	Bishop Bethune Altar[41]			
1927	Salome (fountain)	Marble		
1927	Renewal of Birth			
1927	Torso			
1928	Dancing Baby	Bronze[42]	36.0 cm (d)	
1928	F.C. Loring	Painted Plaster		
1928	Anne Savage	Plaster	51.0 x 32.0 cm	
1928	Baby Fountain, Girl	Plaster Model	97.5 x 48.0 cm	1935 (stone), 1957 (cement)
1928	Baby Fountain, Boy	Plaster Model	95.5 x 45.5 cm	1935 (stone)
1928	Portrait of Lauren Harris	Bronze	41.7 cm (h)	
1928[43]	Young Mother	Bronze	86.0 cm (h)	1958 (5 made available)
1928	Dorothy Stevens (Relief)		45.0 x 32.0 cm	
1928	Mrs. Scott Griffin		58.3 cm	
1928	Huntley Gordon (Relief)		35.4 x 29.5 cm	
1928	Girl with Sickle			
1928	Girl with Grapes			
1928	Woman with Key			
1928	Kneeling Man			
1928	Consolation			

FLORENCE WYLE

Date	Name	Material	Size	Copy (Date)
1928	Child with Flute	Bronze		
1928	Mother and Child			
1928	(Head of) Judas	Plaster		
1928	Chicago	Plaster		
1928–29	Girl with Sparrows (bird bath)			
1928–29	Portrait of A.Y. Jackson	Painted Plaster	49.5 x 34.5 cm	1958 (3 made available)
1929	Deer Panel (section)	Painted Plaster	41.0 cm (h)[44]	1 exists
1929	Deer Panel (section)	Painted Plaster	87.0 x 181.2 cm	
1929	Small Fountainhead Frog	Painted Plaster	71.3 x 40.0 cm	
1929	Allan Burt		16.2 cm (height w/ base)	
1930s?	Shield for Canadian Bank of Commerce		40.5 cm (h)	
1930s?	Drum for Gage Park Fountain			
1930–35	Elaine	Plaster/pottery	Full head	
1930	Seated Female Torso	Plaster	31.8 cm (h)	
1930	Large White Female Torso	Plaster	85.0 cm (h)	
1930	Betty McIvor (Relief)		45.8 x 31.0 cm	
1930	Small Baby (Relief)		25.8 x 24.0 cm	
1930	Betty Clark (Relief)		33.5 x 27.7 cm	
1930	Fountain, Three Women (maquette)		21.4 cm (h)	
1930	Bookends (I and II)		14.5 cm (h)	
1930	Vincent Massey	Plaster	41.7 cm (h)	
1930	Portrait of Woman with Bun		33.5 cm (h)	

FLORENCE WYLE

Date	Name	Material	Size	Copy (Date)
1930	Mary Somerville		48.0 x 33.0 cm	
1930	Indian Baby		34.3 cm (h)	
1930	Male Head		54.0 cm (height w/ base)	
1930	Anne Kinderdine	Plaster Model	38.0 cm (h)	
1930	The Walkinie (torso)			
1931	Blue Heron[45] (fountain figure)	Cast Stone	82.3 cm (height w/ base)	1950, 1960 (x2), 1966 (bronze)
1931	Fountain Figure		91.5 cm (height w/ base)	
1931–32	Torso	Marble	100.6 x 52.3 x 35.0 cm	
1932	Chicago	Painted Plaster	54.0 cm (h)	
1932	Dick Sankey (Relief)			
1932	Head of Baby Davis (Relief)	Plaster	21.0 cm (h)	
1932	Portrait Relief	Plaster		
1932	Reginald de Bruno Austin			
1933	Violinist (Relief)		29.4 x 30.0 cm	
1933	The Violinist[46]	Painted Plaster relief	57.8 cm (d)	
1934	John Goss	Clay/Plaster	56.0 cm (h)	1935 (marble)
1935	Archie Barnes		47.5 cm (h)	
1935	Elizabeth Wyn Wood	Painted Plaster	53.0 cm (height w/ base)	1935 (marble)
1935	Birdbath	Bronze	139.0 cm (h)	
1935	Torso	Wood (Pine)[47]	36.2 cm (h)	
1935	Seated Torso	Plaster/Marble		

FLORENCE WYLE

Date	Name	Material	Size	Copy (Date)
1935	Head	White Wood	12.0 cm (h)	
1935	Woman (maquette)	Plaster	39.7 cm (h)	
1935	Singer (Singing Man)	Marble	93.0 cm	1932, 1958 (2, bronze), 1969
1935–37	Torso (Mother of the Race)			
1936	Workman	Plaster/Stone	36.0 cm (h)	
1936	Head of Esquimau Girl	Pottery		
1936	Penelope	Plaster		
1936	(Modern) Madonna	Clay Pottery		
1936	Head of Woman	Tulip Wood		
1936	Torso	Plaster		
1936	Small Torso	Pottery		
1937	Musician	Plaster		
1937	A Girl			
1937	Elaine (mask)		21.4 cm (h)	
1937–41	The Cellist[48]	Mahogany	37.0 x 29.1 x 19.1 cm	
1938	Charles Goldhammer[49]	Painted Plaster	34.7 cm (height w/out base)	
1938	American Family #1	Painted Plaster	63.7 cm (h)	
1938	American Family #2		63.2 cm (h)	
1938[50]	The Harvester	Painted Plaster	114.5 cm (h)	1984, 1987
1938	Orioles	Painted Plaster	64.4 cm (d)	
1938	Sparrows	Painted Plaster	64.4 cm (d)	

FLORENCE WYLE

Date	Name	Material	Size	Copy (Date)
1938	Wrens (Relief I)	Painted Plaster	64.4 cm (d)	
1938	Seagulls	Painted Plaster	64.4 cm (d)	
1938	Blue Jays	Painted Plaster	64.4 cm (d)	
1938	Indian Boy	Plaster	41.5 cm (h)	
1938	Young Woman[51]	Plaster	121.5 x 30.4 x 35.6 cm	1958 (5 made available, bronze)
1938	Young Girl	Plaster	121.5 x 30.4 x 35.6 cm	1966 (x2), 1969 (x3),
1938	St. Francis (Bird Bath)	Stone	66.7 x 34.5 cm	1958 (5 made available)
1938	Tarzan			
1938–39	Cello			
1939	Draped Torso	Plaster/Aur–Italian	111.8 x 45.7 x 35. 6 cm	1958 (3 made available, marble)
1939	Mrs. Terence McDermott (Relief)		45.7 x 30.1 cm	
1939	Duck	Wood		
1939–40	King George VI and Queen Elizabeth (Relief)[52]	Indiana Limestone		
late 1930s	Various "Indian" and "Eskimo" heads[53]			
1940	Blue Heron[54]	Limestone	92.7 cm (h)	1963
1940	Study for North Country	Plaster	22.0 x 28.5 cm[55]	
1940	Rainbow	Limestone		
1940	Farm	Limestone		

FLORENCE WYLE

Date	Name	Material	Size	Copy (Date)
1940	*Johnny Canuck and Uncle Sam*	Limestone		
1940	*Bus Stop*[56]	Limestone		
1940	*Head of Eskimo Woman*		44.2 x 41.8 cm	
1940	*Wine Makers* (Relief)		25.4 x 28.6 cm	
1940	*Bricklayers* (Relief)		55.4 x 81.0 cm	
1940	*Susannah*	Plaster/Marble	33.5 cm (h)[57]	1958 (5 made available, marble)
1940	*Female Head with Draped Shoulders*		38.0 cm (h)	
1940	*Head of a Boy* (Rond Bas)		22.6 cm (h)	
1940	*Deer Panel Section*		81.4 x 43.8 cm	
1940	*Head of Youth*		30.0 cm (h)	
1940	*Female Worker*		44.5 cm (h)	
1940	*Vincent Massey*[58]	Plaster/Bronze	3/4 life size	
1940–41	*Canadian Coat of Arms*[59]	Limestone		
1941	*Seagulls* (Relief)	Limestone		
1941	*Margot McCurry*		45.3 x 31.3 cm	
1942	*Bain Fountain Figure* (model)	Painted Plaster	133.2 cm (h)	1942 (Indiana limestone), 3 more made available (stone)
1942	*Duck*		12.2 x 20.2 cm	
1942	*Negress*	Plaster	98.8 x 59.5 cm[60]	1958 (5 made available, bronze)

FLORENCE WYLE

Date	Name	Material	Size	Copy (Date)
1943	(Bust of A.Y. Jackson)	Bronze	55.6 x 36.8 x 28.3 cm	1956–early 1960s (bronze)
1943	Wall Fountain	Tennessee Marble		
1944	Nude	Wood	44.4 cm (h)	
1944	Workman		45.7 cm (h)	
1944	Keith Crouch (Relief)		49.5 x 34.0 cm	1969[61]
1945	Violinist (Mask)	Sumac	28.0 cm (h)	
1945	Atlas		21.0 cm (h)	
1945	Jamaican		41.5 cm (h)	
1945	Baby Boy with Cap		28.2 cm (h)	
1945	Bob		33.5 cm (h)	
1945	Charles Comfort (Relief)		52.0 x 53.3 cm	
1946	War Memorial Tablet	Stone		
1946	Keith McIver (Relief)		37.0 cm (h)	
1946	Reclining Woman (Nude)	Plaster	43.8 x 98.0 cm[62]	1958 (5 made available, marble)
1947	Loraine	White Wood	40.8 cm (h)	
1947	Black Cat	Glazed Terracotta	24.1 cm (h)	
1948	New Brunswick[63]	Queenston Limestone		
1948	Prince Edward Island	Queenston Limestone		
1948	Torso	Walnut	41.9 x 10.2 cm (w/out base)	
1948	Margaret Gould Wechsler	Plaster	28.8 cm (h)	

FLORENCE WYLE

Date	Name	Material	Size	Copy (Date)
1948	Japanese Girl (Mask)		20.0 x 22.5 cm	
1948–49	St. Francis (Fountain)	Plaster		
1949	(Head of) Justice	Rama Marble[64]	58.0 cm (h)[65]	1949 (h=64.4 cm), 1969 and 4 others
1949	Torso		49.0 cm (h)	
1949	The Platte[66]	Sumac	38.2 cm (h)	
1949	The Illinois	Sumac	36.6 cm (h)	
1949	The Hudson	Sumac		
1949	The Niagara	Sumac		
1949–50	The Amazon	Sumac		
1949–50	The Mississippi	Sumac		
1949–50	The Missouri	Sumac		
1949–50	The Colorado	Sumac		
1949–50	The Wabash	Sumac		
1949–50	The Potomac	Sumac		
1949–50	Sleeping Cat	Plaster	9.8 x 20.0 cm	1950 (2x, bronze)
1950	Sea and Shore	Plaster model/ Carrara Marble	93.5 x 36.5 cm	1965
1950	Study for Little Blue Boy	Painted Plaster relief	30.0 x 17.6 cm	
1950	Study for Innocence	Painted Plaster relief	30.0 x 17.6 cm	
1950	Child on Tree Stump (Maquette)		17.3 cm (h)	
1950	Child on Tree Stump		47.0 cm (h)	

FLORENCE WYLE

Date	Name	Material	Size	Copy (Date)
1950	Climbing Toad		10.5 cm (h)	
1950	Frog		9.5 cm (h)	1966
1950	Cat		34.0 cm (h)	1950, 1966 (x4, bronze)[67]
1950	Cat's Head		6.3 cm (h)	1969
1950	Isabel McLaughlin (Relief)			1950
1950	Fish Fountainhead		15.3 x 14.7 cm	
1950	Rabbit		50.5 x 42.5 cm	
1950	Male Mask		22.5 cm (h)	
1950	Head of Mamie May		46.3 cm (h)	
1950	Baby with Jug	Plaster		
1950	Night	Plaster		
1951	Spring	Sumac	35.9 cm (h)	1964 (x3, bronze)
1951	Turtle	Painted Plaster	13.0 x 23.4 cm	
1951	Gardenia Bookend		14.5 cm (h)	
1951	Figure in Wood	Wood		
1952	Summer	Sumac	38.7 cm (h)	
1953	Wisdom	Mahogany	63.5 cm (height w/ base)	
1953	Drama	White Wood	81.2 cm (height w/ base)	
1953	Truth	Sumac		
1953	Poetry	Sumac		
1953	Humility	Sumac		
1953	Dr. A.L. MacNabb			

FLORENCE WYLE

Date	Name	Material	Size	Copy (Date)
1953	Humility	Sumac		
1953	Dr. A.L. MacNabb			
1953	Autumn	Sumac	27.7 cm (height w/ base)	
1953	Roland Hayes	Plaster	38.5 cm	
1953	Dancer (Relief)	Pine		1963
1953	Atlas	Sumac		
1953	The Cedars	Wood		
1953	The Pines	Wood		
1953	Pine Trees			
1954	Farm Animals (Relief)	Painted Plaster	152.9 x 399.4 cm	
1954	Large Frog		13.5 cm (h)	
1954	Ducks (Relief)		37.2 x 44.4 cm	
1955	Dryad		33.4 x 30.4 cm	
1955	Clair (Clare) Wood (Fountain Figure)		114.2 cm (h)	1958 (3 made available, stone)
1956	Eskimo Girl		36.2 cm (width w/ base)	
1957	Marjorie Gibbons Counsell Fountain			
1958	Pauline McGibbon	Plaster	45.0 x 37.5 cm	
1958	Young Worker	Mahogany	34.0 x 22.5 cm	
1958	Ira Dilworth	Plaster	1.6 x 53.5 cm	
1958	Dominion Drama Festival Trophy			

FLORENCE WYLE

Date	Name	Material	Size	Copy (Date)
1958	*Draped Torso*	Marble	111.8 cm (h)	
late 1950s	*Torso*	Marble		
late 1950s/ early 1960s	*Barbara Anne Robertson*			
late 1950s/ early 1960s	*Eleanor Sniderman*			
1961	*Wrens* (Relief II)			
1961	*Mrs. Irving Smith*		41.8 x 31.6 cm	
undated	*Head of Young Woman with Draped Shoulder*		43.8 cm (h)	
	The Lily	Beech Wood[68]		
	Naomi	Sumac		
	Dawn	Sumac		
	Madonna	Sumac		
	The Source	Sumac		
	Mother	Pine		
	Ruth	Plaster		1958 (5 made available, marble)
	Girl with Bird Bath (Fountain Piece)	Bronze		1958 (5 made available)
	Kneeling Girl (Fountain Piece)	Stone		1958 (5 made available)
	Girl	Plaster		1958 (5 made available, bronze)

FLORENCE WYLE

Date	Name	Material	Size	Copy (Date)
	Torso[69]	Plaster		1958 (3 made available, stone)
	Babies (Against Background) Fountain[70]	Stone		1958 (2 made available)
	Babies (In Round) Fountain	Stone		1958 (2 made available)
	Mother			1958 (2 cast, 4 more made available)
	Madonna and Child	Bronze	88.9 x 20.3 x 20.3 cm[71]	1969
	Young Girl with Basin	Plaster	116.8 x 83.8 x 73.7 cm	
	Young Woman	Plaster	134.6 x 50.8 x 58.4 cm	
	Garden Baby (Pair)	Plaster	86.4 x 45.7 x 38.1 cm	
	Nora McCullough	Plaster		
	Indian Child	Pottery		
	Mary	Plaster		
	Chinese Girl[72]	Plaster		
	Girl with Birds	Plaster		
	Sylvia	Plaster		
	Wall Fountain — Baby Boy			
	Mary and Son			
	Bird Plaque			
	Bas Relief	Plaster		
	Owl[73]			1969 (x4)

FLORENCE WYLE

Date	Name	Material	Size	Copy (Date)
	Boy with Dolphin[74]			1969 (x3)
	Mother with Cape[75]			1969 (x3)
	Mask			1969 (x2)
	Head with Braids			1969
	Mother and Child[76]			1969 (x3)
	Young Worker Plaque			1969
	Child Resting			1969
	Baby St. Francis[77]			1969
	Heron with Pool			1969
	Ceramic Head	Ceramic		1969
	Girl with Bowl and Gird			1969
	Family Group			1969
	Young Girl-Hand Raised			1969
	Young Girl[78]			1969
	Man with Draped Head			1969
	Reclining Cat	Bronze		1969
	Dog			1969
	Torso of a Woman			
	Nude[79]	Walnut, Pine Base		
	Table Lamp/Female Figure	Plaster		
	Farm Scene (Relief): Barn, Silo etc.	Plaster		
	Farm Scene (Relief): House, Trees etc.	Plaster		

FLORENCE WYLE

Date	Name	Material	Size	Copy (Date)
	Angel (Relief)	Plaster	17.5 x 18.75 cm	
	Female Face (Relief)	Plaster	21.25 x 11.25 x 7.5 cm	
	Child's Head (Margaret Loring)	Plaster	22.5 x 20 cm	
	Aurelia	Plaster	30.0 x 32.5 cm	
	Mother and Child	Bronze	85.0 cm (h)	
	Madonna and Child	Plaster	41.9 x 20.0 cm	
	Portrait of a Woman	Plaster	102.5 cm (h)	

Wyle frequently sculpted small Sumac carvings in the early and mid-1960s. She also recast many old plasters that had become dog-eared. *Sea and Shore*, which was first created in 1950, was carved in marble in 1965 and submitted for an Ontario Society of Arts exhibition; it was not accepted. It would be her final work.

At least one of Wyle's many torsos was cast into bronze in 1966 for a show in Markham; four of these castings were sold. Additionally, another torso was sold in 1969; no year can be traced for this sculpture.

A wood *Turtle* was shown in 1969; it is unclear if *Turtle* is different from *Turtle* (1917) and *Turtle* (1951), or if it is a reproduction of one of the other works. *Frog* was also shown in 1969; again, it is unclear if it was a reproduction of *Frog* (1917), *Frog* (1950), or *Large Frog* (1954), or an entirely different work.

William Colgate's *Canadian Art: Its Origin and Development* (Ryerson Press, 1943) lists both the Victor Ross War Memorial in Pickering, Ontario, and the Queen's University War Memorial, in Kingston, Ontario, as sculptures completed by Wyle. However, there seems to be no record of either sculpture with local library archivists. According to research, the Ross Memorial likely includes a copy of the Blue Heron Fountain.

The Pantazzi Memorial in Hamilton, Ontario has been listed as a Wyle sculpture, but no records can be found.

NOTES TO LIST OF WORKS

1   The location of Loring's earliest works is not known; thus, they are only known through photographs and their sizes and materials cannot be accurately reported. Many of her later works have disappeared as well.

2   Posthumously cast in 1984 for Loring-Wyle parkette; original sculpture was painted plaster and completed by Loring in 1911. *Head of Wyle* was sold in 1969 for $4,000.

3   The CNE *Medal* was co-designed by Miss Loring and Miss Wyle. One side featured a relief of Prime Minister Robert L. Borden, while the other side featured an agricultural emblem. The medal was probably bronze.

4   Sculpture name was interchangeable with Wyle's *Newsboy*. Originally titled by Loring as *The Old One/The Old Jew*, and listed as such in this list.

5   A plaster also exists (likely the maquette) and was exhibited in 1929 at the National Gallery's Annual Exhibition. An inventory of three 1962 exhibitions listed the sculpture as 90.0 x 52.5 x 30.0 cm.

6   *Miss Canada* was co-sculpted by Loring and Margaret Scobie.

7   Originally created as a bronze model in 1917, Loring later had *Dream within a Dream* carved in marble (1938–39) with some of the funds she made from her work on the Harry Oakes Pavilion in Niagara Falls, Ontario. A marble also appeared in 1929 at the National Gallery of Canada's Annual Exhibition of Canadian Art. A marble was also made available for sale in 1936 (at a purchase cost of $750) during the Sculptors' Society of Canada Travelling Exhibition. A personal inventory lists 1910 as the year created.

8   The lioness and cubs used to adorn the Dufferin Gates at the Canadian National Exhibition in Toronto, Ontario. The gates were demolished in 1959. Wyle and sculptor Winnifred Kingsford helped with the technical work.

9   The figure of Christ was completed for St. Mary Magdalene's Church, Toronto. It was designed by William Rae, modelled by Loring, and coloured by Frank Johnston.

10 *Head of Woman* is a cast for Loring's *Mermaid Fountain*.

11 This sculpture was completed for the Byzantine dome of St. Anne's Church in Toronto. Wyle also completed a similar piece.

12 The sculptures of Saints John, Mark, Matthew, and Luke were sculpted for St. Anne's Church, on 270 Gladstone Ave. in Toronto.

13 *Figural Grouping* was a sketch for Loring's submission to the National Commemorative War Monument competition. It was a side grouping, and made up only a small piece of the final submission.

14 A submission for the National Commemorative War Monument competition;

this was co-designed with architect W.L. Somerville, who would later collaborate with Loring on the *Galt War Memorial* (1930), the *Queen Elizabeth Monument* (1939–40) and *St. Michael*, (1940), which was made for St. Michael's Hospital in Toronto.

15   An inventory of three exhibitions in 1962 lists *Ash Man* as 110.0 x 37.5 x 47.5 cm.

16   *War Widow and Children*, along with *Recording Angel*, were designed for the Memorial Chamber, Parliament Buildings in Ottawa, Ontario. The sculptures can be interpreted as two separate works, or two pieces of a larger work. Loring collaborated with architect John Pearson on these pieces.

17   *The Galt War Memorial* was co-designed by Loring and W.L. Somerville. It was very similar to their 1925 submission for the National Commemorative War Monument, but due to financial limitations, the side groupings were eliminated, leaving only parts of the original version.

18   Records from the Art Gallery of Ontario indicate that the maquette for *Three Fountain Figures* may have been sculpted in conjunction with Wyle.

19   A bronze was made available for sale in 1936 (at a purchase cost of $2,000.00) during the Sculptors' Society of Canada Travelling Exhibition.

20   A plaster copy of *Sir Frederick Banting* was shown at an RCA exhibit in Montreal, Quebec, in 1935. Five bronzes were made in 1949, and a sixth was made in 1966.

21   Loring completed a stone replica of *Eskimo Mother and Child* in the early 1960s, despite her illness. Copies were also made in 1958: bronze (104.1 cm h) and stone (182.9 cm h). A personal inventory lists a small *Eskimo Mother and Child*, 1950.

22   Loring and Wyle were commissioned in 1938 to provide decorative sculptures for the Oakes Park Amphitheatre in Niagara Falls, Ontario.

23   These various heads sculpted by Loring were for the National Museum of Man (now the Museum of Civilization) in Hull, Quebec.

24   *The Queen Elizabeth Monument* was co-sculpted by Loring, Wyle, and W.L. Somerville. Originally located at the eastern entrance to the Queen Elizabeth Highway, it has since been moved to Sir Casimir Gzowski Park on Lakeshore Blvd. West in Toronto.

25   *The Canadian Coat of Arms*, which appears on the customs house at the Rainbow Bridge, Niagara Falls, was co-sculpted by Loring and Wyle. It was one of their few collaborations. Some records also list W.L. Somerville contributing to various sculptures done by The Girls in Niagara Falls.

26   The *War Memorial Tablet*, designed for Western Technical School, featured the

quotation, "These laid the world away." Inspired by a Rupert Brooke poem, this quotation first appeared on Loring's *Osgoode Hall War Memorial*.

27 A commission was granted in 1946 for twelve panels. Plaster carver's models were also created.

28 An inventory of three exhibitions in 1962 lists *Refugees* as 90.0 x 45.0 x 52.5 cm. A personal inventory of Loring's work also lists Indiana (limestone) and bronze as materials. It is unclear whether these were only made available for sale, or whether they were actually cast.

29 Loring's *Faun, Invocation, The Dance,* and *Silence* were a part of the Calvert Drama Trophies collection, a series of fourteen trophies awarded to regional dramatic arts festival winners. Wyle's *Wisdom, Truth, Poetry, Drama,* and other sculptures by Sylvia Daoust were also a part of the collection. Wyle added a fifteenth in 1958 when an additional region was added. The festival was renamed the Dominion Drama Festival in 1960 after Calvert Distilleries dropped its sponsorship. One can assume the unknown sizes to be roughly 64.0 cm (h).

30 Loring asked Wyle to sculpt the children for this statue. This sculpture was made from a new material that was weather resistant and permanent. It was a material used in making boats.

31 The location of Wyle's earliest works is unknown; thus, they are only known through photographs and their sizes cannot be accurately reported.

32 Posthumously cast in 1984 for Loring-Wyle parkette; original painted plaster completed by Wyle in 1911. *Head of Loring* was sold in 1969 for $4,000.

33 See endnote 3.

34 See endnote 4.

35 A bronze wreath now appears permanently fastened to the stone below the relief. The wreath was not created by Wyle, who remarked that, "If I'd intended it I'd have done it myself when I made the thing." It mysteriously appeared one day, and the authorities did not wish to interfere.

36 A bronze shown in late 1962 and early 1963 was listed as 40.6 x 33.0 x 30.5 cm. The National Gallery of Canada lists theirs as 37.5 x 20.0 x 22.3 cm (w/out base).

37 This sculpture was completed for the Byzantine dome of St. Anne's Church in Toronto. Loring also completed a similar piece.

38 *Figural Grouping* was a sketch for a war memorial.

39 *Study of a Girl* (1926) shares the same title as another Wyle sculpture completed in 1931. The 1926 piece is the maquette for the later work. The 1931 sculpture was painted plaster and stood 135.5 cm (h).

40 The *Totem* lamp stand was made in large quantities for the commercial market. It is likely that all of the owl bookends and totem lamp stands that were made in 1927 were also produced in large quantities. Wyle made a total of six plaster totem poles and three in iron. The plasters have seemingly been lost over time, but the iron items have remained and are mentioned in this list. Many cast-iron owls are also in existence; a sample size is between 12.0 and 17.0 cm (h).

41 Wyle created the decorative sculpture that appeared on the altar; William Rae designed the altar.

42 A plaster of *Dancing Baby* also exists. The piece was designed as a fountain figure.

43 The sculpture is signed "Wyle 1920," but it is officially dated by Wyle in 1928. Three other plaster casts are also known to exist.

44 A plaster shown in late 1962 and early 1963 was listed as 55.9 x 25.4 x 38.1 cm.

45 Many copies of this sculpture cast. Two models of this piece existed in different sizes (82.3 and 91.5 cm h) in 1931. A limestone copy was made in 1950, which stood 76.2 cm (h). Another stone version dates to the 1960s, while the bronze version was cast in 1966. A limestone version shown in late 1962 and early 1963 was listed as 76.2 x 53.3 x 55.9 cm.

46 Many copies of this sculpture are in existence; however, some feature only a single outer ring.

47 Many plaster versions of this sculpture are in existence.

48 This piece was completed for Wyle's diploma work. A plaster piece is also in existence; it was listed as a part of the catalogue for the Sculptors' Society of Canada Travelling Exhibition, 1936–1937. A bronze copy is in the Loring-Wyle Parkette.

49 A mask of this piece is also in existence. One inventory lists *Goldhammer* as a work completed by Loring. It is unclear if they both sculpted *Goldhammer*, or if the inventory was incorrect.

50 Posthumously cast in 1984 for Loring-Wyle Parkette, and again in 1987 for the Donald Forster Sculpture Park at the University of Guelph. Original painted plaster completed by Wyle in 1938.

51 *Young Woman* (1938) and *Young Girl* (1938) were companion pieces. A *Young Woman* was listed as 134.6 x 50.8 x 58.4 cm; it is unclear whether this is a copy of the original, or a different sculpture altogether. It is likely this piece was made in 1943. A sculpture entitled *Young Woman* was shown in 1937 at the Lyceum Women's Art Association of Canada exhibition. It is possible that this *Young Woman*, 1937 is the same as *Young Women*, 1938.

52 The relief of *King George VI and Queen Elizabeth* appears on the column above the lion on Loring's *The Queen Elizabeth Monument.*

53 These various heads sculpted by Wyle were for the National Museum of Man (now the Museum of Civilization) in Hull, Quebec. A figure of an eight-year-old "Eskimo Girl" was sculpted for the National Museum in Ottawa. Records also show that various "Indian Heads" were sold in 1966. One was done in plaster, the others were plaques. It is unclear when they were first sculpted.

54 It would seem that *Blue Heron* (1940) is different from *Blue Heron* (1931). Records from the AGO: The Canadian Collection, 1970, state that Wyle claims the 1963 copy (shown in the collection) was cast from the original, which was "done about 1940."

55 A larger, more finished study was also made. This was one of three small reliefs for the Rainbow Bridge Garden, Niagara Falls. *Rainbow* and *Farm* are the other reliefs.

56 This piece was the approach to the Rainbow Bridge in Niagara Falls. W.L. Somerville served as the architect for this work.

57 A marble shown in late 1962 and early 1963 was listed as 157.5 x 68.4 x 33.0 cm.

58 A bronze *Vincent Massey Head* was sold to Massey College in Toronto in 1966.

59 See endnote 25.

60 A plaster shown in late 1962 and early 1963 was listed as 99.0 x 38.1 x 43.2 cm.

61 A sculpture entitled *Violinist Head* was sold in 1969.

62 A plaster shown in late 1962 and early 1963 was listed as 99.0 x 48.3 x 45.7 cm.

63 See endnote 27.

64 The *Justice* that was sold in 1969 cost the buyer only $300.00. It is very unlikely that the material used was Rama marble.

65 A marble shown in late 1962 and early 1963 was listed as 30.5 x 55.9 x 43.2 cm.

66 *The Platte* was a part of the *Rivers of America* Collection, a series of ten small torsos carved in sumac beginning in the late 1940s; the series also included *The Amazon, The Hudson, The Mississippi, The Missouri, The Colorado, The Wabash, The Potomac, The Platte, The Illinois,* and *The Niagara.* The sizes could not be located for all the sculptures, but they should be consistent with those that were located (36–39 cm h). A 1950 newspaper refers to a dozen statues, and another publication included *The St. Lawrence* and *The Rio Grande* as sculptures included in the "Rivers" Series. All official records from Miss Wyle's personal

lists, as well as the most notable sources, suggest that only ten sculptures exist.

67 Four bronze cats were sold in 1966. It is likely that these were copies of the original cat from 1950.

68 It is likely that the sculptures made of wood with unknown years, *The Lily*, *Naomi*, *Dawn*, *Madonna*, *The Source*, and *Mother* were sculpted in the late 1940s or early/mid-1950s, a time when Wyle was frequently using wood as a material.

69 It is unclear which of Wyle's many *Torso* sculptures was made available in stone (3 copies only) in November 1958.

70 It is unclear if either of the *Babies* fountain pieces made available in November 1958 were copies of the *Baby Fountain*, *Boy* and *Baby Fountain*, *Girl* pieces originally sculpted in 1958. Copies were made of each piece in 1935, and an additional copy of *Baby Fountain*, *Girl* was made in 1957.

71 *Madonna and Child* was listed as two-and-one-half feet tall (76.2 cm h) in "Fifty Years of Sculpture," 1963. The two 1969 reproductions were sold for $250 each; it is very unlikely that they were cast in bronze.

72 It is possible that this sculpture was mislabelled on an inventory list at some point; Wyle completed a sculpture entitled *Chinese Girl* (date unknown), listed as such in her personal records, as well as a sculpture entitled *Japanese Girl* in 1948.

73 It is unlikely that this *Owl* was one of the owls made by Wyle in 1927. The owls made in 1927 were mass produced for commercial sales; the price paid for each of the five owls sold at an exhibit in 1969 ($75 each) suggests that these were limited reproductions, and not readily available.

74 It is unlikely that this sculpture was the same as *Baby with Dolphin* (1923), which was a bronze fountain piece. The price paid for *Boy with Dolphin* in 1969 ($450) was much less than the 1958 asking price for a bronze *Baby with Dolphin* ($3,500).

75 A maquette of this piece also exists.

76 Wyle sculpted *Mother and Child* in 1910, 1920, and 1928; it is unclear which sculpture the 1969 reproductions are of.

77 *Baby St. Francis* sold for $5,000; it was thus likely a bronze or marble reproduction.

78 *Young Girl* was listed as a companion piece to *Young Girl-Hand Raised*.

79 *Nude* was bought by the National Gallery of Canada in 1951, and they list the year made as unknown. Wyle became increasingly fond of wood sculptures into the late 1940s, and this sculpture is similar in size to the 1948 *Torso*, which was also made of walnut. *Nude* is a sculpture of a torso, and these may be the same pieces.

Bibliography ∽

"200 Guests Attend Lunch of Lyceum Art Association," *Toronto Daily Star* [clipping, 13 Jan. 1937], AGO Archives.

4th Biennial Exhibition, Art Gallery of Ontario, Feb. 1933 (Toronto: Art Gallery of Ontario, 1933).

"A Beautiful Memorial Recently Revealed," *Saturday Night* (23 Apr. 1921), p. 23.

A Century of Canadian Art [catalogue] (London: The Tate Gallery, 1938), p. 34.

"A New QEW Section Opens," *Globe and Mail* (28 May 1974).

"A New Testament Incident in Sculpture," *Current Literature* (Nov. 1905), pp. 522–23.

"A Sculptor Who Thought Big," *Toronto Star* (12 June 1978).

A Sculptor's Scullion, "The School of The Art Institute of Chicago, Il.: The Evening Modelling Classes," *Brush and Pencil* 1.6 (Mar. 1898).

"A Woman Taken in Adultery," *Brush and Pencil* 18.1 (July–Dec. 1906), p. 23.

Abell, Walter. "Some Canadian Moderns," *The Magazine of Art* (American Federation of Arts), 30 (1937), pp. 422–27.

Abell, Walter. "Sculpture," *The Studio*, 119.625 (Apr. 1945), pp. 132–37.

Adilman, Sid. "It was the Salon of Canada's Art World, But Time Seems to Have Passed it By," *Toronto Telegram* [clipping, 1 Feb. 1969], AGO Archives.

"Ages-Old Art of Sculpture Vividly Seen," *Globe* (2 Apr. 1932).

Aitken, Margaret. "Between You and Me," *Toronto Telegram* [clipping, 28 Oct. 1955], AGO Archives.

Aitken, Max. *Canada in Flanders*, intro. Sir Robert Borden (London: Hodder & Stoughton, 1916).

Alfoldy, Sandra. "Eleanor Milne: The Making of an Artist in Canada," essay, 23 June 2005 (access), http://collections.ic.gc.ca/milne/essay.html

"All These Flaming Truths," [clipping, n.d.], AGO Archives.

Allison, Wayne E. "Notes for Lorado Taft's Lectures on Sculpture," [n. d.] Archives, The Art Institute of Chicago.

"An Act Respecting Companies from the Federal Government," *Chapter 27* (1927), SSC papers, LAC.

"An Inspiring Memorial that is Needed at Home," *Mail and Empire* [clipping, 2 Apr. 1925], AGO Archives.

Andrews, Bernadette. "Classic Bronze, Weird Drawings, Mammoth Fields," *Toronto Telegram* (4 June 1969), p. 80.

"Appalled at Poverty, Sculptress Praises Fund," *Toronto Daily Star* [clipping, 17 Aug. 1937], AGO Archives.

Architecture and Allied Arts Exhibit, Feb. 11–27, 1927 [catalogue].

Ardiel, June. *Sculpture/Toronto: An Illustrated Guide to Toronto's Historic and Contemporary Sculpture with Area Maps* (Toronto: Leidra Books, 1994).

Armstrong, Selene Ayer. "Solon H. Borglum: Sculptor of American Life: An Artist Who Knows the Value of 'Our Incomparable Materials,'" *The Craftsman* (July 1907).

"Arrange Studio Tours," *Toronto Daily Star* (20 Apr. 1948).

"Art and Artists," *Globe and Mail* [clipping, 23 Dec. 1917].

"Art and Artists," *Globe and Mail* [clipping, 21 Oct. 1919].

"Art and Artists," *Globe and Mail* [clipping, 8 July 1924].

"Art and Artists," *Globe and Mail* [clipping, 18 Mar. 1925].

"Art and Artists," *Globe and Mail* [clipping, 6 Oct. 1928].

"Art and Artists," *Montreal Herald* (2 Oct. 1920).

"Art at the Exhibition," *Globe* (28 Aug. 1920), p. 31.

"Art Cross-Section of Canadian Life is Fresh and Vital," *Globe* (8 Mar. 1930).

Art Gallery of Ontario: the Canadian Collection (Toronto: McGraw-Hill Co. of Canada, Ltd., 1970).

"Art Gallery Shouldn't Cater to Elite," *Toronto Star* (12 Apr. 1977), p. B4.

"Art in Canada — Promising Development," *Morning Post* (19 Sept. 1924).

"Art is Everywhere," *Globe and Mail* (4 May 1957).

Art News Blog (1 Dec. 2004), AGO Archives.

"Art on a Grand Scale," *Ottawa Journal* (16 May 1969).

Arthur, Eric. "Sculpture in Building," *The Journal of the Royal Architectural Institute of Canada* 15.6 (June 1938).

Arthur, Eric. *Toronto: No Mean City* (Toronto: University of Toronto Press, 1964).

Arthur, Paul. "Editorial," *Canadian Art* 21.4 (July/Aug. 1964), p. 193.

"Artists Entertain in Sculpture Studio," *Toronto Daily Star* (30 Jan. 1933).

"Artists' Exhibition Draws Many Guests," *Toronto Daily Star* (4 Mar. 1947).

"Artists Picture Canada at War," *Ingersoll Daily Sentinel-Review* (13 June 1919), p. 8.

"Artists Whose Work is Shown at O.S.A. Exhibition Today," *Toronto Daily Star* (7 Mar. 1931).

"Assessment Roll for the Municipality of Scarborough, for the year 1945," p. 1528, City of Toronto Archives.

"Athletes as Heroes a Former Staple of the Art World," *Toronto Star* (1 July 2001), p. E8.

"Augustus Saint-Gaudens: The Sculptor Who Has Typified American Character and Has Left Us Noble Memorials of Great Events in American History," (ed.), *The Craftsman* 13 (Oct 1907), pp. 59–67.

Avon, Susan. "The Beaver Hall Group and its Place in the Montreal Art Milieu and the Nationalist Network," M.A. Thesis, The Department of Art History, Concordia University, 1994, 137 pp.

Ayre, Robert. "Lilias Torrance Newton, Painter of the Queen," *The Montrealer* (February 1957).

Ayre, Robert. "Some Extracts," in "Report of the Royal Commission on National Developments in the Arts, Letters, and Sciences," *Canadian Art* 8.4 (1951).

Bach, Ira J. and Mary Lackritz Gray. *A Guide to Chicago's Public Sculpture* (Chicago: The University of Chicago Press, 1983).

Baker, Victoria. *Emanuel Hahn and Elizabeth Wyn Wood: Tradition and Innovation in Canadian Sculpture* [catalogue] (Ottawa: National Gallery of Canada, 1997).

Bale, Doug. "Canadian Women Artists Focus of Shows," *London Free Press* (21 May 1983), p. E6.

Bannerman, Jean. *Leading Ladies, Canada, 1639–1967* (Dundas, ON: Carrswood, 1967).

"Banting Bust May Go to the Medical Academy," *Globe and Mail* (3 Nov. 1962).

Baur, John I.H. *William Zorach* (New York: Frederick A. Praeger and the Whitney Museum of American Art, 1959).

Bayer, Fern. *The Ontario Collection* (Markham: Fitzhenry and Whiteside, 1984).

Bazileva, Irina. "Dossier Moscow," *Sculpture* (July/Aug. 1995), pp. 12–15.

"Beautiful War Memorial Which is Favored for Galt," *Galt Evening Reporter* (10 Nov. 1928).

Beavis, Lynn. *Anne Savage, Aug. 15–Sept. 21, 2002* [catalogue] (Montreal: Concordia University, 2002).

Bedard, Michael, illus. Les Tait. *The Clay Ladies* (Toronto: Tundra Books, 1999).

Bell, Andrew. "An Exhibition of Canadian Sculpture," *Canadian Art* 6.4 (Summer 1949).

Bell, Andrew. "An Exhibition of Contemporary Canadian Art," *Canadian Art* 5.4 (Spring 1950), pp. 153–77.

Bell, Andrew. "Sculpture in Trees — A Successful Innovation," *Canadian Art* 8.2 (Christmas 1950), pp. 66–67.

Bell, Michael and Frances K. Smith, eds. *The Kingston Conference Proceedings* (Kingston: Agnes Etherington Art Gallery, 1991).

Bender, Thomas. *New York Intellect: A History of Intellectual Life in New York City from 1750 to the Beginnings of Our Own Time* (New York: Alfred A. Knopf, 1984).

Bennett, Helen Christine. "Child Figures in Fountains: Good Modelling and Faithful Portrayal of Child Spirit Characteristic of Florence Wyle's Work," *Arts and Decoration* (Feb. 1911) p. 174.

Benzi, Luciana. "The Sculpture of 'the Girl' at the AGO," TAN: Total Art News, Toronto, (Sept 1987), p. 2.

Berger, Carl. *The Sense of Power: Studies in the Ideas of Imperialism, 1867–1914* (Toronto: University of Toronto Press, 1970).

Berger, Carl. "The True North Strong and Free," *Nationalism in Canada*, ed. Peter Russell (Montreal: McGraw-Hill Ryerson, 1966).

"Between You and Me," *The Toronto Telegram* (28 Oct. 1955).

Biéler, André. "Informal Session in Connection with a Loan Exhibition of Canadian Paintings," in *Proceedings: Conferences on Canadian-American Affairs*, ed. Reginald G. Trotter et al. (Montreal: Ginn and Co., 1937).

Biéler, André and Elizabeth Harrison eds. *The Kingston Conference: June 26, 27, 28, 29, 1941* (Kingston: Queen's University, 1941).

Bissell, Claude. *The Imperial Canadian: Vincent Massey in Office* (Toronto: University of Toronto Press, 1986).

Bissell, Claude. *The Young Vincent Massey* (Toronto: University of Toronto Press, 1981).

Bogart, Michele. *Public Sculpture and the Civic Ideal in New York City, 1890–1930* (Chicago: University of Chicago Press, 1989).

Bolotin, Norman and Christine Laing. *The World's Columbian Exposition* (Chicago: The Preservation Press, 1992).

Borden, Henry, ed., *Robert Borden: His Memoirs* (Toronto: Macmillan and Co., 1938).

"Borden Memorial," [clipping, 1957], AGO Archives.

"Borden Statue Jury Denies Prize Promise," [clipping, n.d., ca. 1957], AGO Archives.

Borglum, Gutzon. "Imitation the Curse of American Art," *Brush and Pencil* 19.2 (Feb. 1907).

Bothwell, Robert, Ian Drummond and John English. *Canada 1900–1945* (Toronto: University of Toronto Press, 1987).

Bowdoin, W.G. "S. Borglum and his Work," *The Art Interchange* 46 & 47 (1901), pp. 2–4.

Bowen, Lisa Balfour. "From Sea to Sea: The AGO Celebrates Our Nation's Diversity with the *OH! Canada Project*," *Sunday Sun* (11 Feb. 1996).

Boyanoski, Christine. "AGO Tells Girls' Story with Care and Spirit," *Globe and Mail* (30 July 1987).

Boyanoski, Christine. *Loring and Wyle: Sculptors' Legacy* [catalogue] (Toronto: Art Gallery of Ontario, 1987).

Braz, Robert. *The False Traitor: Louis Riel in Canadian Culture* (Toronto: University of Toronto Press, 2003).

"Breaking Loose from the Rodin Spell," *Current Opinion* 62 (Mar. 1917), pp. 206–208.

Brehl, John. "Medallist's Art Like Short Poems," *Toronto Star* (4 Dec. 1978).

Bridle, Augustus. "Big Crowds, Seven Shows as Art Gallery Reopens," *Toronto Daily Star* [clipping, 6 Oct. 1928], AGO Archives.

Bridle, Augustus. "Canadian Art Tops Music, Plays, Poems," *Toronto Daily Star* (22 Mar. 1944).

Bridle, Augustus. "Eight Art Societies Join in 50th Show at Gallery," *Toronto Daily Star* (11 Mar. 1950).

Bridle, Augustus. "Music, Art, Drama," *Toronto Daily Star* (4 Dec. 1948).

Bridle, Augustus. "Sculptures at Gallery," *Toronto Daily Star* (4 Dec. 1948).

Bridle, Augustus. "Toscanini has 40 Shirts Precede him by Plane," *Toronto Daily Star* (3 June 1950).

Bridle, Augustus. "Work of 4 Women in Sculpture Show," *Toronto Daily Star* [clipping, 13 Mar. 1942], AGO Archives.

Bringhurst, Robert. "Casting of Bronze Statuary," *Brush and Pencil* (1906), pp. 237–39.

Brinton, Selwyn. "The Recent Sculpture of Daniel Chester French," *The International Studio* 59, pp. 17–24.

"British Critics Praise Highly Canada's Art Exhibits at Wembley," *Ottawa Journal* (16 July 1924).

"British Critics Say Canada Developing Own Virile Art," *Toronto Evening Star* (27 May 1924).

Brook, Pamela. "Sculpture in Retrospect," *The Varsity* [clipping, 28 Jan. 1966], AGO Archives.

Brooke, Janet M. *Henri Hébert, 1884–1950, Un Sculpteur Moderne* (Quebec: Museé du Québec, 2000).

Brooker, Bertram. "Sculpture's New Method," *Yearbook of the Arts in Canada 1928–29* (Toronto: Macmillan Co. Of Canada, Ltd., 1929), pp. 102–111.

Brooker, Bertram, ed. *Yearbook of the Arts in Canada, 1936* (Toronto: Macmillan Co. Of Canada, Ltd., 1936).

Broude, Norma and Mary D. Garrard, eds. *Reclaiming Female Agency: Feminist Art History after Postmodernism* (Berkeley: University of California Press, 2005).

Brown, Bill. "Stone Story: Sculpture Project Enhances Toronto's Business District," *Montreal Standard* (1948).

Brown, E.K., *On Canadian Poetry* (Toronto: Ryerson Press, 1943).

Brown, Eric. "Canada's Purchases at Toronto," *Christian Science Monitor* (15 April 1918) pp. 16–17.

Brown, F. Maud. *Breaking Barriers: Eric Brown and the National Gallery* (Ottawa: The Society for Art Publications, 1964).

Brown, F. Maud. "Eric Brown: His Contribution to the National Gallery," *Canadian Art* 4.1 (Nov. 1946), pp. 8–15; 32–33.

Brown, F. Maud. "I Remember Wembley," *Canadian Art* 21.4 (July/Aug. 1964), pp. 210–13.

Brown, Kingsley. "Sculptress Finds Banting, Borden Strong Personalities, 'Fighters,'" *Hamilton Spectator* [clipping, 10 Dec. 1955], AGO Archives.

Brown, Milton W. *The Story of the Armory Show* (New York: Abbeville Press, 1988).

Brown, Robert Craig. *Robert Laird Borden: A Biography*, vol. 1: 1854–1914 (Toronto: Macmillan of Canada, 1975).

Brown, Robert Craig & Ramsay Cook. *Canada 1896–1921: A Nation Transformed* (Toronto: McClelland & Stewart Ltd., 1974).

Bryant, Lorinda Munson. "Bela Lyon Pratt: An Appreciation," *The International Studio* 57, sup. 121 (1908), pp. cxxi–cxxv.

Buchanan, Donald. "A.Y. Jackson — The Development of Nationalism in Canadian Painting," *Geographical Magazine* (June 1946), pp. 284.

Buchanan, Donald. "Canadian Women in the Public Eye/Lilias Torrance Newton," *Saturday Night* 42.52 (12 Nov. 1927), pp. 35.

"Budding Canadian Artists Work Under Disadvantages Born of Lack of Confidence: Frances Loring," *Globe and Mail* (21 Feb. 1939).

Bullough, Vern and Bonnie. "Lesbianism in the 1920s and 1930s: A Newfound Study," *Signs: Journal of Women in Culture and Society* (Summer 1977), pp. 895–904.

Busby, Brian. *Character Parts: Who's Really Who in Canadian Literature* (Toronto: Alfred A. Knopf Canada, 2003).

"Business Proposals," *Toronto Telegram* (17 Sept. 1967).

"Business Proposals," *Toronto Telegram* (18 Sept. 1967).

Cahill, Holger. "Art Goes to the People in the United States," *Canadian Art* 1.5 (Feb./Mar. 1994) pp. 106–07.

Calder-Marshall, Arthur. *The Innocent Eye: The Life of Robert J. Flaherty* (New York: Harcourt, Brace & World, Inc., 1963).

Cameron, Dorothy. "Preface," *Sculpture '67: An Open-Air Exhibition of Canadian Sculpture Presented by the National Gallery of Canada as Part of its Centennial Program* (Ottawa: Queen's Printer, 1968).

Cameron, Elspeth. "Deck the Walls with Wyle and Loring," *Niagara Current* (Summer 2003), pp. 50–55.

"Can't Get Very Far Without Hard Work: Success Secret of Young Sculptress Who Modelled Cavell Memorial Tablet," *Toronto Star Weekly* [clipping, 27 Aug. 1921], AGO Archives, p. 14.

"Canada at War Shown in Pictures," *Daily Mail and Empire* (19 June 1919), p. 10.

"Canada Rightly Proud of Her Younger Artists," *Sunday World*, Toronto (31 August 1924).

"Canadian Academy to Show in Montreal," *Toronto Star* (13 Nov. 1920).

Canadian Art 7.1 (Spring 1950).

"Canadian Art at Wembley," *Daily Telegraph*, England (16 July 1924).

"Canadian Art Now Featured," *Globe* (5 March 1921).

"Canadian Girl Sculptors Do Unique Work," *Toronto Evening Star* [clipping, June 1917], AGO Archives.

Canadian National Exhibition, Catalogue 1918, (Toronto, 1918).

Canadian National Exhibition Fine Art Exhibition, Aug. 25–Sept 9, 1933, [catalogue] (Toronto, 1933).

Canadian National Exhibition Fine Art Exhibition, Aug. 23–Sept. 7, 1935, [catalogue] (Toronto, 1935).

"Canadian Paintings Win Commendation," *Globe* (14 June 1924).

"Canadian Panorama in Carvings for New Bank Building Here," *Globe and Mail* (16 Apr. 1947).

"Canadian Sculptor Frances Loring Dies," *Ottawa Journal* [clipping, 6 Feb. 1968], AGO Archives.

"Canadian Sculptors Achieve Distinction," *Globe and Mail* (3 Apr. 1932).

"Canadian Sculptors Plan Demonstration of Modelling of Head," *London Evening Free Press* (8 May 1942).

"Canadian Sculptors to the Fore," *Saturday Night* (6 Sept. 1924).

"Canadian Sculptors Show Outstanding Work," *Globe* (13 Apr. 1932).

"Canadian Sculptors Strike Sure Note," *Daily Mail and Empire* (8 Oct. 1928).

"Canadian Sculptress Plans Demonstration of Modeling of Head," *London Evening Free Press* (8 May 1942).

"Canadian Sculpture," *Windsor Daily Star*, (4 Apr. 1942).

"Canadian Sculpture (Frances Loring and Florence Wyle)," *Saturday Night* [clipping, n.d.], AGO Archives.

"Canadian Sculpture Makes its First Bow in the U.S.," *Saturday Night* (15 July 1939).

Canadian Section of Fine Arts, British Empire Exhibition (London: 1925), NGC Archives.

"Canadian War Art Exhibition," *Montreal Herald* (25 Sept. 1920), p. 3.

"Canadian War Memorial Show," *American Art News* (14 June 1919).

"Canadian Woman Sculptor Whose Work Shows Distinction," [clipping, ca. 1910–11], AGO Archives.

"Canadian Women Sculptors," *The Dalhousie Review* (Oct. 1949).

Careless, J.M.S. *Toronto to 1918: An Illustrated History* (Toronto: James Lorimer & Co., 1984).

Carr, Emily. *Hundreds & Thousands* (Toronto: Clarke, Irwin & Co. Ltd., 1966).

Carroll, Joy. "Interview," *Canadian Art* 21 (1964), pp. 236–38.

Carson, Fiona and Claire Pajaczkowska, eds. *Feminist Visual Culture* (New York: Routledge, 2001).

"Carving of Galt Statues Cost Three Months' Labor," *Star Weekly* (8 Nov 1930).

Castel, Jane E. *A Walking Tour to Toronto's Public Sculpture: Tour A, St. Clair and Yonge* (Toronto: June E. Castel, 1985), A-14.

Catalogue of the Joint Exhibition of the Royal Canadian Academy of Arts and the Ontario Society of Artists, Opening April the Fourth, 1918 (Toronto: The Art Museum of Toronto, 1918).

Catalogues of The School of the Art Institute of Chicago, 1903–1911.

Chadwick, Whitney. *Women, Art, and Society* (New York: Thames and Hudson, 1992).

Chandler, Clyde G. "Sculpture Exhibit in Humboldt Park," [typescript, 1911], 4 pp., AIC Archives.

Chapman, Christopher. "Frances Loring and Florence Wyle," *Telescope*, CBC film for TV, 30 minutes (May 1965).

Charlesworth, Hector. "Contemporary Canadian Sculpture," *Saturday Night* [clipping, 27 Oct. 1928], AGO Archives.

Charlesworth, Hector. "Reflections," *Saturday Night* (18 Sept. 1920).

Chenier, Nancy Miller. "Canadian Women and War: A Long Tradition," *The Oracle* (Ottawa: National Museums of Canada, 1984), pp. 1–8.

Cherry, Zena. "After a Fashion," *Globe and Mail* (27 May 1974), p. 12.

Cherry, Zena. "King Grooms for Action," *Globe and Mail* (24 Apr. 1973).

Cherry, Zena. "Parked Lion," *Globe and Mail* (5 Aug. 1972), p. 12.

Cherry, Zena. "The Girls," *Globe and Mail* (24 Apr. 1973).

Chevalier, Denys. *Maillol* (Lugano: Ufficipress, 1970).

"Chicago's Dream of Civic Beauty," *The Craftsman* (June 1905).

"Chicago's Newer Sculptured Park Memorials," *Park and Cemetery* 22 (Feb. 1913), pp. 290–91.

"Children That Will Never Grow Old: Illustrated by the Sculpture of Lillian Link," *The Craftsman* 30 (Sept. 1916), pp. 547–53.

Chicago Record Herald, 12 Oct. 1907, Art Institute Scrapbook, 23, microfilm, AIC Archives.

Chicago Tribune, 20 Oct. 1910, Art Institute Scrapbook 27, microfilm, AIC Archives.

Chisholm, Elspeth. "Interview with Frances Loring and Florence Wyle," *Profile*, CBC TV [interview notes and card index] (22 July 1956), AGO Archives.

Chisholm, Elspeth. "Interview with Frances Loring and Florence Wyle," *Telescope*, CBC Radio [interview notes and card index] (22 July 1956), AGO Archives.

Choate, R.H. "Canadian Sculptors Strike Sure Note," *Daily Mail and Empire* [clipping, 8 Oct. 1928], AGO Archives.

"Church, Now Studio, Gives Elbow Room to Two Industrious Sculptors," *Christian Science Monitor* (30 Jan. 1946).

Churchill, Allen. *The Improper Bohemians: A Recreation of Greenwich Village in its Heyday* (New York: E.P. Dutton & Co., 1959).

Cierpik, Anne Felicia. "History of The Art Institute of Chicago from its Incorporation on May 24, 1879 to the Death of Charles L. Hutchinson," M.A. Dissertation, History Dept., De Paul University, Chicago, 1957.

Clapp, Lucretia D. "The Quality of Women's Achievement," *The Craftsman* (1908).

Clark, C.S. *Of Toronto the Good: A Social Study* (Montreal: Toronto Publishing Co., 1898).

Clive, Katharine. "The Canadian Galatea Comes to Life: The Development of a National Movement in Art and Decoration," *Canadian Homes and Gardens* (Feb. 1931), pp. 17–19.

Cloutier, Albert. "Sylvia Daoust, Sculptor," *Canadian Art* 8.4 (1941), pp. 154–57.

Cloutier, Nicole. *Laliberté* (Montreal: Montreal Museum of Fine Arts, 1990).

Coburn, Frederick W. "How Art Importations are Handled," *Brush and Pencil* 13.1 (Oct. 1903), pp. 18–25.

Cohen, Leonard. *Beautiful Losers* (Toronto: McClelland & Stewart, 1966).

Colgate, William. *Canadian Art — Its Origin and Development* (Toronto: McGraw-Hill Ryerson, Ltd., 1943).

"Commemorating Great Canadian," [clipping, 1957], AGO Archives.

"Comstock's Fight for the Fig Leaf," *Brush and Pencil* 18.4 (Oct. 1906), pp. 167–72.

Conde, Valerie. "Canadian Sculptors," *Windsor Daily Star* (4 Apr. 1942).

Connor, Janis and Joel Rosenkranz. *Rediscoveries in American Sculpture: Studio Works, 1893–1939* (Austin: University of Texas Press, 1989).

"Contemporary Canadian Sculpture," *Saturday Night* (27 Oct. 1928).

Contemporary Canadian Sculpture, Sculptors' Society of Canada Exhibit — National Gallery of Canada, 1950, NGC Archives.

"Contemporary Canadian Sculpture Shows More Caution than Experiment," *Canadian Art* 7.3 (Spring 1950), pp. 116–17.

"Contemporary Classical Art Decorates a Bank Building," [clipping, c. 1948], AGO Archives.

"Contest Officials' Remarks 'Quite Unfair' Say Sculptors," [clipping, 12 January 1955], AGO Archives.

Coombe, Rosemary J. "The Properties of Culture and the Possession of Identity: Postcolonial Struggle and the Legal Imagination," *The Canadian Journal of Law and Jurisprudence* 6.2 (1994).

Cooper, A.B. "War Themes in Modern Art," *The Windsor Magazine* 41 (Jan. 1915), pp. 259–74.

Coughtry, Graham. "Our Men in Venice," *The Toronto Daily Star* (21 May 1960), p. 36.

Cousins, Daniel. "The Vogue of Empire: Imperial Spectacle and Modernity at the British Empire Exhibition, 1924," [typescript of lecture presented at Canadian Historical Association Annual Conference, 2006], NGC Archives.

Cousins, M.V. "100 Tons of Stone," *The Ryersonian* (31 Oct. 1973).

Crawford, Lenore. "Dr. Comfort Opens 2-Sculptor Show," *London Free Press* [clipping, 10 Nov. 1962], AGO Archives.

Crawford, Lenore. "Exhibit is Tribute to Two Women Sculptors," *Globe and Mail* (3 Nov. 1962). Reprinted in *Canadian Artists* (10 Nov. 1962).

Crawford, Lenore. "Fifty Years of Sculpture: Loring and Wyle at the London Public Library and Art Museum," *Canadian Art* 20.2 (Mar.–Apr. 1963), p. 79.

Crawley, Radford. *Canadian Landscape: An Intimate Portrait of Group of Seven Painter A. Y. Jackson* (1941), video, 18 min. (Montreal: National Film Board, 1994).

Crean, Susan. *The Laughing One: A Journey to Emily Carr* (Toronto: Harper Flamingo Canada, 2001).

"Creating the Dinner Service: Mary Dignam, Founding President, WAAC," *Civili-*

zation.ca, created 1999, updated 2001, 23 Sept. 2007 (access), http://www.civilization.ca/hist/cadeau/casero3e.html

Cunningham, John J., ed. *José de Creeft*, American Sculptors Series (Georgia: University of Georgia Press, 1950).

"Curator Seeks Works for Exhibit," *Globe and Mail* (26 Oct. 1985).

Curcin, M., ed. *Ivan Meštrović: A Monograph* (London: Williams and Norgate, 1919).

Dale, William S.A. "Sculpture," *The Arts in Canada: A Stocktaking at Mid-Century*, ed. Malcom Ross (Toronto: MacMillan Co. of Canada Ltd., 1958), p. 597.

Dallin, Cyrus Edwin. "American Sculpture: Its Present Aspects and Tendencies," *Brush and Pencil* 2.6 (March 1903), pp. 416–28.

"Dancing on Green at Lyceum Lawns," *Globe and Mail* [clipping, 2 June 1939], AGO Archives.

Dancock, John L. *The Sculpture of Auguste Rodin* (Philadelphia: Philadelphia Museum of Art, 1976).

"Daring Canadian Girl in an Indian Village, *Toronto Star* [clipping, 10 Sept. 1927], AGO Archives.

Dault, Gary Michael. "This City: Artists-in-Residence," *Toronto Life* (Aug. 1985), p. 13.

Davidson, Jo. *Between Sittings: An Informal Autobiography* (New York: The Dial Press, 1951).

Davidson, Jo. "The Extremists: An Interview," *Arts and Decoration* (Mar. 1913), pp. 169–70.

Davies, Blodwen. "Canadian Women of Brush and Chisel," *The Chatelaine* 3.2 (June 1930), pp. 42–43.

Davies, Robertson. *The Cunning Man* (Toronto: McClelland & Stewart, 1994).

Davis, Richard. *Painters and Sculptors of Modern America*, ed. Monroe Wheeler (New York: Thomas Y. Crowell Co., 1942).

Dawson, Michael. *The Mountie: From Dime Novel to Disney* (Toronto: Between the Lines, 1998).

de Pédery Hunt, Dora. "The Sculptors' Lot: The Humiliating Poverty is Gone," *Globe and Mail* (1 Aug. 1970).

de Visser, John. *Toronto*, intro. and notes William Toye (Toronto: Oxford University Press, 1975).

"Dean of the Canadian Sculptors," *The Canadian Scene* 607 (30 Nov. 1962), p. 30.

"Decorative and Memorial Public Fountains," *Park and Cemetery* 25. 6 (June 1908), Lincoln Ill., p. 251.

"Dedication of War Memorial Feature at Augusta Monday," *Portland Sunday Telegram and Sunday Press Herald* [clipping, 10 Nov. 1929], AGO Archives.

Dell, Floyd. *Love in Greenwich Village* (New York: George H. Doran Co., 1926).

Demers, Edgard. "Le rideau se leve," *Ottawa Le Droit* (30 mai 1959).

Dempsey, Lotta. "Person to Person," *Globe and Mail* (7 Oct. 1952).

Dempsey, Lotta. "She's 'mother' to a Colony of Artists," *Toronto Star* [clipping, 12 July 1969], AGO Archives.

Denby, William and William Kilbourn. *Toronto Observed: its Architects, Patrons & History* (Toronto: Oxford University Press, 1986).

"Dennis Burton: Refinement, Often Delight," *Globe and Mail* [clipping, 4 May 1957), AGO Archives.

"Designer of the Centennial Monument is Dead at Chicago" *Chicago, Illinois Examiner* [clipping, 31 Mar. 1916], AIC Archives.

Devrée, Charlotte. *José de Creeft* (The American Federation of the Arts, 1960).

"Dies at 80: Sculptor Frances Loring did Stone Lion on QEW," *Toronto Star* [clipping, 6 Feb. 1968], AGO Archives.

Dillinger, G. "A Sculptor's Dream of Chicago Beautiful," *The Fine Art Journal* 29 (1905), p. 669.

"Distinguished Woman Sculptor Here," *Edmonton Journal* [clipping, 16 Oct. 1952], AGO Archives.

Djwa, Sandra. "*The Canadian Forum*: Literary Catalyst," *Studies in Canadian Literature* 1.1 (1976), http://www.lib.unb.ca/Texts/SCL/bin/get.cgi?directory=vol1-1/&filename=djwa.htm

Dobson, Austin. "The Paradox of Time," [clipping, n.d], AIC Archives.

"Donors and Sculptor of War Memorial Guests at Rotary," *Augusta Portland Star* [clipping, 12 Nov. 1929], AGO Archives.

Downes, William Howe. *The International Studio* 38.149 (July 1909), pp. 3–10.

"Dr. Frances Loring Urges Public Support of Art," *Ottawa Journal* (10 Nov. 1959).

"Dreams in Stone," *Toronto Star Weekly* (14 May 1938).

Drury, John. "Lorado Taft 76; Devotes the Entire Day to His Art," *Chicago Illinois Tribune* [clipping, 28 Apr. 1936], AIC Archives.

Du Bois, Guy Pène. "Art By the Way," *The International Studio* 76 (Nov. 1922), pp. 177–81.

Du Bois, Guy Pène. "Mrs. Whitney's Journey in Art," *The International Studio* 76 (Jan. 1923), pp. 351–54.

Dundas, Verdé V. "The Modelling Class at the Art Institute," *Brush and Pencil* 2.4 (July 1898), pp. 167–76.

Dunington-Grubb, H.B. "Sculpture as Garden Decoration," *Canadian Homes and Gardens* (Mar. 1927).

Dunington-Grubb, H.B. "The Suburban Garden," *The Journal of the Royal Architectural Institute of Canada* (July 1937).

Duval, Paul. "A Monument to Don," *Telegram* (30 Nov. 1963).

Duval, Paul. "Artists Portray Fellow-Artists in O.S.A. Show," *Saturday Night* (8 Apr. 1944), p. 4.

Duval, Paul. "Smaller Works of Sculpture Belong in the Home," *Saturday Night* (27 Apr. 1946).

Dwight, Edward H. "The Armory Show — New York 1913," *Canadian Art* 20.2 (Mar.–Apr. 1963), pp. 118–19.

Dyonnet, Edmond. "French-Canadian Painting and Sculpture," *The Yearbook of Canadian Art*, compiled by The Arts & Letters Club of Toronto (Toronto: J.M. Dent and Sons Ltd., 1913).

"Eaton's Daily Store News," *Globe and Mail* [clipping, 20 Dec. 1929], AGO Archives.

Edgerton, Giles. "Is There a Sex Distinction in Art? The Attitude of the Critic Toward Women's Exhibits," *The Craftsman* 12.2 (June 1908), pp. 239–51.

Edgerton, Giles. "The Quality of Woman's Art Achievement: A Young Austrian Sculptor Who Possesses Both Masculine and Feminine Perception," *The Craftsman* 17.1 (Dec. 1908), pp. 292–300.

E.L., "Sculpture and Poetry," *Winnipeg Free Press* [clipping, 5 Nov. 1959], AGO Archives.

Elsen, Albert E. *The Partial Figure in Modern Sculpture: from Rodin to 1969* (Baltimore: The Baltimore Museum of Art, 1969).

"Emily Carr," biography, 7 July 2005 (access), http://emily-carr.biography.ms/

"Entrance Detail, St. Michael's Hospital, Toronto W.L. Somerville, Architect," *The Journal of the Royal Architectural Institute of Canada* (Oct. 1938).

"Entries So Bad Prizes Cancelled, But Sculptor 'May' Get $600," *Montreal Gazette* [clipping, 4 Jan. 1955], AGO Archives.

"Erecting Monument to Sir Robert Borden," [clipping, 1957], AGO Archives.

Exhibition of Contemporary British Painting, National Gallery of Canada, 1935, Catalogue (Ottawa: NGC, 1935).

"Exhibition Shows Definite Trends in Canadian Arts," *Globe* (3 Dec. 1928).

Exposition d'Art Canadien, Musée du Jeu de Paume, Paris, 10 avril–10 mai, 1927, Catalogue, NGC Archives.

Faderman, Lillian. *Odd Girls and Twilight Lovers: A History of Lesbian Life in Twentieth-Century America* (New York: Columbia University Press, 1991).

Faderman, Lillian. *Romantic Friendship and Love Between Women from the Renaissance to the Present* (New York: Quill William Morrow, 1981).

Faderman, Lillian. *Surpassing the Love of Men* (New York: Quill William Morrow, 1981).

Fairley, Barker. "At the Art Gallery," *The Rebel* 4.3 (Dec. 1919), pp. 123–28.

Fairley, Barker. "Canadian War Pictures," *The Canadian Magazine* 54.1 (Nov. 1919), pp. 2–11.

Fairley, Barker. "What is Wrong with Canadian Art," *Canadian Art* (Autumn 1948).

"False Impression of Poor Lo.," *Saturday Night* (6 Dec. 1924).

"Famed Canadian Sculptress at Brantford Art League," *Brantford Expositor* (9 Mar. 1954), p. 11.

"Famed Sculptress Dies at 80," *Toronto Telegram* (6 Feb. 1968).

"Famous Canadian Artists Lecture in School Auditorium," *Grande Prairie Herald Tribune* [clipping, 13 Nov. 1952], AGO Archives.

Fanton, Mary Annable. "Clio Hinton Bracken, Woman Sculptor and Symbolist of the New Art," *The Craftsman* 8 (July 1905), pp. 472–81.

Farnsworth, P.T. "The Artists' Colony in Macdougal Alley, Where Some of Our Best-known American Painters and Sculptors Live and Work," *The Craftsman* 11.1 (Oct. 1906), pp. 57–69.

Farr, Dorothy. *Lilias Torrance Newton* (Kingston: Agnes Etherington Art Centre, 1981).

Farr, Dorothy and Natalie Luckyj. *From Women's Eyes: Women Painters in Canada* (Kingston: Agnes Etherington Art Centre, 1975).

Farr, Susan. *Sculpture by Sophia Hungerford* (Guelph, ON: Macdonald Stewart Art Centre, 1989).

"Favour Breaking of Rule," *Toronto Telegram* [clipping, 28 May 1930], AGO Archives.

Ferrari, Pepita and Erna Buffie. *By Woman's Hand: A Tribute to Three Women Artists whose Lives and Works were Almost Forgotten*, video, 57 min. (Montreal: National Film Board, 1994).

"Festival Also the Arcade of Sculpture and Paintings," *Globe and Mail* (12 June 1954).

Fetherling, Douglas, ed. *Documents in Canadian Art* (Peterborough: Broadview Press Ltd., 1987).

"Figures by Toronto Sculptors Blend Canadian Themes in Bank Buildings," *Globe and Mail* (3 Sept. 1948).

"Film Challenges Gay-Bashers," *Toronto Star* (27 Apr. 1989), p. C6.

"Fine Arts from Canada," *The Canadian Magazine* 43.3 (July 1924).

"Fine Sculptural Work Executed in Toronto Indicates Canadian Artists Finding Expression in Plastic Art," [clipping, 10 May 1930], AGO Archives.

"Fire-eater, Sculptors and Midgets — the C.N.E. has Them All," *Toronto Daily Star* (25 Aug. 1938).

Fisher, William Murrell. "Sculpture at the Exhibition," (ca. Feb. 1913), p. 168.

Fleming, Marie. "Sculpture: Florence Wyle & Frances Loring," *The Canadian Collector* 1.1 (Apr. 1966).

"Florence Wyle: Human Anatomy Classes Turned her from Medicine to Sculpture," *Globe and Mail* (15 Jan. 1968), p. 15.

"Florence Wyle, New RCA, Finds Abandoned Church is Ideal Studio," *Montreal Gazette* (28 Nov. 1938).

"Florence Wyle: One of Canada's Great Sculptors Dies," *Toronto Telegram* [clipping, 15 Jan. 1968], AGO Archives.

"Florence Wyle — Sculptor," *The Modern Instructor* (June 1958).

Fosdick, J.W. "Émile Antoine Bourdelle: A Modern French Sculptor Who has Been Called a Spiritual Realist," *The Craftsman* 15.2 (Nov. 1908), pp. 159–66.

"Fountain Figure," *Ottawa Citizen* (17 June 1961).

"Frances Loring: A Constant Contributor to Sculpture," *Globe and Mail* [clipping, 6 Feb. 1968], AGO Archives.

"Frances Loring a Gagné le Concours," *Le Droit* (20 Jan. 1955).

"Frances Loring and Her Dreams," *The CBC Times* (22–28 July 1956).

"Frances Loring Back from Trip to Italy: Spent three months there Executing War Memorial for Law Society," *Toronto Star* (28 Aug. 1928).

"Frances Loring: Canada's Grand Dame of Sculpture," *Kitchener-Waterloo Record* [clipping, 16 May 1959], AGO Archives.

"Frances Loring," *Canadian Cancer Society*, Newsletter [clipping, 1960], AGO Archives.

"Frances Loring," *Le Progres du Saguenay-Chicoutimi* (1 juin 1959).

"Frances Loring, Sculptor, Gives Interesting Talk on Art," *Ottawa Evening Journal* [clipping, 8 Feb. 1950], AGO Archives.

"Frances Loring to do Sir Robert Borden Monument," [clipping, c. 1954], AGO Archives.

"Frances Norma Loring and Notable Examples of her Art in Bronze and Stone," *Portland Sunday Telegram and Sunday Press Herald* (10 Nov. 1929).

Francis, Daniel. *The Imaginary Indian* (Vancouver: Arsenal Pulp Press, 1993).

"Francis [sic] Loring, 80, Famed Sculptress Dies," [clipping, 6 Feb. 1968], AGO Archives.

"Francis [sic] Loring/Florence Wyle," *Lesbian and Gay Heritage of Toronto* (Toronto: Canadian Gay Archives, 1982), p. 3.

"Freak Pictures at Wembley," *Saturday Night* (13 Sept. 1924).

Friedman, B.H. *Gertrude Vanderbilt Whitney: A Biography* (New York: Doubleday & Co., 1978).

Fromer, Ann. "At Home with Esther Williams," *Mayfair* 33.8 (Aug. 1959).

Fulford, Robert. "A Generation Gap Too Far to Bridge," *Toronto Star* (12 Sept. 1987), p. M6.

Fulford, Robert. *An Introduction to the Arts in Canada* (Citizenship Branch, Dept. of the Secretary of State of Canada) (Toronto: Copp Clark Publishing, 1977).

Fulford, Robert. "Emma Goldman saw Toronto Harshly," *Toronto Star Weekly* (19 Feb. 1983), p F5.

"Fund for Sculptors Who Helped Others," *Globe and Mail* (25 Sept. 1963).

Gadsby, H.F. "The Hot Mush School," *Toronto Evening Star* [clipping, 12 Dec. 1913], AGO Archives.

"Gave Demonstration: Famed Canadian Sculptress at Brantford Art League," *Brantford Expositor* (9 Mar. 1954).

Genauer, Emily. "The Chicago Art Story," *The Theatre Arts Magazine* (July 1951).

General Conditions for the Guidance of Architects, Artists, Sculptors in Preparing Competitive Designs for the Proposed National Commemorative War Monument for the Dominion of Canada in Ottawa (Ottawa, 12 Feb. 1925), File 9238-1-A. RG 11 Vol. 4004. LAC.

Gibson, Dan, ed. *Fifty Years of Photography by Ashley & Crippen* (Toronto: Ashley & Crippen 1965).

Gillmore, Roger, ed. *Over a Century: A History of the School of the Art Institute of Chicago 1866–1981* (Chicago: The School of the Art Institute of Chicago, 1982).

"Girl Depicts Dreams in Marble and Bronze; Gotham Sculptor Enters the Spokane Contest," *Denver Colorado News* [clipping, 22 Aug. 1911], AGO Archives..

"'Girls were Conservative — and Outrageous," *Toronto Star* (24 July 1987), p. E3.

Globe and Mail [clipping, 7 Aug. 1926], AGO Archives.

Globe and Mail [clipping, 11 Aug. 1926], AGO Archives.

Globe and Mail [clipping, 6 Feb. 1939], AGO Archives.

Globe and Mail (27 Jan. 1958), p. 19.

"Goalie Statue Merits Display," *Toronto Star* (27 May 1983), p. A22.

Goldscheider, Ludwig. *Rodin Sculptures*, intro. Sommerville Story (London: Phaidon Press, 1966).

"Good Progress Being Made on War Memorial," [clipping, c. 1925], AGO Archives.

Gordon, Alan. *Making Public Pasts: The Contested Terrain of Montreal's Public Memories, 1891–1930* (Montreal & Kingston: McGill-Queen's University Press, 2001).

Gosnell, R.E. "Canada's Memorial Hall," *Saturday Night* (1 Dec. 1928), p. 26.

Graham, Mayo. "Introduction," *Another Dimension* (Ottawa: The National Gallery of Canada, 1977).

Grand, Raquel. "Out of History's Closet: Canada's First Gays — Frances Loring & Florence Wyle, 'The Girls,'" *Gaiety* 1.5 (Winter 2004/2005), p. 43.

"'Grandma': Frances Loring," *Toronto Telegram* [clipping, 25 Apr. 1959], AGO Archives.

Greer, H.H. "The Work of Karl Bitter, Sculptor," *Brush and Pencil* 13.5 (Feb. 1904), pp. 466–78.

Grier, E. Wyly. "Canadian Art: A Resumé," *The Yearbook of Canadian Art*, complied by the Arts & Letters Club of Toronto (Toronto: J.M. Dent and Sons Ltd., 1913).

Grier, E. Wyly. "Conclusion," *Yearbook of Canadian Art*, compiled by the Arts & Letters Club of Toronto (Toronto: J.M. Dent and Sons Ltd., 1913).

Groome, L.J. "Florence Wyle, Sculptor," *The Modern Instructor*, Canadian Artist Series [n.d.], AGO Archives.

Gross, Chaim. *Painters and Sculptors of Modern America*, ed. Monroe Wheeler (New York: Thomas Y. Crowell Co., 1942).

Grosse, Ernest. *The Beginnings of Art* (New York and London: D. Appleton & Co., 1914).

Groves, Naomi Jackson. *A.Y.'s Canada* (Toronto: Clarke Irwin & Co. Ltd., 1968).

Gualtieri, Francesco M. "Frances Loring: Artisti Canadesi," *L'Interpetre* [clipping, n.d.], AGO Archives.

Hale, Barry. Exhibition Catalogue. *Toronto Painting: 1953–1965* (Ottawa: National Gallery of Canada, 1972).

Hale, Katherine. "Nymphs and Fauns as Magic Fountains in Canadian Gardens," *Toronto Star Weekly* (1 Aug. 1920).

Hale, William Harlan. *The World of Rodin 1840–1917* (New York: Time-Life Books, 1969).

"Half a Team of Sculptors," *Globe and Mail* [clipping, 28 Jan. 1966], AGO Archives.

Hall, Valerie. "Outlandish Art," *Daily Mercury* (Guelph) (2 June 1994).

Hambleton, Josephine. "Canadian Artists," *Kingston Whig-Standard* (20 Dec. 1947).

Hambleton, Josephine. "Canadian Women Sculptors," *The Dalhousie Review* 29.3 (Oct. 1949), pp. 327–31.

Hambleton, Josephine. "The Memorial Chamber Angel," *Ottawa Citizen* (11 Nov. 1947).

Hammond, M.O. *Painting and Sculpture in Canada* (Toronto: Ryerson Press, 1930).

Hanna, Dierdre. "Loring and Wyle's Legacy," *Now: Toronto's Weekly News and Entertainment Guide* 6 (9–15 July 1987), p. 42.

Harding, Karen Stoskopf. *Sculptors' Society of Canada: 65th Anniversary* (Oakville, ON: Sculptors' Society of Canada & Mosaic Press, 1993).

"Hard to Begin Sculpting Frances Loring Admits," *Toronto Daily Star* (21 Feb. 1939).

Hare, Irene B. "Close-ups of Toronto's Women Artists, No. 1: Miss Frances Loring and Miss Florence Wyle," *The Sunday World* [clipping, 25 May 1924], AGO Archives.

"Harmony in Art Is Emphasized by Miss Loring," *Globe* (15 Feb 1934).

Harper, J. Russell. *Painting in Canada: A History*, 2nd ed. (Toronto: University of Toronto Press, 1977).

Harrington, Lyn. "Church, Now a Studio, Gives Elbow Room to Two Industrious Sculptors" *The Christian Science Monitor* [clipping, 30 Jan. 1946], AGO Archives.

Harrington, Lyn. "Loring and Wyle Canadian Sculpture Team," *Saturday Night* (8 April 1944).

Harrington, Lyn. "Sculptures Form Fine Exhibition," *London Free Press* (13 Jan. 1953).

Harrington, Lyn. "Unique Church-Studio is Home and Workshop for Loring and Wyle," *Saturday Night* 60.11 (18 Nov. 1944), pp. 4–5.

Harrington, Lyn and Richard Harrington. "Living With Sculpture," *Montreal Family Herald and Weekly Star* (18 June 1953), pp. 41–43.

Harris, Lawren S. "The Canadian Art Club," *The Yearbook of Canadian Art*, compiled by the Arts & Letters Club of Toronto (Toronto: J.M. Dent & Sons Ltd., 1913).

Hasbury, Susan. *The Sculpture of Elizabeth Wyn Wood*, M.A. Thesis, Carleton University, Ottawa, 1982.

Haswell, Ernest Bruce. "The Sixteenth Annual Exhibition of the Society of Western Artists," *The International Studio* 57.186 (Aug. 1912).

"Have Proved Equally Successful with Paintings and Sculpture," *Star Weekly* [clipping, 1930], AGO Archives.

Hawthorne, Nathaniel. *The French and Italian Notebooks*, ed. Thomas Woodson, 14, The Centenary Edition of the Works of Nathaniel Hawthorne (Columbus: Ohio State University Press, 1980).

Hayward, Lawrence. *Biographies of Canadian Sculptors* (Walter Allward, Marc-Aurèle de Foy Suzor-Côté, Henri Hébert, Frances Loring, Otto Emanuel Hahn, Louis Hébert, Jacobine Jones), 23 Sept. 2007 (access), http://www.lhaywardcollection.com

"He Writes and Golfs at 90," [clipping, n.d.], AGO Archives.

"Heads Trophy List," *Ottawa Citizen* (18 Jan. 1958).

Hébert, Henri. "Sculptor Gives Discourse on Art," *Montreal Gazette* [clipping, 17 Feb. 1932], AGO Archives.

Heller, Jules and Nancy G. Heller, eds. *North American Women Artists of the Twentieth Century: A Biographical Dictionary* (New York: Garland Publishing, Inc., 1995).

Henson, Leigh. "The Logan County Courtouse, Past and Present," *Mr. Lincoln, Route 66, and Other Highlights of Lincoln, Illinois*, 25 Sept. 2007 (access), http://www.geocities.com/findinglincolnillinois/logancocourthousehistoricarea.html

"Hero of Moose River Mine Dr. David E. Robertson Dies," [clipping, 19 Feb. 1944), AGO Archives.

Hewlett, Bruce. "Put Hockey Player, not Henry Moore, in City Hall Square," letter to the editor, *Toronto Daily Star* [clipping, 9 Sept. 1966], AGO Archives.

Hicks, Wesley. "Skunks are Pretty," *Toronto Telegram* [clipping, 3 Feb. 1950], AGO Archives.

Hill, Charles. *Canadian Painting in the Thirties* (Ottawa: The National Gallery, 1975).

Hill, Charles. *The Group of Seven: Art for a Nation*, National Gallery of Canada, (Toronto: McClelland & Stewart, 1995).

Hill, Charles C. *For the Collection of Later Canadian Art* (Ottawa: The National Gallery of Canada, 10 August 1993).

Hill, Mary Brawley. *The Woman Sculptor: Malvina Hoffman and her Contemporaries* (New York: Berry-Hill Galleries, Inc., 1984).

"Historical Plaque to Commemorate Loring-Wyle Studio," News Release, Ontario Heritage Foundation, (22 Oct. 1976), 4 pp., AGO Archives.

Hoffman, Malvina. *Heads and Tales* (New York: Garden City Publishing Co., Inc., 1943).

Hoffman, Malvina. *Sculpture Inside and Out* (New York: Bonanza Books, 1939).

Hoffman, Malvina. *Yesterday is Tomorrow: A Personal History* (New York: Crown Publishers, Inc., 1965).

"Hon. H. S. Beland Officially Opens Exhibit War Memorials," *Ottawa Citizen* [clipping, 6 Jan. 1923], AGO Archives.

"Honor Tire Firm Founder," *Toronto Daily Star* (28 April 1959).

"Honorary Doctorates of Law," *Globe and Mail* (23 Apr. 1955).

"Honorary LL.D," *Globe and Mail* (3 Aug. 1956).

"Honoring a Great Canadian," [clipping, 1957], AGO Archives.

Hopkins, Jeanne. "Looking Back: Deer Park's Christ Church was Established by a Group of Neighbours," *Post Newspapers* (June 1993), p. 30.

Hopkins, Jeanne. "Road Built for Depression Relief," *Toronto Star* (9 May 1991).

Hopkins, Sis. "Song of the 1907 Initiates," in *'Art Throbs: An Annual by the Normal Students of The Art Institute of Chicago* (1908–1909).

Horne, Cleeve. "Bank of Montreal Building, Toronto ... and Sculpture," *The Journal of the Royal Architectural Institute of Canada* 26.11 (Nov. 1949).

House of Commons Debates, Official Report, 8 January 1957.

Housser, F.B. *A Canadian Art Movement: The Story of the Group of Seven* (Toronto: The Macmillan Co. of Canada, Ltd., 1926).

Hubbard, R.H. ed. *The Development of Canadian Art* (Ottawa: The National Gallery of Canada, 1964).

Hubbard, R.H. ed. *The National Gallery of Canada: Catalogue of Paintings and Sculpture*, vol. 1: Older Schools (Toronto: University of Toronto Press, 1961).

Hubbard, R.H. ed. *The National Gallery of Canada: Catalogue of Paintings and Sculpture*, vol. 2: Modern European Schools (Toronto: University of Toronto Press, 1959).

Hubbard, R.H. ed. *The National Gallery of Canada: Catalogue of Paintings and Sculpture*, vol. 3: Canadian School (Ottawa: The National Gallery of Canada, 1960).

Hubbard, R.H. and J.R. Ostiguy. *Three Hundred Years of Canadian Art* (Ottawa: The National Gallery of Canada/ Queen's Printer, 1967).

Huebner, Jeff. "Can This Patient Be Saved," *Chicago Reader* (6 Dec. 2002), pp. 1, 30–33.

Hughes, Talbot. *Dress Design: An Account of Costumes for Artists & Dressmakers* (London: Sir Isaac Pitman & Sons, Ltd., 1920).

Hume, Christopher. "A Monument to the Girls," *Toronto Star* (24 July 1987).

Huneault, Kristina. "Heroes of a Different Sort: Gender and Patriotism in the War Workers of Frances Loring and Florence Wyle," *The Journal of Canadian Art History* 15.2 (1993), pp. 26–45.

Hunter, Louis V. "Her Studio in Small Unused Toronto Church," *Timmins Press* (26 Nov. 1938).

Hunter, Louis V. "New Woman Academician has her Studio in an Abandoned Church," *Ottawa Evening Citizen* [clipping, 24 Nov. 1938], AGO Archives.

Hurder, Steven. "Frank Lloyd Wright in Oak Park, Illinois (1899–1909)," *Oak Park Tourist*, updated Oct. 2003, 23 Sept. 2007 (access), http://www.oprf.com/flw/

Illustrated Catalogue: Seventy-Second Annual Exhibition — The Ontario Society of Artists (Toronto: The Art Gallery of Ontario, March 18–April 9, 1944).

"In Memory of Law Society Members Who Lost Their Lives," *Globe* (22 Oct. 1928).

"In Society," *Saturday Night* (23 Apr. 1923).

"In the Studios of Toronto Artists," *Toronto Daily Star* [clipping, 8 June 1912], AGO Archives.

"Invitation to Memorial Service for Florence Wyle," AGO Archives.

"Invocation," *Charlottetown Patriot* (2 March 1959).

Isaak, Jo Anna. *Feminism and Contemporary Art: the Revolutionary Power of Women's Laughter* (London and New York: Routledge, 1996).

Ivan Meštrović: A Monograph (London: Williams & Norgate, 1919).

"Ivan Meštrović — The Greatest Sculptor Since the Renaissance," *Tesla Memorial Society of New York*, 23 Sept. 2007 (access), http://www. teslasociety.com/ivan.htm

Jackson, A.Y. *A Painter's Country: The Autobiography of A.Y. Jackson* (Toronto: Clarke, Irwin & Co., Ltd., 1958).

Jackson, A.Y. *Banting as an Artist* (Toronto: Ryerson Press, 1943).

"Jackson, Loring to Speak in North," *Lethbridge Herald* (22 Oct. 1952).

James, Philip, ed. *Henry Moore on Sculpture* (London: Macdonald, 1966).

Janvier, T. "Greenwich Village," *Harper's Magazine* 87 (1893).

Jarvis, Alan. *"Faces of Canada Exhibit a Modest Social History,"* *Canadian Art* 21.5 (Sept./Oct. 1964).

Jarvis, Alan. *Frances Loring-Florence Wyle* [introduction to catalogue] (Toronto: Pollock Gallery, 1968).

Jarvis, Alan, ed. "Sculpture in Canada," *Canadian Art* 19.80 (Jul.–Aug. 1962).

J.C. "Chronique d'Art: La Société des Sculpteurs du Canada," *La Revue Populaire* (June 1929).

J.C. "La Société des Sculptures du Canada," *La Revue Populaire* (July 1929), p. 9.

"John Cage," *Wikipedia*, http://en.wikipedia.ord/wiki/John_Cage

John Lyman (Montreal: Montreal Museum of Fine Arts), [clipping, 1963], AGO Archives.

Jones, Donald. "Loring-Wyle Memorial Park Honors Odd-Couple Sculptors," *Toronto Star* (18 June 1983), p. F10.

Jones, Donald. "'Lost' Treasures of The Group of Seven," *Toronto Star* (4 Dec. 1993).

Jones, Donald. "The Story of the Queen, the Lion and the Old Church Schoolhouse," *Toronto Star* [clipping, 30 June 1979], AGO Archives.

Jones, Donald. "Walter Allward's Great Work is Monument to Canadian Dead," *Toronto Star* [clipping, n.d.], AGO Archives.

Joynes, Agnes. "Among Canadian Sculptors: Florence Wyle, A.R.C.A.," [clipping, 27 Nov. 1932], AGO Archives.

Joynes, Agnes. "Loring the Sculptor," *Saturday Night* 53.60 (15 Oct. 1938), p. 2.

Joynes, Agnes. "Sculpture in Canada," *Saturday Night* (1920).

Joynes, Agnes. "The Sculptor at Work," *The Challenge* (8 Nov. 1936).

Kerr, Estelle M. "Peace and Victory to Guard Memory of Galt's War Dead," *Toronto Star Weekly* [clipping, Oct. ca. 1930].

Kerr, Estelle M. "The Etcher's Point of View," *Canadian Magazine* (Dec 1916).

Kerr, Estelle M. "Women Sculptors of Canada," *Women's Saturday Night* [clipping, 20 June 1914], AGO Archives.

Kilbourn, Elizabeth. "Painter-Sculptors," *Canadian Art* 19 (1962), pp. 272–75.

Kilbourn, William, ed. *The Toronto Book: An Anthology of Writings Past and Present* (Toronto: Macmillan of Canada, 1976).

Kilbourn, William. *Toronto in Words & Pictures* (Toronto: McClelland & Stewart, 1997).

Kitchener-Waterloo Record [clipping, 16 May 1957], AGO Archives.

Kritzwiser, Kay. "A Constant Contributor to Sculpture," *Globe and Mail* (2 June 1969).

Kritzwiser, Kay. "Different Labour of Love for Sculptor," *Globe and Mail* (21 July 1973), p. 24.

Kritzwiser, Kay. "Hands That Mold Beauty: In a Former Church, Sculptors Wyle and Loring Create Ageless Art," *Globe Magazine* (7 Apr. 1962), pp. 9–11, 14, 16–17.

Kritzwiser, Kay. "Homage to Hands in Slender Handset Book," *Globe and Mail* (7 Apr. 1976).

Kritzwiser, Kay. "Sculpture Goes Back to Bronze," *Globe and Mail* (29 Sept. 1970).

Kritzwiser, Kay. "Seventies Art May Be Pure Concept," *Globe and Mail* (3 Jan. 1970).

Kritzwiser, Kay. "Sold: $12,000 Worth of Wyle and Loring," *Globe and Mail* (29 Jan. 1966).

Kritzwiser, Kay. "The Girls Show to Foster Young Talent," *Globe and Mail* (2 June 1969), p. 15.

Kritzwiser, Kay. "The 'Terrible Beauty' of Women in Wartime," *Globe and Mail* [clipping, 21 Nov. 1964], AGO Archives.

Kritzwiser, Kay. "Valedictory in Studio-Church," *Globe and Mail* [clipping, 2 Feb. 1968], AGO Archives.

La Société des Sculpteurs du Canada/The Sculptors' Society of Canada, Catalogue 1951 (Quebec: Musée de la Province Québec, 1951).

Laliberté, Alfred. "Existe-t-il au Canada français une sculpture d'interpretation spécifiquement canadienne-français?" *Culture* (June 1942), pp. 328–30.

Lampert, Catherine. *Rodin: Sculpture and Drawings* (New Haven: Yale University Press/The Arts Council of Great Britain, 1986).

Lankevich, George J. and Howard B. Furer. *A Brief History of New York City* (New York: National University Publications, 1984).

"Law Society Memorial," *Toronto Evening Star* (7 Nov. 1928).

Lawrence, A.W. *Greek and Roman Sculpture* (London: Jonathan Cape, 1972).

"Lawrence Hayward," http://collections.ic.gc.ca/sculpture/text/hay/html

L.C., "Sculptures Form Fine Exhibition," *London Free Press* (13 Jan. 1953), p. 26.

Leacock, Stephen. "The Woman Question" (1915), *The Social Criticism of Stephen Leacock*, ed. Alan Bowker (Toronto: University of Toronto Press, 1973), pp. 51–60.

"Leading Sculptors to design Drama Festival Trophies," *Ottawa Journal* (15 Jan. 1953).

LeBourdais, D.M. "Hahn and Wife, Sculptors," *MacLean's* (1 Nov. 1945), pp. 19–20.

"Lecture Given by Sculptress," *London Evening Free Press* [clipping, 11 May 1942], AGO Archives.

Lemon, James. *Toronto Since 1918: An Illustrated History* (Toronto: James Lorimer & Co. and National Museum of Man, 1985).

Lewis, John R. "Why Would a Woman Want to be a Sculptor?" *Star Weekly Magazine* (2 Jan. 1960), pp. 19, 37.

"Link Between Business, Art Seen by Premier as Exhibition Opened," *Globe and Mail* (28 Nov. 1956), p. 5.

Linton, Marilyn. "AGO Celebrates the 'Odd Couple,'" *Leaside Town Crier* (Aug. 1987).

Lisburn, Henry. "The Art of Ivan Meštrović," *Saturday Night* 42.24 (30 Apr. 1927), p. 28.

"List of Fund Contributors," (1962), AGO Archives.

"Literature, Music, Life and Art," *Toronto Daily Star* (18 July 1931).

"Little Interest or Knowledge of Art," *Daily Mail and Empire* [clipping, n.d.], AGO Archives.

Littler, William. "Canadian Classics Take Off: Eleanor Sniderman Becomes a One-Woman Music Industry," *Toronto Star* (28 Aug. 1976), p. H3.

Littman, Sol. "Feminists Challenge Male Art Values," *Toronto Star* (2 June 1973), p. 79.

"Local Art Examined," *Ottawa Citizen* (22 Mar. 1967), p. 22.

"Local Artists Show Sculptory: Splendid Exhibition is Now on View at the Grange," *Mail and Empire* (27 Nov. 1915).

Longstreth, T. Morris. "When Canadian Art Arrived in Europe," *Saturday Night* (8 April 1933).

"Lorado Taft: A Retrospective Exhibition: Jan. 16 to Feb. 20, 1983," *The Bulletin*, Krannert Art Museum, University of Illinois, Urbana-Champaign, 8.2 (1983), pp. 1–34.

"Lorado Taft 76: Devotes his Entire Day to his Art," *Chicago Tribune* (28 Apr. 1936).

"Lorado Taft and the Western School of Sculptors," *The Craftsman* (Apr. 1908), p. 22.

Lord, Barry. *The History of Painting in Canada: Toward a People's Art* (Toronto: NC Press, 1974).

Lorimer, James. *The Ex: A Picture History of the Canadian National Exhibition* (Toronto: James Lewis & Samuel, 1973).

Loring and Wyle Sculptors' Legacy, Invitation to Opening, 23 July 1987 (Toronto: Art Gallery of Ontario, 1987).

Loring, Frances. "Bronze Casts Equal in Value, Says Sculptor," [clipping re: CBC Radio lecture on Rodin, 1948], AGO Archives.

Loring, Frances. CBC Radio (interview, n.d.), CBC Archives.

Loring, Frances. "Experiments in Sculpture Must Go On," [clipping, write-up of CBC Radio program, 1939], AGO Archives.

Loring, Frances. "Frances Loring, Sculptor, Gives Interesting Talk on Art," *Ottawa Evening Journal* (8 Feb. 1950).

Loring, Frances. "How to Carve Soap," (Talk to the CBC's national radio network in the series "Fireside Fun"), *The Canadian Red Cross Junior* 21.6 (June 1942) pp. 9–10.

Loring, Frances. *How to Get Started: Wood Carving for Pleasure* (Ottawa: Canadian YMCA War Services and Canadian Legion Educational Services, 1939), 16 pp.

Loring, Frances. "Introduction," *S.S.C. Cont. Can. Sculpting, 1950* (Toronto: S.S.C., 1950).

Loring, Frances. Lecture at the Women's Association of Hamilton [clipping, Nov. 1954], AGO Archives.

Loring, Frances. "Meštrović's Style Natural Outcome of Boyhood Factors," (CBC Radio lecture, 1948).

Loring, Frances. "Perfect Harmony In White Shrine By Great Sculptor Meštrović," (CBC Radio lecture, May 1939).

Loring, Frances. "Sculptural Sense Owned by Epstein," (CBC Radio lecture 1948), AGO Archives.

Loring, Frances. "Sculpture in the Garden," *Canadian Art* 1.2 (Dec.–Jan. 1943–44), pp. 64–67.

Loring Frances. "St. Gaudens Dominating Figure Among American Sculptors," (CBC Radio lectures, 1948), AGO Archives.

Loring, Frances. "Sympathy With Oppressed Stands Out in Epstein's Work," (CBC Radio lecture, 1948), AGO Archives.

Loring, Frances. "Walter Allward's Sculpture Wins Lecturer's Praise" [CBC Radio or other lecture, clipping, n.d.], AGO Archives.

"Loring, Wyle Sculpture," *Windsor Daily Star* (6 Dec. 1952).

"Love Affair Pays Off!" *Sarnia Gazette* (30 Jan. 1964).

Lowery, Susan J. "The Art Gallery of Toronto: Pattern and Process of Growth, 1872 to 1966," M.A. Thesis (Montreal: Concordia University, 1985).

Luckyj, Natalie. "Visions and Victories: Canadian Women Artists, 1914–1945," *ArtsWest* 8.10 (Nov. 1983).

Luckyj, Natalie. *Visions and Victories: Ten Canadian Women Artists May 1983–July 1984* [catalogue] (London: Regional Art Gallery, 1983).

"Lyceum Club — History," based on Constance Smedley, *Crusaders: The Reminiscences of Constance Smedley* (London: Duckworth, 1929), 2004, 23 Sept. 2007 (access), http://www.lyceumclub.org/en/history.htm

"Lyceum Women Hold Gay Garden Festival," *Toronto Daily Star* (18 June 1930).

Lyle, John M. "The Allied Arts at the Recent Toronto Chapter Exhibition," *The Journal of the Royal Architectural Institute of Canada* (May 1927), pp. 62–64.

MacCarthy, Hamilton. "The Development of Sculpture in Canada," *Canada: An Encyclopedia of the Country*, ed. J. Castell Hopkins, vol. 5 (Toronto: Linscott Publishing Co., 1898), pp. 371–82.

MacDonald, Colin. *A Dictionary of Canadian Artists* 4 (Ottawa: Canadian Paperbacks Publishing Ltd., 1967).

MacDougall, Isabel, "Leonard Crunelle, Sculptor of Children," *The Craftsman* 15 (Oct. 1908), pp. 26–33.

MacIntosh, Barb. "RPI Gets Art Works in Purchase of Brewery," *Daily Ryersonian* (3 Mar. 1967).

MacKay, James A. *The Animaliers: The Animal Sculptors of the 19th and 20th Centuries* (London: Ward Lock, 1973).

MacKinnon, John S. "A Canadian's View of the Empire as Seen from London," Empire Club Speech, Toronto (18 Mar. 1926).

Mackenzie, Susan. "Forgotten Treasures Grace Public Squares," *Kitchener-Waterloo Record* (21 Apr. 1973).

MacTaggart, Kenneth W. "Dr. D.E. Robertson Dies; Moose River Survivor's Skill Saved Thousands," [clipping, 21 Feb. 1944], AGO Archives.

MacTavish, Newton. *The Fine Arts in Canada* (Toronto: Macmillan Co. of Canada, Ltd., 1925).

Magner, Brian. "The Artist Who Captured Canada," *Globe Magazine* (27 Aug. 1960), pp. 7–8; 42–44.

"Many Interesting Works on View at RCA Show," *Toronto Daily Star* (3 Dec. 1953).

Martin, Denis. *Portraits des Héros de la Nouvelle-France: Images d'un culte historique* (Quebec: Hurtibise HMH Cahiers de Québec/Album, 1988).

Martin, Elizabeth and Vivian Meyer. *Female Gazes: Seventy-Five Women Artists* (Toronto: Second Story Press, 1997).

Martyn, Lucy Booth. *The Face of Early Toronto: An Archival Record 1797–1936* (Sutton West & Santa Barbara: The Paget Press, 1982).

"Mary Ella Williams Dignam," *Museum of London*, LRAHM, 23 Sept. 2007 (access), http://www.londonmuseum.on.ca/Historical/First_Ren/dignam.html

Mavor, James. "Walter Allward, Sculptor," *The Yearbook of Canadian Art*, compiled by The Arts & Letters Club of Toronto (Toronto: J.M. Dent & Sons Ltd., 1913).

Mayer, David. "Loring, Wyle Sculpture," *Windsor Daily Star* (6 Dec. 1952).

Mays, John Bentley. "AGO Tells Girls' Story with Care and Spirit," *Globe and Mail* [clipping, 31 July 1987] AGO Archives.

Mays, John Bentley. "Singing the Praises of St. Anne's Interior," *Globe and Mail* (15 Apr. 1995).

McCarthy, Pearl. "Art and Artists," *Globe and Mail* [clipping, 28 Nov. 1936], AGO Archives.

McCarthy, Pearl. "Art and Artists," *Globe and Mail* [clipping, 14 Oct.1939], AGO Archives.

McCarthy, Pearl. "Art and Artists," *Globe and Mail* [clipping, 7 Mar. 1942], AGO Archives.

McCarthy, Pearl. "Art and Artists," *Globe and Mail* [clipping, 1 Aug. 1942], AGO Archives.

McCarthy, Pearl. "Art and Artists," *Globe and Mail* [clipping, 13 Aug. 1942], AGO Archives.

McCarthy, Pearl. "Art and Artists," *Globe and Mail* [clipping, 15 Mar. 1952], AGO Archives.

McCarthy, Pearl. "Art and Artists," *Globe and Mail* [clipping, 5 Dec. 1953], AGO Archives.

McCarthy, Pearl. "Art Association Honors Noted Sculptor," *Globe and Mail* (13 Oct. 1955).

McCarthy, Pearl. "Art is Everywhere," *Globe and Mail* [4 May 1957], AGO Archives.

McCarthy, Pearl. "Bank of Montreal Panels Soon Adopted by Citizens," *Globe and Mail* (3 Sept. 1949).

McCarthy, Pearl. "Canadian Sculptors Achieve Distinction: Exhibition at Art Gallery Provides Credible Standard 54 Pieces Shown," *Mail and Empire* (8 Apr. 1932).

McCarthy, Pearl. "Contest-Winning Sculptor to Model Borden," *Globe and Mail* [clipping, 29 Dec. 1954], AGO Archives.

McCarthy, Pearl. "Eskimo Sculptress is Honoured by Sculptors' Group," *Globe and Mail* [clipping, 5 May 1958], AGO Archives.

McCarthy, Pearl. "Festival Trophies — a Cause for Rejoicing," *Globe and Mail* [clipping, 21 Mar. 1953], AGO Archives.

McCarthy, Pearl. "Florence Wyle's Sculpture Excels in the Counsell Garden," *Globe and Mail* (10 Aug. 1957), p. 15.

McCarthy, Pearl. "Gallery to Seek Extra $50,000 for Year's Work," *Globe and Mail* (25 Oct. 1955).

McCarthy, Pearl. "Her Hope: To Die Standing," *Globe and Mail* [clipping, 16 Dec. 1961], AGO Archives.

McCarthy, Pearl. "New Plastic Material in a Loring Sculpture," *Globe and Mail* (29 June 1957).

McCarthy, Pearl. "New Sculpture at the OVC Sets an Example of Service," *Globe and Mail* (5 Dec. 1953).

McCarthy, Pearl. "Ontario Artists Show Individualistic Work," *Globe and Mail* (4 Mar. 1938).

McCarthy Pearl. "Preserving the Native Work Among a Gallery's Functions," *Globe and Mail* (15 Nov. 1952).

McCarthy, Pearl. "Sculptor Offered Award for Service to the Arts," *Globe and Mail* (21 June 1954), p. 19.

McCarthy, Pearl. "Sculptors Find Public Designers Score Well," *Globe and Mail* (2 Sept. 1950).

McCarthy, Pearl. "Sculptors' Large Exhibition to be Held in Quebec City," *Globe and Mail* (24 Mar. 1951).

McCarthy, Pearl. "Sculpture to Enhance Busy Street," *Globe and Mail* [clipping, 22 May 1948], AGO Archives.

McCarthy, Pearl. "Sculpture Works," *Globe and Mail* (15 Mar. 1952).

McCarthy, Pearl. "Watch the Youngsters Among the Sculptors," *Globe and Mail* (10 May 1956).

McCarthy, Pearl. "Works of Ontario Artists Display Catholicity," *Mail and Empire* (7 Mar. 1931).

McCarthy, Pearl. "Y.M.C.A. Exhibits Travel to Camps," *Globe and Mail* (22 May 1963).

McCaughey, Claire. *A Survey of Arts Audience Studies: A Canadian Perspective* (Ottawa: Research & Evaluation, Canada Council, 1984).

McCauley, Lena M. "An Epoch in National Art," *Brush and Pencil* 14.5 (Dec. 1904).

McCulley, Joseph. letter to the editor, *Globe and Mail*, (23 Aug. 1969).

McCullough, Norah. *The Beaver Hall Hill Group/Le Groupe de Beaver Hall Hill* (Ottawa: The National Gallery of Canada, 1966).

McCurry, H.O. "Foreword," *S.S.C. Cont. Can. Sculpting, 1950* (Toronto: S.S.C., 1950).

McDougall, Anne. *Anne Savage: The Story of a Canadian Painter* (Montreal: Harvest House, 1977).

McFarlane, Arthur E. "Art Awakes in a Forgotten Church," *Toronto Star Weekly* (1 Aug. 1925), p. 59.

McFarlane, Arthur E. "Two Toronto Sculptors," *Toronto Star Weekly* (19 Aug. 1923), p. 4.

McFarlane, Arthur E. "Two Toronto Sculptors," *Toronto Star* (1 Aug. 1925).

McGinnis, Rick. "Historic Statue Stands Forgotten," *National Post* [clipping, 22 May 1948], AGO Archives.

McInnes, C. Graham. "A Century of Canadian Art: Exhibition at the Tate Gallery, London," *The Studio* (Dec. 1938), pp. 294–96.

McInnes, C. Graham. *A Short History of Canadian Art* (Toronto: Macmillan Co. of Canada, Ltd., 1939).

McInnes, C. Graham. *Canadian Art* (Toronto: Macmillan Co. of Canada Ltd., 1950).

McInnes, G. Campbell. "Thoughts on Canadian Art," *Saturday Night* [clipping, 1 Aug. 1936], AGO Archives.

McInnes, G. Campbell. "World of Art," *Saturday Night* 51.1 (7 Dec. 1935).

McKay, Ian. *The Quest of the Folk: Antimodernism and Cultural Selection in Twentieth-Century Nova Scotia* (Montreal & Kingston: McGill-Queen's University Press, 1994).

McKelvey, Margaret and Merilyn McKelvey. *Toronto: Carved in Stone* (Toronto: Fitzhenry and Whiteside, 1984).

McKenzie, Karen and Larry Pfaff. "The Art Gallery of Ontario, Sixty Years of Exhibitions, 1906–1966," *RACAR*, VII (1980): 62–91.

McKinley, Barry. "The Art Scene." *Toronto Sun* (10 July 1977).

McLennan, Gordon. "Loring and Wyle to be Re-released after 10 Years," *The Art Magazine* 7.24 (Dec./Jan. 1975).

McLuhan, Marshall. *The Mechanical Bride: Folklore of Industrial Man* (New York: Vanguard Press, 1951).

McMann, Evelyn de Rostaing. *Royal Canadian Academy of Arts/Académie Royale des Arts du Canada: Exhibitions and Members, 1880–1979* (Toronto: University of Toronto Press, 1981).

McPherson, Hugo. "The Scope of Sculpture in '64," *Canadian Art* 21 (1964), pp. 224–25.

Meadowcroft, Barbara. *Painting Friends: The Beaver Hall Women Painters* (Montreal, Véhicule Press, 1999).

Mellon, Peter. *The Group of Seven* (Toronto: McClelland and Stewart, 1970).

"Memorial Exhibit Includes Works of Women Artists," *Montreal Herald* (2 Oct. 1920), p. 3.

"Memorial Fountain, Kew Gardens, Toronto," [clipping, Aug. 1920/1921], AGO Archives.

"Memorial Unveiled to Galt War Dead by Militia Minister," [clipping (Galt), 10 Nov. 1925], AGO Archives.

Merrill, Anne. "Sculptor from Paris," *Mail and Empire* (4 Sept. 1920), p. 23.

Merrill, Anne. "The Average Woman," *Mail and Empire* (4 Sept. 1920).

"Meštrović, Ivan," *Answers.com, Columbia University Press Encyclopedia*, 2003, 23 Sept. 2007 (access), http://www.answers.com/topic/ivan-mestrovic

Millar, Joyce. "Lawrence Hayward," ca. 1992 [based on a 1992 essay by Millar], 22
Apr. 2005 (access), http://collections.ic.gc.ca/sculpture/text/hay.html

Millar, Joyce. "The Girls: Canadian Sculptors Francis [sic] Loring and Florence
Wyle," *Gallerie: Women's Art* 1.4 (Spring 1988), pp. 4–8.

Millar, Joyce. "The Sculptors' Society of Canada: 65 Years of Sculpture in Canada,"
Le Revue Espace Magazine 29, pp. 34–36.

Millar, Joyce. "The Sculptors' Society of Canada: The First Fifty Years, 1928–1978,"
M.A. Thesis, Art History Dept., Concordia University, Montreal, QC, 1992,
230 pp.

Miller, Ian Hugh Maclean. *Our Glory and Our Grief: Torontonians and the Great War*
(Toronto: University of Toronto Press, 2002).

Miller, Sandra. *Constantin Brancusi: A Survey of his Work* (Oxford: Clarendon Press,
1995).

"Miss Canada in Yonge St.: Heroic Figure of Lady of Confederation in Front
of T. Eaton Co. Store," *Globe and Mail* [clipping, 20 June 1917], AGO
Archives.

"Miss Loring Succeeds," (Italian paper in New York), [clipping, ca. 1910], AGO
Archives.

Moffat, W.D. "The Open Letter," *The Mentor* 6.24, p. 12.

Moffat, W.D. "Women Sculptors of America," *The Mentor* 6.24, pp. i–xi.

Monroe, Lucy B. "Art In Chicago," *The New England Magazine* 6.4 (June 1892),
pp. 1–44.

Monteglas, Albrecht. "Tribute Paid to Mulligan by Taft," *Chicago Illinois Examiner*
[clipping, 31 Mar. 1916], AIC Archives.

"Montrealers Hysterical, Is Toronto View," [clipping, n.d.], AGO Archives.

"Monument to Borden," [clipping, 1957], AGO Archives.

Moodie, Sheila. "Noted Toronto Sculptress Finds Canada a Challenge," *Ottawa
Citizen* [clipping, 10 Jan. 1957], AGO Archives.

Moon, Diana. "Francis [sic] & Florence: A Love Story," *The Siren* 6.2 (June–July
2001), pp. 16–17.

"More Paintings of War Activities," *Daily Mail and Empire* [clipping, 20 Oct. 1919],
AGO Archives.

Moritz, Albert and Theresa Moritz. *The World's Most Dangerous Woman* (Toronto:
Subway Books, 2001).

Morris, R. Schofield. "Bank of Montreal Building, Toronto," *The Journal of the
Royal Architectural Institute of Canada* 26 (Nov. 1949), pp. 365–78.

"Mother and Child Find Gallery Home," *Edmonton Journal* [clipping, 21 Feb.
1964], AGO Archives.

Moulton, Robert H. "Chicago's Dream of Civic Beauty Realized in the Symbolic Marble of Lorado Taft," *The Craftsman* 25 (1904), pp. 123–30.

Munk, Linda. "A Talk with Miss Loring and Miss Wyle," *Women's Globe and Mail* [clipping, 6 May 1965], AGO Archives.

Murray, Alice. *Egyptian Sculpture* (Westport, Connecticut: Greenwood Press, 1930).

Murray, Joan. *Ontario Society of Artists: 100 Years, 1872–1972* (Toronto: Art Gallery of Ontario, 1972).

Murtha, Edwin. *Paul Manship* (New York: Macmillan, 1957).

Musgrove, Alex J. "Sculpture Show Fine Attraction at Art Gallery, Works of Canadian Artists Show Deft Craftsmanship and Artistic Expressiveness," *Winnipeg Free Press* (6 Feb. 1937).

Naismith, Cecilia. "Frances Gage: Creator of the WREN Memorial," *Cobourg Daily Star* (11 Nov. 2005).

Nasby, Judith M. *The University of Guelph Art Collection: A Catalogue of Paintings, Drawing, Prints and Sculpture* (Guelph: University of Guelph, et al., 1980).

"National Gallery Lending Encouragement to Sculptors," [clipping, 16 June 1939], AGO Archives.

"National Monument Designed in Toronto," *Toronto Star* (17 July 1925).

"Native Sculpture in Canadian Galleries," *Saturday Night* (13 Jan. 1923).

Nelles, H.V. *The Art of Nation-Building: Pageantry and Spectacle at Quebec's Tercentenary* (Toronto: University of Toronto Press, 1999).

Nelson, Eric. "How a Streetcar Loop Became an Art Park," *Leaside Town Crier* [clipping, Aug. 1987], AGO Archives.

"New Home for Landmark," *The Globe and Mail* [clipping, 21 Nov. 1972], AGO Archives.

"New York Critics Praise Canadian Art at the Fair," *Toronto Daily Star* (30 June 1939), p. 24.

Newton, Eric. *British Sculpture, 1944–1946* (London: John Tiranti Ltd., 1947).

Newton, Lilias T. "Canadian Women in the Public Eye," *Saturday Night* (12 Nov. 1927), p. 35.

Nichols, K.L. "Canadian Women Painters: 1893 Exposition," 29 May 2007, 23 Sept. 2007 (access), http://members. cox.net/academia2/cassatt9e.html

"No Takers for Sculpture so Goalkeeper's on Ice," *Toronto Star* [clipping, 26 May 1983], AGO Archives.

Nobbs, Percy E. *Design: A Treatise on the Discovery of Form* (London: Oxford University Press, 1937).

"Noted Artist Puts Life into Stone and Bronze," *The Canadian Tribune: a Journal of Democratic Opinion* (15 June 1946), p. 11.

"Noted Sculptor to Lecture at Gallery," *Ottawa Evening Citizen* (3 Feb. 1950).

"Noted Woman Sculptor to Receive Degree," *St. Catharines Standard* (5 May 1955).

"Novel Studio for Sculptors," *Mail and Empire* [clipping, 20 Nov. 1920], AGO Archives.

Nurse, Andrew. *A Confusion of Values: Artists and Artistic Ideologies in Modern Canada, 1927–1952*, M.A. Thesis, Queen's University, Kingston, ON, 1991.

Nurse, Andrew. "Sculpting Canada: The Art of Frances Loring," *Woman* (Spring 2000), p. 35.

Nurse, Andrew. *Tradition and Modernity: The Cultural Work of Marius Barbeau*, PhD. Thesis, Queen's University, Kingston, ON, 1997.

"Nymphs and Fauns as Magic Fountains," *Toronto Star Weekly* (11 Aug. 1923).

"Obituary of Frances Norma Loring, obituary of Florence Wyle," http://www.ogs.on.ca/ogspi/2000w/2005w034.htm

"Old Monument in New Spot," *Toronto Star* (27 Aug 1974).

Oliver, Maude I.G. "Recent Work at the Art Institute of Chicago," *The International Studio* 29.113-16 (Jul., Aug., Sept., & Oct., 1906), pp. cv–cix.

Ollie, Jennifer. "Art and Architecture: Toronto Between the Wars," *Vanguard* 11.2 (March 1982).

"On Current Art," *New York Times* (2 Nov. 1919).

Ontario Society of Artists, Membership (Toronto: OSA, 1933).

"Opening on Royal Academy," [clipping, n.d.], AGO Archives.

"O.S.A. Exhibition Off to New York," *Globe and Mail* (14 July 1952).

"Osgoode Hall Memorial to be Unveiled Nov. 10," *Toronto Star* (8 Nov. 1928).

Ostiguy, Jean-René. *Modernism in Quebec Art, 1916–1946* (Ottawa: National Gallery of Canada, 1982).

"Ottawa Scene," *Globe and Mail* (28 Mar. 1953).

"Our Civilized Politics," [clipping, n.d.], AGO Archives.

Paine, Robert T. "How the Sculptor's Model is Enlarged," *Brush and Pencil* 13.3 (Dec. 1903), pp. 184–89.

"Paint, Not Politics, Stuff for Artists," *Toronto Daily Star* (10 Dec. 1932).

"Painter Says Abstracts Doomed [A.Y. Jackson]," [clipping, 22 Mar. 1967], AGO Archives.

"Painting and Sculpture Exhibit Opens Today," *Toronto Daily Star* (5 Nov. 1942).

Pantazzi, Sybille. "Foreign Art at the Canadian National Exhibition 1905–1938," *NGC Annual Bulletin*, 22 (1973), 31 pp. Full text at: http://national.gallery.ca/bulletin/num22/pantazzi1.html

"Park and Park Work: Chicago's Newer Sculptured Park Memorials," *Park and Cemetery* 22.12 (Feb. 1913).

Park, Julian, ed. *The Culture of Contemporary Canada* (Ithaca, New York: Cornell University Press, 1957).

Parr, Roger. "A Woman of Value," *Country Beautiful* 2.8 (May 1963).

Parr, Roger. "The Uses of Simplicity," *Country Beautiful* 2.8 (May 1963).

"Part III: The British Empire Exhibit at Wembley," [clipping, 1929], NGC Archives.

"Pauline McGibbon Unveils Sculpture," *Globe and Mail* (7 May 1980).

Payne, Frank Owen. "The Tribute of American Sculpture to Labor," *Art and Archaeology* 6 (Aug. 1917), pp. 83–93.

Payne, Henry Charles. "Fine Work in Chicago Sculpture Exhibit," *Monumental News* 20 [Mar. 1908], pp. 196–99.

Peattie, Elia W. "The Artistic Side of Chicago," *The Atlantic Monthly* 84 (Dec. 1899), pp. 828–34.

"Permanent Collection," *Art Gallery of Ontario*, 23 Sept. 2007 (access), http://www.ago.net/info/collection/collection.cfm?collection-id=4

Pevsner, Nickolaus. *Academies of Art: Past and Present* (Cambridge: Cambridge University Press, 1940).

"Pictures at Exhibition of Royal Canadian Academy," *Globe* (24 Nov. 1914).

"Pictures by Canadian Artists to be Sent to the Soviet Union," *Toronto Daily Star* (6 Sept. 1944).

"Pioneer Canadian Sculptor was also a Published Poet," *Toronto Star* (11 June 1973), p. C5.

"Plan Fashion Show," *Toronto Daily Star* [22 Sept. 1937], AGO Archives.

"Plan Tea Entertainment," *Toronto Daily Star* [clipping, 5 Feb. 1935], AGO Archives.

Plaskett, Joseph. *A Speaking Likeness*, foreword by George Woodcock (Vancouver: Ronsdale Press, 1999).

"Pleasing Innovation is 'Open Studio Day,'" *Toronto Daily Star* (7 June 1924).

Poole, Lucianne. "Stolen Chances," *Kingston Whig-Standard* (17 July 1999), p. 3.

"Popular Palace of Arts—Empire Impressions at Wembley," *The Times*, London England (18 June 1924).

Powell, S. Morgan. "The Montreal Art Association: Spring Exhibit," *The Yearbook of Canadian Art*, compiled by The Arts & Letters Club of Toronto (Toronto: J.M. Dent & Sons Ltd., 1913).

"Price List—Florence Wyle," (12 May 1964), AGO Archives.

"Proposed Memorial, Kew Gardens, Toronto," [clipping, 1919–1921], AGO Archives.

Purdie, James. "Scouts Who Cleared the Underbrush," *Globe and Mail* (23 July 1977), p. 31.

Purser, Mona. "Films of Cultural Arts Bring Thrill to Viewer," *Globe and Mail* (10 Feb. 1948), p. 11.

Putnam, Brenda. *The Sculptor's Way: A Guide to Modelling and Sculpture* (New York: Farrar & Rinehart, Inc., 1939).

"QEW Widening Costs Lion his Post," *Toronto Star* (17 June 1971).

Quan, Betty. "Radio drama based on The Girls," *Morningside*, CBC Radio, 9 Dec. 1991.

Rasby, Brian. *Character Parts: Who's Who in Can Lit* (Toronto: Alfred A. Knopf, 2003).

Rather, Susan. "The Past Made Modern: Archaism in American Sculpture," *The Arts Magazine* 59.3 (Nov. 1984), pp. 111–19.

R.C.A. Annual Exhibition, Nov. 5–27, 1943, Catalogue (Toronto: R.C.A., 1943).

R.C.A. Annual Report, 1916, AGO Archives.

R.C.A. Report, 1969–70, AGO Archives.

Read, Herbert. *The Art of Sculpture*, the A.W. Mellon Lectures in the Fine Arts 1954, National Gallery of Art, Washington, Bollingen Series XXXV, 3 (Princeton: Princeton University Press, 1956).

Reade, R.C. "Art Grange in Readiness for Annual Fall Exhibit," *Toronto Daily Star* (4 Oct. 1928).

Reade, Winwood. *The Martyrdom of Man* (London: Jonathan Cape, 1927).

Regan, Edward. "Group of Seven's Angel at Work," *Globe and Mail* (19 Feb. 1999).

Reid, Dennis R. *A Concise History of Canadian Painting* (Toronto: Oxford University Press, 1973).

"Remarks made by Prof. Woodside — Convocation — University of Toronto," (27 May 1955), AGO Archives.

"Renovations Elevate CE to New Heights: Historic Building to Grow Outward, Upward," *The Forum/Ryerson Polytechnic University* 28.4 [clipping, Mar. 2003], AGO Archives.

Report of the Royal Commission on National Development in the Arts, Letters and Sciences, 1949–1951 (Ottawa, 1951).

"Rhythm Band Wins House, Ontario Art Show Opens," *Toronto Daily Star* (7 Mar. 1952).

Richards, A.G. "Father Love in Art," *The Fine Arts Journal* 36 (Mar. 1918), pp. 21–25.

Richman, Michael. *Daniel Chester French: An American Sculptor* (New York: Metropolitan Museum of Art, 1977).

"Right Statuary in the Garden is Important," *London Free Press* (18 Sept. 1948).

Robert Flaherty Photographer/Filmmaker: The Inuit 1910–1922 (Vancouver: The Vancouver Art Gallery, 1980).

Robertson, Heather and Joan Murray. *A Terrible Beauty: The Art of Canada at War* (James Lorimer & Co., The Robert McLaughlin Gallery, Oshawa and The National Museum of Man, Ottawa, 1977).

Robinson, John, ed. *Once Upon a Century: 100 Year History of the 'Ex'* (Toronto: J.H. Robinson Publishing Ltd., 1978).

Rockwell, Edwin A. "Daniel Chester French," *The International Studio* 41.163 (Sept. 1910), pp. 55–60.

Rooney, Frances. "Loring and Wyle, Sculptors," *Pink Ink* 1.1 (July 1983), pp. 18–20.

Rooney, Frances. "Loring and Wyle, Sculptors," *Resources for Feminist Research* 13.4 (Dec. 1984/Jan. 1985), pp. 21–23.

"Rosa Bonheur," http://www.nmwa.org/collection/Profile.asp?LinkID=95

Roseborough, Everett. "Frances Loring, Dean of Canadian Sculptors," *The Canadian Scene* 607 (30 Nov. 1962), p. 30.

Ross, Malcolm, ed. *The Arts in Canada: A Stocktaking at Mid-Century* (Toronto: The Macmillan Company of Canada, Ltd., 1958).

Ross, Malcolm, ed. *Our Sense of Identity: A Book of Canadian Essays* (Toronto: Ryerson Press, 1954).

Ross, Val. "Artistic Heritage Feared Crumbling along with Church Ceiling," *Globe and Mail* (23 July 1998).

Rubenstein, Charlotte Streifer. *American Women Sculptors: A History of Women Working in Three Dimensions* (Boston: G. K. Hall & Co., 1990).

Rudin, Ronald. *Founding Fathers: The Celebration of Champlain and Laval in the Streets of Quebec, 1878–1908* (Toronto: University of Toronto Press, 2003).

Sabbath, Lawrence. "Modellers," *Canadian Art* 1980, pp. 290–95.

Sabbath, Lawrence. "Painter-Sculptors," *Canadian Art* 1980, pp. 296–104.

"Sale of Canvasses Put Toronto on the Map," *Toronto Daily Star* [clipping, 25 Mar. 1922], AGO Archives.

Salinger, Jehanne Bietry. "Elizabeth Wyn Wood Hahn," *The Canadian Forum* III.128 (1931), pp. 17–21.

Salinger, Jehanne Bietry. "Women Sculptors Prominent at OSA: Superior sculpture present but rare at 58th exhibition," *Mail and Empire* (22 Mar. 1930).

Saltmarche, Kenneth. "Sculpture Exhibit," *Windsor Star* (12 Jan. 1963).

Sandburg, Carl. *Chicago Poems* (New York: Henry Holt and Co., 1916).

Sargent, Charles Chapin. "Sculptor and Student," *Munsey's Magazine* [clipping], AIC Archives.

"Says Good Education is Important for Artist," *London Evening Free Press* [clipping, 14 Apr. 1943], AGO Archives.

"Says Paintings from Canada Are Most Vital of Century," *Toronto Star* (5 July 1924).

Scaravaglione, Concetta, in *Painters and Sculptors of Modern America*, ed. Monroe Wheeler (New York: Thomas Y. Crowell Co., 1942).

Schafer, D. Paul and André Fortier. *Review of Federal Policies for the Arts in Canada (1944–1988)*, Department of Communications (Ottawa: Canadian Conference of the Arts, 1989).

Schmeckebier, Laurence. *Ivan Meštrović: Sculptor and Patriot* (Syracuse: Syracuse University Press, 1959).

Schnier, Jacques. *Sculpture in Modern America* (Berkeley: University of California Press, 1948).

Scudder, Janet. *Modeling My Life* (New York: Harcourt, Brace and Co., 1925).

Scudder, Janet. "Why so Few Women are Sculptors," *New York Times* (18 Feb. 1912), p. SM13.

"Sculptor Champions Honesty of Thought," (Loring lecture to Heliconian Club), [clipping, n.d.], AGO Archives.

"Sculptor gives Discourse on Art," *Montreal Gazette* [clipping, 17 Feb. 1932], AGO Archives.

"Sculptor Gives Lecture on Sculpture at Gallery," *Ottawa Evening Citizen* (8 Feb. 1950).

"Sculptor Issues Call for Support," *Kitchener-Waterloo Record* [clipping, 16 Jan. 1960], AGO Archives.

"Sculptor of the Rural Tradition: Alfred Laliberté," *About Sculpture*, Sculptors' Society of Canada, 2 June 2005 (access), http://collections.ic.gc.ca/sculpture/text/laliberte.html

"Sculptor Offered Award for Service to the Arts," *Globe and Mail* (21 June 1954).

"Sculptor Plans Exhibit Talk: Miss Loring will Give Lecture," *Windsor Daily Star* (20 Nov. 1952).

"Sculptor Speaks to Coste House," *Calgary Herald* (4 Nov. 1952).

"Sculptor Urges: Support the Arts — As Well as Sports," [clipping, ca. 1959], AGO Archives.

"Sculptors' Models of Sir Robt. Borden on Exhibition," *Ottawa Evening Journal* (12 Mar. 1955).

Sculptors' Society of Canada — 1944 Exhibit, Catalogue.

Sculptors' Society of Canada — Contemporary Canadian Sculpture, 1950, Catalogue.

Sculptors' Society of Canada — Exhibition at the Art Gallery of Ontario, Oct. 5–Nov. 1, 1928, Catalogue (Toronto: Art Gallery of Toronto, 1928).

Sculptors' Society of Canada — Exhibition at the Art Gallery of Ontario, April 1932, Catalogue (Toronto: Art Gallery of Toronto, 1932).

Sculptors' Society of Canada Travelling Exhibition: 1936–1937 (Ottawa: The National Gallery of Canada, 1936).

"Sculptors Tell Canada's Story in Bank's Stone Carvings," *Toronto Evening Telegram* (18 Sept. 1948).

"Sculptors Would Rather Work than Pursue Hobbies," *Toronto Evening Telegram* (1 Aug. 1947).

"Sculptress Addresses Art Guild, Stresses Quiet Dignified Work," *Lindsay Daily Post* (20 May 1953).

"Sculptress At Home is Merry Girl," [clipping, 1921], AGO Archives.

"Sculptress Awarded LL.D. at Varsity Graduation," *Toronto Star* (28 May 1955), p. 5.

"Sculptress Finds Banting, Borden Strong Personalities, 'Fighters,'" *Hamilton Spectator* [clipping, 10 Dec. 1955], AGO Archives.

"Sculptress Says Memorial of War 'Cheap Melodrama,'" *Toronto Star* (11 Apr. 1946), p. 19.

"Sculpture," *The Studio*, special Canadian issue (Apr. 1945), pp. 132–37.

"Sculpture — Canvas Exhibit By Five Canadian Women," *Globe and Mail* (Dec. 1936).

"Sculpture — Canvas Exhibit By Five Canadian Women: Malloney Gallery shows notable assembly of exquisite pieces," *Mail and Empire* (Dec. 1932).

"Sculpture Exhibit Open at Art Gallery," *Toronto Daily Star* (8 Jan. 1942).

"Sculpture Exhibition at Stratford Festival Draws Gazes, Giggles," *Globe and Mail* (15 June 1965), p. 10.

"Sculpture from 110 Glenrose Ave., to Robertson Gallery, Ottawa," typescript (March 1953), AGO Archives.

"Sculpture Important in the National Academy Exhibition for the Winter of Nineteen Hundred and Ten," *The Craftsman* 19.5 (Feb. 1911), pp. 452–45.

"Sculpture in Canada," *The Canadian Geographical Journal* 43 (Dec. 1951), pp. 268–71.

"Sculpture in Canada," *Canadian Life* 1.4 (Spring 1950), pp. 13–15.

"Sculpture is Topic at Fine Art Club," *Varsity* (4 Feb. 1945).

"Sculpture Show," *North Bay Nugget* (17 Jan. 1950).

"Sculpture Show at Art Gallery," *Montreal Gazette* (or *Herald*)[clipping, 1929], AGO Archives.

"Sculpture Show at Art Gallery Open All Month," *Winnipeg Tribune* (5 Feb. 1937).

"Sculptures by Florence Wyle and Frances Loring at U of G," *Guelph Mercury* (14 Aug. 1978).

"Sentinel of Parking Lot," [clipping, n.d.], AGO Archives.

Sewell, John. *Doors Open Toronto: Illuminating the City's Great Spaces* (Toronto: Alfred A. Knopf, 2002).

Shanes, Eric. *Constantin Brancusi* (New York: Abbeville Press, 1989).

Sherman, Leah. *Anne Savage, 1896–1971* (Montreal: Leah and Bina Ellen Art Gallery, 2002).

Shields, Roy. "Did You See?" CBC *Times* [clipping, 8 May 1965], AGO Archives.

Shipley, Robert. *To Mark Our Place: A History of Canadian War Memorials* (Toronto: NC Press, Ltd., 1987).

Silcox, David P. "Carvers," *Canadian Art* 19.80 (July/Aug. 1962), pp. 284–89.

"Silence," *La Presse* (30 Jan. 1958).

"Sir Robert Borden Statue Lowered Into Position," [clipping, 1957], AGO Archives.

"Sir Robert Comes Back to Parliament Hill," *Montreal Star Weekend Magazine* 7.11 (1957).

Sisler, Rebecca. *Art for Enlightenment: A History of Art in the Toronto Schools*, intro. Timothy Findley (Toronto: Fitzhenry & Whiteside, the Learnxs Foundation, and the Board of Education for the City of Toronto, 1993).

Sisler, Rebecca. "Florence Wyle (1881–1968)," *Lives and Works of the Canadian Artists*, series ed. R.H. Stacey, 20 (Toronto: Dundurn Press, 1978).

Sisler, Rebecca. "Frances Loring (1887–1968)," *Lives and Works of the Canadian Artists*, series ed. R.H. Stacey, 18 (Toronto: Dundurn Press, 1978).

Sisler, Rebecca. Letter to the editor, *Globe and Mail* [clipping, 16 Dec. 1972], AGO Archives.

Sisler, Rebecca. *Passionate Spirits: A History of the Royal Canadian Academy of the Arts, 1880–1980* (Toronto: Clarke, Irwin & Co. Ltd., 1980).

Sisler, Rebecca. *The Girls: A Biography of Frances Loring and Florence Wyle* (Toronto: Clarke, Irwin & Co., 1972).

"Six Honorary Degrees are Conferred at 'T' Convocation," [clipping, 1955], AGO Archives.

"Six Sculptors Design Canadian Panorama in Carvings for New Bank Building Here," *Globe and Mail* (16 Apr. 1947).

"Sketch Room Exhibition," Hart House (University of Toronto), notice 1926. Papers UT Archives, Hart House, A73-0050, 1925–26.

Smith, Alson J. *Chicago's Left Bank* (Chicago: Henry Regnery Company, 1953).

Smith, Bertha H. "Two Women Who Collaborate in Sculpture," *The Craftsman* 8 (June–Sept. 1905), pp. 623–33.

Smith, Mariann. "Rosa Bonheur, French, 1822–1899," *Albright-Knox Art Gallery*, 25 Oct. 2005 (access), Art Index A-L, http://albrightknox.org/ArtStart/Bonheur.html

Smith, Mariann. "Rosa Bonheur, French, 1822–1899" *National Museum of Women in the Arts, 2007*, 23 Sept. 2007 (access), http://www.nmwa.org/collection/Profile.asp? LinkID=95

"Social and Personal," *Toronto Daily Star* (20 Nov. 1914), p. 11.

"Social and Personal Notes," *Globe and Mail* (9 June 1953).

"Social and Personal Notes," *Globe and Mail* (3 May 1954).

"Social Events," *Globe and Mail* (9 Feb. 1931), p. 14.

"Social Notes," *Toronto Daily Star* [clipping, 2 Aug. 1932], AGO Archives.

"Social Notes," *Toronto Daily Star* [clipping, 30 Aug. 1935], AGO Archives.

Solender, Katie. *The American Way in Sculpture, 1890–1930* (Cleveland: Cleveland Museum of Art, 1986).

Souhami, Diana. *Wild Girls: Paris, Sappho, and Art: The Lives and Loves of Natalie Barney* (New York: McArthur & Co., 2006).

Stacey, Col. C.P. *A Date with History: Memoirs of a Canadian Historian* (Ottawa: Deneau Publishers, 1982).

Stacey, Col. C.P. "Nationality: The Experience of Canada," *Historical Papers* (Canadian Historical Association, 1967).

Stamp, Robert M., *Kings, Queens and Canadians* (Toronto: Fitzhenry & Whiteside, 1987).

Stapleton, Betty. "See Favorite Artists at Work on Studio Tour," *Toronto Daily Star* (26 Aug. 1958).

"Statues for the Garden Exhibited Outdoors at CNE," *Globe and Mail* (2 Sept. 1953).

"Stone Carvings on Expressway to Ruin," *Toronto Star* (19 Aug. 2000), p. N9.

"Stone Figures by Toronto Sculptors Blend Canadian Theme in Bank Building," *Globe and Mail* (3 Sept. 1948).

Strachey, Lytton. "Introduction," *Eminent Victorians* (London: Penguin Books, 1986).

Stuber, Irene. "Women of Achievement and Herstory," (Margaret Anderson and Florence Wyle) http://www.undelete.org/woa/woa11-24.html

"Subtleties of Human Emotions Shown in the Sculpture of Chester Beach," *The Craftsman* 30 (1909), pp. 350–55.

Summers, Claude J. *The Queer Encyclopedia of the Visual Arts* (San Francisco: Cleis Press, Inc., 2004).

"Supper Dance and Bridge by Lyceum, Women's Art Club an Event of Monday Evening," *Globe and Mail* [clipping, 27 Jan. 1939], AGO Archives.

"Support for Sculptors Urged in Gallery Panel," *Kitchener-Waterloo Record* (16 May 1959).

"Support for Sculptors Urged in Gallery Panel," *Ottawa Citizen* (20 May 1959).

"Survey of Canadian Sculpture Given in Art Gallery Lecture," *Globe* (13 Mar. 1928), p. 14.

"Swift Fire in the Ontario Art Gallery," *Toronto Evening Star* [clipping, 19 April 1909], AGO Archives.

Swift, Samuel. "Americanism in Art," *Brush and Pencil* 15.1 (Jan. 1905), pp. 51–57.

Sydney, Norman. "A Dean Among Mining Engineers Pays Tribute to the Prospectors," *Globe and Mail* [clipping, 22 Apr. 1938], AGO Archives.

Sykes, A.R. "Best of Canadian Sculptors Sought for Borden's Statue," [clipping, 4 Apr. 1953], AGO Archives.

Sylvester, David, ed. *Henry Moore, Complete Sculpture, vol. 1, Sculpture 1921–1948* (London: Lund, Humphries, 1988).

"Symphony Concert Massey Hall," *Toronto Daily Star* [clipping, 22 Nov. 1933], AGO Archives.

Taft, Lorado. "Exhibition of Statuary, Art Institute, Chicago," *The Sketchbook* 5.10 (Aug. 1906).

Taft, Lorado. "Sculptors of the World's Fair — A Chapter of Appreciations," *Brush and Pencil* 13.3 (Dec. 1903), pp. 199–236.

Taft, Lorado. "That Fountain," *Brush and Pencil* (Aug. 1899), pp. 248–54.

Taft, Lorado. "The Exhibition of the National Sculpture School," *Brush and Pencil* (July 1898), pp. 151–54.

Taft, Lorado. *The History of American Sculpture* (New York: Macmillan, 1903).

Taft, Lorado. *The History of American Sculpture, rev.* (New York: Arno Press, 1969).

Taft, Lorado. "Women Sculptors of America," *The Mentor* 6.24 (1 Feb. 1919), pp. I–II.

"Talented Artists Will Tour Area," *Fairview Post* (26 Oct. 1952).

Tancock, John L. *The Sculpture of Auguste Rodin* (Philadelphia: David R. Godine and the Philadelphia Museum of Art, 1976).

Tarbell, Ida M. "Lorado Taft and the Western School of Sculpture: A Group of Men and Women who are Finding a New and Vital Expression in Art by Recording the Simplest Phases of Life and of Work," *The Craftsman* 13.1 (Apr. 1908), pp.12–26.

"Technical School Students Compete in Statuettes," *Toronto Star* [clipping, 21 Nov. 1929], AGO Archives.

"Telescope will Visit Sculptors," *Halifax Chronicle-Herald* (1 May 1965).

The Art Gallery of Toronto: Exhibition of Canadian Sculpture, Spanish Paintings, Water Colours by Robert Riggs, Woodblocks by Elizabeth Keith, Etchings by Emil Fuchs, Batiks by Arthur and Lawrence Smith (Toronto: Art Gallery of Toronto, 1928).

"The Art of Canada," *The Studio* 129.625 (Apr. 1945).

"The Art of Canada," *Winnipeg Free Press* (20 Nov. 1924).

"The Art Scene," *Toronto Sun* (10 July 1977).

"The Blind: Lorado Taft," 12th *Annual Exhibition Catalogue of Work by artists of Chicago and Vicinity 1908*, The Art Institute of Chicago, Krannert Gallery (Urbana: University of Illinois, 1988), pp. 1–18.

"The Cult of the Unworthy," *Brush and Pencil* 17.5 (May 1906).

"The Girls," editorial, *Globe and Mail* (7 Feb. 1968).

"The Girls," *Globe and Mail* (24 Apr. 1973).

"The Group of Seven and Their Contemporaries," *McMichael Canadian Collection of Art*, 23 Sept. 2007 (access), http://mcmichael.com/webl/our-collection/group.shtml

The International Society of Women Painters and Sculptors at the Lyceum Women's Art Association of Canada, February 8th to February 25th, 1937 [program] (Toronto, 1937).

"The Memorial Chamber Angel," *Ottawa Citizen* (11 Nov. 1947).

The National Gallery of Canada: Annual Exhibition of Canadian Art, Ottawa 1929 (Ottawa: The National Gallery, 1929).

The National Gallery of Canada: Sculptors' Society of Canada Travelling Exhibition, 1936–1937 (Ottawa: The National Gallery, 1936).

"The National Gallery of Canada at Ottawa," *Globe* (12 Nov. 1927).

The New World Illustrated (Feb. 1942), p. 28.

"The New York Armory Show of 1913," *AskArt*, 2006–07, 23 Sept. 2007 (access), http://www.askart.com/AskART/interest/new_york_armory_show_of_1913s_1.aspx?id=15

The Ontario Society of Artists and the Arts and Letters Club, Executive Meeting Minutes (6 Mar. 1962), AGO Archives.

"The Osgoode Hall War Memorial," *Globe* (22 Oct. 1928).

"The Other Sections," *Mail and Empire* (8 Oct. 1927).

"The Recent Exhibition of Chicago Artists," *The Bulletin of the Art Institute of Chicago* 1 (Apr. 1908).

"The Rood at St. Mary Magdalen's Anglican Church, Toronto," *Saturday Night* (11 Mar. 1922).

"The Sculptor and the Garden: Another Chance for the Fairies," *The Craftsman* 30 (June 1916).

"The Seven Arts," *Ottawa Evening Citizen* (20 Sept. 1930).

"The Story of a Waverly Artist," *Waverly Journal* [clipping, 21 Dec. 1945], AGO Archives.

"The Toronto Art Gallery: New Extensions to be Opened Shortly Bring it to Metropolitan Dimensions," *Saturday Night* (9 Jan. 1926), p. 5.

The Year Book of Canadian Art, 1913, The Arts & Letters Club of Toronto (London and Toronto: J.M. Dent & Sons, 1913).

Third Dimension, Directed by Laurence Hyde; National Film Board of Canada (Featuring sculptors: Jacobine Jones, Frances Loring, Florence Wyle, Donald

Stewart, Elford Cox, Dora Weshler, Emanual Hahn and Elizabeth Wyn Wood), 16 minutes, 1947.

Thompson, Francis. *The Hound of Heaven*, intro. Katherine Brégy (Philadelphia: Peter Reilly, 1916).

Thomson, Hugh. "Comedy, Romance, Poetry in Sculptors' Exhibition," [clipping, n.d.], AGO Archives.

Thomson, Hugh. "Eglinton Gallery Holds First Show," *Toronto Daily Star* (13 Mar. 1954), p. 12.

Thomson, Hugh. "Loring, Wyle Influence Lives on in Sculpture," *Globe and Mail* (8 Apr. 1967), p. 28.

Thomson, Hugh. "Many Interesting Works on View at RCA Show," *Toronto Daily Star* (3 Dec. 1953).

Thomson, Hugh. "Miss Loring a Laisse un Oeuvre Considérable," *La Presse* [clipping, 8 Feb. 1968], AGO Archives.

"Thoughts on Canadian Art," *Saturday Night* [clipping, n.d.], AGO Archives.

"Three Artists Join in Exhibit of Recent Work," *Montreal Gazette* [clipping, 18 Nov. 1931], AGO Archives.

"Three Elements in Sculpture: Line and Form, Mood and Silence Needed," *Windsor Daily Star* (21 Nov. 1952).

"Three Women Sculptors on Canadian Scene," *Saturday Night* (20 June 1914).

Tincombe-Fernandes, W.G. "The Anarch-Sculptor — Rodin," *Brush and Pencil* 15.1 (Jan. 1905), pp. 109–21.

Tippett, Maria. *Art at the Service of War: Canada, Art, and the Great War* (Toronto: University of Toronto Press, 1984).

Tippett, Maria. *By a Lady: Celebrating Three Centuries of Art by Canadian Women* (Toronto: Viking/Penguin, 1992).

Tippett, Maria. *Emily Carr, A Biography* (Toronto: Oxford University Press, 1979).

Tippett, Maria. *Making Culture: English-Canadian Institutions and the Arts before the Massey Commission* (Toronto: University of Toronto Press, 1990).

Tippett, Maria. *The Making of English-Canadian Culture, 1900–1939: The External Influences* (Toronto: ECW Press, 1987) and (Robarts Centre for Canadian Studies Lecture Series, York University, 1988).

"To The Winner," *Charlottetown Patriot* (2 Mar. 1959).

Toles, Page. "Sculptors' Society Exhibition," *Canadian Art* 1.5 (June/July 1944), pp. 190–93.

"Toronto City Hall," *Wikipedia*, 23 Sept. 2007 (access), http://en.wikipedia.org/wiki/Toronto_City_Hall

"Toronto Heliconian Club (1909–)," *Music Division Archival Guide*, National Library of Canada, created 14 May 2001, updated 15 Mar. 2006, http://www.collectionscanada.ca/4/7/m15-503-e.html

"Toronto Sculptors Spring a Surprise," *Globe and Mail* (15 Nov. 1915), p. S7.

Toronto Star [clipping, 19 Nov. 1929], AGO Archives.

Toronto Star [clipping, 1936], AGO Archives.

Toronto Star [clipping, 11 Apr. 1946], AGO Archives.

Toronto Star [clipping, 28 Apr. 1959], AGO Archives.

"Toronto Three Win Awards of Alberta University," *Globe and Mail* (29 Jun. 1954).

"Toronto Woman to Design Augusta War Memorial Gift of the Macombers," *Augusta Portland Star* [clipping, 10 Nov. 1929], AGO Archives.

Townsend, W., ed. *Canadian Art Today* (London: Studio International, 1970).

Toye, William. "Introduction," to John Visser, *Toronto* (Toronto: Oxford University Press, 1975).

"Transaction Papers," signed by Optimers, a geologist and land broker, 12 Dec. 1963, AGO Archives.

Trotter, Reginald G. et al., eds. *Proceedings: Conference on Canadian-American Affairs* (Montreal: Ginn and Co., 1937).

Turnbull, Grace H. *Chips From My Chisel: An Autobiography* (Rindge, New Hampshire: R.R. Smith, 1953).

Turner, Evan H. "Welders," *Canadian Art* 19.80 (July/Aug. 1962), pp. 276–83.

Turner, Linda. "Niagara-on-the-Lake: Jacobine Jones more than Forty Years of Sculpting," *The Art Magazine* 1.15 (1973), pp. 31.

"Turn Unused Church into Sculptor's Studio — Ladies Show Resource in Obtaining Place with Required Headroom," *Toronto Daily Star* (27 Nov. 1920), p. 22.

"Unique Church-Studio is Home and Workshop for Loring and Wyle," *Saturday Night* (18 Nov. 1944), p. 4.

"University Women Hear Dr. McCurdy," *Toronto Daily Star* [clipping, 25 Nov. 1939], AGO Archives.

"Untitled," [clipping, n.d., after 1949], p 101, AIC Archives.

"Untitled," *Globe and Mail* (24 March 1951), NGC Archives.

"Untitled," *Le Progress de Saguenay* (27 mai 1959), AGO Archives.

"Unveil Statute of Former War Leader," *Kingston Whig-Standard* [clipping, 19 Jan. 1957], AGO Archives.

"Uplands Lady Golfers Elect Officers at Dinner-Bridge," *Toronto Daily Star* [clipping, 28 Nov. 1932], AGO Archives.

"Upside-Down Party — Mr. Meighen Said — What Artists Wore at Lunch," *Toronto Daily Star* [clipping, 11 Mar. 1932], AGO Archives.

"Urge More Artists be Given War Jobs," *Toronto Daily Star* (2 May 1942).

"Urges Canadians Pursue Sculpture with Sports Spirit," *Sarnia Observer* [clipping, ca. 1959], AGO Archives.

Urquhart, Jane. *The Stone Carvers* (Toronto: McClelland & Stewart, 2001).

Usher, Edna. "K–W Art Fans Visit 4 Toronto Studios," *Kitchener-Waterloo Record* (30 April 1959).

Usher, Edna. "We're All in Debt to These Women," *Toronto Telegram* (25 Apr. 1959).

Vance, Jonathan F. *Death So Noble: Memory, Meaning and the First World War* (Vancouver: UBC Press, 1997).

Vancouver Art Gallery: All-Canadian Exhibition [catalogue] (May–July, 1932).

"Vandals and a Treasure," *Globe and Mail* [clipping, 4 May 1972], AGO Archives.

Vanderpoel, J.H. *The Human Figure* (New York: Bridgeman Publishers Inc., 1935).

Vickers, G. Stephen. "The Architecture in Sculpture," *The Journal of the Royal Architectural Institute of Canada* 26.1 (Jan. 1949), pp. 28–31.

"Vigor and Fine Taste Seen in Work of Local Sculptors: Exhibition by Florence Wyle and Frances Loring at Hart House Sketch Club Reveals Marked Progress of Delicate Art in Canada," *Globe and Mail* (23 Mar. 1926).

"Village Chapter I.O.D.E. Completes Dance Details," *Toronto Daily Star* [clipping, 2 Nov. 1937], AGO Archives.

Villeneuve, René. *Baroque to Neo-Classical: Sculpture in Quebec* (Montreal: Véhicule Press, 1997).

"Vimy Monument Urged for Canada, French Don't Seem to Want it: Florence Wyle," *Toronto Star* (15 Feb. 1934).

"Vimy Ridge," *Canadian Geographic* [n.d.], AGO Archives.

Walchuk, Bradley. *Telescope* CBC TV (typescript interview, n.d.) CBC Archives.

Wallace, Claire. "Stockingless Limbs Scorned as Ridiculous, Hideous," *Toronto Daily Star* (15 May 1934), p. 26.

Wallace, W. Stewart. *The Growth of National Feeling* (Toronto: MacMillan and Co. of Canada Ltd., 1927).

"Walter S. Allward, Sculptor and Architect of Vimy Memorial," *The Journal of the Royal Architectural Institute of Canada* 14.3 (Mar. 1937), p. 39.

"Wanted: A Borden Biography," [clipping, n.d.], AGO Archives.

"War Memorial of Law Society," *Toronto Daily Star* (7 Feb. 1928.) Reprinted in *Toronto Telegram*.

Ware, Caroline F. *Greenwich Village, 1920–1930: A Comment on American Civilization in the Post-war Years* (Boston: Houghton Mifflin Company/The Riverside Press, 1935).

Warneke, Heinz. *Painters and Sculptors in Modern America*, ed. Monroe Wheeler (New York: Thomas Y. Crowell, 1942).

Warrack, John. *Greek Sculpture* (London: Simpkin, Marshall, Hamilton, Kent & Co Ltd., printed by Turnbull & Spears, Edinburgh, n.d.).

Watson, Sheila. *The Double Hook* (Toronto: McClelland & Stewart, 1959).

"Waverly Girl Chosen to Execute Memorial Statue by Canadian Government," [clipping], Canadian Artists file, Metropolitan Toronto Library Board.

Weller, Allen S. "Foreword, Lorado Taft: A Retrospective Exhibition: January 16 to February 20, 1983," *The Bulletin*, Krannert Art Museum 8.2 (Urbana-Champaign: University of Illinois, 1983), pp.1–6.

Weller, Allen S. "Lorado Taft, 1860–1936," in "Lorado Taft: A Retrospective Exhibition: January 16 to February 20, 1983," *The Bulletin*, Krannert Art Museum 8.2 (Urbana-Champaign: University of Illinois, 1983).

Wells, Anna Mary. *Miss Marks and Miss Woolley* (Boston: Houghton Mifflin Co., 1978).

Wells, Karen. "Interview with Frances Gage," *Arts National*, CBC Radio, 12 July 1978.

"What is Modern?" *Modernity and Modernism: French Painting in the Nineteenth Century*, ed. Nigel Blake, et al. (New Haven: Yale University Press, 1993).

"What Women Are Doing," *Globe and Mail* [clipping, 30 Sept. 1918], AGO Archives.

"What Women Are Doing," *Globe and Mail* [clipping, 25 Mar. 1919], AGO Archives.

"What Women Are Doing," *Globe and Mail* [clipping, 25 Apr. 1919], AGO Archives.

"What Women Are Doing," *Globe and Mail* [clipping, 28 Apr. 1919], AGO Archives.

"What Women Are Doing," *Globe and Mail* [clipping, 6 Nov. 1920], AGO Archives.

"Whatever Happened to Frances Loring and Florence Wyle," *Toronto Telegram* (17 Mar. 1967).

"What's the Fate of Pity?" *Lake Simcoe Advocate* (9 Mar. 1967).

Wheeler, Monroe, ed. *Painters and Sculptors of Modern America* (New York: Thomas Y. Crowell Co., 1942).

Whittaker, Herbert. "Is Stratford Too English?" *Globe and Mail Weekly* (4 May 1957), p. 65.

Whitton, Charlotte. *Opening of the Chamber by The Prime Minister of Canada, Armistice Day, 1928*, (Toronto: British Book Service (Canada) Ltd., 1961).

"Who's Who In Ontario Art — Frances Norma Loring," (November 1948).

Wieselberger, Carl. "Talks About Art [Loring: *Eskimo Mother And Child*]," *The Ottawa Citizen* (7 Jan. 1961), p. 10.

Wilkinson, Alan G. *Henry Moore Remembered* (Toronto: Key Porter Books and The Art Gallery of Ontario, 1987).

William Zorach, Whitney Museum of American Art Catalogue (Frederick A. Prager, Inc., n.d.).

Williams, Talcott. "Augustus Saint-Gaudens," *The International Studio* 33.132 (Feb. 1908), pp. 123–38.

Withrow, William. *Contemporary Canadian Painting* (Toronto: McClelland & Stewart, 1972).

Withrow, William. "Miss Florence Wyle," speech, 2 pp., AGO Archives.

Wittig, Monique. "The Straight Mind," *Feminist Issues* 1.1 (1980), pp. 106–11; reprinted in *Gender in/of Culture* (Winter 1981), pp. 37–41.

Wittkower, Rudolf. *Sculpture: Processes and Principles* (New York: Harper & Row, 1977).

Wodehouse, R.F. *A Check List of The War Collections of World War I, 1914–1918 and World War II, 1039–1945* (Ottawa: The National Gallery of Canada/Queen's Printer, 1968).

"Woman Wins Contest for Memorial Design," *Ottawa Citizen* (30 Dec. 1954).

"Women Artists' Work Exhibited," *Montreal Daily Star* (2 Oct. 1920), p. 30.

"Women Sculptors Prominent at O.S.A.," *Globe and Mail* (22 Mar. 1930).

"Women With Mallets: Loring and Wyle complete three decades of partnership in sculpture," *The New World Illustrated* (Feb. 1942), pp. 27–28.

"Women's Art Group Holds Garden Fete," *Toronto Daily Star* (19 June 1930), p. 28.

"Women's Daily Interests at Home and Abroad," *Toronto Daily Star* (24 Dec. 1930), p. 16.

"Work of 4 Women in Sculpture Show," *Toronto Star* (13 Mar. 1942).

"Works of Ontario Artists Offer Display Catholicity," *Globe and Mail* (7 Mar. 1931).

Worthington, Helen. "Sculptors Hope Toronto Will Be Known for its Art," *Toronto Star* [clipping, 6 Oct. 1972], AGO Archives.

Wuorio, Eva-Lis. "Careers for Women," *Globe and Mail* (1 June 1946).

Wuorio, Eva-Lis. "Sculpture a Lifetime Job, View of Frances Loring," *Globe and Mail* (1 June 1946), p. 13.

Wuorio, Eva-Lis. "Visitors See How It's Done," *Toronto Telegram* (1 June 1946).

Wyer, R. "A New Message in Sculpture," *The Fine Arts Journal* 26 (1912), pp. 263.

"Wyle and Loring: the Olympian Sculptors Talk About their Sorrows and their Joys," *Globe Magazine* (7 Apr. 1962).

Wyle, Florence. "An Inspiring Memorial that is Needed at Home," letter to the editor, *Globe* (2 Apr. 1925).

Wyle, Florence. *Poems*, foreword by Ira Dilworth (Toronto: The Ryerson Press, 1959).

Wyle, Florence. "Sculpture and the People," [unpublished] for *Canadian Art* (Dec. 1943), AGO Archives.

Wyle, Florence. "Sculpture Appreciation," ms., AGO Archives.

Wyle, Florence. "Sketchbook," NGC Archives.

Wyle, Florence. "Tarzan," ms. attached to "Sculpture Appreciation," AGO Archives.

Wyle, Florence. *The Shadow of the Year* (Toronto: Aliquando Press, 1976).

"Wyle, Florence: Works Sold as of Feb. 22, 1966," The Pollack Gallery, AGO Archives.

Wyle, Florence. "Young Women," *The New World Illustrated* (June 1943).

Wylie, Betty Jane. "Winnipeg's Cenotaph," *The Manitoba Pageant* 8.2 (Jan. 1963), http://www.mhs.mb.ca/docs/pageant/08/winnipegcenotaph.shtml

Wyn Wood, Elizabeth. "A National Program for the Arts in Canada," *Canadian Art* 1.3 (1943–44), pp. 93–95.

Wyn Wood, Elizabeth. "Art and the Pre-Cambrian Shield," *The Canadian Forum* 16.193 (Feb. 1937), pp. 13–15.

Wyn Wood, Elizabeth. "Art Goes to Parliament," *Canadian Art* 2.1 (1944–45), pp. 3–5; 41–42.

Wyn Wood, Elizabeth. "Observations on a Decade, 1938–48: Ten Years of Canadian Sculpture," *The Journal of the Royal Architectural Institute of Canada* 25.1 (Jan.1948), pp. 15–19; 30.

York, Karen. "Fantastic Garden Rooted in Reality," *Globe and Mail* (26 Aug. 1995).

Zerilli, Linda M. "Rememoration or War? French Feminist Narrative and the Politics of Self-Representation," *differences: A Journal of Feminist Cultural Studies* 3.1 (1991).

Permissions ∾

Grateful acknowledgment is made for permission to reprint from material under copyright and for permission to use materials held in public and private archives from the following:

E.P. Taylor Library and Archives, Art Gallery of Ontario
Archives of Ontario
Art Institute of Chicago
Canadian Broadcasting Corporation
Canadian Gay & Lesbian Archives
Canadian National Exhibition Archives
Canadian War Museum
City of Toronto Archives
Library and Archives Canada
Metropolitan Toronto Library Board
National Gallery of Canada
Sears Canada Inc.

The Women's Art Association of Canada
University of Toronto
University of Illinois
Globe and Mail
The (Montréal) Gazette
Toronto Star Newspapers Ltd.
Qennefer Browne
Dale Fehr
Frances Gage
Rebecca Sisler
Rosalind Went
Ashley & Crippen Photography
Don Foley Studio of Professional Photography Services
Transcript from Telescope CBC TV, 7 May 1965
Used with permission of the CBC.

Index

About the Author

Elspeth Cameron is the author of three award-winning biographies: *Hugh MacLennan: A Writer's Life* (1981), *Irving Layton: A Portrait* (1985), and *Earle Birney: A Life* (1994). Her 1997 memoir *No Previous Experience* won the W.O. Mitchell Literary Prize. She was the recipient of the UBC Medal for Canadian Biography in 1981 and the City of Vancouver Book Award in 1995. Her biography of Hugh MacLennan was a finalist for the Governor General's Literary Award. She has written numerous profiles of Canadian cultural figures such as Peter Newman, Jack McClelland, Veronica Tennant, Anne Murray, Howard Engel, Janette Turner Hospital, and Timothy Findley, winning several journalism awards. Her work has appeared in *Saturday Night*, *Chatelaine*, *Maclean's*, *Leisureways*, and in a number of academic journals. In addition, she has edited seven books, including *Great Dames*, a collection of biographical sketches, memoirs, and essays about twentieth-century Canadian women from all walks of life. She has taught English and Canadian Studies at Concordia University and the University of Toronto, and is currently an adjunct professor in the English Language and Literature Department at Brock University. Elspeth now lives in St. Catharines, Ontario, and is at work on a biography of Group of Seven member, A.Y. Jackson.

The publication of
And Beauty Answers: The Life of Frances Loring and Florence Wyle
is in honour of the 50th anniversary of the establishment of
The Canada Council for the Arts.